Macroeconomic Challenges to Structural Reform and Industrial Development

Oytun Meçik
Eskişehir Osmangazi University, Turkey

IGI Global
Publishing Tomorrow's Research Today

Published in the United States of America by
IGI Global
701 E. Chocolate Avenue
Hershey PA, USA 17033
Tel: 717-533-8845
Fax: 717-533-8661
E-mail: cust@igi-global.com
Web site: https://www.igi-global.com

Copyright © 2025 by IGI Global. All rights reserved. No part of this publication may be reproduced, stored or distributed in any form or by any means, electronic or mechanical, including photocopying, without written permission from the publisher.
Product or company names used in this set are for identification purposes only. Inclusion of the names of the products or companies does not indicate a claim of ownership by IGI Global of the trademark or registered trademark.

Library of Congress Cataloging-in-Publication Data

CIP Pending
ISBN: 979-8-3693-5508-4
EISBN: 979-8-3693-5510-7

Vice President of Editorial: Melissa Wagner
Managing Editor of Acquisitions: Mikaela Felty
Managing Editor of Book Development: Jocelynn Hessler
Production Manager: Mike Brehm
Cover Design: Phillip Shickler

British Cataloguing in Publication Data
A Cataloguing in Publication record for this book is available from the British Library.

All work contributed to this book is new, previously-unpublished material.
The views expressed in this book are those of the authors, but not necessarily of the publisher.

Editorial Advisory Board

Hazal Duman Alptekin, *KTO Karatay University, Turkey*
Murat Atan, *Ankara Hacı Bayram Veli University, Turkey*
Üzeyir Aydın, *Dokuz Eylül University, Turkey*
Ercan Bahtiyar, *Uşak University, Turkey*
Feride Hayırsever Baştürk, *Bilecik Şeyh Edebali University, Turkey*
Fatih Ceylan, *Uşak University, Turkey*
Erdal Demirhan, *Afyon Kocatepe University, Turkey*
Mehmet Dinç, *Ağrı İbrahim Çeçen University, Turkey*
Onur Dirlik, *Eskişehir Osmangazi University, Turkey*
Başak Özarslan Doğan, *İstanbul Gelişim University, Turkey*
Emrah Doğan, *İstanbul Gelişim University, Turkey*
Fatma Doğruel, *Marmara University, Turkey*
Yahya Can Dura, *Union of Municipalities of Turkey, Turkey*
Burhan Durgun, *Dicle University, Turkey*
Elif Erer, *Manisa Celal Bayar University, Turkey*
Etem Hakan Ergeç, *İstanbul Medeniyet University, Turkey*
Birol Erkan, *İskenderun Technical University, Turkey*
Erdinç Gülbaş, *İstanbul Esenyurt University, Turkey*
Gülçin Gürel Günal, *Ege University, Turkey*
Şafak Gündüz, *Yeditepe University, Turkey*
Süleyman Gürbüz, *Yozgat Bozok University, Turkey*
Yeşim Üçdoğruk Gürel, *Dokuz Eylül University, Turkey*
Hakan Kahyaoğlu, *Dokuz Eylül University, Turkey*
Fatih Kaplan, *Tarsus University, Turkey*
Oğuz Kara, *Düzce University, Turkey*
Mustafa Karabacak, *Uşak University, Turkey*
Can Karabıyık, *Manisa Celal Bayar University, Turkey*
Hakan Deniz Karakoç, *Başkent University,* Turkey
Esin Kılıç, *Eskişehir Osmangazi University, Turkey*

Mustafa Kırca, *Ordu University, Turkey*
Berna Kırkulak, *Dokuz Eylül University, Turkey*
Esra Koç, *Artvin Çoruh University, Turkey*
Özge Kozal, *Ege University, Turkey*
Onur Lakeç, *Anadolu University, Turkey*
Süleyman Emre Özcan, *Manisa Celal Bayar University, Turkey*
Onur Özdemir, *İstanbul Gelişim University, Turkey*
Şükriye Gül Reis, *Gaziantep University, Turkey*
Selim Şanlısoy, *Dokuz Eylül University, Turkey*
Deniz Timurçin, *Small and Medium Enterprises Development Organization of Turkey Turkey*
Ünal Töngür, *Akdeniz University, Turkey*
Osman Tüzün, *Uşak University, Turkey*
Mert Ural, *Dokuz Eylül University, Turkey*
Abdullah Yalaman, *Eskişehir Osmangazi University, Turkey*

Table of Contents

Preface xxii

Chapter 1
The Origins of Structural Reform: Structural Adjustment, What and Where Did It Come From? 1
    Sureyya Yigit, New Vision University, Georgia

Chapter 2
Unlocking Potential: Overcoming Structural Reform Roadblocks in International Economic Governance 33
    Özden Sevgi Akıncı, Independent Researcher, Turkey

Chapter 3
An Analysis on the Determinants of Global Inflation 61
    Öznur Taşdöken, Antalya Chamber of Commerce and Industry, Turkey

Chapter 4
Causality Relationship between Inflation and Interest Rate: A Research for 20 Developed Countries 99
    Fatih Ceylan, Uşak University, Turkey
    Birol Erkan, İskenderun Technical University, Turkey

Chapter 5
Financial and Human Capital Awareness in Industrialized Countries 123
    Ezgi Kopuk, Eskişehir Osmangazi Universty, Turkey
    Hasan Umutlu, Düzce University, Turkey

Chapter 6
Quality or Quantity? The Role of Human Capital on Sustainable Growth 157
    Ozlem Inanc, Isik University, Turkey

Chapter 7
Is There a Relationship between Financial Stability and Macroeconomic Variables? OECD Example 185
    Burcu Savaş Çelik, İstanbul Gelişim Üniversitesi, Turkey

Chapter 8
The Role of Sustainable Finance in the Transition to the Post-Growth
Economy 207
    Aynur Yilmaz Ataman, Post Growth Institute, UK

Chapter 9
Which Fiscal Instruments Do Corrupt Governments Prefer During Fiscal
Consolidation Episodes? 241
    Kerim Peren Arin, Zayed University, UAE & CAMA, Australia
    Elif Boduroğlu, Atilim University, Turkey
    Esref Ugur Celik, Atilim University, Turkey
    Nicola Spagnolo, Brunel University London, UK & University of
        Campania "Luigi Vanvitelli", Italy

Chapter 10
Understanding Trends in Economic Development and Financial Dynamics ... 259
    Feyza Ozdinc, Gaziantep University, Turkey
    Sukriye Gul Reis, Gaziantep University, Turkey

Chapter 11
Quantitative Measures and Moderating Power of Monetary Policies: Insight
from the Analysis of the Link between Equity Sector Indices with Money
Supply 283
    Orhan Özaydın, İstanbul Medipol University, Turkey
    Edmund Ntom Udemba, Shanxi Technology and Business University,
        China

Chapter 12
Fostering Prosperity: Unveiling the Impact of Governance Quality on GDP
per Capita in OECD Nations... 313
    İhsan Erdem Kayral, Başkent University, Turkey
    Hacer Pınar Altan, Atılım University, Turkey
    Tiago Silveira Gontijo, Federal University of São João del-Rei, Brazil

Chapter 13
The Impact of Trade and Financial Globalization on Cross-Border
Investments: Perspective of Newly Industrialized Countries............................. 331
    Sinem Atıcı Ustalar, Ataturk University, Turkey

Chapter 14
Uneven Human Development: Revisiting Economic, Environmental, and
Political Determinants in OECD 361
    Özge Kozal, Ege University, Turkey

Chapter 15
Sustainable Finance Practices for Handling Climate Change: The Case of
Türkiye 387
    Bakhtiyar Garayev, Anadolu University, Turkey
    Aslı Afşar, Anadolu University, Turkey

Chapter 16
Spatial Analysis of Environmental Degradation: The Role of International
Trade and Democracy 419
    Elif Korkmaz Tümer, Ege University, Turkey
    Erol Türker Tümer, Dokuz Eylul University, Turkey

Chapter 17
Green Industrial Policies and Sustainable Economy Approaches Ensuring
Industrial Growth and Environmental Balance 447
    Tuğba Koyuncu Çakmak, İstanbul Esenyurt University, Turkey

Chapter 18
Environmental Policies in Global Economies and Environmental Concern in
Regional Sustainable Production: Environmental Sustainable Production 463
    Aslı Öztopcu, Maltepe University, Turkey

Chapter 19
Empirical Analysis of the Relationship Between Inclusive Green Growth and
Agricultural Added Value: The Case of Türkiye 493
    Başak Özarslan Doğan, Gelisim University, Turkey

Chapter 20
Sustainable Development and Ecological Footprint in Türkiye 513
    Hüseyin Naci Bayraç, Faculty of Economics and Administrative
        Sciences, Eskisehir Osmangazi University, Turkey
    Fatih Çemrek, Faculty of Science, Eskisehir Osmangazi University,
        Turkey

Chapter 21
Structural, Configurational, Relational, and Instrumental Dimensions of
Entrepreneurship Ecosystems 533

    José G. Vargas-Hernandez, Tecnológico Nacional de México, ITS
        Fresnillo, Mexico
    Francisco J. González-Ávila, Tecnológico Nacional de México, ITS
        Fresnillo, Mexico
    Omar C. Vargas-González, Tecnológico Nacional de México, Ciudad
        Guzman, Mexico
    Selene Castañeda-Burciaga, Universidad Politécnica de Zacatecas,
        Mexico
    Omar A. Guirette-Barbosa, Universidad Politécnica de Zacatecas,
        Mexico

About the Contributors 563

Index 571

Detailed Table of Contents

Preface xxii

Chapter 1
The Origins of Structural Reform: Structural Adjustment, What and Where
Did It Come From? 1
    Sureyya Yigit, New Vision University, Georgia

The 1970s witnessed economic programs aimed to help governments refinance their debts owed to the American international banking system by ending the Bretton Woods system and the gold-dollar peg. These programs required debtor states to open up their markets and privatize state-owned companies, ultimately strengthening the power of international financial institutions and promoting a more neoliberal economic approach in many parts of the world. As part of these efforts, many laws restricting the private sector were repealed, government spending was curbed and refinanced through credit policy, trade restrictions were reduced, and the exchange rate was devalued. This period also saw the abolishment of collective labour rights, introducing or increasing subsidies for companies, and tax relief for these businesses with deregulated pricing policies. International financial institutions such as the World Bank and the International Monetary Fund advocated structural adjustment for developing countries to overcome economic distress. This chapter focuses on the origin of these policies.

Chapter 2
Unlocking Potential: Overcoming Structural Reform Roadblocks in
International Economic Governance.. 33
    Özden Sevgi Akıncı, Independent Researcher, Turkey

Focusing on the International Monetary Fund, the study underscores the profound impact of the international institutions on the global economy and the interconnected nature of their operations. It emphasizes overcoming common barriers to reform, such as disparities in representation and decision-making power, to promote more inclusive and effective governance. Reform of the international institutions is essential to prevent or mitigate global crises and to promote equitable and sustainable development worldwide. A comprehensive literature review was conducted, followed by data interpretation through visual analysis, observation, and evaluation. The findings were subjected to an assessment, after which recommendations were presented. The study concludes with a call for structural reforms to enhance the resilience, responsiveness, and fair distribution of electoral power. This would facilitate effective structural reforms and promote sustainable economic development.

Chapter 3
An Analysis on the Determinants of Global Inflation 61
    Öznur Taşdöken, Antalya Chamber of Commerce and Industry, Turkey

The volatilities observed in different markets have an impact on global inflation. The persistent upward trend in inflation forms the basis of economic challenges experienced in all countries. Therefore, especially considering recent developments and events, inflation stands out as one of the most researched topics. In this contextthis, this study analyzes the relationship between global inflation, global food price, Brent oil price, global energy prices, the global supply chain, and global geopolitical risks variables using monthly data from 2004:08 to 2023:10. In this analysis, the Dynamic Wavelet Correlation Analysis For Multivariate (WLMC) approach is employed to examine the dynamic correlation relationship between variables across time and frequency dimensions. Considering the findings from the study, it can be stated that strong correlation relationships among variables have been found after the year 2021 in all analyses. This suggests a stronger economic integration across different global markets, especially in recent years.

Chapter 4
Causality Relationship between Inflation and Interest Rate: A Research for 20
Developed Countries.. 99
    Fatih Ceylan, Uşak University, Turkey
    Birol Erkan, İskenderun Technical University, Turkey

The study aims to reveal the causality relationship between inflation and interest rates in general and for G20 countries in particular. In this context, the study analyses the bidirectional relationship between inflation and interest rates using monthly data for the period 2000-2022, using causality methods based on traditional and Fourier functions that capture structural breaks gradually or smoothly. According to the test results of the traditional Granger causality analysis, while there is a bidirectional causality relationship between inflation and real interest rates in the panel data of G-20 countries, causality relationships change when structural breaks based on Fourier functions are taken into account. With the increasing global inflation in recent years, it is considered important for central banks aiming for price stability to take into account the changing relationship between inflation and interest rates.

Chapter 5
Financial and Human Capital Awareness in Industrialized Countries 123
    Ezgi Kopuk, Eskişehir Osmangazi Universty, Turkey
    Hasan Umutlu, Düzce University, Turkey

The study examines the financial and human resources in the industrial sectors of the industrialized countries (Germany, China, Ireland, South Korea, America, Switzerland, Japan, Singapore and the Netherlands) that provide the highest efficiency, income and sustainability from financial and human capital. It is aimed to examine capital developments. For this purpose, firstly, the definition of financial and human capital, its economic effects, its importance in the industrial sector, and the financial and human capital policies and competitiveness of the industrialized countries implemented by the industrial sector were evaluated. In order to make a unique inference for this purpose and evaluation, another aim of the study was to investigate the effect of financial and human capital in the industrial sector of industrializing countries. In this regard, the aim was tested by panel data analysis covering the period 2005-2021. It was determined that the variables had different effects on a country basis, and human capital indicators were found to have a higher positive effect.

Chapter 6
Quality or Quantity? The Role of Human Capital on Sustainable Growth 157
Ozlem Inanc, Isik University, Turkey

This study examines the link between human capital and sustainable economic growth, highlighting the contradiction of rising university education without improved graduate employability in Turkiye from 2014 to 2023. It notes high unemployment among university graduates, indicating a disconnect between the skills provided by educational institutions and job market demands. The rapid growth in universities and graduates has not matched the increase in high-skilled job opportunities, leading to skill mismatches and underemployment, especially during economic downturns. The paper calls for a reassessment of educational strategies towards a quality-focused education that prioritizes practical skills and market needs, emphasizing university-industry collaborations to boost graduate employability and ensure higher education's role in fostering economic resilience and growth.

Chapter 7
Is There a Relationship between Financial Stability and Macroeconomic Variables? OECD Example... 185
Burcu Savaş Çelik, İstanbul Gelişim Üniversitesi, Turkey

Financial stability has many determinants. These include various macroeconomic variables, the soundness and infrastructure of financial institutions, and the monetary policies pursued. This study aims to examine the relationship between financial stability and economic growth, interest rates, inflation rates, and interest rates of OECD member countries Z-score provides important information about the financial stability of a country's banking system by comparing its capital and returns and the volatility of returns. The study's data set consists of 15 OECD constituent countries. The data range of the study was determined as the period 2000 - 2021. Panel data analysis is used in this study. Dumitrescu and Hurlin causality test results from gross domestic, inflation, and interest rate variables to the Z-score. Also, there is bi-causality from the Z-score to gross domestic, inflation, and interest rate variables.

Chapter 8
The Role of Sustainable Finance in the Transition to the Post-Growth
Economy 207
    Aynur Yilmaz Ataman, Post Growth Institute, UK

In light of the urgent ecological and social challenges facing our world, there has been a noticeable shift in focus towards exploring economic models that prioritise ecological constraints and societal well-being over the pursuit of continuous growth and profit maximisation. These alternative perspectives collectively fall under the overarching term of post-growth economic models and the financial sector has significant influence over the real economy, and the investments made within it can either perpetuate destructive traditional practices or contribute to the construction of sustainable, regenerative, and inclusive economic and social structures. Therefore, this chapter aims to delve into the role of existing sustainable investment strategies, such as ESG (Environmental, Social, and Governance) Investment and Impact Investment, in the transition to a post-growth era. It also aims to examine the new transformative investment frameworks that have emerged in response to the shortcomings of current investment models in facilitating this transition.

Chapter 9
Which Fiscal Instruments Do Corrupt Governments Prefer During Fiscal
Consolidation Episodes? 241
    Kerim Peren Arin, Zayed University, UAE & CAMA, Australia
    Elif Boduroğlu, Atilim University, Turkey
    Esref Ugur Celik, Atilim University, Turkey
    Nicola Spagnolo, Brunel University London, UK & University of
       Campania "Luigi Vanvitelli", Italy

This study investigates the fiscal policy choices of corrupt governments during periods of fiscal consolidation. By using the same dataset by Arin et al. (2011), our analysis of pooled observations for 18 OECD countries reveals two key findings: (i) corrupt governments tend to raise indirect taxes rather than reduce expenditures during fiscal adjustments, and (ii) they yield to political lobbying and pressure by lowering corporate taxes and increasing social benefits and subsidies during substantial fiscal adjustment episodes.

Chapter 10
Understanding Trends in Economic Development and Financial Dynamics ... 259
Feyza Ozdinc, Gaziantep University, Turkey
Sukriye Gul Reis, Gaziantep University, Turkey

Since economic activities require funds, the financial system is a crucial component of the economic system, with the development of the financial sector having a significant impact on an economy's overall financial health. This study focuses on the intersection of economic development and finance and identifies significant themes and new research directions in the distribution of articles on finance and economic development. It reviews 296 articles from the Web of Science and Scopus databases, focusing on the dynamic fields of economic development and finance. The data shows an increasing trend after 2013, with 101 articles on this issue between 2015 and 2021 and 99 between 2022 and 2024. The results offer new perspectives on how economic development and finance are changing, offering light on both historical precedents and future directions.

Chapter 11
Quantitative Measures and Moderating Power of Monetary Policies: Insight from the Analysis of the Link between Equity Sector Indices with Money Supply 283
Orhan Özaydın, İstanbul Medipol University, Turkey
Edmund Ntom Udemba, Shanxi Technology and Business University, China

Re-evaluation of the critical macroeconomic indices behind the movement of money and other financial assets with respect to the flow and supply of money for the case of Türkiye is essential at this present economic situation of Türkiye. Türkiye's economic activities have been, and still passing through unstable development due to excessive inflation and poor performance of the foreign exchange rate. To this end, authors applied the monthly end price data from 2005 December to 2022 March to researched 10 different Istanbul Equity Indices (IEI) as dependent variable, to see whether they are related with Money supply for the case of Türkiye. From the quantitative analysis of the indices, all control variables including USD/TRY and BOND2Y coefficients are negatively correlated with equity indices and statistically significant. Furthermore, the impact of Central Bank reserves and deposits to the Central Bank (M1) and term deposits at banks (M2 minus M1) on sector indices is found to vary significantly across different sectors.

Chapter 12
Fostering Prosperity: Unveiling the Impact of Governance Quality on GDP
per Capita in OECD Nations... 313
    İhsan Erdem Kayral, Başkent University, Turkey
    Hacer Pınar Altan, Atılım University, Turkey
    Tiago Silveira Gontijo, Federal University of São João del-Rei, Brazil

This study aims to investigate the influence of the quality of governance on economic development among 38 OECD countries using a panel data approach. The data was gathered from the World Bank database for the period of 2002-2021 and consists of six governance indicators and two macroeconomic variables. The independent variables are the six governance indicators (WGI): control of corruption (CC), government effectiveness (GE), political stability and absence of violence/terrorism (PS), rule of law (RL), regulatory quality (RQ), and voice and accountability (VA). The dependent variable is the natural logarithm of GDP per capita, and inflation and real interest rates are control variables. The research identifies a direct and significant relationship between GDPPC and GE, PS, RL, RQ, and VA in OECD countries. These findings suggest that the existence of mechanisms for GE, PS, RL, RQ, and VA contribute positively to economic development. Moreover, interest rates and inflation are found to be significant and negatively related to GDPPC.

Chapter 13
The Impact of Trade and Financial Globalization on Cross-Border
Investments: Perspective of Newly Industrialized Countries............................ 331
    Sinem Atıcı Ustalar, Ataturk University, Turkey

This study analyzes the impact of Newly Industrialized Countries (NICs) trade and financial globalization on bilateral financial asset trade. The analysis is carried out using the financial gravity model. The model is estimated with the PPML estimator using bilateral portfolios, debt securities, and equity investments of 120 countries between 2001-2022. De facto and de jure trade and financial openness variables are used to control globalization in model estimation. Estimation results show that the impact of trade and financial openness on financial asset trade in NICs is higher than the world average. When compared with G7 countries, show that the openness of NICs' goods and capital markets is not yet at the level of industrialized countries.

Chapter 14

Uneven Human Development: Revisiting Economic, Environmental, and
Political Determinants in OECD 361

Özge Kozal, Ege University, Turkey

This study examines the factors influencing uneven human development in OECD countries from 1995 to 2021, focusing on industrial structure, governance, and environmental degradation while controlling for income inequality, trade openness, and unemployment. The MMQR analysis reveals that increasing industrial output alone does not enhance human development; however, medium and high-technology manufacturing exports significantly boost HDI. Additionally, CO2 emissions per capita negatively impact HDI, highlighting the need for zero-carbon industrialization. Democracy improves HDI in lower quantiles, while income inequality negatively affects HDI, particularly in higher quantiles. Trade openness supports HDI. The study suggests that OECD countries should pursue high-tech industrialization, reduce CO2 emissions, strengthen democratic governance, address income inequality, and manage trade openness for sustainable and equitable human development, requiring integrated policies to connect economic, social, and environmental aspects.

Chapter 15

Sustainable Finance Practices for Handling Climate Change: The Case of
Türkiye 387

Bakhtiyar Garayev, Anadolu University, Turkey
Aslı Afşar, Anadolu University, Turkey

Global climate change has emerged as one of the world's most urgent issues, with climatic catastrophes having significant economic and environmental impacts. These challenges play a crucial role in Türkiye's development strategies and policies. Financing the necessary transformation to reduce carbon emissions and adapt is vital in the fight against climate change. Integrating environmental, social, and governance (ESG) criteria into investment processes promotes sustainable development and the achievement of environmental goals. Consequently, sustainable finance practices have gained importance, supported by good practices from various organizations and banks in Türkiye. This research examines Türkiye's position in international climate agreements and its actions aligned with sustainable development goals. Additionally, the study analyzes the integrated reports of eight banks that are members of the UN Global Compact, exploring their sustainability strategies.

Chapter 16
Spatial Analysis of Environmental Degradation: The Role of International
Trade and Democracy 419
    Elif Korkmaz Tümer, Ege University, Turkey
    Erol Türker Tümer, Dokuz Eylul University, Turkey

This paper explores the drivers of environmental degradation by using spatial panel data models to account for spatial interdependence among countries. Despite a large body of literature investigating the relationship between international trade, democracy, and the environment, previous studies have produced mixed results, partly due to the conceptualizations of variables and methodological limitations. This paper addresses these limitations by proposing alternative measures of trade openness and democracy while accounting for spatial dependence between countries. The results reveal that income, economic complexity, democracy, energy intensity, and agricultural land contribute to CO_2 emissions, while forest area is negatively associated with environmental degradation. The results also reveal that while trade openness has statistically significant and positive direct effects, there are strong spillover effects as well. Indeed, the negative spillover effects of trade openness outweigh the direct effects, leading to a mitigating impact on environmental degradation.

Chapter 17
Green Industrial Policies and Sustainable Economy Approaches Ensuring
Industrial Growth and Environmental Balance 447
Tuğba Koyuncu Çakmak, İstanbul Esenyurt University, Turkey

The aim of this chapter is to analyses the effects of industrial growth on environmental degradation in terms of green industrial policies. The relationship between environmental pollution and economic growth has been explained from two different perspectives. The first approach points to the existence of a potential duality between economic growth and environmental protection and the existence of a trade-off relationship in terms of achieving economic growth or reducing environmental pollution. The second approach claims that the negative impact of economic growth on environmental pollution can be corrected by green industrial policies. Numerous empirical studies and country-level data in the literature suggest that economic growth also stimulates the development of sustainable technologies and innovations that can enhance environmental protection. Recent evidence, especially from developed countries, shows that there is a decoupling between environmental pollution and economic growth, and, thanks to green industry policy measures, between economic growth and emissions. This draws attention to the fact that while economic growth increases thanks to green policy measures, environmental pollution decreases at the same time. Therefore, it is pointed out that it is possible to reduce carbon emissions without compromising economic growth. Therefore, it is very important for policy makers and decision makers to support green industrial policies in the fight against climate change and global warming.

Chapter 18
Environmental Policies in Global Economies and Environmental Concern in
Regional Sustainable Production: Environmental Sustainable Production 463
    Aslı Öztopcu, Maltepe University, Turkey

Today, rapidly growing population, industrialization, and urbanization are causing global environmental problems to become an ever-greater threat. Globally, there is an increasing demand for sustainable development due to issues including air pollution, water resource depletion, biodiversity reduction, and climate change. This chapter looks at how regionally implemented environmental policies contribute to the global economies' sustainable development objectives. With examples from projects in developed and developing countries, this article tries to understand the environmental policies and practices implemented for sustainable development. The findings demonstrate that international cooperation is necessary to ensure the world's sustainability. Nonetheless, a significant determinant of the sufficiency of efforts is a nation's degree of social and economic development. The outputs of this study can provide insights into regional environmental problems, cooperation against environmental risks, and the global implications of advances in environmental sustainability.

Chapter 19
Empirical Analysis of the Relationship Between Inclusive Green Growth and
Agricultural Added Value: The Case of Türkiye 493
    Başak Özarslan Doğan, Gelisim University, Turkey

In this study, the relationship between inclusive green growth and agricultural added value in Türkiye for the period 1990-2020 was examined with the help of the ARDL bounds test. In order to represent inclusive green growth, the inclusive green growth index was created using the Principal Component Analysis method. In addition, the effects of inclusive green growth, as well as the effects of total labor force and temperature increase on agricultural added value, were also examined in the study. According to the findings, inclusive green growth in Türkiye positively affects agricultural added value and the coefficient is statistically significant. In addition, in the study, the effect of the total labor force on agricultural added value was found to be positive and the coefficient was statistically significant. While the effect of temperature increase on agricultural added value is found to be negative, the coefficient is statistically insignificant.

Chapter 20
Sustainable Development and Ecological Footprint in Türkiye 513
    Hüseyin Naci Bayraç, Faculty of Economics and Administrative
        Sciences, Eskisehir Osmangazi University, Turkey
    Fatih Çemrek, Faculty of Science, Eskisehir Osmangazi University,
        Turkey

The ecological footprint serves as a devised methodology aimed at quantifying the impact of human endeavors on ecosystems. Sustainability, in this context, entails the augmentation of biologically productive areas, fortification of their capacity for self-regeneration, and preservation thereof. The ecological footprint framework emerges as a numerical tool pivotal for fostering the sustainable utilization of resources. The principal objective of this research is to identify the determinants contributing to the ecological footprint within the framework of sustainable development, focusing on selected indicators for Türkiye, namely Ecological Footprint per Capita, CO_2 Emissions per Capita, GDP per Capita, Energy Consumption per Capita. The chapter aims to explore the interrelationships among these variables through cointegration and causality analyses.

Chapter 21
Structural, Configurational, Relational, and Instrumental Dimensions of
Entrepreneurship Ecosystems 533

    José G. Vargas-Hernandez, Tecnológico Nacional de México, ITS Fresnillo, Mexico
    Francisco J. González-Ávila, Tecnológico Nacional de México, ITS Fresnillo, Mexico
    Omar C. Vargas-González, Tecnológico Nacional de México, Ciudad Guzman, Mexico
    Selene Castañeda-Burciaga, Universidad Politécnica de Zacatecas, Mexico
    Omar A. Guirette-Barbosa, Universidad Politécnica de Zacatecas, Mexico

This study aims to analyze the structural, configurational, relational, and instrumental dimensions of entrepreneurship ecosystems. The analysis departs from the assumption that the entrepreneurship ecosystem is a focal multidimensional paradigm including several dimensions in its formation. The method employed is the meta-analytical descriptive and reflective based on conceptual, theoretical, and empirical literature review. The study concludes that the formation of any entrepreneurship ecosystem incorporates several dimensions, among others, the configurational, structural, relational, instrumental, and operational.

About the Contributors 563

Index 571

Preface

In the ever-evolving landscape of global economics, the interplay between structural reform and industrial development stands as a pivotal axis upon which nations chart their course towards prosperity. *Macroeconomic Challenges to Structural Reform and Industrial Development* delves deep into this intricate relationship, offering a comprehensive exploration of the hurdles, strategies, and implications inherent in this dynamic domain.

At its core, this book is a testament to the enduring quest for economic advancement and societal progress. It navigates through the complexities of macroeconomic policies and structural reforms, unraveling the intricate web of challenges that confront policymakers, economists, and industrialists alike. Through meticulous analysis and insightful perspectives, it sheds light on the nuanced interconnections between macroeconomic stability, structural transformation, and industrial growth.

Drawing upon a rich tapestry of theoretical frameworks, empirical evidence, and real-world case studies, this volume transcends conventional boundaries to offer a holistic understanding of the forces shaping economic landscapes across the globe. From the imperative of fostering innovation and technological advancement to the need to address income inequality and environmental sustainability, each chapter embarks on a journey of discovery, unraveling the multifaceted dimensions of macroeconomic challenges and their profound implications for structural reform and industrial development.

Chapter 1

This chapter delves into the pivotal economic transformations of the 1970s, marked by the dismantling of the Bretton Woods system and the severance of the gold-dollar peg. These changes were not merely technical adjustments; they were part of a broader strategy to strengthen the influence of international financial institutions and promote a neoliberal economic framework globally. The chapter explores how debtor states were compelled to open their markets, privatize state assets, and repeal laws restricting the private sector, leading to widespread economic liberalization. This era also witnessed the erosion of collective labor rights, the introduction of corporate subsidies, and the implementation of deregulated pricing policies. The World Bank and the International Monetary Fund (IMF) emerged as key advocates of structural adjustment programs, particularly in developing countries, as a means to navigate economic crises.

Chapter 2

This chapter underscores the profound impact of international financial institutions like the IMF on the global economy, particularly their role in shaping economic governance. The study advocates for structural reforms within these institutions to address disparities in representation and decision-making power, which are crucial for promoting inclusive and effective governance. The chapter is grounded in a comprehensive literature review, supplemented by data interpretation through visual analysis and observation. The findings emphasize the need for reforms that enhance the resilience and responsiveness of these institutions, thereby supporting equitable and sustainable global development.

Chapter 3

Inflation, a persistent economic challenge, is intricately linked to various global market volatilities. This chapter offers an in-depth analysis of the relationships between global inflation, food and energy prices, geopolitical risks, and supply chain dynamics, using data spanning from 2004 to 2023. Employing the Dynamic Wavelet Correlation Analysis For Multivariate (WLMC) approach, the study reveals that since 2021, there has been a significant increase in the correlation between these variables, indicating stronger economic integration across global markets. This analysis is particularly relevant in understanding the complex interdependencies that shape global inflationary trends.

Chapter 4

This chapter explores the intricate causality relationship between inflation and interest rates, with a particular focus on the G20 countries. Using monthly data from 2000 to 2022 and employing advanced causality methods, including Fourier functions that account for structural breaks, the study finds a bidirectional causality between inflation and real interest rates in the G20. However, this relationship evolves when structural breaks are considered, highlighting the need for central banks to factor in these changing dynamics in their pursuit of price stability, especially in the face of rising global inflation.

Chapter 5

This chapter investigates the critical role of financial and human capital in driving industrial efficiency, income, and sustainability across leading industrialized nations, including Germany, China, and the United States. The study evaluates the economic impacts of financial and human capital policies, using panel data analysis from 2005 to 2021. It reveals that while the effects of these variables vary across countries, human capital consistently exerts a significant positive influence on industrial performance. This analysis underscores the importance of strategic investments in human and financial capital to sustain industrial competitiveness in the global market.

Chapter 6

The rapid expansion of university education in Türkiye since 2014 has not been matched by an increase in high-skilled job opportunities, leading to high unemployment among graduates. This chapter examines the disconnect between the skills provided by educational institutions and the demands of the job market, highlighting the need for a shift towards a quality-focused education that emphasizes practical skills. The study calls for stronger university-industry collaborations to enhance graduate employability and ensure that higher education contributes meaningfully to economic resilience and growth in Türkiye.

Chapter 7

Financial stability is a cornerstone of economic health, influenced by various macroeconomic variables. This chapter examines the relationship between financial stability and economic growth, interest rates, and inflation in OECD countries, using Z-scores as a measure of banking system stability. The study, based on data from 2000 to 2021, employs panel data analysis and the Dumitrescu and Hurlin causality test, revealing significant bidirectional causality between these macroeconomic variables and financial stability. These findings highlight the importance of robust macroeconomic policies in maintaining financial stability across OECD countries.

Chapter 8

As the world faces ecological and social challenges, there is a growing shift towards economic models that prioritize sustainability over continuous growth. This chapter explores the role of sustainable investment strategies, such as ESG (Environmental, Social, and Governance) and Impact Investment, in facilitating the transition to a post-growth era. It also examines emerging transformative investment frameworks designed to address the shortcomings of traditional investment models. The chapter argues that the financial sector has a crucial role in promoting sustainable and regenerative economic and social structures.

Chapter 9

This chapter investigates how corrupt governments manage fiscal policy during periods of fiscal consolidation. Using data from 18 OECD countries, the study finds that corrupt governments are more likely to raise indirect taxes rather than cut expenditures during fiscal adjustments. Additionally, they often succumb to political pressure by lowering corporate taxes and increasing social benefits during significant fiscal adjustments. These findings shed light on the interplay between corruption and fiscal policy, particularly in the context of economic crises and adjustments.

Chapter 10

This chapter reviews the dynamic relationship between economic development and finance, based on an analysis of 296 articles from the Web of Science and Scopus databases. The study identifies key themes and emerging research directions in this field, highlighting the increasing trend in scholarly interest after 2013. The findings offer new insights into how financial systems influence economic development, providing a foundation for future research and policy development aimed at fostering sustainable economic growth.

Chapter 11

This chapter focuses on the critical macroeconomic indices that influence the flow and supply of money in Türkiye's economy, particularly in the context of its ongoing economic challenges. Using data from 2005 to 2022, the study analyzes the relationship between these indices and the financial stability of Türkiye, with a specific focus on equity indices and exchange rates. The findings reveal significant correlations, offering insights into the economic dynamics that drive financial stability in Türkiye.

Chapter 12

Governance quality is a key determinant of economic development, as demonstrated in this chapter's analysis of 38 OECD countries. Using panel data from 2002 to 2021, the study examines the relationship between six governance indicators and GDP per capita, with inflation and real interest rates as control variables. The findings suggest that strong governance mechanisms, including political stability, regulatory quality, and accountability, are positively associated with economic development. These insights underscore the importance of good governance in fostering sustainable economic growth.

Chapter 13

This chapter explores the impact of trade and financial globalization on bilateral financial asset trade in Newly Industrialized Countries (NICs), using the financial gravity model and data from 2001 to 2022. The study finds that the openness of NICs' goods and capital markets significantly influences financial asset trade, although it has not yet reached the level of industrialized countries. These findings highlight the growing integration of NICs into the global financial system and the challenges they face in achieving full globalization.

Chapter 14

This chapter examines the factors contributing to uneven human development across OECD countries from 1995 to 2021. The study focuses on the impact of industrial structure, governance, and environmental degradation, while controlling for income inequality, trade openness, and unemployment. The findings reveal that high-technology manufacturing exports significantly enhance human development, while CO_2 emissions per capita negatively impact it. The chapter advocates for policies that promote high-tech industrialization, democratic governance, and environmental sustainability to achieve equitable human development.

Chapter 15

In the context of global climate change, this chapter examines Türkiye's sustainable finance practices and its alignment with international climate agreements. The study analyzes the integrated reports of Turkish banks that are members of the UN Global Compact, exploring their sustainability strategies and contributions to reducing carbon emissions. The findings highlight the importance of integrating

Environmental, Social, and Governance (ESG) criteria into investment processes to promote sustainable development and support Türkiye's climate goals.

Chapter 16

This chapter investigates the drivers of environmental degradation, focusing on the role of trade openness and democracy. Using spatial panel data models, the study reveals that while trade openness has positive direct effects on environmental degradation, there are significant negative spillover effects that mitigate these impacts. The findings suggest that environmental policies need to account for both the direct and indirect effects of trade and democracy on environmental outcomes, emphasizing the importance of sustainable trade practices.

Chapter 17

The relationship between industrial growth and environmental protection is explored in this chapter, which examines the potential duality between economic growth and environmental sustainability. The chapter argues that while economic growth can lead to environmental degradation, green industrial policies can mitigate these effects by promoting sustainable technologies and innovations. Recent evidence from developed countries suggests a decoupling between economic growth and emissions, driven by green industry policy measures. The chapter calls for the continued implementation of such policies to achieve both economic and environmental goals.

Chapter 18

This chapter focuses on the role of regional environmental policies in achieving global sustainability objectives. By examining case studies from both developed and developing countries, the study highlights the importance of international cooperation in addressing global environmental challenges. The findings suggest that regional policies, when effectively coordinated, can contribute significantly to global sustainability efforts, particularly in the areas of climate change mitigation and biodiversity conservation.

Chapter 19

This chapter explores the concept of Economic Policy Uncertainty (EPU) and its effects on global markets, particularly in the context of trade, investment, and financial stability. Using data from 1997 to 2022, the study analyzes the impact of EPU on both developed and emerging economies, revealing that heightened uncertainty can lead to significant volatility in financial markets and slow down economic growth. The chapter also discusses policy measures that can mitigate the adverse effects of EPU, emphasizing the importance of transparent and stable economic policies.

Chapter 20

This chapter examines the impact of the global energy transition on industrial competitiveness, particularly in energy-intensive industries. As countries shift towards renewable energy sources, there are significant implications for industries that rely heavily on fossil fuels. The study assesses the readiness of various industries to adapt to these changes, analyzing the potential costs and benefits of transitioning to cleaner energy. The chapter argues that while the energy transition poses challenges, it also presents opportunities for innovation and long-term competitiveness in a low-carbon economy.

Chapter 21

The final chapter focuses on the role of structural reforms in enhancing economic resilience in the aftermath of the COVID-19 pandemic. The pandemic exposed vulnerabilities in global supply chains, labor markets, and healthcare systems, prompting calls for comprehensive reforms. This chapter analyzes the effectiveness of various policy responses implemented during and after the pandemic, with a focus on labor market flexibility, healthcare reform, and digital transformation. The study concludes that countries that successfully implement structural reforms will be better positioned to recover and thrive in the post-pandemic global economy.

Moreover, this book serves as a timely call to action, advocating for a paradigm shift in economic governance and policy-making. It underscores the necessity of fostering synergies between macroeconomic stability and microeconomic dynamism, creating an environment conducive to innovation, entrepreneurship, and inclusive growth. Through a blend of theoretical insights and practical wisdom, it offers a roadmap for policymakers, businesses, and stakeholders to navigate the turbulent waters of economic transformation with resilience and foresight.

As we stand at the cusp of a new era defined by rapid technological advancements, geopolitical shifts, and environmental imperatives, *Macroeconomic Challenges to Structural Reform and Industrial Development* emerges as an indispensable compass, guiding us towards a future of sustainable prosperity and shared progress. It is not merely a book; it is a manifesto for change, a catalyst for innovation, and a beacon of hope in an ever-changing world of economic possibilities.

Editor

Oytun Meçik
Eskisehir Osmangazi University, Türkiye

Chapter 1
The Origins of Structural Reform:
Structural Adjustment, What and Where Did It Come From?

Sureyya Yigit
https://orcid.org/0000-0002-8025-5147
New Vision University, Georgia

ABSTRACT

The 1970s witnessed economic programs aimed to help governments refinance their debts owed to the American international banking system by ending the Bretton Woods system and the gold-dollar peg. These programs required debtor states to open up their markets and privatize state-owned companies, ultimately strengthening the power of international financial institutions and promoting a more neoliberal economic approach in many parts of the world. As part of these efforts, many laws restricting the private sector were repealed, government spending was curbed and refinanced through credit policy, trade restrictions were reduced, and the exchange rate was devalued. This period also saw the abolishment of collective labour rights, introducing or increasing subsidies for companies, and tax relief for these businesses with deregulated pricing policies. International financial institutions such as the World Bank and the International Monetary Fund advocated structural adjustment for developing countries to overcome economic distress. This chapter focuses on the origin of these policies.

DOI: 10.4018/979-8-3693-5508-4.ch001

INTRODUCTION

In the past half-century, around fifty countries, more than half of them in Africa, have implemented structural adjustment programs (SAP). However, although the term is used more and more frequently in Third World countries, associating it with debt strategy, it needs to be understood in all its dimensions. For example, denouncing structural adjustments – negative - social impacts is common without defining this beforehand. Likewise, the International Monetary Fund (IMF) and the World Bank (WB) are often presented as the main actors responsible for the increase in poverty globally, notably due to their role in the adjustment. However, this role is rarely explained and placed in a more global context. What is a structural adjustment, and what are its origins? What is it about? Why and what to adjust to? Who requires this adjustment? For what purposes? These are some of the questions one needs to answer in this chapter.

The strategic goals of the WB and IMF are set out in their Articles of Agreement. The IMF should mainly intervene to support short-term balance of payments imbalances and pursues precisely defined goals:

- restrict the money supply and thus reduce inflation;
- reduce government spending;
- increase exports and thus government revenues.

The IMF's decisions and programs not only have domestic political consequences for the countries taking out loans. They also have an important signalling function for other lenders, especially private commercial banks. For example, a country that does not sign the IMF's letter of intent will also have difficulty obtaining loans on the private capital market at all, or if it does, then only under harsh conditions. The financial situation of many developing countries is often so precarious that new loans are usually only granted with high interest rates and strict conditions. If a country in financial difficulties refuses to allow the IMF to impact its internal affairs, it can immediately be subject to sanctions, which can lead to the freezing of funds and even a trade boycott.

The World Bank was given the task of promoting long-term development projects through advice and technical support, for which it provides loans directly to the governments of its member countries. This originally intended division of tasks no longer exists in this form today. The IMF now grants longer-term loans, while the World Bank in turn also provides (short-term) balance of payments assistance. At the time the organizations were founded, two areas were in the foreground. Firstly, the reconstruction of Europe after the Second World War; the consolidation of the interests of the USA as an emerging economic and leading power of the western industrialized countries. The loan policy of the IMF and World Bank is still essentially based on the statutes from the 1940s, which largely reflect the interests of US post-war planning.

It was already clear during the planning phase that the desired capacities could not be achieved or maintained through private investment and consumption alone. It was assumed that considerable external subsidies, far beyond the capabilities of the private sector, would be necessary to maintain economic performance. The economic plan presented by the National Planning Association (NPA) in 1944 advocated an increase in state-supported foreign investment and justified this primarily with domestic political requirements on the part of the USA (Jones, 1972). The members of the NPA also concluded that private entrepreneurs did not have sufficient capital at their disposal to be able to maintain economic performance at a level anywhere near the high post-war level. The NPA therefore put forward a series of proposals on how private investment could be supported and the necessary securities guaranteed. Accordingly, the US government should primarily promote the establishment of the World Bank and the IMF, as well as secure private exports and foreign investments through sureties and security guarantees.

LITERATURE REVIEW

Sullivan and Hickel critically evaluate assertions positing that prior to the 19th century, approximately 90% of the global populace endured severe poverty, characterized by the lack of access to essential goods, and assert that the amelioration of global human welfare commenced only concomitant with the ascendancy of capitalism (Sullivan & Hickel,2023). These assertions rely heavily on national accounts and PPP exchange rates, which inadequately encapsulate shifts in individuals' access to essential goods. The authors cross-examine this narrative against extant data about three empirical benchmarks of human welfare: actual wages (about a basic sustenance basket), human stature, and mortality rates. They inquire into whether these benchmarks manifested improvement or regression with the rise of capitalism across five global regions - Europe, Latin America, sub-Saharan Africa, South Asia, and China – aligning with the chronology advanced by world systems theorists. The evidence assessed presents three conclusions:

1. The likelihood that 90% of the human population experienced severe poverty before the 19th century appears dubious. Historically, unskilled urban labourers in all regions commonly commanded wages of sufficient magnitude to sustain a family of four above the poverty threshold by working 250 days or 12 months

per annum, barring periods of profound societal upheaval, such as famines, conflicts and institutionalized dispossession – particularly under colonial rule.
2. The advent of capitalism precipitated a marked deterioration in human welfare. Across all scrutinized regions, integration into the capitalist global system correlated with descent in wages beneath subsistence levels, a regression in human physical stature, and a spike in premature mortality. Fundamental welfare indices have yet to recuperate in South Asia, sub-Saharan Africa, and Latin America.
3. In instances where advancement materialized, noteworthy enhancements in human welfare were inaugurated several centuries after the rise of capitalism. Progress was initiated within the core realms of Northwest Europe during the 1880s. By contrast, within the periphery and semi-periphery, progress commenced during the mid-20th century, a period typified by the ascent of anti-colonial and socialist political movements that redistributed incomes and established communal provisioning systems.

Reinsberg, Stubbs and Bujnoch assert that the IMF is renowned for its implementation of structural adjustment programs, which provide fresh credit to borrowing governments in exchange for market-liberalizing policy reforms and that while academic research has identified a causal relationship between structural adjustment and political instability, the precise mechanisms underlying this relationship remain understudied (Reinsberg, Stubbs & Bujnoch, 2023). It is generally acknowledged that IMF policy conditions precipitate material hardship, thereby inciting political instability. They propose an additional pathway, contending that instability is also driven by alienation effects stemming from the foreign imposition of policies. Through a rigorous analysis of data pertaining to up to 168 countries from 1980 to 2014, they conducted tests to ascertain the presence of both mechanisms. Their findings, which are the result of a comprehensive and meticulous research process, suggest that alienation effects persist, as evidenced by the inclination of IMF program participation to provoke protests, particularly in instances involving left-wing governments and non-repeat borrowers. Additionally, they identified evidence supporting hardship effects, as manifested by a positive association between the intensity of fiscal austerity measures and the frequency of protests. These findings held significant implications for the intersection of structural adjustment, contentious politics, and the role of international organizations in influencing domestic policy reform.

Malah Kuete and Asongu highlight the crucial role of infrastructure development in driving long-term and sustainable economic growth in African countries (Malah Kuete & Asongu, 2023). They specifically focus on the importance of infrastructure in reducing poverty, promoting employment, and facilitating structural change. Their paper aims to analyse the impact of infrastructure quality, with a particular emphasis on energy and information and communication technologies, on the growth of the manufacturing sector in 52 African countries from 2003 to 2018. Their study utilizes fixed effects models to ensure accurate analysis, and their results, which control for institutional dynamics and the natural resource curse hypothesis, emphasize the significant positive effect of infrastructure development on African structural change, particularly in energy and information and communication technologies. Their findings suggest important policy implications, such as the recommendation to establish partnership projects with developed countries to support industrialization.

In his analysis, Peters briefly explores three significant moments in contemporary neoliberalism: Milton Friedman's early statement, the Colloque Walter Lippman, and the Mt Perelin Society (Peters, 2023). His examination acknowledges the diverse institutional landscape and gives deeper insight into the early developments in political philosophy during the revival of liberalism following the perceived threat of fascist and communist forms of statism in the postwar context. Such a historical and political complexity is essential for revisiting questions about the origins of neoliberalism, which continue to be of enduring relevance even after the decline of neoliberalism. Peters believes that addressing these questions could lead to a revival of the tradition of state interventionism, offering a hopeful perspective for the future.

Boone and Wilse-Samson examined the sectoral labour reallocation and the reversal of urbanization during the Great Depression in the United States (Boone & Wilse-Samson, 2023). Their findings have significant implications, as they observed that a significant migration of individuals to farms occurred as a form of migratory insurance during the crisis, with a notable preference for farms characterized by low levels of mechanization. Conversely, the mechanized agricultural sector experienced a reduced workforce, leading to the relocation of numerous workers to low-productivity or subsistence farming. The abnormal restructuring of the labour market, influenced by macroeconomic fluctuations, disrupted the conventional process of structural change, wherein workers displaced by agricultural machinery typically transition to more productive occupations. This underscores the influential role of macroeconomic fluctuations in shaping the labour market outcomes of technological advancements.

International Organisations and Structural Adjustment

Reviewing official texts from the Organization for Economic Cooperation and Development (OECD), the IMF, and the World Bank, as well as the academic literature and works related to structural adjustment, convinces us that this vast and eminently complex question deserves to be explored in more depth in more than one aspect. Still, we will approach the content below with three complementary angles corresponding to this chapter's three main sections.

First, a historical overview is an essential step to grasping the logic of structural adjustment to better situate, in the following section, the strategic role of the IMF and the World Bank in an international system where the interdependence of OECD member countries prevails. The central focus point is the Third World. Above all, this reminder will be founded on the documents of the OECD, in which we find all -or almost all the main international institutions' main concepts and policy rationale.

The historical perspective also explains that structural adjustment has many dimensions. To adequately understand structural adjustment, it was appropriate to address the activities of the IMF simultaneously with the World Bank. According to such an approach, as the world is always evolving, we will situate the role of the IMF and the World Bank in context. This will also allow us to clarify concepts like stabilisation. During the 1980s, faced with the infernal cycle of debt, international lenders suddenly lost confidence and refused to fuel the flow of capital to indebted countries. This was followed by the massive intervention of multilateral financial organisations, led by the IMF and the World Bank, both lenders and guarantors of the world trade system, as we will see. This more recent period is the most fertile in reflections and developments, but it can only be understood with an overview of previous events and decisions.

Considering the structural adjustment and close connections with the country's debt strategy in development put forward in recent years, it is important to recall the various phases that have marked the global economic situation over the last three or four decades. At least, on this question of the economic environment, a consensus was agreed to. The OECD defined the first period, from 1940 to 1970, as the "Golden Age" (Glyn, Hughes, Lipietz & Sigh, 1988). After the post-war reconstruction phase, the question must be raised: Who favoured the launch of the trade liberalisation movement? The period in question witnessed a spectacular expansion of world trade. OECD member countries experienced surprisingly vigorous growth to the point where, by the late 1960s, this sustained expansion was taken for granted. The OECD partly explains this growth as the need to adapt to international competition and the high profits that it then appeared possible for this adaptation (Høj et al., 2007). The earnings of the highest productivity levels were achieved in the exporting sectors. Besides that, the work characterised by a low level of unemployment and fairly high internal and external mobility was auspicious, as their growth is sustainable in terms of their productivity and structural changes without clashes.

Obstacles began to arise when performance was at its best. From the end of the 1960s, the beneficial effects of economic performance began to fade, disappearing almost completely after 1973, the first turning point (Jiménez-Rodríguez & Sánchez, 2005). The analysis of this second period proves decisive for understanding the present period. According to the Organization, the weakening of inflation and the decline in the prices of energy products and raw materials traded on international markets have once again released a margin capable of increasing incomes and creating jobs. Rapid technological progress has opened the way to many new products and processes. At the same time, a decade of profound structural changes in the industry has made many companies more efficient. However, although uneven, the reaction of economies remained mediocre and far from corresponding to expectations.

The changes of the 1970s were part of macroeconomic origin. Stabilisation policies have given rise to successive waves of inflation and recessionary movements, creating market confusion. Convinced that politicians could effectively guarantee full employment, businesses and workers undoubtedly felt a feeling which slowed down their adaptation to new conditions and accentuated inflationary increases in wages and prices. It must also be said that governments and observers had remained excessively optimistic about the results expected from policies: strong pressures were exercised to continue increasing public expenditure (Joumard, Kongsrud, Nam & Price, 2004).

The OECD also saw obstacles to resuming economic growth in inadequate microeconomic policies. There was an obvious need for coherence between macro-economic and micro-economic policies: results obtained at the level of the former risk being compromised if governments allow micro-economic policies to contribute to preserve inefficient economic structures, hindering the play of market forces on which, to a large extent, the success of macroeconomic policy depends.

From the beginning of the 1970s, the dynamic of trade liberalisation initiated after the war was blunted. If the first oil shock of 1973 were related to the initial reduction in oil supplies and a subsequent quadrupling of oil prices, leading to a loss of real income, it would be linked to the deterioration of the terms of trade at the international level. In other words, the oil crisis came to amplify the inflationary pressures which already existed, which led to a severe recession in the industrial world, the consequences of which were damaging for the economies of developing countries, all the more so since the brutal increases and unprecedented global energy prices and other products of the base have occurred then that the international monetary system was strongly shaken (Vázquez-Fariñas, 2023).

According to the World Bank, it was easy to define to which corpus the theoretical underpinnings of the recommended reforms belong: these are divided, concretely, between the economic theory of well-being in partial equilibrium within the framework of dependent economy models and liberal political economy (Crawford, 2012). However, comparing these demonstrations with academic reference texts shows very clearly that:

Only part of the theories mentioned are used;

Only certain conclusions are retained;

There is constant recourse to empirical evidence and other practical considerations in deciding between various solutions. Hence, one cannot speak of theories underlying the recommended reforms but rather of a discussion which inspires economic policies. The discussions proposed by the Bretton Woods institutions are built around three more or less implicit principles:

i. The introduction of the liberal norm of the minimal state and, in particular, the free trade norm.
ii. The search for simplicity at all costs.
iii. The desire to circumscribe politics.

Focusing only on external liberalisation reforms, the most widespread measure of adjustment programs. However, other readings suggest that this point has general value. Contrary to what the World Bank literature suggests, there is not one economic theory but many of them; similarly, models do not provide one solution but an infinity of solutions, depending on the hypotheses and constraints chosen. It is even one of the popular criticisms against economists, who are accused of being able to say everything and its opposite. The discussion and debate on the political economy is normative and political since a national economy is a political space transformed by the state. Weber has demonstrated the dependence of knowledge, and therefore of analysis, of an object on the society in which it finds itself (Wallace, 1990). Knowledge of reality necessarily introduces values through indicators and analysis instruments. This banality is important to remember at a time when donors tend to want to impose their perception and their economic policy with arguments which are scientific and apolitical. However, the analysis of the texts and documents mentioned above highlights that the donors' views and arguments are highly normative (the standards chosen to be, unsurprisingly, free trade, the ideology of the minimal state and the absence of political and social considerations at the heart of economic analysis). At least four processes feed into this construction:

i. Choice of some models.
ii. Oversight some instructions for the selected models.
iii. The introduction of certain hypotheses is used to arrive at a unique solution.
iv. Rejection, explicit or not, of certain theories.

Oil Shocks

The second oil crisis in 1979 highlighted the constraints faced by the economy. However, in 1977-78, the OECD believed that a return to growth was possible, as indicated in the McCracken report (Keohane, 1978). A stricter attitude led to responsible monetary policies aimed at controlling inflation and reducing the gap between the effective progression of wages and their growth justified by the evolution of productivity. As inflation subsided, international policy inconsistency became more apparent, distorting competitive structures and introducing uncertainty. Exceptions to the rule of free trade, such as non-tariff barriers on imports from industrial countries, continued to grow. At the same time, governments introduced restrictive measures on internal markets, such as those affecting workforce reductions in large companies (Jackman, Pissarides & Savouri, 1990). In summary, changes in labour market microeconomic characteristics segmented employment opportunities and increased the difficulties for businesses in adjusting their workforce. Efficiency in resource use has been particularly evident in the public sector, directly and indirectly influencing the economy as a whole.

A reform program was implemented to enhance competition in product markets, improve the flexibility of factor markets, and enhance the efficiency of the public sector. It was necessary to alleviate the constraints that had hindered better performance and introduce more flexibility into all economic operations. The alternative was (and remains) the virtuous circle of macroeconomic stability and microeconomic flexibility or the vicious circle of instability and rigidity. The OECD guidelines for implementing positive adjustment policies, adopted in 1978, emphasised the need to avoid and gradually eliminate the use of internal measures likely to hinder or delay adaptation to lasting transformations in product and factor markets (Beroud, 2017). Rigidities in advanced industrial societies stemming from achieving legitimate social objectives and accumulating inefficiencies can impede growth and jeopardise their adaptability.

In 1982, the OECD reiterated the same elements but acknowledged even more explicitly the structural nature of the "deep and lasting crisis" (Rubenson, 2008). The approach recommended since 1978 has been to promote adjustment to new economic conditions while preserving the strengths of existing measures as much as possible to encourage labour and capital to move towards the most productive jobs. The issue is that one can no longer be clear about whether the goal is "economic efficiency," "non-inflationary growth," or "sustainability."

Need For Adjustment

In order to achieve sustainable and well-balanced growth in the global economy, it is essential for both OECD member countries and developing nations to work together. The OECD recognises that although competition from developing countries is not a major factor, their exports to OECD countries are crucial to them. It is also acknowledged that developing countries are particularly vulnerable to protectionist measures taken by industrialised nations (Wade, 2010). Consequently, policies for adjustment have become an important topic in the North-South dialogue, and it is important to consider the interests of developing countries in this regard.

Upon first reading, this may seem surprising if separated from the issue of debt and the ultimate goal: maintaining the good health of the international economic system, which relies on growth and economic sustainability. Notably, developing countries that are oil importers have been the most affected by economic shocks, and oil-dependent economies have suffered due to both their trade deterioration and the overall global economic changes. It has been observed that since the early 1980s, most countries have experienced persistent high inflation without any signs of improvement, declining growth rates, and increased external imbalances. These challenges, which have slowed economic growth, pose a risk to the necessary expansion of global trade, potentially steering the international economy towards another general recession. Many developing countries dealt with the aftermath of the disruptions of the first half of the 1970s: current account deficits have risen, which hindered international payments, particularly for oil-importing countries (Sachs, Cooper & Fischer, 1981). The Debtor countries' successful implementation of structural adjustment policies will play a crucial role. Increasing revenues from raw and processed products makes improving African countries' development prospects more feasible. However, this is contingent on the OECD countries maintaining a faster growth rate and being willing to open their markets. Therefore, effectively addressing the international debt problem requires us to consistently consider the essential connections between trade, financing, structural adjustment policies (by debtors and creditors), and development cooperation.

The IMF emphasises that trade liberalisation is essential for improving internal efficiency and creating a healthier global economic environment (Santos-Paulino, 2005). It is also a prerequisite for the success of structural adjustments. The IMF states that opening markets and accelerating growth rates in industrialised countries is necessary for the structural adjustments made by developing countries to have the desired positive effects (Summers & Pritchett, 1993). Therefore, the World Bank's and the IMF's actions towards developing countries are significantly influenced by the global economic environment, although there is room for improvement in their adaptability. One must define structural adjustment to understand the institution's interventions comprehensively.

During the early 1980s, numerous developed countries grappled with economic issues. These included an overabundance of demand, an excessive reliance on imports for consumption and investment, low export prices, high debts, a lack of economic efficiency, and an inadequate focus on exports. These factors culminated in chronic and severe deficits in the current account balances of several nations. According to the World Bank, two types of responses, known as adjustment, have been implemented: stabilisation (reducing spending to systematically adjust domestic demand at a lower level of external resources) and structural adjustment - making changes in relative prices and institutions to increase economic efficiency, flexibility, and the ability to utilise resources for sustainable long-term growth (Hermes & Schilder, 1997).

While external borrowing can be a means to finance deficits, it may not necessarily address the root cause. This approach can lead to deferred tough decisions, perpetuating a lifestyle beyond means and exacerbating fundamental imbalances. However, external borrowing can facilitate the necessary structural changes for economic growth. As key players, the World Bank and the IMF have attached conditions to structural adjustment loans to ensure their utilisation. The ongoing discussions revolved around the resolution of these imbalances through structural adjustments.

Defining the adjustment structure in the context of stabilisation is a complex task. These two terms are increasingly used interchangeably, reflecting a shift in the discourse, particularly within the International Monetary Fund. This change resulted from the growing convergence in the roles of the IMF and the World Bank. Furthermore, since 1980, the IMF has been replacing stabilisation with adjustment, particularly as it directed its loans and activities towards developing countries (LDCs) significantly impacted by the deteriorating global economic conditions.

In the 1970s, stabilisation programs were financial programs countries requested funding from the IMF and committed to implementing. At that time, adjustment was the international process of offsetting surplus and deficit balances of the balance of payments, notably due to the rise in oil prices and the financial flows which were the counterpart thereof (Tandon, 1986). However, the IMF's stabilisation programs have expanded and begun to be designated as adjustment programs. This change is not trivial. By designating them under this term, the IMF has thus agreed to place its policies in a longer-term perspective, as claimed elsewhere by developing countries. It is no longer just a matter of adjusting balances of payments to each other but "of adjusting the countries themselves, their policies and their social structures to a global context that, by definition, they do not control." The adjustment has also become "national".

The IMF explained structural adjustment as a response to the realisation that traditional macroeconomic management tools such as budgetary, monetary, and income policies had not effectively maintained non-inflationary economic growth and full employment in the 1980s (Levitt, 1992). As a result, economic managers sought to improve their country's economic performance in the medium term by using these traditional macroeconomic policy instruments from a medium-term perspective and enhancing overall economic operations. It underscored the significance of taking a long-term approach to economic progress, highlighting the crucial role of production capacity and the importance of implementing measures to enhance production potential and improve the adaptability of factor and goods markets.

As per the IMF, structural measures can be classified into two categories. The first category includes measures that optimise resource utilisation, allowing for swift adjustment to technological advancements, fluctuations in relative prices, and the opening up of foreign trade (Logan & Mengisteab, 1993). This also encompasses measures that aim to eliminate barriers to labour mobility. The second category focuses on initiatives that aim to bolster production potential by creating additional productive resources (such as capital and labour) and enhancing overall productivity (Vreeland, 2002).

The concept described here, similar to the perspective of the OECD, is complex. This term more explicitly indicates that IMF stabilisation programs often require significant shifts in the economy's trajectory and sectoral and institutional priorities. This change in discussion and perception reflects the complexity and depth of the global disorder, which demands our utmost attention and understanding.

The World Bank's perspective aligns more closely with the traditional definition when distinguishing between structural adjustment and macroeconomic stabilisation. The former aims to address immediate problems that require intervention, such as inflation, depletion of exchange rate reserves, capital flight, and serious current account deficits. On the other hand, structural adjustment aims to eliminate obstacles to future growth, such as distortions in production incentives (e.g., overvalued real exchange rates), price controls, interest and credit rate controls, high customs duties, import restrictions, and excessive subsidies.

According to the World Bank, structural adjustment is rarely as urgent as emergency interventions, as its effects are less visible and more gradual (Heinrich, 1985). However, this does not diminish the importance of economic restructuring. It necessitates long-term planning and a strategic approach. Key elements of such restructuring include tax system reform, financial sector reform, and the regulatory framework for economic activities, all crucial for an economy's long-term stability and growth.

The two concepts have different objectives and methods, but they are complementary. This complementarity is due to the close collaboration between the Bank and the Fund, which has made it difficult to distinguish between the two institutions. They agree with the perspective that the economic shocks of the past two decades have forced them to significantly change their programs and approaches, leading to an overlap in their responsibilities. The World Bank presents a more comprehensive definition of adjustment, which includes policies aimed at changing internal and external balances and changes in the structure of instigators and institutions (Corbo & Fischer, 1992). This "elastic" definition encompasses stabilisation, which emphasises changes in internal and external balances, and structural adjustment, which emphasises changes in the structure of instigators and institutions.

According to this definition, stabilisation and structural adjustment coexist, with the IMF supporting stabilisation programs and the World Bank supporting structural adjustment (Rodrik, 1990). The World Bank's structural adjustment programs have two key components. The first aspect is primarily macroeconomic, with a rapid impact on the balance of payments in the context of IMF stabilisation programs. The second aspect is microeconomics, which aims to adjust the economic structure to enhance efficiency. The World Bank's loans for adjustment specifically target structural and sectoral adjustment.

In brief, an institution with a developmental focus, such as the World Bank, inherently adopts a long-term approach. Despite contentions by various authors regarding the increasing convergence of activities between these two institutions, leading to ambiguity, one can maintain that they diverge fundamentally in their method of assisting others, highlighting the primary challenge faced by the World Bank as the perpetually unfilled financial gap between the Fund's available finances and the Bank's required finances. This constitutes the principal problem for the Bank, a complex issue that requires careful consideration and innovative solutions.

The criticism against the IMF's SAPs is growing increasingly vehement. Detractors argue that the reduction in public spending proposed by SAPs results in declining health and education standards (Mlambo, (1995). They argue that SAPs focus on promoting economic growth through imports, often neglecting the country's internal needs. As a result, SAPs are believed to have largely negative social effects and exacerbate poverty. Critics emphasise the need for SAPs to consider the unique social and political contexts of the countries they affect.

The IMF recommends compensatory measures to soften the impact of economic adjustments on particularly vulnerable social groups (Goldstein, Geithner, Keating & Park, 2003). On the other hand, the World Bank, which claims poverty reduction as its primary focus, established a committee on poverty reduction in 1988 and dedicated its 1990 World Development Report to this theme (Crawford & Abdulai, 2009). Both institutions acknowledge the significant risk that many poor people face due to economic adjustments, particularly in Africa, where evidence confirms the severity of poverty. However, the Bank argues that ongoing economic adjustments are necessary.

There needs to be more understanding of the overall impact of economic adjustment programs on poverty, largely due to the challenge of separating the effects of a recession caused by external factors from those resulting from policies and programs designed to address them. Nonetheless, past experiences have demonstrated that failure to adjust is likely to harm individuals with low incomes, and a systematic adjustment process is deemed crucial for long-term improvement in their situation.

The IMF and the World Bank acknowledge the importance of a favourable economic environment for the success of adjustment programs. However, they do not consider it the sole condition for success. Sub-Saharan Africa is an example of the World Bank's emphasis on internal factors in implementing adjustment programs and explaining the region's challenging situation. The Bank's publications rightly point out that countries that react quickly, such as Indonesia, tend to fare better (Ravallion & Huppi, 1991). They also suggest that developing countries can significantly influence their economic outlook, especially in public finances, regardless of the international economic environment.

In sub-Saharan Africa, studies conducted by the Bank show that the countries (such as Burundi, Congo, Malawi, Niger, and Nigeria) that have implemented vigorous adjustment and economic reform programs are displaying some signs of recovery, despite the numerous difficulties experienced in the region (Noorbakhsh & Paloni, 2001). The region must adapt its economy to external and unfavourable factors at a pace aligned with other developing countries. Accordingly, the crisis in Africa can only be partially attributed to an adverse international economic climate or low prices of primary products. They assert that endogenous factors, such as strong and accelerating demographic growth in sub-Saharan Africa, have played a significant role. Additionally, challenging conditions such as high infant mortality and low literacy rates make it even more difficult to achieve structural adjustment through economic reforms. The region's structural economic problems, including institutional weaknesses, have hindered its ability to adapt to external factors. The mixed assessment from the two multilateral institutions shows how fragile the argument for market liberalisation can be. While the World Bank, IMF, and OECD still see market liberalisation as desirable in the long term, the challenge lies in determining the right pace and steps for this process.

There is a widely known argument that liberalising market forces is the best way to address the major imbalances and structural problems in the international economy that emerged in the early 1980s (Edwards, 1997). This argument is based on the historical success of the 'newly industrialised countries', particularly those in East Asia, such as Korea, Taiwan, South Korea, Singapore, and Hong Kong. It is argued that the economic policies recommended by the IMF and the World Bank are applicable and have been proven successful by these countries.

The Bank acknowledges that its adjustment programs differ from the experiences of Asian countries, where the state has played a pivotal role in guiding, developing, and safeguarding industrial strategy (Edwards, 1997). However, criticisms persist on this matter. One may censure the IMF and the Bank for their attempt to apply the unique Asian model to Africa, particularly by basing comparative advantage on products that have little long-term effects. This raises a significant question about the effectiveness of SAPs that promote exporting products with limited future potential, such as cocoa and peanuts.

It is hard not to question SAP's blind faith in the global economy, especially in the context of Africa. This is due to these countries' unfavourable external conditions and the failure of GATT negotiations on agriculture. Even the IMF expresses concern about environmental degradation and the growing dependence of developing countries (Girdner & Siddiqui, 2008). It is evident that while the IMF and the World Bank acknowledge the significance of external factors in theory, internal factors still exert the most significant influence on a country's growth or lack thereof. Surprisingly, the performance indicators used to evaluate the SAPs must consider the country's domestic social situation. They do not factor in indicators such as public health, education levels, or income distribution. This disregard for social factors impedes the potential for more equitable income distribution in developing countries and poses a barrier to growth. The focus on monetary policies and institutional aspects overlooks the substantial impact of robust social and domestic policies and geopolitical interests within countries. This narrow focus on growth, primarily defined by exchange rates, credit availability, tax policies, and export prices, neglects crucial social and geopolitical factors.

The proposed economic growth in the SAP framework is not related to development. When organisations or researchers criticise SAPs, it is essentially a clash of two development models. The OECD emphasised the importance of the support of social groups for the success of adjustment measures (Kalisch, Aman & Buchele, 1998). The IMF and the World Bank also significantly influence this success. Surprisingly, these institutions refuse to consider the type of political regime, claiming it would be internal interference. However, with increasing pressure for respect for human rights, they will have to change their approach at some point. Furthermore, have they started doing so concerning SAPs and poverty?

Intervention

The World Bank's interventions have brought about significant economic changes and marked a crucial shift in Africa's economic history. This shift underscores that the implications of liberalisation reforms are more than just economic; they are deeply social and political. The World Bank's lack of comprehension of the unique nature of African states and politics has played a significant role in this shift. It is important to note that the nature of the state in Africa is a well-documented item in international discussion. However, it is widely accepted within the African community that the state is not 'imported'. However, it has had historical development in Africa, even in unique and original forms, with the formation process continuing today, particularly through crises and wars (Cohen, 1984). The lack of awareness of these debates and studies has significant implications for the political economy. In the process of state formation in Africa, the political class sees any opportunity as valuable, which plays a pivotal role in shaping the political landscape.

In essence, the formation of the state and the national economy are closely connected. Pursuing economic, financial, political, or social resources is essential when everything is negotiated, and conflicts are ongoing. This environment is characterised by another layer to the "politics of the stomach", extending beyond mere enrichment and corruption. Recent instability stemming from independence, economic crises, and, in some cases, war or increased violence has strengthened long-term trends towards the proliferation of social and economic networks and various affiliations. In this context, enhancing one's ability to participate, influence negotiations, and compromise is more important, mobilising potential supporters rather than obtaining immediately profitable and inflexible resources. Therefore, acquiring wealth depends less on cumulative accumulation and more on a "compositional" mode, accumulating different values in different registers, ultimately favouring human capital accumulation, as only humans can transcend the different value registers.

What matters for elites is not the accumulation of physical wealth (economic and financial) but rather the control of social and political capital. Factional struggles reflect this: the lack of homogeneity in the "rhizome state" and the fragmentation of power is revealed through conflicts, negotiations, and compromises over opportunities for gaining wealth and sources of wealth (Baker, 2015). This is evident in struggles over privatising public companies or marketing boards, efforts to combat smuggling or corruption, and socio-political conflicts, as seen in Liberia, Sierra Leone, Somalia, and Zaire (Reno, 2000).

The liberalisation reforms can only be understood within the context of the specificity of the liberalisation, which explains the need for compliance with models and the socio-political significance of the reforms in sub-Saharan Africa. The changes in economic policy promoted by the World Bank call into question not just the economic mechanisms, modes of production, or the quality of the state's economic interventions but also the conditions in which the search for resources—economic, financial, political, and social—takes place. Privatisations are not just a shift in management methods from "economic nationalism" to exploitative privatisation opportunities, but also a shift in the methods of the "looting economy" (from siphoning public resources by the elites to sharing the national cake through the purchase or participation in private companies by these same elites). Trade liberalisation is not just a shift in development strategy from import-substitution to export-driven development but also a change in the modalities of accessing liberalisation (from protected rents such as licenses, quotas, and currency restrictions under public monopolies to annuities of trade liberalisation: control of private monopolies or oligopolies, access to "informal" networks, and access to credit).

Given the unique nature of the state and politics in Africa, economic reforms have a greater impact on the liberalisation of political factors than economic effects. Liberalisation functions as a mechanism for social transformation by altering access to resources. Amid economic and particularly political crises, liberalisation frequently leads to exclusion. Despite their good intentions, the World Bank's actions have unintended consequences. Even if unintentional, involvement in the political sphere often ends up supporting the current structures and institutions, thereby preserving the power of elites and governments. This unintended support reinforces the state's 'informal' and underground aspects, a key point to consider in our analysis.

The introduction of political economy into the economic teachings and the push to end the African exception by promoting "economic rationality" acknowledges the importance of politics in Africa. Reforms and political conditions related to good governance are part of a project to minimise political influence and prioritise the economy. However, the focus on issues such as rents, corruption, and separating the state from the market is ineffective and insufficient because it overlooks the underlying depth of socio-political conflicts, the impact of social structures on different economic sectors, the political influence on economic activities, and the socio-political reasoning behind economic policies.

When donors act without understanding the environment they are operating in, such as conflicts in social policies, the social organisation of economic sectors, and political influences, they may not realise the true effects of their actions (Yigit, 2024b). Inadvertently, they influence politics and involve themselves in local dynamics, especially if their behaviour is easily understood. Each donor follows their logic, which may differ from their African partners, leading to biased perceptions. As a result, the misunderstandings arising from this are often only relevant to actors already well-integrated into the African socio-political context. Therefore, purely technical measures aimed at combating customs fraud, such as computerisation, administrative restructuring, and private surveillance companies, have proven ineffective in addressing the social and political factors that underlie this issue.

These technical measures favour the most capable actors who understand new methods of accumulating wealth, wielding political influence, and shifting fraudulent techniques. This can include displacing the under-invoicing of "purchase" by customs officers with similar actions involving suppliers abroad, targeting repression towards smaller competitors or political rivals, delaying the implementation of new laws, or exploiting regional agreements in an abusive manner (Ayogu, 2021).

Implementing these intentionally apolitical reforms unintentionally strengthens the position of the economic elites. The repression and denouncement of practices central to the political sphere lead those in power to shift their accumulation strategies towards more covert methods. Liberalisation and privatisation reforms end up favouring clandestine networks and power structures (Hibou, 2016). In the current political landscape, these groups are the only ones capable of navigating the spaces between political demands and economic constraints. In contrast to the 1960s and 1970s, where accumulation involved public job distribution, obtaining privileges, and benefiting from advantages such as import licenses or preferential access to currencies, these activities now tend to occur at the edge of legality: through protection or access to informal trade, control of criminal activities, control of violence for economic gain, and the proliferation of frauds and scams.

The World Bank's role is paradoxical: it implements reforming actions and supports the existing elites, whose management it criticises. This duality contributes to the erosion of traditional material bases of government and its capacity to implement reforms and inadvertently pushes economic activities towards illegality. These ambiguities resonate with the concerns raised by the rulers of North Africa on the eve of colonisation, underscoring the intricate nature of the issue. The economic teachings have played a significant role in delegitimising and privatising the government's mode of operation. The World Bank's focus on results rather than the methods used to achieve them has led to unintended outcomes. Prioritising objectives such as more market - less state and reforms at all costs over the means to achieve them represents a major shortcoming (Reisman, 1991). The World Bank and other donors have shown a high tolerance for African countries' methods to liberalise and privatise. They believe that the concentration of wealth and the rise of an entrepreneurial bourgeoisie would promote the emergence of capitalism. However, this approach has resulted in unintended consequences, particularly in African countries, that require attention.

In the African context, it is clear that there can be socio-political consequences from the particular methods used to implement reforms. These consequences can arise from neglecting the role of public policies and economic behaviour in forming the state, underestimating the administration's weakness and sometimes its decline, and not addressing the deficiencies of African taxation from a broader perspective. Also, by solely focusing on the economic performance of privatised companies, the World Bank may inadvertently contribute to two concerning movements in the region: the loss of legitimacy of public authorities, if not its disappearance, and the privatisation of the state and modes of government. This is an urgent issue that requires immediate attention. The loss of legitimacy of public authorities is primarily an internal process. However, donors contribute involuntarily in at least four ways.

First, the World Bank is increasingly involved in defining economic policies and the modalities of state action through its expertise and conditionalities. Its intrusion into the shaping of public finances, the design of public services, and the definition of public sectors is a fundamentally political act.

Secondly, the World Bank contributes to the fragmentation of state decision-making centres with other donors, which affects the administration's effectiveness and legitimacy. Furthermore, by reinforcing the fragmentation of the administration, the World Bank contributes to restricting centralised policy power.

Thirdly, implementing "good governance," accountability, and institutionalisation of the government often has negative effects. The World Bank considers these concepts as instruments for delegitimising the state.

Fourthly, the World Bank's influence is more persuasive in the short term than in the long term, particularly regarding economic reforms. This leads to "good" management practices taking precedence over archaic and corrupt methods.

The influence and instrumentalisation of external organisations are limited in their effectiveness. On the one hand, some interventions contribute to the informal strengthening of existing regimes, which are often illegitimate. On the other hand, the World Bank's actions weaken public administration through the adoption of liberal and anti-statist norms, neglect of the majority of the administration in favour of small cells working with external experts, and the proliferation of reforms that cannot be effectively implemented. Additionally, the external legitimacy of the government, compared to its internal legitimacy, is particularly harmful. Rulers tend to prioritise the financial demands of international donors over the economic and political demands of citizens, leading to concerns about external respectability and neglect of internal legitimacy, especially during economic crises.

The political consequences of a reversal of legitimacy are very important. When external legitimacy is primarily economic and financial, it reduces the importance of seeking political and social legitimacy. This external focus accelerates the decline of the legitimacy of public authorities. This reaction is not unique to Africa, as it has also been replicated in Eastern Europe (Andreev, 2008). Such examples demonstrate how building political and economic societies on an inverted pyramid of legitimacy (where economic actors are more legitimate than economic institutions and the latter are more legitimate than political institutions) has damaging consequences for democratisation.

The fragmentation and loss of legitimacy of power are not isolated occurrences but rather global phenomena that drive the privatisation of the sovereign functions of the state and modes of government. This process, which has extended beyond the classic transfer of public companies' operations to private interests, now takes on more diffuse forms. These include the private appropriation of natural and economic resources in general, privatisation of development, and privatisation of sovereign functions, including coercion control.

The significant role of private interests characterises the nature of these different processes. Regardless of the policymaking scale, these interests are the same in all sectors. This shift towards deregulation policy, away from economic deregulation, is a common thread. These changes contribute to a significant shift in governance, with a growing influence of private interests closely connected to power. These interests are often hidden and involved in parallel and sometimes criminal economies, leading to the development of indirect, fragmented, and focused private governance.

The process of privatisation mainly involves the transfer of economic resources from public to private ownership. This transfer is becoming increasingly common in African countries, often due to pressure from donors and the influence of certain elites. Some privatisations represent a genuine shift in economic management, especially when the buyers are foreign. However, many privatisations are driven by political motives beyond personal enrichment. They are used as a power tool, both directly and indirectly (such as through tacit agreements with foreign buyers and local elites). Apart from the formal privatisation of public companies, there are also unofficial and often secretive forms of privatisation involving the illegal appropriation of natural resources such as wood, precious stones, oil, mines, ivory, and wildlife, as well as theft of land, art objects, and economic exploitation (Schoneveld & Zoomers, 2015).

Resources are appropriated through power and violence to benefit the main political actors, especially members of secret power structures who lead the parallel economy. Additionally, development is privatised. In this scenario, external funding is monopolised and used for economic and political purposes; elites or certain political factions privatise these development projects for their benefit.

Privatising sovereign functions of the state, such as customs, has become a growing concern. The World Bank has been promoting the delegation of customs operations to private foreign organisations, akin to the system of rents in the Ancien Régime (Parthiban, Murali & Subramanian, 2020). Despite customs revenue constituting a significant portion of tax revenue in African countries, privatisation has not led to a significant increase in revenue. Furthermore, the private companies taking on these public services become entangled in the socio-political dynamics of the countries in which they operate. Additionally, these delegations can inadvertently encourage unregulated privatisations. The essential element of taxation, which plays a central role in defining political power and the formation of the state, is left at the mercy of local leaders, influential figures in power, and even private companies.

For example, in Cameroon, public services are increasingly managed by private individuals rather than civil servants (Warai, 2021). This is evident when citizens have to pay for forms or stamps, civil servants have to pay to receive their salaries, or ministers have to use their budgets to cover expenses. This trend reflects a shift from mere corruption to privatising public services. Similarly, private companies are taking the initiative to build roads in neglected regions, further blurring the principle of the monopoly of public services. The violation of this principle is also seen in the rise of private militias, security services, and surveillance companies, as well as the emergence of a "mercenary market" that exploits violence for political and economic gains (Rosky, 2003). These trends are not only observed in countries at war but are also becoming prevalent in other contexts.

Privatising the state and economic governance are specific features of the subcontinent. It represents a new stage in the ongoing process of state formation. This trend reflects a reduced socio-political space and increased political control of economic society. Furthermore, there is a deepening of the indirect government mode due to the administrative system's disintegration. Additionally, society is experiencing greater fragmentation alongside increased political control of wealth, leading to a rise in violence, particularly for economic gain.

The prevailing economic crisis, escalating political volatility, and the escalating material requisites necessary for the sustenance of the ruling class have prompted established authorities to seize dominion over specific sectors of the national economy. Consequently, resources are being redirected to encircle a significantly smaller political nucleus. Against the backdrop of interconnected networks and politico-economic strife, the clash between the ongoing political restructuring—marked by the pursuit of authority over dwindling resources—and the economic constraints resultant from liberalisation and diminished public interventions actively facilitates the course of privatisation (Van de Walle, 1989).

The reconfiguration of power within the new global context manifests through novel modalities and iterations, echoing historical legacies of indirect governance, the strategic use of coercion for economic ends, and the significance of covert influences. Once again, the international banking sector emerges as a central protagonist in this transformative process. Notably, in nations like Cameroon, a climate of arbitrary governance prevails alongside continual negotiations involving key contributors and select holders of public authority, including the head of state and his close associates, albeit within private realms across all the mentioned countries (Njoh, 2015). Indigenous actors further distort advocated measures by international entities, employing tactics such as engaging non-governmental organisations, advocating for decentralisation, enlisting private oversight entities, prioritising fiscal aspects, and advocating for the elimination of public entities and interventions, in addition to clamping down on confluence between public and private sectors. Assimilation of beliefs, such as positivist apoliticism, simplicity, adherence to a simplistic liberal standard, and notably, tolerance for specific methodologies, provided they advance reforms, significantly contribute to this paradigm shift.

CONCLUSION

The 1997 World Development Report marked a significant shift in the World Bank's thinking. After focusing on human capital in the sixties and seventies and economic policies in the eighties, the report emphasised the role of institutions, particularly the state. The report discusses what the state should prioritise and how it should operate globally (Wade, 2003). One needs to query whether the World Bank's arguments have changed and if the characteristics ascribed to it (minimal state intervention, pursuit of simplicity at all costs, and avoidance of politics) are still relevant today. Given the crucial role of state ignorance in creating problems, are these issues more than remnants of a bygone era?

The 1997 Report acknowledges the importance of the state and the challenges posed by its collapse rather than focusing solely on the problems caused by excessive state intervention. The report admits to needing a more complex view of the state's role in implementing reforms and acknowledges the limitations of technical support, particularly in administration. Importantly, it recognises that donors may have contributed to the institutional deterioration of countries, especially by exacerbating the fragmentation of central power.

The World Bank has published an insightful analysis of the situation in Africa, providing a more accurate depiction than previous documents (Harrison, 2005). Their report sheds light on the alarming increase in crime, escalating violence driven by economic motives, and the unfortunate collapse of a significant number of African states. It emphasises the adverse effects of the state's inability to safeguard property rights, ensure judicial fairness, and uphold stable governance. Additionally, the analysis recognises corruption's varying impact and prevalence across different regions. This fresh perspective in the World Bank's viewpoint showcases its ability to acknowledge and integrate constructive criticism.

This suggests that the World Bank has long been developing good governance, capacity building, and civil society analyses, particularly in Africa (Yigit, 2024). Their publications expand and systematise these themes, extending their application to other continents. However, it does not represent a fundamental departure from the Bank's established ideological framework. Historically, the core principles that have underpinned the Bank's arguments and views persist, albeit articulated in a modified fashion. Notably, the analysis of behaviours continues to exhibit a deterministic and culturalist orientation, treating "culture" as a static and singular entity, as evidenced by its treatment of ethnic groups. Furthermore, the portrayal of civil society as distinct from the state endures despite acknowledging certain shortcomings through the activities of non-governmental organisations.

The World Bank's approach to countries undergoing reform, particularly African nations, needs more clarity as it overlooks the analysis of the underlying mechanisms generating these results (Yigit, 2024a). Rather than understanding the root causes, the Bank views these issues as dysfunctional symptoms. Accordingly, the crisis is often attributed solely to the state's incapacity and inefficiency, which is more of a description than an explanation. The World Bank's worldview needs to better engage in the discussion on the nature and functioning of the state, and it must be better equipped to integrate socio-political data, the involvement of various actors, and the numerous overlapping practices into its analysis of the state's role in the economy. The principle of being apolitical is even more evident in these analyses than in reports on economic policies.

Although the role of policies and social factors in the economic performance of countries is acknowledged, political and economic analyses remain separate. The principle of recommended economic policies such as liberalisation and privatisation is not questioned, even if it is recognised that the advantages of the Asian privatisation strategy cannot be extended to other developing countries, especially in Africa. Politics is consistently approached in a technical and deterministic manner. Once a country is classified as a "low-capacity state," the World Bank asserts what that country should and should not do; it sets priorities and defines the functions of the state (Rajagopalan & Tabarrok, 2021). The interference of the World Bank in the sovereignty of the state is evident, and its consequences in terms of the centrality of power and, most importantly, the inversion of the hierarchy of legitimacy seem likely to remain relevant today.

The pivotal year of 1997 mirrored the shift towards good governance in the late eighties. Although the discussions and debates evolved, the fundamental philosophy and goals remained unchanged. The transformation of government practices, characterised by the privatisation of state functions and the transfer of responsibilities from public authorities to state interests, was the outcome of various complex issues: escalating economic crises, administrative decline, political instability, social fragmentation, and a concerted effort by a select few to control economic resources. In this light, the influence of the World Bank and other donors may seem insignificant as historical patterns resurface exploiting economic dependence for internal political control, resorting to violence for political and economic gain, and organising society around illicit economies.

REFERENCES

Andreev, S. (2008). Corruption, legitimacy and the quality of democracy in Central and Eastern Europe and Latin America. *Review of Sociology*, 14(2), 93–115. DOI: 10.1556/RevSoc.14.2008.2.4

Ayogu, M. D. (2021). Challenges for Governance. On the Trail of Capital Flight from Africa: The Takers and the Enablers, 193.

Baker, J. (2015). The rhizome state: Democratizing Indonesia's off-budget economy. *Critical Asian Studies*, 47(2), 309–336. DOI: 10.1080/14672715.2015.1041282

Beroud, S. (2017). "Positive Adjustments": The Emergence of Supply-Side Economics in the OECD and G7, 1970–1984. *The OECD and the International Political Economy Since*, 1948, 233–258. DOI: 10.1007/978-3-319-60243-1_10

Boone, C. D., & Wilse-Samson, L. (2023). Structural change and internal labor migration: Evidence from the great depression. *The Review of Economics and Statistics*, 105(4), 962–981. DOI: 10.1162/rest_a_01116

Cohen, R. (1984). Warfare and state formation: Wars make states and states make wars. Warfare, culture, and environment, 329-358.

Corbo, V., & Fischer, S. (1992). Adjustment programmes and World Bank support: rationale and main results. In *Development Finance and Policy Reform: Essays in the Theory and Practice of Conditionality in Less Developed Countries* (pp. 157–175). Palgrave Macmillan UK. DOI: 10.1007/978-1-349-22219-3_8

Crawford, G. (2012). The World Bank and good governance: rethinking the state or consolidating neo-liberalism? In *The IMF, World Bank and policy reform* (pp. 109–134). Routledge.

Crawford, G., & Abdulai, A. G. (2009). The World Bank and Ghana's Poverty Reduction Strategies: Strengthening the State or Consolidating Neoliberalism? *Labour Capital and Society. Travail Capital et Société*, 82–115.

Di Maio, M. (2009). Industrial policies in developing countries: history and perspectives. Industrial policy and development, 13, 107-143.

Edwards, S. (1997). Trade liberalization reforms and the World Bank. *The American Economic Review*, 87(2), 43–48.

Girdner, E. J., & Siddiqui, K. (2008). Neoliberal globalization, poverty creation and environmental degradation in developing countries. *International Journal of Environment and Development*, 5(1), 1–27.

Glyn, A., Hughes, A., Lipietz, A., & Sigh, A. (1988). The rise and fall of the golden age.

Goldstein, M., Geithner, T. F., Keating, P., & Park, Y. C. (2003). IMF structural programs. In *Economic and financial crises in emerging market economies* (pp. 363–458). University of Chicago Press. DOI: 10.7208/chicago/9780226241104.003.0006

Harrison, G. (2005). The World Bank, governance and theories of political action in Africa. *British Journal of Politics and International Relations*, 7(2), 240–260. DOI: 10.1111/j.1467-856X.2005.00175.x

Heinrich, T. J. (1985). Adjustment or Structural Change in Crisis Management Policy of Tanzania. Verfassung und Recht in Übersee/Law and Politics in Africa, Asia and Latin America, 195-207.

Hermes, N., & Schilder, A. (1997). Setting priorities: The IMF and World Bank and structural adjustment programmes. In *Public priority setting: Rules and costs* (pp. 39–60). Springer Netherlands. DOI: 10.1007/978-94-009-1487-2_3

Hibou, B. (2016). The 'privatization' of the state: North Africa in comparative perspective. In *The Dynamics of States* (pp. 81–106). Routledge.

Høj, J., Jimenez, M., Maher, M., Nicoletti, G., & Wise, M. (2007). Product market competition in the OECD countries: Taking stock and moving forward.

Jackman, R., Pissarides, C., Savouri, S., Kapteyn, A., & Lambert, J.-P. (1990). Labour market policies and unemployment in the OECD. *Economic Policy*, 5(11), 449–490. DOI: 10.2307/1344483

Jiménez-Rodríguez, R., & Sánchez, M. (2005). Oil price shocks and real GDP growth: empirical evidence for some OECD countries. Applied economics, 37(2), 201-228.

Jones, B. L. (1972). The role of Keynesians in wartime policy and postwar planning, 1940-1946. *The American Economic Review*, 62(1/2), 125–133.

Joumard, I., Kongsrud, P. M., Nam, Y. S., & Price, R. (2004). Enhancing the effectiveness of public spending: experience in OECD countries.

Kalisch, D. W., Aman, T., & Buchele, L. A. (1998). Social and health policies in OECD countries: a survey of current programmes and recent developments.

Keohane, R. O. (1978). Economics, inflation, and the role of the state: Political implications of the McCracken Report. *World Politics*, 31(1), 108–128. DOI: 10.2307/2009969

Levitt, K. P. (1992). IMF Structural Adjustment: Short-Term Gain for Long-Term Pain? *Economic and Political Weekly*, •••, 97–102.

Logan, I. B., & Mengisteab, K. (1993). IMF-World Bank adjustment and structural transformation in sub-Saharan Africa. *Economic Geography*, 69(1), 1–24. DOI: 10.2307/143887

Malah Kuete, Y. F., & Asongu, S. A. (2023). Infrastructure development as a prerequisite for structural change in Africa. *Journal of the Knowledge Economy*, 14(2), 1386–1412. DOI: 10.1007/s13132-022-00989-w

Mlambo, A. S. (1995). Towards an analysis of IMF structural adjustment programmes in Sub-Saharan Africa (SSA): The case of Zimbabwe 1990-94. *Africa Development. Afrique et Developpement*, 77–98.

Njoh, A. J. (2015). The meta indigenous politico-administrative system, good governance, and the modern republican state in Cameroon. *Journal of Asian and African Studies*, 50(3), 305–324. DOI: 10.1177/0021909614528772

Noorbakhsh, F., & Paloni, A. (2001). Structural adjustment and growth in sub-Saharan Africa: The importance of complying with conditionality. *Economic Development and Cultural Change*, 49(3), 479–509. DOI: 10.1086/452512

Parthiban, M. M., Murali, T. S., & Subramanian, G. K. (2020). World Customs Organisation and Global Trade: Imprints and Future Paradigms. *World Customs Journal*, 14(2), 157–176. DOI: 10.55596/001c.116425

Peters, M. A. (2023). The early origins of neoliberalism: Colloque Walter Lippman (1938) and the Mt Perelin Society (1947). *Educational Philosophy and Theory*, 55(14), 1574–1581. DOI: 10.1080/00131857.2021.1951704

Rajagopalan, S., & Tabarrok, A. (2021). Simple rules for the developing world. *European Journal of Law and Economics*, 52(2), 341–362. DOI: 10.1007/s10657-021-09716-3

Ravallion, M., & Huppi, M. (1991). Measuring changes in poverty: A methodological case study of Indonesia during an adjustment period. *The World Bank Economic Review*, 5(1), 57–82. DOI: 10.1093/wber/5.1.57

Reinsberg, B., Stubbs, T., & Bujnoch, L. (2023). Structural adjustment, alienation, and mass protest. *Social Science Research*, 109, 102777. DOI: 10.1016/j.ssresearch.2022.102777 PMID: 36470630

Reisman, K. (1991). The World Bank and the IMF: At the Forefront of World Transformation. *Fordham Law Review*, S349, 60.

Reno, W. (2000). Clandestine economies, violence and states in Africa. *Journal of International Affairs*, 433–459.

Rodrik, D. (1990). How should structural adjustment programs be designed? *World Development*, 18(7), 933–947. DOI: 10.1016/0305-750X(90)90077-B

Rosky, C. J. (2003). Force, inc.: The privatization of punishment, policing, and military force in liberal states. *Connecticut Law Review*, 36, 879.

Rubenson, K. (2008). OECD education policies and world hegemony. The OECD and transnational governance, 242-259.

Sachs, J. D., Cooper, R. N., & Fischer, S. (1981). The current account and macroeconomic adjustment in the 1970s. *Brookings Papers on Economic Activity*, 1981(1), 201–282. DOI: 10.2307/2534399

Santos-Paulino, A. U. (2005). Trade liberalisation and economic performance: Theory and evidence for developing countries. *World Economy*, 28(6), 783–821. DOI: 10.1111/j.1467-9701.2005.00707.x

Schoneveld, G., & Zoomers, A. (2015). Natural resource privatisation in Sub-Saharan Africa and the challenges for inclusive green growth. *International Development Planning Review*, 37(1), 95–118. DOI: 10.3828/idpr.2015.10

Sullivan, D., & Hickel, J. (2023). Capitalism and extreme poverty: A global analysis of real wages, human height, and mortality since the long 16th century. *World Development*, 161, 106026. DOI: 10.1016/j.worlddev.2022.106026

Summers, L. H., & Pritchett, L. H. (1993). The structural-adjustment debate. *The American Economic Review*, 83(2), 383–389.

Tandon, R. (1986). Balance-of-Payments Adjustment and Financing in Developing Countries: Scenarios for the 1980s. *Foreign Trade Review*, 21(2), 193–204. DOI: 10.1177/0015732515860209

Van de Walle, N. (1989). Privatization in developing countries: A review of the issues. *World Development*, 17(5), 601–615. DOI: 10.1016/0305-750X(89)90062-4

Vázquez-Fariñas, M. (2023). Major economic recessions in the last quarter of the 20th century: The oil crisis (1973–1980). In *The Age of Global Economic Crises* (pp. 56–81). Routledge. DOI: 10.4324/9781003388128-3

Vreeland, J. R. (2002). The effect of IMF programs on labor. *World Development*, 30(1), 121–139. DOI: 10.1016/S0305-750X(01)00101-2

Wade, R. (2010). After the Crisis: Industrial policy and the developmental state in low-income countries. *Global Policy*, 1(2), 150–161. DOI: 10.1111/j.1758-5899.2010.00036.x

Wade, R. H. (2003). What strategies are viable for developing countries today? The World Trade Organization and the shrinking of 'development space'. *Review of International Political Economy*, 10(4), 621–644. DOI: 10.1080/09692290310001601902

Wallace, W. L. (1990). Rationality, human nature, and society in Weber's theory. *Theory and Society*, 19(2), 199–223. DOI: 10.1007/BF00137258

Warai, M. T. (2021). Informal Practices in Public Administrations in Cameroon. *Journal of Public Administration and Governance*, 11(1), 65–84. DOI: 10.5296/jpag.v11i1.17986

Yigit, S. (2024). Pan-African Unity, in 3. INTERNATIONAL CANKAYA SCIENTIFIC STUDIES CONGRESS February 28-29, 2024 / Ankara-TÜRKİYE, THE PROCEEDINGS BOOK, EDITOR Prof. Dr. Gökhan ACAR, IKSAD Publications, Issued: 15.03.2024 ISBN: 978-625-8254-35-8, p.108-124.

Yigit, S. (2024a). States, Sustainable Development, and Multilateral Environmental Agreements. In Ordóñez de Pablos, P. (Ed.), *Digital Technologies for a Resource Efficient Economy* (pp. 88–106). IGI Global., DOI: 10.4018/979-8-3693-2750-0.ch005

Yigit, S. (2024b). Water as Life for Susceptible Sustainability and Dithering Development. In Baporikar, N. (Ed.), *Infrastructure Development Strategies for Empowerment and Inclusion* (pp. 409–431). IGI Global., DOI: 10.4018/979-8-3693-2917-7.ch019

ADDITIONAL READINGS

Bayliss, K., & Cramer, C. (2023). Privatisation and the post-Washington consensus: Between the lab and the real world? In *Development Policy in the Twenty-First Century* (pp. 52–79). Routledge. DOI: 10.4324/9781003419563-3

Francis, A. (2023). The concept of competitiveness. In *The competitiveness of european industry* (pp. 5–20). Routledge. DOI: 10.4324/9781003369820-2

Harsono, I., Indrapraja, R., Kusnadi, I. H., & Rohman, S. (2024). Application of Dynamic Structural Model to Identify Factors That Influence Capital Adjustments in The National Manufacturing Industry. Jurnal Informasi Dan Teknologi, 29-33.

Niu, Y., Wang, S., Wen, W., & Li, S. (2023). Does digital transformation speed up dynamic capital structure adjustment? Evidence from China. [Opoku-Mensah, E., Chen, W., Tuffour, P., Agozie, D. Q., Gyamfi, B. A., & Mahmoud, A. Toward sustainable energy transition: Unveiling the synergies of democracy, energy justice, and structural adjustment on emissions in West Africa. Sustainable Development.]. *Pacific-Basin Finance Journal*, 79, 102016. DOI: 10.1016/j.pacfin.2023.102016

Rietveld, P., & Shefer, D. (Eds.). (2024). *Regional development in an age of structural economic change*. Routledge.

KEY TERMS AND DEFINITIONS

Bretton Woods System: The Bretton Woods Agreement resulted from global cooperation involving representatives from 44 nations. It established a system for creating fixed currency exchange rates using gold as the universal standard and led to the formation of the IMF and the World Bank. Although the fixed currency exchange rate system eventually failed, it provided much-needed stability when it was created. The Bretton Woods System provided the necessary framework for creating fixed international currency exchange rates, with the newly formed IMF being entrusted with determining the fixed exchange rate for currencies worldwide.

External Borrowing: A country's gross external debt is the total amount it owes to foreign creditors, including the government, corporations, and citizens. Net external debt is calculated by subtracting any external assets as debt instruments from the gross external debt.

Free Trade: A type of trade relationship between countries, the main barrier to free trade being tariffs, which are taxes people must pay when importing goods into another country. Free trade involves flowing goods and services across national borders without being hindered by laws, tariffs, quotas, or other restrictions.

Good Governance: Good governance has eight important characteristics. It involves people's participation, building agreement, being accountable and open, and being responsive, effective, and fair. It also follows the law. Good governance helps reduce corruption, considers the opinions of minorities, and hears the voices of society's most vulnerable people. It also responds to society's current and future needs.

International Organisations: Usually refer to international governmental organisations or organisations with a universal membership of sovereign states. Due to their universal membership, international organisations differ from similar institutions that are open only to member states from a particular region.

Minimal State: A minimal state is a government with a very limited role in the lives of its citizens. Its main job is to protect individuals from force, fraud, and theft and ensure contracts between individuals are followed. Proponents argue against government involvement in the economy, the lives of its citizens, and providing social services, believing the only legitimate role of government is to protect individual rights, such as the rights to life, liberty, and property.

Privatisation: The government's process of selling off industries, companies, or services to private investors. The fundamental change in this process is the transfer of ownership and control from the government to the private sector.

Structural Adjustment: Set of measures implemented by the International Monetary Fund and the World Bank in loans to Third World countries. These policies focus on three main components: stabilisation, which involves controlling inflation by limiting the increase of the money supply through the budget deficit; liberalisation, which aims to reduce government intervention in product and factor markets to bring domestic prices more in line with world prices; and privatisation of public-sector institutions to improve the technical efficiency of production. In the short term, these policies have caused negative distributive effects due to high prices and increased unemployment, with inconsistent long-term impacts.

Washington Consensus: A set of economic policies promoting free trade, changing exchange rates, a free market, and macroeconomic stability. Renowned economists and international organisations such as the IMF, the European Union, the United States, and the World Bank support it. In 1989, economist John Williamson introduced the term "Washington Consensus" to explain the policies that gained support from Latin American policymakers in response to macroeconomic difficulties and debt crises in the early to mid-1980s, with the backing of the IMF, the World Bank, and the US Treasury.

Chapter 2
Unlocking Potential:
Overcoming Structural Reform Roadblocks in International Economic Governance

Özden Sevgi Akıncı
https://orcid.org/0000-0002-9250-4446
Independent Researcher, Turkey

ABSTRACT

Focusing on the International Monetary Fund, the study underscores the profound impact of the international institutions on the global economy and the interconnected nature of their operations. It emphasizes overcoming common barriers to reform, such as disparities in representation and decision-making power, to promote more inclusive and effective governance. Reform of the international institutions is essential to prevent or mitigate global crises and to promote equitable and sustainable development worldwide. A comprehensive literature review was conducted, followed by data interpretation through visual analysis, observation, and evaluation. The findings were subjected to an assessment, after which recommendations were presented. The study concludes with a call for structural reforms to enhance the resilience, responsiveness, and fair distribution of electoral power. This would facilitate effective structural reforms and promote sustainable economic development.

INTRODUCTION

The International Monetary Fund (IMF) has long been a central pillar in the global economic architecture, with a mandate to promote international monetary cooperation and ensure financial stability. However, over the decades, the IMF's role has under-

DOI: 10.4018/979-8-3693-5508-4.ch002

gone a significant transformation, giving rise to critical discourse surrounding its efficacy and the necessity for substantial reforms. A review of the literature reveals a consensus among scholars and policymakers on the necessity of comprehensive reforms within the IMF. Notable critiques include Stiglitz's (2010) advocacy for deep structural changes, Helleiner's (2011) call for more inclusive governance, and Truman's (2010) emphasis on enhanced surveillance and expanded functions for the IMF. These critiques identify systemic deficiencies that impede the institution's capacity to effectively safeguard global financial stability and address contemporary economic challenges. As a consequence of the increasing interconnectedness of the global economy, the governance structures of the IMF have been subjected to intensifying scrutiny. The historical legacies of colonialism and imperialism have exerted a profound influence on the current governance framework, resulting in the disproportionate representation of certain countries and the inadequate inclusivity of developing nations. This imbalance has given rise to debates concerning the legitimacy of the IMF's decision-making processes, particularly in the context of its interventions in economically distressed countries.

This study aims to contribute to the ongoing discourse surrounding the IMF's governance structure by providing a detailed analysis of the current issues and proposing actionable reforms. To this end, a comprehensive literature review was conducted, and methods such as visual analysis, observation, and evaluation were employed. The study identified key areas where the IMF's governance structure can be improved. The findings highlight the necessity of reallocating quotas, increasing basic votes, and establishing group voting systems to enhance the representation and decision-making power of developing countries. These recommendations are essential for aligning the IMF's governance practices with the evolving economic realities of the 21st century, ensuring that it can effectively support the diverse needs of its member countries.

Furthermore, the study examines how past financial crises, including the East Asian Crisis and the 2007-2009 Global Financial Crisis, have illustrated the limitations of the IMF's traditional methodologies. These crises underscored the need for a more agile and flexible IMF, equipped to tackle the unique challenges posed by member countries in an increasingly volatile global economy. In addition, the study will present a succinct examination of particular case studies for Argentina and Türkiye, elucidating the triumphs and shortcomings of IMF programs and reinforcing the case for comprehensive governance reforms.

Although the study proposes specific reforms designed to enhance transparency, inclusivity, and equitable representation within the IMF, it also acknowledges the significant challenges to implementing these reforms. The study identifies three significant obstacles to implementing the proposed reforms: political resistance, institutional inertia, and the complexities of achieving consensus among member countries. Overcoming these governance challenges would enhance the IMF's legitimacy and credibility as a global financial institution, enabling it to play a more effective role in promoting international economic cooperation, stability, and development. This would contribute to a welfare-oriented global economy.

1. THE IMF'S INADEQUACIES IN PREVENTING CRISES AND THE NEED FOR REFORM

The following literature review critically examines the IMF's surveillance practices, shedding light on prevalent critiques and proposals for reform. From Stiglitz's (2010) advocacy for comprehensive structural changes to empirical analyses revealing disparities in governance, the review underscores the urgent need for a more inclusive and effective IMF. Through a thorough exploration of scholarly discourse, this review aims to stimulate discussions aimed at enhancing global financial governance.

1.1 Critical Views in the Literature

The IMF's surveillance practices have been the subject of numerous critiques in the literature, which underscore systemic weaknesses that impede the institution's effectiveness in safeguarding global financial stability. Stiglitz (2010), in "The Stiglitz Report," advocates for comprehensive reform of the IMF, arguing that deep structural changes are necessary to better address the challenges of the global economic and financial architecture. He critiques the IMF's policies, particularly in the wake of financial crises, and calls for a new approach to ensure greater stability.

Helleiner (2011) and Obstfeld (2013) both emphasize the need for reforms in global financial governance, focusing on more inclusive and representative governance structures within the IMF to better reflect shifting global economic power dynamics. Helleiner highlights the importance of adapting IMF governance to these changes, while Obstfeld argues for enhancing the IMF's crisis prevention and management tools to improve global economic stability.

Other scholars, such as Irwin (2011) and Acemoğlu (2005), bring historical and institutional perspectives to the discussion. Irwin draws lessons from the IMF's past policies, suggesting that structural reforms are essential to address contemporary economic challenges, while Acemoğlu's analysis implies that effective economic outcomes are closely linked to the nature of political institutions and governance structures, including those of the IMF.

Rodrik (2014) advocates for a reorientation of global economic governance, proposing that the IMF move away from promoting uniform economic models towards developing more context-specific and adaptable policy frameworks. This approach, he argues, would more effectively address the distinctive needs of different countries. Similarly, Gabor (2016) critiques the IMF's surveillance practices for failing to translate critical theoretical insights, such as the role of global banks as "super-spreaders" of systemic risk, into practical policy advice at the country level. Vines and Gilbert (2004) add to this critique by suggesting that the IMF's interventions may inadvertently encourage countries to take greater risks, thereby exacerbating financial vulnerabilities.

Given these critiques, scholars have increasingly called for structural reforms within the IMF to address underlying governance issues. Truman (2010) underscores the pivotal role of Asian leaders in facilitating economic recovery and advocates for substantial reforms within the IMF, including expanded functions as a lender of last resort and enhanced surveillance measures. His recommendations also include comprehensive prequalification for IMF assistance, increased financial resources, and reforms to IMF quotas and executive board representation, all aimed at enhancing global economic governance and promoting more equitable international financial cooperation.

Eichengreen and Woods (2016) highlight the limitations of the IMF's perceived competence and impartiality, attributing these shortcomings to failures in surveillance, conditionality, debt management, and governance. They argue that these limitations undermine the IMF's effectiveness and credibility, necessitating significant reforms. Similarly, Gola and Spadafora (2009) point out persistent gaps in the IMF's Financial Sector Surveillance (FSS), particularly in its ability to address risks within advanced economies.

A critical aspect of governance reform within the IMF is the distribution of voting rights, which currently disproportionately favors advanced economies. Empirical studies, such as those by Dreher and Jensen (2007), support the argument for governance reforms within international financial institutions (IFIs). They analyze the impact of U.S. interests on IMF conditions, highlighting the undue influence of powerful member states on IMF decision-making processes. These scholars suggest that reforms should aim to mitigate this influence, fostering greater equity and transparency in IMF governance.

Bird and Rowlands (2002) discuss potential options for the future of the IMF, emphasizing the need for a restructuring of its governance mechanisms to enhance representation from developing countries. Such restructuring would ensure a fairer distribution of voting rights and decision-making authority, aligning the IMF more closely with the economic realities of its diverse membership.

Oatley (2011) and Woods (2006) offer comprehensive analyses of international institutions like the IMF, contributing both theoretical insights and empirical evidence to the discourse on governance issues. They advocate for reforms that promote greater accountability, transparency, and inclusivity within the IMF, enabling it to better address the diverse needs and concerns of its member countries.

While criticisms of IMF surveillance practices are well-founded, addressing underlying governance issues, particularly regarding voting distribution, is essential for enhancing the institution's effectiveness and reliability. By embracing structural changes that empower developing countries and better align voting rights with economic realities, the IMF can strengthen its legitimacy and credibility as a global financial institution.

1.2 Case Studies: Argentina and Türkiye

This section provides an overview of IMF interventions in Argentina and Türkiye, emphasizing the necessity for reforms. The 2001 crisis in Argentina and the economic issues in Türkiye in the late 1990s demonstrate the shortcomings of a one-size-fits-all IMF policy and the value of more flexible strategies.

Argentina represents a pivotal case study for elucidating the consequences of IMF involvement. The country's 2001 economic crisis constituted one of the most severe financial collapses in modern history, and the IMF's involvement was both substantial and controversial. The IMF provided substantial financial assistance to Argentina, but the associated conditionality policies—which focused on fiscal austerity, privatization, and labor market reforms—had mixed outcomes (Nemiña, 2013). While these policies were designed to stabilize the economy, they also resulted in significant social unrest, accompanied by rising unemployment and poverty levels (Cooper, 2002). The inflexible implementation of IMF conditionality, without sufficient consideration of the socio-economic circumstances on the ground, intensified the crisis rather than resolving it (Daseking et al., 2005). This event significantly undermined Argentina's economy and strained its relationship with the IMF for years to come (Setser & Gelpern, 2006).

The Argentine case highlights the necessity for comprehensive reforms within the IMF's governance structures. As observed by scholars such as Stiglitz (2010) and Helleiner (2011), and other academics referenced above, there is a growing consensus that the IMF must adopt a more context-sensitive and adaptable approach, aligning its policies with the specific needs of member countries. The case of Argentina illustrates the potential negative consequences of the IMF's current governance structures, which often favor uniform policy prescriptions. This example supports the argument for reforms that would enable the IMF to implement more inclusive and flexible policies, thereby enhancing its ability to safeguard global financial stability.

Similarly, Türkiye provides an illustrative case of IMF intervention, particularly during the financial crises of the late 1990s and early 2000s. In response to the 2000-2001 financial crisis, the International Monetary Fund (IMF) implemented a series of structural adjustment programs in Türkiye. These programs placed an emphasis on fiscal discipline, privatization, and structural reforms designed to stabilize the economy (Miller, 2006). In the short term, Türkiye experienced economic stabilization, with inflation rates declining and the fiscal deficit being brought under control. However, the long-term impacts of the IMF's intervention were more complex. The stringent austerity measures contributed to social and economic difficulties, including increased unemployment and income inequality (Öniş, 2009).

The experience of Turkiye serves to illustrate the potential drawbacks of a one-size-fits-all approach to economic stabilization. The lack of flexibility in IMF policies and the emphasis on uniform economic models failed to fully account for Türkiye's unique economic and social context (Ghoshal, 2006). This case study underscores the necessity for reforms within the IMF's governance structure that would facilitate the development of more nuanced and context-specific policy frameworks. Such reforms are vital for the IMF to more effectively address the distinctive requirements of disparate countries and to more effectively promote global economic stability (Lipscy & Lee, 2018).

The case studies presented here illustrate the vital necessity for reforming the IMF's governance structures in order to enhance the institution's adaptability and inclusivity. By addressing the systemic weaknesses identified in these examples, the IMF can enhance its effectiveness in managing global financial stability and better serve the diverse needs of its member countries.

1.3 The Impact of Global Economic Crises and the Unlearned Lessons

The global health crisis caused by the novel coronavirus (COVID-19) has served as a stark reminder to nations around the world that the challenges facing humanity cannot be solved by individual countries acting in isolation. This is a lesson that was also learned during the 2007-2009 global financial crisis (OECD, 2020).

Prior to the global financial crisis, significant shortcomings were evident in the structures of international financial supervision, including those of the IMF. Despite its mandate to oversee global financial stability, the IMF was unable to anticipate the full range of vulnerabilities that ultimately led to the financial catastrophe. This deficiency underscores the necessity for substantial governance reforms within the IMF to enhance its effectiveness. The reform of the international monetary system is intrinsically linked to broader changes in the global financial architecture, with the objective of better intercepting and managing future crises (Obstfeld & Rogoff, 2010).

1.3.1 The East Asian Crisis: International Institutional Failure

The East Asian Crisis, which originated in Thailand in July 1997, precipitated a global financial collapse, resulting in substantial capital outflows and a financial cost of $260 billion in the initial year alone, equating to the annual income of sub-Saharan Africa (Ongun, 2012). The crisis revealed the shortcomings of international institutions, particularly the IMF's inability to anticipate the crisis and its post-crisis policies, which were criticized for failing to consider country-specific conditions. This resulted in a significant loss of credibility (Çelik, 2007).

The Asian financial crisis originated from a combination of flawed financial strategies and the disproportionate responses of overseas creditors to transient imbalances in global liquidity. Rather than being driven by deep-rooted structural issues or excessive debt, the crisis initially manifested as a liquidity squeeze, which subsequently cascaded into insolvencies due to ill-judged interventions, notably those by the IMF (Akyüz, 2017).

Joseph Stiglitz, then Vice President of the World Bank, criticized IMF policies and advocated for the "Post-Washington Consensus," emphasizing the need for long-term development strategies, locally owned reforms, and market interventions to address failures. He stressed the importance of institutional frameworks, social norms, and power dynamics in implementing liberalization and privatization measures (Ongun, 2012).

As a result, in the wake of the crisis, the efficacy and legality of IFIs came under scrutiny, prompting calls for the establishment of a novel global organization as an alternative to the IMF. In response, the IMF adopted a strategy centered on the prevention of future crises through the provision of long-term credits to support the growth of healthy economies.

1.3.2 2007-2009 Crisis: IMF Failures and Reform Calls

Critics argue, as evidenced by the literature review, that the IMF's surveillance mechanisms and economic models failed to anticipate the risks accumulating in the global financial system, particularly within the US financial sector. These criticisms draw on insights from various financial crises and the IMF's responses to them. The 2007-2009 Global Financial Crisis starkly exposed significant shortcomings in the IMF's crisis prevention and management capabilities, notably in developed economies such as the US financial sector. This period underscored the imperative for substantial reforms within the IMF.

The global financial crisis, originating in the United States, revealed notable deficiencies in the IMF's ability to foresee and prevent major financial disruptions (Griesgraber, 2009). Moreover, the crisis highlighted significant weaknesses in financial risk management and regulation in advanced economies, emphasizing the urgent need for reforms in global financial regulatory frameworks. This necessitated increased collaboration among IFIs, including the IMF and the Financial Stability Board (Knight, 2015).

The crisis underscored the necessity for governance reforms within the IMF to enhance its legitimacy and effectiveness. This included calls for more representative quota and voting systems to reflect the changing economic weights in the global economy (Cooper, 2009). The IMF faced significant pressure to reform its surveillance processes and improve its crisis management capabilities. This involved developing new financial instruments and providing more flexible and substantial financial support to crisis-hit countries (Moschella, 2012).

In response to these mounting pressures, the IMF implemented a series of operational changes following the crisis. These changes included the revision of its lending instruments and the augmentation of its financial resources. The reforms were designed to enhance the IMF's capacity to address future crises and to improve its crisis response mechanisms (Schinasi & Truman, 2010).

1.3.3 Recession Persists: Amid Promised Reform

In the wake of financial crises, as was the case following the 2007-2009 crisis, there has consistently been a consensus on the necessity to adapt the international monetary system and governance to the evolving realities. However, despite initial indications of recovery, enthusiasm for reforms has abruptly declined. Unfortunately, with the advent of the next crisis, the world has once again mobilized. Consequently, the consequences of the crisis itself have tended to become more severe, and the challenges in front of reforms have become much more complex (Mminele, 2015).

Similarly, despite the IMF's commitments to reform following the 2007-2009 global financial crisis, the institution's obstacles to implementing substantial changes in governance, policy flexibility, and structural reforms have hindered its effectiveness in addressing the ongoing global recession.

Although the crisis heightened awareness of the necessity for reforms, changes in IMF governance have been limited (Bird & Rowlands, 2010). The 2010 Quota and Governance Reform aimed to enhance the voice of emerging markets and developing countries, yet the results fell short of expectations. The reforms did not sufficiently alter the power dynamics within the IMF, leaving major decisions still heavily influenced by advanced economies (Lesage et al., 2013). The subsequent modifications were similarly inadequate to alter the fundamental configuration of the electoral system and the way decisions are reached.

The IMF continued to promote conventional policy targets such as low inflation and fiscal consolidation, often at the cost of inducing recessions in borrowing countries. This was despite some initial moves towards more flexible approaches to crisis management. The adherence to these traditional policies limited the effectiveness of IMF interventions in fostering sustainable economic recovery (Broome, 2010).

The IMF's efforts to reform its lending and surveillance practices were insufficient to address the deep-seated issues revealed by the crisis. The financial system's instability and the IMF's limited capacity to manage systemic risks persisted, making it difficult to prevent or mitigate the effects of ongoing economic downturns (Akyüz, 2006).

The IMF's operations continued to be influenced by political considerations, leading to asymmetrical treatment of member countries. Politically influential countries received more favorable terms, which contributed to moral hazard and reduced the credibility of IMF conditionality. This imbalance undermined the effectiveness of IMF policies in promoting stable economic environments (Lipscy & Lee, 2019).

The structural reforms needed to address long-term economic weaknesses were not fully implemented. The IMF's focus remained on short-term stabilization rather than long-term structural changes, which are essential for sustained economic growth and recovery. This lack of deeper reform limited the IMF's ability to support countries in overcoming the persistent recession (Bird, 2000).

2. IMPORTANCE OF DECISION-MAKING IN KEY ISSUES

Daniel Mminele, who was Deputy Governor of the South African Reserve Bank at the time, discusses significant governance issues in the IMF from an academic standpoint. Even though BRICS countries represent approximately a quarter of the global economy and population, their collective voting power within the IMF remains relatively modest, at around 10% (following the 2014 reforms, it was around 14%). Moreover, 53 Central African countries, which comprise 25% of IMF members, hold only two seats on the 24-member IMF Executive Board. This underscores the inadequacy of the system to adapt to global changes. In essence, Mminele argues that without reforms, efforts to address global imbalances and enhance resilience against future crises will be ineffective, thereby hindering efforts for sustainable growth (Mminele, 2015).

As argued in their study by Bordo & Eichengreen (2015), it is challenging to envision the IMF assuming a more prominent global role without substantial governance reform. The United States must determine whether it desires and possesses the capacity (not merely financial capability but also competence) to act as a global crisis manager, or whether it prefers this responsibility to be entrusted to a relevant multilateral institution.

2.1 The Significance of Fair Voting Distribution

The current voting distribution in the IMF has the effect of exacerbating inequalities among member countries, particularly disadvantaging developing nations. The United States' veto power and the influential positions of major economies serve to illustrate a system that is skewed towards the interests of powerful nations. This imbalance results in a lack of representation for the least developed and developing economies in crucial decision-making processes within the IMF, perpetuating a cycle where their voices are often marginalized in shaping global economic policies. The participation of developing countries in the decision-making processes of IFIs, such as the IMF, is significant for a number of reasons.

2.1.1 Representation and Fairness

It can be argued that ensuring that developing countries have a voice in the IMF will lead to more equitable policies and decisions that better reflect their needs and circumstances. Research indicates that fair representation enhances the legitimacy and acceptance of IMF policies among member countries (Woods & Lombardi, 2006).

2.1.2 Policy Relevance

The participation of developing countries in decision-making processes is associated with the formulation of policies that are more likely to be relevant and effective in addressing their unique economic conditions. This inclusivity can result in the design of more tailored and impactful financial assistance programs (Bird, 1996).

2.1.3 Economic Stability

Greater involvement of developing countries in the IMF can lead to improved global economic stability. By addressing the specific challenges and vulnerabilities of developing economies, the IMF can implement measures that prevent financial crises from spreading and affecting global markets (Rapkin & Strand, 2005).

2.1.4 Capacity Building

Participating in IMF decision-making processes helps build the institutional and financial capacities of developing countries. This involvement fosters better governance and stronger economic frameworks within these nations, contributing to their long-term development (Muhumed & Gaas, 2016).

2.1.5 Addressing Inequalities

IMF programs have often been criticized for favoring developed nations, but increased participation from developing countries can help address these inequalities. This shift can lead to more balanced and fair economic policies globally (Jain & Gupta, 2018).

2.2 Current Voting Distribution and Power Asymmetry

The current voting distribution in the IMF perpetuates power asymmetries that favor developed countries, particularly the United States and European nations, while marginalizing developing and least developed countries. This imbalance impedes the IMF's capacity to create fair and effective policies that address the needs of all member states.

2.2.1 Dominant Positions of Large Economies

The quotas at the IMF, which determine the contributions and voting power of member states, are a source of contention. The United States, with approximately a 17% voting share, exerts significant control due to its veto power, which necessitates an 85% supermajority for major decisions. This enables the United States to unilaterally block any reforms or decisions requiring such a majority, thereby undermining the collective decision-making process (Lesage et al., 2015). But China, the second-largest economy, seeks more influence. The last major quota adjustment, agreed in 2010 and ratified in 2016, shifted significant voting power from the U.S. and Europe to China, now the third-largest IMF shareholder. Given the continued growth of China, India, Brazil, and other emerging markets, there is pressure for further adjustments (IMF, 2022a, 2022b, 2022c).

As is the case with all quota reforms, a significant number of crucial votes requiring 85% of the vote have thus far been dominated by US domestic politics, resulting in lengthy delays in the implementation of the regulations. In particular, the US has consistently opposed quota reviews, upgrades, and allocations. Of particular note are the seventh, eighth, and ninth quota increases and reforms, which occurred concurrently with US elections or were made a domestic political issue. These reforms were long awaited by the international community, including the United Nations, and were ultimately decided upon by the US Congress (Boughton, 2001).

Large economies like those in Europe are overrepresented in the IMF's Executive Board. This overrepresentation skews decision-making in favor of developed countries, leaving developing nations with less influence (Lipscy & Lee, 2019). However, every quota review faces a stalemate requiring high-level political concessions. This deadlock impacts the IMF's ability to assist distressed countries, potentially pushing more nations towards Chinese loans. Additionally, it reduces pressure on borrowing countries to implement policy reforms for sustainable recovery and stability, as China's lending conditions are less transparent than the IMF's.

2.2.2 Implications for Global Economic Cooperation

The BRICS acronym, representing Brazil, Russia, India, China, and South Africa, was established in 2009. It encompasses a population of 3.27 billion people, constituting approximately 41.13% of the global population. China and India, as the world's most populous nations, jointly dominate BRICS with an 87% share of its population. At the 15th summit, BRICS members agreed to extend invitations to six new countries—Egypt, Ethiopia, Iran, Saudi Arabia, and the United Arab Emirates—on January 1, 2024. While an official name for the expanded group has yet to be announced, it is tentatively referred to as BRICS+ (Klomegah, 2024).

This recent expansion is viewed as a strategic move to foster a more equitable global order by amplifying the voices of the Global South and integrating them more prominently into international dialogues. Therefore, placing BRICS+ within the broader context of multilateral frameworks becomes essential for understanding its evolving role.

The utilization of PPP (Purchasing Power Parity) Gross Domestic Product (GDP) data is of paramount importance for the analysis of the global economy. This data adjusts for differences in price levels and cost of living across countries, thereby providing a more accurate comparison of economic productivity and living standards. PPP-based GDP data avoids distortions caused by fluctuating market exchange rates, ensuring that economic comparisons reflect real output and income levels (Karacan & Kiliçkan, 2018). This method is essential for understanding global inequality, developing economic policies, and conducting reliable international comparisons of economic aggregates (Gulde & Schulze-Ghattas, 1992; Rao, 2013; Ivanov & Khomenko, 2021).

Figure 1. Voting Power Distribution in the IMF, A Global Perspective, Including PPP-GDP

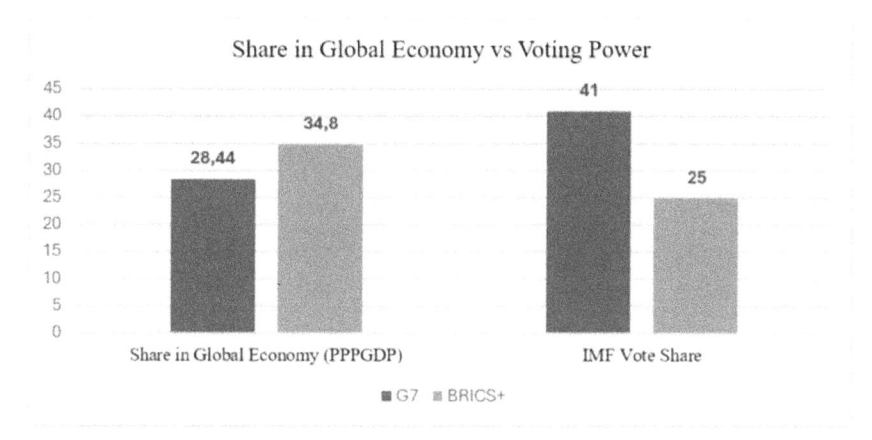

Note. Author's Result, based on the IMF database in the World Economic Outlook, April 2024. Units are in percent.

As illustrated in Figure 1, the combined BRICS+ countries account for a 34.80% share of the global economy, while the G7 countries represent a 28.44% share. This evidence suggests that the expanded BRICS have a higher share in the global economy than the G7. However, when we examine the IMF voting rates, we observe that the G7 countries collectively possess 41% of the total voting power, while the BRICS+ countries account for 25% of the total. This indicates that the BRICS+ countries are underrepresented in the IMF relative to their proportion of the global economy.

2.2.3 Weak Representation of Least Developed and Developing Economies

The voting power of developing countries is disproportionately low compared to their population and economic contributions. This results in policies that often do not reflect or prioritize the needs of these countries (Wei, 2017). Figure 2 illustrates the evolution of the shares of developing and least developed countries, in addition to those of advanced economies, within the global economy from the 1980s to 2022. This unequal framework results in underdeveloped and developing countries being marginalized in decision-making processes, subjecting them to the priorities and choices of developed nations with greater voting power. As illustrated in Figure 2, there has been a striking reversal from the 1980s, with developing and least developed economies now commanding a significant 62% share of the global economy, surpassing advanced economies. This marked reversal marks a stark departure from the trends observed in the 1980s. Despite these advancements, developing and least developed economies continue to be inadequately represented in global decision-making mechanisms, underscoring the need for equitable recognition of their rightful place in the global political and economic order.

Figure 2. The shift in the shares of developing and least developed countries, alongside those of advanced economies, in the global economy from the 1980s to 2022.

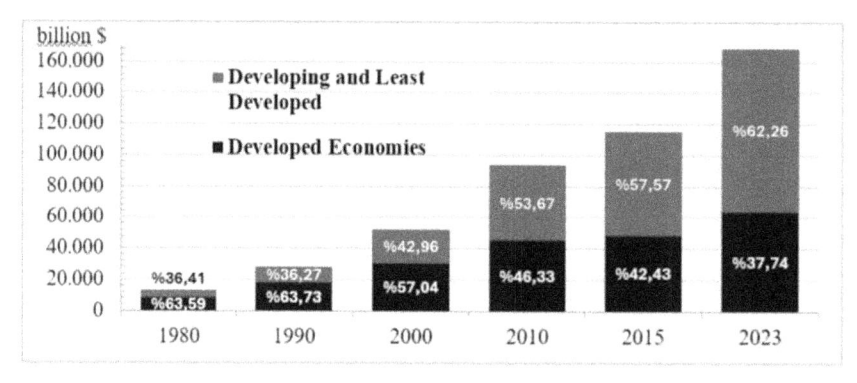

Note: Author's Result, based on the IMF database in the World Economic Outlook, April 2024.

The system of weighted voting in the IMF, which ties voting power to financial contributions (quotas), inherently disadvantages developing nations that have lower quotas. This further entrenches their marginalization in decision-making processes (Clark, 2017).

2.3 Benefits of Fair Voting Distribution

Fair voting distribution in the International Monetary Fund (IMF) can significantly contribute to achieving global economic balance, alongside positive effects on legitimacy, transparency, and accountability. These benefits contribute to achieving a more balanced and equitable global economy.

A fair voting distribution in the International Monetary Fund (IMF) serves to enhance the legitimacy, transparency, and accountability of the organization. The equal representation of all member countries, regardless of their economic size, ensures that each country has a voice in decision-making processes, thereby enhancing the IMF's legitimacy and global acceptance of its policies (Lesage et al., 2015). A transparent voting system fosters accountability by allowing for the scrutiny of IMF operations and the reduction of corruption risks (Lipscy & Lee, 2019). This accountability ensures that the IMF addresses the needs of smaller and developing countries, thereby promoting equitable policies (Clark, 2017). Inclusive decision-making involving small and developing countries leads to balanced policies that support global economic stability and growth (Wei, 2017). Furthermore, fair voting enables developing countries to advocate for policies addressing infrastructure, education, and healthcare, thereby accelerating economic development (Broz & Hawes, 2006). Moreover, the involvement of developing countries fosters the implementation of sustainable practices that reconcile economic growth with environmental protection (Lesage et al., 2015).

3. BARRIERS TO REFORMS

The resistance from major economies to IMF reforms is driven by their desire to maintain control and influence over the institution, which complicates efforts to achieve a fairer and representative governance structure within the IMF. This hinders the implementation of necessary reforms.

In June 2009, the BRIC countries called for reforms to the IMF, including increased voting rights for developing countries (G77) and a fairer global financial system with better representation. They emphasized predictability, diversity, and balance in the international monetary system, promoting a cooperative, pluralistic international order. The United Nations (UN) backed these reforms at the IMF and World Bank, approving a global financial system action plan in June 2009. Nevertheless, some developed countries, most notably the United States, were reluctant to implement significant changes, thereby maintaining their influence and the status of the US dollar as a global reserve currency (Özkan, 2010).

3.1 Resistance of the US and Other Developed Countries

The current voting and quota system in the IMF benefits the United States and other developed nations by affording them substantial influence over the Fund's policies and decisions. For instance, the United States possesses veto power due to its significant voting share, enabling it to block major reforms that might diminish its sway (Lesage et al., 2015). Developed countries have been reluctant to implement reforms that would increase the voting power of emerging markets and developing countries. They have expressed concerns that such changes could result in policies that are less favorable to their economic interests. These nations have also argued that reforms might jeopardize the stability and predictability of the IMF (Bhasin & Gupta, 2018).

3.2 Concerns that Reforms Would Contradict the Interests of Major Economies

The key global economies express concern that the proposed reforms could diminish their influence over IMF policies, which they view as essential for shaping international financial regulations and crisis response strategies aligned with their economic priorities (Weisbrot et al., 2009). They argue that such reforms might empower developing and least developed countries, potentially leading to policies that prioritize development needs in these regions at the expense of strategic interests held by developed nations (Hawkins, 1991).

3.3 Historical and Geopolitical Factors

The historical and geopolitical legacies, notably colonialism and imperialism, have significantly shaped the inequities within the decision-making structures of international economic institutions. These legacies persistently influence power dynamics and economic policies, typically favoring developed nations at the expense of developing and post-colonial states.

3.3.1 Colonial Past and Power Dynamics

The legacy of colonialism and imperialism continues to influence the structure of international economic institutions, perpetuating persistent inequalities. Colonial powers structured economies to extract resources and wealth, benefiting themselves and leaving colonies underdeveloped (Alemazung, 2010). Imperialism further solidified global power dynamics, directing investments to serve colonial interests and perpetuate economic disparities (Frieden, 1994).

These historical dynamics shape decision-making in institutions like the IMF, where former colonial powers wield significant influence, while developing countries often face underrepresentation (Reynaud & Vauday, 2009). Post-colonial states continue to grapple with economic dependency and structural inequalities, which are further exacerbated by international policies that inadequately address their unique contexts (Quijano, 2007). Despite reform efforts, these inequalities persist, indicating that equity-focused initiatives in international economic governance have had only a limited impact.

4. REFORM PROPOSALS AND SOLUTIONS

Reforming the IMF's voting system to increase the representation of developing countries requires adjusting quotas, adopting group voting systems, and increasing the number of basic votes. The evaluation of consensus versus majoritarian decision-making mechanisms underscores the importance of balanced strategies that promote inclusiveness, efficiency, and fairness in global economic governance.

4.1 Proposals for Increasing Voting Rights of Developing Countries

Various proposals have been put forth with the aim of reforming the IMF's quota determination process and voting regime in order to enhance the representation of developing countries. The reform of the IMF's voting system to enhance the representation of developing countries necessitates the reallocation of quotas to reflect the prevailing economic circumstances, thereby affording greater weight to the economic contributions and needs of developing countries (Rapkin & Strand, 2006). The implementation of a group voting system, wherein developing countries vote collectively, can augment their collective influence. Furthermore, the number of basic votes allotted to each member country can be increased to ensure that smaller and less economically powerful nations have a greater voice (Weisbrot & Johnston, 2016).

4.2 Comparison of Consensus and Majority-Based Decision-Making Mechanisms

Consensus-Based Decision-Making is a process that promotes inclusivity and ensures that all voices, especially those from smaller and developing countries, are heard before decisions are made. However, it can lead to delays in decision-making due to the need for unanimous or near-unanimous agreement, which may hinder timely responses to urgent issues. Best practices involve structured negotiations and mediation to facilitate agreement while maintaining transparency and accountability (Aleskerov et al., 2008).

Majority-Based Decision-Making allows for more efficient decision-making processes, as decisions can be made without requiring total agreement. However, this approach may marginalize smaller or less powerful countries if their votes do not carry significant weight. To ensure fairness, it is necessary to implement supermajority rules for critical decisions and safeguard mechanisms to protect the interests of minority stakeholders (Wei, 2017).

4.3 Ensuring Equal Representation: Proposals for Increasing the Voting Rights of Developing Countries

Ensuring equal representation entails proposals for increasing the voting rights of developing countries by reallocating quotas to better reflect current global economic realities. This entails increasing the quotas of developing countries based on their economic growth and contributions, thus enhancing their voting power within the IMF (Rapkin & Strand, 2006). Furthermore, the distribution of additional basic votes, which are allocated equally among all member countries, can facilitate the assertion of a more robust voice by smaller and less economically powerful nations (Weisbrot & Johnston, 2016).

4.4 Concrete Steps for Making International Organizations More Democratic and Equitable

It is of the utmost importance for international organizations such as the IMF to adopt transparent procedures in order to implement transparent decision-making processes. This entails publicly disclosing the rationale behind decisions, making meeting minutes available, and providing comprehensive reports on the outcomes of discussions and voting records (Truman, 2010). Furthermore, the establishment of independent evaluation offices can serve to enhance transparency and accountability by ensuring unbiased assessments of organizational policies and actions. It is recommended that these offices conduct regular audits and evaluations, with the results made publicly accessible (Weaver, 2010). To foster greater stakeholder engagement, mechanisms such as advisory panels or forums should be created to involve NGOs, civil society, and the private sector in providing input and feedback on policies and decisions (Gartner, 2013). It is also essential to strengthen surveillance and compliance mechanisms within the IMF, ensuring that member countries adhere to agreed norms and standards. This includes the development of norms and a transparent peer review process to effectively monitor and assess compliance (Truman, 2010).

5. CONCLUSION

This study underscores the critical need for structural reforms within the IMF to enhance its effectiveness and legitimacy in safeguarding global financial stability. Our findings reveal persistent governance issues, particularly the disproportionate influence of developed countries, such as the United States and European nations. This aligns with critiques from Dreher and Jensen (2007), who highlight how powerful member states exert undue influence on IMF decision-making. Addressing this imbalance through a more equitable distribution of voting rights is crucial.

The legacy of colonialism and imperialism continues to affect power dynamics within international economic institutions, contributing to persistent inequalities. This is consistent with the observations of Helleiner (2011) and Truman (2010), who emphasize the necessity for inclusive and representative governance structures to reflect changing global economic power dynamics. Major economies' reluctance to embrace reforms, due to the benefits they derive from the current system, further complicates efforts to enhance the participation of developing countries.

Our research supports Stiglitz's (2010) call for comprehensive structural changes within the IMF. The reallocation of quotas, the increase of basic votes, and the establishment of group voting systems are potential avenues for enhancing the representation and decision-making processes of developing countries. These measures could facilitate a fairer distribution of power and resources, aligning with Rodrik's (2014) advocacy for context-specific and adaptable policy frameworks.

Reforming the IMF's governance structure is crucial for achieving a more balanced and equitable global economic system. Eichengreen and Woods (2016) highlight the limitations of the IMF's perceived competence and impartiality, particularly in surveillance and conditionality. Our findings suggest that governance reforms would enhance the legitimacy, transparency, and accountability of the IMF, leading to policies that better reflect the needs of all member countries, especially developing nations.

To promote transparency, it is essential for international organizations to implement clear decision-making processes. Truman (2010) suggests publicly disclosing the rationale behind decisions, making meeting minutes available, and providing comprehensive reports on discussions and voting records. Establishing independent evaluation offices, as proposed by Weaver (2010), can ensure impartial assessments through regular audits and evaluations, with findings made accessible to the public.

Enhancing stakeholder engagement is also critical. Gartner (2013) emphasizes creating mechanisms such as advisory panels or forums that involve NGOs, civil society, and the private sector in policy discussions and decision-making processes. Strengthening the IMF's surveillance of member countries' economic policies, including developing transparent peer review processes, is necessary for effective monitoring and compliance, as highlighted by Truman (2010).

To achieve more equitable global economic governance, several reform proposals are beneficial:

Adjusting quotas to more accurately reflect the current economic realities and contributions of developing countries. Amplifying the voice of smaller and less economically powerful nations in IMF decisions. Allowing developing countries to vote as a bloc to enhance their combined influence. Implementing transparent decision-making processes, independent evaluations, and fostering greater stakeholder engagement.

Developing countries can improve their participation in IMF decision-making processes by addressing key challenges and implementing strategic measures. This includes pushing for increased representation on the IMF's Executive Board through quota reforms and the use of basic votes (Stiglitz & Charlton, 2005; Van Houtven, 2002; Woods, 2006). Participating in capacity-building initiatives to enhance understanding of IMF decision-making processes and improve negotiation skills can help bridge the knowledge gap between developed and developing countries (Van Houtven, 2002).

Advocating for consensus decision-making, which protects minority interests and ensures more inclusive decisions, is also vital (Stiglitz & Charlton, 2005; Vanko, 2006; Woods, 2006). Pushing for greater transparency and accountability in IMF decision-making, including the publication of minutes of informal meetings and detailed information on technical details and political compromises, is crucial.

Forming coalitions with other countries can amplify the voices of developing nations and counterbalance the influence of major economies. This ensures that developing countries' interests are represented. Additionally, advocating for institutional reforms that enhance their representation and influence in the IMF, such as modifications to the consensus principle and increased transparency, is essential.

Implementing reforms incrementally can help mitigate both political resistance and institutional inertia. By starting with smaller, less contentious reforms, it is possible to build momentum for larger changes over time, reducing the likelihood of encountering significant opposition.

A gradual rollout of reforms can also facilitate consensus-building among member countries. Pilot programs or phased implementation can serve as a testing ground, allowing for adjustments and increasing the likelihood of broader acceptance.

Active participation in the Development Committee, which advises the Boards of Governors on economic issues in developing countries, provides a platform for developing countries to engage in discussions and shape policies that affect them.

In conclusion, this study underscores the urgent need for structural reforms within the IMF to address governance issues and enhance its effectiveness and reliability. By embracing changes that empower developing countries and align voting rights with economic realities, the IMF can strengthen its legitimacy and credibility as a global financial institution, ultimately contributing to better global financial stability.

REFERENCES

Acemoğlu, D. (2005). Politics and economics in weak and strong states. *Journal of Monetary Economics*, 52(7), 1199–1226. DOI: 10.1016/j.jmoneco.2005.05.001

Akyüz, Y. (2006). Reforming the IMF: Back to the drawing board. *Iktisat İşletme ve Finans*, 21(39), 5–45. DOI: 10.3848/iif.2006.239.1836

Akyüz, Y. (2017). The Asian financial crisis: Lessons learned and unlearned. *Ekonomi-Tek*, 6(2), 1–11.

Alemazung, J. (2010). Post-Colonial Colonialism: An analysis of international factors and actors marring African socio-economic and political development. *The Journal of Pan African Studies*, 3, 62.

Aleskerov, F. T., Kalyagin, V. A., & Pogorelskiy, K. (2008). Actual voting power of the IMF members based on their political-economic integration. *Mathematical and Computer Modelling*, 48(9-10), 1554–1569. DOI: 10.1016/j.mcm.2008.05.020

Bhasin, N., & Gupta, S. (2018). Reforms in International Monetary Fund (IMF): Challenges and the road ahead. *Management and Economics Research Journal*, 4(S1), 19–29. DOI: 10.18639/MERJ.2018.04.520665

Bird, G. (1996). The International Monetary Fund and developing countries: A review of the evidence and policy options. *International Organization*, 50(3), 477–511. DOI: 10.1017/S0020818300033452

Bird, G. (2000). Reforming the IMF: Long term lessons from short term crises. *Zagreb International Review of Economics and Business*, 3, 1–24.

Bird, G., & Rowlands, D. (2002). Do IMF programmes have a catalytic effect on other international capital flows? *Oxford Development Studies*, 30(3), 229–249. DOI: 10.1080/1360081022000012671

Blomberg, S. B., & Broz, J. L. (2007). The political economy of IMF voting power and quotas. *Political Economy: International Political Economy eJournal*. DOI: 10.2139/ssrn.1080316

Bordo, M., & Eichengreen, B. (2015). Twenty years after fifty years after Bretton Woods. In Uzan, M. (Ed.), *Bretton Woods: The Next 70 years* (pp. 51–61). Reinventing Bretton Woods Committee.

Boughton, J. M. (2001). *The silent revolution: The International Monetary Fund, 1979–1989*. International Monetary Fund Publications.

Broome, A. (2010). The International Monetary Fund, crisis management and the credit crunch. *Australian Journal of International Affairs*, 64(1), 37–54. DOI: 10.1080/10357710903460006

Çelik, F. (2007). Gelişmekte olan ülkelerde uygulanan IMF programları ve refah devleti anlayışı. *Uluslararas Insan Bilimleri Dergisi*, 4(2), 1–16.

Clark, R. (2017). Quotas Operandi: Examining the distribution of voting power at the IMF and World Bank. *The Sociological Quarterly*, 58(4), 595–621. DOI: 10.1080/00380253.2017.1354735

Cooper, R. (2009). Necessary reform? The IMF and international financial architecture. *Harvard International Review*, 30(4), 52–55.

Cooper, R. N., & Mussa, M. (2002). Argentina and the Fund: From Triumph to Tragedy. *Foreign Affairs*, 81(6), 185–186. DOI: 10.2307/20033366

Daseking, C., Ghosh, A. R., Lane, T. D., & Thomas, A. H. (2005). *Lessons from the crisis in Argentina* (IMF Occasional Paper No. 2005/003). International Monetary Fund.

Dreher, A., & Jensen, N. M. (2007). Independent actor or agent? An empirical analysis of the impact of US interests on International Monetary Fund conditions. *The Journal of Law & Economics*, 50(1), 105–124. DOI: 10.1086/508311

Eichengreen, B., & Woods, N. (2016). The IMF's unmet challenges. *The Journal of Economic Perspectives*, 30(1), 29–52. DOI: 10.1257/jep.30.1.29

Frieden, J. (1994). International investment and colonial control: A new interpretation. *International Organization*, 48(4), 559–593. DOI: 10.1017/S0020818300028319

Gabor, D. (2016). A step too far? The European financial transactions tax on shadow banking. *Journal of European Public Policy*, 23(6), 925–945. DOI: 10.1080/13501763.2015.1070894

Gartner, D. (2013). Uncovering Bretton Woods: Conditional transparency, the World Bank, and the International Monetary Fund. *Geo. Wash. Int'l L. Rev.*, 45, 121.

Gola, C., & Spadafora, F. (2009). Financial Sector Surveillance and the IMF. IMF Working Paper WP/09/247.

Griesgraber, J. M. (2009). Reforms for major new roles of the International Monetary Fund? The IMF post–G-20 summit. *Global Governance*, 15(2), 179–185. DOI: 10.1163/19426720-01502003

Gulde, A.-M., & Schulze-Ghattas, M. (1992). Aggregation of economic indicators across countries: Exchange rate versus PPP based GDP weights. *International Monetary Fund, Working Paper WP/92/36*, May.

Hawkins, J. J.Jr. (1991). Understanding the failure of IMF reform: The Zambian case. *World Development*, 19(7), 839–849. DOI: 10.1016/0305-750X(91)90137-7

Helleiner, E. (2011). Understanding the 2007–2008 Global Financial Crisis: Lessons for Scholars of International Political Economy. *Annual Review of Political Science*, 14(1), 67–87. DOI: 10.1146/annurev-polisci-050409-112539

International Monetary Fund. (2022a). How the IMF makes decisions. Retrieved from https://www.imf.org/en/About/Factsheets/Sheets/2022/How-the-IMF-makes-decisions

International Monetary Fund. (2022b). IMF decisions. Retrieved from https://imf.md/imfdecis.html

International Monetary Fund. (2022c, November 9). IMF quota and governance publications. Retrieved from https://www.imf.org/external/np/fin/quotas/pubs/#section1

International Monetary Fund. (2024). *World economic outlook, April 2024*. Retrieved from https://www.imf.org/en/Publications/WEO/Issues/2024/04/16/world-economic-outlook-april-2024

Irwin, D. A. (2011). *Trade policy disaster: Lessons from the 1930s*. MIT Press. DOI: 10.7551/mitpress/8886.001.0001

Ivanov, Y., & Khomenko, T. (2021). On the global international comparison of GDP for reference year 2017. *Voprosy statistiki*, 28(1), 80-87. DOI: 10.34023/2313-6383-2021-28-1-80-87

Karacan, R., & Kiliçkan, Z. (2018). Investigation the correlation between purchasing power parity, per capita gross domestic product and the price level indices with panel data analysis: Evidence from New Zealand, USA, Germany, Canada and Turkey. *International Journal of Economics and Financial Issues*, 8(6), 15–19.

Klomegah, K. K. (2024, January 6). BRICS: Definition, meaning and usage - Modern Diplomacy. Retrieved from https://moderndiplomacy.eu/2024/01/06/brics-definition-meaning-and-usage/

Knight, M. D. (2015). *Reforming the global architecture of financial regulation: The G20, the IMF and the FSB. Special Papers (No. 6)*. Systemic Risk Centre, The London School of Economics and Political Science., Retrieved from http://eprints.lse.ac.uk/id/eprint/61213

Lesage, D., Debaere, P., Dierckx, S., & Vermeiren, M. (2013). IMF reform after the crisis. *International Politics*, 50(4), 553–578. DOI: 10.1057/ip.2013.17

Lesage, D., Debaere, P., Dierckx, S., & Vermeiren, M. (2015). Rising powers and IMF governance reform. In Lesage, D., & Van de Graaf, T. (Eds.), *Rising powers and multilateral institutions* (pp. 153–174). Palgrave Macmillan.

Lipscy, P. Y., & Lee, H. N. (2019). The IMF as a biased global insurance mechanism: Asymmetrical moral hazard, reserve accumulation, and financial crises. *International Organization*, 73(1), 35–64. DOI: 10.1017/S0020818318000371

Miller, C. (2006). Pathways through financial crisis: Turkey. *Global Governance*, 12(4), 449–464. DOI: 10.1163/19426720-01204008

Mminele, D. (2015). Perspectives on the global financial architecture and the future of the international monetary system. In Uzan, M. (Ed.), *Bretton Woods: The Next 70 years* (pp. 231–237). Reinventing Bretton Woods Committee.

Moschella, M. (2012). IMF surveillance in crisis: The past, present and future of the reform process. *Global Society*, 26(1), 43–60. DOI: 10.1080/13600826.2011.629987

Muhumed, M. M., & Gaas, S. A. (2016). The World Bank and IMF in developing countries: Helping or hindering? *International Journal of African and Asian Studies*, 28, 39–49.

Nemiña, P. (2013). Dominación, confrontación y acuerdo: La intervención del FMI en la crisis Argentina durante 2002. *Conjuntura Austral*, 4(19), 11. DOI: 10.22456/2178-8839.36773

Oatley, T. (2011). The reductionist gamble: Open economy politics in the global economy. *International Organization*, 65(2), 311–341. DOI: 10.1017/S002081831100004X

Obstfeld, M. (2013). The International Monetary System: Living with Asymmetry. NBER Working Paper No. 19677.

Obstfeld, M., & Rogoff, K. (2010). Global imbalances and the financial crisis: Products of common causes. In R. Glick & M. M. Spiegel (Eds.), *Asia and the Global Financial Crisis*. Asia Economic Policy Conference. San Francisco, CA: Federal Reserve Bank of San Francisco. Retrieved from https://scholar.harvard.edu/rogoff/publications/global-imbalances-and-financial-crisis-products-common-causes

OECD. (2020, November 10). The territorial impact of COVID-19: Managing the crisis across levels of government. Retrieved from https://www.oecd.org/coronavirus/policy-responses/the-territorial-impact-of-covid-19-managing-the-crisis-across-levels-of-government-d3e314e1/

Ongun, M. T. (2012). 1980'lerden küresel krize dünya ekonomisi. *Ekonomik Yaklaşım*, 23(Special Issue), 39–76. DOI: 10.5455/ey.20007

Öniş, Z. (2006). Varieties and crises of neoliberal globalisation: Argentina, Turkey and the IMF. *Third World Quarterly*, 27(2), 239–263. https://www.jstor.org/stable/4017673. DOI: 10.1080/01436590500432366

Öniş, Z. (2009). Beyond the 2001 financial crisis: The political economy of the new phase of neo-liberal restructuring in Turkey. *Review of International Political Economy*, 16(3), 409–432. DOI: 10.1080/09692290802408642

Özkan, G. (2010). 'Uluslararası güç dengeleri bağlamında uluslararası finans sisteminin yeniden yapılandırılması: Disiplinlerarası bir değerlendirme'. *Uluslararası İlişkiler*, 7(27), 3–26.

Quijano, A. (2007). Coloniality and Modernity/Rationality. *Cultural Studies*, 21(2-3), 168–178. DOI: 10.1080/09502380601164353

Rao, D. S. P. (2013). The framework of the International Comparison Program. In *Measuring the real size of the world economy: The framework, methodology, and results of the International Comparison Program—ICP* (pp. 13–45). World Bank. DOI: 10.1596/9780821397282_CH01

Rapkin, D. P., & Strand, J. (2005). Developing country representation and governance of the International Monetary Fund. *World Development*, 33(12), 1993–2011. DOI: 10.1016/j.worlddev.2005.07.008

Rapkin, D. P., & Strand, J. R. (2006). Reforming the IMF's weighted voting system. *World Economy*, 29(3), 305–324. DOI: 10.1111/j.1467-9701.2006.00784.x

Reynaud, J., & Vauday, J. (2009). Geopolitics and international organizations: An empirical study on IMF facilities. *Journal of Development Economics*, 89(1), 139–162. DOI: 10.1016/j.jdeveco.2008.07.005

Rodrik, D. (2014). *The globalization paradox: Democracy and the future of the world economy*. W. W. Norton & Company.

Schinasi, G. J., & Truman, E. M. (2010, September 14). Reform of the global financial architecture. Peterson Institute for International Economics Working Paper No. 10-14. DOI: 10.2139/ssrn.1692186

Setser, B. W., & Gelpern, A. (2006). Pathways through financial crisis: Argentina. *Global Governance*, 12(4), 465–487. DOI: 10.1163/19426720-01204009

Stiglitz, J. E. (2010). *The Stiglitz Report: Reforming the international monetary and financial systems in the wake of the global crisis*. The New Press.

Stiglitz, J. E., & Charlton, A. (2005). Improving IMF governance and increasing the influence of developing countries in IMF decision-making. In Buira, A. (Ed.), *Reforming the Governance of the IMF and the World Bank* (pp. 149–170). Cambridge University Press., DOI: 10.7135/UPO9780857288189.008

Truman, E. M. (2010). The G-20 and international financial institution governance (Working Paper Series WP10-13). Peterson Institute for International Economics.

Van Houtven, L. (2002). *Governance of the International Monetary Fund (IMF): Decision Making, Institutional Oversight, Transparency and Accountability.* International Monetary Fund, Pamphlet Series No. 53.

Weaver, C. (2010). The politics of performance evaluation: Independent evaluation at the International Monetary Fund. *The Review of International Organizations*, 5(3), 365–385. DOI: 10.1007/s11558-010-9094-1

Wei, H. (2017). Calculable power: A case study of IMF quotas and voting rights reform. *Social Sciences in China*, 38(4), 45–66. DOI: 10.1080/02529203.2017.1376951

Weisbrot, M., Cordero, J., & Sandoval, L. (2009). *Empowering the IMF: Should reform be a requirement for increasing the fund's resources? CEPR Reports and Issue Briefs 2009-15.* Center for Economic and Policy Research. CEPR.

Weisbrot, M., & Johnston, J. (2016). Voting share reform at the IMF: Will it make a difference? *CEPR Reports and Issue Briefs*. Center for Economic and Policy Research (CEPR). Retrieved from https://cepr.net/report/voting-share-reform-at-the-imf-will-it-make-a-difference/

Woods, N. (2005). Making the IMF and the World Bank more accountable. In Buira, A. (Ed.), *Reforming the Governance of the IMF and the World Bank* (pp. 149–170). Anthem Press., DOI: 10.7135/UPO9780857288189.008

Woods, N., & Lombardi, D. (2006). Uneven patterns of governance: How developing countries are represented in the IMF. *Review of International Political Economy*, 13(3), 480–515. DOI: 10.1080/09692290600769351

KEY TERMS AND DEFINITIONS

Governance Reform: Governance reform refers to the systematic changes and improvements proposed or implemented within an institution, like the IMF, to enhance transparency, accountability, and inclusivity. In the context of the IMF, governance reform addresses the disparities in representation and decision-making power, aiming to create a more equitable and effective global financial system.

Institutional Inertia: Institutional inertia describes the resistance to change within an organization due to established practices, norms, and power structures. This concept is crucial in understanding the challenges faced by the IMF in implementing reforms, as existing power dynamics and long-standing procedures can slow down or prevent necessary changes.

Quota System: The quota system in the IMF determines a member country's financial contribution, voting power, and access to financial resources. Quotas are crucial in influencing the balance of power within the institution, and debates around quota reform often focus on increasing the representation of developing countries.

Voting Power: Voting power in the IMF is linked to the quota system, where a country's influence in decision-making processes is proportional to its financial contribution. This system has been criticized for favoring wealthier nations and contributing to power imbalances within the institution.

Representation and Fairness: Representation and fairness refer to the equitable participation of all member countries in the IMF's governance. This concept highlights the need for reforms that ensure developing nations have a more significant voice and influence in the institution's decisions, promoting a more just and balanced global financial system.

Power Asymmetry: Power asymmetry in the IMF refers to the unequal distribution of influence among member countries, often favoring developed nations over developing ones. This imbalance can lead to policies that disproportionately benefit the more powerful members, making the case for reforms that address these disparities.

Power Dynamics: Power dynamics within the IMF involve the interactions and relationships between member countries, particularly how power and influence are distributed and exercised. Understanding these dynamics is essential for analyzing the institution's decision-making processes and the need for governance reforms.

Global Cooperation: Global cooperation in the context of the IMF involves collaboration among member countries to address international financial challenges. Effective global cooperation is critical for ensuring that the IMF can fulfill its mandate of promoting global economic stability and development.

Decision-making Processes: Decision-making processes in the IMF refer to the procedures and mechanisms through which policies are formulated and implemented. These processes are influenced by the quota system and voting power, and reforms are often proposed to make them more transparent, inclusive, and equitable.

Chapter 3
An Analysis on the Determinants of Global Inflation

Öznur Taşdöken

Antalya Chamber of Commerce and Industry, Turkey

ABSTRACT

The volatilities observed in different markets have an impact on global inflation. The persistent upward trend in inflation forms the basis of economic challenges experienced in all countries.Therefore, especially considering recent developments and events, inflation stands out as one of the most researched topics. In this contextthis, this study analyzes the relationship between global inflation, global food price, Brent oil price, global energy prices, the global supply chain, and global geopolitical risks variables using monthly data from 2004:08 to 2023:10. In this analysis, the Dynamic Wavelet Correlation Analysis For Multivariate (WLMC) approach is employed to examine the dynamic correlation relationship between variables across time and frequency dimensions. Considering the findings from the study, it can be stated that strong correlation relationships among variables have been found after the year 2021 in all analyses. This suggests a stronger economic integration across different global markets, especially in recent years.

1. INTRODUCTION

In recent years, wars, pandemics, and terrorist incidents that have had a global impact have led to disruptions in the global supply chain, problems in global supply, fluctuations in crude oil prices, changes in global energy prices, increases in global food prices, geoeconomic problems and rising geopolitical risks. The volatilities or

DOI: 10.4018/979-8-3693-5508-4.ch003

Copyright © 2025, IGI Global. Copying or distributing in print or electronic forms without written permission of IGI Global is prohibited.

shocks occurring in different markets spread to other markets, with some countries becoming exporters of the shock while others become importers. This situation leads to the diffusion of the shock across all markets (Taşdöken & Kahyaoğlu, 2023a).

In recent years, one of the most significant factors affecting national economies has been geopolitical issues. The raw material resources a country possesses highlight its foremost geo-economic power in international relations. Considering recent global events affecting global markets, it can be argued that geopolitical influence, which has traditionally held significant importance in international trade, is now evolving toward geo-economic influence.

Since World War II, there have been various periods globally and in many countries where there has been a continuous upward trend in the general price level for different reasons (Taşdöken & Kahyaoğlu, 2023b). Although the reasons for the increasing trend in inflation have varied, central banks have implemented tight monetary and fiscal policies to repress the resulting increase in domestic demand. The policies implemented by central banks to slow down the increase in inflationary tendencies have an impact on savings and investment decisions.

After the Covid-19 pandemic began in 2019, numerous disruptions and issues occurred in global markets. These global disruptions and issues have led to both supply and demand-side changes in many countries. Changes in supply and demand also contribute to a continued upward trend in inflation and introduce uncertainties in inflation. To mitigate the rising trend in inflation and prevent potential recessionary issues, central banks have begun implementing disinflationary policies. In other words, policies aimed at raising interest rates to reduce domestic demand have been initiated. The increase in interest rates affects the economy through two different macroeconomic channels. As interest rates rise, borrowing costs for households and firms increase (Örn, 2017), leading to reduced consumer spending by households (Weller & Chaurushiya, 2004), changes in economic preferences among households (Taşdöken & Kahyaoğlu, 2022), and influencing investment and saving decisions.

Despite disinflationary policies implemented by all countries, there has been a continued upward trend in inflation in recent years. In other words, despite tight monetary policies being implemented in countries, inflation expectations have been slow to respond to these policies. The persistent upward trend in inflation, despite central banks raising interest rates, indicates that domestic demand has not been sufficiently suppressed, and supply and demand shocks continue to be effective in markets due to the current global economic conditions. This situation leads to persistence of inflation in many countries (Canepa, 2024). In other words, the effectiveness of tight monetary policies implemented due to the continuing upward trend in countries' inflation affects markets (Sun & Dimiski, 2024). Therefore, instead of standard monetary policies aimed at reducing the effectiveness of supply and demand shocks on markets, a monetary policy may be required that also considers households' inflation expectations (Dietrich, 2024; Beckworth & Horan, 2024). Thus, it can be said that changes in inflation expectations will have an impact on the monetary transmission mechanism.

The continuing upward trend in inflation also shapes household inflation expectations (Beaudry & Carter, 2023; Adams & Barrett, 2024; Stanislawska & Paloviita, 2024), leads to income inequalities (Hu et al., 2024), affects consumer spending depending on households' incomes (Ampudia et al., 2024), influences capital flows to developing countries (Ogrokhina & Rodriguez, 2024), impacts actions of financial market participants (Pedersen, 2024), affects uncertainty in trade policies (Q. Wang & Weng, 2024), and involves inflation expectations in wage and price-setting processes.

High inflation expectations during the wage-setting process also lead to an upward trend in prices. Due to the continuous upward trend in the general price level, workers demand higher wages to maintain their purchasing power. When workers demand wage increases, they form future wage expectations based on past inflation, future inflation expectations, and past wages. Accordingly, high inflation expectations will lead to higher wage demand (Jordà & Nechio, 2023). In this context, if the wage price spiral occurs, it can be said that tight monetary policies implemented in many countries may fail to meet inflation expectations.

When considering variables related to inflation within the economic theoretical framework, inflation has a direct or indirect impact on the fundamental dynamics of a economy. This situation enhances the influence of monetary policy on the economy's fundamental dynamics. In other words, it demonstrates that inflation is a crucial parameter for assessing the entire economic structure and determining the effectiveness of policies across different markets. Therefore, policies aimed at reducing the upward trend in inflation significantly affect macroeconomic stability and economic resilience.

When global geopolitical risks (GPRT) begin to rise, they directly impact global energy supply due to increases in oil and natural gas prices (Lee et al., 2023; Zheng et al., 2023; Lu et al., 2024). In other words, shocks occurring in the global supply chain (GSCPI), Brent crude oil prices (BP), or global energy prices (WEP) lead to general price pressures, disruptions in production processes, and logistical sector problems (Andriantomanga et al., 2022; Diaz et al., 2023; Aharon et al., 2023; Bouri et al., 2023). The irregular development of demand and unexpected supply interruptions resulting from these issues also contribute to the stronger transmission of cost-driven shocks to global inflation (Taşdöken & Kahyaoğlu, 2023:68). Therefore, the volatility occurring in different markets causing imbalances in supply and demand can be said to transform into significant macroeconomic shocks globally and at the national level. Considering high economic integration among countries, volatility originating in one market affects the markets of other countries. In other words, shocks starting in one market spread to others (Taşdöken & Kahyaoğlu, 2023; Jiang et al., 2024).

In recent years, global events such as geopolitical risks have caused problems in container shipping and global trade routes. These issues have increased insurance costs for containers, extended shipping times, and led to higher transportation costs. Consequently, they have caused delays and disruptions in production in many countries. Imbalances in supply and demand due to external and internal shocks have resulted in persistent upward pressure on the inflation (Ha et al., 2023). This situation can also be said to lead to increased inflation expectations, issues with chronic inflation in some countries, and problems in the monetary transmission mechanism.

In recent years, considering the global events and their impact on national economies, numerous studies have been conducted on inflation. The majority of these studies investigate the impact of external and internal shocks on countries' inflation. As a result of these studies, findings have been obtained that can help reduce risks and uncertainties that may arise in future markets and enhance the effectiveness of monetary policy (Finck & Tillmann, 2022; Giovanni et al., 2022; Shahzad et al., 2024). This study examines the effect on disruptions in the global supply chain (GSCPI), volatility in global energy prices (WEP), fluctuations in Brent crude oil prices (BP), geopolitical risks (GPRT), and volatility in global food prices on global inflation pass-through. The primary objective of this study is to analyze the effect of changes in BP, WEP, GPRT, global food prices, and GSCPI between 2004:8 and 2023:10 on global inflation. There are many studies in the literature on this topic. Most of the analytical methods used in these studies consider the relationship between variables over time dimensions. However, there is a lack of analysis considering the dynamic correlation relationship between variables in both time and frequency dimensions. Therefore, this study analyzes the dynamic correlation relationship between variables considering both time and frequency dimensions.

This analysis will expand upon previous studies in the following aspects. Firstly, it examines the dynamic correlation relationship between GPRT and global inflation rates. Thus, it investigates the impact of events such as civil conflicts, international wars, political unrest, and terrorist attacks occurring in different geopolitical regions on markets. Secondly, it analyzes the dynamic correlation relationship in the time-frequency domain between global inflation rates and global food prices. It explores the effect of changes in food prices due to climate crises and global crises on global inflation. Thirdly, it investigates the dynamic correlation relationship in the time and frequency domains between global inflation rates and WEP. Hence, it examines the impact of the global energy crisis arising from events such as COVID-19 and the Russia-Ukraine war during the studied period on global inflation rates. Fourthly, it analyzes the dynamic correlation relationship in the time-frequency domain between global food prices and BP. Thus, it explores the dynamic correlation between changes in BP prices, representing transportation costs, and global inflation rates. Fifthly, it examines the dynamic correlation relationship between global inflation rates and GSCPI. This analysis investigates the impact of disruptions in global trade represented by GSCPI issues on the correlation relationship with global inflation.

The relationship between global inflation rate and global food prices, BP prices, WEP, GPRT, and GSCPI is being analyzed in this study. Firstly, each variable influencing global inflation rate is individually analyzed for correlation in time and frequency domains. For instance, the dynamic correlation relationship between GSCPI and global inflation rate has been analyzed in the time-frequency domain separately for each variable. Secondly, an analysis is conducted considering all variables that influence global inflation rate together. In other words, the dynamic correlation relationship in time and frequency domains has been analyzed for changes in global food price index, BP, WEP, GPRT, and GSCPI affecting global inflation rate. This allows for the analysis of the total impact of changes occurring in different time periods across various markets on the global inflation rate. Changes in global inflation rate, global food prices, BP price, WEP, GPRT, and GSCPI affect commodity prices both in terms of supply and demand. This study aims to contribute to the research on global inflation and expand the existing literature on its analysis.

In the continuation of the article, Section-2 provides a brief review of the relevant literature. Section-3 explains the data and the approach used in the study. Section-4 presents the analysis results. Section-5 is the conclusion.

2. RECENT STUDIES RELATED TO THE TOPIC

This section of the study includes research on factors affecting global inflation rates

2.1. Recent Studies on Factors Influencing Inflation

Changes in macroeconomic variables affect inflation through various transmission channels. A shock in one macroeconomic variable causes fluctuations in others, thereby impacting both global and domestic inflation. Particularly high interdependencies among macroeconomic variables amplify the effect of a shock in one market on others. Therefore, shocks in macroeconomic variables have significant effects on inflation, often leading to the emergence of chronic inflation or inflationary pressures. To mitigate these pressures, both developed and developing economies implement tight monetary and fiscal policies. This typically results in higher borrowing costs due to increased interest rates, influencing firms' investment decisions and household consumption behaviors. Accordingly, Considering the impact of price stability across all transmission channels, the economics literature has extensively studied inflation-related issues.

Volatilities in GSCPI, BP, and GPRT significantly impact global shipping costs. These volatilities also affect global and domestic inflation. For instance, disruptions in GSCPI account for approximately 30% of the upward trend in inflation in the Euro area. A shock in the supply chain in the Euro area leads to a roughly 1% decline in industrial production and a 0.3% increase in consumer prices. This situation has persistent effects on inflation, reaching its peak seventeen months later (Finck & Tillmann, 2022:4). Giovanni et al. (2022) concluded in their study that the primary reasons for the inflationary trend in the Euro area during 2020-2021 were external shocks and disruptions in the global supply chain. In the study by Platitas & Ocampo (2024), it was found that disruptions in the supply chain in the Philippines, Republic of Korea, Thailand, and Singapore lead to increases in inflation. Ascari et al. (2024), using a Bayesian VAR approach for the period from 2005M4 to 2023M8, concluded that GSPCI shocks dominate Eurozone inflation and have persistent effects. Diaz et al. (2023) found, using an SVAR model for the years 1995-2021, that each commodity and disruptions in the supply chain affect inflation in the United States. Andriantomanga et al. (2022), in their study covering monthly data from 2000 to 2022 for 29 Sub-Saharan African countries, highlighted the significant impacts of supply chain disruptions on inflation in these countries. Anderl and Caporale (2024), using a VAR model, found that shocks in global shipping costs affect inflation in all countries and exhibit strong pass-through effects. Considering these studies in the literature, disruptions in the global supply chain have been identified as a key factor contributing to the recent upward trend in inflation.

Volatility in oil prices also influences global shipping costs. Since oil to use as a fundamental input for many companies or as a commodity, shocks in oil prices affect production costs. Changes in oil prices asymmetrically impact global inflation, commodity prices, and crude oil prices (Taşdöken & Kahyaoğlu, 2023). Li et al. (2023) In their study using weekly data from 2018 to 2023 in China employed the TVP-VAR approach and concluded that there is a mutually dependence relationship between crude oil, commodity markets, and inflation. The correlation among variables varies across different quantile values. Cheikh et al. (2023) used the VSTR approach to investigate the effects of oil price shocks on inflation in the Eurozone for the period 1999-2022. Aharon et al. (2023), in their analysis spanning from 1987 to 2022, found that in Malaysia, Singapore, Thailand, the Philippines, and Japan, increases in inflation are largely attributed to shocks from oil prices and shocks originating from total demand. Thus, countries react differently to oil shocks (Wen et al., 2021), indicating that supply shocks in oil impact inflation and vary across countries (Bjørnland, 2022). The differing impacts of factors affecting inflation in countries also influence the tendency and persistence of domestic inflation.

Therefore, it is evident that Europe shows high sensitivity to oil price fluctuations concerning geopolitical events, which can increase inflationary pressures in Europe due to heightened geopolitical risks.

Another factor affecting global shipping costs arises from global geopolitical risks. Negative geopolitical events lead to changes in international capital flows and trade routes, impacting all countries and causing disruptions in global trade. Lee et al. (2023), using non-parametric quantile causality (NPQC), found that increasing geopolitical risks as a result of events occurring in different periods affect inflation in the ABD and China. Shahbaz et al. (2023), employing Granger causality-in-quantile, established evidence of bidirectional causality linking changes in geopolitical risks with fluctuations in oil prices in countries such as Thailand, Argentina, Israel, China, Mexico, India, South Korea, Indonesia, South Africa, Turkey, the Philippines, Venezuela, and Ukraine. Yang et al. (2023), using the TVP-SV-VAR model, determined that volatilities in GPRT and oil prices affect inflation in China, the United States, and 27 European countries. Bouri et al. (2023), using the connectedness approach, examined the transmission relationship between inflation and GPRT for North American and European countries, finding a strong relationship between inflation and GPRT during periods of high GPRT. Considering findings from the literature, geopolitical risks create uncertainty and risk in the future, leading to deviations or volatilities in macroeconomics and markets. This situation particularly facilitates the transmission of risk to markets in countries with high economic integration, thereby increasing financial and economic vulnerabilities in these countries.

Global energy supply issues arising from geopolitical risks have led to increased production costs and the emergence of supply-demand imbalances in many countries. Geopolitical risks particularly have a significant impact on energy supply security. Zheng et al. (2023) utilized data from Europe, Asia, and the ABD using the TVP-VAR model, finding heterogeneous effects of energy price fluctuations on inflation across countries. Shahzad et al. (2024) investigated inflation expectations and energy shocks for the United States using the ARDL and QARDL models, revealing that changes in inflation rates and energy shocks significantly affect inflation expectations. Lu et al. (2024) employed a macro-econometric model to demonstrate the short- and long-term impacts of energy shocks on the economy of the United Kingdom. Bednář et al. (2022) concluded from their regression model that electricity prices have significant effects on inflation in EU countries and anticipated potential future increases in energy price shocks. Fazal et al. (2022), using the GTA model, found a positive relationship between inflation rates, energy prices, and interest rates in Pakistan. Saeed et al. (2023) examined the relationship between inflation in G-7 countries and China and energy commodities using the WTC model, revealing heterogeneous behavior of countries' inflation in response to changes in energy commodities. Considering findings from the literature, geopolitical risks significantly affect energy supply security. Therefore, countries need to diversify their energy sources, as energy diversification is crucial in mitigating the increase in cost inflation. Transitioning a significant portion of energy supply from coal, gas, and petroleum to renewable energy sources can help mitigate the potential impacts of future energy price volatility.

Another factor influencing global inflation is fluctuations in food prices. In recent years, geopolitical events, global climate crises, and volatility in energy prices have been fundamental drivers of volatility in food prices. Particularly, changes in food prices due to climate crises and energy price volatility are among the most significant contributors to inflation. Therefore, Soliman et al. (2023) investigated the relationship between energy prices and food prices using the NARDL and SVAR models for the United Kingdom, finding that the continuous upward trend in energy prices adversely affects agricultural production and inflation. Pan et al. (2024) examined the relationship between inflation and global commodity prices for the ABD using an asymmetric Granger causality approach, revealing bidirectional causality between the variables. Ha et al. (2023) used the FAVAR approach to study global factors affecting inflation across 55 countries, noting that global shocks explain approximately 26% of inflationary changes and their impact on inflation has increased in recent years. AL-Rousan et al. (2024) examined the impact of geopolitical events on global food prices using Pearson correlation, linear regression, and SARIMA approaches, finding that uncontrolled increases in food prices contribute to higher global inflation. Durevall et al. (2013) found a strong relationship between global food prices and domestic food prices in Ethiopia, indicating that global shocks affect food prices in the long term due to this strong relationship. Considering studies in the literature, the high sensitivity of developing countries to global shocks significantly influences the pass-through of changes in global inflation to domestic inflation. This highlights the importance of investing in food security in developing countries.

Considering the findings from recent studies in the literature regarding fundamental macroeconomic variables, firstly, the most significant impacts of the Covid-19 pandemic on the global economy include disruptions in global supply chains and imbalances in global commodity markets. These disruptions have led to labor shortages arising from quarantine measures, disruptions in the logistics sector, extended waiting times at ports, and increased global shipping costs. These increases have escalated firms' input costs and intensified the effects of supply-side shocks. Secondly, the outbreak of the Ukraine-Russia war in 2022 has led to increased volatility in the global energy and agricultural markets, contributing to approximately a 1.3 percentage point increase in global inflation (Caldara et al., 2022). In other words, restrictions implemented by Russia, the largest natural gas producer, in the natural gas sector have raised global energy prices. Simultaneously, disruptions in the agricultural sector due to the war in Ukraine, the world's largest grain producer, have caused increases in agricultural product prices. Thus, since 2022, the increases in both global energy prices and global agricultural product prices have resulted in supply-side shocks affecting economies worldwide. Thirdly, disruptions in the supply of goods traded in global commodity markets have led to production challenges and increased input costs. During this period, production difficulties have resulted in demand shocks, while disruptions in the global supply chain have caused supply shocks. Moreover, the combination of shocks emerging through different economic channels has had significant economic implications. Therefore, both supply-side and demand-side shocks have altered the dynamics of economies during this period (Baba et al., 2023). Fourthly, disruptions in the global supply chain and the increase in global shipping costs have led to significant economic consequences in economies with strong economic integration. One of these consequences is the occurrence of cyclical fluctuations in economies, leading to increased unemployment rates (Blinova et al., 2021) and fluctuations in production quantities. Another consequence is the inadequacy in meeting strong demand for goods due to disruptions in the logistics sector during quarantine periods. These developments have resulted in relative price changes and pushed prices upwards. The fundamental reason for price changes is fluctuations in basic input prices, primarily due to increases in energy prices and transportation costs, which have led to higher food prices and increased core inflation rates (Bolhuis et al., 2023). This situation has caused inflation issues in all countries due to the increase in global inflation affecting local inflation rates.

2.2. Research Gaps in Determinants of Global Inflation

The changing linearity and stationarity characteristics of macroeconomic variables indicate a tendency to exhibit different behaviors in different time periods. Therefore, the temporal variation of spectral properties of macroeconomic indicators necessitates examination across various frequency components of these variables.

Macroeconomic variables can exhibit different structural characteristics at different frequencies over time. Thus, changes in variables over time also affect the overall behavior of the series. From this perspective, analyzing series at the frequency level contributes to obtaining important information about how relationships between variables have changed and how parameters and long-term trends have varitation. In this context, using this approach in the study;

- Analyzing time series in both time and frequency domains contributes to analyzing the long-term trends of variables at different frequencies in different time periods. Therefore, in this study, key macroeconomic variables affecting global inflation are analyzed at different frequencies over the long term. This approach also contributes to obtaining detailed information regarding dynamic correlation relationships that vary among variables across different periods. Therefore, it has also been used to analyse the dynamic correlation relationship between different macroeconomic variables (Bouri et al., 2023;Phiri & Anyikwa, 2024;Kartal et al., 2024).

- There are studies in the literature that examine the relationship between GSCPI, global food prices, BP, WEP, GPRT, and global inflation in the time domain. However, there is currently no research that examines the relationship between these variables considering both time and frequency domains. This situation has motivated our research.
- When considering studies in the literature related to key macroeconomic variables, the relationship between variables is analyzed over time using time series analysis methods in different time periods. In our study, however, we focus on the current time period and analyze the relationship between variables in both time and frequency domains.
- Considering the non-stationary, linear, and non-linear nature of financial and macroeconomic time series, employing suitable methods for analyzing these variables is crucial. Therefore, WLMC approach is used in this study instead of traditional wavelet and other statistical methods.

There are many approaches developed to analyze relationships between variables in either the time or frequency domain. These approaches include Fourier-based methods and wavelet-based methods for time series analysis. Traditional time series approaches consider the temporal dimension of series, while Fourier analysis examines the frequency domain of series. Wavelet analysis, on the other hand, considers both the time and frequency dimensions in its analysis. A general limitation of correlation analyses developed using wavelet approaches in the literature is that they typically focus on analyzing relationships between two variables. However, the WLMC approach developed by Fernández-Macho (2012, 2018) differs significantly from other approaches by enabling simultaneous analysis of relationships among more than two variables. This approach facilitates dynamic analysis of multivariate time series across different time periods and frequency domains. Additionally, considering the non-stationary, linear, and non-linear nature of financial and macroeconomic time series, the WLMC approach is suitable for analyzing these variables. Due to these advantages, this study employs the WLMC approach instead of traditional wavelet and other statistical methods.

There are studies analysing the relationship between GSCPI, global food prices, BP, WEP, GPRT and global inflation. However, there is currently no research that investigates this relationship considering in time and frequency domains. This gap has motivated our research. This study employs the WLMC approach developed by

Fernandez-Macho (2018) to examine factors influencing global inflation in time and frequency domains. This analysis examines the changes over time and frequency in the variables BP, WEP, GPRT, GSCPI, and global food prices, which are influential on global inflation. In other words, it investigates the dynamic correlation relationship between these variables, analyzing both bivariate and multivariate aspects. Therefore, it is expected to provide further insights into the relationships between variables and contribute to the relevant literature.

3. ECONOMETRIC METHODOLOGY AND DATASET

This section of the study discusses the dataset and econometric methodology.

3.1. Dynamic Wavelet Correlation Analysis For Multivariate Test

The WLMC approach analyzes dynamic correlation relationships among multivariate datasets. In this analysis, it is used to examine the dynamic correlation relationship at different scales of stationary or non-stationary time series. Therefore, it can be said that it is an appropriate approach for analyzing relationships between economic variables that vary with conjunctural movements (Polanco-Martínez et al., 2020).

In the WLMC approach, dynamic correlation relationships between variables are analyzed in both time and frequency domains by combining wavelet analysis and multivariate correlation analysis. Wavelet analysis estimates the spectral properties of signals as a function of time. Thus, *"the spectrum of a variable is defined by the decomposition of the series' variance as a function of frequency"* (Schulte, 2016:257). In other words, changes in the frequencies of macroeconomic variables affect their variances, thereby altering their spectral properties. Consequently, changes in the series' frequency lead to changes in its spectral properties, indicating shifts in the signals provided by economic indicators. Therefore, analysing the series in both time and frequency dimension with newly developed econometric approaches provides important contributions to the related literature.

There are various approaches developed in the literature to analyze the correlation relationship between variables in terms of time and frequency dimensions. These approaches include the wavelet multiple correlation (WMC), vector wavelet coherence (VWC), and wavelet multiple cross-correlations (WMCC) methods. The WMC approach analyzes the common movements of variables across time scales to examine correlations (Bouri, Nekhili, et al., 2023:2). Additionally, both the WMCC and WMC approaches *"implicitly assume that time series follow difference-stationary processes, thereby eliminating non-stationarity from the data with a sufficiently long wavelet filter, similar to standard bivariate wavelet correlations. Consequently, only a single global correlation per scale is required"* (Fernández-Macho, 2018:1227). The VWC approach analyzes the correlation relationship between two time series using wavelet phase coherence, employing continuous wavelet transform to ensure analysis without any loss of information in the variables (Phiri & Anyikwa, 2024:3). The arrows obtained from the analysis indicate positive or negative correlation relationships between variables at different times and frequencies (Kalmaz & Kirikkaleli, 2019; Adebayo, 2020; Wang et al., 2022). The WLMC approach, on the other hand, analyzes the correlation relationship between variables in a multi-variate dataset in both time and frequency dimensions. In other words, the WLMC approach examines the common movements between variables across time varying at different frequencies.

In the WLMC approach,

$$X_t = x_{1t} + x_{2t} + ... + x_{nt} \qquad (1)$$

is a multivariate stochastic process, and

$$W_{jt} = (w_{1jt}, x_{2jt}, ..., w_{njt}) \qquad (2)$$

the scale wavelet coefficients (λ_j) are obtained as a result of the maximum overlap discrete wavelet transform (MODWT) applied to each process x_{it}. The wavelet multiple correlation (WMC) $\varphi_X(\lambda_j)$ can be defined as a single set of multiscale correlations calculated from X_t given in equation 1. We calculate the square root of the regression coefficient of determination in the linear combination of variables w_{ijt}, i=1,2,...,n, where the coefficient of determination is maximum at each wavelet scale λ_j. The coefficient of determination corresponding to the regression of a variable z_i on a set of regressors $\{z_k, k \neq i\}$ can be obtained as

$$R_i^2 = 1 - \frac{1}{p^{ii}} \qquad (3)$$

The parameter p^{ii} given in equation (3) is the i-th diagonal element of the inverse of the full correlation matrix P. In this context, WMC is shown in Equation 4.

$$\varphi_{X,s}(\lambda_j) = \sqrt{1 - \frac{1}{\max diag P_{j,s}^{-1}}} \quad s = 1, 2, ..., T \qquad (4)$$

When the parameter $P_{j,s}$ given in Equation (4) is an (n×n) correlation matrix with weights W_{jt} and $\theta(t-s)$, the maxdiag(.) operator selects the largest element in the diagonal of the argument. The regression coefficient of determination, $\varphi_{X,s}(\lambda_j)$, obtained as the square of the correlation between the observed values and the fitted values can be obtained as in equation (5).

$$\varphi_{X,s}(\lambda_j) = Corr\left(\theta(t-s)^{1/2} w_{ijt}, \theta(t-s)^{1/2} \widehat{w}_{ijt}\right)$$
$$= \frac{Cov\left(\theta(t-s)^{1/2} w_{ijt}, \theta(t-s)^{1/2} \widehat{w}_{ijt}\right)}{\sqrt{Var\left(\theta(t-s)^{1/2} w_{ijt}\right) Var\left(\theta(t-s)^{1/2} \widehat{w}_{ijt}\right)}} \quad s = 1,2,...,T \tag{5}$$

The parameter w_{ij} given in Equation (5) is chosen to maximise the value of $\varphi_{X,s}(\lambda_j)$ and the parameter $\widehat{w}_{ij}$ is the appropriate values in the local regression of w_{ij} on the remaining wavelet coefficients at scale λ_j. In a multivariate setting, we apply MODWT to a multivariate time series X of degree J and obtain the MODWT coefficient $\widetilde{W}_j = \left(\widetilde{W}_{j0}, \widetilde{W}_{j1},...,\widetilde{W}_{j,T-1}\right)$ for j=1,2,...,J for J number of lengths T. From Equation (4), the WLMC of scale λ_j is a non-linear function of all W_{jt} weighted correlations of $n(n-1)/2$. Alternatively, it can be expressed in terms of all weighted covariances and variances of WW as in Equation (5). Therefore, a consistent WLMC estimator based on MODWT is given by;

$$\widetilde{\varphi}_{X,s}(\lambda_j) = \sqrt{1 - \frac{1}{\max diag \, \widetilde{P}^{\wedge -1}_{j,s}}} = Corr\left(\theta(t-s)^{1/2} \widetilde{w}_{ijt}, \theta(t-s)^{1/2} \widehat{\widetilde{w}}_{ijt}\right)$$
$$= \frac{Cov\left(\theta(t-s)^{1/2} \widetilde{w}_{ijt}, \theta(t-s)^{1/2} \widehat{\widetilde{w}}_{ijt}\right)}{\sqrt{Var\left(\theta(t-s)^{1/2} \widetilde{w}_{ijt}\right) Var\left(\theta(t-s)^{1/2} \widehat{\widetilde{w}}_{ijt}\right)}} \quad s = 1,2,...,T \tag{6}$$

Weighted wavelet covariances and variances can be estimated as follows.

$$Var(\widetilde{w}_{ijt}) = \sum_{t=L_j-1}^{T-1} \theta(t-s) \widetilde{w}^2_{ijt}; \quad s = 1,2,...,T \tag{7a}$$

$$Var(\widehat{\widetilde{w}}_{ijt}) = \sum_{t=L_j-1}^{T-1} \theta(t-s) \widehat{\widetilde{w}}^2_{ijt}; \quad s = 1,2,...,T \tag{7b}$$

$$Cov(\widetilde{w}_{ijt}, \widehat{\widetilde{w}}_{ijt}) = \gamma_{j,s} = \sum_{t=L_j-1}^{T-1} \theta(t-s) \widetilde{w}_{ijt} \widehat{\widetilde{w}}_{ijt}; \quad s = 1,2,...,T \tag{7c}$$

The parameter $\widetilde{w}_{ij}$ given in Equation (7) is such that the local regression of $\widetilde{w}_{ij}$ on the regressor set $\{\widetilde{w}_{kj}, k \neq i\}$ maximises the corresponding coefficient of determination. $\widehat{\widetilde{w}}_{ij}$ denotes the fitted values and $L_j=(2^j-1)(L-1)+1$ is the number of boundary-affected wavelet coefficients associated with a wavelet filter of length L at scale λ_j (Fernández-Macho, 2018:1229-1230).

3.2. Data Set Used In The Study

In this study, monthly data from 2004:08 to 2023:10 are used. Data for Brent oil (BP) Price and MSCI World Energy Price Index (WEP) were obtained from Investing.com. The Food Commodity Price Index data is sourced from the Food and Agriculture Organization database. Global inflation rates were sourced from the IMF database. Global Supply Chain Pressure Index (GSCPI) data was obtained from the FED. Geopolitical Risk (GPRT), developed by Dario Caldara and Matteo Iacoviello, was used (https://www.matteoiacoviello.com/gpr.htm). GPRT index is determined using automated text searches of leading newspapers' electronic archives in the US, UK, and Canada, focusing on articles discussing negative geopolitical events and related threats (Caldara & Iacoviello, 2022). The study utilized the 'wavemulcor' R package. Additionally, all variables in the study are used in their raw form.

The primary reason for starting the dataset used in the study from the year 2004 is that the MSCI World Energy Price Index variable obtained from the investing site begins its series from 2004. Therefore, the year 2004 was chosen as the common time period for analyzing all variables.

4. EMPIRICAL RESULTS AND DISCUSSION

This section presents the analysis results of the WLMC approach used for analyzing variations in BP, WEP, GPRT, GSCPI, and global food prices, which are effective on global inflation at different times and frequencies. Preliminary tests are conducted before analyzing the dynamic correlation relationship between variables. The analysis results of the preliminary tests are shown in Table 1 and Table 2. Table 1 presents the Spearman's Correlation Matrix analysis results for the variables, while Table 2 provides the Unit Root Test analysis results. In the pre-tests and WLMC approach used to analyze the dynamic correlation relationship between variables, the variables were used as raw data.

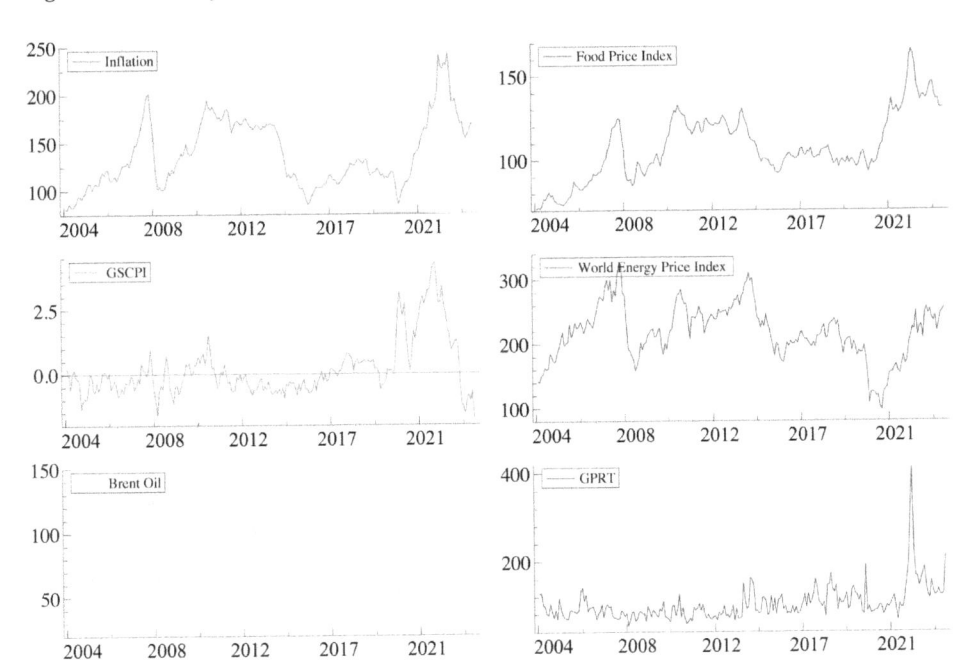

Figure 1. Monthly time trend of İnflation, Food Price, WEP, GPRT, GSCPI and BP

Figure 1 depicts graphs showing the trend changes of all series across different time periods. All variables exhibit volatility trends across various time frames. However, volatility in all markets has increased after 2020-2021.

Table 1. Spearman's Correlation Matrix

Variable	WEP	Inflation	Food Price	BP	GPRT	GSCPI
WE	1	0.6279***	0.4040***	0.7903***	-0.0698	-0.2805***
Inflation	0.6279***	1	0.8425***	0.9107***	0.0495	0.2157***
Food Price	0.4040***	0.8425***	1	0.6615***	0.1813***	0.2855***
BP	0.7903***	0.9107***	0.6615***	1	-0.0756	-0.0279
GPRT	-0.0698	0.0495	0.1813***	-0.0756	1	0.1991***
GSCPI	-0.2805***	0.2157***	0.2855***	-0.0279	0.1991***	1

Note: * $p<0,1$; ** $p<0.05$ and *** $p<0.001$. 95% confidence interval was used statistically.

Table 1 displays the results of Spearman correlation coefficients. The correlation relationships among the variables Inflation, Food price, GSCPI, WEP, GPRT, and BP vary due to being either positive or negative. Example, there is a positive correlation between Inflation and Food price variables with GSCPI, WEP, BP, and

GPRT variables. This finding indicates that certain variables have a significant impact on changes in global inflation. Specifically, there is a high and positive correlation between global inflation, food price, and BP.

Table 2. Unit Root Test

Unit Root Test	Inflation	Food Price	WEP	GPRT	GSCPI	BP
ADF Test						
Intercept	-2.4925	-2.4011	-2.7665	-5.7775***	-2.5711	-2.9842**
Trend and intercept	-2.4866	-2.8252	-2.9195	-6.9383***	-2.6515	-3.0001
KPSS Test						
Intercept	0.244179***	0.7939	0.3238***	1.036718	0.683802*	0.207578***
Trend and intercept	0.171238*	0.1869*	0.1453**	0.170764*	0.132734**	0.188562**
Zivot-Andrew Test						
Intercept	-4.2816***	-4.4848**	-3.6914***	-7.3429	-3.3756***	-5.1060*
Break Point Date	2014M7	2014M5	2014M10	2008M1	2019M6	2014M10
Trend and intercept	-4.2075***	-4.3864***	-4.1205***	-7.5603	-5.4829*	4.9249**
Break Point Date	2014M7	2014M5	2020M2	2020M2	2020M11	2014M10

Note: * $p<0,1$;** $p<0.05$ and *** $p<0.001$. 95% confidence interval was used statistically.

Table 2 presents the results of stationarity tests for the variables. The ADF unit root test, the variables inflation, WEP, GSCPI, and food price contain with a unit root at intercept with intercept and trend levels. The GPRT variable is stationary with intercept and trend terms. The KPSS test indicates that the variables Inflation, WEP, and BP are stationary, while food price, GPRT, and GSCPI are non-stationary. Zivot-Andrew test, Inflation, food price, WEP, and GSCPI variables are stationary at the intercept level, whereas GPRT and BP variables are non-stationary. At the trend and intercept levels, Inflation, food price, WEP, and BP variables are stationary, while GPRT and GSCPI variables are non-stationary.

4.1. Model Analysis for Wavelet Local Multiple Correlation

Many of the approaches used to analyze the correlation relationship between variables conduct static analysis, as they do not consider changes occurring in different time periods. Therefore, various approaches have been developed to analyze the dynamic correlation relationship between variables. Accordingly, in this study, the WLMC approach has been used to estimate the dynamic correlation relationship between variables.

The WLMC approach is estimated based on 231 monthly observations with a Gauss window length. The wavelet filter used has a Daubechies LA(8) at level J = 8. *"The vertical axis represents frequencies, and the horizontal axis represents time intervals. The periods shown on the vertical axis range from period 1 (months) to period 32 (months). The wavelet periods are defined as follows: 2–4 months, 4–8 months, 8–16 months, and 16–32 months. Periods beyond 32 months are labeled as 'Smooth'. The correlation relationship between variables is depicted in the figures with black lines. Wavelet local multiple correlations illustrate the regions where two variables are dependent in the time-frequency domain. Areas where there is no correlation between variables are shown as empty. High correlation between variables is represented in red, while low correlation is represented in blue. The vertical side bar indicates the value of the spectral correlation relationship between variables"* (Shah et al., 2022:7)

Figure 2a. Inflation and Food Price

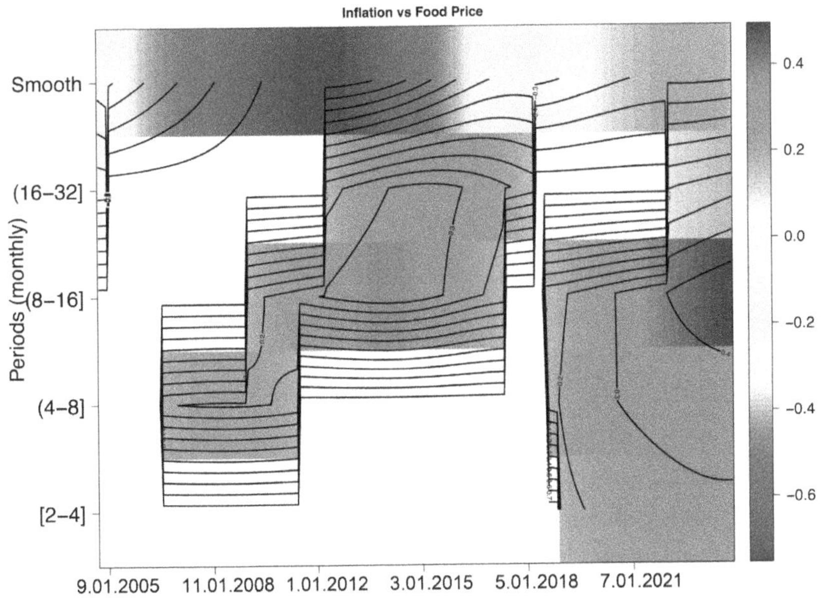

Note: *parameters: window=Gaussian, M=231/6=38 (days), Wf= "la8".*

In **Figure 2a**, the correlation relationship between global inflation and global food prices is desplayed. Between the two variables, the longest period [Smooth] from 2005 to 2018 shows a negative correlation (-0.5). From 2012 to 2018, the shortest period [2-4 months] exhibits a strong correlation (within the range of 0.2-0.4). After 2018, there is no correlation among the variables in the shortest period [2-4 months]. The shortest period [2-4 months] and the period (8-16 months] after 2018 indicate a strong positive correlation among the variables, which is consistent with the Spearman correlation (0.8425).

Figure 2b. Inflation and GSCPI

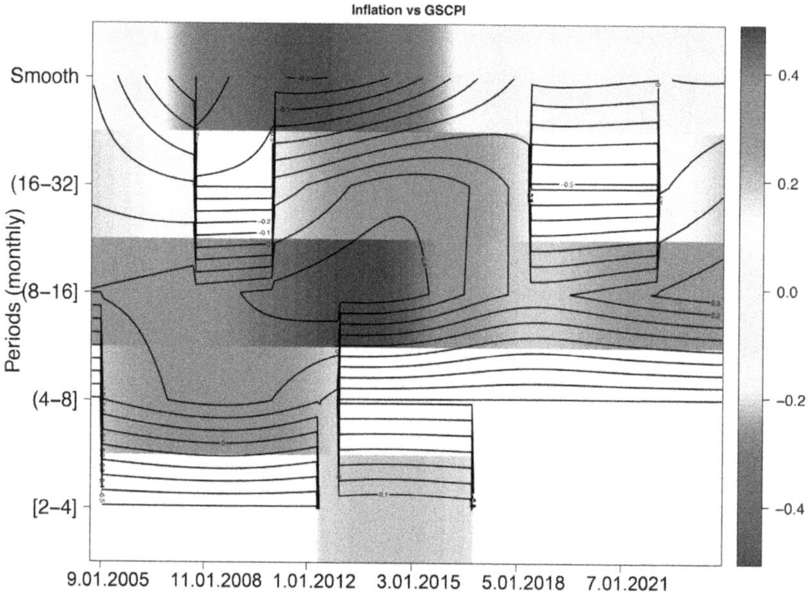

Note: *parameters: window=Gaussian, M=231/6=38 (days), Wf= "la8".*

In **Figure 2b**, the correlation relationship among global inflation and GSCPI is examined. The spectral correlation relationship among the two variables changes from negative to positive correlation towards the highest period [Smooth] and after 2018. This variability suggests that disruptions in global trade have different effects on global inflation across different time and frequency dimensions. This finding is consistent with the Spearman correlation (0.2157) obtained. Particularly in recent periods, it can be said that the correlation relationship has changed due to global events and shocks occurring in different markets.

Figure 2c. Inflation and BP

[Figure: Inflation vs BP spectral correlation plot. X-axis: dates from 9.01.2005 to 7.01.2021. Y-axis: Periods (monthly) with levels [2–4], (4–8], (8–16], (16–32], Smooth. Color scale from -0.4 to 0.4.]

Note: *parameters: window=Gaussian, M=231/6=38 (days), Wf= "la8".*

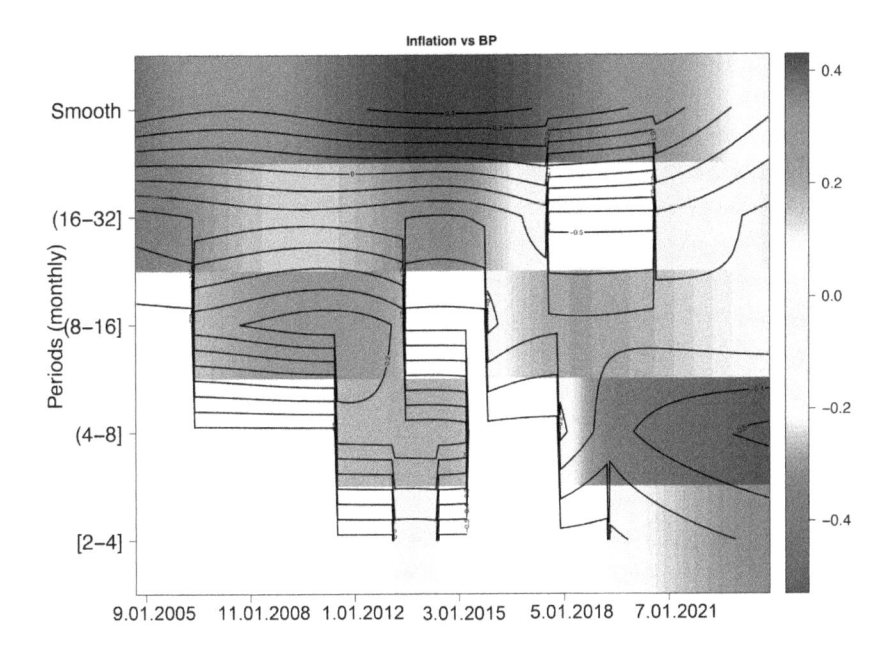

In **Figure 2c,** the relationship among global inflation and BP is desplayed. The spectral correlation relationship among the two variables shows a strong and positive correlation (0.4) up to the longest period [Smooth] and until 2018, whereas after 2018, a positive and weaker correlation (0.2-0) is observed. This indicates that the correlation relationship among the variables varies across different periods and time frames. The highest period results are consistent with the Spearman correlation (0.8425) obtained. At the lowest period, a correlation relationship among the variables is observed after 2018, while generally, there is no correlation relationship among the variables before 2018.

Figure 2d. Inflation and WEP

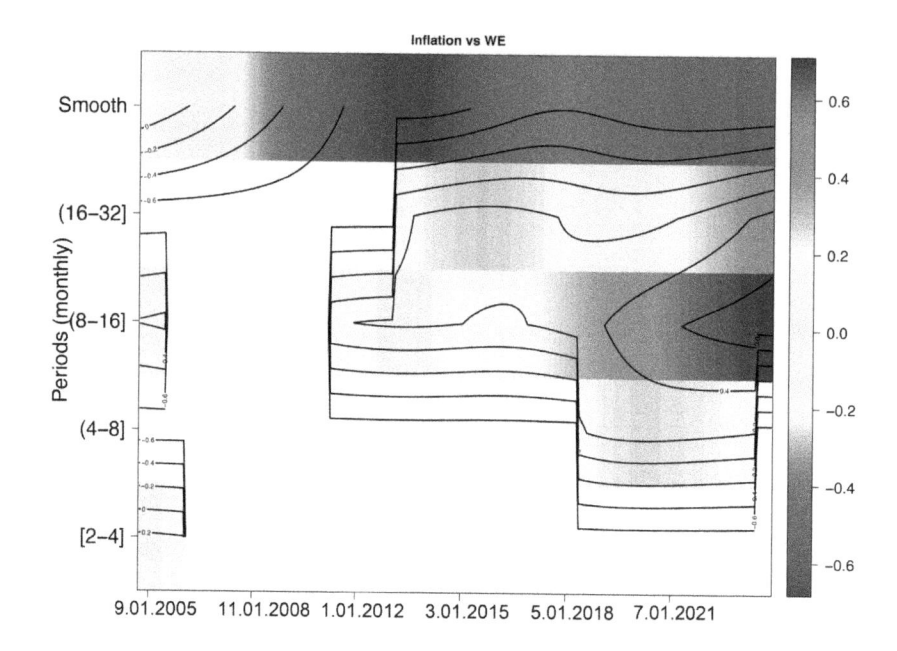

Note: *parameters: window=Gaussian, M=231/6=38 (days), Wf= "la8".*

Figure 2d, the relationship among global inflation and WEP is desplayed. The spectral correlation relationship among the variables shows a negative correlation since the longest period [Smooth] and after 2008. However, there is no correlation relationship among the variables at the shortest period (2-4 months] after 2005. The spectral correlation relationship among the variables generally does not align with the Spearman correlation (0.6279). There is a positive correlation relationship between the variables among (4-8 months] and (16-32 months] periods after 2012, but it can be noted that the highest period shows a negative correlation.

Figure 2e. Inflation and GPRT

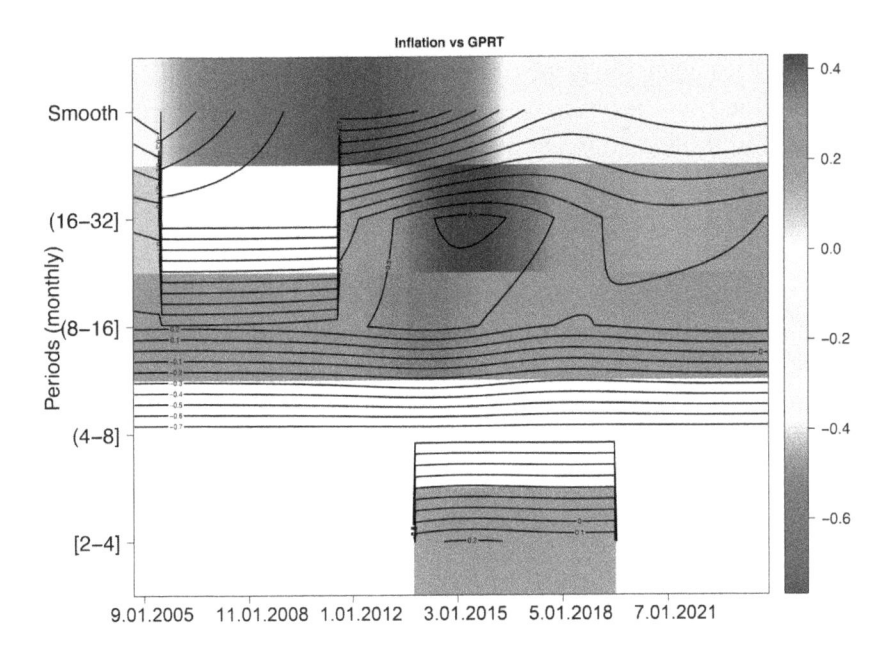

[Figure: Inflation vs GPRT contour plot. Y-axis: Periods (monthly) with levels Smooth, (16–32], (8–16], (4–8], [2–4]. X-axis: dates from 9.01.2005 to 7.01.2021. Color scale from -0.6 to 0.4.]

Note: *parameters: window=Gaussian, M=231/6=38 (days), Wf= "la8".*

Figure 2e, the relationship among global inflation and GPRT is desplayed. The spectral correlation relationship among the variables shows a negative correlation during the longest period [Smooth] and among 2005-2015, while generally, there is no correlation relationship among the variables at the shortest period (2-4 months]. According to the Spearman correlation, there is no correlation relationship among the variables.

Bivariate model analysis for WLMC; Considering the findings from the two-variable analysis, the correlation relationship among variables varies across different periods and time periods. There is no correlation among the variables during the shortest period [2-4 months] and before 2018, whereas a correlation relationship exists among the variables after 2018 at the longest period. This relationship shows a weak correlation at the highest period. However, it can be noted that before 2018, there was a high correlation among global inflation and BP at the highest period. Particularly, the occurrence of high correlation among variables at high frequencies after 2018 may be attributed to recent events such as wars, pandemics, and economic crises.

Since 2018, a strong correlation relationship among variables has been observed at high frequencies. In other words, the presence of a robust correlation between inflation and key macroeconomic variables can be said to be a fundamental cause of inflationary tendencies in many countries (Bank of England, 2022). Particularly, European Union countries have been among the most affected by the continuous upward trend in inflation, largely due to issues and price increases in the energy market. While these countries implement a common monetary policy, the lack of a common fiscal policy to support these monetary policies affects their effectiveness on the markets. This is because each country's different institutional and socio-economic structures influence the effectiveness of implemented monetary policies, thereby contributing to changes in inflationary trends across all countries (Taşdöken & Kahyaoğlu, 2023b). Another significant factor is the impact of Russia imposing restrictions on gas sales to Europe due to the Russia-Ukraine war, leading to increased energy prices and household energy consumption costs in Europe (Abbas & Lan, 2020; Abubakar et al., 2024). Considering all these factors, it can be generally stated that a persistent inflation problem has emerged across all countries.

Figure 3a. Inflation,FoodPrice,GPRT

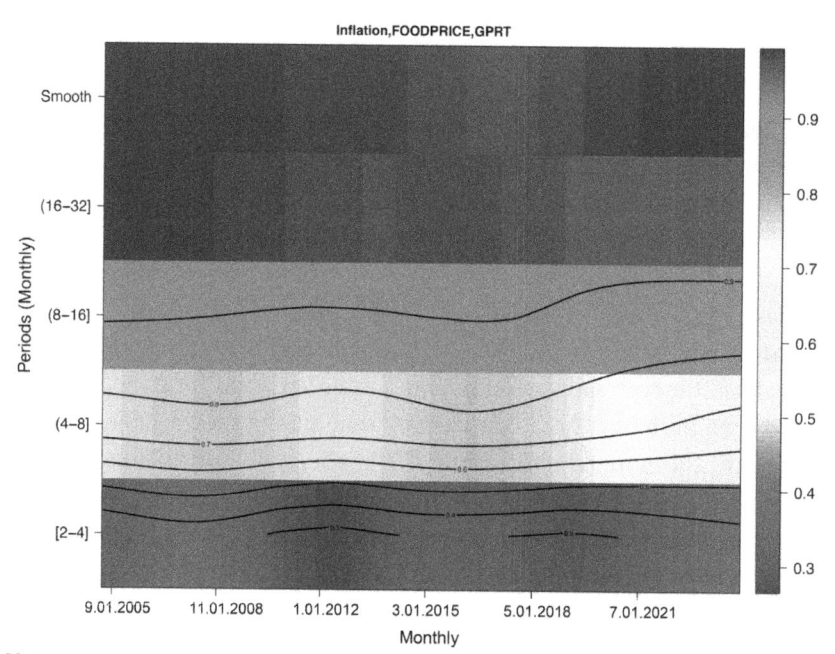

Note: *parameters: window=Gaussian, M=231/6=38 (days), Wf= "la8".*

Figure 3a, the relationship among global inflation, global food prices, and GPRT variable is desplayed. There is a spectral correlation relationship among the variables, with the longest period [Smooth] showing a positive and high correlation among 2005-2023, whereas the shortest period [2-4] exhibits a negative and low correlation over the same period.

Figure 3b. Inflation, GPRT,GSCPI

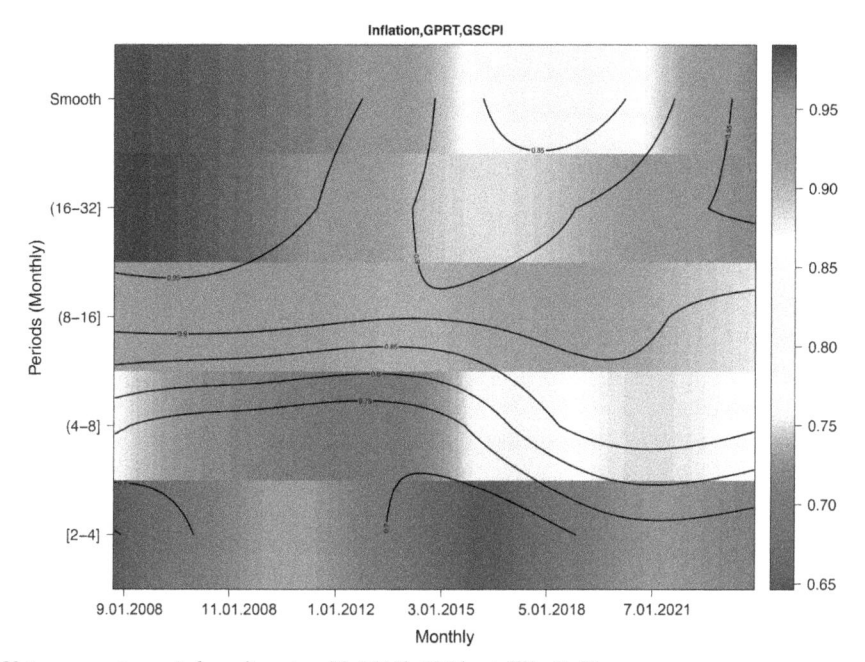

Note: *parameters: window=Gaussian, M=231/6=38 (days), Wf= "la8".*

Figure 3b, the relationship among inflation and GPRT, GSCPI variables is desplayed. There is a weak correlation among the variables with a [2-4 month] period after 2012, whereas there is no correlation relationship before 2012. The correlation relationship varies among the variables with a [Smooth] period among 2005-2021, particularly showing a strong correlation relationship after 2021.

Figure 3c. Inflation,GSCPI,BP

Note: *parameters: window=Gaussian, M=231/6=38 (days), Wf= "la8".*

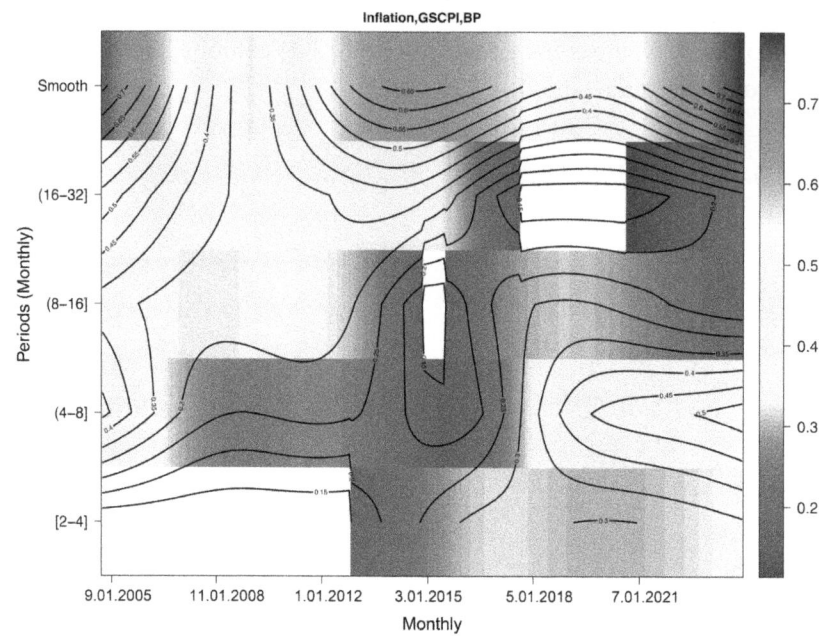

Figure 3c, the relationship among global inflation, GSCPI, and BP variable is desplayed. There is a weak correlation among the variables at the [2-4 month] period among 2005-2015, while no correlation relationship exists between 2015-2021. The correlation relationship varies with the [Smooth] period and different years. After 2021, a positive correlation is observed among the variables at this period, showing a higher correlation compared to other years

Figure 3d. Inflation,BP,WEP

Note: *parameters: window=Gaussian, M=231/6=38 (days), Wf= "la8".*

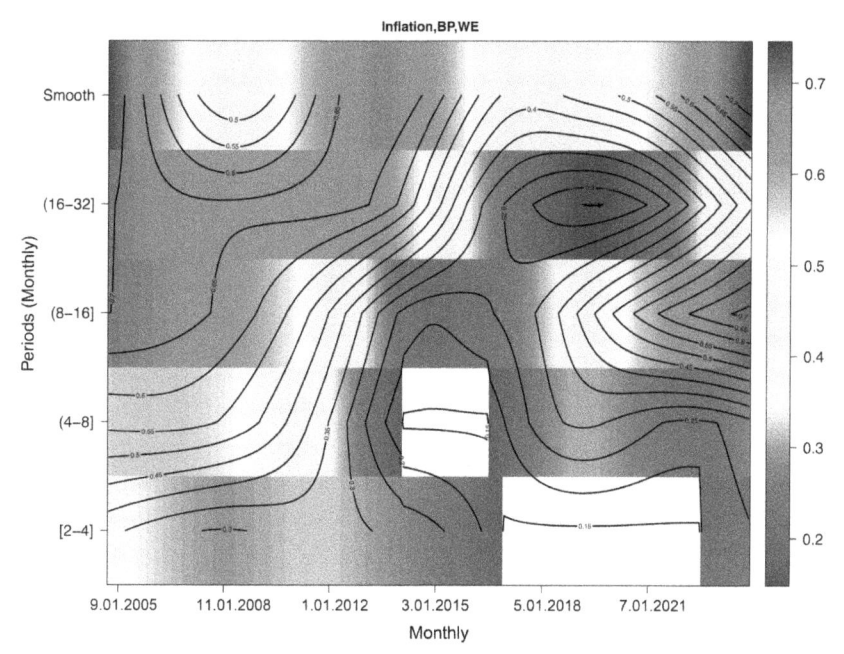

Figure 3d, the relationship among global inflation, BP and WEP variable is desplayed. There is a correlation relationship among the variables across all different years and periods. The highest correlation relationship among the variables occurred with the [Smooth] period between 2005-2015 and after 2021. Across all different years, a weak and positive correlation relationship is observed with the [2-4 month] period.

Figure 3e. Inflation, GPRT,BP

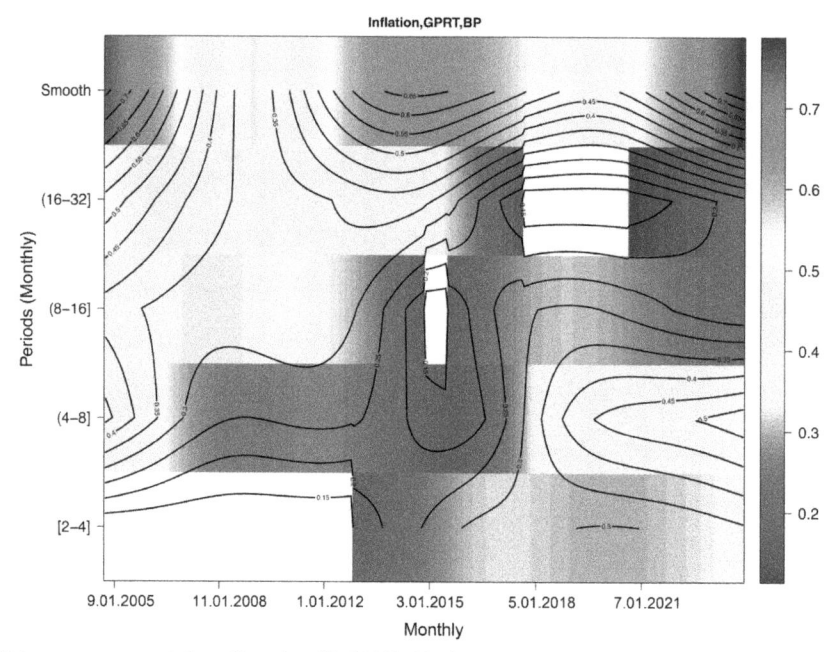

Note: *parameters: window=Gaussian, M=231/6=38 (days), Wf= "la8".*

Figure 3e, the relationship among global inflation, BP, and GPRT variable is desplayed. There is no correlation relationship among the variables at the [2-4 month] period between 2005-2012. However, a weak and positive correlation relationship is observed among the variables after 2012. Across different time periods, both the [2-4 month] and (16-32 month) periods exhibit positive and weak correlation relationships. With the [Smooth] period between 2005-2012 and 2016-2018, a positive and weak correlation relationship is found, while in all other years, a positive and strong correlation relationship is observed among the variables.

Figure 3f. Inflation,WEP,GPRT

[Figure: Wavelet coherence plot titled "Inflation,GPRT,WE" showing periods (Monthly) on y-axis with levels Smooth, (16-32], (8-16], (4-8], [2-4], and dates from 9.01.2005 to 7.01.2021 on x-axis. Color scale 0.2 to 0.8.]

Note: *parameters: window=Gaussian, M=231/6=38 (days), Wf= "la8".*

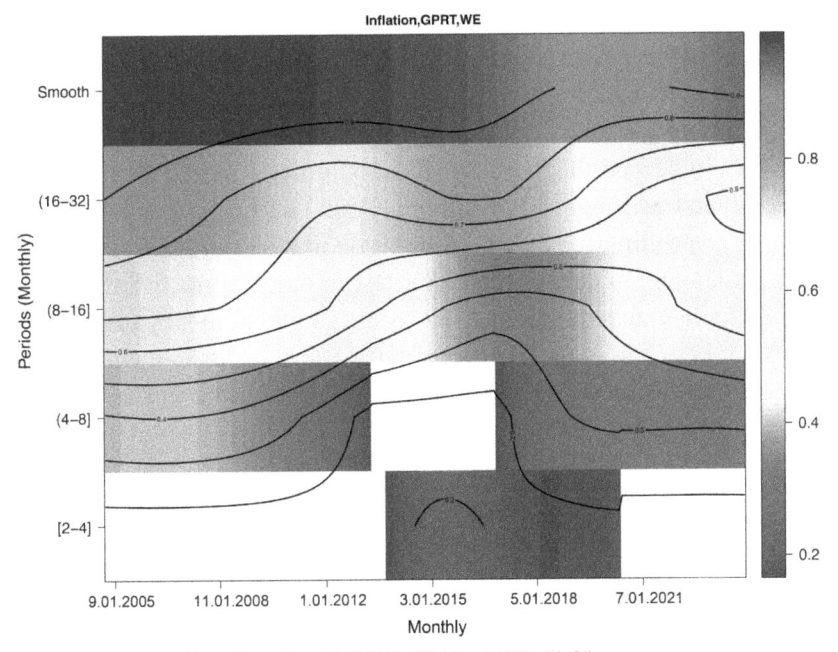

Figure 3f, the relationship among global inflation, WEP, and GPRT variable is desplayed. There is no correlation relationship between the variables at the [2-4 month] period between 2005-2012 and after 2018. However, in other years, there is a positive and weak correlation relationship between the variables. Across all years, a positive and high correlation relationship is found with the [Smooth] period. The correlation relationship among the variables varies across different years as much as between the [2-4 month] period and the [Smooth] period.

Considering the findings, the correlation relationship among variables varies across different periods and time spans. Particularly, all analyses indicate a high correlation between variables after 2021 with the [Smooth] period. Triple analyses involving variables influencing inflation also indicate strong concurrent movements occurring at different periods. Strong concurrent movements between variables notably increase, especially with the [Smooth] period and after 2021.

The Multivariate Model Analysis for WLMC; Figure 4, the relationship among global inflation, GPRT, GSCPI, WEP, BO, food price variable is desplayed. The correlation relationship among variables varies across different periods and time frames. Specifically, there is a negative and weak correlation between the variables at the (2-4 month] period and across all years, while a positive and high correlation emerges with the [Smooth] period between 2005-2023. In this context, the multivariate model analysis suggests that the dynamic correlation between variables is irregular across different times and frequencies. Especially in recent times, events occurring in different global markets are noted to have simultaneous impacts on other markets. In this context, considering the heterogeneous effects of volatilities occurring in different markets on developed and developing country markets and economies, it can be said that the normalization process in economic structure in developing country markets will be different from that in advanced country economies. While controlling the effects of inflation is easier in developed countries, it is more challenging in developing countries. In other words, it can be said that the economic policy uncertainty that may occur in global money markets and the inflation shock in global trade are fundamental determinants in the markets of developing countries where the dollar is used as a reserve currency (Thac et al., 2024).

Figure 4. Inflation <− GPRT,GSCPI,WEP,BO, Food Price

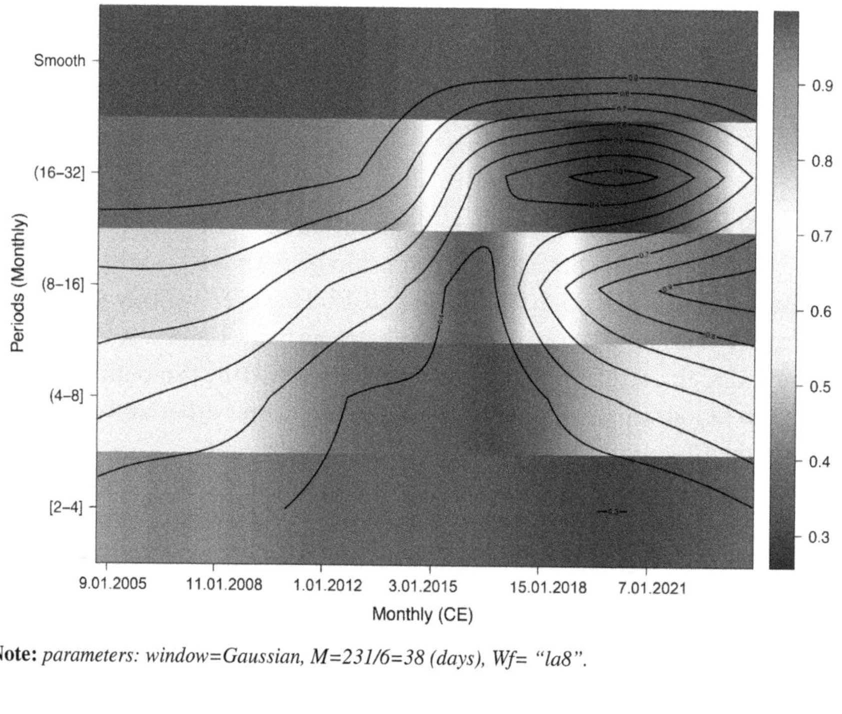

Note: *parameters: window=Gaussian, M=231/6=38 (days), Wf= "la8".*

5. CONCLUSION

This study analyzes the relationship among global inflation, global food price, BP, WEP, GSCPI, and GPRT variables using monthly data from 2004:08 to 2023:10. In this analysis, the WLMC approach is employed to examine the dynamic correlation relationship between variables across time and frequency dimensions.

The study, firstly, it is observed that the correlation relationship in time and frequency dimensions varies across different time periods among the variables. This indicates heterogeneous relationships among the variables over different periods. Secondly, it is concluded that there are varying annual and period correlations among all variables. In this context, economic variables and markets are generally interrelated, and increased economic integration also influences the correlation relationship between variables. Thirdly, it can be stated that strong correlation relationships among variables have been found after the year 2021 in all analyses. In this context;

- The finding indicates that in recent years, there has been stronger economic integration across different global markets. Despite various adversities globally between 2019 and 2023, it can be said that a global recession did not occur. This situation suggests that the banking sector and different markets have become less vulnerable to potential crises, and policies implemented by central banks to mitigate the impact of possible shocks on markets have been effective.
- The continuous increase in global production costs also indicates a persistent upward trend in living costs. Additionally, it can be stated that inflation expectations were high during the period under consideration. Therefore, in many countries, various financial supports have been provided to reduce household living costs to prevent a pass-through from prices to wages. In this context, the absence of wage-price spirals in countries has enhanced the effectiveness of policies implemented on markets.
- Strong economic integration among global markets also affects the transmission of global economic shocks to local economies depending on the monetary policies implemented in different countries.
- Strong economic integration among different markets also tends to increase long-term financial and fiscal risks, and economic uncertainties for national economies. In this context, central banks have significant responsibilities to eliminate current volatilities across all markets and to ensure stability.

Considering the findings from this study, policies aimed at reducing the upward trend in global inflation;

- The slow impact of central banks' tight monetary policies during this period indicates the need for central banks to carefully calibrate their periods of monetary easing.
- Between 2019 and 2024, the strong measures and reforms implemented by central banks to combat disinflation are expected to gradually reduce domestic demand and thereby slow down inflationary trends. However, ongoing geopolitical issues and global supply-side shocks continuing to impact local economies will predominantly contribute to inflationary pressures stemming from supply-side shocks. This situation may lead countries to shift their external trade partners, adopt new trade routes, implement stringent protectionist measures, and witness a shift in global trade towards neighboring countries.
- Disinflation policy applied under disinflation policies increase borrowing costs, leading to increased public and household debt in all countries implementing tight monetary policies. This situation is likely to increase countries' financial risks and economic vulnerabilities.
- Considering the current global economic conditions and market situation between 2019 and 2024, it can be said that there has been a decrease in direct foreign investments and a slowdown in capital flows from advanced economies to developing economies. Therefore, it can be stated that this has been effective in creating favorable economic conditions for ensuring financial and economic stability in developing countries.
- The high economic dependency among countries and the strong economic integration of different markets lead to the transmission of shocks occurring in one market or country to other countries and markets. Therefore, central banks' monetary policies have varying impacts on other economies and markets depending on the strength of economic integration. This phenomenon tends to manifest as an economic trend from developed country economies towards developing country economies. Hence, while living costs may decrease in developed countries, it can be said that living costs in developing country economies may continue to rise.
- Increasing investment in green energy policies aimed at reducing volatility in the global energy market, which has a significant impact on the upward trend of global inflation, will help mitigate supply shocks. This approach contributes to reducing energy dependence, implementing net-zero carbon emission policies, and reducing environmental pollution.
- The increasing external dependency on and consumption of petroleum by all countries affects the effectiveness of policies aimed at achieving economic stability. In this context, countries can increase investments in renewable energy sources to reduce volatility in oil prices (Zhang et al., 2024). Such

investments not only decrease countries' reliance on oil but also contribute to mitigating the upward trend of inflation against supply shocks.

Taking into account the findings from this study, central banks can help reduce future risks and uncertainties by investigating the relationships among macro-economic variables affecting global inflation. Specifically, it is expected that the insights gained could assist monetary policy decisions in addressing the persistence of general price levels.

6. LIMITATIONS OF THE STUDY

Limitations of the study analyzing the dynamic correlation relationship between global inflation and global food price, BP, WEP, GSCPI, and GPRT variables are as follows:

- The analysis focuses on fundamental economic variables that influence volatility in global inflation. However, it does not consider other economic variables that directly or indirectly affect the volatility of these fundamental variables. This omission constitutes one of the major limitations of the study. Future research could expand the scope by including these variables.
- The study does not include global climate change as a variable, despite its significant influence on global food prices. This omission is primarily due to the focus on analyzing global inflation using fundamental macroeconomic variables. Including climate change as a variable in future studies could enhance the comprehensiveness of the analysis.

REFERENCES

Abbas, S. K., & Lan, H. (2020). Commodity price pass-through and inflation regimes. *Energy Economics*, 92, 104977. DOI: 10.1016/j.eneco.2020.104977

Abubakar, A. B., Karimu, S., & Mamman, S. O. (2024). Inflation effects of oil and gas prices in the UK : Symmetries and asymmetries. *Utilities Policy*, 90(July), 101803. DOI: 10.1016/j.jup.2024.101803

Adams, J. J., & Barrett, P. (2024). Review of economic dynamics shocks to inflation expectations. *Review of Economic Dynamics, 54*(October 2022), 101234. DOI: 10.1016/j.red.2024.101234

Adebayo, T. S. (2020). Revisiting the EKC hypothesis in an emerging market: An application of ARDL-based bounds and wavelet coherence approaches. *SN Applied Sciences*, 2(12), 1–15. DOI: 10.1007/s42452-020-03705-y

Aharon, D. Y., Azman Aziz, M. I., & Kallir, I. (2023). Oil price shocks and inflation: A cross-national examination in the ASEAN5+3 countries. *Resources Policy, 82*(December 2022), 103573. DOI: 10.1016/j.resourpol.2023.103573

AL-Rousan, N., AL-Najjar, H., & AL-Najjar, D.AL-Rousan. (2024). The impact of Russo-Ukrainian war, COVID-19, and oil prices on global food security. *Heliyon*, 10(8), e29279. DOI: 10.1016/j.heliyon.2024.e29279 PMID: 38638981

Ampudia, M., Ehrmann, M., & Strasser, G. (2024). Shopping behavior and the effect of monetary policy on inflation heterogeneity along the income distribution. *Journal of Monetary Economics, September 2023*, 103618. DOI: 10.1016/j.jmoneco.2024.103618

Anderl, C., & Caporale, G. M. (2024). Shipping cost uncertainty, endogenous regime switching and the global drivers of inflation. *International Economics, 178*(November 2023), 100500. DOI: 10.1016/j.inteco.2024.100500

Andriantomanga, Z., Bolhuis, M. A., & Hakobyan, S. 2022. Global supply chain disruptions: Challenges for inflation and monetary policy in Sub-Saharan Africa. Technical report, International Monetary Fund, Working Paper WP/23/39. https://www.imf.org/en/Publications/WP/Issues/2023/02/24/Global-Supply-Chain-Disruptions-Challenges-for-Inflation-and-Monetary-Policy-in-Sub-Saharan-530156

Ascari, G., Bonam, D., & Smadu, A. (2024). Global supply chain pressures, inflation, and implications for monetary policy. *Journal of International Money and Finance*, 142(February), 1–25. DOI: 10.1016/j.jimonfin.2024.103029

Baba, C., Duval, R., Lan, T., & Topalova, P. (2023). *The 2020-2022 Inflation surge across Europe : A Phillips-Curve-Based Dissection* (WP/23/30).

Beaudry, P., Carter, T., & Lahri, A. (2023). "The Central Banker's Dilemma: Look through supply shocks or control inflation expectations?", NBER Working Paper 31741

Beckworth, D., & Horan, P. J. (2024). A Two-for-One Deal: Targeting nominal GDP to create a supply-shock robust inflation target. *Journal of Policy Modeling*, 1–22. DOI: 10.1016/j.jpolmod.2024.05.014

Bednář, O., Čečrdlová, A., Kadeřábková, B., & Řežábek, P. (2022). Energy prices impact on inflationary spiral. *Energies*, 15(9), 3443. Advance online publication. DOI: 10.3390/en15093443

Ben Cheikh, N., Ben Zaied, Y., & Mattoussi, W. (2023). Oil price shocks in the age of surging inflation. *Energy Economics*, 128(January), 107128. DOI: 10.1016/j.eneco.2023.107128

Bjørnland, H. C. (2022). The effect of rising energy prices amid geopolitical developments and supply. In *CAMP Working Paper Series* (Issue 7/2022).

Blinova, T. V., Rusanovskii, V. A., & Markov, V. A. (2021). Estimating the impact of economic fluctuations on unemployment in Russian regions based on the Okun Model. *Studies on Russian Economic Development*, 32(1), 103–110. DOI: 10.1134/S1075700721010032 PMID: 33642848

Bolhuis, M., Hakobyan, S., & Andriantomanga, Z. (2023). Global supply chain disruptions: Challenges for inflation and monetary policy in Sub-Saharan Africa. *IMF Working Paper*, 2023(039), 1. DOI: 10.5089/9798400235436.001

Bouri, E., Gabauer, D., Gupta, R., & Kinateder, H. (2023). Global geopolitical risk and inflation spillovers across European and North American economies. *Research in International Business and Finance*, 66(March), 102048. DOI: 10.1016/j.ribaf.2023.102048

Bouri, E., Nekhili, R., & Todorova, N. (2023). Dynamic co-movement in major commodity markets during crisis periods: A wavelet local multiple correlation analysis. *Finance Research Letters, 55*(PB), 103996. DOI: 10.1016/j.frl.2023.103996

Caldara, D., Conlisk, S., Iacoviello, M., & Penn, M. (2022). The Effect of the War in Ukraine on Global Activity and Inflation. In *FEDS Notes*. Board of Governors of the Federal Reserve System. [date of access:28.07.2024], https://www.federalreserve.gov/econres/notes/feds-notes/the-effect-of-the-war-in-ukraine-on-global-activity-and-inflation-20220527.html DOI: 10.17016/2380-7172.3141

Canepa, A. (2024). Inflation dynamics and persistence: The importance of the uncertainty channel. *North American Journal of Economics and Finance, 72*(March 2023), 102135. DOI: 10.1016/j.najef.2024.102135

Diaz, E. M., Cunado, J., & de Gracia, F. P. (2023). Commodity price shocks, supply chain disruptions and U.S. inflation. *Finance Research Letters*, 58, 1–7. DOI: 10.1016/j.frl.2023.104495

Dietrich, A. M. (2024). Consumption categories, household attention, and inflation expectations : Implications for optimal monetary policy. *Journal of Monetary Economics*, 103594(April), 103594. DOI: 10.1016/j.jmoneco.2024.103594

Durevall, D., Loening, J. L., & Ayalew Birru, Y. (2013). Inflation dynamics and food prices in Ethiopia. *Journal of Development Economics, 104*(December 2012), 89–106. DOI: 10.1016/j.jdeveco.2013.05.002

England, B. (2022). *Monetary policy summary and minutes of the monetary policy committee meeting ending on 15 june 2022*. Bank of England.

Fazal, R., Rehman, S. A. U., & Bhatti, M. I. (2022). Graph theoretic approach to expose the energy-induced crisis in Pakistan. *Energy Policy, 169*(October 2021), 113174. DOI: 10.1016/j.enpol.2022.113174

Fernández-Macho, J. (2012). Wavelet multiple correlation and cross-correlation: A multiscale analysis of Eurozone stock markets. *Physica A*, 391(4), 1097–1104. DOI: 10.1016/j.physa.2011.11.002

Fernández-Macho, J. (2018). Time-localized wavelet multiple regression and correlation. *Physica A*, 492, 1226–1238. DOI: 10.1016/j.physa.2017.11.050

Finck, D., & Tillmann, P. The Macroeconomic effects of global supply chain disruptions (February 6, 2023). BOFIT Discussion Paper No. 14/2022, Available at *SSRN*: https://ssrn.com/abstract=4349825 or DOI: 10.2139/ssrn.4349825

Giovanni, D. J., Kalemli Özcan, Ş., Silva, A., & Yildirim, A. M. (2022). *Global supply chain pressures, international trade and inflation* (No. 30240). https://www.nber.org/papers/w30240

Ha, J., Kose, M. A., Ohnsorge, F., & Yilmazkuday, H. (2023). Understanding the global drivers of inflation: How important are oil prices? *Energy Economics, 127*(PA), 107096. DOI: 10.1016/j.eneco.2023.107096

Hu, R., Wang, J., Yang, Y., & Zheng, Z. (2024). Journal of International Money and Finance Inflation and income inequality in an open-economy growth model with liquidity constraints on R & D. *Journal of International Money and Finance*, 147(July), 103127. DOI: 10.1016/j.jimonfin.2024.103127

Jiang, Y., Qu, B., Hong, Y., & Xiao, X. (2024). Dynamic connectedness of inflation around the world: A time-varying approach from G7 and E7 countries. *Quarterly Review of Economics and Finance, 95*(August 2022), 111–125. DOI: 10.1016/j.qref.2024.03.006

Jordà, Ò., & Nechio, F. (2023). Inflation and wage growth since the pandemic. *European Economic Review, 156*(March 2020), 104474. DOI: 10.1016/j.euroecorev.2023.104474

Kalmaz, D. B., & Kirikkaleli, D. (2019). Modeling CO2 emissions in an emerging market: Empirical finding from ARDL-based bounds and wavelet coherence approaches. *Environmental Science and Pollution Research International*, 26(5), 5210–5220. DOI: 10.1007/s11356-018-3920-z PMID: 30604366

Kartal, M. T., Taşkın, D., & Kılıç Depren, S. (2024). Dynamic relationship between green bonds, energy prices, geopolitical risk, and disaggregated level CO2 emissions: Evidence from the globe by novel WLMC approach. *Air Quality, Atmosphere & Health*. Advance online publication. DOI: 10.1007/s11869-024-01544-z

Lee, C. C., Olasehinde-Williams, G., & Özkan, O. (2023). Geopolitical oil price uncertainty transmission into core inflation: Evidence from two of the biggest global players. *Energy Economics*, 126(August), 106983. Advance online publication. DOI: 10.1016/j.eneco.2023.106983

Li, H., Huang, X., & Guo, L. (2023). Extreme risk dependence and time-varying spillover between crude oil, commodity market and inflation in China. *Energy Economics, 127*(PB), 107090. DOI: 10.1016/j.eneco.2023.107090

Lu, S., Coutts, K., & Gudgin, G. (2024). Energy shocks and inflation episodes in the UK. *Energy Economics, 129*(December 2022), 107208. DOI: 10.1016/j.eneco.2023.107208

Ogrokhina, O., & Rodriguez, C. M. (2024). Inflation targeting and capital flows : A tale of two cycles in developing countries. *Journal of International Money and Finance*, 146(June), 1–27. DOI: 10.1016/j.jimonfin.2024.103121

Örn, M. N. (2017). *Negative interest rate & the level of household debt*. OAI: oai:DiVA.org:umu-132005. [date of access:28.07.2024] https://www.diva-portal.org/smash/get/diva2:1077817/FULLTEXT01.pdf

Pan, Z., Bai, Z., Xing, X., & Wang, Z. (2024). US inflation and global commodity prices: Asymmetric interdependence. *Research in International Business and Finance, 69*(November 2023), 102245. DOI: 10.1016/j.ribaf.2024.102245

Pedersen, M. (2024). The effect of monetary policy on inflation expectations : Evidence from a financial traders survey. *Economic Modelling*, 137(April), 106778. DOI: 10.1016/j.econmod.2024.106778

Phiri, A., & Anyikwa, I. (2024). A multiscale analysis of returns and volatility spillovers in cryptocurrency markets: A post-COVID perspective. *The Investment Analysts Journal*, 1–21. Advance online publication. DOI: 10.1080/10293523.2024.2333069

Platitas, R. J. C., & Ocampo, J. C. G. (2024). Latin American Journal of Central Banking From bottlenecks to inflation : Impact of global supply-chain disruptions on inflation in select Asian economies. *Latin American Journal of Central Banking, May*, 100141. DOI: 10.1016/j.latcb.2024.100141

Polanco-Martínez, J. M., Fernández-Macho, J., & Medina-Elizalde, M. (2020). Dynamic wavelet correlation analysis for multivariate climate time series. *Scientific Reports*, 10(1), 1–11. DOI: 10.1038/s41598-020-77767-8 PMID: 33277562

Saeed, A., Chaudhry, S. M., Arif, A., & Ahmed, R. (2023). Spillover of energy commodities and inflation in G7 plus Chinese economies. *Energy Economics, 127*(PA), 107029. DOI: 10.1016/j.eneco.2023.107029

Schulte, J. A. (2016). Wavelet analysis for non-stationary, nonlinear time series. *Nonlinear Processes in Geophysics*, 23(4), 257–267. DOI: 10.5194/npg-23-257-2016

Shah, M. I., Foglia, M., Shahzad, U., & Fareed, Z. (2022). Green innovation, resource price and carbon emissions during the COVID-19 times: New findings from wavelet local multiple correlation analysis. *Technological Forecasting and Social Change, 184*(September 2021), 121957. DOI: 10.1016/j.techfore.2022.121957

Shahbaz, M., Sharif, A., Soliman, A. M., Jiao, Z., & Hammoudeh, S. (2023). Oil prices and geopolitical risk: Fresh insights based on Granger-causality in quantiles analysis. *International Journal of Finance and Economics, June 2020*, 1–17. DOI: 10.1002/ijfe.2806

Shahzad, U., Orsi, B., & Sharma, G. D. (2024). Managing inflation expectations and the efficiency of monetary policy responses to energy crises. *Energy Economics*, 133(March), 107474. DOI: 10.1016/j.eneco.2024.107474

Soliman, A. M., Lau, C. K., Cai, Y., Sarker, P. K., & Dastgir, S. (2023). Asymmetric effects of energy inflation, agri-inflation and CPI on agricultural output: Evidence from NARDL and SVAR models for the UK. *Energy Economics, 126*(December 2022), 106920. DOI: 10.1016/j.eneco.2023.106920

Stanislawska, E., & Paloviita, M. (2024). Heterogeneous responsiveness of consumers ' medium-term inflation expectations. *Economics Letters*, 237(March), 5–8. DOI: 10.1016/j.econlet.2024.111629

Sun, Y., & Dimiski, A. (2024). Exploring inflation dynamics in Canada: A threshold vector autoregressive approach. *Journal of Economic Asymmetries*, 30(May), e00364. DOI: 10.1016/j.jeca.2024.e00364

Taşdöken, Ö., & Kahyaoğlu, H. (2022). Davranışsal makroekonomi çerçevesinde hane halkı borçluluk düzeyinin analizi. *Selçuk Üniversitesi Sosyal Bilimler Meslek Yüksekokulu Dergisi*, 25(1), 156–174. DOI: 10.29249/selcuksbmyd.1061507

Taşdöken, Ö., & Kahyaoğlu, H. (2023a). Analysis of the global food crisis in international markets by the asymmetric tvp-var method. *Eurasian Research Journal*, 5(1), 59–71. DOI: 10.53277/2519-2442-2023.1-04

Taşdöken, Ö., & Kahyaoğlu, H. (2023b). EURO bölgesi enflasyon oranında şokların kalıcılığı üzerine bir inceleme. *Eskişehir Osmangazi Üniversitesi Sosyal Bilimler Dergisi*, 2023(3), 622–641. DOI: 10.17494/ogusbd.1290193

Thac, T., Nguyen, T., Duy, S., Li, X., & Xuan, H. (2024). Does the U. S. export inflation? Evidence from the dynamic inflation spillover between the U. S. and EAGLEs. *International Review of Economics & Finance*, 94(April), 103427. DOI: 10.1016/j.iref.2024.103427

Wang, Q., & Weng, C. (2024). Two-way risk : Trade policy uncertainty and inflation in the United States and China. *Finance Research Letters, 62*(PA), 105154. DOI: 10.1016/j.frl.2024.105154

Wang, Y., Wei, M., Bashir, U., & Zhou, C. (2022). Geopolitical risk, economic policy uncertainty and global oil price volatility—An empirical study based on quantile causality nonparametric test and wavelet coherence. *Energy Strategy Reviews*, 41(April), 100851. DOI: 10.1016/j.esr.2022.100851

Weller, C. E., & Chaurushiya, R. (2004). *Payment Due: The effects of higher interest rates on consumers and the economy.* www.americanprogress.org

Wen, F., Zhang, K., & Gong, X. (2021). The effects of oil price shocks on inflation in the G7 countries. *North American Journal of Economics and Finance, 57*(June 2020), 101391. DOI: 10.1016/j.najef.2021.101391

Yang, T., Dong, Q., Du, M., & Du, Q. (2023). Geopolitical risks, oil price shocks and inflation: Evidence from a TVP–SV–VAR approach. *Energy Economics, 127*(PB), 107099. DOI: 10.1016/j.eneco.2023.107099

Zhang, L., Padhan, H., Kumar, S., & Gupta, M. (2024). The impact of renewable energy on inflation in G7 economies : Evidence from artificial neural networks and machine learning methods. *Energy Economics*, 136(January), 107718. DOI: 10.1016/j.eneco.2024.107718

Zheng, T., Gong, L., & Ye, S. (2023). Global energy market connectedness and inflation at risk. *Energy Economics, 126*(December 2022), 106975. DOI: 10.1016/j.eneco.2023.106975

KEY TERMS AND DEFINITIONS

Brent Crude Oil: Brent oil is recognised as one of the main indicators used in the pricing of crude oil on a global scale.

Dynamic Wavelet Correlation Analysis for Multivariate (WLMC): The WLMC approach, on the other hand, analyzes the correlation relationship between variables in a multivariate dataset in both time and frequency dimensions. In other words, the WLMC approach examines the common movements between variables across time varying at different frequencies.

Global Geopolitical Risks (GPRT): 43 countries are taken into account and developed based on text searches from newspapers published in the US, UK and Canada. This index is developed by Dario Caldara and Matteo Iacoviello based on geopolitical events and threats published in newspapers.

Spearman's Correlation Matrix: The correlation relationship between the variables is analysed.

The Global Supply Chain: The GSCPI index was developed by the Federal Reserve Bank of New York. This index combines global transport costs and production indicators using data from the Baltic Dry Index (BDI) and the Harpex index.

The Wavelet Multiple Correlation (WMC) Methods: The WMC approach analyzes the common movements of variables across time scales to examine correlations.

Vector Wavelet Coherence (VWC) Methods: The VWC approach analyzes the correlation relationship between two time series using wavelet phase coherence, employing continuous wavelet transform to ensure analysis without any loss of information in the variables. The arrows obtained from the analysis indicate positive or negative correlation relationships between variables at different times and frequencies.

Chapter 4
Causality Relationship between Inflation and Interest Rate:
A Research for 20 Developed Countries

Fatih Ceylan
Uşak University, Turkey

Birol Erkan
İskenderun Technical University, Turkey

ABSTRACT

The study aims to reveal the causality relationship between inflation and interest rates in general and for G20 countries in particular. In this context, the study analyses the bidirectional relationship between inflation and interest rates using monthly data for the period 2000-2022, using causality methods based on traditional and Fourier functions that capture structural breaks gradually or smoothly. According to the test results of the traditional Granger causality analysis, while there is a bidirectional causality relationship between inflation and real interest rates in the panel data of G-20 countries, causality relationships change when structural breaks based on Fourier functions are taken into account. With the increasing global inflation in recent years, it is considered important for central banks aiming for price stability to take into account the changing relationship between inflation and interest rates.

DOI: 10.4018/979-8-3693-5508-4.ch004

INTRODUCTION

Especially after the 2008 global economic crisis, the importance of economic policies increased with fiscal policies all over the world. In this context, the effects of the central banks, the boss of monetary policies on economics and monetary policies, have increased further over time. In fact, in case of monetary policies failure, central banks and presidents have become more questionable. Major central banks such as Federal Reserve (FED), the European Central Bank (ECB), the Central Bank of the UK (BOE) and the Central Bank of Japan (Boj), the main determinant of the monetary policies of the world countries, were strictly monitored. The monetary policy board meetings carried out by the major central banks in a routine were the effect of announcement by relatively small central banks in the context of their global influences. In this perspective, all countries started to use policy interest rates effectively in order to eliminate the inflation problem that emerged from time to time and to become stable at acceptable levels. Accordingly, this study aims to reveal the causal relationship between the inflation rate and the interest rate in the 20 largest economies of the world (Argentina, Australia, Brazil, Canada, China, France Dec, Germany, India, Indonesia, Italy, Japan, Mexico, Republic of Korea, Russia, Saudi Arabia, South Africa, Turkey, the United Kingdom and the United States, the European Union Commission) in the period 2000-2022.

The extensive literature research conducted by us shows that many scientific studies have been conducted on the subject. A significant portion of the studies for both developed and developing countries have focused on the Fisher effect in the relationship between inflation rate and interest rate. Among these studies, Mahdi and Masood (2011), Gocer and Ongan (2019), Abasız, Akbarelieve and Bulut (2024), Dritsaki (2017), Crowder and Hoffman (1996) stated that the Fisher effect is valid in the long term. Mahdi and Masood (2011) used the Johansen's Co-Integration test in her work on Iran (Mahdi & Masood, 2011). Gocer and Ongan worked on the UK and used the Nonlinear Ardl model (Gocer & Ongan, 2019). Abasız, Akbarelieve and Bulut tested E7 countries with Engle & Granger Causality and LM (Abasız, Akbarelıeve, & Bulut, 2024). Dritsaki used ARDL and Toda and Yamamoto test in his study on Germany, UK and Switzerland countries (Dritsaki, 2017). Crowder and Hoffman covered the USA with the Johansen Cointegration test and the Dickey-Fuller test (Crowder & Hoffman, 1996).

Levi and Makin (1978), Makin (1978), Bhar and Mallik (2012), Clemente et al. (2017), Ahmed and Abdelsalam (2017), Sánchez-Fung (2019), Kumar and Kaushal (2023), Ito (2016), Ongan and Gocer (2020), Hartman and Makin (1982) investigated the existence of the Fisher effect only. Ahmed and Abdelsalam used the Autoregressive Conditional Heteroscedasticity (ARCH) model in their study on Egypt and found that there was no clear Fisher effect (Ahmed & Abdelsalam,

2018). Levi and Makin discussed the US economy using the General Equilibrium model and revealed the existence of the Fisher effect (Levi & Makin, 1978). Makin also examined the Canadian economy with the same model and reached the same conclusion (Makin, 1978). Bhar and Mallik used the Generalized Autoregress Conditional Changeable Variation (Garch) model in their study on the countries of Australia and New Zealand and revealed the existence of the Fisher effect in both countries (Bhar & Mallik, 2012). Clemente et al., used the Dickey-Fuller (ADF) test and the Generalized Least Squares (GLS) method and proved the Fisher effect in the G7 countries (Clemente, Gadea, Montañés, & Reyes, 2017). Ongan and Gocer used the NARDL model (Ongana & Gocer, 2020), and Sánchez-Fung used Ordinary Least Squares (OLS) method (Sánchez-Fung, 2019). They stated that the Fisher effect was valid in the Chinese economy. Kumar and Kaushal used the OLS Simple Regression model and Panel Data method and covered Southeast Asian countries. They mentioned the existence of the Fisher effect in these countries (Kumar & Kaushal, 2023). Ito examined the Swedish economy with the help of the Engle and Granger test and came to the conclusion that changes in inflation had an effect on long-term interest rates (Ito, 2016). Hartman and Makin covered the US economy and revealed the effect using the ABIIA model (Hartman & Makin, 1982).

In addition, the studies examining the causality relationship between inflation rate and interest rate variables and the direction of this relationship are also available in the literature. Kılcı (2019), Çiğdem (2019), Teker, Elçin Alp and Kent (2012) conducted research on Turkey. Kılcı revealed that there was a one-way relationship from the interest rate to inflation by using the Fourier Granger Causality test (Kılcı, 2019). Çiğdem determined that there was a bilateral relationship between the two variables by using the Granger Causality test (Çiğdem, 2019). Teker, Elçin Alp and Kent used the Threshold Vector Error Correction (T-VEC) method and stated that the increase in interest rates was the result of an increase in inflation rates (Teker, Alp, & Kent, 2012).

Olayinka did a study on Nigeria, used the Johansen Decoupling test and found that there was a weak relationship between the two variables in the short term and a strong relationship in the long term (Olayinka, 2021). Christopoulos, McAdam and Tzavalis used the Threshold vector autoregression model in their work for the USA and discussed interest rate policy to reduce inflation. They stressed that interest rates should be kept higher for a long time to bring inflation back to its low level (below 4 percent) (Christopoulos, McAdam, & Tzavalis, 2023). Kasibhatla also used the Gaussian Vector Autoregressive (VAR) model in his work on the US economy. He revealed that the two variables were related and that the inflation rate affected the interest rate (Kasibhatla, 2011). Asgharpur, Kohnehshahri and Karami used the Hsiao Causality and Panel Data method in their study on 40 Islamic Countries. They emphasized that there was only one relationship from the interest rate to inflation and that interest rates should be lowered in order to reduce inflation (Asgharpur, Kohnehshahri, & Karami, 3-5 December 2007). Jaradat and AI-Hhosban used Augmented Dickey-Fuller and Granger Causality tests in their studies examining Jordan. They reached the conclusion that there was a bidirectional relationship between the two variables (Jaradat & AI-Hhosban, 2014). Munir et al. covered Pakistan and used the regression method. They examined the effect of interest rates on inflation and as a result, they stated that the interest rate had an effect on inflation (Munir, Arshad, Saleem, Majeed, & Hassan, 2023). Akoto conducted a correlation analysis in his study on Ghana and revealed that there was a positive correlation between the two variables (Akoto, 2021).

AMPIRICAL ANALYSIS

Data

The G-20 group of countries consists of 19 independent countries, namely Argentina, Australia, Brazil, Canada, China, France, Germany, India, Indonesia, Italy, Japan, Mexico, the Republic of Korea, Russia, Saudi Arabia, South Africa, Turkey, the United Kingdom and the United States of America, together with the European Union Commission representing many European countries. In this study, the two-way causality relationship between inflation and real interest rates is analyzed by taking G-20 countries into account. Using monthly data for the period 2000:01-2022:12, the study analyzed the two-way causality using time series and panel data causality methods. The inflation and interest rate data used in the study are obtained from the central banks of the countries, International Monetary Fund (IMF) and Bank for International Settlements (BIS) databases. The interest rate variable is inflation-adjusted and realized.

METHODOLOGY

Cross-sectional Dependence Test

Cross-sectional dependence plays an important role in determining the causality relationship between economic variables in panel data models. Especially in the globalizing world, a high degree of economic integration in developing countries may increase the probability of spillovers of shocks occurring in a country. If the spillover effect of shocks across countries is not taken into account, the estimation results may be misleading. Pesaran (2006) emphasizes that when cross-country dependence is ignored in a panel data study, the estimation results may be biased, thus emphasizing the importance of testing for cross-country dependence (Pesaran, 2006: 970). Cross-sectional dependence is necessary both in determining the unit root test in panel data models and in selecting the appropriate test model for panel causality analysis. Therefore, this study will first test whether there is cross-sectional dependence among countries.

For cross sectional dependence, the Lagrange Multiplier (LM) test developed by Breusch and Pagan (1980), which is frequently used in empirical studies, is applied. The LM test first requires the estimation of the panel data model:

$$y_{it} = \alpha_i + \beta_i x_{it} + \epsilon_{it}, \quad i = 1, 2, \ldots N; t = 1, 2, \ldots T \tag{1}$$

Where i is the cross-sectional dimension and, t is the time dimension and x_{it} vector of explanatory variables α_i and β_i are the constant term and the slope coefficient varying across countries, respectively. In the *LM* test;

H_0 = There is no cross-sectional dependence,
H_a = There is cross-sectional dependence

To test the null hypothesis from the *LM* test;

$$LM = T \sum_{i=1}^{N-1} \sum_{j=i+1}^{N} \hat{\rho}_{ij}^{2} \tag{2}$$

$\hat{\rho}_{ij}^{2}$ is the sample estimate of the pairwise correlations of the error terms from the least squares estimator for each country in equation (1). The *LM* is valid in samples for relatively small N and sufficiently large T. When the time (T) and country (N) dimension are both large, CD_{LM} test developed by Pesaran (2004) can be used to test for cross-sectional dependence. The CD_{LM} is as follows:

$$CD_{LM} = \left(\frac{N}{N-1}\right)^{1/2} \sum_{i=1}^{N-1} \sum_{j=i+1}^{N} (T \hat{\rho}_{ij}^{2} - 1) \sim N(0,1) \tag{3}$$

The CD_{LM} test may be subject to size distortions when N is large and T is small. Pesaran (2004) develops a more general *CD* test statistic. The *CD* test is as follows:

$$CD = \sqrt{\frac{2T}{N(N-1)}} \sum_{i=1}^{N-1} \sum_{j=i+1}^{N} \hat{\rho}_{ij}^{2} \sim N(0,1) \tag{4}$$

Pesaran (2004) shows that the *CD* test has zero mean for fixed T and N and is robust to heterogeneous dynamic models with multiple breaks in slope coefficients and/or error variances.

Testing For Slope Homogeneity

Another important issue in panel data analysis is to decide whether the slope coefficients are homogeneous or not. In other words, country-specific heterogeneity should be taken into account before estimating panel data (Pesaran and Yamagata, 2008). Moreover, the homogeneity assumption for the parameters fails to capture heterogeneity due to country-specific characteristics (Breitung, 2005).

It is possible to test slope homogeneity with the standard F test. Accordingly, for all countries, the null hypothesis $H_0 = \beta_i = \beta$ nd the alternative hypothesis $H_a = \beta_i \neq \beta_j$. However, the F test is valid for T>N panel data, where the explanatory variables are exogenous and the error terms are constant variance. Swamy (1970) developed a new slope homogeneity test by extending the condition of constant variance of error terms. Nevertheless, both F and Swamy's test require panel data models where N is small relative to T. Pesaran and Yamagata (2008) develop the delta test ($\tilde{\Delta}$) as a standardized version of the Swamy (1970) test for large panels. The delta test is valid without any restrictions in the case of relative expansion of the country (N) and time (T) dimension. In the delta test approach, we first compute the following modified version of the Swamy test:

$$\tilde{S} = \sum_{i=1}^{N} (\hat{\beta}_i - \tilde{\beta}_{WFE})' \frac{x_i' M_\tau x_i}{\tilde{\sigma}^2} (\hat{\beta}_i - \tilde{\beta}_{WFE}) \tag{5}$$

The standardized version of the Swamy (1970) test by Pesaran and Yamagata (2008) is as follows:

$$\tilde{\Delta} = \sqrt{N} \frac{N^{-1}\tilde{S} - k}{\sqrt{2k}} \tag{6}$$

The Delta test ($\tilde{\Delta}$) is asymptotically normally distributed due to its large sample properties. However, in small samples, under the constraint of the normal assumption of errors, an adjusted version of the statistic ($\tilde{\Delta}_{adj}$) can be used. Accordingly, the adjusted Delta test ($\tilde{\Delta}_{adj}$) version is calculated as follows:

$$\tilde{\Delta}_{adj} = \sqrt{N} \left(\frac{N^{-1}\tilde{S} - E(\tilde{z}_{it})}{\sqrt{Var(\tilde{z}_{it})}} \right) \tag{7}$$

Hypotheses of the delta test:

$H_0 = \beta_i = \beta$ (Slope coefficients are homogeneous.)
$H_a = \beta_i \neq \beta_j$ (Slope coefficients are heterogeneous.)

Unit Root Tests

In this study, different unit root tests were applied to investigate the degree of integration for all countries. Since the variables used in the model have cross-sectional dependence and the slope coefficients are heterogeneous, second-generation unit root tests were applied to investigate the degree of integration.

The equation for real interest and inflation rates is as follows.

$$\alpha_{it} = d'_{it}\delta_i + \tau_{it} + \varepsilon_{it} \tag{8}$$

$$\tau_{it} = \tau_{it-1} + u_{it} \tag{9}$$

α_{it} enotes real interest and inflation rates in $i=1,\ldots,N$ cross-section and $t=1,\ldots,T$ time dimension. u_{it} variance σ^2_{ui} is used to test the stationarity of the series. The null hypothesis states that all G20 countries are stationary and the alternative hypothesis states that there are differences among countries and some countries are stationary (Hadri and Rao, 2008, p. 248; Nazlıoglu et al., 2021, p.5).

$$H_0 : \sigma^2_{ui} = 0 \tag{10}$$

$$H_1 : \sigma^2_{ui} > 0 \tag{11}$$

In the second-generation panel unit root tests, the error term allows for a factor structure.

$$\varepsilon_{it} = \gamma'_i F_t + e_{it} \tag{12}$$

In Equation (12), F_t is an f-dimensional vector of unobserved common factors, γ'_i is the loading weights and e_{it} is the error term. When Equation (8) is re-write within the framework of the factor model, it is expressed as follows.

$$\alpha_{it} = d'_{it}\delta_i + \tau_{it} + \gamma'_i F_t + \varepsilon_{it} \tag{13}$$

Bai and Ng (2005) F_t stimates the unobserved common factors using principal component analysis (PCA) based on the PANIC procedure of Bai and Ng (2004).

In this study, Pesaran (2007) and Hadri and Kurozumi (2011) panel unit root tests that take into account the common factor structure were also applied to test the stationarity of the variables. Hadri and Kurozumi (2011) used Pesaran's (2007) cross-section-averaged augmented (CA) approach to remove the common factor and proposed the group-averaged panel stationarity test, which is an extended version of the Hadri (2000) test expressed in terms of the common factor (Nazlioglu et al., 2021).

In the period used in the study, structural changes such as the global financial crisis and the pandemic have occurred, affecting all countries. However, real interest rates and inflation rates may not be linear in the period analyzed. For this reason, Nazlıoğlu and Karul (2017) panel stationarity test based on the Fourier approach, which takes into account the possible nonlinearity of the variables and models multiple structural breaks as a gradual process, was appliedNazlioglu and Karul (2017) define the deterministic term $d_i(t)$ as a function of time, and allow for a common factor based on the CA approach. In the regression model in the framework of this test, $d(t) = \left(1, \sin\left(\frac{2\pi kt}{T}\right), \cos\left(\frac{2\pi kt}{T}\right)\right)'$ is defined as the level change model $d(t) = \left(1, t, \sin\left(\frac{2\pi kt}{T}\right), \cos\left(\frac{2\pi kt}{T}\right)\right)'$ enotes the model of both level and trend change, and, k idenotes the Fourier frequency. Nazlıoğlu and Karul (2017) present a standardized statistic with mean $m_{LM(k)}$ and variance $v^2_{LM(k)}$ in the following equation.

$$W(k) = \sqrt{N}\left(LM(k) - m_{LM(k)}\right)/v_{LM(k)} \qquad (14)$$

Where k sed to indicate that the asymptotic distribution of the panel statistic depends on the Fourier frequency.

Causality Analysis

Due to the cross-sectional dependence and country-specific heterogeneity detected in the a priori tests, the bootstrap panel causality analysis proposed by Emirmahmutoğlu and Köse (2011), which takes into account both cross-sectional dependence and slope heterogeneity, is used to determine the causality test. This test also does not require a pre-test for cointegration except for the lagged structure. Variables can be used in their level form without taking any difference.

Emirmahmutoğlu and Köse (2011) causality test includes a Granger causality test procedure combined with Toda and Yamamoto's (1995) LA-VAR approach for heterogeneous panels. The Fisher test statistic is used to test the hypothesis of Granger causality in heterogeneous panels. The Fisher test statistic (λ) defined as follows:

$$\lambda = -2\sum_{i=1}^{N} ln(\rho_i) \quad i = 1,....,N \tag{15}$$

According to equation (15), ρ_i represents the probability values (p-value) of the Wald statistic values for each country. This test statistic has a chi-square distribution with 2N degrees of freedom. However, the limit distribution of the Fisher test statistic is no longer valid in the presence of cross-sectional dependence across countries.. Therefore, Bootstrap Granger causality methodology is proposed for panel data models with horizontal cross-section dependence. For panel data models with heterogeneous variables with different degrees of integration, the VAR model with $k_i + d\,max_i$ lags is as follows:

$$x_{i,t} = \mu_x^i + \sum_{j=1}^{k_i+d\,max_i} A_{11,ij} x_{i,t-j} + \sum_{j=1}^{k_i+d\,max_i} A_{12,ij} y_{i,t-j} + u_{i,t}^x \tag{16}$$

$$y_{i,t} = \mu_y^i + \sum_{j=1}^{k_i+d\,max_i} A_{21,ij} x_{i,t-j} + \sum_{j=1}^{k_i+d\,max_i} A_{22,ij} y_{i,t-j} + u_{i,t}^y \tag{17}$$

Where, $d\,max_i$ is the maximum degree of integration expected in the system for each i (country). Equations (16) and (17) are estimated without any parameter restrictions and then the null hypothesis of causality for each country is estimated for each country separately using Wald statistics. The Fisher test statistic is then calculated by equation (16). While Equation (16) tests the causality from x to y, Equation (17) tests the causality from y to x. In case of cross-sectional dependence, Equations (16) and (17) are tested with bootstrap methodology.[1]

As of the periods analyzed in this study, there have been many developments that may cause structural changes in real interest rates and inflation rates both on a country-specific and global scale. Therefore, as noted by Enders and Jones (2016), inferences from a standard Granger causality analysis can be misleading not only when structural breaks in the VAR model are ignored but also when breaks are modeled incorrectly. Dummy variables are used to capture breaks as a sharp process, but structural changes can be gradual and/or smooth in nature. The Fourier approach is used to capture structural changes as a gradual process without a priori information on the shape and number of breaks (Enders and Jones, 2016). For this reason, the Fourier Toda-Yamamoto causality approach developed by Nazlıoğlu et al. (2016), which also takes structural changes into account, is used to analyze the causality between real interest rates and inflation rates.

Nazlıoğlu et al. (2016) extend the Toda-Yamamoto framework to include the VAR($p+d$) model and the Fourier approach as follows:

$$y_t = \alpha_0 + \sum_{k=1}^{n}\alpha_{1k}\sin\left(\frac{2\pi kt}{T}\right) + \sum_{k=1}^{n}\alpha_{2k}\cos\left(\frac{2\pi kt}{T}\right) + \Pi_1 y_{t-1} + \ldots + \Pi_{p+d} y_{t-(p+d)}\,\epsilon_t \quad (18)$$

In equation (18), n is the number of frequencies, α_{1k} and α_{2k} measure the amplitude and displacement of the frequency, respectively. The null hypothesis of Granger causality is based on the zero restriction of the initial p parameters. The null hypothesis $H_0 = \Pi_1 = \ldots = \Pi_p = 0$ is tested by the chi-square Wald statistic with p degrees of freedom. The optimal frequency components and lag lengths in the Fourier Toda-Yamamoto approach are determined using the Schwarz information criterion (SIC).

EMPIRICAL RESULTS

In order to select the appropriate estimation method, a priori tests were conducted. First, slope homogeneity specific to the variables used in the study was tested. Accordingly, in both $\tilde{\Delta}$ and $\tilde{\Delta}_{adj}$ slope homogeneity tests, the null hypothesis that slope coefficients are homogeneous is rejected for all variables for both tests. Thus, there is country-specific heterogeneity in all variables used in the study.

Another important issue in panel data is the cross-sectional dependence test for variables. According to the LM (Breusch and Pagan 1980), CD_{LM} (Pesaran 2004) and CD (Pesaran 2004) test test results, the null hypothesis of no horizontal cross-section dependence is rejected for inflation and real interest rate variables. Horizontal cross-section dependence and slope homogeneity test results of the variables are shown in Table 1.

Table 1. Cross-sectional Dependence and Slope Homogeneity Test Results

	INF	RIR
Breusch-Pagan LM	10169.19***	3485.603***
Pesaran scaled LM	511.9215***	169.0609***
Pesaran CD	72.53200***	27.95661***
The Delta test (Δ)	10.46***	165.48***
The Delta test (Δ_{adj})	10.52***	166.39***

Notes: ***,**,* indicate significance at 1%, 5%, 10% level, respectively.

Panel unit root tests may differ according to the characteristics of the horizontal cross-sectional units forming the panel. First-generation unit root tests are preferred if there is no dependence between the cross-sections forming the panel, and second-generation unit root tests are preferred if there is dependence between the cross-sections. Since country-specific heterogeneity was detected in all variables used in the study, homogeneous panel unit root tests were not preferred. Accordingly, second-generation panel unit root tests were applied since the cross-sectional dependence specific to the variables could not be strongly rejected. For the second-generation panel unit root tests, CIPS (Pesaran, 2007), P_{PCi} (Bai ve Ng, 2005) and W_{CA} (Hadri ve Kurozumi, 2011) tests are used to determine the level of integration in panel data. Although CIPS (Pesaran, 2007) and W_{CA} (Hadri ve Kurozumi, 2011) panel panel unit root tests are two tests that apply the cross- sectional averaging procedures, CIPS (Pesaran, 2007) tests the null hypothesis that the variable contains a unit root, i.e. is non-stationary, while, W_{CA} (Hadri ve Kurozumi, 2011) ests the null hypothesis that the variable is stationary, i.e. does not contain a unit root. Thus, it can be stated that these two unit root tests applying similar procedures are robust to each other. P_{PCi} (Bai ve Ng, 2005) test tests the null hypothesis that the variable is stationary using the principal components procedure.

According to the results in Table 2, the panel unit root tests excluding structural breaks differ for the real interest rate and inflation rate variables. In the CIPS (Pesaran, 2007) panel unit root test, the null hypothesis that the inflation rate contains unit root is rejected. However, according to the results of P_{PCi} (Bai ve Ng, 2005) and W_{CA} (Hadri ve Kurozumi, 2011) panel unit root tests, the null hypothesis is rejected. Similar results are also valid for the real interest rate variable. CIPS (Pesaran, 2007) panel unit root test rejects the null hypothesis that real interest rate contains unit root. The results of P_{PCi} (Bai ve Ng, 2005) panel unit root test support the results of CIPS (Pesaran, 2007) panel unit root test for the real interest rate variable, while W_{CA} (Hadri ve Kurozumi, 2011) anel unit root test rejects the null hypothesis that the real interest rate is stationary in the level state. Similar findings are valid for country-specific unit root test results.

Table 2. Panel Unit Root Test Results

	CADF (2007)		Bai and Ng-PANIC (2005)		Hadri and Kurozumi-CA(2011)	
Country	INF	RIR	INF	RIR	INF	RIR
Germany	-2.63	-4.70***	0.19***	0.03	0.23***	0.03
Argentina	-4.78***	-4.20**	0.04	0.05	0.07	0.14**
Australia	-4.38***	-3.48*	0.07	0.13*	0.09	0.18**
Brazil	-3.50*	-2.90	0.01	0.05	0.03	0.05
Canada	-4.90***	-7.58***	0.12*	0.05	0.04	0.04
China	-4.61***	-5.69***	0.06	0.06	0.06	0.03
The United Kingdom	-1.55	-1.50	0.03	0.06	0.05	0.16**
Indonesia	-4.98***	-5.20***	0.10	0.03	0.24***	0.31***

continued on following page

Table 2. Continued

	CADF (2007)		Bai and Ng-PANIC (2005)		Hadri and Kurozumi-CA(2011)	
Country	INF	RIR	INF	RIR	INF	RIR
France	-2.76	-4.85***	0.13*	0.10	0.06	0.06
India	-4.92***	-6.10***	0.04	0.07	0.15**	0.02
Italy	-0.61	-3.33	0.07	0.07	0.09	0.07
Japan	-2.35	-16.84***	0.03	0.11	0.03	0.06
Republic of Korea	-3.17	-3.11	0.06	0.03	0.09	0.04
Mexico	-4.20**	-2.78	0.10	0.03	0.05	0.04
Russia	-3.64*	-2.77	0.06	0.04	0.04	0.04
Saudi Arabia	-2.49	-9.42***	0.06	0.11	0.12*	0.10
Turkey	-3.74**	-3.09	0.10	0.074	0.20**	0.06
The United States	-3.62*	-3.10	0.20***	0.14*	0.03	0.14
European Union	-3.14	-4.50***	0.06	0.03	0.10	0.03
South Africa	-3.77**	-5.34***	0.16**	0.07	0.10	0.07
CIPS	-3.49***	-4.29***				
P_{PCi}			61.39**	48.72		
W_{CA}					3.37***	2.25**

Notes: ***,**,* indicate significance at 1%, 5%, 10% level, respectively. CADF unit root test critical values are -4.32(1%),, -3.71(5%) and -3.41(10%) respectively. CIPS unit root test critical values are -2.85(1%), -2.70(5%) and -2.63(10%). Critical values for the individual statistics. Bai and Ng (2005) and Hadri and Kuyozumi (2011) unit root tests are 0.119 (10%), 0.146 (5%), 0.216 (1%) (see, Kwiatkowski et al., 1992, p.166). P_{PCi} and W_{CA} panel unit root tests critical values are obtained by Nazlıoğlu et. al. (2021)[2]. AIC was used to determine the number of lags.

The results of three different second-generation panel unit root tests used to determine the degree of integration of the variables show that nonlinearity and structural breaks are effective in both panel data and country-specific variables in the period under consideration as well as the application of different procedures. Therefore, in order to determine the maximum degree of integration of real interest rates and inflation rates, the Fourier panel unit root test developed by Nazlıoglu and Karul (2017), which takes structural breaks into account gradually, is applied.

Fourier panel unit root test results are shown in Table 3. Accordingly, the null hypothesis of inflation and real interest rate at Fourier frequency two and three in the panel data is rejected. Therefore, considering the gradual breaks in G20 countries, real interest rate and inflation rate contain unit root in their level states. Moreover, according to the country-specific process test results, when the Fourier frequency is one, the null hypothesis that the inflation rate is stationary in Germany, Australia and Turkey is rejected. When the Fourier frequency is two and three, the null hypothesis that the inflation rate is stationary in Germany, Indonesia, India and Turkey is rejected. When the Fourier frequency of the real interest rate variable is one, the null hypothesis that the real interest rate is stationary in Indonesia and the United States is rejected. When the Fourier frequency is two and three, the null hypothesis that the real interest rate is stationary in Argentina, Australia, the United Kingdom, Indonesia and the United States is rejected. Although the findings obtained in this framework differ, the highest level of integration (dmax) of the variables of the countries in the VAR system before causality analysis can be expressed as I(1).

Table 3. Fourier Panel Unit Root Test Results

	Nazlıoglu and Karul (2017) Fourier Panel Unit Root Test					
	INF			RIR		
Country	K=1	K=2	K=3	K=1	K=2	K=3
Germany	0.06**	0.10*	0.17**	0.02	0.02	0.03
Argentina	0.01	0.05	0.07	0.04	0.12*	0.13*
Australia	0.07***	0.03	0.09	0.03	0.19**	0.18**
Brazil	0.01	0.03	0.03	0.04	0.01	0.04
Canada	0.01	0.04	0.04	0.02	0.03	0.04
China	0.01	0.05	0.06	0.01	0.02	0.02
The United Kingdom	0.01	0.04	0.06	0.02	0.19**	0.17**
Indonesia	0.01	0.18**	0.25***	0.07***	0.27***	0.28***
France	0.03	0.07	0.06	0.02	0.06	0.06
India	0.03	0.13**	0.16**	0.02	0.02	0.02
Italy	0.01	0.08	0.09	0.01	0.07	0.07
Japan	0.01	0.05	0.03	0.02	0.05	0.06
Republic of Korea	0.01	0.08	0.09	0.02	0.04	0.05
Mexico	0.02	0.06	0.05	0.02	0.06	0.05
Russia	0.02	0.03	0.05	0.02	0.04	0.05
Saudi Arabia	0.01	0.07	0.11*	0.03	0.09	0.10
Turkey	0.05**	0.19**	0.19**	0.04	0.02	0.06
The United States	0.01	0.02	0.03	0.06**	0.16**	0.16**
European Union	0.01	0.09	0.09	0.02	0.02	0.03
South Africa	0.02	0.10*	0.08	0.03	0.08	0.09
W(k)	-1.20	3.17***	3.76***	0.93	3.58***	3.11***

Note: ***,**,* indicate significance at 1%, 5%, 10% level, respectively. Critical values for the individual statistics are 0.0471 (10%), 0.0546 (5%), 0.0716 (1%) for k =1; 0.1034 (10%), 0.1321 (5%), 0.2022 (1%) for k = 2; 0.1141 (10%), 0.1423 (5%), 0.2103 (1%) for k = 3 (see, Becker et al., 2006, p.389).

Considering the a priori test results and the sample structure, the Granger causality test developed by Emirmahmutoğlu-Köse (2011) is used in this study. This test, which uses Toda-Yomamato's (1995) LA-VAR approach in heterogeneous panels using meta-analysis, does not require a pre-test for cointegration except for determining the lagged structure (the highest degree of integration of variables). Variables can be used in their level form without taking any difference. Moreover, Monte Carlo simulation results show that the LA-VAR approach is robust under both cross-sectional dependence and cross-sectional independence even when N and T are small (Emirmahmtuoğlu-Köse, 2011:875). Bootstrap p-value is used in panel data due to cross-country dependence. In the period under consideration, both the effects of country-specific dynamics and the effects of structural breaks due to the country-specific effects of global developments were tested with causality analysis based on Fourier functions. Thus, the causality relationship between inflation and real interest rates in G-20 countries is analyzed in a multidimensional manner. Accordingly, the causality test results between inflation and real interest rate variables are shown in Table 4.

According to the test results of the Granger causality analysis, which ignores breaks and assumes linearity of the variables, the null hypothesis that the inflation rate is not the cause of the real interest rate in G-20 countries is rejected. Therefore, in these countries, inflation rates are the cause of real interest rates in panel data. Similarly, the null hypothesis that real interest rates are not the cause of inflation rates in panel data is rejected. Therefore, according to the Granger causality test results that do not take breaks into account, there is a reciprocal causality relationship between inflation and real interest rates in panel data in G-20 countries.

The null hypothesis that country-specific inflation rates are not the cause of real interest rates is rejected for Argentina and South Korea without structural breaks and for Germany, China and France with structural breaks. Therefore, when structural breaks are taken into account, inflation rates are not the cause of real interest rates in Argentina and South Korea. However, when breaks are taken into account, inflation is the cause of real interest rates in Germany, China and France. Considering both methods, the null hypothesis that inflation rates do not cause real interest rates cannot be rejected in Australia, the United Kingdom, Japan and Saudi Arabia. However, the null hypothesis that inflation rates are not the cause of real interest rates is rejected in Brazil, Canada, Indonesia, India, Italy, Mexico, Russia, Turkey, the United States, the European Union and South Africa. Therefore, inflation rates are strongly the cause of real interest rates in these countries.

The null hypothesis that real interest rates are not the cause of inflation rates is rejected in Argentina and the United Kingdom when structural breaks are not taken into account, while real interest rates are not the cause of inflation rates when structural breaks are taken into account. In Brazil and Mexico, the null hypothesis that real interest rates are not the cause of inflation rates cannot be rejected when structural breaks are not taken into account, while real interest rates are the cause of inflation rates when structural breaks are taken into account. Therefore, it is seen that structural changes in inflation and real interest rates are effective in causality relations in these countries.

Table 4. Causality Tests Results

Country	Emirmahmuoglu and Kose (2011)		Fourier Toda-Yomamato								Fourier Toda-Yomamato Cumulative						
	INF ≠> RIR	RIR ≠> INF	INF ≠> RIR				RIR ≠> INF				INF ≠> RIR				RIR ≠> INF		
	Wald St.	Wald St.	Wald St.	k	lag		Wald St.	k	lag		Wald St.	k	lag		Wald St.	k	lag
Germany	2.91	1.01	11.16**	1	4		5.08	1	4		14.61**	3	4		5.11	3	4
Argentina	47.58***	78.24***	0.27	1	2		0.26	1	2		0.43	3	2		0.40	3	2
Australia	1.80	0.62	2.82	1	7		5.41	1	7		2.14	3	7		7.50	3	7
Brazil	5.36*	3.69	30.07***	2	12		40.68***	2	12		28.64***	3	12		40.01***	3	12
Canada	20.05***	7.95	12.24**	1	4		7.38	1	4		15.21***	3	4		6.25	3	4
China	0.58	3.02	39.82***	1	12		7.30	1	12		36.31***	3	12		6.71	3	12
The United Kingdom	14.86	22.45**	2.90	1	12		8.68	1	12		4.19	3	12		8.57	3	12
Indonesia	10.09*	4.49	19.70**	1	8		7.35	1	8		58.07***	3	12		18.18	3	12
France	1.12	1.48	8.47**	1	2		3.16	1	2		61.46***	3	12		14.26	3	12
India	26.25***	6.97	33.57***	1	5		6.13	1	5		47.94***	3	4		1.91	3	4
Italy	16.81*	19.43**	17.21*	1	9		23.31**	1	9		20.37**	3	9		18.90*	3	9
Japan	2.48	2.62	2.99	3	2		2.01	3	2		3.69	3	2		1.84	3	2
Republic of Korea	18.76***	19.27**	16.16	1	10		18.70*	1	10		12.76	3	10		20.04**	3	10
Mexico	29.75***	2.49	33.66***	2	11		27.35***	2	11		41.30***	3	12		21.71*	3	12
Russia	46.87***	132.8***	42.70***	3	3		134.90***	3	3		37.59***	3	3		135.56***	3	3
Saudi Arabia	0.05	0.12	1.08	2	4		0.66	2	4		1.38	3	5		1.35	3	5

continued on following page

Table 4. Continued

Country	Emirmahmuoglu and Kose (2011)		Fourier Toda-Yomamato						Fourier Toda-Yomamato Cumulative					
	INF ≠> RIR	RIR ≠> INF	INF ≠> RIR			RIR ≠> INF			INF ≠> RIR			RIR ≠> INF		
	Wald St.	Wald St.	Wald St.	k	lag	Wald St.	k	lag	Wald St.	k	lag	Wald St.	k	lag
Turkey	37.61***	27.26***	38.89***	1	12	26.26*	1	12	27.60*	3	12	23.91	3	12
The United States	44.34***	34.29***	43.57***	2	12	21.60*	2	12	44.96***	3	11	38.42***	3	11
European Union	28.62***	19.40**	41.64***	3	8	22.78***	3	8	61.37***	3	9	25.87**	3	9
South Africa	34.12***	14.81*	37.95***	1	7	13.26*	1	7	45.95***	3	12	12.76	3	12
Bootstrap p-value	227.13***	274.46***												

Note: ≠> denotes the null hypothesis of no Granger causality. ***,**,* indicate significance at 1%, 5%, 10% level respectively. Akaike Information Criterion (AIC) is used to determine the lags. Critical values are based on 1000 bootstrap replications.

When both methods are considered together, the null hypothesis that real interest rates are not the cause of inflation rates cannot be rejected in Germany, Australia, Canada, China, Indonesia France, India, Japan and Saudi Arabia. The null hypothesis that real interest rates do not cause inflation rates is rejected in Italy, Republic of Korea, Russia, Turkey, United States, Eurpean Union and South Africa. Therefore, in these countries, real interest rates are strongly the cause of inflation. According to the findings, there is a feedback causality between inflation and real interest rates in Italy, Russia, Turkey, the United States, the Europena Union and South Africa. There is no causality relationship between inflation and real interest rates in Australia, Japan and Saudi Arabia.

CONCLUSION

Inflation ceased to be a problem in the world, especially in the developed countries of the world, and on the contrary, countries had to fight deflation. In almost all of the developed countries, inflation rates remained close to zero, and even in some countries, especially Japan, negative inflation rates became stable. Therefore, the interest rates in the countries were in parallel to this at very low levels. In some countries, nominal interest rates remained negative for many years due to the high dimensions of deflation and economic stagnation. However, the Covid-19 pandemis and the subsequent Ukraine-Russia War, the problems arising from the global diameter supply front, along with the problems of inflation reminded itself even in developed countries. In fact, in some of the developed countries, the inflation rate reached double-digit levels after many years. This revealed the need for these countries to raise their policy interest rates in a planned manner.

The relationship between inflation and interest rates has been the subject of research all over the world with its Fisher influence and causality dimensions and is still being investigated today. In this context, some research shows that the existence of the Fisher effect and the inflation rate is the determinant of the interest rate, while others indicate that interest rates are the determinant of changes in inflation rate. In some studies, both economic variables argue that they are in a bidirectional causal relationship with each other. In this perspective, this study aims to determine the relationship between mutual causality between inflation rate and interest rates in the world's most developed 20 countries. In this respect, this study aims to reveal the existence and direction of the causality relationship between inflation and interest rates in these countries by applying causality tests based on traditional and Fourier functions. According to the test results of the traditional panel data causality analysis of the world's 20 largest economies, the existence of a bidirectional causality relationship between the inflation rate and real interest rate variables has been shown.

Although the results of the causality test based on Fourier functions differed according to the traditional causality methods, bidirectional causality relations were generally detected. Therefore, we can talk about a chain relationship between inflation and interest rates that feeds each other.

Due to the global supply shocks that have emerged in recent years, extraordinary price increases in goods markets have emerged and increase inflationary tendencies and threats all over the world. For this reason, whether the monetary policy decisions of all countries, whether developed or developing countries, must be determined within the framework of scientific and rational parameters. In this context, the central banks of the country should determine the policy interest rates in a way that indicates positive real interest rates and should not go to any reduction in nominal interest rates until local and/or global inflationary threats disappear. Thus, countries that can stabilise their monetary policies will contribute to further structural reforms and therefore to the realisation of industrial development.

REFERENCES

Abasız, T., Akbarelıeve, M., & Bulut, B. (2024). Dynamics of the Relationship between Inflation and Interest Rates: Testing For the Fisher Hypothesis with Structural Break(S) and Parameter Stability. *Journal of Economics. Finance and Management Studies*, 7(1), 540–550. DOI: 10.47191/jefms/v7-i1-56

Ahmed, D. A., & Abdelsalam, M. A. (2018). Inflation Instability Impact on Interest Rate in Egypt: Augmented Fisher Hypothesis Test. *Applied Economics and Finance*, 5(1), 2332–7308.

Akoto, D. (2021). The Relationship between Interest Rates and Inflation in Ghana and Their Impact on Economic Growth for the Period 2006-2019. *Journal of Financial Economics*, 9(1), 34–41.

Asgharpur, H., Kohnehshahri, L. A., & Karami, A. (3-5 December 2007). The Relationships Between Interest Rates and Inflation Changes: An Analysis of Long-Term Interest Rate Dynamics In Developing Countries. *InInternational Economic Conference on Trade and Industry (IECTI)*, (s. 1-8).

Bai, J., & Ng, S. (2004). A PANIC attack on unit roots and cointegration. *Econometrica*, 72(4), 1127–1177. DOI: 10.1111/j.1468-0262.2004.00528.x

Bai, J., & Ng, S. (2005). *A new look at panel testing of stationarity and the PPP hypothesis*. Cambridge University Press. DOI: 10.1017/CBO9780511614491.019

Becker, R., Enders, W., & Lee, J. (2006). A Stationarity Test in the Presence of an Unknown Numberof Smooth Breaks. *Journal of Time Series Analysis*, 27(3), 381–409. DOI: 10.1111/j.1467-9892.2006.00478.x

Bhar, R., & Mallik, G. (2012). Components of Inflation Uncertainty and Interest Rates: Evidence from Australia and New Zealand. *Economic Analysis and Policy*, 42(1), 39–49. DOI: 10.1016/S0313-5926(12)50003-2

Breitung, J. (2005). A parametric approach to the estimation of cointegration vectors in panel data. *Econometric Reviews*, 24(2), 151–173. DOI: 10.1081/ETC-200067895

Breusch, T. S., & Pagan, A. R. (1980). The Lagrange Multiplier test and its applications to model specification in econometrics. *The Review of Economic Studies*, 47(1), 239–253. DOI: 10.2307/2297111

Christopoulos, D., McAdam, P., & Tzavalis, E. (2023). *Do the Effects of Interest Rate Changes Depend on Inflation?* Economic Review, Fourth Quarter. DOI: 10.18651/ER/v108n4ChristopoulosMcAdamTzavalis

Çiğdem, G. (2019). A Paradox: An Empiric Approach to Inflation-Interest Rates Relationship: Evidence from Turkey. *Research in Applied Economics*, 11(3), 1948–5433. DOI: 10.5296/rae.v11i3.15171

Clemente, J., Gadea, M. D., Montañés, A., & Reyes, M. (2017). Structural Breaks, Inflation and Interest Rates. *Econometrics*, 5(11), 1–17.

Crowder, W. J., & Hoffman, D. L. (1996). The Long-Run Relationship between Nominal Interest Rates and Inflation: The Fisher. *Journal of Money, Credit and Banking*, 28(1), 102–118. DOI: 10.2307/2077969

Dritsaki, C. (2017). Toda-Yamamoto Causality Test between Inflation and Nominal Interest Rates: Evidence from Three Countries of Europe. *International Journal of Economics and Financial Issues*, 7(6), 120–129.

Emirmahmutoglu, F., & Kose, N. (2011). Testing for Granger causality in heterogeneous mixed panels. *Economic Modelling*, 28(3), 870–876. DOI: 10.1016/j.econmod.2010.10.018

Enders, W., & Jones, P. (2016). Grain Prices, Oil Prices, and Multiple Smooth Breaks in a VAR. *Studies in Nonlinear Dynamics and Econometrics*, 20(4), 399–419. DOI: 10.1515/snde-2014-0101

Gocer, I., & Ongan, S. (2019). The Relationship between Inflation and Interest Rates in the UK: The Nonlinear ARDL Approach. *Journal of Central Banking Theory and Practice*, 3, 77–86.

Granger, C. W. J. (1969). Investigating causal relations by econometric models and cross-spectral methods. *Econometrica*, 37(3), 424–438. DOI: 10.2307/1912791

Hadri, K. (2000). Testing for stationarity in heterogeneous panel data. *The Econometrics Journal*, 3(2), 148–161. DOI: 10.1111/1368-423X.00043

Hadri, K., & Kurozumi, E. (2011). A locally optimal test for no unit root in cross-sectionally dependent panel data. *Hitotsubashi Journal of Economics*, •••, 165–184.

Hadri, K., & Rao, Y. (2008). Panel stationarity test with structural breaks. *Oxford Bulletin of Economics and Statistics*, 70(2), 245–269. DOI: 10.1111/j.1468-0084.2008.00502.x

Hartman, R., & Makin, J. H. (1982). *Inflation Uncertainity and Interest Rates: Theory And Empirical Tests*. National Bureau of Economic Research. DOI: 10.3386/w0906

Ito, T. (2016). Does the Fisher Hypothesis Hold in Sweden? An Analysis of Long-Term Interest Rates under the Regime of Inflation Targeting. *Review of Integrative Business and Economics Research*, 5(3), 283–295.

Jaradat, M. A., & Al-Hhosban, S. A. (2014). Relationship and Causality Between Interest Rate and Inflation Rate Case of Jordan. *IJCRB, 6*(4), s. 54-65.

Kasibhatla, K. M. (2011). The Relationship Between Inflation and Interest Rates: A Co-integration Analysis. *The International Journal of Finance, 23*(4), 7034–7044.

Kılcı. (2019). Analysis of the Relationship Between Inflation and Central Bank Interest Rates In Turkey: Fourier Approach. *UİİİD, 22*, 135–146.

Kumar, A., & Kaushal, D. S. (2023). Real Interest Rates-Inflation Relation in South Asian Countries. *Asia Pacific Economic Review, 16*(1), 1435–1449.

Levi, M. D., & Makin, J. H. (1978). Anticipated Inflation and Interest Rates: Further Interpretation of Findings on the. *The American Economic Review, 68*(5), 801–812.

Mahdi, S., & Masood, S. (2011). The long run relationship between interest rates and inflation in Iran: Revisiting Fisher's hypothesis. *Journal of Economics and International Finance, 3*(14), 705–712.

Makin, J. H. (1978). Anticipated Inflation and Interest Rates In an Open Economy. *Journal of Money, Credit and Banking, 10*(3), 275–289. DOI: 10.2307/1991508

Munir, S., Arshad, M. A., Saleem, S., Majeed, M. I., & Hassan, F. (2023). Interest Rate Impact on Monetary Policy in Pakistan. *The International Journal of Interdisciplinary Organizational Studies*, s. 476-487.

Nazlıoğlu, S., Gormus, A., & Soytas, U. (2016). Oil prices and real estate investment trusts (reits): Gradual shift causality and volatility transmission analysis. *Energy Economics, 60*, 1–28. DOI: 10.1016/j.eneco.2016.09.009

Nazlioglu, S., & Karul, C. (2017). A panel stationarity test with gradual structural shifts: Re-investigate the international commodity price shocks. *Economic Modelling, 61*, 181–192. DOI: 10.1016/j.econmod.2016.12.003

Nazlioglu, S., Payne, J. E., Lee, J., Rayos-Velazquez, M., & Karul, C. (2021). Convergence in OPEC carbon dioxide emissions: Evidence from new panel stationarity tests with factors and breaks. *Economic Modelling, 100*, 105498. DOI: 10.1016/j.econmod.2021.105498

Olayinka, M. S. (2021). Interest Rates and Inflation Rate Interplay: Impact on Policy Decision in Nigeria Since Year 2000. *International Journal of Economics. Management and Accounting, 29*(1), 129–166.

Ongana, S., & Gocer, I. (2020). The Relationship between Interest Rates and Inflation: Examining the Fisher Effect in China. *Frontiers of Economics in China, 15*(2), 247–256.

Pesaran, M. H. (2004). General diagnostic tests for cross section dependence in panels. CESifo Working Paper 1229. IZA Discussion Paper, 1240.

Pesaran, M. H. (2006). Estimation and inference in large heterogeneous panel with a multifactor error structure. *Econometrica*, 74(4), 967–1012. DOI: 10.1111/j.1468-0262.2006.00692.x

Pesaran, M. H. (2007). A simple panel unit root test in the presence of cross section dependence. *Journal of Applied Econometrics*, 22(2), 265–312. DOI: 10.1002/jae.951

Pesaran, M. H., Ullah, A., & Yamagata, T. (2008). A bias-adjusted LM test of error crosssection independence. *The Econometrics Journal*, 11(1), 105–127. DOI: 10.1111/j.1368-423X.2007.00227.x

Sánchez-Fung, J. R. (2019). Interest rates, inflation, and the Fisher effect in China. *Macroeconomics and Finance in Emerging Market Economies*, 12(2), 124–133. DOI: 10.1080/17520843.2019.1592206

Swamy, P. A. V. B. (1970). Efficient inference in a random coefficient regression model. *Econometrica*, 38(2), 311–323. DOI: 10.2307/1913012

Teker, D., Alp, E. A., & Kent, O. (2012). Long-Run Relation between Interest Rates and Inflation: Evidence from Turkey. *Journal of Applied Finance & Banking*, 2(6), 41–54.

Toda, H. Y., & Yamamoto, T. (1995). Statistical inference in vector autoregressions with possibly integrated processes. *Journal of Econometrics*, 66(1-2), 225–250. DOI: 10.1016/0304-4076(94)01616-8

ENDNOTES

[1] Detailed information "Emirmahmutoğlu, F. and N. Köse (2011) "Testing for Granger Causality in Heterogeneous Mixed Panels", Economic Modelling, 28, 870-876."

[2] For detailed information see "Nazlioglu, S., Payne, J. E., Lee, J., Rayos-Velazquez, M., & Karul, C. (2021). Convergence in OPEC carbon dioxide emissions: Evidence from new panel stationarity tests with factors and breaks. Economic Modeling, 100, 105498."

Chapter 5
Financial and Human Capital Awareness in Industrialized Countries

Ezgi Kopuk
https://orcid.org/0000-0001-7242-1160
Eskişehir Osmangazi Universty, Turkey

Hasan Umutlu
https://orcid.org/0000-0002-2604-3573
Düzce University, Turkey

ABSTRACT

The study examines the financial and human resources in the industrial sectors of the industrialized countries (Germany, China, Ireland, South Korea, America, Switzerland, Japan, Singapore and the Netherlands) that provide the highest efficiency, income and sustainability from financial and human capital. It is aimed to examine capital developments. For this purpose, firstly, the definition of financial and human capital, its economic effects, its importance in the industrial sector, and the financial and human capital policies and competitiveness of the industrialized countries implemented by the industrial sector were evaluated. In order to make a unique inference for this purpose and evaluation, another aim of the study was to investigate the effect of financial and human capital in the industrial sector of industrializing countries. In this regard, the aim was tested by panel data analysis covering the period 2005-2021. It was determined that the variables had different effects on a country basis, and human capital indicators were found to have a higher positive effect.

DOI: 10.4018/979-8-3693-5508-4.ch005

1. INTRODUCTION

Capital is generally defined as physical tools such as tools, equipment, factories, and machines that increase the productivity of labor in production. Financial capital is a means of exchange that enables the purchase and exchange of these physical tools. Financial capital generally constitutes the unconsumed part of income. These savings are transferred to institutions that perform financial intermediation and are loaned to investors from there (Yazıcı, 2020: 187). In general, financial capital consists of the total financial assets of an individual or a business. These resources can consist of various sources such as bonds, stocks, cash, funds and real estate. Financial capital is used to ensure the growth of a business, maintain its sustainability and support the strengths of the business. Financial capital must be used effectively in order to use the working capital structure in the most appropriate way.

The developments in terms of financial capital since the 1980s have had a global impact on the world economy. In this period, the increase in international capital inflows and outflows and the disappearance of borders and restrictions separating national financial markets from each other were effective. Especially the developments in the field of international private financial capital left their mark after 1980 (Ongun, 1993: 35).

Human capital is generally expressed as the sum of knowledge and skills in the workforce (Easterly and Wetzel, 1989: 4). Investment in human capital such as education and health is not only related to production, but also increases the quality of life of the individual and affects social relations. Therefore, the way an educated individual perceives and lives life may be different than uneducated people. Therefore, human capital has a dynamic structure, unlike physical capital. This is due to the fact that human capital is in a variable state. In this context, changes in the quality and quantity of the country's people have an impact. These features of human capital have led to the understanding of the importance of human capital in cases where classical production factors are insufficient. Due to the contribution made to production, dynamism, knowledge, skill and experience have been the components that make human capital come to the fore. Developing and using human capital effectively is important for developing countries (Karagül, 2003: 82-88).

Researching the use, development and transformation of human and financial capital, which constitute the basic factor of economic growth and production, into a source of income in economies is very important for the sustainability of economic existence. Examining the developments in the industrial sectors of industrialized countries that can use these two factors most efficiently and integrate them into high added value production is of particular importance in benefiting both the new opportunities that may arise and the developing countries. In line with this importance, the study aims to investigate the definition of human and financial capital, its economic effects, its importance in the industrial sector, human and financial policy applications and competitiveness in the industrial sectors of industrialized countries (Germany, China, Ireland, South Korea, America, Switzerland, Japan, Singapore and the Netherlands). The second aim of the study was to determine the effect of human and financial capital on the industrial value added of industrialized countries in order to make an econometric inference. Panel data analysis was used in the study covering the period 2005 -2021. According to the analysis results, it was observed that ECI, EE and GFCF variables positively affected the development of the industrial sector in the panel overall. When the country-specific results are examined, different results are obtained, and while it is concluded that the GFCF variable has a positive effect in the countries in general, it is observed that the ECI and EE variables have different effects in countries with statistical significance. In line with the results obtained, although human and financial capital have effects in the industrial sector, it has been determined that human capital has a more positive effect in almost all countries.

2. ECONOMIC IMPACTS OF FINANCIAL AND HUMAN CAPITAL: THEIR IMPORTANCE IN THE INDUSTRIAL SECTOR

The economy generally consists of a dynamic structure consisting of goods, services and financial markets. The goods and services markets within the scope of this structure constitute real markets. Financial markets constitute money and capital markets. Real and financial markets play a complementary role in the current economic environment. The fact that the balances formed in the real and financial markets reflect the optimum level will cause the general balance in the economy to reflect the optimum level (Uslu, 2002: 106).

2.1. Financial Capital

The financial system is directly related to capital accumulation. Capital accumulation is the saving of a portion of income and turning it into investment to increase future income and production. Differences in economic growth rates of countries are closely related to their efficient use of their natural resources. In this context, its relationship with the financial system is important. The financial system accelerates economic growth by increasing average investment efficiency and providing more investment. The development of the financial system not only increases savings but also encourages technological development (Afşar, 2007: 189-190).

In the globalizing world, international capital accumulation is increasing at a very high rate. This situation has caused international capital movements to turn to emerging markets with the expectation of high returns. Globalization in financial markets, along with the development of technology, has led to an increase in international capital mobility and its transformation into a speculative character after the 1980s. Financial liberalization and the economic crises experienced in countries with different political, social and economic structures have brought capital movements and financial liberalization movements to the fore. In this context, economic measures regarding controls on issues such as foreign exchange transactions, tax transactions, international capital movements have begun to be frequently included in studies. However, speculative money inflow and outflow can harm the economy of countries. For this reason, speculative movements can be the main element of crises, as well as a triggering role for crises (Aytekin, 2018: 191).

In modern economies, industry is a tool in the production of goods and services, but also plays an important role in increasing wealth, sustainable development and reducing unemployment. The industrial sector also serves as a catalyst for increasing the pace of diversification of the economy and achieving structural transformation. Therefore, governments implement various strategies and support the industrial sector to increase industrial production and capacity. Despite these supports from governments, the industrial production of most developing countries has followed a fluctuating trend recently. The most important reason for this situation is the countries' lack of access to finance. Because financial risks are high in these countries and there are restrictive rules for the construction sector in the funds coming from the banking sector. Inadequate capital formation and lack of access to funds have led to increases in resource costs and interest rates. Thus, it has become difficult to access machines and information technologies, which play an active role in reducing production costs and increasing competitiveness and productivity of developing industries. As a result, there were increases in producers' costs and decreases in their capacity utilization (Güngör et al., 2020: 120-121).

The increase in economic relations in the globalizing world has brought about the financial liberalization process. This has led to the elimination of restrictions such as capital controls and capital account restrictions. In this process, international investments increased, new investment opportunities emerged, and the profitability rates of the countries increased. This has had a significant impact on the growth and development of countries. External financing sources are important to meet the financing needs and eliminate capital insufficiency in the process of economic growth and development. However, the increase in short-term capital movements, especially in developing countries, may cause economic negativities and even financial crises (Aytekin, 2018: 192).

2.2. Human Capital

With each passing period, new technological tools enter our lives and change the known things. The industrial revolution, which started 200 years ago with the mechanization of looms, has today turned into a revolution characterized by cyber-physical systems. Human capital has an important position in terms of the success, future and continuity of the sectors in the industry 4.0 revolution, where technological change and artificial intelligence in life and production have become important. In order to achieve this sustainability and success, progress must be made in human capital as well as in the technological field. It is especially important to invest in education, knowledge and experience. Human capital theory reveals that knowledge provides individuals with cognitive skills and thus affects their productivity and productivity potential (Gürün, 2019: 69).

In order to realize production in the economy, inputs such as labor force, natural resources, human, financial and physical capital are brought together. The qualification of the workforce is improved through education in workplaces and schools. Thus, the country's human capital also increases. In this context, human capital can be defined as the knowledge and skills of the workforce. In order for human capital to contribute effectively to production, it depends on establishing a balance between physical and human capital. For a production, physical and human capital must first come together at a certain rate. Therefore, the complementary element between human and physical capital has two different dimensions. The first is that physical and human capital can balance each other in quantity. The second is the qualitative adaptation of physical and human capital. A business can have employees who have human capital. However, if the technical equipment cannot be established so that these employees can use their human capital effectively, human capital may be wasted. Because employees cannot find an environment where they can use their human capital, it leads to waste of human capital (Karataş and Çankaya, 2010: 30-31).

Human capital is defined as the sum of qualities such as knowledge and skills that people have regarding economic activities. Today, human capital is accepted as one of the main determinants of economic development. In this context, it is stated that showing the development levels of countries only with income indicators will not be considered sufficient. It is noteworthy in terms of the importance of the issue that health and education indicators should also be evaluated along with income indicators. Different definitions are made in terms of the importance of the educated population and information as the highest stage of economic development, and the use of the concept of information society is generally seen as meaningful in this context. One of the characteristics of the information society is that it has a qualified population and human capital that can produce and use information (Yumuşak, 2008: 5-6).

Talent, knowledge, in-service training, school education, observation, social interaction, and learning by doing are among the sources of human capital accumulation. A well-educated society also brings social advantages. For example, as the duration of education increases and the literacy rate increases, the flexibility to adapt to changes in business life also increases. Therefore, human capital investments are beneficial to society because their future benefits will offset their costs. Insufficient human capital investments can disrupt the income distribution in society. This problem can be overcome in the long term by increasing human capital investments. While carrying out production, human capital is needed along with traditional production factors. Developing countries that do not have sufficient human capital may not be able to produce some products even if they have sufficient physical capital and labor. Developed countries with relatively strong human capital can produce these goods that require advanced technology. Therefore, human capital investments are needed as much as physical capital investments in an economy. Concepts such as education and health have been evaluated within the scope of human capital as a growth-development indicator in the information society process. In this context, making remedial investments in areas such as education and health has positive results in terms of the development of economies. The critical point here is that education and health are included in the investment simultaneously. Thus, efforts will be made to accelerate development by creating synergy between the two sectors. The main purpose of investing in two sectors simultaneously is that healthy people can receive better education (Özyakışır, 2011: 54-59).

3. DEVELOPMENT OF FINANCIAL AND HUMAN CAPITAL AND INDUSTRIALIZATION RESULTS IN INDUSTRIALIZED COUNTRIES: STATISTICAL DATA AND ECONOMIC RESULTS

In industrialized countries, the development of financial and human capital is pivotal in the industrialization process. Financial development accelerates both industrialization and economic growth. Consequently, it is imperative to invest in human capital and prioritize financial capital, particularly in developing countries. The established positive relationship between financial development, human capital, and economic growth underscores the critical importance of investments in these areas (Sarwar et al., 2020).

The advancement of new technologies in the realm of information and communication significantly impacts the performance, profitability, and development of financial capital. Additionally, the growth of human capital and R&D activities positively influence financial development. Consequently, it is imperative for countries to enhance investments in financial and human capital and prioritize R&D expenditures to foster industrialization and economic growth (Gu et al., 2021).

Figure-1 examines the financial capital data of the countries analyzed in the study for the period 1970-2022. Although there are different data on financial capital, personal remittances were selected as financial capital data in order to make the data accessible and to make comparisons for selected countries. It is seen that America and South Korea, primarily China and Germany, differ significantly in terms of financial capital. While Japan, Switzerland and the Netherlands have increased in financial capital over the years, Ireland has increased relatively less in financial capital than other countries. It is seen that Singapore does not have any income in personal remittances, which are selected as financial capital data.

Figure 1. Financial Capital Data for Selected Countries: Personal Remittances - Current Dollar

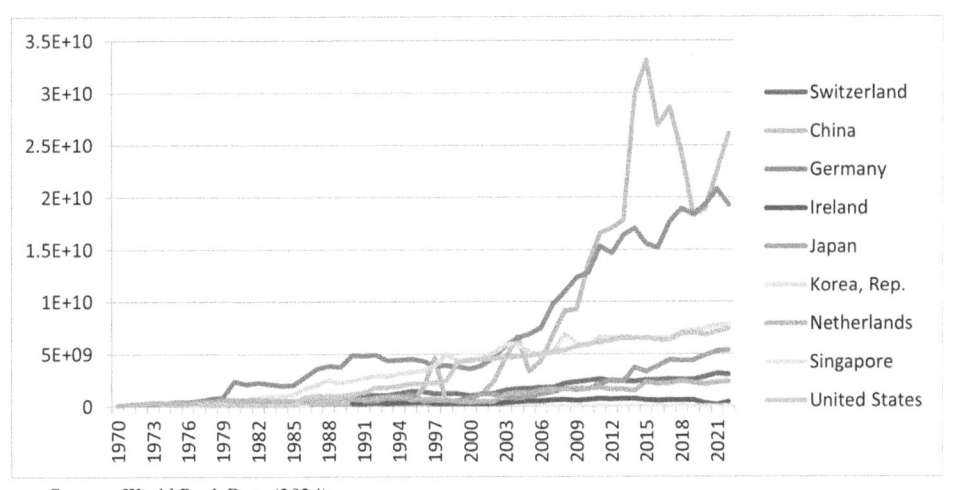

Source: *World Bank Data (2024)*

Figure 2 shows government expenditures on education as a percentage of GDP as human capital data for selected countries in the period 1970-2022. Among these ratios, there have been fluctuations in the percentage of GDP of government expenditures on education over the years. It can be seen that the Netherlands, America,

Ireland and Germany differ from the other 4 countries. It is seen that China's government expenditures on education as a percentage of GDP spend relatively less than other countries.

Figure 2. Human Capital Data for Selected Countries: Education Expenditures

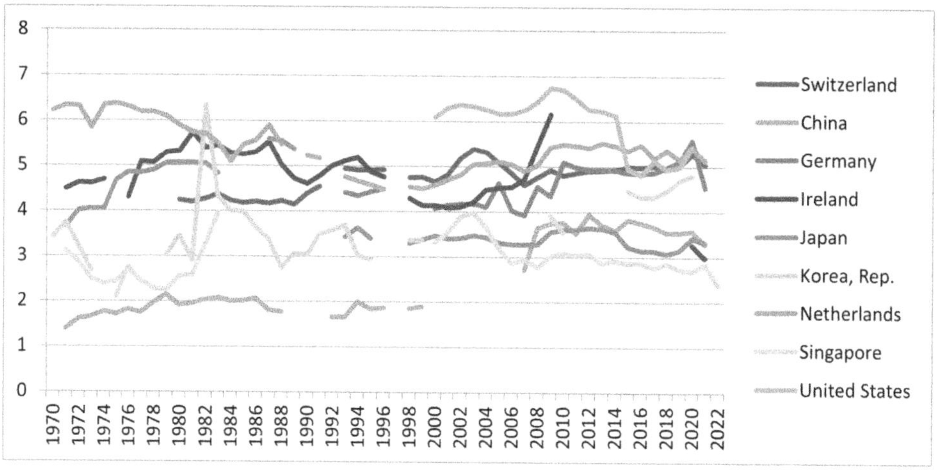

Source: *World Bank Data (2024)*

Figure 3 shows health expenditure data as human capital data for selected countries in the period 1970-2022. Health expenditures Current health expenditures are considered as a percentage of GDP. It can be seen that America differs from other countries in terms of education expenditures and financial capital expenditures. While it is seen that Germany, the Netherlands, Switzerland and Japan also increased their health expenditures as a percentage of GDP, Ireland differs negatively from this group. It is seen that South Korea has increased its health expenditures as a percentage of GDP, especially in the recent period, while Singapore and China are the countries that spend the least on health as a percentage of GDP compared to other countries.

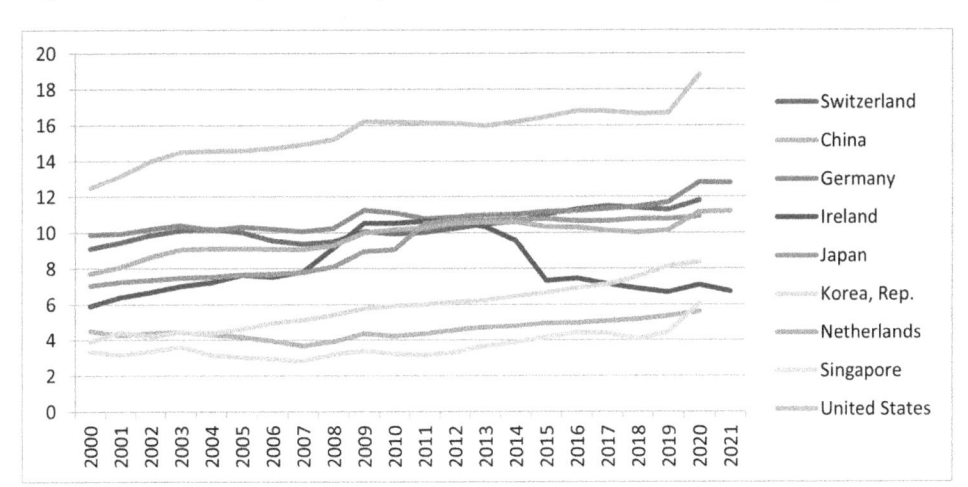

Figure 3. Human Capital Data for Industrialized Countries: Health Expenditures

Source: *World Bank Data (2024)*

Figure 4 shows industry data as a percentage of GDP for selected countries. Accordingly, while the share of industry in GDP has decreased over the years in the Netherlands and America, China and especially recently Ireland differ from other countries in this area. Again, it is seen that especially South Korea and Japan stand out compared to other countries.

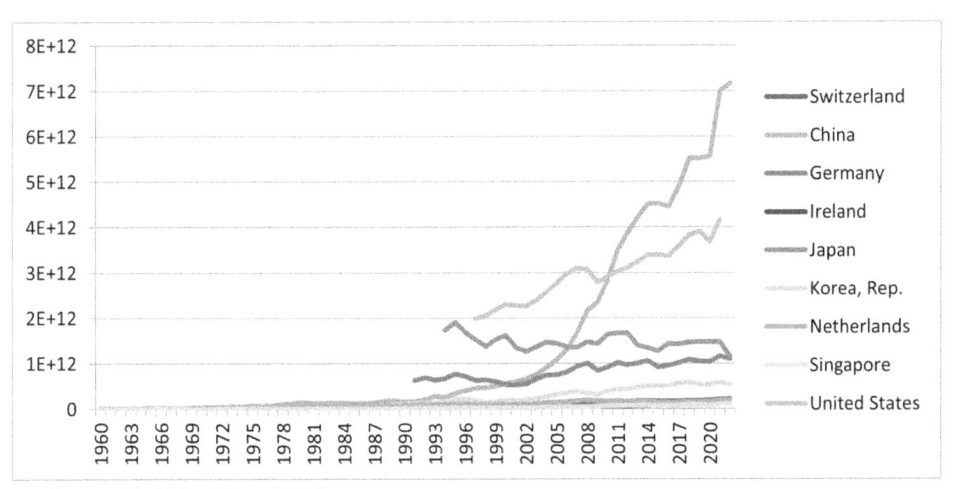

Figure 4. Industrial Sector Data for Selected Countries

Source: *World Bank Data (2024)*

4. POLICIES AND REGULATIONS FOR STRENGTHENING FINANCIAL AND HUMAN CAPITAL IN INDUSTRIALIZED COUNTRIES

Economy lies at the basis of the global existence of countries. Any country that is not economically strong cannot develop in political, social and cultural areas. In order to prevent this negative cycle from occurring, economies primarily attach importance to their monetary development. In this direction, country economies are turning to the management of factors that will increase income with the motivation of monetary strengthening. Capital and labor, known as factors of production, do not constitute the two basic elements of income increase. Without financial structuring, qualified labor cannot be produced, and without qualified labor, products with high added value cannot be produced. Therefore, in order to ensure the sustainability of economic existence, obtaining and managing these two elements in an efficient manner becomes an issue that all societies focus on (Afşar, 2007: 188). On the other hand, human capital enables the economy to remain in a dynamic structure and income increases in terms of the emergence of new inventions, the production of high value-added products and the creation of new professional fields as a result of increasing the productivity of the labor force that carries out production with knowledge, skills and experience (Eser and Gökmen, 2009: 42).

4.1. Financial Capital Policies and Regulations

The intense impact of financial and human capital on the economy is known by all countries. Especially in industrialized and high-income countries, financial and human capital are carried out in a systematic structure. In the early 2000s, Germany moved its financial structuring from a bank-based system to a capital market-based system and adapted its financial structuring according to current economic and commercial conditions. However, capital-based pension reform has developed a financial system based on investment awareness with capital market options such as stocks and salary payments. This system, which was developed with a focus on the stock market, had negative consequences with the decrease in the values of stocks (Hackethal, Schmidt and Tyrell, 2006: 445-446). These negativities and crisis environments led to the development of a more protective and secure financial system in Germany. With the crisis caused by the 2020 Covid-19 epidemic, Germany has implemented financial policies such as the Economic Stability Fund, fiscal and federal budget plans, borrowing limits and financial transaction limits with legal regulations to protect the economy. In addition to macroeconomic protection policies, the country has adopted a financial system establishment depending on the special conditions of the field in many areas such as energy, climate, sectoral, individual investment, employment, education and research, family and social life, health, security, taxation (Federal Ministry of Finance, 2023: 15-35). Similar to Germany, Ireland has created its financial system with policies that protect financial stability. Within the scope of macroprudential policies, it is aimed to increase the efficiency of financial capital through national and international financial cooperation coordinating organizations such as the Central Bank Financial Stability Directorate, Macroprudential Measures Committee and Financial Stability Group. At the same time, the EU has implemented macroprudential measures for non-bank institutions with the AIFMD regulation (International Monetary Fund, 2022: 33-34). Unlike Germany and Ireland, China has developed financial policies aimed at the value of the local currency and inflation in financial capital markets. In addition, financial payment conditions have been simplified along with financial regulations aimed at increasing commercial activity (Monetary Policy Analysis Group of the People's Bank of China, 2023: 28-29). However, as a result of the crisis caused by the pandemic, the government turned to the creation of a new system to increase financial stability and efficiency. In this direction, it has implemented export-based growth and investment-enhancing policies with financial support. At the same time, exchange rate management and restrictions were taken into account to protect the value of the domestic currency (Adams, Jacobs, Kenny, Russell and Sutton, 2021: 74-75).

South Korea is currently implementing policies aimed at reducing the public debt of its financial system and preventing irregularities that may arise in the capital market due to fluctuations in the exchange rate. Korea, which has restricted its budget expenditures, has also restricted its R&D expenditures. However, with the thought that this would have a negative impact in the long term, it was financed together with risky investment expenditures. In addition, South Korea has developed a financial system that acts with monetary policies (International Monetary Fund, 2023a: 10-12). America, on the other hand, directs the financial system with the Federal Reserve in order to determine financial fragility, risks and action plans and to ensure appropriate policy management. The Federal Reserve implements these initiatives towards financial stability together with local institutions through the Financial Stability Oversight Council. On the other hand, it provides information flow to the circular capital buffer (CCyB) designed to increase efficiency. In general, the country's current financial system focuses on eliminating and protecting the risks and irregularities that may arise in the capital market and encouraging credit supply in terms of sustainability of the economic cycle (Financial Stability Report, 2023a: 6). Switzerland is one of the countries with the lowest inflation and interest rates. These low rates led to a decrease in the prices of many investment instruments, especially housing, and to an economic recession. However, the country's banking system is quite developed. This banking system includes a wide financial structure, including globally operating banks, domestic banks and specialized banks, as well as branches and subsidiaries of foreign banks. The country is secured by a financial legal regulation and institutions with "too big to fail" (TBTF) regulations in case of failure in any of the banks operating on a global or local basis. In this respect, it has a reliable and up-to-date financial system (Financial Stability Report, 2023b: 19-33).

Japan's financial system is currently focused on the expansion of consumption and investment based on incentives and subsidies. As a result of the depreciation of the Yen and the resulting bubble in the value of stocks, a large financial incentive package was prepared and the aim of this incentive was to reduce financial distress. It has also pursued policies to increase household consumption by limiting the expansion of structural reforms related to digital and climate change (International Monetary Fund, 2023b: 11; Financial System Report, 2023c: 12). In Singapore, the Singapore Institute of Banking and Finance (IBF), which it established in 1974, implemented a policy of protecting the interests of nearly 200 financial institutions such as banks, insurance companies, securities brokerages and asset management firms. At the same time, the IBF aims to expand Singapore's financial system together with the financial sector, government institutions, education providers and unions. In Singapore, the development of financial competence has been achieved through the Skills Framework for Financial Services within the scope of IBF. In line with these institutions, Singapore has made financial capital dynamic with reskilling policies in order for the financial system to have a global, up-to-date and efficient future (The Institute of Banking and Finance, 2023: 3). Among these countries, the Netherlands has demonstrated very good resilience in banking and liquidity management despite successive shocks. The decrease in the country's non-performing loans during this period also reduced the country's financial irregularity risk. The country's security is generally based on high customer deposits. Interest rates, which have increased since 2021, have started to decrease and the way for investments has been opened (Monetary and Capital Markets Department, 2024: 20-23).

4.2. Human Capital Policies and Regulations

Human capital, for which economically usable behavior, competencies, skills and knowledge are a prerequisite, constitutes Germany's basic production factor. As a matter of fact, the Human Capital Management (HCM) institution has addressed the development of the skills and abilities of all employees within the framework of a systemic structuring (Stein, 2007: 296). The country's overall human capital policy is based on the German national spirit and compulsory education, world-leading scientific research talents, advanced university education, and a unique and system-based vocational training consciousness. In this direction, private investments in human capital, social security institutions and education reform are kept up to date and advanced in the light of science (Chunyang, Ke and Chen, 2021: 230-232).

Ireland, on the other hand, has carried out studies in economic, social, technological, professional, cultural and demographic areas for the last 60 years. Especially in the field of education, it has carried out educational reforms with strategic, national vision, programs and structural curricula. After 2013, the education system was designed in line with the country's foreign direct investment and export-based industrial policies. Later, it prepared employment guidance programs within the scope of the skill needs of the economy (Building Human Capital, 2021: 59-61). In addition to the structural reforms of Germany and Ireland, China has carried out human capital management with rural, urban and regional policies. In this way, it tends to provide many opportunities such as laboratories, research institutes, social norms, government investments, and corporate boards of directors to eliminate the problem of inequality and provide equal qualifications to every citizen living in China. The education system has implemented specific policy regulations such as early childhood development, the Hukou system (which is a system of minimizing the qualitative distinction between rural and urban citizens by making a qualitative distinction) and domestic mobility, ethnic inequality and minority policies, limits of innovation, strategic talent development lines, in the context of the principle of equality (Boland, Dong, Blanchette and Hass, 2022: 2-5).

South Korea has adopted a management approach that takes into account principles such as education based on the awareness of the technological development and growth engine of human capital, R&D, physical capital, and talent development in line with newly developing employment conditions. In addition, China has developed policies based on a similar principle of equality through strategic plans and programs. With these policies taken into consideration, Korea's human capital development has progressed with a focus on general education, vocational training and the development of skills directly proportional to innovations (UNDP, 2017: 1-2). Unlike these countries, America follows a more innovative, rational and scientific approach in the development of human capital. In the strategic plans and programs it has prepared, it has created activity areas to expand the activities of individuals educated within the scope of STEM (science, technology, engineering and mathematics) and to subsidize doctoral and post-doctoral activities in these fields. It has established R&D, laboratories and training centers directly proportional to these activities. The human capital management that America takes into consideration generally progresses in a competitive and leading attitude based on innovation (Van Reenen, 2021: 9-10). The Japanese government, on the other hand, evaluates its human capital policy within the scope of the principles of developing skills, increasing human capital accumulation and producing advanced technology, with the prediction that the workforce will decrease depending on the population in the future. In line with these principles, with the awareness that creating intellectual property that takes new inventions into account is a great condition for economic development, it has allocated large amounts of funds to technology and R&D studies. At the same time, it has established a systemic structure with private and public collaborations (Ministry of Foreign Affairs of Japan, 2023: 1-8).

Singapore, which is in a rapid and technology-based growth, has established Singapore's Ministry of Manpower (MOM) for many reasons such as control, assurance and regulation of human capital and has developed a system for the development of human resources, including a tripartite and multi-part approach that includes all relevant government institutions. established. While the triple approach, one of the systems it has established, takes into account strategies and practices aimed at the development of national human capital, the other approach includes activities that take into account the national human capital agenda, innovations and the knowledge-based growth model. Singapore's basic human capital policy is aimed at reskilling the workforce, as well as investments that enable the creation of human capital through national councils (Konishi, 2014: 69-70). Similar to the policies implemented by these countries, the Netherlands has enabled the support of human capital by facilitating the dialogue between education and research institutions within the framework of the economic development and resilience plan. New skill policies have been implemented to eliminate the imbalance of special investment and talent in needed areas of employment (European Commission, 2023: 43). Switzerland's human capital policy approach progresses educationally in addition to other countries. As a matter of fact, Switzerland has an advanced education system that is registered worldwide. In this context, it aims to further increase the quality of human development and education with the International Cooperation Strategy 2021-24 (IC Strategy 2021-24) with an innovative knowledge and scientific awareness approach (Switzerland's Voluntary National Review, 2022: 23).

5. HUMAN AND FINANCIAL CAPITAL COMPETITION FOR THE DEVELOPMENT OF THE INDUSTRIAL SECTOR IN INDUSTRIALIZED COUNTRIES

Technological and digital life, which develops by increasing the efficiency of human capital, has shown its impact in every field. The areas where this development was most effective were observed in human capital, as well as in the functioning of financial capital. In particular, developments in information-based transactions and telecommunications have paved the way for reduced costs, increased circulation speed of financial capital, ease of transportation, time savings and financial innovation developments. With this new situation, both human capital and financial capital, which have gained a global character, have become a matter of international competition (Demirci and Özyakışır, 2017: 26). Human capital, which acts in direct proportion to financial capital, is the most needed production factor in the industrial sector, and this creates new production conditions and directs the future of competition. Production techniques differentiated by these two production factors have expanded the scope of sustainability of economic existence of countries, especially production, consumption, investment, employment and marketing, with the use of physical and cyber technologies. Therefore, countries' competitive awareness has turned towards the efficient use of financial capital, which allows the development of human capital and support of development (T.C. Sanayi ve Teknoloji Bakanlığı, 2019: 69).

Today, where information is a strategic source of competition, both the private sector and the public sector have adopted an organizational management approach in order to increase the quality of human capital and reskill, as well as raising the level of competence and efficiency to the highest level, as well as basic skills. A similar structuring was also implemented to make financial capital efficient and accessible (Savitri and Syahza, 2019: 88). Therefore, systematically managed human and financial capital has paved the way for new inventions and formations. The development of human and financial capital, which is especially felt in the industrial sector, has brought technological structuring and digital transformation. Each newly developing process has brought the need for new and differentiated human capital and financial capital to the agenda. The development of these production factors, which have a great impact on production, have also had a great impact on employment and financial markets. The increase in mechanization within the scope of Industry 4.0 has restricted the labor-intensive production approach and created the need for a qualified and inventive labor force. This change observed in employment has developed a system that adopts the use of advanced technology such as automation, mass production and digitalization. In this case, countries have adopted a competitive economic policy approach that aims to enable those with the most financial capital to qualify their human capital and to increase the financial capital of countries with qualified human capital (İlhan, 2021: 263-264).

Table 1. Human and Financial Development Indicators of Industrialized Countries

Countries	Financial Development Index (2021)	Financial Institutions Efficiency Index (2021)	Financial Markets Index (2021)	Human Development Index (2022)	Human Capital and Research Index (2023)	Skills of Current Workforce Index (2019)
Germany	0.70	0.54	0.78	0.95	61.1	79.9
Ireland	0.62	0.40	0.65	0.95	45.2	65.4
Switzerland	0.94	0.62	0.92	0.96	59.8	78.2

Countries	Financial Development Index (2021)	Financial Institutions Efficiency Index (2021)	Financial Markets Index (2021)	Human Development Index (2022)	Human Capital and Research Index (2023)	Skills of Current Workforce Index (2019)
Netherlands	0.74	0.73	0.68	0.94	55.7	72.9
Korea of Rep.	0.82	0.72	0.78	0.92	66.9	62.8
Japan	0.89	0.72	0.86	0.92	53.8	61.7
China	0.63	0.61	0.74	0.78	49.8	59.4
Singapore	0.70	0.70	0.64	0.94	63.2	73.1
USA	0.92	0.65	0.90	0.92	56.5	71.7

Source: WIPO, IMF, WEF ve UNDP, 23.04.2024.

Note: While Human Capital and Research Index and Skills of Current Workforce Index values are determined between 0 and 100, other indicators are determined between 0 and 1.

Table 1 shows the latest human and financial development indicators of the countries. When the table is examined, the highest success in the financial development index is America and Japan, especially Switzerland; Netherlands, Korea and Japan in the financial institutions efficiency index; Switzerland and America in the financial markets index; All countries except China in the human development index, Korea and Singapore in the human capital and research index; Finally, Germany, Sweden and Singapore achieved success in the working day skills index. In terms of performance across indicators, Switzerland has reached an advanced level in terms of the development, management, efficiency and returns of both financial and human capital. On the other hand, it is observed in the table that the success of industrialized countries in the human development index is that these countries have human capital-based growth and development.

6. ECONOMETRIC ANALYSIS

6.1. Literature Research

In the literature review, it was found that human capital positively affects the industrial sector (Arık and Erdem, 2019) or economic growth (Baharumshah and Almasaied, 2009; Evans et al., 2002, Kargbo et al., 2016; Mahmood and Alkahtani, 2018; Oyinlola and Adedeji, 2019). While there are studies that affect it negatively, there are also studies that affect it negatively (Hünerli et al., 2022). While there are studies in which a causality relationship from financial development to the industrial sector has been determined, it has also been determined that the increase in the industrial sector affects financial development (Öztürk, 2020). There are studies that human capital affects economic growth, as well as studies that financial development affects economic growth (Baharumshah, and Almasaied, 2009; Evans et al., 2002, Kargbo et al., 2016; Mahmood and Alkahtani, 2018; Oyinlola and Adedeji, 2019) also available. While there are studies that financial development and economic growth positively affect human capital, there are also studies that financial capital indirectly affects economic growth through human capital (Abubakar et al., 2015).

Significant findings have been obtained in studies demonstrating that human capital influences the industrial sector and economic growth. In their 2019 study, Arık and Erdem concluded that human, institutional, innovative, and infrastructure initiatives positively affect manufacturing industry competitiveness for 31 selected countries during the 2000-2016 period. In their 2009 study, Baharumshah and Almasaied investigated the relationship between financial capital, human capital, and economic growth in Malaysia from 1974 to 2004 using the ARDL bounds test approach, revealing that both human and financial capital significantly enhance economic growth. Furthermore, in their 2002 study, Evans et al. examined the relationship between financial capital, human capital, and economic growth for 82 selected countries during the 1972-1992 period using OLS and panel GLS methods, concluding that financial development is as impactful as human capital on economic growth. Kargbo et al. (2016) examined the relationship between financial development, human capital, and economic growth in Sierra Leone for the period 1980-2012 using the OLS regression estimator. Their findings indicated that financial development and human capital accumulation positively affect economic growth. In a 2018 study, Mahmood and Alkahtani explored the relationship between financial capital, human capital, and economic growth in Saudi Arabia for the period 1970-2017 using the ARDL bounds test method, concluding that the interaction between financial market development and human capital positively contributes to economic growth. Similarly, Oyinlola and Adedeji (2019) analyzed the relationship between financial development and human capital for 19 Sub-Saharan African countries for the period 1999-2014 using the System GMM method, finding that both financial development and human capital have a direct positive effect on economic growth. Conversely, some studies have found that human capital negatively impacts industrialization. Hünerli et al. (2022) examined the effect of human capital on the industrial sector for 34 OECD member countries during the period 1996-2018 using the Driscoll-Kraay standard errors estimator, concluding that increased human capital expenditures negatively affected the share of the industrial sector.

In the literature, there are studies that identify the relationship between financial development and the industrial sector (Güngör et al., 2020) and from the industrial sector to financial development (Öztürk, 2020). Güngör et al. (2020) examined the relationship between financial development and industrialization in Turkey using quarterly data for the period 2005-2018. The causality results indicated a unidirectional causality from the M2/GDP ratio to industrial production and from industrial production to the loans provided to the industrial sector/GDP ratio. In his 2020 study, Öztürk concluded that development in the industrial sector leads to an increase in financial capital through Panel Regression Analysis, using data for the period 1995-2012 for 24 selected OECD countries. Among the studies investigating the impact of financial development on economic growth, Uç (2019) examined the relationship between financial development and economic growth in Turkey for the period 1986-2017 and concluded that financial development affects economic growth in the short run.

In their 2017 study, Sehrawat and Giri examined the relationship between financial development, human capital, and economic growth in Asian countries for the period 1984-2013. They found a long-run relationship between financial development, economic growth, and human capital. According to the PDOLS and FMOLS results, financial development indicators and economic growth are significant drivers of human capital growth. The panel Granger causality results indicated a causality relationship from financial development, public education expenditure, and economic growth to human capital. Additionally, financial capital indirectly affects economic growth through human capital. In 2015, Abubakar et al. examined the relationship between financial capital, human capital, and economic growth for the Economic Community of West African States (ECOWAS) for the period 1980-2011. Their study concluded that financial capital affects economic growth both directly and through human capital.

In their 2023 study, Aktürk et al. examined the relationship between human capital and physical capital in Turkey for the period 2000-2014 using the Driscoll-Kraay fixed effects model with standard errors. They concluded that the share of human capital in manufacturing goods imports is negative, while the share of manufacturing goods exports in total exports is positive. Qamruzzaman et al. (2021) investigated the relationship between human capital, financial development, and economic growth in Bangladesh, India, Pakistan, Sri Lanka, Nepal, and Bhutan for the period 1982-2016 using quarterly data. The analysis revealed a long-run relationship between human capital, financial development, and economic growth in these countries. Both in the short and long run, there is a reciprocal relationship between financial development and economic growth, and between human capital and economic growth.

In his 2016 study, Işık examined the relationship between financial capital and industrial production in Turkey for the period 1994-2014 using the Generalized Method of Moments (GMM). The relationship between financial capital and firms in the manufacturing industry was analyzed using three different models. The research findings indicated that, although different results were obtained across the three models, the manufacturing industry and financial capital moved in the same direction in two of the models.

6.2. Data and Model

The aim of the study is to determine the impact of financial and human capital on the industrial added value of industrializing countries (Germany, China, Ireland, South Korea, America, Switzerland, Japan, Singapore and the Netherlands). The countries included in the research are the best performers according to the Competitive Industrial Performance Indexes (https://stat.unido.org/database/CIP%20%20 Competitive%20Industrial%20Performance%20Index) using the United Nations Industrial Development Organization (UNIDO) resource. It covers countries. The aim is for these researched countries to serve as an example to other countries. The time period in the econometric model established for the purpose of the study includes the years 2005 and 2021, which includes the 2007-2008 global crisis period.

The econometric equation of the study was determined as follows.

$$IVA_t : \beta_0 + \beta_1 ECI_t + \beta_2 EE_t + \beta_3 EI_t + \beta_4 FDI_t + \beta_5 FMEI_t + \beta_6 GCFC_t + \varepsilon_t \quad (1)$$

Table 2. Information on Variables

Değişkenler	Değişkenlerin Nitelikleri	Kaynak
Industry (including construction), Value Added (Current US$)- **(IVA)**	The Industry Sector	The World Bank World Development Indicators
Education Expenditure (Current US$)- **(EE)**	Human Capital	The World Bank World Development Indicators
Employment in Industry (% of total employment)- **(EI)**	Human Capital	The World Bank World Development Indicators
Economic Complexity Indeks - **(ECI)**	Human Capital	Atlas Of Economy Complexity
Gross Fixed Capital Formation (Current US$) – **(GFCF)**	Finacial Capital	The World Bank World Development Indicators
Financial Development Index – **(FDI)**	Financial Capital	IMF Finacal Development Index Database
Financial Markets Efficiency Index – **(FMEI)**	Financial Capital	IMF Finacal Development Index Database

continued on following page

Table 2. Continued
6.3. Econometric Findings

Before making econometric analysis, determining the horizontal coefficient dependence of the variables and the distribution functions of the slope coefficients is very important for appropriate test selection. In this context, firstly, it was determined whether the model included a horizontal section and the structure of the slope coefficients, and the test results are given in Table 3.

Table 3. Cross-Section Dependency and Homogeneity Test of the Model

Test	Test Statistic	Probability Value	Result
Cross Section Dependency			
LM (Breusch and Pagan (1980)	46.55	0.11	There is no cross-sectional dependency.
LM adj (Pesaran vd. (2008)	-5.00	0.00*	There is no cross-sectional dependency.
LM CD (Pesaran (2004)	2.38	0.01**	There is no cross-sectional dependency.
Homogeneity Test			
Delta_tilde	2.53	0.01**	Heterogeneous.
Delta_tilde_adj	3.48	0.00*	Heterogeneous.

Note: * and ** signs indicate 1% and 5% significance level, respectively.

According to the cross-sectional dependency test results used to determine the tests to be used in the analysis, it was determined that the model contained cross-sectional dependency because the probability value of the LM CD and LM adj tests was lower than the 5% significance level. On the other hand, the probability values of homogeneity tests, which help determine appropriate tests by calculating the slope coefficients of the variables, were lower than the 5% significance level, and the slope coefficients of the variables were found to be heterogeneous.

According to cross-sectional dependence and homogeneity tests, second generation panel data tests will be used in the analysis because the model includes cross-sectional dependence and is heterogeneous.

Table 4. Second Generation CADF Unit Root Test Results

Variables	Constant – I(0)	Constant – I(1)	Critical Values
IVA	-1.900	-3.090*	%1 / -2.21
EI	-2.055	-2.382*	%5 / -2.34
GFCF	-1.879	-2.983*	%10 / -2.06
EE	-1.345	-3.098*	
FDI	-2.424*	-4.390*	
FMEI	-0.510	-2.170***	
ECI	-2.047	-3.994*	

Note: * and *** signs indicate 1% and 10% significance level, respectively.

According to the CIPS statistical values obtained from the CADF unit root test, only the FDI variable was found to be stationary at the I(0) level, while all differenced variables were found to be stationary at the I(1) level. In this regard, the analysis will be carried out by taking into account the levels at which the variables to be included in the analysis are stationary.

Table 5. Second Generation Westerlund Cointegration Test

IVA	Statistic	Value	Z-Value	Probability Value	Bootstrap p Value
ECI	Gt	-2.792	-3.372	0.000*	0.680
	Ga	-14.812	-4.214	0.000*	0.662
	Pt	-4.460	-0.036	0.486	0.698
	Pa	-19.739	-10.058	0.000*	0.442
EE	Gt	-3.416	-5.477	0.000*	0.367
	Ga	-15.265	-4.464	0.000*	0.738
	Pt	-11.758	-7.240	0.000*	0.430
	Pa	-14.087	-6.362	0.000*	0.353
EI	Gt	-3.197	-4.738	0.000*	0.530
	Ga	-21.240	-7.772	0.000*	0.720
	Pt	-11.771	-7.253	0.000*	0.550
	Pa	-34.977	-20.021	0.000*	0.620
FDI	Gt	-4.732	-9.919	0.000*	0.300
	Ga	-26.963	-10.939	0.000*	0.098***
	Pt	-11.913	-7.398	0.000*	0.450
	Pa	-34.771	-13.340	0.000*	0.330

continued on following page

Table 5. Continued

IVA	Statistic	Value	Z-Value	Probability Value	Bootstrap p Value
FMEI	Gt	-3.481	-5.696	0.000*	0.495
	Ga	-16.409	-5.097	0.000*	0.393
	Pt	-6.372	-1.923	0.027**	0.433
	Pa	-19.524	-9.924	0.000*	0.258
GFCF	Gt	-3.031	-4.177	0.000*	0.562
	Ga	-12.936	-3.175	0.001*	0.480
	Pt	-10.253	-5.754	0.000*	0.200
	Pa	-21.910	-11.477	0.000*	0.008*

Note: *, ** and *** signs indicate 1%, 5% and 10% significance level, respectively.

Since the slope coefficients of the variables in the model are heterogeneous, Gt and Ga test statistics should be taken into account in the Westerlund cointegration test. In this context, it was observed that all variables had asymptotic probability values of 1% significance level in all test statistics. Therefore, a long-term relationship was detected between the dependent and independent variables within the scope of asymptotic probability. On the other hand, it has been observed that there is no long-term relationship between the dependent and independent variables, since the probability values of all test statistics, except the Pa bootstrap probability value of the FDI Ga and GFCF variables, are greater than 0.05 probability value, according to the bootstrap probability values, which should be taken into consideration since the model contains cross-sectional dependence (Doğanay and Değer, 2017: 137-138).

Table 6. Augmented Mean Group Estimator (AMG) - Long-Term Cointegration Coefficient Estimates

IVA	Coefficient	Standard Error	Z-Value	P > |z|	95% Confidence Interval Lower GS / Upper GS
Long-Term Cointegration Coefficient Estimates of the Panel					
ECI	1.01e+11	4.82e+10	2.09	0.036**	6.50/1.95
EI	7.74e+90	5.45e+09	1.42	0.155	-2.93/1.84
FDI	2.24e+10	1.29e+11	0.17	0.863	-2.31/2.76
EE	5.27081	2.685095	1.96	0.050**	0.00/10.53
GFCF	0.5347273	0.1631993	3.28	0.001*	0.21/0.85
FMEI	2.44e08	6.97e+09	0.04	0.972	-1.34/1.39
Long-Term Cointegration Coefficient Estimates by Country					
Germany					

continued on following page

Table 6. Continued

IVA	Coefficient	Standard Error	Z-Value	P > |z|	95% Confidence Interval Lower GS / Upper GS
ECI	9.56e+10	6.39e+10	1.50	0.135	-2.96/2.21
EI	3.07e+10	1.92e+10	1.60	0.110	-6.98/6.83
FDI	-4.85e+10	2.59e+11	-1.88	0.061***	-9.93/2.20
EE	-4.85e+11	0.7689402	-1.71	0.087***	-2.82/0.19
GFCF	1.328673	0.1198872	11.08	0.000*	1.09/1.56
FMEI	-3.58e+10	4.47e+10	-0.80	0.424	-1.23/5.19
Chine					
ECI	3.70e+11	2.73e+11	1.36	0.174	-1.64/9.04
EI	3.87e+11	1.70e+10	2.27	0.025**	5.31/7.20
FDI	4.57e+11	6.86e+11	0.67	0.505	-8.87/1.80
EE	20.55856	4.550092	4.52	0.000*	11.64/29.47
GFCF	0.2518319	0.1309596	1.92	0.054***	-0.00/0.50
FMEI	-1.18e+10	7.85e+10	-0.15	0.881	-1.66/1.42
Ireland					
ECI	-1.84e+10	3.34e+10	-0.55	0.583	-8.39/4.72
EI	6.49e+09	5.00e+09	1.30	0.195	-3.32/1.63
FDI	-5.12e+10	1.42e+11	-0.36	0.719	-3.30/2.27
EE	0.2280951	4.626129	0.05	0.961	-8.83/9.29
GFCF	-0.2256529	0.1537036	-1.47	0.142	-0.52/0.07
FMEI	4.01e+10	4.82e+10	0.83	0.406	-5.44/1.35
Sounth Korea					
ECI	9.55e+10	4.14e+10	2.31	0.021**	1.45/1.77
EI	-4.48e+09	9.78e+09	-0.46	0.647	-2.37/1.47
FDI	1.06e+11	2.18e+11	0.49	0.627	-3.21/5.32
EE	2.023714	0.6637787	3.05	0.002*	0.72/3.32
GFCF	0.9331811	0.1433256	6.51	0.000*	0.65/1.21
FMEI	0	0	0	0	0.0/0.0
America					
ECI	5.21e+10	2.24e+11	0.23	0.820	-3.89/4.91
EI	1.02e+09	7.45e+10	0.01	0.989	-1.45/1.47
FDI	-4.92e+11	1.66e+12	-0.30	0.766	-3.74/2.75
EE	0.9355443	0.6188436	1.51	0.131	-0.27/2.14
GFCF	0.721442	0.1769785	4.08	0.000*	0.37/1.06

continued on following page

Table 6. Continued

IVA	Coefficient	Standard Error	Z-Value	P > |z|	95% Confidence Interval Lower GS / Upper GS
FMEI	0	0	0	0	0.0/0.0
Switzerland					
ECI	6.75e+09	1.22e+10	0.55	0.579	-1.71/3.06
EI	6.81e+09	3.77e+09	1.80	0.071***	-5.86/1.42
FDI	-2.55e+10	2.80e+10	-0.91	0.364	-8.04/2.95
EE	2.41797	1.063008	2.27	0.023**	0.33/4.50
GFCF	0.6037955	0.2175793	2.78	0.006*	0.17/1.03
FMEI	4.61e+09	3.78e+09	1.22	0.223	-2.80/1.20
Japan					
ECI	3.16e+11	8.99e+10	3.51	0.000*	1.40/4.92
EI	-1.11e+10	5.46e+10	-0.20	0.838	-1.18/9.59
FDI	7.08e+10	2.69e+10	2.63	0.009*	1.81/1.24
EE	1.914999	2.532924	0.76	0.450	-3.04/6.87
GFCF	0.7050527	0.3493837	2.02	0.044**	0.02/1.38
FMEI	0	0	0	0	0.0/0.0
Singapore					
ECI	-2.38e+10	9.63e+09	-2.47	0.013**	-4.27/-4.92
EI	2.37e+09	1.20e+90	1.98	0.048**	2.41/4.71
FDI	5.47e+10	5.40e+10	1.01	0.311	-5.12/1.61
EE	17.9692	3.804956	4.72	0.000*	10.51/25.42
GFCF	-0.0965709	0.2169625	-0.45	0.656	-0.52/0.32
FMEI	1.73e+10	9.18e+09	1.89	0.059***	-6.86/3.52
Holland					
ECI	1.56e+10	4.04e+10	0.38	0.700	-6.37/9.48
EI	-7.05e+10	6.67e+09	-0.11	0.916	-1.38/1.24
FDI	-6.97e+10	7.10e+10	-0.98	0.326	-2.09/6.94
EE	2.70532	0.8490741	3.19	0.001*	1.04/4.39
GFCF	0.590793	0.1429144	4.13	0.000*	0.31/0.87
FMEI	-1.22e+10	3.19e+10	-0.38	0.701	-7.49/5.04

Note: *, ** and *** signs indicate 1%, 5% and 10% significance level, respectively.

According to the long-term coefficient estimation results given in Table 6, a 1% increase in the gross fixed capital formation variable, which is a financial indicator for the panel in general, increases the industrial added value by 0.53%, while a 1% increase in the economic complexity index and education expenditures, which are human capital indicators, increases the value added by 0.53%. It was determined that it increased the industrial added value by 1.01% and 5.27%, respectively. No statistical significance was encountered for other variables. However, when the results are examined on a country-specific basis, the developments observed in the GFCF variable, which is among the financial indicators, increased the industrial added value in Germany, China, South Korea, America, Switzerland, Japan and the Netherlands by 1.32%, 0.25, 0.93, 0.72, 0.60, 0.70 and 0.59, respectively. It has not been determined to have a positive effect. 1% increases in the FMEI variable, which is considered as a financial indicator, increased the industrial value added by 1.73% in Singapore, and 1% increases in the FDI variable increased the industrial value added by 7.08% in Japan. The only financial variable that negatively affects industrial value added is FDI, and it has been determined that it causes a 4.85% decrease in Germany's industrial value added.

When the human capital variables, which are of great importance in the development of the industry, are examined, it is observed that the activities carried out for the development of the education expenditure variable have a positive impact on the development of the industry in China, South Korea, Switzerland, Singapore and the Netherlands by 20.55%, 2.02, 2.41, 17.96 and 2.70%, respectively. However, in Germany, the return of investments made in the education expenditure variable to the industrial value added was negative by 4.85%. It has been observed that increases in the industrial employment rate, another human capital indicator, positively affect the development of industry by 3.87% in China, 6.81% in Switzerland and 2.37% in Singapore. It was determined that 1% increases in the ECI variable increased the industrial value added by 9.55% in South Korea and 3.16% in Japan, and decreased it by 2.38% in Singapore.

Generally speaking, it can be said that gross fixed capital formation among financial indicators and education expenditure, which is a human capital indicator, have a simultaneous effect on the development of countries' industrial sectors. Although this result shows that there is a balanced recycling between financial capital and human capital, industrialized countries have been able to maintain both their monetary and development policies on this balance, with the awareness that there can be no human capital without financial capital, and there can be no financial capital without human capital.

7. CONCLUSION

To achieve economic growth, countries must establish conditions for high value-added production. Designing production factors and processes in an innovative, dynamic manner that aligns with living standards will pave the way for economic growth by enhancing efficiency. Financial and human capital are the primary drivers in creating products and production processes with high added value, which are essential for achieving economic growth. These two factors, which play complementary roles, are not only crucial for development across all sectors but also play a key role in ensuring high quality and income within the industrial sector.

In light of this importance, the study aims to examine the management and efficiency of financial and human capital in the industrial sectors of industrialized countries. Another objective is to assess the impact of financial and human capital on the industrial sectors of these countries and to draw specific conclusions. To achieve these goals, the study first analyzes the development of human and financial capital in industrialized countries, focusing on their economy, industrial sector, and global competitiveness. It then determines the effect of financial and human capital indicators on the industrial added value of the countries included in the research.

The research findings indicate that industrializing countries place significant emphasis on developing plans, policies, and tools specifically tailored to human and financial capital, in line with innovation. These countries have also achieved their goals of advancing their current development and enhancing global competitiveness through collaboration in general economic, sectoral, or micro-based work areas. According to the panel data analysis conducted in the study, the ECI, EE, and GFCF variables were found to positively impact the industrial sectors of the countries across the entire panel. These results underscore the importance of human capital for the entire panel.

On a country-specific level, the GFCF variable, representing financial capital, was found to have a statistically significant and positive effect in all countries except Singapore and Ireland. Although the human capital indicators EE, EI, and ECI showed varying effects, the EE variable had the highest positive impact in China and Singapore, at 20% and 17%, respectively. The analysis also revealed that Germany's FDI and EE variables, as well as Singapore's ECI variable, negatively affected industrial value added.

Overall, the analysis suggests that human capital has greater potential in the industrial sector. When compared with other studies in the literature, the positive impact of human capital in the industrial sector was consistently found, with the exception of the study by Hünerli et al. (2022). Specifically, Aktürk et al. (2023) and Arık and Erdek (2019) found a positive effect of human capital in the industrial sector, while Işık (2016), Öztürk (2020), and Uç (2019) found that financial capital positively affected the industry. Contrary to these studies, research by Qamruzzaman et al. (2021), Oyinlola and Adedeji (2019), Mahmood and Alkahtani (2018), Sehrawat and Giri (2017), Abubakar et al. (2015), Baharumshah and Almasaied (2009), and Evans et al. (2002) highlighted that financial and human capital are major drivers of income growth.

The research and analysis results conclude that human and financial capital are the most important elements of industrialization. The efficient utilization of available human and financial capital has enhanced the competitiveness of countries and enabled them to reach a global industrial environment. Financial and human capital are not only considered economic policy tools but also strategic instruments in the economic, industrial, and digital transformation of industrializing countries. The countries examined in this study have used financial and human capital as tools by leveraging or creating opportunities in their national and international activities. Industrialized countries that differentiate their production processes by adhering to local policies and continuing their development have transformed these two factors into strategic elements in their global connections.

In this context, developing countries that are still in the process of industrialization should strengthen their political and economic ties with experienced industrialized nations. These countries should also demonstrate a commitment to adopting and implementing the national policies of industrialized countries and capitalize on opportunities by recognizing financial and human capital as strategic tools in their global economic activities. Developing nations that approach financial and human capital as key elements of development in the industrialization process will gain insights into global competition, its mechanisms, innovations, and new market formations. This approach will foster a dynamic development process for both industrialized and developing countries.

This study emphasizes the pivotal role of financial and human capital in the process of industrialization. For developing countries, it is particularly critical to enhance investments in human capital, especially in areas such as education, healthcare, and vocational training. The development of a skilled labor force is expected to increase the competitiveness of the industrial sector, thereby fostering long-term economic growth. Additionally, expanding and improving financial systems in developing countries is essential for broadening access to financial capital for businesses and individuals. This is especially important for supporting the growth of small and medium-sized enterprises (SMEs) and facilitating the implementation of innovative initiatives.

REFERENCES

Abubakar, A., Kassim, S. H., & Yusoff, M. B. (2015). Financial development, human capital accumulation and economic growth: Empirical evidence from the Economic Community of West African States (ECOWAS). *Procedia: Social and Behavioral Sciences*, 172, 96–103. DOI: 10.1016/j.sbspro.2015.01.341

Adams, N., Jacobs, D., Kenny, S., Russell, S., & Sutton, M. (2021). China's Evolving Financial System and Its Global Importance. *Reserve Bank of Australia*, 72-85.

Afşar, A. (2007). Finansal gelişme ile ekonomik büyüme arasındaki ilişki. *Muhasebe ve Finansman Dergisi*, (36), 188–198.

Aktürk, E., Akan, Y., & Gültekin, S. (2023). "İmalat Sanayi İthalat ve İhracatı İle Beşerî Sermayenin Türk İmalat Sanayi Üzerine Etkisi: 2000-2014 Dönemi. Pamukkale Sosyal Bilimler Enstitüsü Dergisi(56), 343-356. https://dergipark.org.tr/tr/download/article-file/2485189 adresinden alındı

Arık, Ş., & Erdem, M. Ş. (2019). İmalat Sanayi Rekabet Gücünün Yapısal Belirleyicileri. Akdeniz İİBF Dergisi, 455-488. https://dergipark.org.tr/en/download/article-file/859161 adresinden alındı

Aytekin, G. K. (2018). Uluslararası Sermaye Hareketleri Kapsamında Sıcak Para Akımlarının Ekonomik Etkileri ve Spekülasyon. *Uluslararası Beşeri Bilimler ve Eğitim Dergisi*, 4(7), 184–207.

Baharumshah, A. Z., & Almasaied, S. W. (2009). Foreign direct investment and economic growth in Malaysia: Interactions with human capital and financial deepening. *Emerging Markets Finance & Trade*, 45(1), 90–102. DOI: 10.2753/REE1540-496X450106

Boland, B., Dong, K., Blanchette, J., & Hass, R. (2022). How China's Human Capital Impacts Its National Competitiveness. CSIS BRIEFS, 1-15. https://csis-website-prod.s3.amazonaws.com/s3fs-public/publication/220516_Boland_China_HumanCapitalImpacts.pdf?VersionId=5I44COiOIVbdFmZlL_IT9LbTW6BZbbCC adresinden alındı

Building Human Capital. (2021). *Ireland's Human Capital: The Contribution of Education and Skills Development to Economic Transformation*. International Bank for Reconstruction and Development / The World Bank.

Chunyang, L., Ke, G., & Chen, Y. (2021). Education and Technology for Industrial Power: The German Experience of Human Capital Accumulation. *International Journal of Economics. Finance and Management Sciences*, 9(4), 128–133.

Demirci, N. S., & Özyakışır, D. (2017). Finansal Gelişmişlik ve Beşeri Sermaye Arasındaki İlişki: Türkiye için Zaman Serileri Analizi (1971-2013). *Finans Politik & Ekonomik Yorumlar*, 54(624), 25–39.

Doğanay, M. A. and Değer, M. K., (2017). Yükselen piyasa ekonomilerinde doğrudan yabancı yatırımlar ve ihracat ilişkisi: panel veri eşbütünleşme analizleri (1996-2014). Çankırı Karatekin Üniversitesi İktisadi ve İdari Bilimler Fakültesi Dergisi, 7(2), 127-145.

Easterly, W. R., & Wetzel, D. L. (1989). *Policy determinants of growth: survey of theory and evidence* (Vol. 343). World Bank Publications.

Eser, K., & Gökmen, Ç. E. (2009). Beşeri sermayenin ekonomik gelişme üzerindeki etkileri: Dünya deneyimi ve Türkiye üzerine gözlemler. *Sosyal ve Beşeri Bilimler Dergisi*, 1(2), 41–56.

Europen Commission. (2023). *2023 Country Report: The Netherland*. Office of the European Union.

Evans, A. D., Green, C. J., & Murinde, V. (2002). Human capital and financial development in economic growth: New evidence using the translog production function. *International Journal of Finance & Economics*, 7(2), 123–140. DOI: 10.1002/ijfe.182

Federal Ministry of Finance. (2023). *German Stability Programme*. Federal Ministry of Finance.

Gu, J., Gouliamos, K., Lobonţ, O. R., & Nicoleta-Claudia, M. (2021). Is the fourth industrial revolution transforming the relationship between financial development and its determinants in emerging economies? *Technological Forecasting and Social Change*, 165, 120563. DOI: 10.1016/j.techfore.2020.120563

Güngör, S., Şahin, E., & Karaca, S. S. (2020). Finansal Serbestleşme İle Sanayi Üretimi Arasındaki İlişkinin Fourier Temelli Yaklaşımlar İle Test Edilmesi Türkiye Örneği. *Maliye ve Finans Yazıları*, (113), 119–138. DOI: 10.33203/mfy.570314

Gürün, F. (2019). Endüstri 4.0 ve beşeri sermayenin geleceği. In Journal of Social Policy Conferences (No. 76, pp. 67-88). Istanbul University.

Hackethal, A., Schmidt, R. H., & Tyrell, M. (2006). The Transformation of the German Financial System. *Revue d'Économie Politique*, 116(4), 431–456. DOI: 10.3917/redp.164.0431

Hünerli, Ö. C., Bilik, M., & Aydın, Ü. (2022). Fiziksel ve Beşeri Sermaye İyileştirmelerinin Sanayi Sektörü Katma Değerine Etkisi. *EKEV Akademi Dergisi*, 0(92), 193–205. DOI: 10.17753/sosekev.1107759

İlhan, Ü. D. (2021). Gaining Financial Competitive Power Through Human Capital: An Evaluation of Turkey. *Financial Strategies in Competitive Markets: Multidimensional Approaches to Financial Policies for Local Companies* (s. 263-276). içinde Switzerland: Springer.

IMF. (2021). *Financial Development Index, Financial Institutions Efficiency Index, Financial Markets Index.*https://data.imf.org/?sk=f8032e80-b36c-43b1-ac26-493c5b1cd33b

IMF. (2022). *Irland: Financial System Stabilitty Assessment.* International Monetary Fund.

IMF. (2023a). *Republic of Korea.* International Monetary Fund.

IMF. (2023b). *Japan.* Washington: IMF Country Report No. 23/127.

Işık, M. (2016). *Finansal Piyaslardaki Gelişmelerin İmalat Sanayi Firmaları Üzerindeki Etkisi: Türkiye Örneği (Cilt Yüksek Linsas Tezi).* Nevşehir Hacı Bektaş Veli Üniversitesi- Sosyal Bilimler Enstitüsü.

Karagül, M. (2003). Beşeri Sermayenin Ekonomik Büyümeyle İlişkisi ve Etkin Kullanımı. *Akdeniz Üniversitesi İktisadi ve İdari Bilimler Fakültesi Dergisi,* 3(5).

Karataş, M., & Çankaya, E. (2011). Türkiye'de Beşeri Sermaye ve Ekonomik Büyüme İlişkisinin Analizi. *Journal of Management & Economics*, 18(1).

Kargbo, A. A., Ding, Y., & Kargbo, M. (2016). Financial development, human capital and economic growth: New evidence from Sierra Leone. *Journal of Finance and Bank Management*, 4(1), 49–67.

Konishi, N. (2014). Human Resources Development Initiatives in Singapore: Investing in Sustainable Global Competitiveness. *Journal of Policy Studies*, 67-76. https://core.ac.uk/download/pdf/143637516.pdf adresinden alındı.

Mahmood, H., and Alkahtani, N. S. (2018). Human resource, financial market development and economic growth in Saudi Arabia: a role of human capital. *Economic annals-XXI*, (169), 31-34.

Ministry of Foreign Affairs of Japan. (2023). Trade Policy Review of Japan 2023. *Ministry of Foreign Affairs of Japan*, 1-10. https://www.mofa.go.jp/mofaj/files/100469410.pdf adresinden alındı.

Monetary and Capital Markets Department. (2024). *Kingdom of the Netherlands: Financial System Stability Assessment*. International Monetary Fund.

Monetary Policy Analysis Group of the People's Bank of China. fco(2023). *China Monetary Policy Report*. China: Monetary Policy Analysis Group of the People's Bank of China.

Ongun, M. T. (1993). Finansal Globalleşme. *Ekonomik Yaklaşım*, 4(9), 35–46. DOI: 10.5455/ey.10148

Oyinlola, M. A., & Adedeji, A. (2019). Human capital, financial sector development and inclusive growth in sub-Saharan Africa. *Economic Change and Restructuring*, 52(1), 43–66. DOI: 10.1007/s10644-017-9217-2

Öztürk, A. İ. (2020). *Sanayi Sektörünün Finansal Gelişme Üzerindeki Etkisinin Panel Veri Analizi ile İncelenmesi (Cilt Yüksek Lisans Tezi)*. İstanbul Üniversitesi-Sosyal Bilimler Enstitüsü.

Özyakışır, D. (2011). Beşeri sermayenin ekonomik kalkınma sürecindeki rolü: Teorik bir değerlendirme. *Girişimcilik ve Kalkınma Dergisi*, 6(1), 46–71.

Qamruzzaman, M., Jianguo, W., Jahan, S., & Yingjun, Z. (2021). Financial innovation, human capital development, and economic growth of selected South Asian countries: An application of ARDL approach. *International Journal of Finance & Economics*, 26(3), 4032–4053. DOI: 10.1002/ijfe.2003

Report, F. S. (2023a). *Financial Stability Report*. Federal Reserve Board.

Report, F. S. (2023b). *Financial Stability Report 2023*. Swiss National Bank.

Report, F. S. (2023c). *Financial System Report 2023*. Tokyo: Bank of Japan. https://www.boj.or.jp/en/research/brp/fsr/data/fsr231020a.pdf adresinden alındı

Sanayi ve Teknoloji Bakanlığı. (2019). *2023 Sanayi ve Teknoloji Stratejisi*. Ankara: T.C. Sanayi ve Teknoloji Bakanlığı. https://www.sanayi.gov.tr/assets/pdf/SanayiStratejiBelgesi2023.pdf adresinden alındı.

Sarwar, A., Khan, M. A., Sarwar, Z., & Khan, W. (2020). Financial development, human capital and its impact on economic growth of emerging countries. *Asian Journal of Economics and Banking*, 5(1), 86–100. DOI: 10.1108/AJEB-06-2020-0015

Savitri, E., & Syahza, A. (2019). Effect Of Human Capital And Competitive Strategies Against The Financial Performance Of Small And Medium Enterprises. *International Journal of Scientific & Technology Research*, 8(4), 86–92.

Sehrawat, M., & Giri, A. K. (2017). An empirical relationship between financial development indicators and human capital in some selected Asian countries. *International Journal of Social Economics*, 44(3), 337–349. DOI: 10.1108/IJSE-05-2015-0131

Stein, V. (2007). Human capital management: The German way. [ZfP]. *Zeitschrift für Personalforschung*, 21(3), 295–321.

Switzerland's Voluntary National Review. (2022). *Implementing the 2030 Agenda for Sustainable Development: Voluntary National Review of Switzerland 2022*. Bern: Swiss Federal Council. https://www.sdgital2030.ch/docs/CountryReport/country-report-switzerland-2022_en.pdf adresinden alındı.

The Atlas Of Economy Complexity. (2023). *Economic Complexity Indeks*.https://atlas.cid.harvard.edu/

The Institute of Banking & Finance. (2023). *Event Management Services for 2023 Singapore Financial Leaders'*. Shenton Way: IBF.

The World Bank. (2024). *Personal Remittances - Current Dollar, Education Expenditures, Health Expenditures, Industrial Sector*. https://data.worldbank.org/

The World Bank World Development Indicators. (2023) *Industry (including construction), Value Added (Current US$), Education Expenditure (Current US$), Employment in Industry (% of total employment), Gross Fixed Capital Formation (Current US$)*.https://databank.worldbank.org/source/world-development-indicators

Uç, K. (2019). *Finansal Gelişme ve Ekonomik Büyüme Arasındaki İlişkinin Ekonometrik Bir Analizi: Türkiye Örneği (Cilt Yüksek Lisans Tezi)*. Afyon Kocatepe Üniversitesi, Sosyal Bilimler Enstitüsü.

UNDP. (2017). *Achieving Inclusive Growth and Prosperity by Bolstering Human Capital: Lessons from Korea*. Seoul: United Nations Development Programme. https://www.undp.org/sites/g/files/zskgke326/files/migration/seoul_policy_center/Human-Capital-report-policy-brief-8.pdf adresinden alındı.

UNDP. (2022). Human Development Index. *Human Development Reports*.https://hdr.undp.org/data-center/human-development-index#/indicies/HDI

Uslu, N. Ç. (2002). Finansal Sistemin Gelişiminin Reel Ekonomi Üzerine Olası Etkileri. *Anadolu Üniversitesi İktisadi ve İdari Bilimler Fakültesi Dergisi*, 18(1), 105–116.

Van Reenen, J. (2021). Innovation and Human Capital Policy. *National Bureau of Economic Research*, 1-30. https://www.nber.org/system/files/working_papers/w28713/w28713.pdf adresinden alındı.

WEF. (2019). Skills of Current Workforce Index. The Global Competitiveness Report (2022). Geneva Switzerland.

WIPO. (2023). Human Capital and Research Index (2023). *Global Innovation Index 2023.* Geneva, Switzerland.

Yazıcı, R. (2020). Finansal Sermaye İsrafının Önlenebilmesinde Katılım Finans Sisteminin Geliştirebileceği Faizsiz Araçlar/Interest Free Tools That Can Be Developed By The Participation Finance System In Order To Prevent Financial Capital Waste. *Uluslararası Ekonomi İşletme ve Politika Dergisi*, 4(1), 185–204. DOI: 10.29216/ueip.679403

Yumuşak, İ. (2008). Beşeri sermayenin iktisadi önemi ve Türkiye'nin beşeri sermaye potansiyeli. In Journal of Social Policy Conferences (No. 55). Istanbul University.

KEY TERMS AND DEFINITIONS

Competition: Competition is a struggle for superiority.

Economic Development: Economic development is the increase in a country's income and welfare as a result of goods and services produced in a certain period.

Financial Capital: Financial capital is the monetary values necessary for an economic unit to maintain its economic existence.

Human Capital: Human capital is the state of labor qualified by knowledge, experience and skills.

Industrial Policies: Industrial policies are plans and strategies that will improve the products and production processes of countries and companies.

Industrial Sector: The industrial sector is the sector where mass production is carried out using machines to produce finished products using raw materials.

Industrialized Countries: Industrialized countries are countries that have reached high technology and production in the industrial sector.

Chapter 6
Quality or Quantity?
The Role of Human Capital on Sustainable Growth

Ozlem Inanc
Isik University, Turkey

ABSTRACT

This study examines the link between human capital and sustainable economic growth, highlighting the contradiction of rising university education without improved graduate employability in Turkiye from 2014 to 2023. It notes high unemployment among university graduates, indicating a disconnect between the skills provided by educational institutions and job market demands. The rapid growth in universities and graduates has not matched the increase in high-skilled job opportunities, leading to skill mismatches and underemployment, especially during economic downturns. The paper calls for a reassessment of educational strategies towards a quality-focused education that prioritizes practical skills and market needs, emphasizing university-industry collaborations to boost graduate employability and ensure higher education's role in fostering economic resilience and growth.

1. INTRODUCTION

In this study, while analyzing the relationship between human capital and sustainable economic growth, the subject will be evaluated for Turkey as an example of a country in the transition process to an innovation-oriented economy.

Sustainable development aims to meet the needs of the present generation without compromising the ability of future generations to meet their own needs. To achieve sustainable development, three interconnected pillars must be addressed: economic, social, and environmental. (Armeanu et al., 2018). The 2030 Agenda for Sustainable

DOI: 10.4018/979-8-3693-5508-4.ch006

Development, adopted by all member states in 2015, provides a blueprint for prosperity for people and the planet. At its center are the 17 Sustainable Development Goals (SDGs), which call for action by all countries in a global partnership. They recognize that ending poverty and other deprivations must be paired with strategies that improve health, education, reduce inequality, and promote economic growth, while also addressing climate change and preserving the environment. Similar to this, goals of Europe 2020 strategy includes fighting poverty, increasing education, employment and rate of innovation (Armeanu et.al., 2018).

Goal eight in the 2030 Agenda focuses on promoting sustained, inclusive, and sustainable economic growth, full and productive employment, and decent work for all through diversification, technological upgrading, and innovation. In this regard, Hanushek and Woessmann (2021) mention that to reach the SDGs, countries need to ensure a high and strong rate of economic growth. One of the most important requirements to achieve this targeted economic growth rate is strong and productive human capital, as the skills of individuals are the source of economic growth.

Goal 4 of the 2030 Agenda emphasizes ensuring inclusive and equitable quality education and promoting lifelong learning opportunities for all. According to this goal, by 2030, countries should provide equal access to affordable technical, vocational, and tertiary education, including universities, for everyone. Hanushek and Woessmann (2021) argues that increasing the knowledge and skills of the population is a key element for achieving inclusive and sustainable development. Armenau et al. (2018) analyze the drivers of sustainable economic growth in EU-28 countries for the period 2002-2012 using panel data regression. Regarding higher education, the results indicate that expenditure per student in higher education is positively linked with sustainable economic growth. Expanded skills also enhance the nation's innovative capacity and productivity, making knowledge-led growth possible. The data indicate that countries with less skilled populations and lower knowledge capital will find it difficult to improve productivity. Consequently, these countries will experience lower economic growth rates (Hanushek and Woessmann, 2021).

According to Kopuk (2024), countries that frequently experience significant innovations must continually develop new ideas, products, production processes, and economic structures to sustain their development and maintain a competitive advantage. Innovation capacity is very crucial in gaining competitive advantage especially for high value added production.Therefore, investing in a human capital is a priority to learn and implement new ideas.

There appears to be broad agreement that education, as one of the main determinants of human capital, benefits society in numerous ways, including better health, reduced fertility, improved ability to cope with economic shocks, enhanced research and development (R&D) capacity, and adoption of new technologies. As a result, education increases labor productivity and contributes to sustainable economic growth (Orazem and King, 2007). In R&D activities, which are particularly important for high value-added sectors, both the quantity and quality of human capital are of great importance. Countries that lead in this area also determine the competitiveness, which is a key factor in economic growth. R&D activities, which enhance the competitiveness of countries, inherently require a high-skilled workforce; therefore, universities play a crucial role in R&D efforts. In his study, Krastic (2021) analyzed the relationship between the Global Competitiveness Index, as determined by the World Economic Forum (WEF), and higher education. The results of the study indicate a positive relationship between the variables.

In light of these discussions, this study aims to analyze the relationship between human capital and economic growth. In today's knowledge-led growth world, where the impact of high-tech sectors is rapidly increasing, it will be beneficial to discuss the concepts of R&D and innovation, and consequently, the structure of universities and the higher education system as producers of a high-skilled labor force in the analysis of this relationship.

In the second section of the study, relation between R&D and economic growth will be discussed. In the third section, the literature on the impact of human capital on economic growth will be analyzed. The fourth section will provide an evaluation of Turkey, and the fifth section of the study concludes.

2. A DISCUSSION ON THE DETERMINANTS OF ECONOMIC GROWTH

In the current era, competition between countries is increasing, and achieving high, stable, and sustainable economic growth rates has become one of the important factors that enhance welfare levels. In this context, it is vital for economies to enhance their global competitiveness, and the competitiveness of countries is measured by productivity, which forms the foundation of economic growth (Krugman, 1996; Porter and Ketel, 2003; Global Competitiveness Index, 2017). The necessity of increasing the competitiveness of stakeholders in national economies has recently become a frequently emphasized topic. For example, in the European Union (EU), it is observed that policies enhancing competitiveness are being implemented to ensure social and economic cohesion among member countries and to reduce the "competitiveness gap" between the EU and the USA. The importance of R&D investments is increasing every day in achieving stable economic growth rates, enhancing global competitiveness through the production and marketing of high value-added products, and consequently reaching the targeted increase in welfare.

In the Global Competitiveness Index rankings, innovative economies that produce and export high value-added products are at the top, indicating that R&D and innovation activities have a positive impact on productivity and competitiveness. It is crucial to follow global developments, select appropriate ones, and clearly define goals when determining R&D policies. To stay competitive internationally, it is not only essential to focus on R&D expenditure amounts but also on the chosen fields, strategies, and quality. Conducting "basic and applied research" (R&D) aimed at technology development rather than merely "product development" (Product Development) activities form the basis for increasing productivity and competitiveness. The conversion of R&D activities into innovation and the launch of marketable, high value-added products are also important. All these requirements can be met by stakeholders progressing together on a common roadmap.

Countries like Turkey, in the transition process to an innovation-oriented economy, face some structural challenges in their R&D policies. In this situation, inefficiencies arise in meeting societal demands and the effective use of public resources. Therefore, it is crucial to establish R&D and innovation strategies based on reliable data, considering Turkey's priorities, ensuring the effective use of limited resources, determining sectors accordingly, and making planned investments based on needs, accessibility, and feasibility.

The results of studies investigating the relationship between R&D expenditures and/or R&D intensity with productivity and, ultimately, economic growth vary. According to the most recent research in this field, productivity starts to be positively affected only after a certain threshold level of knowledge and technology stock is exceeded. In other words, the R&D-productivity relationship is non-linear, resulting in the differentiation of each sector's R&D strategy. Therefore, it is important to define sector-specific threshold values and determine competitive R&D and innovation policies, rather than presenting a general R&D strategy and policy analysis and policy recommendations based on the results of this analysis.

The relationship between R&D activities and sustainable growth is also included in the 2030 Agenda. The Goal 9 of the Agenda, which is "***Build resilient infrastructure, promote inclusive and sustainable industrialization and foster innovation,***" underscores the importance of increasing scientific research and technological capacity, particularly for developing countries, by 2030. It also emphasizes the need for all countries to promote innovation and increase the share of workforce and expenditures in the R&D field.

3. THE EFFECTS OF HUMAN CAPITAL ON ECONOMIC GROWTH

It has been observed that the slowdown in economic growth rates is more pronounced in countries with lower levels of education and insufficient shares in the export of high-tech products. The most critical issue concerning the problem of limited resources in countries undergoing a transition process is the "qualified human capital" resource.

The effects of human capital on economic growth are significant and multidimensial. Firstly, an educated and skilled workforce enhances productivity, increasing the efficiency of economic activities. Investments in human capital develop individuals' knowledge and skills, which in turn fosters innovation and accelerates technological progress. A healthy workforce boosts productivity by reducing sick leave and increasing work capacity. Furthermore, human capital improves social welfare by reducing income inequality and strengthening social cohesion. These elements form the foundation for sustainable economic growth and ensure long-term economic stability. Regardless of the sector, any infrastructure established will not operate efficiently without a sufficient number of qualified workforces, leading to the wastage of resources. In other words, increasing productivity and economic growth will be possible by improving the production of high-tech products and innovation capacity, simultaneously with improvements in the quantity and quality of human capital defined by knowledge, skills, and competencies.

In innovation-oriented economies, human capital is the main driver of sustainable economic growth. Skilled and educated individuals are essential for fostering innovation, enabling economies to develop new technologies and improve productivity. Human capital investment enhances creativity and problem-solving abilities, which are crucial for adapting to rapidly changing market demands. Moreover, a well-developed human capital base supports research and development activities, leading to breakthroughs that sustain long-term growth. For countries transitioning to innovation-focused economies, policies prioritizing education, continuous professional development, and health are vital. Such investments ensure a capable workforce, driving sustainable growth through constant innovation and improved economic resilience.

For sustainable growth, a balance between the quality and quantity of human capital is essential. A larger quantity of human capital ensures a sufficient labor force to support economic activities. This is particularly important in labor-intensive industries and for maintaining overall economic activity. In addition to this, A larger workforce can help achieve economies of scale in production, leading to lower costs and higher output. Studies, such as those by Barro and Lee (2013), have shown a positive correlation between the level of education and economic growth.

But simply increasing the number of workers without improving their skills and education may lead to underemployment and low productivity. Therefore, countries with a goal of sustainable growth should focus not only on the quantity of human capital but also on its quality. Moreover, Hanushek and Woessmann (2008) have shown that cognitive skills, more than mere years of schooling, are crucial for economic growth. De Muelemeester and Rochat (1995) investigate the causal effect of higher education on economic growth in Japan, the UK, France, and Sweden. Their results suggest that education can stimulate growth only if its curriculum is designed with that purpose in mind, and if the social, political, and economic structures, as well as the technological level of the society, enable graduates to effectively utilize their knowledge. Likewise, Hanushek and Woessmann (2021), highlighting the limitations of the schooling variable, which is commonly used as a proxy for the quantity of human capital in the literature, propose using a different human capital variable that includes skill levels. The variable suggested by the authors involves the use of International Large-Scale Assessments (ILSA) scores. ILSA exams, such as PISA and TIMSS, which are administered to a wide range of countries, can help measure the impact of the skill variable when analyzing differences in growth rates between countries.

Higher quality human capital, which includes education, skills, and experience, tends to enhance productivity and innovation. Well-educated and skilled workers are more capable of developing new technologies, improving processes, and increasing efficiency and maintain a competitive advantage in high-tech and high-value industries, which are often key drivers of sustainable economic growth. Furthermore, high-quality human capital is more adaptable to changing economic conditions and technological advancements. This adaptability is crucial for sustaining growth in a rapidly changing global economy.

University education plays an important role in enhancing both the quantity and quality of human capital, which are critical factors for economic development and sustainable economic growth. By providing individuals with advanced knowledge and specialized skills, college education not only increases the overall size of the educated workforce but also significantly improves its efficiency and productivity. Therefore, it would be reasonable to argue that increasing access to higher education is crucial to increasing the quantity of human capital. Higher participation rates in college education mean a larger number of individuals obtaining advanced skills, thereby contributing to a more productive labor force. Advanced knowledge and specialized skills acquired through higher education are crucial for high-level professions and industries such as engineering, medicine, science, and technology One can argue that, college education fosters critical thinking, analytical skills, and problem-solving abilities, which are essential for innovation. These skills enable individuals to adapt to new challenges, drive technological advancements, and improve productivity in many sectors.

Higher education is also associated with better health outcomes, as educated individuals are more likely to make informed health choices, leading to a healthier population, which contributes to higher productivity and lower healthcare costs. On the other hand, it should be noted that, having a highly educated workforce with limited job opportunities can result in brain drain or educated unemployment. Therefore, matching higher education system with current and future labor market needs is essential to ensure that graduates possess relevant skills and knowledge. Collaboration between higher education institutions and industries can help design the system that meet the demands of the job market and enhancing the employability of graduates.

One of the outcomes of supply and demand mismatches in the labor market is overeducation. Overeducation refers to a situation where individuals possess more education than is required for their current job and cause a mismatch between the skills and education of the labor force and the requirements of available employment opportunities, in other words it is basically a mismatch between an individual's education and skill level and the requirements to perform the job that he or she employed. Several factors contribute to overeducation, including labor market dynamics, higher education system policies, and decisions of individuals. A mismatch of supply and demand in the labor market is a primary cause, particularly when the supply of college graduates exceeds the demand for highly skilled jobs. This can happen due to the rapid expansion of higher education without a corresponding growth in high-skilled job opportunities, or during economic downturns when job opportunities decrease, forcing highly educated individuals to take lower-skilled jobs to avoid unemployment.

Overeducation appears in various ways, such as college graduates working in positions that do not require a college degree or individuals with advanced degrees performing tasks that could be done by individuals who has high school degree or lower. Although there have been dramatic increases in the education of the labor force in the past years in both developed and many developing countries, the debate on the economic returns to extra years of education rises questions on higher education expansion and capability of the labor markets to provide relevant job opportunities to highly educated workforce (Capsada-Munsech, 2017). According to Freeman (1976) and Rumberger (1981), one of the possible consequences of overeducation is the declining economic returns to education Policies aimed at increasing access to higher education can result in a larger number of college graduates than the labor market can absorb. Moreover, if the education system does not move together with the needs of the labor market, graduates may find themselves overeducated for the available jobs. From an individual's perspective, overeducated workers may also have lower motivation towards work and thus have negative impact on their efficiency. Individual decisions, such as career aspirations and a lack of career guidance, can further exacerbate the issue. Many individuals pursue higher education with the expectation of better job prospects and higher earnings but may end up in jobs that do not fully utilize their qualifications.

Especially for developing countries, "qualified human capital" is the most important of the limited resources, and new infrastructure and R&D investments will not be efficient without sufficient qualified labor, leading to the wasteful use of already limited resources. Studies in the relevant literature show that the number and quality of an educated workforce are critical for total factor productivity, which is the key to economic growth. Among the first studies examining the contributions of human capital to productivity and economic growth are Schultz (1960), Becker (1964), and Nelson and Phelps (1966). Particularly with the addition of Endogenous Growth Theories to the literature in the 1980s, the concept of human capital came to the forefront, and the impact of an educated human capital on economic performance became even more significant (Yalçınkaya and Kaya, 2017). According to endogenous growth models, an educated workforce, on which technological development depends, is more effective in innovation and technological applications, thus contributing to economic growth. Lucas (1990) states that educated human capital can directly affect productivity by increasing the capacity to implement new technologies.

Numerous studies using various educational variables and different econometric analyses have examined the relationship between education and economic growth. Models investigating the relationship between human capital and economic growth do not assume that individuals need to be excessively educated; however, human capital increases with the level of education and is a fundamental determinant of economic growth and productivity. Mankiw, Romer, and Weil (1992) explained income differences across countries using the extended Solow Growth Model, while Benhabib and Spiegel (1994) analyzed the impact of education duration on growth rates. In these models, human capital affects growth rates directly and through technological convergence. Countries with high stocks of human capital assume a position of technological leadership and maintain this position as long as the superiority in human capital levels continues. However, considering human capital as a homogeneous variable has revealed some limitations of these studies. Vandenbussche et al. (2006) and Wang and Liu (2016) showed that qualified labor is effective in economic growth and productivity increase, whereas unqualified labor has no significant impact. Acemoğlu and Zilibotti (2001) emphasized that productivity gains in developing countries that cannot adapt to the technology of developed countries will remain limited.

De la Fuente and Ciccone (2003) stated that education has a significant impact on individuals' incomes and overall productivity, but the effect of increasing education durations will be limited in the long term due to diminishing returns, and therefore, countries should focus on the quality of education.

The demand for university graduates is determined by various factors such as the country's growth rate, labor force distribution among sectors, the growth rate of knowledge and technology-intensive sectors using qualified labor, and the number of individuals leaving the workforce. The supply of university graduates to the market is determined by the proportion of the adult population of university education age, the number of graduates, and the expected increase in income levels after university education (Shelley, 1992). Today, as both developed and developing countries increasingly recognize the growing importance of qualified human capital to achieve sustainable economic growth targets, individuals also aim to mitigate risks through higher education considering economic changes and increasing risks.

There are those in the studies who argue that university education is not aligned with the labor market and that it can lead to problems of educated unemployment and underemployment. For instance, Bowers-Brown and Harvey (2004) state that easing university entrance conditions can increase the imbalance of supply and demand in the labor market. On the other hand, there are views emphasizing that higher education should be accessible to everyone and highlighting the societal benefits of education. Bennet (1999) and Follows and Steven (2000) emphasize the importance of universities undertaking curriculum innovations to improve the quality of education and the employability of graduates. Brown et al. (2003) suggest that candidates with diverse education will benefit more. When the choice of departments and career planning are not made according to the expectations of the labor market and changing global conditions, the increase in the number of individuals educated and graduated in areas with low labor market demand, combined with an unplanned university system, inevitably results in qualified labor unemployment and wage disparities (Andrews et al., 2022). Additionally, the lack of emphasis on personal competencies (soft skills) in university education, such as analytical and creative thinking, communication, resilience, problem-solving, curiosity, leadership, and teamwork, also results in failing to meet the expectations of the labor market (WEF, 2023).

As it is discussed in the previous part of this study, in the past decades the expansion of higher education and the demand structure of the labor market have advanced in different rates, and this resulted into a suboptimal match between the supply and demand in the labor markets. (Capsada-Munsech, 2024). This mismatch called overeducation and discussed in the literature from different perspectives (Bauer, 2002; Hartog, 2000; Green and Zhu, 2010; Capsada-Munsech, 2017; Kupets, 2024). The results of the studies vary depending on the country of focus, the time-period, and the variables considered. For instance, according to Grrot and van den Brink (2000), overeducation has positive results on earnings of the individuals. On the other hand, Eguia et.al (2023) findings indicate that the wages of those who manage to overcome an initial situation of overeducation do converge but very slowly to the respective wages of those others that entered the labor market correctly matched from the beginning. Allen and van der Velden (2001) reports negative impact on the motivation and the productivity on the individuals. However, by using aggregate data, Plesca and Summerfield (2023) find productivity-enhancing effects in Canadian data by province and industry spanning 1997–2015.

Overeducation is closely associated with having too many college graduates relative to the demand for high-skilled jobs. When the education system produces more graduates than the economy can absorb, it leads to a situation where many graduates cannot find jobs that match their level of education. This mismatch can result in underemployment, where graduates take jobs that do not require a college degree, leading to potentially lower earnings than expected. Additionally, the mismatch between the skills possessed by graduates and the skills required by employers can result in economic inefficiencies as resources spent on higher education are not fully utilized in the labor market.

The World Economic Forum's 2020 competitiveness report emphasizes the need for countries to focus on revitalizing and transforming human capital activities in the wake of the crisis caused by the Covid-19 pandemic. It is stated that this transformation will occur by focusing on transitioning to new labor market opportunities, re-evaluating active labor market opportunities, and expanding reskilling and upskilling programs. The same report underscores the necessity of updating curricula in education and renewing them to equip individuals with skills suitable for future jobs and professions. Peters and Jandric's (2019) studies point to the mismatch between the expectations of the labor demand market and the competencies of university graduates. The education models of the past do not meet today's needs. Jung (2020) argues that education models need to be updated in line with technological developments. Higher education programs that ignore the demand side may increase the number of qualified unemployed and fail to meet the needs of the labor market. Therefore, it is emphasized that university-industry collaborations play a critical role in shaping the current economy and that curricula prepared jointly by supply and demand will meet both academic requirements and labor market expectations, facilitating the transition from education to employment. The real question that needs to be asked is not whether there is an excess of qualified labor in the labor market but whether there are sufficient employment opportunities for qualified labor, and solutions should be sought from this perspective (Bowers-Brown and Harvey, 2004).

Although there are uncertainties about the future professions that will exist and disappear in the labor market, all parties agree that the skills and competencies individuals will possess, rather than a diploma, will support their employability. The 2023 report of the French Business School INSEAD, which has been publishing the Global Skills Competitiveness report since 2013, also emphasizes this issue. The report highlights that countries able to employ competent individuals in their economy (through immigration and/or human capital development) increase their competitive advantages in global markets. To support countries' improvement policies on the subject, the 2023 report compares 134 countries, and Switzerland, which has ranked first every year since the report started being published in 2013, again ranks first in skills competitiveness. Switzerland is followed by Singapore, the USA, Denmark, the Netherlands, Finland, Norway, Australia, Sweden, and the UK, with 17 European countries in the top 25 being noteworthy. Another noteworthy point in the 2023 report is that countries like the United Arab Emirates and Israel have also risen and managed to enter the top 25 countries. Turkey ranks 81st among 134 countries in the report.

The high proportion of university graduates in Switzerland's labor force and the shaping of education policies according to the expectations of the business world are seen as significant factors in its leadership. Singapore also scores highly on education quality and labor supply-demand matching issues.

In short, relevant literature indicates that increasing competitiveness is important for countries to achieve sustainable economic growth rates and improve welfare levels because of productivity increases. It is observed that education and competencies, in other words, human capital, are among the most important factors for countries to advance to the forefront in this race, and that countries experiencing problems in these areas will find it difficult to shape their industrial and production structures in line with future expectations (WEF Future Job Reports, 2023).

4. HUMAN CAPITAL, UNIVERSITY EDUCATION AND GROWTH: AN ANALYSIS FOR TURKIYE

In the past few decades, there have been dramatic increases in the education of the workforce. In the group of OECD countries, the proportion of university graduates in the 25-34 age group rose from 23.6% in 1998 to 47.1% in 2021 (OECD, 2023). It is particularly emphasized that countries caught in the middle-income trap can escape this situation through technological advancement and innovation (Eichengreen et al., 2013). Various steps have been taken in our country over the years to increase the educated workforce as a way out of the middle-income trap. Significant transformations have occurred in higher education in Turkey since the

1930s. Thanks to the state universities established in 1982, the number of universities increased to twenty-seven, and with the establishment of the first foundation university in 1984, this number continued to grow. Although there was no change in the number of state universities between 1992 and 2006, there were significant increases in the number of foundation universities (Günay and Günay, 2011). The number of higher education institutions, which was 165 in 2011, increased to 208 in 2022 due to the policy of having at least one university in each city. This increase in the number of universities has also led to a significant rise in the number of students and graduates in higher education. Between 2013 and 2021, the number of students graduating from higher education programs increased substantially, with the number of graduates exceeding one million by 2021, up from less than 700,000 in 2013. The goal of having at least one university in each province has been achieved, and with the inclusion of private universities, the number has surpassed 200. This growth has increased the number of university graduates, but it has also brought up issues that need to be discussed, such as the quality of human capital and the balance of supply and demand in the labor market.

Post-Covid-19 pandemic, unemployment has become one of the significant issues in Turkey. According to Turkish Statistical Institute (TURKSTAT) data, the unemployment rate was measured at 9.6% in August 2022. Among the youth, this rate is 18% When we come to March 2023, the unemployment rate was 10% and among the youth the rate was measured at 20.1%. Due to individual and family decisions affected by economic and social conditions, as well as state policies, the increase in the number of university graduates has also increased the proportion of this group among young unemployed individuals. Unemployment, especially when high among young people, is a problem that can have long-term negative effects on national income.

Figure 1 summarizes the youth unemployment rates across various educational levels between the years 2014-2023 in Turkiye. From 2014 to 2023, unemployment rates by education level reveal a concerning trend for university graduates, whose unemployment rates have consistently been the highest among all educational groups. Starting at 28.3% in 2014, these rates peaked at 35.8% in 2020, reflecting significant economic challenges, possibly highlighted by global events such as the COVID 19 pandemic. Although there was a slight improvement to 25.1% by 2023, the data underscores a persistent issue where higher education does not necessarily correlate with better employment prospects. This paradox highlights a critical mismatch between the skills taught in universities and the demands of the modern job market, emphasizing the need for educational reforms to better align with industry needs.

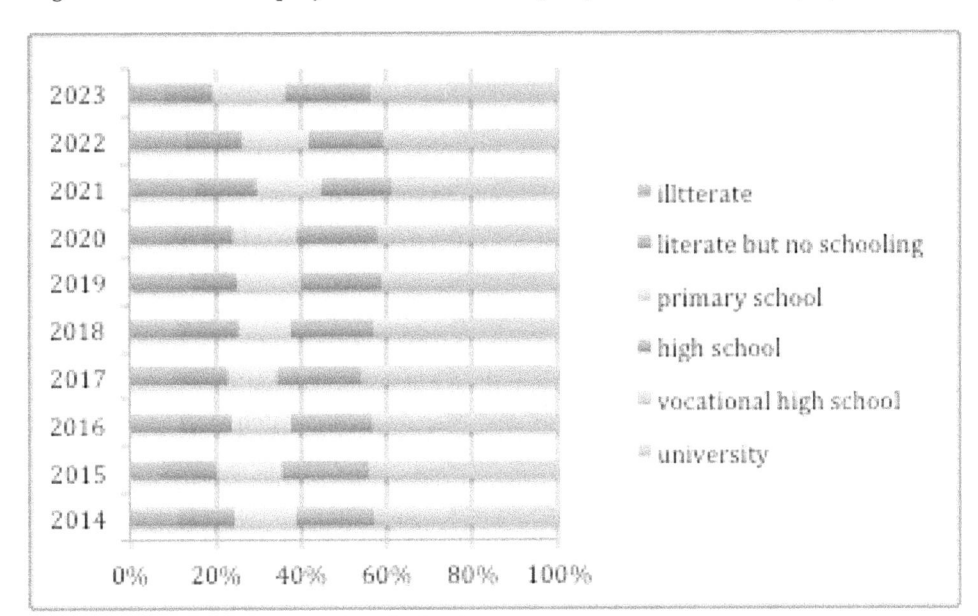

Figure 1. Youth Unemployment Rate in Turkiye by Education Level (%)

[Bar chart showing youth unemployment rates from 2014 to 2023 by education categories: illiterate, literate but no schooling, primary school, high school, vocational high school, university]

Source: TURKSTAT Laborforce Statistics Database

While there is generally a negative relationship between the level of education and unemployment in Europe, this relationship is measured as positive in Turkey. In other words, university graduates hold a significant place among young unemployed individuals. Therefore, it would be useful to conduct a supply-demand analysis for educated and qualified individuals in the labor market. When we consider graduates working in jobs that require fewer skills than they acquired during their university education, the imbalance of supply and demand in the job market becomes more evident. The contribution of education to the acquisition of human capital, one of the main sources of productivity and economic growth, is questioned, and the need to reassess the university system in Turkey arises. The increase in the educated workforce also brings the issue of qualified unemployment. With the rise in the number of universities in Turkey and the rapid increase in the number of graduates, the proportion of unemployed university graduates has increased. Despite the increase in the supply of highly educated labor, firms still report difficulties in filling their vacancies on the demand side of the market. In this context, according to the Talent Shortage Survey conducted by Manpower Group covering 39,000 employers in 41 countries, firms reported difficulties in hiring in 2023. This effect is felt most strongly in Taiwan, Germany, and Hong Kong, with rates of 90%, 86%, and 85%, respectively, while the rate in Turkey is 72% as of 2023.

Due to high number of university graduates that added to the job candidates each year, overeducation also becomes an unwanted reality oh young college graduates in Turkiye. In the analysis conducted by the Presidential Human Resources Office of Turkiye examining the employment status of graduates by field between 2010 and 2022, the levels of mismatch experienced by graduates were calculated. The skills mismatch indicator, which arises when jobs require lower or higher qualifications than the individual's education level, is based on the education and employment information of individuals under the age of 35 who graduated from universities in Turkey and found employment between 2010 and 2022. This data was calculated by the Republic of Turkey Human Resources Office using the International Labour Organization's (ILO) standard occupation (ISCO) and skill set classifications. This indicator shows whether graduates from the 81 examined departments are working in jobs appropriate to their qualifications. The skills mismatch in graduates' first jobs was examined and reported in four groups. The group with a mismatch level of 0 was defined as "Workers in Jobs Matching Their Qualifications," the group with a mismatch level of 1 as "Low Skills Mismatch," the group with a mismatch level of 2 as "Medium Skills Mismatch," and finally, the group with a mismatch level of 3 as "High Skills Mismatch." The data shows that a significant portion of university graduates in almost all fields experience medium to high levels of skills mismatch. This problem is observed at a rate of 60% in fields such as Economics and Business Administration, and even graduates from more specific departments like Engineering experience this issue at a rate of 20%. In summary, despite the presence of a highly educated workforce, the data highlights difficulties in filling vacant positions and a skills mismatch in the labor market. Additionally, it shows potential income loss for young individuals who remain unemployed after leaving education and potential output loss due to long-term vacant positions. For example, 15% of computer engineering graduates, 35% of fine arts graduates, and approximately 60% of economics-business graduates experience a high level of mismatch. Considering the opportunity cost of university education, it is concluded that the human capital investments of these individuals are not being used efficiently, and the negative impacts of this on both individual and societal levels should be evaluated.

Moreover, Turkey has the highest rate of young people who are neither in employment nor in education (NEET) among OECD countries. Figure 2 shows a comparison between the OECD NEET average and the figures for Turkey for the age group 20-24, which is the typical university student age. Although the NEET rate in Turkey has decreased over the years, it remains significantly higher than the OECD average. The situation becomes even more dramatic when looking at the female group. The NEET rate among women in this age range in Turkey is much higher than the OECD average. Furthermore, while the NEET rate for women calculated for the OECD is very close to the overall average, unfortunately, the NEET rate for women in Turkey is significantly higher than the overall calculated value.

Figure 2. NEET Rate in Turkiye and OECD by (%)

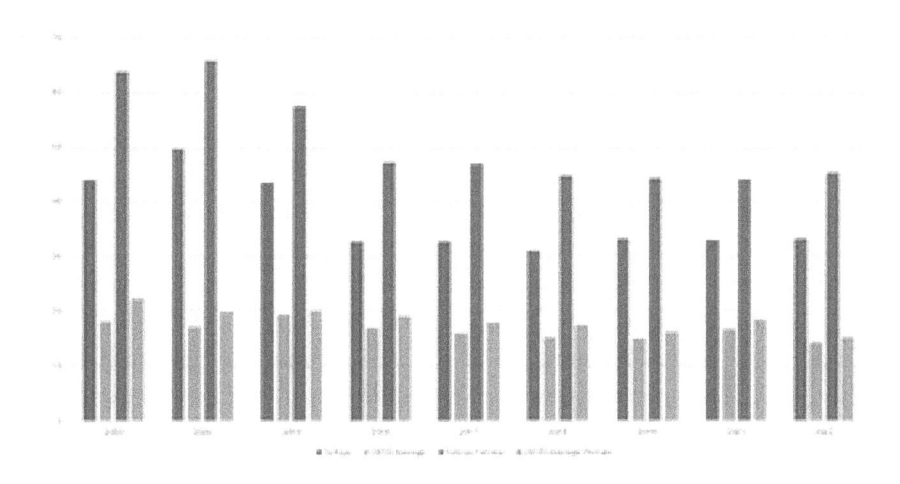

Source: OECD Statistics Database

Moreover, as it is summarized in Table 1 below, although the relevant literature indicates that this group generally has low education and skill levels, it was observed that about 30% of the young people defined as NEET in Turkey in 2023 were higher education graduates. This high rate points to potential problems in the transition from education to the labor market, making it difficult to achieve growth targets due to productivity loss, and analyzing this problem to develop policy recommendations would be beneficial.

While the share of university graduates in the unemployed population is increasing, it cannot be said that the applied education policy has contributed to solving the current problem. The "A University in Every City" policy has led to a significant increase in the number of university graduates entering the labor market in recent years. However, the lack of a proportional increase in job opportunities suitable for qualifications has resulted in deferred unemployment for university education. Therefore, the importance of conducting necessary analyses and developing policy recommendations to determine an education policy that meets the needs of the labor market is clearly evident.

Table 1. Educational Level of Young People Neither In Employment Nor in Education or Training in Turkiye (%)

	Total Population between aged 15 – 24 (NEET (%))	Illeterate (NEET (%))	Less than high school (NEET (%))	High school (NEET (%))	Vocational high school (NEET (%))	Higher education (NEET (%))
2020	28.4	80.6	23.3	26.8	34.1	41.8
2021	24.7	82.9	19.9	23.3	29.1	36.7
2022	24.2	79.5	18.6	26.4	27.8	33
2023	22.5	83	17.5	24.6	25.5	29.2

As highlighted in reports published by the World Economic Forum and in the Global Competence Index study reports published by INSEAD, the proportion of skilled labor is of great importance for countries to achieve sustainable growth rates by adapting to increasing and intensifying competition conditions in future periods. However, an increase in numbers should not be seen as a guarantee for countries to achieve their targeted outcomes. For example, while the high proportion of university graduates in the workforce is considered an advantage for Switzerland, which has been the leading country in the Global Competence Competitiveness Index for ten years since 2013, Turkey has not been able to utilize this advantage. In 2020, while Turkey was ranked 78th in the list, despite being third in the world in the number of university graduates, by 2023, Turkey rose to second place among 134 countries analyzed in terms of the number of university graduates but fell to 81st place in the index ranking. Therefore, an increase in the number of university graduates not aligned with the demands of the business world does not guarantee an increase in the competitiveness of countries. According to Cunedioğlu (2023), the structural transformation in Turkey that would result in an increase in activities requiring high skill levels has not occurred. According to 2021 data, while 8.6% of jobs in the EU27 average are low-skilled and 48.3% are semi-skilled, these rates are 15.5% and 60.6% in Turkey, respectively. With this employment structure, Turkey is the country with the highest proportion of low-skilled jobs in Europe. While the share of highly skilled jobs in total employment is 17.6% in Romania and 21.4% in Poland, this rate is only 12.2% in Turkey.

Although the share of highly skilled jobs in total employment in Turkey has been on an upward trend since 2014, the increase has remained below the EU27 average. From 2014 to 2022, the share of highly skilled jobs in total employment increased by 4.1 points in the EU27, while this increase was only 2.9 points in Turkey.

In a period when skilled labor is needed, one of the factors influencing individuals' education decisions is undoubtedly the wage premium, which can be considered the return on education. According to human capital theories, skilled labor should receive a higher wage compared to unskilled labor. However, in Turkey, especially due to the increasing number of university graduates and the rising minimum wage, some graduates are employed by employers at or very close to the minimum wage level. Employer representatives state that the increasing minimum wage level, which is approaching the average wage level, reduces the country's competitiveness, increases informal employment, and decreases the attractiveness of education (Cunedioğlu, 2023). In Turkey, while the share of faculty and/or vocational school graduates in total employment was 34.3% in 2021, 38.1% of the total workforce earns income at the minimum wage level. Since 2014, the average wage of higher education graduates aged 20-24 working full-time as paid or daily wage earners has approached the minimum wage. In this category, the average wages of male workers have decreased from 1.73 times the minimum wage to 1.32 times, and the average wages of female workers have decreased from 1.56 times the minimum wage to 1.18 times during the 2014-2022 period (Cunedioğlu, 2023). The employment of newly graduated young people at these low wage levels or their unemployment is a topic discussed in both academic studies and the media. According to Cunedioğlu (2023), this situation may be due to two reasons: The first reason is that there has not been a quantitative increase in education, and the signaling effect of graduates from new universities on the labor market remains low. The second possible reason is that there has been no planning considering education, and the problem of skills mismatch triggered in the market following the expansion of higher education without considering employment connections.

The subject of university education in Turkiye is one of the emphasized subjects under the heading of developing a qualified workforce in the 12th Development Plan. The 12th Development Plan, covering the period between 2024-2028, emphasizes that Turkey will follow an approach of 'focusing on a production structure that centers productivity and competitiveness, with the industrial sector taking a leading role in growth by increasing interaction with the agricultural and services sectors, utilizing the demographic opportunity window to the fullest to create employment, and providing quality financing opportunities with a healthy balance of payments structure, based on export-oriented stable growth'. The plan also highlights that during this process, a qualified workforce will be one of the key elements of the anticipated stable growth. Priorities include enhancing the qualifications of the workforce, directing them towards more productive sectors and areas, considering the relationship between education and employment, and integrating women and youth into the labor market with the necessary professional skills.

The plan states, *"The share of higher education graduates in the labor force will approach 55% by 2053 with the faster increase of qualified employment, and the rate of those aged 15-24 who are not in education or employment will be reduced to single digits. ... It is important for our country to become an attraction center for scientists in critical areas both regionally and globally. Turkey's 2053 vision is to become a hub of advanced technologies by fostering an ecosystem that leaves no one behind in science and technology, internalizes innovation, and promotes technology ventures and R&D investments. By 2053, it is aimed that at least 5 of our universities will be among the top 100 universities in the world, our country will rank among the top 10 in the global innovation index, and the share of R&D expenditures in national income will rise to 4%.*" The document emphasizes increasing the scientific research capacity of universities to support high value-added production by strengthening the research university program and increasing the capacities of universities included in this program through special supports.

While it is highlighted that youth employment will be increased and working conditions improved, and the effectiveness of programs supporting the employment access of young people who are not in education or employment will be enhanced, it is emphasized in terms of competencies that:

-The loss of qualified workforce will be prevented, and mechanisms will be developed to strengthen the ties of qualified citizens working abroad with Turkey, facilitating the transfer of professional knowledge and experience.
-The reasons for the migration of qualified workforce related to the labor market will be identified, and steps will be taken to prevent mass workforce loss by sector.
-The employment of qualified foreign workforce in areas needed by the country will be increased.

Additionally, the report emphasizes that higher education quotas should be determined based on the capacities of universities, in alignment with the current and projected sectoral labor supply and demand and considering regional needs.

5. CONCLUSION

One of the most important building blocks of human capital is education. Considering that the most important sectors that will provide countries with a competitive advantage are high value-added, technology-intensive sectors, the importance of university education in training personnel for these sectors becomes apparent. The Sustainable Development Goals (SDGs), adopted by all United Nations Member States in 2015, provide a comprehensive framework aimed at addressing global challenges and promoting prosperity while protecting the planet. Among the 17 SDGs, Goal 4 focuses on ensuring inclusive and equitable quality education and promoting lifelong learning opportunities for all. According to this target, countries shall substantially increase the number of youth and adults who have relevant skills, including technical skills, for employment, decent jobs and entrepreneurship by 2030. This goal is intrinsically linked to economic growth, as education is a fundamental driver of development. Similarly, Goal 8, which states the importance of inclusive and sustainable economic growth, full employment and decent work for all mentions the reduction of the proportion of youth not in employment, education or training.

Quality education not only empowers individuals with knowledge and skills but also fosters innovation and productivity, which are crucial for sustainable economic growth. Educational improvements support employability, decrease poverty and stimulates the R&D activities which increase competitiveness of the country and creates more employment opportunities. So, we can argue that A smart and sustainable economic growth strategy is essential for developing an economy that thrives on knowledge and innovation. This approach necessitates more effective investments in education, R&D, and innovation. Investing in these areas is not only beneficial but also critical for building a robust economic foundation that can adapt to changing global dynamics and technological advancements.

Education, particularly at the university level, plays a critical role in this framework. Higher education institutions are the source for skilled labor force who drive innovation and technological progress. Universities provide the advanced training and knowledge necessary for students to excel in high-skilled occupations that are essential for R&D activities. These activities, in turn, are the engines of innovation, leading to the development of new products, processes, and technologies that can enhance productivity and economic growth.

However, despite the increasing level of education among new entrants to the workforce over time, employers increasingly report that they are unable to find the skills they need.

It proves that university education policies aimed solely at increasing the number of graduates without responding to the needs of the labor market increase the rates of unemployment and skills mismatch among the educated workforces. Consequently, a decline in the productivity of university graduates who are forced to work at minimum wage levels is observed, and the wage premium expected from the periods individuals spend in educational institutions gradually decreases and overeducation problem occurs in the job market. Policies aimed at increasing access to higher education can result in a larger number of college graduates than the labor market can absorb. Moreover, if the education system does not move together with the needs of the labor market, graduates may find themselves overeducated for the available jobs. Individual decisions, In the end, many individuals pursue higher education with the expectation of better job prospects and higher earnings but may end up in jobs that do not fully utilize their qualifications and can result in underemployment, where graduates take jobs that do not require a college degree, leading to potentially lower earnings than expected. Additionally, the mismatch between the skills possessed by graduates and the skills required by employers can result in economic inefficiencies as resources spent on higher education are not fully utilized in the labor market.

The consequences of overeducation are different, affecting both economic and social dimensions. Economically, overeducated individuals often face wage penalties, earning less than their appropriately educated counterparts in similar positions. Additionally, the underutilization of skills can result in lower productivity and inefficiencies in the labor market. Socially, overeducated individuals may experience lower job satisfaction and motivation, impacting their overall well-being.

To alleviate the effects of overeducation, several strategies can be considered. Aligning education with labor market needs is crucial. This involves developing curricula and educational programs that are closely aligned with the needs of the labor market and encouraging collaboration between educational institutions and industry to ensure that graduates have relevant skills. Providing students with accurate information about labor market trends and career prospects through career guidance and counseling is also essential. Offering career counseling services can help students make informed educational and career choices. In addition to this, promoting lifelong learning and continuous education can help workers adapt to changing job requirements, supporting vocational and technical education as viable alternatives to traditional college education. Economic policies that stimulate job creation, particularly in high-skilled sectors, are also important. Encouraging entrepreneurship and innovation can create new opportunities for highly educated individuals.

The swift advancement of technology has outpaced the current educational frameworks, which are predominantly diploma focused. For a pivotal shift towards a knowledge-based economy where skills, rather than mere qualifications, dictate one's success in the workforce. This new vision of education advocates for a balance between hard skills, like technical abilities, and soft skills, which include emotional intelligence and creativity.

Considering the rising unemployment among the educated workforce, the disconnect between existing educational outputs and market demands has never been clearer. This highlights the importance of adaptability, problem-solving capabilities, and lifelong learning as essential competencies for today's graduates. Colleges and universities are encouraged to adopt real-world applications in their curricula, promote interdisciplinary approaches, and implement project-based learning to better prepare students for the complexities of modern job environments.

New technologies such as artificial intelligence (AI) and automation. are set to replace routine tasks, creating uncertainty about future occupations and potentially increasing the ranks of the educated unemployed. However, this technological disruption also brings opportunities for innovation and emphasizes the unique human abilities to empathize, lead, and innovate. Educational institutions must, therefore, focus on nurturing these irreplaceable human skills.

New higher education system should concern quality more than the quantity of graduates by focusing the needs of the new era in the labor market and interdisciplinary learning as an engine of change. By fostering a robust connection between academia and the business sector, universities can evolve into not just centers of learning but also hubs of innovation. This collaboration will equip students with a flexible, enduring mindset and a comprehensive thought process that are imperative in today's dynamic professional landscape.

As the number of universities and graduates increases, employers are struggling to find graduates with the qualities they need, and the shortage of intermediate staff emerges as a serious problem. This situation underscores the importance of aligning the education system with the requirements of the job market. Ensuring the accumulation of qualified human capital should not come at the expense of a shortage of intermediate staff. Instead of four-year university education, vocational schools offering technical education and vocational skills can be an alternative path for individuals with lower academic orientation. This approach can contribute to economic growth by increasing the total accumulation of human capital without reducing the potential additional benefits of university education. Higher education institutions should focus more on developing practical and technical skills in addition to theoretical knowledge. Particularly, expanding programs integrated with the business world and internship opportunities could increase graduates' chances of finding employment. This trend necessitates that educational reforms address not only quantity but also quality.

As we stand at the crossroads of a significant educational transformation, there is an urgent need for educational institutions to reevaluate and revamp their teaching methodologies and curricula. The goal is to cultivate a workforce that is not only skilled and knowledgeable but also adaptable and innovative, capable of navigating the uncertainties of the future with integrity and insight. By embracing this new vision of education, we can ensure that our educational institutions remain relevant and effective in preparing individuals for the evolving demands of the global job market.

REFERENCES

Acemoglu, D., & Zilibotti, F. (2001). Productivity Differences. *The Quarterly Journal of Economics*, 116(2), 563–606. DOI: 10.1162/00335530151144104

Allen, J., & Van der Velden, R. (2001). Educational mismatch versus skill masmatch: Effects on wages, job satisfaction, and on-the-job search. *Oxford Economic Papers*, 53(3), 434–452. DOI: 10.1093/oep/53.3.434

Allen, J., & Van der Velden, R. (2011). *The Flexible Professional in the Knowledge Society*. Springer. DOI: 10.1007/978-94-007-1353-6

Andrews, R. J., Imberman, S. A., Lovenheim, M. F., & Stange, K. M. (2022). The Returns to College Major Choice: Average and Distributional Effects, Career Trajectories and Earning Variability, NBER Working Paper, August, No:w30331

Armeanu, D. S., Vintila, G., & Gherghina, S. C. (2018). Emprical Study Towards the Drivers of Sustainable Growth in EU-28 Countries. *Sustainability (Basel)*, 10(1), 4. DOI: 10.3390/su10010004

Bauer, T. K. (2002). Educational mismatch and wages: A panel analysis. *Economics of Education Review*, 21(3), 221–229. DOI: 10.1016/S0272-7757(01)00004-8

Becker, G. S. (1964). *Human Capital: A Theoretical and Empirical Analysis, with Special Reference to Education*. University of Chicago Press.

Benhabib, J., & Spiegel, M. (1994). The role of human capital in economic development: Evidence from aggregate cross-country and regional US data. *Journal of Monetary Economics*, 34(2), 143–173. DOI: 10.1016/0304-3932(94)90047-7

Bennet, N., Dunne, E., & Carre, C. (1999). Patterns of core and generic skill provision in higher education. *Higher Education*, 37(1), 71–93. DOI: 10.1023/A:1003451727126

Bound, J., & Johnson, G. (1995). What are the Causes of Rising wage inequality in the United States? *Economic Policy Review*, 1, 1.

Bowers-Brown, T., & Lee, H. (2004). Are There too Many Graduates in the UK? A Literature Review and an Analysis of Graduate Employability. *Industry and Higher Education*, 18(4), 152–161. DOI: 10.5367/0000000041667538

Brown, P., Hesketh, A., & Williams, S. (2003). Employability in a knowledge-driven economy. *Journal of Education and Work*, 16(2), 107–126.

Caner, A., Demirel-Derebasoglu, M., & Okten, C. (2022). Higher Education Expansion and College Wage Premium: Evidence from Turkey. *Sixth Annual Istanbul Meeting on Human Capital: Economics of Education, Health and Worker Productivity*

Capsada-Munsech, Q. (2017). Overeducation: Concept, theories, and empirical evidence. *Sociology Compass*, 11(10), e12518. DOI: 10.1111/soc4.12518

Capsada-Munsech, Q. (2024). Do secondary education systems influence the overeducation risk of university graduates? A cross-national analysis by field of study and social background. *International Journal of Comparative Sociology*, 65(1), 63–89. DOI: 10.1177/00207152241228148

Crivellaro, E. (2014). College Wage Premium Over Time: Trends in Europe in the last 15 Years, University of Venice. Tech.Rep. Department of Economics Working Paper 03.

Cumhurbaşkanlığı Strateji ve Bütçe Başkanlığı. (2023). On ikinci Kalkınma Planı 2024-2028. URL:https://onikinciplan.sbb.gov.tr/wp-content/uploads/2023/11/On-Ikinci-Kalkinma-Plani_2024-2028.pdf

Cunedioğlu, H.E.(2023). Turkey's Wage Issue: Why Do We Talk About the Minimum Wage So Much?, TEPAV Değerlendirme Notu, Temmuz, No:202328.

De la Fuente, A., & Ciccone, A. (2003). Human capital in a global and knowledge-based economy. Working Paper, Barcelona School of Economics, No: 70.

De Muelemeester, J. L., & Rochat, D. (1995). A Causality Analysis of the Link Between Higher Education and Economic Development. *Economics of Education Review*, 14(4), 351–361. DOI: 10.1016/0272-7757(95)00015-C

Eguia, B., Gonzalez, C. R., & Serrano, F. (2023). Overeducation and scarring effects on the wages of young graduates. [February.]. *International Journal of Manpower*, 44(4), 755–771. DOI: 10.1108/IJM-02-2022-0075

Eichengreen, B., Park, D., & Shin, K. (2013). Growth Slowdowns Redux: New Evidence on the Middle-Income Trap, NBER Working Paper, No:18673

Fallows, S., & Steven, C. (2000). Building Employability Skills into the Higher Education Curriculum: A University-Wide Initiative. *Education + Training*, 42(2), 75–82. DOI: 10.1108/00400910010331620

Green, F., & Zhu, Y. (2010). Overqualification, job dissatisfction, and increasing dispersion in the returns to graduate education. *Oxford Economic Papers*, 62(4), 740–763. DOI: 10.1093/oep/gpq002

Groot, W., & van den Brink, H. M. (2000). Overeducation in the labor market: A meta-analysis. *Economics of Education Review*, 19(2), 149–158. DOI: 10.1016/S0272-7757(99)00057-6

Günay, D., & Günay, A. (2011). 1933'ten Günümüze Türk Yükseköğretiminde Niceliksel Gelişmeler. *Yükseköğretim ve Bilim Dergisi*, 1(1), 1–22.

Hanushek, E.A., Woessmann, L. (2008). The Role of Cognitive Skills in Economic Development, Journal of Economic Literature, V:46, No:3, September

Hanushek, E. A., & Woessmann, L. (2021). The Political Economy of ILSAs in Education: The Role of Knowledge Capital in Economic Growth,(Nilsen, T. et al. (eds.)), International Handbook of Comparative Large-Scale Studies in Education,Springer International Handbooks of Education, Springer.

Hartog, J. (2000). Over-education and earnings: Where are we, where should we go? *Economics of Education Review*, 19(2), 131–147. DOI: 10.1016/S0272-7757(99)00050-3

Hedvicakova, M. (2018). Unemployment and effects of the first work experience of university graduates on their idea of a job. *Applied Economics*, 50(31), 3357–3363. DOI: 10.1080/00036846.2017.1420895

INSEAD. (2023). *The Global Talent Competitiveness Index: What a Difference Ten Years Make, What to Expect fort he Next Decade* (Larvin, B., & Monteiro, F., Eds.). Human Capital Leadership Institute.

Jung, J. (2020). The fourth industrial revolution, knowledge production and higher education in South Korea. *Journal of Higher Education Policy and Management*, 42(2), 134–156. DOI: 10.1080/1360080X.2019.1660047

Katz, L. F., & Murphy, K. M. (1992). Changes in Relative Wages,1963-1987: Supply and demand factors. *The Quarterly Journal of Economics*, 107(1), 1. DOI: 10.2307/2118323

Kettunen, J. (1997). Education and unemployment duration. *Economics of Education Review*, 16(2), 163–170. DOI: 10.1016/S0272-7757(96)00057-X

Kivinen, O., & Ahola, S. (1999). Higher Education as Human Risk Capital. *Higher Education*, 38(September), 191–208. DOI: 10.1023/A:1003788929925

Kopuk, E. (2024). Development of Skills Reacquisition in Industry Sector and Employment in Turkey, Meçik, O. (eds.) Reskillingthe Workforce in the Labor Market: The Country Cases, IGI Global, March.

Kristic, M. (2021). Higher Education as Determinants of Competitiveness and Sustainable Economic Growth, (Topic, M., Lodorfor, G. eds.) The Sustainability Debate (Critical Studies on Corporate Responsibility, Governence and Sustainability) V:14, Emerald Publishing Limited, Leeds, 15-34.

Krugman, P. (1996). *Pop Internationalism*. MIT Press.

Kupets, O. (2016). Education-job mismatch in Ukraine: Too many people with tertiary education or too many jobs for low-skilled? *Journal of Comparative Economics*, 44(1), 125–147. DOI: 10.1016/j.jce.2015.10.005

Lauder, H., Mayhew, K. (2020). Higher Education and the Labor Market: An Introduction. Oxford Review of Education, V:46, Issue:1.

Li, H., Liang, J. Wu,B. (2022). Labor Market Experience and Returns to College Education in Fast Growing Economies. The Journal of Human Resources, 0421-11629R2, June.

Li, S., Whalley, J., & Xing, C. (2014). China's higher education expansion and unemployment of college graduates. *China Economic Review*, 30, 567–582. DOI: 10.1016/j.chieco.2013.08.002

Lovenheim, M. F., & Smith, J. (2022). Returns to Different Postsecondary Investment: Institution Type, Academic Programs and Credential. NBER Working Paper, April, No: w29933.

Lucas, R. E.Jr. (1990). Why Doesn't Capital Flow from Rich to Poor Countries? *The American Economic Review*, 80(2), 92–96.

Mankiw, N. G., Romer, D., & Weil, D. N. (1992). A Contribution to the Empirics of Economic Growth. *The Quarterly Journal of Economics*, 107(2), 407–437. DOI: 10.2307/2118477

Manpower Group (2023). Employment Outlook Survey-Global Findings

Mincer, J. (1989). Education and Unemployment. NBER Working Paper, No:3838.

Mora, J. G., Garcia-Montalvo, J., & Garcia-Aracil, A. (2000). Higher education and graduate employment in Spain. *European Journal of Education*, 35(2), 229–237. DOI: 10.1111/1467-3435.00021

Moreau, M. P., & Leathwood, C. (2006). Graduates' employment and the discourse of employability: A critical analysis. *Journal of Education and Work*, 19(4), 305–324. DOI: 10.1080/13639080600867083

Nelson, R., & Phelps, E. (1966). Investment in Humans, Technological Diffusion, and Economic Growth. *The American Economic Review*, 56, 69–75.

OECD. (2020). Population with tertiary education. URL:https://data.oecd.or/eduatt/population-with-tertiary-education.html

OECD (2023). Education at a Glance 2023

Orazam, P., & King, E. M. (2007). Schooling in Developing Countries: The Roles of Supply, Demand and Government Policy, Handbook of Development Economics, 4, 3475-3559.

Oreopolos, P., & Petronijevic, U. (2013). Making College Worth It: A Review of Research on the Returns to Higher Education. NBER Working Paper, No: w19053

Peters, M. A., & Jandriü, P. (2019). Education and technological unemployment in the Fourth Industrial Revolution. In *The Oxford Handbook of Higher Education Systems and University Management*. Oxford University Press. DOI: 10.1093/oxfordhb/9780198822905.013.27

Plesca, M., Summerfield, F. (2023). The Productivity Benefits of Overeducation. Journal of Human Capital, 17(4), winter

Porter, M. E., & Ketel, C. H. M. (2003). *UK Competitiveness: Moving to the Next Stage, DTI Economics Paper*. Department of Trade and Industry.

Psacharopoulos, G., & Patrinos, H. A. (2018). Returns to Investment in Education: A Decennial Review of the Global Literature, WorldBank Policy Research Working Paper, No: 8402, April.

Riddell, W. C., & Song, X. (2011). The impact of education on unemployment incidence and re-employment success: Evidence from the US labour market. *Labour Economics*, 18(4), 453–463. DOI: 10.1016/j.labeco.2011.01.003

Schomburg, H. (2000). Higher education and graduate employment in Germany. *European Journal of Education*, 35(2), 189–200. DOI: 10.1111/1467-3435.00017

Schultz, T. P. (1960). The Role of Education and Human Capital in Economic Development: An Empirical Assessment, IPR Working Paper Series, No:039.

Shelly, K.J. (1992). The Future Jobs for College Graduates. Monthly Labor Review, July.

Simionescu, M., Naro, M. S. (2019). The Unemployment of Highly Educated People in Romania. A Panel VAR Approach. Studia Universitatis "Vasile Goldis". *Arad–Economics Series*, 29(3), 20–37.

Taber, C. R. (2001). The rising college premium in the eighties: Return to college or return to unobserved ability? *The Review of Economic Studies*, 68(3), 3. DOI: 10.1111/1467-937X.00185

Tasci, H. M., & Tansel, A. (2005). Unemployment and transitions in the Turkish labor market: evidence from individual level data. SSRN Working paper, No:756385.

The Global Competititveness Index. (2017). World Economic Forum.

The Global Competititveness Index. (2019). World Economic Forum.

The Global Competititveness Index. (2020). World Economic Forum.

ÜNİ-VERİ. (2024). Cumhurbaşkanlığı İnsan Kaynakları Ofisi, URL: https://www.cbiko.gov.tr/projeler/uni-veri

Vandenbussche, J., Aghion, P., & Meghir, C. (2006). Growth, Distance to Frontier and Composition of Human Capital. *Journal of Economic Growth*, 11(2), 97–127. DOI: 10.1007/s10887-006-9002-y

Walker, I., & Zhou, Y. (2008). The college wage Premium and the expansion of Higher Education in the UK. *The Scandinavian Journal of Economics*, 110(4), 4. DOI: 10.1111/j.1467-9442.2008.00557.x

Wang, Y., & Liu, S. (2016). Education, Human Capital and Economic Growth: Empirical Research on 55 Countries and Regions (1960-2009). *Theoretical Economics Letters*, 6(2), 347–355. DOI: 10.4236/tel.2016.62039

Wolbers, M.H.J. (2000). The Effects of Level of Education on Mobility Between Employment and Unemployment in the Netherlands. European Sociological Review, V:16, Issue:2, June.

World Economic Forum. (2023). The Future of Jobs Report 2023. Insight Report, May.

Yalçınkaya, Ö., & Kaya, V. (2017). The Effects on Economic Growth of Education: An Application on The PISA Participants (1990-2014). *Sosyoekonomi*, 25(33), 11–35.

KEY TERMS AND DEFINITIONS

Demand for Labor: Number of workers who wish to be employed by the firms.
NEET: It stands for "Not in Employment, Education, or Training" and it refers to individuals, typically between the ages of 15 and 29, who are not currently engaged in education, employed in a job, or involved in a training program.

Overeducation: A situation where an individual possesses more education, qualifications, or skills than are required for their job.

Quality of Human Capital: Level of skills and competencies ownwd by the workers in the labor force.

Quantity of Human Capital: The number of workers available labor force, including their education and skills.

Skills: Abilities and knowledge that individuals accumulate, which enhance their productivity and efficiency in various tasks and professions.

Supply of Labor: Number of workers in the labor market who wants to participate.

Unemployment: The condition of someone who 16 years old or older actively searching for employment but unable to find work.

Chapter 7
Is There a Relationship between Financial Stability and Macroeconomic Variables?
OECD Example

Burcu Savaş Çelik
https://orcid.org/0000-0002-3896-5858
İstanbul Gelişim Üniversitesi, Turkey

ABSTRACT

Financial stability has many determinants. These include various macroeconomic variables, the soundness and infrastructure of financial institutions, and the monetary policies pursued. This study aims to examine the relationship between financial stability and economic growth, interest rates, inflation rates, and interest rates of OECD member countries Z-score provides important information about the financial stability of a country's banking system by comparing its capital and returns and the volatility of returns. The study's data set consists of 15 OECD constituent countries. The data range of the study was determined as the period 2000 - 2021. Panel data analysis is used in this study. Dumitrescu and Hurlin causality test results from gross domestic, inflation, and interest rate variables to the Z-score. Also, there is bi-causality from the Z-score to gross domestic, inflation, and interest rate variables.

DOI: 10.4018/979-8-3693-5508-4.ch007

1. INTRODUCTION

The liberalization of financial markets and globalization have contributed to the deepening and adequacy of national economies. However, countries' different levels of development and various financial system structures have affected financial stability differently. Because of this, how the central bank and other intermediary institutions—actively involved in the financial markets—address financial stability has grown increasingly significant, particularly during the 1990s (Allen & Wood, 2006). Instability in financial institutions affects other sectors directly and indirectly. This is demonstrated by the U.S. financial crisis in 2008, which eventually extended to different industries and nations and sparked the global Crisis.

This study aims to examine the relationship between financial stability and economic growth, interest rates, inflation rates, and interest rates of OECD member countries. It is assumed that there is a causality between financial stability and economic growth (Manu et al., 2011; Creel et al., 2015; Karim et al., 2016; Akram & Eitrheim, 2008) The most important reason for this is that economic growth in countries will lead to financial stability by providing a more secure and peaceful environment in financial markets. Inflation, considered one of the most important indicators of financial stability (Chandrashekar, 2014), is expected to have a causality between financial stability and inflation (Akram & Eitrheim, 2008). A review of the literature price stability is the economic variable that influences the purchasing decisions of producers and consumers. Uncertainty in prices affects the purchasing decisions of producers and consumers. price increases may cause interest rates to rise, which may have a destabilizing effect on financial stability. Interest rate: the long-term government bond yield, one of the important applications for the banking sector, is another macroeconomic variable that effectively determines financial stability. As with the inflation variable, causality is expected between financial stability and interest rates. The study has many contributions to the literature. Firstly, the literature does not study the relationship between financial stability (Z-score) and OECD countries' economic growth, inflation, and interest rates. Secondly, it is expected to contribute to the literature as an inclusive study with all data from 2000, when financial stability started to be calculated, until 2021.

The study consists of four stages. In the second stage, the importance of financial stability and the basic concepts of measuring financial stability are emphasized, and the relationship between financial stability and various macroeconomic variables is discussed. There are many economic variables that affect financial stability. However, there is no study in which variables such as economic growth, interest rate and inflation rate of OECD constituent countries are considered together. Because of that in third stage the relationship between financial stability (Z-score) indicators and economic growth, interest rates, and inflation rates of OECD founding members is analyzed. In the last section, the results obtained are compared with the empirical literature, and political and economic recommendations are made regarding the financial stability of OECD countries.

2. FINANCIAL STABILITY

Although the Bank of England first introduced the concept of financial stability in 1994, there is still no clear definition today. The most important reason for this situation is that the expectations of the Central Bank and/or other researchers from the concept of financial stability vary. Each country and institution has various definitions of the concept of financial stability.

According to the European Central Bank (2024), financial stability is defined as the state in which the financial system is resilient to shocks and financial imbalances, while the TCMB (2024) describes it in the same terms. The FED (2023) sets out qualities similar to economic stability. Accordingly, a reliable and sound banking system, full employment, stable prices, and an efficient payment system are the key elements of financial stability. However, the Bank of England (2024) defines it as a system that can absorb shocks, such as economic downturns, rather than exacerbate them.

Financial stability has many determinants. These include various macroeconomic variables, the soundness and infrastructure of financial institutions, and the monetary policies pursued. The World Bank (2024) establishes eight sub-categories within the scope of financial stability. These categories are shown in Table 1.

Table 1. World Bank Financial Stability Indicators

Indicator Name	Short Definition
Bank Z-score	It expresses the likelihood that the nation's commercial banking system may fail. The Z-score contrasts the volatility of yields with the buffer (capitalization and yields) of a nation's commercial banking system.
The ratio of non-performing loans to gross loans (%)	The ratio of defaulted loans to total gross loans.
The ratio of bank capital to total assets (%)	The ratio of bank capital and reserves to total assets.
The ratio of bank loans to bank deposits (%)	Financial resources provided by domestic money banks to the private sector as a share of total deposits
The ratio of regulatory capital to risk-weighted assets (%)	Capital adequacy of deposit-taking institutions.

continued on following page

Table 1. Continued

Indicator Name	Short Definition
The ratio of liquid assets to deposits and short-term funding (%)	The ratio of the value of liquid assets to short-term funding plus total deposits.
Provisions for non-performing loans (%)	Provisions for non-performing loans.
Stock price volatility	Stock price volatility is the average 360-day national stock market index volatility.

Resource: World Bank, Global Financial Development (2021)

The Z-score, one of the financial stability indicators, is frequently preferred because it reveals the probability of bankruptcy of financial institutions and the relationship between asset values and debt values. Z-score keeps at least five banks in a country under observation. The following formula shows the Z-score financial stability calculation method;

$$z - score\ (z) \equiv \frac{k+\mu}{\sigma}$$

k = equity
μ = returns
σ = standard deviation of asset return

The Z-score provides important information about the financial stability of a country's banking system by comparing its capital and returns and the volatility of returns (World Bank, 2021). Higher values of the Z-score indicate a lower risk of bankruptcy and failure. Table 2 shows the bank-z score by country. According to the table, Iceland has the lowest bank z-score with a score of 1.28, while New Zealand has the highest bank z-score with a value of 44.78.

Table 2. Bank Z-score by Country

Afghanistan 24.92 Score	Angola 15.55 Score	Albania 19.06 Score	Andorra 29.14 Score	United Arab Emirates 22.29 Score	Brunei 9.95 Score
Argentina 9.08 Score	Armenia 12.32 Score	Australia 14.15 Score	Austria 30.91 Score	Guatemala 30.72 Score	Bhutan 12.46 Score
Burundi 18.7 Score	Belgium 15.45 Score	Benin 11.9 Score	Burkina Faso 9.56 Score	South Africa 15.46 Score	Botswana 9 Score

continued on following page

Table 2. Continued

Bulgaria 7.87 Score	Bahrain 7.81 Score	Bahamas 13.23 Score	Barbados 13.96 Score	Dominican Republic 32.58 Score	Canada 13.85 Score
Belize 6.77 Score	Bermuda 18.73 Score	Bolivia 8.32 Score	Brazil 16.35 Score	Gibraltar 7.52 Score	Switzerland 15.34 Score
Chile 7.45 Score	China 25.02 Score	Ivory Coast 19.02 Score	Cameroon 10.59 Score	Czech Republic 10.34 Score	Denmark 26.42 Score
Bangladesh 12.78 Score	Colombia 4.32 Score	Cape Verde 27.09 Score	Costa Rica 19.61 Score	Cuba 22.45 Score	Belarus 17.12 Score
Curacao 11.01 Score	Cyprus 6.07 Score	Congo 5.64 Score	Germany 16.05 Score	Djibouti 16.97 Score	Algeria 24.82 Score
Ecuador 9.51 Score	Egypt 20.6 Score	Spain 16.92 Score	Estonia 8.42 Score	Ethiopia 11.56 Score	Finland 17.11 Score
France 19.98 Score	Micronesia 23.41 Score	Gabon 16.63 Score	Uganda 16.68 Score	Georgia 7.91 Score	Ghana 13.92 Score
Bosnia and Herzegovina 15.29 Score	New Zealand 44.78 Score	Sierra Leone 6.34 Score	Guinea Bissau 7.08 Score	St Vincent and the Grenadines 10.99 Score	Republic of the Congo 6.3 Score
Guyana 26.12 Score	Hong Kong 19.75 Score	Honduras 28.6 Score	Croatia 7.39 Score	Haiti 11.55 Score	Hungary 7.07 Score
Indonesia 5.27 Score	India 19.44 Score	Ireland 10.99 Score	Iran 2.99 Score	Iraq 37.25 Score	Iceland 1.28 Score
Israel 29.3 Score	Italy 13.17 Score	Jamaica 15.48 Score	Jordan 50.11 Score	Japan 12.86 Score	Kazakhstan 2.95 Score
Kenya 23.23 Score	Kyrgyzstan 14.62 Score	Cambodia 26.77 Score	South Korea 10.19 Score	Kuwait 16.58 Score	Laos 19.48 Score
Lebanon 20.19 Score	Liberia 9.72 Score	Libya 32.05 Score	St Lucia 4.9 Score	Sri Lanka 35.09 Score	Uruguay 6.08 Score
Lesotho 16.92 Score	Madagascar 14.06 Score	Maldives 14.79 Score	Mexico 23.75 Score	Malawi 14.51 Score	Nicaragua 25.13 Score
U.S. 31.06 Score	Uzbekistan 11.21 Score	Zambia 8.86 Score	Venezuela 12.7 Score	Vietnam 14.66 Score	Montenegro 8.93 Score
Yemen 17.67 Score	Greece 6.64 Score	Malta 18.41 Score	Zimbabwe 8.08 Score	Macedonia 9.52 Score	Mali 12.83 Score
Mauritania 23.53 Score	Myanmar 7.59 Score	Mongolia 36.25 Score	Mozambique 7.06 Score	Niger 14.38 Score	Mauritius 10.95 Score
Malaysia 20.72 Score	Namibia 23.72 Score	Nepal 28.87 Score	Nigeria 12.19 Score	Oman 19.64 Score	Netherlands 13.04 Score
Norway 12.57 Score	Peru 16.94 Score	Guinea 25.44 Score	Poland 7.05 Score	Pakistan 8.85 Score	Panama 40.39 Score
Qatar 18.46 Score	Philippines 24.13 Score	Russia 6.87 Score	Portugal 16.09 Score	Paraguay 17.13 Score	Senegal 15.87 Score

continued on following page

Table 2. Continued

Romania 10.34 Score	Gambia 10.93 Score	Rwanda 21.42 Score	Saudi Arabia 24.37 Score	South Sudan 8.1 Score	Singapore 28.63 Score
Slovakia 18.93 Score	El Salvador 20.57 Score	Serbia 10.35 Score	Swaziland 24.42 Score	Suriname 8.66 Score	Syria 8.79 Score
Slovenia 4.49 Score	Sweden 39.35 Score	Tajikistan 15.34 Score	Seychelles 10.41 Score	Trinidad and Tobago 21.36 Score	Togo 9.57 Score
Tunisia 38.68 Score	Thailand 7.88 Score	Tanzania 22.18 Score	Turkmenistan 40.62 Score	U.K. 18.11 Score	Türkiye 7.29 Score
Ukraine 5.18 Score					

Source: tradingeconomics Bank Z-score By Country Retrieved from: https://tradingeconomics.com/country-list/bank-z-score-wb-data.html Retrieved date:03.06.2024

There are various studies in the literature on the relationship between financial stability and macroeconomic variables. At the same time, the results obtained from these studies are quite different. One of the most important reasons for this is the other development levels of countries. The economic growth variable, one of the elements of the development level, is shown as an example (Nasren & Anwar, 2018). The studies on the relationship between economic growth and financial stability found that the relationship between variables varies according to the developmental status of countries, the type of analysis, and the data range. In addition, the effect of the Central Bank's monetary policy on inflation and interest rates also affects financial stability. Many variables, such as employment (Asongu et al., 2021; Carney, 2024), foreign debt (Amjad, 2022), and the exchange rate (Eichengreen,1998) are among macroeconomic variables and have an impact on financial stability.

The study hypothesizes a relationship between financial stability and macroeconomic variables. The basis of analyzing this hypothesis is to identify the variables that play a role in determining financial stability. Systematic financial markets lead to efficient resource allocation. On the other hand, significant losses in resource allocation happen if the operation of financial markets is interfered with or if financial instability arises.

GDP, Interest rate and Inflation ↔ OECD countries' z-scores.

In this study, GDP and inflation are two very popular macroeconomic variables in terms of the financial stability of countries. Economic growth and low inflation rates are the basic assumptions that the market mechanism is functioning properly and that the country is stable. The reason for using interest rate: long-term government bond yields are based on the assumption that the interest rate that countries apply to bonds is directly related to the financial market. High or low interest rates provide information on financial stability. Therefore, this study aims to investigate whether the GDP, interest rate and inflation rates of OECD countries impact financial stability.

3. LITERATURE REVIEW

In the literature, while the intensity of studies on the relationship between financial development and economic growth is noteworthy, it is observed that there are not many empirical studies on the relationship between financial stability and economic growth. In addition, studies on the relationship between financial stability, inflation, and interest rates are limited. Table 3 presents the studies on the relationship between financial stability and economic growth.

Table 3. Relationship between Financial Stability and Gross Domestic Product

Author	Period	Country	Method	Result
Manu et al. (2011)	1996-2006	29 Africa countries	Dynamic fixed-effect panel analysis	Positive relationship between F.S. and GDP
Enowbi & Mlambo (2012)	1985-2010	41 Africa Countries	Dynamic panel regression analysis	Positive relationship between F.S. and GDP
Creel et al. (2014)	1998-2011	21 European countries	Dynamic panel regression analysis	Positive relationship between z-score and GDP
Valverde & Sancez (2013)	1980-2009	Germany, Norway, and Spain	VAR analysis	Positive relationship between z-score and GDP for Germany, Spain. No relationship for Norway
Dhal et al. (2011)	1995-2012	India	VAR analysis	Positive relationship between F.S. and GDP
Gezer (2019)	2004-2017	Türkiye	ARDL analysis	Positive relationship between F.S. and GDP
Karamelikli & Bayar (2016)	2005-2015	Türkiye	ARDL analysis	Positive relationship between F.S. and GDP
Karim et al. (2016)	1999-2013	Indonesia	ARDL and IRF analysis	Positive relationship between F.S. and GDP (except Islamic Banks)
Akram & Eitrheim (2008)	1970-2001	Norway	Sensitivity analysis	Positive relationship between F.S. and GDP

Table 4 presents the studies on the relationship between financial stability and inflation. It is seen that the studies are quite limited.

Table 4. Relationship between Financial Stability and Consumer Price Index

Author	Period	Country	Method	Result
Karim et al. (2016)	1999-2013	Indonesia	ARDL IRF analysis	Positive relationship between F.S. and CPI(except Islamic Banks)
Akram & Eitrheim (2008)	1995-2000	Norway	Sensitivity analysis	Positive relationship between F.S. and CPI
Awdeh & Moussawi (2024)	1999-2021	MENA	GMM analysis	Positive relationship between F.S. and CPI
Fazio et al. (2018)	1998-2014	66 countries	Cross country analysis	Negative relationship between inflation target and F.S. in low levels of institutional quality
Boyd et al. (2001)	1960-1995	65 countries	Panel data analysis	Negative relationship between F.S. and inflation
Blot et al. (2015)	1993-2012 (U.S.) 1999-2012 (E.Z.)	U.S. and Eurozone	VAR DCC analysis	No relationship between F.S. and inflation

Table 5 presents the studies on the relationship between financial stability and interest rates. When the literature is reviewed, it is seen that the studies in this field are quite limited.

Table 5. Relationship between Financial Stability and Interest Rate

Author	Period	Country	Method	Result
Blot et al. (2015)	1993-2012 (U.S.) 1999-2012 (E.Z.)	U.S. and Eurozone	VAR and DCC analysis	No relationship between F.S. and Central Bank i
Mukhlis et al. (2020)	2005-2017	Indonesia	SVAR, IRF and VD analysis	The change in interest rate leads to financial instability

4. DATA SET AND METHODOLOGY

The study's data set consists of OECD constituent countries (15 countries). The 15 OECD countries, namely Austria, Belgium, Canada, France, Germany, Ireland, Italy, Luxembourg, Norway, Portugal, Spain, Switzerland, Sweden, United Kingdom, and the United States, are selected for the empirical estimation based on data availability. Denmark, Holland, Iceland, Greece, Greece, and Türkiye could not be subjected to the analysis due to insufficient and missing data. The data range of the study was determined as the period 2000 - 2021. The z-score data for countries are obtained from https://databank.worldbank.org/source/global-financial-development database, gross domestic product variables are selected from the IMF database, and interest rate: long-term government bold yields (10 years-including benchmarks) and inflation data are selected from https://fred.stlouisfed.org.

Panel data analysis is used in this study. The reasons for using panel data analysis in this study structural characteristics of the data set. These problems may arise from omitted variables and the possibility of reducing estimation biases. The study's biggest limitation is that the data set started to be reported in 2000. Secondly, due to insufficient and incomplete data, Denmark, Holland, Iceland, Greece, Greece and Türkiye could not be analyzed. Thirdly, although there are eight sub-categories to measure financial stability, only the Z-score financial stability ratio has been evaluated due to insufficient data.

4.1. Correlation Between Units (Horizontal Cross Section Dependence)

Inter-unit correlation implies a correlation between the residuals obtained from the models estimated for the units in the model. Second-generation unit root tests should be used if there is horizontal cross-section dependence between the series. Therefore, inter-unit correlation should be preferred before proceeding to unit root analysis. (Yerdelen Tatoğlu, 2017).

There are many proposed tests for inter-unit correlation. Time (T) and unit/group (N) values should be considered here. For the case where T>N, the Breusch Pagan (1980) L.M. test is appropriate for the analysis.

4.2. Breusch and Pagan LM Tests

This test, used for correlation between units in the fixed effects model, can be used to test whether there is the correlation between the residuals of the cointegration or error correction model for each unit. Main hypothesis;

$H_0: cor(u_{it}, u_{jt}) = p_{ij} = 0$ i≠j No interdependence between units
$H_1: cor(u_{it}, u_{jt}) = p_{ij} \neq 0$ There is interdependence between units
L.M. test statistic;

$$LM = T\sum_{i=1}^{N-1}\sum_{j=i+1}^{N} p_{ij}^2 \qquad (1)$$

is calculated with the formula. p_{ij}^2: i,j are the correlation coefficient of the residue.

4.2.1. CD Test

The CD test proposed by Pesaran (2004) to test the correlation between units uses the residuals from the estimation of the ADF regression. The correlation of each unit with all units other than itself is calculated. Its hypotheses are as follows;

$$H_0: p_{ij} = 0$$
$$H_1: p_{ij} \neq 0$$

Pesaran for the balanced panel to test for inter-unit correlation,

$$CD = \left(\sqrt{\frac{2T}{N(N-1)}}\right)\left(\sum_{i=1}^{N-1}\sum_{j=i+1}^{N} \dot{p}_{ij}\right) \qquad (2)$$

for the unbalanced panel to test for inter-unit correlation,;

$$CD = \left(\sqrt{\frac{2}{N(N-1)}}\right)\left(\sum_{i=1}^{N-1}\sum_{j=i+1}^{N} T_{ij}\dot{p}_{ij}\right) \qquad (3)$$

have developed statistics.

4.2.2. NLM Test

Pesaran, Ullah, and Yamagata (2008) adapt the Breusch Pagan (1980) L.M. test, which is valid when N is small, and T is sufficiently large but inappropriate when N goes to infinity, for the cases where N and T are large.

$$NLM = \left(\sqrt{\frac{1}{N(N-1)}}\right)\left(\sum_{i=1}^{N-1}\sum_{j=i+1}^{N} T\dot{p}^2_{ij} - 1\right) \qquad (4)$$

it is calculated as. Under hypothesis H_0, NLM~N(0,1)) as T, then N goes to infinity respectively.

4.3. Homogeneity Test

Cointegration tests and estimation methods are selected according to whether the constant and slope parameters are homogeneous or heterogeneous across units. Therefore, it is important to conduct homogeneity tests before choosing the methods to be used (Yerdelen Tatoğlu, 2017). Various homogeneity tests are used in the literature. Paseran, Yamagata (2008) test is used to detect slope homogeneity in large panels.

4.3.1. Paseran, Yamagata (2008) Homogenity Test

The homogeneity of the slope coefficients is tested using the delta test developed by Pesaran and Yamagata (2008) and calculated as follows.

$$\tilde{\Delta} = \sqrt{N}\frac{N^{-1}\tilde{S} - K}{\sqrt{2k}} \qquad (5)$$

The equation below gives the adjusted delta test statistic

$$\tilde{\Delta}_{adj} = \sqrt{N}\frac{N^{-1}\tilde{S} - E(\tilde{Z}_{it})}{\sqrt{VAR(\tilde{Z}_{it})}} \qquad (6)$$

The hypotheses for the delta test are as follows:

H_0: Eğim katsayısı homojendir
H_1: Eğim katsayısı homojen değildir

If the probability value of the test statistics obtained from Equations (5) and (6) is less than 10%, the H_0 hypothesis is rejected, and the slope coefficients are accepted to be heterogeneous.

4.4. Second-Generation Unit Root Tests

As an alternative to the first group of panel unit root tests, heterogeneous panel unit root tests were developed. In the second-generation unit root tests, the assumption that the series of all units have a common autoregressive parameter is made more flexible. In this way, each individual can have its own autoregressive parameter instead of a common one (Yerdelen Tatoğlu, 2017). Second-generation panel unit root tests are unit root analyses developed against the absence of horizontal cross-section dependence in the first-generation panel unit root tests. They are produced to eliminate the problems that may occur in the case of dependence between cross-sectional units. These tests address the series' stationarity by considering the horizontal cross-sectional dependence between units.

The hypotheses of the second group of unit root tests are as follows.

H_0 : no unit is stationary

H_1: at least one of the units is stationary

4.4.1. Im, Pesaran and Shin (CIPS) Panel Unit Root Test

Pesaran (2007) adds lagged levels and cross-sectional means of first differences as factors in the D.F. or ADF regression. Therefore, this method eliminates inter-unit correlation using an extended ADF regression with lagged cross-sectional means. This test is called "cross-sectional extended Dickey-Fuller (CADF)" and is expressed in equation (7).

$$\Delta Y_{it} = a_i + p_i Y_{it-1} + \gamma_i f_t + \varepsilon_{it} \tag{7}$$

4.4.2. Second-Generation Panel Cointegration Tests

Like panel unit root tests, first-generation panel cointegration tests are insufficient if a correlation exists between units. Second-generation cointegration tests that consider the relationship between the units should be used in this case.

4.4.2.1. Gengenbach, Urbain and Westerlund Panel Cointegration Test

An error correction-based panel cointegration test was developed by Gengenbach, Urbain, and Westerlund (2016). Using the error correction model, this test allows for heterogeneity and inter-unit correlation, unbalanced panel and unequal lag lengths across units. This test is based on the error correction model (8).

$$\Delta_{yi} = d\delta_{yx_i} + a_{yi} y_{i,-1} + \omega_{i,-1} \gamma_i + \mu_i \pi_i + \varepsilon_{yx_i} = a_{yi} y_{i,-1} + g_i^d \lambda_i + \varepsilon_{yx_i} \tag{8}$$

The hypotheses of the panel cointegration test tests are as follows.

$H_0: a_{y1} = \ldots = a_{yN} = 0$
$H_1: a_{y1} < 0$

4.5. Dumitrescu and Hurlin Panel Causality Test

Dumitrescu and Hurlin (2012) extend the Granger causality test for heterogeneous panels. Taking the first equation of the panel VAR model in equation (9) below,

$$Y_{it} = a_i + \sum_{k=1}^{K} \gamma_i^{(k)} Y_{it-k} + \sum_{k=1}^{K} \beta_i^{(k)} X_{it-k} + \varepsilon_{it} \qquad (9)$$

In the equation, the lag length (k) is the same for each unit of the panel, and the panel is balanced, while the autoregressive parameter $\gamma_i^{(k)}$ and the slopes $\beta_i^{(k)}$ vary across units.

$H_0: \beta_i = 0 \; i = 1, ..., N$ (doesn't Granger cause)
$H_1: \beta_i \neq 0 \; i = N_1 + 1, N_2 + 2, ..., N$ (does Granger cause)

The test statistic for N<T is shown in equation (10).

$$Z_{N,T}^{HNC} = \sqrt{\frac{N}{2K}} \left(W_{N,T}^{HNC} - K \right)$$

When the panel regression is not homogeneous, parameter estimates vary across units, but causality is observed for all units. If the null hypothesis is rejected, variable X is the cause of Y for all panel units.

5. RESULTS

5.1. Descriptive Analysis

Before testing the relationship between OECD financial stability and macroeconomic variables, the descriptive statistics of each series are analyzed. Descriptive statistical information is given in Table 6.

Table 6. Descriptive Statics

Variable	Obs	Mean	Std. Dev.	Min	Max
Country	0				
id	330	8	4.327055	1	15
Years	330	2010.5	6.353923	2000	2021
Z	330	18.30499	10.06016	.0173334	57.44071
IR	330	2.953968	1.91436	-.5238333	10.5475
GDP	330	27.59482	10.22004	13.48132	64.10049

5.2. Correlation between Units (Horizontal Cross Section Dependence)

The model for panel data analysis is based on the assumption that there is no horizontal cross-sectional dependence between units. In the study, horizontal cross-section dependence was first questioned to ensure the analysis's reliability. The results are presented in Table 7.

Table 7. Results of Correlation between Units

Test	Statistic	p-value
LM	324.4	0.0000*
LM adj*	32.29	0.0000*
LM CD*	9.004	0.0000*

Note: *** indicates rejection of hypothesis H_0 at 1% statistical significance.

According to the obtained result, the H_0 hypothesis that no horizontal cross-sectional dependence between units is rejected. In the next step, the homogeneity of the series should be determined. The homogeneity status of the series is shown in Table 8.

Table 8. Results of Homogeneity

	Delta	p-value
$\tilde{\Delta}$	10.006	0.0000***
$\tilde{\Delta}_{adj}$	11.382	0.0000***

Note: *** indicates rejection of the hypothesis H_0 at 1% statistical significance.

According to the result obtained, the slope coefficient is heterogeneous. A second-generation unit root analysis is required since cross-sectional dependence and heterogeneity among the units exist. Therefore, it was deemed appropriate to perform CADF unit root analysis first. The test results are shown in Table 9. According to the results of the analysis, Z and Inf series are stationary at level, while I.R. and GDP series are stationary at first difference.

Table 9. Unit Root Analysis Results

	Constant		Constant and Trend	
	Z(t-bar)	p-value	Z(t-bar)	p-value
Z	-2.500	0.006***	-2.500	0.023

continued on following page

Table 9. Continued

	Constant		Constant and Trend	
	Z(t-bar)	p-value	Z(t-bar)	p-value
Inf	-2.672	0.004**	-1.782	0.037
ΔIR	-8.495	0.000***	-6.776	0.000***
ΔGDP	-2.342	0.010**	-0.918	0.179

Note: *** indicates that the null hypothesis H_0 is rejected at 1%, ** at 5%, * at 10% statistical significance, Δ: indicates that the series are stationary at 1st difference.

Table 10 presents the results of the Gengenbach, Urbain, and Westerlund Panel Cointegration Test. The table shows that Pesaran CD Test values are not significant at 0.01% level. In short, it is accepted that there is no cointegration relationship between the variables. Therefore, the next step is to determine whether there is causality between the variables.

Table 10. Gengenbach, Urbain and Westerlund Panel Cointegration Test

d.y	Coef.	T-bar	p-value*
Y(t-1)	-0.875	-2.075	>0.1

Table 11 presents the Dumitrescu and Hurlin causality test results for the relationship between Z-score, economic growth, inflation, and interest rate: long-term government bond yields. The table shows causality from gross domestic, inflation, and interest rate variables to the Z-score. Also, there is causality from the Z-score to gross domestic, inflation, and interest rate variables.

Table 11. Dumitrescu and Hurlin Panel Causality Test

Variables	w-bar	z-bar	z-bar (p-value)
GDP→ Z	2.296	3.550	0.0004**
Z→ GDP	11.602	8.086	0.0000***
Inf→ Z	9.947	6.058	0.0000***
Z→ Inf	8.536	4.364	0.0000***
IR→ Z	11.919	10.865	0.0000***
Z→ IR	11.341	7.766	0.0000***

CONCLUSION AND DISCUSSION

Financial and macroeconomic stability are different, but at the same time, they are important indicators of the economy that feed each other. A negative impact on macroeconomic stability may also affect financial stability. The World Bank calculates financial stability using Bank Z-score, Bank NPLs to gross loans (%), Bank capital to total assets (%), Bank loans to bank deposits (%), Bank regulatory capital to risk-weighted assets (%), Liquid assets to deposits and short-term funding (%), Provisions for non-performing loans (%) and Stock price volatility variables.

In this study, the effect of economic growth, inflation, and interest rate: long-term government bold yields variables on the Z-score prepared by the IMF based entirely on banking accounting data is evaluated using the Dumitrescu and Hurlin Panel Causality Test for OECD countries in the period 2000-2021.

The study results show that economic growth, inflation, interest rate, and long-term government bold yield variables have a significant causality on the Z-score. According to these results, economic growth, inflation, and interest rate: long-term government bold yields variable affect financial stability and also Z-score affects economic growth, inflation, and interest rate: long-term government bold yield.

The result obtained from the study shows that there is causality towards the Z-score, a financial stability indicator, in OECD countries where economic growth is realized. Economic growth indicators are an important determinant of countries' financial stability (Ozili, 2024). Factors such as imports, exports, foreign direct investment, capital investment, and labor force participation rate affect economic growth. Increases in foreign direct investment and capital investment, the ratio of exports to imports, and the rise in labor force participation lead to economic growth and stability in the financial market. The causality relationship between GDP and z-score is consistent with Creel (2014), Valverde and Sanchez (2013). It is also found that there is a causality from Z-Score to GDP. As a result of financial instability in countries, it may affect domestic and foreign investors and cause a decrease in the volume of transactions in stock markets, disruption of import and export regimes and damage to economic growth. the results obtained are in line with the literature.

In the study, bidirectional causality was found between CPI and Z-score. It has been revealed that the inflation phenomenon impacts financial stability. Inflation is an important determinant of the stability of countries. Therefore, the results obtained from this study are supported by Akram and Eitrheim (2008) and Awdeh & Moussawi (2024). Monetary policy tools that central banks implement to ensure price stability are also aimed at providing financial stability. However, the study's results by Blot et al. (2015) reveal different results, although they cover countries similar to the study. The most important reason for this is the methodology and time period used. It is also found that there is a causality from Z-score to CPI. As a result of financial instability in countries, it may affect domestic and foreign investors and cause a decrease in the volume of transactions in stock markets, disruption of import and export regimes and damage to economic growth. the results obtained are in line with the literature. The wrong monetary and fiscal policies implemented in countries have the power to directly affect financial instability and inflation. To elaborate, wrong monetary policies can lead to wrong interest rate targeting. these interest rates affect the investment decisions of consumers and producers, leading to a change in the market equilibrium and the emergence of the inflation phenomenon.

When the causality relationship between interest rate, long-term government bond yields, and Z-score is analyzed, quite different results are obtained from other studies since the existing studies in the literature are quite limited, and the interest rate variable used in this study is different from the interest rate variable used in other studies. The relationship between bond interest rates and financial stability is multifaceted. High and low interest rates are very important for financial stability. High interest rates do not pose a significant risk to financial stability because monetary policy normalization increases credibility and stabilizes the financial system (Abbasi and Schmidt, 2019). However, low interest rates can lead to financial instability. Therefore, establishing bidirectional causality from bond interest rates to financial stability is consistent with monetary policy implications.

Finally, financial markets and institutions, financial instruments, investors, fund suppliers, and demanders represent a link in the economic chain. Since financial markets and stability do not depend on a single variable, they should be considered whole. In particular, the decisions taken by policymakers and officials involved in the financial market affect the economic system as a whole. It is not correct for monetary and fiscal policy makers to address only one economic variable in order to ensure financial stability. All variables that ensure financial stability need to be addressed in a multifaceted and integrated manner. Otherwise financial stability will be replaced by financial instability.

REFERENCES

Abbassi, P., & Schmidt, M. (2019). Financial Stability Effect of Yield-Oriented Investment Behaviour. *Available at SSRN* 3250799., doi: DOI: 10.2139/SSRN.3250799

Akram, Q. F., & Eitrheim, Ø. (2008). Flexible inflation targeting and financial stability: Is it enough to stabilize inflation and output? *Journal of Banking & Finance*, 32(7), 1242–1254. DOI: 10.1016/j.jbankfin.2007.10.008

Allen, W. A., & Wood, G. (2006). Defining and achieving financial stability. *Journal of Financial Stability*, 2(2), 152–172. DOI: 10.1016/j.jfs.2005.10.001

Amjad, A. (2022). Foreign Debt, Financial Stability, Exchange Rate Volatility and Economic Growth in South Asian Countries, *MPRA*, Paper No. 116328. Retrieved from: https://mpra.ub.uni-muenchen.de/116328/1/MPRA_paper_116328.pdf

Asongu, S. A., Nounamo, Y., Njangang, H., & Tadadjeu, S. (2021). Gender Inclusive Intermediary Education, Financial Stability and Female Employment in the Industry in Sub-Saharan Africa. *Finance Research Letters*, 43, 101968. DOI: 10.1016/j.frl.2021.101968

Awdeh, A., El Moussawi, C., & Hamadi, H. (2024). The impact of inflation on bank stability: evidence from the MENA banks. *International Journal of Islamic and Middle Eastern Finance and Management*. DOI: 10.1108/IMEFM-10-2023-0388

Bank of England. (2024). Financial Stability. Retrieved from: https://www.bankofengland.co.uk/financial-stability

Blot, C., Creel, J., Hubert, P., Labondance, F., & Saraceno, F. (2015). Assessing the link between price and financial stability. *Journal of Financial Stability*, 16, 71–88. DOI: 10.1016/j.jfs.2014.12.003

Boyd, J. H., Levine, R., & Smith, B. D. (2001). The Impact of Inflation on Financial Sector Performance. *Journal of Monetary Economics*, 47(2), 221–248. DOI: 10.1016/S0304-3932(01)00049-6

Breusch, T. S., & Pagan, A. R. (1980). The Lagrange Multiplier Test and Its Applications to Model Specification in Econometrics. *The Review of Economic Studies*, 47(1), 239–253. DOI: 10.2307/2297111

Carney, M. (2024). Globalisation, Financial Stability and Employment. *Methods (San Diego, Calif.)*, 1–10. https://www.bankofcanada.ca/wp-content/uploads/2012/08/remarks-220812.pdf

Chandrasekhar, C. P. (2014). Off-target on Monetary Policy. *Economic and Political Weekly*, •••, 27–30. https://www.jstor.org/stable/24479171

Creel, J., Hubert, P., & Labondance, F. (2015). Financial Stability and Economic Performance. *Economic Modelling*, 48, 25–40. DOI: 10.1016/j.econmod.2014.10.025

Dhal, S., Kumar, P., & Ansari, J. (2011). Financial Stability, Economic Growth, Inflation and Monetary Policy Linkages in India: An Empirical Reflection. *Reserve Bank of India Occasional Papers, 32*(3), 1-35. Retrieved from: https://www.semanticscholar.org/paper/Financial-Stability%2C-Economic-Growth%2C-Inflation-and-Dhal-Kumar/8b12f49fe526afd0ddc61f9667b225724aecbf41

Dumitrescu, E. I., & Hurlin, C. (2012). Testing for Granger Non-Causality in Heterogeneous Panels. *Economic Modelling*, 29(4), 1450–1460. DOI: 10.1016/j.econmod.2012.02.014

Eichengreen, B. (1998). Exchange Rate Stability and Financial Stability. *Open Economies Review*, 9(1+), 569–608. DOI: 10.1023/A:1008373022226

Enowbi, B. M., & Mlambo, K. (2012). Financial Instability, Financial Openness and Economic Growth in African Countries. MPRA, Paper No.43340. Retrieved from: https://mpra.ub.uni-muenchen.de/43340/1/final_version_Financial_Instability_Financial_Openness_and_Economic_Growth_in_African_Countries_Final.pdf

Eurupean Central Bank. (2024). Retrieved from: https://www.ecb.europa.eu/paym/financial-stability/html/index.en.html#:~:text=Financial%20stability%20can%20be%20defined,the%20unravelling%20of%20financial%20imbalances

Fazio, D. M., Silva, T. C., Tabak, B. M., & Cajueiro, D. O. (2018). Inflation Targeting and Financial Stability: Does The Quality Of Institutions Matter? *Economic Modelling*, 71, 1–15. DOI: 10.1016/j.econmod.2017.09.011

FED. (2024). What is Financial Stability. Received from: https://www.federalreserve.gov/faqs/what-is-financial-stability.htm

Federal Reserve Bank of St. Louıs. (2024). Retrieved from: www.fred.stlouisfed.org

Gengenbach, C., Urbain, J. P., & Westerlund, J. (2016). Error Correction Testing in Panels With Common Stochastic Trends. *Journal of Applied Econometrics*, 31(6), 982–1004. DOI: 10.1002/jae.2475

Gezer, M. A. (2019). Finansal İstikrar ve Reel Ekonomi Arasındaki İlişki: Türkiye Örneği.(Doctorate Thesis), Kütahya Dumlupınar University, Institute of Social Sciences.

Karamelikli, H., & Bayar, Y. (2016). Makroekonomik ee Finansal İstikrarin Ekonomik Büyüme Üzerindeki Etkisi: Türkiye Örneği. *Uluslararası Yönetim İktisat ve İşletme Dergisi, 12*(12), 225-236. https://dergipark.org.tr/en/download/article-file/1125568

Karim, N. A., Al-Habshi, S. M. S. J., & Abduh, M. (2016). Macroeconomics Indicators and Bank Stability: A Case of Banking in Indonesia. *Bulletin of Monetary Economics and Banking*, 18(4), 431–448. DOI: 10.21098/bemp.v18i4.609

Manu, L. P., Adjasi, C. K., Abor, J., & Harvey, S. K. (2011). Financial Stability and Economic Growth: A Cross-Country Study. *International Journal of Financial Services Management*, 5(2), 121–138. https://ideas.repec.org/a/ids/ijfsmg/v5y2011i2p121-138.html. DOI: 10.1504/IJFSM.2011.041920

Mukhlis, I., Hidayah, I., & Retnasih, N. R. (2020). Interest Rate Volatility of The Federal Funds Rate: Response of the Bank Indonesia and Its Impact on the Indonesian Economic Stability. *Journal of Central Banking Theory and Practice*, 9(1), 111–133. DOI: 10.2478/jcbtp-2020-0007

Nasreen, S., & Anwar, S. (2018). How Financial Stability Affects Economic Development in South Asia: A Panel Data Analysis. *European Online Journal of Natural and Social Sciences, 7*(1), pp-54. ISSN:1805-3602.

Ozili, P. K. (2024). Impact of Financial Stability on Economic Growth in Nigeria. In *Blockchain Applications for Smart Contract Technologies* (pp. 177–187). IGI Global. DOI: 10.4018/979-8-3693-1511-8.ch008

Pesaran, M. H. (2007). A Simple Panel Unit Root Test in The Presence of Cross-Section Dependence. *Journal of Applied Econometrics*, 22(2), 265–312. DOI: 10.1002/jae.951

Pesaran, M. H., Ullah, A., & Yamagata, T. (2008). A Bias-Adjusted L.M. Test of Error Cross-Section Independence. *The Econometrics Journal*, 11(1), 105–127. DOI: 10.1111/j.1368-423X.2007.00227.x

Pesaran, M. H., & Yamagata, T. (2008). Testing Slope Homogeneity in Large Panels. *Journal of Econometrics*, 142(1), 50–93. DOI: 10.1016/j.jeconom.2007.05.010

Peseran, M. (2004). General Diagnostic Tests for Corss Section Dependence in Panels. *IZA Discussion Paper*, 1240. DOI: 10.17863/CAM.5113

TCMB. (2024). Finansal İstikrar. Retrieved from: https://www.tcmb.gov.tr/wps/wcm/connect/TR/TCMB+TR/Main+Menu/Temel+Faaliyetler/Para+Politikasi/Finansal+Istikrar/

Tradingeconomics (2024). Bank Z-score By Country. Retrieved from: https://tradingeconomics.com/country-list/bank-z-score-wb-data.html

Valverde, C. S., & Sánchez, L. P. (2013). Financial Stability and Economic Growth. In *Crisis, risk and stability in financial markets* (pp. 8–23). Palgrave Macmillan UK., DOI: 10.1057/9781137001832_2

World Bank. (2021). Global Financial Development. Retrieved from: https://www.worldbank.org/en/publication/gfdr/data/global-financial-development-database

Yerdelen Tatoğlu, F. (2017). Panel Zaman Serileri Analizi Stata Uygulamalı (3. Baskı 2020).

Chapter 8
The Role of Sustainable Finance in the Transition to the Post-Growth Economy

Aynur Yilmaz Ataman
https://orcid.org/0000-0001-6678-7908
Post Growth Institute, UK

ABSTRACT

In light of the urgent ecological and social challenges facing our world, there has been a noticeable shift in focus towards exploring economic models that prioritise ecological constraints and societal well-being over the pursuit of continuous growth and profit maximisation. These alternative perspectives collectively fall under the overarching term of post-growth economic models and the financial sector has significant influence over the real economy, and the investments made within it can either perpetuate destructive traditional practices or contribute to the construction of sustainable, regenerative, and inclusive economic and social structures. Therefore, this chapter aims to delve into the role of existing sustainable investment strategies, such as ESG (Environmental, Social, and Governance) Investment and Impact Investment, in the transition to a post-growth era. It also aims to examine the new transformative investment frameworks that have emerged in response to the shortcomings of current investment models in facilitating this transition.

DOI: 10.4018/979-8-3693-5508-4.ch008

Copyright © 2025, IGI Global. Copying or distributing in print or electronic forms without written permission of IGI Global is prohibited.

1. INTRODUCTION

Amid challenging times where we have been experiencing the limits of planetary boundaries in various ways such as climate crisis that is manifesting itself with increased frequency of extreme weather events, biodiversity loss, pollution, land conversion, resource scarcity and deterioration in social and cultural structures reflecting in various ways, such as widening inequality across and within countries, the coexistence of overconsumption and lack of access to basic necessities within the same territory, various number of initiatives, policies, targets and technologies have been introduced to mitigate the detrimental impacts of our current way of living and to keep the humanity within the safe ecological and social boundaries.

In this context, to alleviate the pressure on the planet, support the regenerating nature of Earth systems and enhance social welfare, various economic approaches have been proposed to mitigate or undo the adverse impacts of current growth-oriented and linear economic model based on extracting finite natural resources with an unsustainable rate and producing a vast amount of harmful waste. Some discourses, like green growth (Hallegatte et al., 2012) and inclusive growth (OECD, 2015), advocate for economic growth as the primary goal of economic policies and argue that by considering environmental and social concerns and creating opportunities for all segments of the population, it is possible to mitigate the negative impacts of industrial activities and ensure prosperity for everyone while staying within the planet's biophysical limits.

On the other hand, other approaches that can be categorised as post-growth alternatives in very general terms, suggest a shift in focus from economic growth. These approaches emphasise that there is no conclusive evidence of permanent decoupling of economic growth from environmental degradation (Parrique et al., 2019) and advocate placing ecological and human well-being at the core of economic and social policies. In addition to detrimental environmental outcomes, targeting constant economic growth is also stated to be the cause of various adverse impacts on society, and it has been found to be unsustainable due to various macro-economic parameters. Among numerous research in this field, Jackson (2018) focuses on exploring the dynamics of secular stagnation experienced in many advanced economies after the 2008 financial crisis and shows that growth-oriented economic policies in the course of declining labour productivity are leading to the rise in social and financial instability. Additionally, as the role of new technologies in rising labour productivity remains uncertain, lower growth rates are stated to be inevitable and a "new normal" to which particularly advanced economies need to adopt.

In this regard, the steady-state economy has been one of the concepts proposed as an alternative to continuous growth. It was revived by Herman Daly in the late 1970s, drawing on the pioneering works of Georgescu-Roegen (1977) and Meadows et al., (1972). These works show that economic growth rates cannot continue indefinitely as population growth, industrialisation, pollution, food production, and resource depletion surpass biophysical limits and continuous growth per se violates the laws of thermodynamics. The concept is associated with a macroeconomic model of a zero-growth economy, advocating for stabilised population and per capita consumption levels while maintaining a throughput of energy and materials within the biosphere's regenerative capacity and minimising waste (Daly, 2008). The degrowth approach, initially launched as a project of voluntary societal shrinking of production and consumption to ensure social and ecological sustainability in the early 2000s (Demaria et al., 2013) takes a more proactive stand by proposing the inevitability of scaling down the material and energy throughput, with a focus on high-income countries with high levels of consumption, to realign the economy with Earth systems in a way that reduces inequality and improves human well-being. Degrowth proponents advocate for a planned reduction in material output through a series of integrated policy reforms, transitioning from environmentally harmful and socially unnecessary industries to those creating more social value. Possible increases in unemployment are argued to be mitigated through reduced working hours and a just transition to supported industries, with governments playing a crucial role in financing and organising these reforms, as outlined by Hickel (2021). The well-being economy, offering another alternative to the mainstream economic paradigm, argues that simply reducing material consumption does not necessarily lead to increased human and planetary well-being. Instead, it suggests focusing on increasing these parameters rather than solely discussing changes in production and consumption and proposes adopting more comprehensive indicators to measure human and planetary well-being (Fioramonti, 2024; WeAll, 2022). On the other hand, the circular economy approach offers a tool to keep economic activities within the planet's capacity by proposing the circulation of products and materials to eliminate waste and regenerate nature (European Parliament, 2023). A recently emerged economic concept, known as "Doughnut Economics," also suggests shifting the focus away from economic growth that may not necessarily benefit humanity (Raworth, 2017). Instead, there is an emphasis on social and ecological boundaries, and the space between these boundaries is described as a safe and just place for humanity to thrive as illustrated in Figure 1. As alternative perspectives have also begun to attract more attention in the financial system, a new discourse, named as "Regenerative Economics", proposing eight critical principles around which the economy should be redesigned to support human prosperity and wellbeing within the planet's capacity, explicitly considers the finance sector and proposes a policy agenda to direct investments toward regenerative activities and reduce income inequality (Fullerton, 2015).

Figure 1. Doughnut Economics

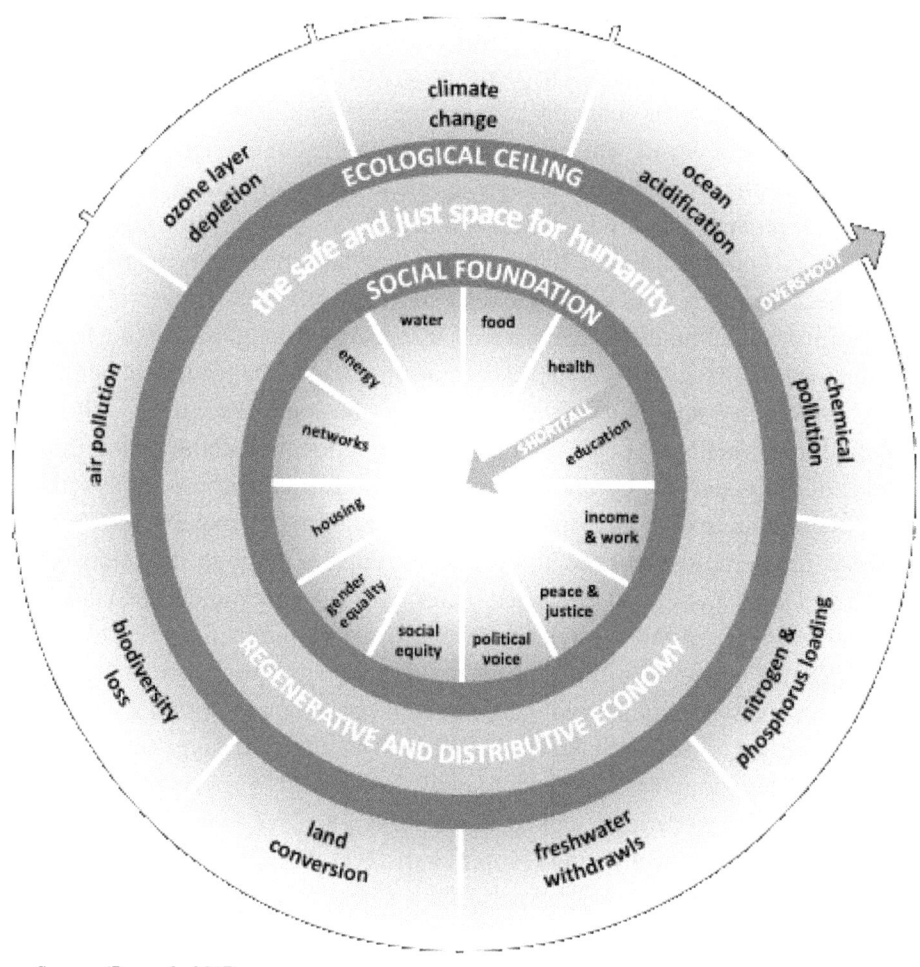

Source: (Raworth, 2017)

These approaches recognise the biophysical limits on economic activities, offer frameworks and tools to keep human activity within these limits and provide essential perspectives that contribute to reshaping the economy in the transition towards an economic system operating within the planetary boundaries. In the meantime, these efforts have led the way to envision the new social conditions and their economic implications where the constant pursuit of economic growth is left behind, and instead, all social and ecological values are prioritised over it. While in some studies "post-growth" term has begun to be used to cover all growth-critical approaches (Fioramonti, 2024; Hinton, 2021) it is also used to define a worldview indicating to a society operating better without the demand of constant economic growth, thus serve to the economic justice, social well-being and ecological regeneration (PGI, 2018) Similarly, Cassiers & Maréchal (2018; p.2) use the term "post-growth" to define *"an era that we are entering and yet are unable to define precisely, other than by reference to what we are leaving behind, (....)* and *"in which the societal project is redefined beyond the pursuit of economic growth"*. In this regard, in a system where economic growth is left as a target per se, Cassiers & Maréchal (2018) explain that three core principles, which are connected to each other and thus should be implemented together, can be guidance: ecological limits, the equity in the distribution of wealth and of the right to a good life, and the autonomy in a sense that to include all parties in the establishment of socio-political norms. In a recent study comparing three post-growth theories, Fioramonti (2024) identifies four policy tools that have emerged as common in the context of the post-growth economy: determination of broader economic indicators beyond GDP, a tax reform, including taxing consumption and wealth rather than just income, the expansion of the concept of work to include all paid and unpaid activities that provide social benefits and the redistribution that involves the localisation and regionalisation of all heavy industrial activities.

While the term refers to a worldview on a global and national economic scale, inevitably, it has implications for businesses as key economic actors. In this regard, as described in (Prophil, 2022), developing a post-growth approach for a company involves pursuing fully sustainable[1] activities in environmental, social, and economic aspects. This includes respecting planetary boundaries to ensure environmental sustainability, upholding the social foundation for social sustainability, and generating prosperity for economic sustainability. In that regard, as a first step, the company is expected to ensure that the human and natural resources it is able to conserve and regenerate by its activities outweigh those depleted as a result of these activities. For this reason, companies are required to redefine their development strategy based on qualitative targets, focusing on growth in other areas rather than sales, assets and financial worth. In that regard, this includes setting limits on its growth to keep its economic activity in line with the goal of sustainability. The post-growth approach for a company also includes redefining its purpose of existence in a way to give up any unsustainable activities and promote ecological and social values and adopting a system of evaluation and accounting to measure its sustainability and overall performance in financial, social and environmental aspects, and take informed decisions. However, it is also acknowledged that not all existing and new businesses can operate fully compatible with this perspective. Therefore, Hinton (2021) provides a five-dimension framework (size-scope, strategy, governance structure, incorporation structure, and relationship to profit) that can be helpful for assessing how and why different types of businesses might be compatible with post-growth transition and categorising them based on their compatibility.

However, the ongoing cycle of unsustainable living practices in our societies is also connected to the global financial system comprising various institutions, organisations, regulations and practices along with business models that function with the narrow definition of efficiency and focus on profit-maximisation and short-term returns for shareholders often at the expense of a broader economic, environmental, social and cultural impacts for all stakeholders. Therefore, it is important to acknowledge the role of finance sector in driving ecological and social transitions by funding initiatives that lead to necessary structural changes and shift from harmful practices to sustainable ones. A number of examples have already been established, and they are becoming increasingly widespread within the financial sector, where regulations, agencies, organisations, and practices are moving away from short-termism towards long-term value creation that takes into account social and environmental factors.

As the flow of money within the finance system has the potential to shape the real economy and society, it is considered important to explore the motivations, strategies, and perspectives driving these financial flows. They can either perpetuate destructive traditional practices or contribute to building sustainable, regenerative, and inclusive economic and social structures. Therefore, it is crucial to delve into the current perspectives guiding investment decisions and their effectiveness, as well as to explore newly emerging innovative perspectives. This exploration will offer valuable insights and lay the groundwork for further theoretical and empirical studies. Therefore, the primary objective of this study is to examine investment approaches and their potential contributions to the inevitable and required transition to a post-growth era considering that this shift necessitates a fundamental transformation in economic and social structures as well as embedded mindsets. Although there is extensive literature on how investments can safeguard and generate social and environmental values, their role in the post-growth transition is not commonly evaluated. Similarly, there is limited research on the role of the finance sector and investment practices in the growing literature on the post-growth economy. Consequently, this chapter aims to offer a distinctive and constructive perspective on investment approaches.

Investment practices that consider non-financial factors fall under the umbrella term of sustainable finance. Although they are not mutually exclusive, they differ in the areas they focus on and how they are implemented. There are various terms to describe investment approaches that consider non-financial factors, but in this chapter, the term of sustainable investment will be used to encompass all perspectives that take into account environmental, social, and governance-related issues to varying extents in investment decisions.

In that regard, the environmental, social, and governance (ESG) investment and impact investment are the two main approaches covered by the term sustainable investment. The ESG investment approach, which is currently the most widespread practice and refers to integrating ESG criteria into financing and investment decisions and shielding portfolios from sustainability-related risks by excluding funding for specific activities and practices that are known to be harmful to society and the environment, implicitly and indirectly creating a positive impact. However, the impact investment approach explicitly aims to make a positive impact by allocating funds to specific projects and activities, taking a proactive stance by taking a step further from minimising the negative effects to actively seeking to create a positive outcome for the planet and all living beings. It is only recently that the necessity of a more transformative approach and practices have begun to be expressed as a remedy for the driving factors of the planetary crisis, aiming for structural and long-term systemic changes that would help the society and economy transform in a fundamental and desired way by considering social, environmental, and cultural impacts as non-financial returns, prioritising long-term impact over solely financial returns.

In this context, the first part of this chapter will provide a brief account of the emergence of these approaches as well as available data on sustainable investment, while the next part will delve into them more deeply, also addressing the factors that hinder their implementation and effectiveness in addressing the current polycrisis. The final part will focus on new perspectives that can be classified as transformative investment approaches.

2. A BRIEF BACKGROUND OF SUSTAINABLE INVESTMENT

Although some studies trace the origins of sustainable investment perspectives back to faith-based investing in the early 1800s, the emergence of the early examples of sustainable investment approaches similar to the way it is practiced today dates back to the 1950s (IFC, 2019). Based on a historical analysis, Penna et al. (2023) identify four distinctive waves in sustainable investing each of which have had different characteristic. Exclusion of companies conducting morally and religiously unreliable activities from the portfolios of investors was the first example of investment approaches concerning with non-financial parameters and observed in the first period between 1950-1970s. In the second wave, covering the 1980s and 1990s, religious and moral bases were mostly replaced with a combination of social and environmental goals while preserving financial returns. In that period, social concerns were more on the focus, and Sparkes (2001) further explains that environmental concerns, which were also named as "green investment" or "green ethic" at that time, focusing mainly on the sustainability objectives, were later on added to the ethical criteria of the existing funds due to their low financial performance and investor preferences who want both types of criteria to be included together. Penna et al. (2023) use the term "socially responsible investing" to describe the investment strategy in this second period and explain that directing financial resources to assets that displayed better performance on ESG issues, investing in companies that follows certain norms or a part of sustainability or market index such as Domini 400 Social (now the MSCI KLD 400 Social Index), Dow Jones Sustainability Index or FTSE4Good Index were the main strategies applied. The late 1990s and early 2000s are categorised as the third wave of sustainable investing and characterized by the integration of ESG values into investment decisions with the aim to achieve higher returns on investments which was popularized by the launch of UN's initiative Principles of Responsible Investment (UNPRI) in 2006. [2] As the focus is more on financial returns than ethical values, this new trend is named by as "responsible investment" omitting the "socially" segment. The last wave in sustainable investing covering the period after the late 2000s, is categorised as the "sustainable and impact investing" due to the emergence of impact investing and thematic investing as the new and alternative approaches with more focus on creating positive social and environmental impacts. While thematic investment refers to the investments focusing on certain trends such as climate change, circular economy or artificial intelligence etc. to capture the structural changes that may affect the entire industry, impact investing refers to investments made with the intention to generate positive environmental and social impacts.

Despite the fact that social and environmental concerns have long influenced investment decisions, generating comprehensive, consistent and comparable data and indicators to capture the magnitude of these investments has still remained to be a challenging issue. These challenges were addressed at the 2021 International Conference on Statistics of Sustainable Finance, co-organized by the Bank of France and Deutsche Bundesbank, and were summarized in three main categories. Incomplete firm-level data, fragmented reporting standards, and the lack of adequate metadata were included in the first category as factors which hinder standardized data production in sustainable finance. Furthermore, the need for statistical methodological guidance to establish standardized definitions and classifications were highlighted in the second category. Lastly, the necessity of an improved international cooperation to address these analytical complexities were emphasised (BIS, 2022).

Currently, data on sustainable finance is being provided by different initiatives, institutions and private data companies, and the amount provided varies according to the scope of sustainable finance concept as well as the strategies and instruments included. An example of the regional-level efforts of official institutions is the step taken by the European Central Bank and the national central banks of all EU members to develop indicators on climate-related risks and sustainable finance and the first set of experimental indicators on the issuance and holdings of sustainable debt securities was developed in November 2023 (ECB, 2024). At the global level, the Global Sustainable Investment Alliance (GSIA), an international membership-based collaboration consisting of sustainable investment organizations, have been publishing biennial reviews based on regional data from across the United States, Canada, Japan, Australia, New Zealand and Europe. According to the fifth edition of its Global Sustainable Investment Review (GSIR), covering the period 2018-2020 and-global sustainable investment amount reached to USD 35.3 trillion assets under management (AUM)[3] at the start of 2020, increasing 15% in the previous two-year period and constituting a total of 35.9% of all AUM. However, at the beginning of 2022, the total amount of sustainable investment finance decreased to USD 30.3 trillion AUM, mainly due to an update in the calculation methodology of the US Sustainable Investment Forum, the member institution providing the US sustainable finance data to the GSIA, and as a result, the share of sustainable investment assets in total global AUM decreased to 24.4% (Figure 2).

Figure 2. Global Sustainable Investment Assets 2012-2022 (AUM USD trillions)

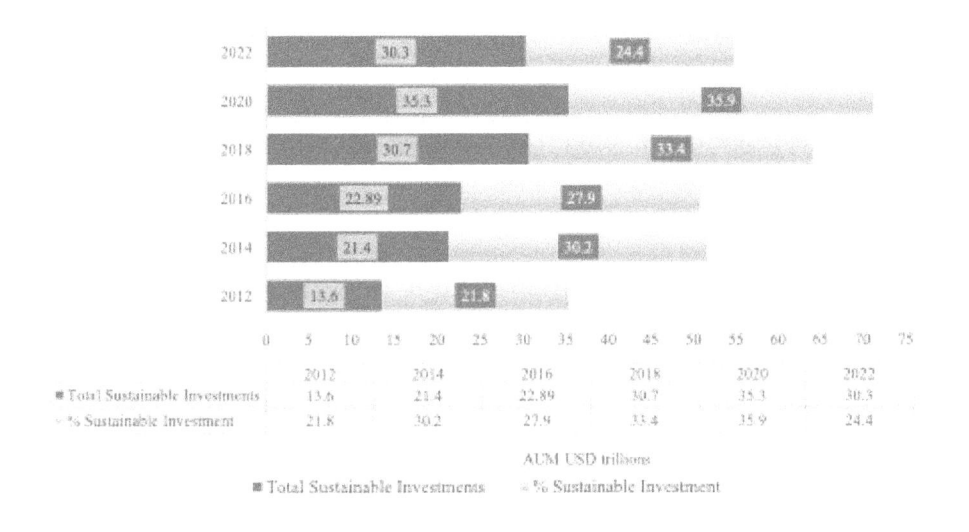

	2012	2014	2016	2018	2020	2022
Total Sustainable Investments	13.6	21.4	22.89	30.7	35.3	30.3
% Sustainable Investment	21.8	30.2	27.9	33.4	35.9	24.4

However, as an example of the challenges mentioned earlier regarding the lack of methodological guidance on gathering data for sustainable finance, it is important to note that, while the GSIA is the primary source of global-level data, each regional data source covered in the main report uses a different methodology to generate the relevant regional data. This diversity in methodologies poses a risk of weaknesses in consolidating the data. Moreover, until very recently, surveys have been allowing the selection of sub-strategies more than once. making it difficult to observe the share of different strategies. Additionally, since the European member institution of the GSIA stopped collecting data for these sub-strategies, this information could not be included in the last report. Thus, these structural parameters regarding to the surveys makes the comparison of the amount of sustainable finance provided each year and its subcomponents impossible.

In an effort to standardize the definitions of common sustainable finance-related terms, the Chartered Financial Analyst Institute (CFA), GSIA, and the Principles for Responsible Investment (PRI) grouped these different approaches under the umbrella term "responsible investment" into five categories, four of which covered under the term of ESG investment in the following section, while the fifth strategy, impact investment will be the subject of a separate examination in the subsequent section due to its focus on creating a positive impact and thus the potential for contributing to the transition to post-growth era (CFA Institute et al., 2023).

3. ESG INVESTMENT

The four different responsible investment strategies covered by (CFA Institute et al., 2023) consist of *Screening*, *ESG integration*, *Thematic Investing* and *Stewardship*. Screening refers to the process of deciding on investments based on pre-defined qualitative and quantitative ESG criteria, such as whether the investee is a part of a specific ESG index or whether a percentage of its revenues from the production/consumption of banned products go beyond the permitted levels or achieve a given gender diversity performance score. Screening also can be grouped into five categories: *exclusionary*, *negative*, *positive*, *best-in-class*, and *norms-based* screening, depending on how screening rules are applied. Exclusionary and negative screenings involve excluding investments based on ESG and undesirable ESG criteria. In many places, these two terms are used interchangeably. On the other hand, positive screening involves including investments that meet positive ESG criteria. Best-in-class screening directs investments to companies that outperform their peers in meeting certain desirable ESG criteria. Lastly, norms-based screening is based on compliance with relevant international conventions. ESG integration, on the other hand, denotes the inclusion of ESG-related qualitative and quantitative information into the investment and decision-making analysis to make an improved risk and return analysis, as it is believed that asset prices do not reflect the impact of all of the ESG-related factors. Stewardship, also known as corporate engagement and shareholder actions, includes direct engagement such as communication with senior management and/or board of companies, co-filling shareholder proposals and proxy voting. Thematic investment points out to the selection of assets linked to the economic, technological, political, environmental, social and regulatory dynamics, such as climate change, circular economy or ageing population, as it is believed that these dynamics are the main determinants of the investment risks and return. Based on the sustainable investment reviews by the GSIA, it was found that negative screening used to be the primary method of ESG investments, followed by ESG integration and stewardship (Figure 3). However, stewardship has recently emerged as the leading strategy, followed by ESG integration. Impact investments, which will be discussed further in the following section, constitute less than 1% of all sustainable investment assets in the covered regions, such as the United States, Canada, Japan, Australia, and New Zealand in 2022 (CFA Institute et al., 2023; GSIA, 2020, 2022).

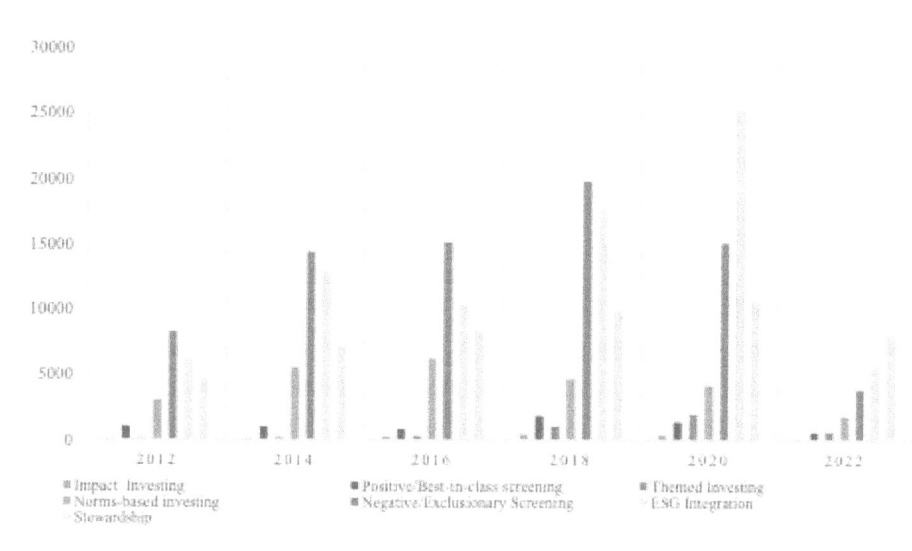

Figure 3. Sustainable Investment Assets by Strategy, 2012-2022

Source: (GSIA, 2012, 2014, 2022)

As the figures indicate, ESG investment is a widely recognised sustainable investment approach. There is also great potential for further growth due to escalating environmental concerns and the increasing focus on climate-related policies at national and international levels. Additionally, ESG investments have the potential to encourage greater public advocacy by requiring companies to track and report their actions on various issues, which can prompt corporate leaders to modify their behaviours (Hornberger, 2023). However, the ability of ESG investing to produce positive ESG outcomes remains limited, as environmental and social factors are often viewed primarily as risks, and investors' primary objective is often to enhance their assets' performance and mitigate these risks. As stated in the OECD report on ESG investing (Boffo & Patalano, 2020), ESG investments aim to maximise financial returns by using ESG factors to assess medium and long-term risks and opportunities. Investor surveys referred in the same report also emphasise that the pursuit of maximising financial returns and enhancing risk-management systems are key motivating factors for integrating ESG factors. Hornberger (2023) illustrates this with examples from energy companies, where efforts to reduce carbon emissions are primarily motivated by the desire to protect financial interests rather than by environmental concerns, as climate change poses a significant threat to their bottom line.

In addition, although they have a relatively long history, challenges on the operational side impede ESG investments from performing better in serving the sustainable business practices. One of the important challenges has been the fact of green-washing, where companies, even larger and reputable ones, tend to create a positive ESG facade while continuing to engage in harmful practices that ultimately bolster their financial performance (Ma, 2024) . One of the reasons for greenwashing is the lack of sufficient control mechanisms regarding the generation and disclosure of information related to ESG criteria. Carbon emissions of companies are one of the most readily available pieces of information in ESG-related factors. In a study by In & Schumacher (2021) attention is drawn to the increasing prevalence of carbon-washing as a result of the fragmented regulations and proliferation of actors involved in the regulation and governance of climate action. It is noted that companies themselves are the primary generators of their carbon data, and its disclosure is not subject to regulation. The lack of regulation leads to the dissemination of false and manipulative information through various marketing mechanisms for public relations purposes, in order to continue selling their services/products and to meet funding requirements (Guo et al., 2020; In & Schumacher, 2021). As a matter of fact, numerous greenwashing cases are brought to the public attention each year (AKEPA, 2023; Robinson, 2022). Also, an analysis of net-zero targets of all companies in the Forbes Global 2000 list and their relevant managerial actions show that only 66% of companies have a relevant reporting mechanism in place, and only 50% of the companies have published plans outlining the steps they would take to meet these targets (Black et al., 2021).

Additionally, discrepancies between methodologies used in calculating the ESG ratings and indices by the third-party data providers, resulting in different ratings for the same companies, constitute a misleading factor hindering investors' sound assessment of the ESG performance of companies and funds. Difference in ratings arise from a number of factors, including differences in frameworks used by rating providers, prioritisation of sub-categories, incorporation of events/cases indicating to the incapability of the companies dealing with certain ESG issues, weightings, indicators and expert judgements (Boffo & Patalano, 2020). In a study based on the data from six established rating agencies, Berg et al. (2022) find the correlation between different ESG ratings change from 0.31 to 0.71 and utilisation of different indicators for the same attributes is found to be the main and most difficult factor to be solved, with being other two are the usage of different sets of attributes and divergence in their relative weights. As these ratings and indices help to turn the ESG disclosures and reporting into inputs that direct and shape investment decisions, the differences in the scoring for the same company can be quite misleading. Additionally, it is suggested there is an ESG scoring bias in favour of large companies and developed economies against SMEs and emerging markets resulting from the lack of technical and financial resources and experience (Boffo & Patalano, 2020).

The lack of standardisation in reporting has posed another challenge that needs to be addressed to enhance the transparency and the impact of ESG investing practices. Efforts have been made to address this issue, such as the Global Reporting Initiative (GRI), founded in 1997, setting global standards for sustainability reporting in 2016 and continuing to provide standards for companies in this field. Other reporting initiatives have recently been consolidated into the International Financial Reporting Standards (IFRS) Foundation, which supports the establishment of the International Sustainability Standards Board (ISSB).[4] However, according to the latest sustainability survey by World of Federation of Exchanges in 2024, in which 44 exchanges participated, a lack of consensus regarding the reporting standards is still observed; as 66% of the respondents encouraged or required the GRI, which is followed by the ISSB, the Task Force on Climate related Financial Disclosures (TFCD)[5] and others (WFE, 2024).

In a study examining the effectiveness of different ESG investment strategies, Kölbel et al. (2020) first differentiate the investor impact and company impact and points out that investors can only have an indirect impact (*investor impact*) on social and environmental parameters through the companies they invest in and whose activities can actually contribute (*company impact*) to the desired changes. They highlight three main strategies for investor impact: shareholder engagement, capital allocation, and indirect impacts. Shareholder engagement, which includes activities such as voting on proposals and discussions with management, is considered the most reliable strategy, while capital allocation is not found equally effective and the effectiveness of indirect impacts remained unproven. Also, the impact of shareholder engagement is found to be positively influenced by the investor's involvement and the company's experience in ESG issues, whereas it is negatively affected by the cost of requested changes, suggesting that even the most effective ESG investment strategy has the potential to bring about incremental improvements in environmental and social issues rather than fundamental and long-term changes.

4. IMPACT INVESTMENT

The concept of impact investing emerged in 2007[6] to characterize an investment approach that seeks to produce positive, quantifiable social and environmental effects alongside financial returns (GIIN, 2023) and is perceived to hold greater potential for addressing societal and environmental challenges compared to investments based solely on ESG criteria.

Grabenwarter & Liechtenstein (2011) identify five key features of the impact investing: a profit objective, a positive correlation between the intended social impact and the financial return of the investment, an intentional and measurable social impact, and a result that brings about a net positive change to society. The GIIN definition aligns with these characteristics, except for the positive correlation sought between the intended social impact and the financial return. (Schlütter et al., 2023), based on a systematic literature review, expand this definition to include professional investors engaging in impact investing in companies, organizations, and funds with the intention to create a measurable social and/or environmental impact alongside a financial return paid by the investee.

Figure 4. Comparison of the ESG and Impact Investment

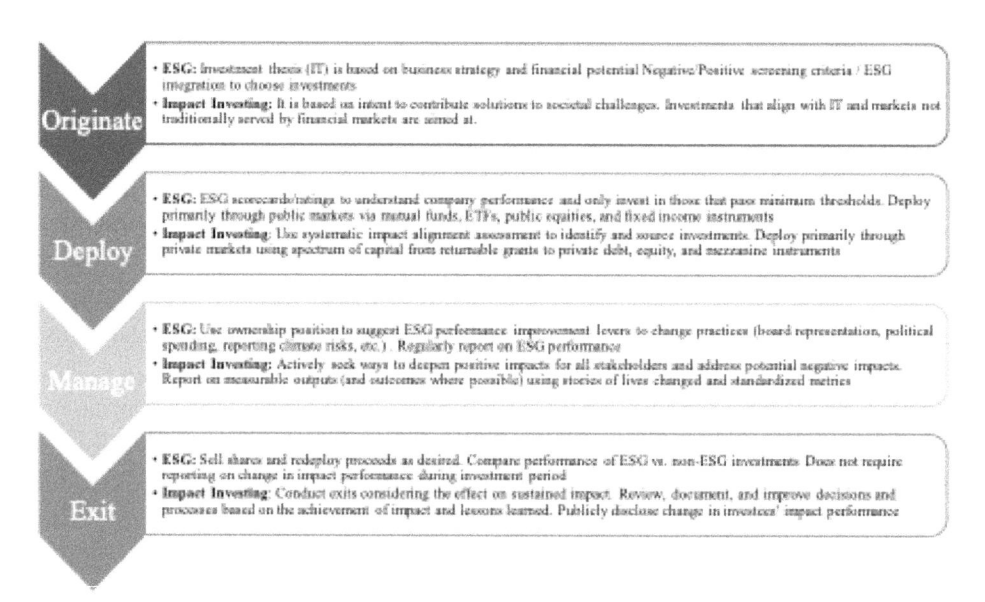

Originate
- **ESG:** Investment thesis (IT) is based on business strategy and financial potential Negative/Positive screening criteria / ESG integration to choose investments
- **Impact Investing:** It is based on intent to contribute solutions to societal challenges. Investments that align with IT and markets not traditionally served by financial markets are aimed at.

Deploy
- **ESG:** ESG scorecards/ratings to understand company performance and only invest in those that pass minimum thresholds. Deploy primarily through public markets via mutual funds, ETFs, public equities, and fixed income instruments
- **Impact Investing:** Use systematic impact alignment assessment to identify and source investments. Deploy primarily through private markets using spectrum of capital from returnable grants to private debt, equity, and mezzanine instruments

Manage
- **ESG:** Use ownership position to suggest ESG performance improvement levers to change practices (board representation, political spending, reporting climate risks, etc.). Regularly report on ESG performance
- **Impact Investing:** Actively seek ways to deepen positive impacts for all stakeholders and address potential negative impacts. Report on measurable outputs (and outcomes where possible) using stories of lives changed and standardized metrics

Exit
- **ESG:** Sell shares and redeploy proceeds as desired. Compare performance of ESG vs. non-ESG investments. Does not require reporting on change in impact performance during investment period
- **Impact Investing:** Conduct exits considering the effect on sustained impact. Review, document, and improve decisions and processes based on the achievement of impact and lessons learned. Publicly disclose change in investees' impact performance

Hornberger (2023) differentiates impact investment and ESG investment throughout the four stages of an investment; initial stage, deployment, management and exit (Figure 4). In the initial stage, investment thesis differs considerably as it is based on a business strategy and financial potential of the investment, whereas in the impact investment it is based on intention to contribute solution to societal and environmental challenges and in that regard, impact investments are considered to be serving markets otherwise not funded by the traditional markets. Also, the assessment of potential investments differs, as well as the instruments used in each investment approach. In terms of management, on the other hand, ownership position is stated to be the most implemented strategy applied by ESG investors, whereas impact investors ideally are expected to seek different ways to increase the desired impacts for all stakeholders. In terms of reporting, ESG investments rely on reporting on ESG performance, whereas measurable outputs and, if possible, outcomes are the subjects of impact reporting. At the final stage, ESG investments do not require reporting on the realization of an impact led by the investors, whereas, in impact investment, public disclosure of the impact performance of investees is necessary.

As stated earlier, impact investments' market size is relatively small compared to ESG investments, partly due to their relatively recent emergence. The Global Impact Investing Network (GIIN) provides data about the global market size for impact investment meeting the GIIN's criteria. According to the latest data, as of December 2021, the market size of the impact investment is estimated to reach USD 1.164 trillion AUM, covering 3.349 organizations located in both developed and emerging markets and including but not limited to fund managers, development finance institutions, pension/retirement funds, foundations (Hand et al., 2022)[7]. International Financial Institution (IFC), on the other hand, provides two different estimates for the market size for impact investment. The first segment represents market with impact measurement systems in place and estimated to be USD 505 billion AUM as of 2019 covering private funds and development finance institutions[8]. The second segment, on the other hand, represents a broader scope of assets managed with the intent for impact but do not have any measurement system in place, and estimated to be equal USD 2.1 trillion AUM (IFC, 2020).

Considering that fact that the cost of achieving sustainable development goals is estimated to be between $5.4 and $6.4 trillion annually until 2030 and private sector support is essential for governments to meet these financial needs, the current market size of impact investment falls short of supplying these necessary funds (UNCTAD, 2023).

Despite the limited size of the market, the role of impact investments is considered to be very important in addressing the environmental challenges and, as can be seen in the impact value chain demonstrated in Figure 5. This consideration arises from the difference between the outcome and final impact, as the latter one refers to the long-term social and environmental impact that the investment is expected to generate.

Figure 5. Impact Value Chain

	Input	Activity	Output	Outcome	Impact
Definition	Resources that are deployed in service of a certain (set of) activity.	Actions, or tasks, that are performed in support of specific impact objectives	Tangible, immediate practices, products and services that result from the activities that are undertaken	Changes, or effects, on individuals or the environment from the products and services	Changes, or effects, on society or the environment that follow from outcomes that have been achieved
Illustrative Example	Investments to an impact organization (e.g., in a microfinance institution)	Actions by an impact organization to attract clients (e.g., campaigns)	Number of clients served by an impact organization (e.g., pans extended)	Changes among clients (e.g., doubling of household income among MFI clients)	Changes in broader environment of the impact organization (e.g., less crime)
Illustrative Insight for Investors	Capital deployed (i.e., initial investment)	Activities undertaken Services rendered to deliver on impact through impact goals capital provided	Services rendered through impact capital provided	Income generated by beneficiaries due to impact capital	Impact on society due to impact capital

As impact investing becomes more popular, there is a growing variety of reporting methods and institutions dedicated to measuring the outcomes of impact investments. Many impact investors have developed their own metrics to track social and environmental performance, and there are numerous tools and platforms aimed at improving impact measurement and reporting developed by different institutions, such as Acumen Fund, GIIN, B Lab, and Social Value. The IRIS+ system, launched by GIIN as an updated version of Impact Reporting and Investment Standards (IRIS), has been a widely adopted tool, along with other metrics, to measure the outputs of impact investments (Bymolt, 2019; Hornberger, 2023).

However, while the intention to create a positive impact and its measurement are crucial aspects of impact investing, other essential factors, such as engaging with stakeholders to enhance the positive impacts for them, as stated in the above comparison with ESG investments, appear to be not common in current investment practices. In a recent report of a leading impact auditing company, it is stated that stakeholders' perspectives are generally overlooked in the impact reports of companies, and only 28% of verified investors now included the engagement of key affected stakeholders in their impact management systems. Also, there is a lack of a unified approach in determining ex-ante impact targets, resulting in underperformance in setting and assessing realised impacts against these targets, with only 22% of verified investors performing these practices well (BlueMark, 2022). Similarly, reporting unintended negative impacts is not a common practice, undermining the quality of impact reporting systems and raising concerns about this strategy's overall credibility and transparency (Hornberger, 2023).

Additionally, focusing on investors' motivations and willingness to pay, (Heeb et al. 2023) examines the sensitivity of their willingness to pay to the level of impact as an indicator of how much these investors are willing to create an impact. The study finds that investors are willing to pay for sustainable investments. However, their level of willingness does not increase with the level of the impact of these investments indicating to the financial limitations on creating impact. They also find that emotions play an important role in investors' approaches to impact, and their decisions are resulting more from being emotionally drawn to these particular targets rather than the impact itself, and that increases the risk of green/impact washing by making positive impact statements about investment assets while these statements are not backed by the investment strategy and asset portfolio. These concerns are confirmed by a study on SDG funds. Balitzky & Mosson (2024) focus on these funds to examine if they can have a positive and tangible impact by examining whether they are more invested in companies participating in the United Nations Global Compact (UNGC) initiative and countries with high SDG index scores. The study found that these funds do not significantly invest in more companies within the UNGC initiative or those targeting specific SDGs. This indicates that SDG funds claiming to contribute to SDGs do not seem more closely aligned with the UN SDGs than non-SDG funds.

In that regard, in terms of how effective these impact funds in realizing their expected benefits Cole et al. (2023) focus on the impact of impact investors and find that they mainly invest in disadvantaged areas, build new industries and markets, and are willing to provide more risk-tolerant and patient capital regarding traditional investors. However, it is also found that impact investing is not effective in helping new enterprises that could not otherwise attract capital from other investors, and in the post-investment period, employee welfare declines significantly, even more than following a comparable traditional investment.

In addition, although impact investments have the motivation to create a certain impact, it is important to note that this motivation is always combined with a financial return. In this context, in the 2019 IFC survey of 50 impact investors, 84% of respondents reported aiming for risk-adjusted market-rate returns, while only 15% indicated that target returns were not a single choice (IFC, 2019). According to the latest investor survey of GIIN, 74% of investors aim for market-rate returns adjusted for risk, while the rest strive for returns that are either below market rate but closer to market rate or capital preservation. The return expectations also vary by investor type, with 90% of institutional asset owners targeting market-rate returns, whereas 56% of development financial institutions and only 38% of foundations aim for market-rate returns (Hand et al., 2023). The findings clearly demonstrate that although impact investing is a more positive tool than traditional and ESG investments due to its ability to create positive value, its potential stays limited due to the important role that expected financial returns play in investment decisions.

5. TRANSFORMATIVE INVESTMENT APPROACHES

The inadequacy of ESG and impact investment in producing the expected positive effects has also faced structural criticisms and been the subject of numerous studies. Amongst them, Utz & Wimmer (2014), based on a comprehensive analysis of socially responsible funds in the US, found that these funds do not guarantee the exclusion of unethical companies and do not significantly increase ethical assets. This undermines the premise that ESG investing approaches socially outperform traditional funds. Additionally, in a study focusing on divestments in agricultural and renewable energy sectors, Neville (2020) argues that while divestments are crucial, a lack of scrutiny on reinvestments and the current economic order can result in reinforcing the same system. Based on the analysis of a sample of 50 divestment announcement between 2014-2022, Dordi & Weber (2019) provides an example of the inadequacy of the divestments on the fossil fuel sector finding that these announcements do not have a statistically measurable effect on the stock price of fossil fuel companies. Also, the voluntary nature of sustainable investment strategies has sparked criticism for being limited reformist concessions, rather than transformative measures that could bring about real change to the current system which is considered the root cause of the current environmental crisis (Reynolds & Ciplet, 2023). In a study conducted between 2009-2013, covering 22 semi-structured interviews conducted with US-based shareholder activists, King & Gish.E (2015) observed the evolution of social movements advocating for better corporate practices and noted the potential risk of these movements turning into "hybrid" for-profit businesses while still aiming for change, citing examples such as fair trade and organic agriculture. In this context, Penna et al. (2023) state that that these sustainable investment approaches only serve to optimize the system, rather than transforming it.

The criticisms have given rise to a new wave of investment strategies. In the meantime, some financial institutions have also begun to acknowledge the need for a systemic change, in some cases using the term "post-growth" in their reports to describe the economy they are aiming to operate and live in the future (Aviva Investors, 2022; Triodos Investment Management, 2024).

In this context, Reynolds & Ciplet (2023) proposes a new framework for transformative investment based on environmental justice and neo-Gramscian theories. This framework is anchored by three fundamental principles. The first principle, *"cumulative responsibility"*, seeks to eradicate the environmental and social damage caused by an investment by preventing the replacement of one harm with another. In this regard, this principle mainly strives for a holistic investment approach across all sectors and impacts, covering the entire value chains of corporations and eliminating trade-offs between harmful industries. Thus, it is argued that investors should focus on investing in companies that actively promote environmental justice rather than just avoiding those companies engaging in environmentally and socially awful business practices. As an example of this approach, it is suggested that rather than simply excluding companies from investment portfolios based on limited or no reinvestment criteria, a comprehensive screening process should be applied. This screening should consider the full impact of investments across time and space and include criteria for reinvesting money in companies and projects that align with social, economic, and environmental justice.

The second principle, *"embedded accountability"*, entails restructuring top-down decision-making processes within companies to include direct engagement with affected communities and enhanced accountability. In this regard, the voices of these communities should be central to the decision-making processes of projects that might affect them, and their knowledge and identities should be acknowledged as crucial to the success of those processes. By granting impacted community members formal decision-making authority over screening criteria and in shareholder meetings, this principle aims to transfer the control of investment measures from small groups of financial experts to those who are most susceptible to the negative effects of the investment.

Lastly, the framework underscores the necessity of a comprehensive strategy and movement aimed at challenging the existing structure rooted in oppressive and exploitative practices (*"counter-hegemonic practices"*). To tackle the lack of collective action and challenges arising from the profit-focused approach of current sustainable investment methods, this principle acknowledges the limitations of market-based solutions in addressing systemic inequalities. It calls for regulatory systems that can significantly restrict corporate activities to support social and environmental protections, in order to drive widespread and structural changes across the global economy. Examples aligned with this principle include advocating for broader regulations of the financial industry, supporting grassroots justice efforts, and addressing structural barriers to systemic change.

Another approach that offers a new investment framework, also named as *"transformative investment"* as an alternative to existing approaches and aiming for a system transformation towards the solution of the environmental and social crises we are going through is based on the deep transition thinking, which provides a theoretical framework to understand how systems change unfolds over time. Recognizing the long historical perspective of contemporary problems integrated into the socio-technical systems established by the Industrial Revolution, referred to as the "First

Deep Transition," it is believed that a fundamental system change is necessary to overcome these challenges, which may lead to the "Second Deep Transition". In this regard, after an extensive and structured dialogue between sustainability transitions experts and a global Deep Transition Panel of investors over a year, it was affirmed that the deep transitions theory is applicable to investment practices, leading to the articulation of an investment philosophy based on 12 transformative investment principles summarized in Table 1 (Schot et al., 2022; Schot & Kanger, 2018). These principles are regarded to surpass the definitions of impact investing and ESG investing while still sharing common elements with both investment approaches.

Table 1. Principles of "Transformative Investment"

Goal Setting	a. Transforming the system Rather than optimising specific impact outcomes or ESG criteria, aiming for the transformative potential of the investments as systems change is the only way to achieve a sustainable and desirable future.
	b. Thinking long term Investment structures like evergreen funds or those incentivizing long-term holding align more with long-term change. While achieving system change impacts may take years, financial returns are expected to materialize sooner as markets anticipate future financial flows.
	c. Including and giving voice Engaging local communities and key stakeholders in assessing significant transformations and involve them in decision-making. Encourage transparent dialogue and discussions to enhance stakeholder and community participation.
Investment strategy-related	a. Visualise desirable futures Defining the key characteristics of the desired future world and integrating these traits into investment strategies.
	b. Enhancing portfolio synergies Designing a portfolio approach allows for implementing various system changes, such as introducing investment tools or policy programs to establish a new meta-regime (such as circular economy) across multiple systems centred around coordinated production, consumption, and distribution practices.
	c. Embracing uncertainty Anticipating a high level of investment risk and recognizing the need for experimental capital, as it has the potential to create transformative investment opportunities that will appeal to market-driven investors. Additionally, funding can be in the form of donations, concessional capital, public funding, or in-kind support.

continued on following page

Table 1. Continued

Investment process-related	a. Contextualising in transition dynamics Investments alone cannot create or steer a deep transition process. However, they can contribute to ongoing change processes and potentially influence their direction. Therefore, it is recommended to consider each investment in relation to ongoing deep transition dynamics.
	b. Avoiding lock-in solutions, impeding deeper system change Avoiding solutions that could prevent deeper systemic change, by blocking potential transformation and locking systems into unsustainable paths, while providing optimizing the system
	c. Fostering collective action among related actors Partnerships and collaborations among investors, policy makers, and other stakeholders to have better influence on a system at various levels. Examples include partnerships between investors with different risk-reward expectations, such as through blended finance structures, as well as collaborations between investors and policy makers, along with buyers, suppliers, intermediaries, and other market participants.
Experimentation	a. Experimenting with transformative tools Exploring transformative investment tools and methods from the Deep Transitions framework and contributing to their development over time.
	b. Fostering interdisciplinary research Ongoing interdisciplinary collaboration to assess, measure, and monitor the transformational potential and performance of investments over time, including learning and unlearning processes by all stakeholders involved.
	c. Sharing Learnings Sharing lessons, data, insights, successes, and failures among stakeholders, while encouraging open-source materials to enable replication and adoption of transformative investment practices.

Source: (Schot et al., 2022)

Within this general framework, Penna et al. (2023) further outlines a set of four rules based on these principles. In the first rule, financial return from investing in system change is prioritised; however, it is proposed that instead of focusing on non-financial values contributing to financial return, this approach emphasises that maximising financial return should stem from its impact on system change, recognising the necessity for a legal mandate for assessing whether financial return is coming from investments contributing to the system change or not. In the second rule, the definition of fiduciary duty is broadened in recognising the importance of change in the system in ensuring the creation/protection of long-term value and in that regard, legislative changes to realign the obligation of investment fiduciary, promotion of legal reforms and guidelines for incorporating and aligning investments with system change scenarios and future shock considerations as well as equivalent revisions in the internal policies, norms and risk assessment tools and cultural changes are proposed. The third rule involves mapping out unquantifiable systemic uncertainties, including those related to societal challenges, broader consequences, and rebound effects, by integrating future scenarios into investment decisions. This rule also recognises the importance of multi-stakeholder forums or working groups, which provide diverse perspectives for scenario and uncertainty analysis and allow for input from affected individuals and organizations. The final rule aims to maximise the impact of system change with a long-term focus. Sustainable investing strategies should prioritise advancing activities, projects, and companies that have the potential to drive system change and contribute to long-term transformations. This can be achieved by developing new portfolio management strategies, system change impact metrics, regulatory reforms, and initiatives to change investors' mindset through programs like new training curricula.

In this regard, as the comparison of this "transformative investment" framework with ESG and impact investment practices is provided in Table 2 for a better illustration of the implications on current investment practices. With the aim to create systemic changes, this new perspective aims to invest in areas and practices that trigger changes in other areas along the impact chain, whereas ESG and impact investments are defined as helpful only to fix the problems (symptoms) arising from the current economic model. In this regard, the outcome of the investment in this framework would be the change in a living practice or a consumption model as opposed to the improvements in certain indicators related to a certain activity. Instead of individual sectors and industries, this approach also proposes to invest in multiple sectors and systems, considering the interlinkages between them. Additionally, collaboration among investors and other relevant actors is emphasised and regarded as necessary in order to act jointly in areas that will create targeted systemic effects, develop new methods and produce solutions.

Table 2. A Comparison of of ESG/Impact Investment and "Transformative Investment"

ESG and Impact Investing Practices	"Transformative Investment"
Aims for short-term positive impact with at least market rate return. Functions as a symptomatic (global warming, biodiversity loss) treatment rather than targeting systemic changes to eliminate the rooted causes. Such as reducing emissions and increasing efficiencies in an manufacturing industry or providing access to clean water in an underdeveloped region	Aims to enhance positive impact within multiple dynamic systems. Investment is considered a means to accelerate transformation processes by strategically targeting key leverage points in single or multiple systems. For example, the transition to a production and consumption model of more durable and shared-use goods.
Consider the risks and outcomes of an investment in terms of set, easily measurable ESG factors, such as CO_2 emissions avoided, areas reclaimed for forest or the number of people given access to power	Considers the investment's outcome in terms of its impact on the underlying and guiding rules embedded within a system. For instance, replacing individual car ownership with shared mobility services, or shifting from centralized energy production to decentralized renewable energy systems.

continued on following page

Table 2. Continued

ESG and Impact Investing Practices	"*Transformative Investment*"
Invest in specific industry sectors and tackle specific challenges within single systems, such as deep engagement with agri-tech or renewable energy but in separate efforts.	Investing across various sectors and systems, aiming to comprehend new innovations, products, and solutions as opportunities that exist within a broader interconnected network of systems
Investors usually work independently based on the investment opportunities that are presented to them.	Investors are encouraged to collaborate with each other and other stakeholders, such as the public sector and organizations, to create solutions and investment opportunities.

Source: (Deep Transitions Lab, 2022)

6. DISCUSSION AND CONCLUDING REMARKS

As finance sector has the potential to shape the real economy and society, this study focuses on investment approaches to explore their role and contribution to addressing the complex environmental, social, and economic challenges we have been experiencing. Since the environmental and social problems grow unnoticed, related concerns have gradually been integrated into investment strategies. However, as the current growth-oriented economic model is proven to be unsustainable in many aspects, a transition into a post-growth era where economic policy no longer prioritises continuous growth but instead focuses on maintaining social and environmental stability and well-being considering the planetary boundaries seems inevitable. In that regard, traditional sustainable investment approaches have proven inadequate in triggering this transition. This is not solely due to the need for improvements, such as standardised reporting and measurements, inadequate mechanisms to prevent deceptive practices such as greenwashing, but also stems from the prioritisation of financial returns over long-term value creation/protection, the absence of a holistic impact perspective, and the lack of legislative infrastructure enforcing this perspective as well as its implementation. In other words, these approaches are still rooted in a growth-oriented perspective that is believed to be one of the fundamental causes of the polycrisis we are living in now. Thus, while they are, to a varying extent, trying to reduce harm and create positive impacts, they promote the continuation of the same economic model and serve to the root of our long-existing problems. Even the most successful examples of impact investment eventually compensate for the harm given by the current economic system rather than transforming it in a sustainable, regenerative and inclusive way.

As a result, new perspectives have emerged, aiming to uncover the transformative power of investments and provide a roadmap for the necessary steps. While these perspectives do not explicitly advocate moving away from the growth-oriented economic system, they do stress the importance of creating long-term and systemically transformative impacts. They advocate for abandoning short-termism and profit-oriented approaches, increasing stakeholder engagement in decision-making processes, and establishing the necessary legislative and regulatory background. Both approaches also acknowledge that fully implementing these principles is challenging and requires international consensus, ownership, and embodiment of this mindset by all economic actors.

While adopting these principles and their full implementation may take time, there are innovative investment tools and business models that can be useful and viable in fuelling the targeted transformation of the system. In this regard, revenue-based and profit-share finance models, where the investor receives a certain percentage of the revenue/profit generated by the enterprise until a certain level of return expectation of the investor is met, prevent the enterprises from being forced for rapid and destructive growth and provide them with a non-dilutive capital option without making changes to the ownership structure. Redeemable equity constitutes another funding model functioning similarly in the sense that it provides a flexible repayment plan and less/non-dilutive capital for the investees (Haumann & Feldthus, 2023). Additionally, fund management companies that move away from profit-oriented structures operate as perpetual purpose trusts and make venture capital investments without applying a specific exit date, which also contributes to the long-term goals of the invested companies (Ekeland, 2022). Moreover, the not-for-profit economic model (Hinton, 2020; Hinton & D. Maclurcan, 2017) offers a concrete and applicable example of where to invest in to create a long term and structural change, and how the companies in which investments are made can carry forward systemic transformation through their operational models. Indeed, investing in areas, activities, and business models that create transformative effects within the system's operation and/or contribute to these effects represents one of the viable paths to transitioning to a post-growth economy.

These innovative financial tools will no doubt be more effective in the shift to a post-growth era within a supportive regulatory environment and a business mindset. It is equally important to consider the change in the economic system, shifting the focus from growth to establishing a regenerative, sustainable, and inclusive system to address the current complex challenges. This transformation should be embraced by all economic actors, including large corporations, SMEs, start-ups, and individuals, as our consumption-oriented society is a significant product of the continuous growth-focused system. This shift in mindset is perhaps the most significant challenge in this transition and requires a sufficient amount of time. However, these gradual changes progress quickly when implemented from top to bottom. Governments and policymakers, in that sense, have a pivotal role in shaping, regulating, and promoting this transformation.

It should also be noted that abandoning profit maximisation does not mean not making any profit or not expecting a return from investments. Rather, it refers to making investments not for the sole purpose of making profit, but rather to achieve certain targets. When economic policy focuses on maintaining social and environmental stability, economic growth becomes a tool for achieving these objectives. As a result, profits and returns, acting as a catalyst for growth, ultimately help to establish socio-economic equilibrium by breaking away from the pattern of earning more, producing more, and generating more profit.

This study aimed to establish the foundation for future theoretical and empirical research on the role of current sustainable investment practices and new transformative investment approaches in the transition to a post-growth era, despite some limitations. The primary limitation is the lack of comparable, standardized, and comprehensive qualitative and quantitative data on various sustainable investment practices, as well as their performance and impacts. Once improvements in their collection and standardization are achieved, further research can be conducted to assess the scale of different investment strategies and models, their impacts, taking this study to the next level.

Additionally, the legislative and regulatory framework was not within the scope of this study. However, there are existing gaps in regulations that need to be addressed to increase the effectiveness of traditional sustainable investment practices and to allow investments to be more transformative.

Moreover, further empirical research can be conducted to explore the role of new innovative investment models in supporting enterprises and projects with the potential to contribute to the post growth transition. Finally, of course, more theoretical, regulatory, and empirical work on transformative investment perspectives is needed to accelerate their implementation.

REFERENCES

AKEPA. (2023, July 21). *Greenwashing: 14 recent stand-out examples.* https://thesustainableagency.com/blog/greenwashing-examples/#delta

Anderson, K. (2024, April 27). *The International Integrated Reporting Council (IIRC).* Greenly.Institute. https://greenly.earth/en-gb/blog/company-guide/the-international-integrated-reporting-council-iirc

Aviva Investors. (2022, September 22). *The Levers of Change A systems approach to reconcile finance with planetary boundaries.* The Macro Stewardhip Edition.

Balitzky, S., & Mosson, N. (2024). *Impact investing – Do SDG funds fulfil their promises?* https://www.esma.europa.eu/sites/default/files/2024-02/ESMA50-524821-3098_TRV_article_-_Impact_investing_-_Do_SDG_funds_fulfil_their_promises.pdf

Berg, F., Kölbel, J. F., & Rigobon, R. (2022). Aggregate Confusion: The Divergence of ESG Ratings. *Review of Finance*, 26(6), 1315–1344. DOI: 10.1093/rof/rfac033

BIS. (2022). *IFC Bulletin No 56 Statistics for Sustainable Finance.* https://www.bis.org/ifc/publ/ifcb56.htm

Black, R., Cullen, K., Fay, B., Hale, T., Lang, J., Mahmood, S., & Smith, S. (2021). *Taking Stock: A global assessment of net zero targets.* https://eciu.net/analysis/reports/2021/taking-stock-assessment-net-zero-targets

BlueMark. (2022). *Making the Mark June 2022 Spotlighting Leadership in Impact Management.* https://bluemark.co/app/uploads/2024/01/bluemark-making-the-mark-2022-spotlighting-leadership-in-impact-management.pdf

Boffo, R., & Patalano, R. (2020). *ESG Investing: Practices, Progress and Challenges.* www.oecd.org/finance/ESG-Investing-Practices-Progress-and-Challenges.pdf

Bymolt, R. (2019). *Measuring what matters : The pathway to success in impact investment.* https://www.kit.nl/institute/publication/measuring-what-matters/

Cassiers, I., & Maréchal, K. (2018). The Economy in a Post Growth Era: What project and what philosophy? In Cassiers, I., Maréchal, K., & Méda, D. (Eds.), *Post-growth Economics and Society Exploring the Paths of a Social and Ecological Transition* (1st ed.). Routledge.

CFA Institute. PRI, & GSIA. (2023). *Definitions for Responsible Investment Approaches.* https://rpc.cfainstitute.org/-/media/documents/article/industry-research/definitions-for-responsible-investment-approaches.pdf

Cole, S., Jeng, L., Lerner, J., Rigol, N., & Roth, B. N. (2023). *What do impact investors do differently?* (31898). https://www.nber.org/papers/w31898

Daly, H. E. (2008). *Towards A Steady-State Economy Essay commissioned by the Sustainable Development Commission, UK*. the Sustainable Development Commission. https://is.muni.cz/el/1423/jaro2015/ENS242/um/55677449/3_Daly_2008_Towards_a_Steady_State_Economy.pdf

Deep Transitions Lab. (2022). *Unleashing the Power of Capital Transformative Investment*. https://www.transformativeinvestment.net/transformative-investment-3

Demaria, F., Schneider, F., Sekulova, F., & Martinez-Alier, J. (2013). What is Degrowth? From an Activist Slogan to a Social Movement. *Environmental Values*, 22(2), 191–215. DOI: 10.3197/096327113X13581561725194

Dordi, T., & Weber, O. (2019). The Impact of Divestment Announcements on the Share Price of Fossil Fuel Stocks. *Sustainability (Basel)*, 11(11), 3122. DOI: 10.3390/su11113122

ECB. (2024). *Experimental indicators on sustainable finance*. https://www.ecb.europa.eu/stats/all-key-statistics/horizontal-indicators/sustainability-indicators/data/html/ecb.climate_indicators_sustainable_finance.en.html

Ekeland, M. (2022). Post-Growth Finance: Crafting a New Economy. In Prophil (Ed.), *Post-Growth for Business* (Vol. 3, pp. 46–49). https://prophil.eu/wp-content/uploads/2022/04/PROPHIL_study_PostGrowthBusiness_COMPLET-WEB_EN_27-04-21_page-a-page.pdf

European Parliament. (2023, May 24). *Circular economy: definition, importance and benefits*. https://www.europarl.europa.eu/topics/en/article/20151201STO05603/circular-economy-definition-importance-and-benefits

Fioramonti, L. (2024). Post-growth theories in a global world: A comparative analysis. *Review of International Studies*, 1–11. DOI: 10.1017/S0260210524000214

FSB. (2023, July 23). *FSB Plenary meets in Frankfurt*. https://www.fsb.org/2023/07/fsb-plenary-meets-in-frankfurt/

Fullerton, J. (2015). *Regenerative Capitalism: How Universal Principles And Patterns Will Shape Our New Economy*. https://capitalinstitute.org/wp-content/uploads/2015/04/2015-Regenerative-Capitalism-4-20-15-final.pdf

Georgescu-Roegen, N. (1977). Inequality, Limits and Growth from a Bioeconomic Viewpoint. *Review of Social Economy*, 35(3), 361–375. DOI: 10.1080/00346767700000041

GIIN. (2023). *Impact Investing A Guide to this Dynamic Market*. https://thegiin.org/publication/post/about-impact-investing/#what-is-impact-investing

Grabenwarter, U., & Liechtenstein, H. (2011). In Search of Gamma - An Unconventional Perspective on Impact Investing. SSRN *Electronic Journal*. DOI: 10.2139/ssrn.2120040

GSIA. (2020). *Global Sustainable Investment Review 2020*. https://www.gsi-alliance.org/trends-report-2020/

GSIA. (2022). *Global Sustainable Investment Review 2022*. https://www.gsi-alliance.org/members-resources/gsir2022/

Guo, T., Zha, G., Lee, C. L., & Tang, Q. (2020). Does corporate green ranking reflect carbon-mitigation performance? *Journal of Cleaner Production*, 277, 123601. DOI: 10.1016/j.jclepro.2020.123601

Hallegatte, S., Heal, G., Fay, M., & Treguer, D. (2012). *From Growth to Green Growth- A Framework* (17841; NBER Working Papers).

Hand, D., Ringel, B., & Danel, A. (2022). *Sizing the Impact Investing Market : 2022*. https://thegiin.org/publication/research/impact-investing-market-size-2022/

Hand, D., Sunderji, S., & Pardo, N. M. (2023). *2023 Market GIINsight : Impact Investing Allocations*. Activity & Performance.

Haumann, O., & Feldthus, M. (2023). *The guide to alternative funding : 7 funding options relevant for a Post Growth Business*. https://postgrowthguide.notion.site/Open-Hub-7ff04fa753a644609e8ca98cdd594b2e?p=8dca0fbc0322414b91dfb4ba2848efbd&pm=s

Heeb, F., Kölbel, J. F., Paetzold, F., & Zeisberger, S. (2023). Do Investors Care about Impact? *Review of Financial Studies*, 36(5), 1737–1787. DOI: 10.1093/rfs/hhac066

Hickel, J. (2021). What does degrowth mean? A few points of clarification. *Globalizations*, 18(7), 1105–1111. DOI: 10.1080/14747731.2020.1812222

Hinton, J. (2020). Fit for purpose? Clarifying the critical role of profit for sustainability. *Journal of Political Ecology*, 27(1). Advance online publication. DOI: 10.2458/v27i1.23502

Hinton, J. (2021). Five key dimensions of post-growth business: Putting the pieces together. *Futures*, 131, 102761. DOI: 10.1016/j.futures.2021.102761

Hinton, J., & Maclurcan, D. (2017). A not-for-profit world beyond capitalism and economic growth? *Ephemera*, 17(1), 147–166.

Hornberger, K. (2023). *Scaling Impact: Finance and Investment for a Better World* (2023rd ed.). Palgrave Macmillan.

IFC. (2019). *Creating Impact: The Promise of Impact Investing*. https://www.ifc.org/en/insights-reports/2019/promise-of-impact-investing

IFC. (2020). *Growing Impact New Insights into the Practice of Impact Investing*. 04/06/2024https://www.ifc.org/en/insights-reports/2020/growing-impact

In, S. Y., & Schumacher, K. (2021). Carbonwashing: ESG Data Greenwashing in a Post-Paris World. In *Settling Climate Accounts* (pp. 39–58). Springer International Publishing. DOI: 10.1007/978-3-030-83650-4_3

Jackson, T. (2018). *The Post-Growth Challenge: Secular Stagnation, Inequality and the Limits to Growth* (12; CUSP Working Paper). https://cusp.ac.uk/themes/aetw/wp12/

King, L., & Gish, E. (2015). Marketizing social change: Social share- holder activism and responsible investing. *Sociological Perspectives*, 58(4), 711–730. DOI: 10.1177/0731121415576799

Kölbel, J. F., Heeb, F., Paetzold, F., & Busch, T. (2020). Can Sustainable Investing Save the World? Reviewing the Mechanisms of Investor Impact. *Organization & Environment*, 33(4), 554–574. DOI: 10.1177/1086026620919202

Ma, M. (2024). A Study on the Impact of ESG Greenwashing on Listed Companies — A Case Study of Volkswagen Group. *Advances in Economics. Management and Political Sciences*, 59(1), 315–322. DOI: 10.54254/2754-1169/59/20231139

Meadows, D., Meadows, D., Randers, J., & Behrens, W. W.III. (1972). *The Limits to Growth* (5th ed.). Universe Books.

Mudaliar, A., & Dithrich, H. (2019). *Sizing the Impact Investing Market 2019*. https://thegiin.org/publication/research/impinv-market-size/

Neville, K. J. (2020). Shadows of Divestment: The Complications of Diverting Fossil Fuel Finance. *Global Environmental Politics*, 20(2), 3–11. DOI: 10.1162/glep_a_00555

OECD. (2015). *All on Board : Making Inclusive Growth Happen*. OECD., DOI: 10.1787/9789264218512-

Parrique, T., Barth, J., Briens, F., Kuokkanen, A., & Spangenberg, J. H. (2019). Decoupling Debunked - Evidence and arguments against green growth as a sole strategy for sustainability. *European Environmental Bureau*. https://eeb.org/wp-content/uploads/2019/07/Decoupling-Debunked.pdf

Penna, C. C. R., Schot, J., & Steinmueller, W. (2023). Transformative investment: New rules for investing in sustainability transitions. *Environmental Innovation and Societal Transitions*, 49, 100782. DOI: 10.1016/j.eist.2023.100782

PGI. (2018). *What is post-growth economics and why is it necessary?* https://postgrowth.org/post-growth-economics/

PRI. (2017). *What are the principles for responsible investment?* https://www.unpri.org/about-us/what-are-the-principles-for-responsible-investment

Prophil. (2022). *Post-Growth for Business Rethinking Accounting, Governance And Business Models* (C. Houzelot & M. Deguet, Eds.; Vol. 3). Prophil. https://prophil.eu/wp-content/uploads/2022/04/PROPHIL_study_PostGrowthBusiness_COMPLET-WEB_EN_27-04-21_page-a-page.pdf

Raworth, K. (2017). *Doughnut Economics: Seven Ways to Think Like a 21st Century Economist*. Random House Business.

Reynolds, D., & Ciplet, D. (2023). Transforming Socially Responsible Investment: Lessons from Environmental Justice. *Journal of Business Ethics*, 183(1), 53–69. DOI: 10.1007/s10551-022-05070-9 PMID: 35287286

Robinson, D. (2022). *10 Companies Called Out For Greenwashing* (Pollution). https://earth.org/greenwashing-companies-corporations/

Schlütter, D., Schätzlein, L., Hahn, R., & Waldner, C. (2023). Missing the Impact in Impact Investing Research – A Systematic Review and Critical Reflection of the Literature. *Journal of Management Studies*. Advance online publication. DOI: 10.1111/joms.12978

Schot, J., Benedetti del Rio, R., Steinmueller, E., & Keesman, S. (2022). *Transformative Investment in Sustainability: An Investment Philosophy for the Second Deep Transition*.

Schot, J., & Kanger, L. (2018). Deep transitions: Emergence, acceleration, stabilization and directionality. *Research Policy*, 47(6), 1045–1059. DOI: 10.1016/j.respol.2018.03.009

Sparkes, R. (2001). Ethical investment: Whose ethics, which investment? *Business Ethics (Oxford, England)*, 10(3), 194–205. DOI: 10.1111/1467-8608.00233

The IFRS Foundation. (2023). *Consolidated Organisations (CDSB & VRF)*. https://www.ifrs.org/about-us/consolidated-organisations/

The Rockefeller Foundation. (2015). *The Rockefeller Foundation: Building a backbone to accelerate impact investing*. https://engage.rockefellerfoundation.org/story-sketch/the-rockefeller-foundation-weaving-ties-and-building-a-backbone-to-accelerate-impact-investing/

Triodos Investment Management. (2024). *Pathways to post-growth Long-term Investment Outlook 2024*. https://www.triodos-im.com/binaries/content/assets/tim/shared/investment-outlook/outlook-2024/long-term-outlook-2024.pdf

UNCTAD. (2023). *The costs of achieving the Sustainable Development Goals*. https://unctad.org/sdg-costing?utm_source=UNCTAD+Media+Contacts&utm_campaign=b0c0110038-EMAIL_CAMPAIGN_2020_06_10_02_38_COPY_01&utm_medium=email&utm_term=0_1b47b7abd3-b0c0110038-64981361

Utz, S., & Wimmer, M. (2014). Are they any good at all? A financial and ethical analysis of socially responsible mutual funds. *Journal of Asset Management*, 15(1), 72–82. DOI: 10.1057/jam.2014.8

WeAll. (2022). *What is a Wellbeing Economy?* https://weall.org/what-is-wellbeing-economy

WFE. (2024). *The WFE's Annual Sustainability Survey 2023: Exchanges' collective effort for a global transition to a sustainable economy*. https://www.world-exchanges.org/our-work/articles/wfe-10th-annual-sustainability-survey

KEY TERMS AND DEFINITIONS

ESG Factors: The term refers to the criteria that are used to assess a company's environmental and social impacts and governance practices.

ESG Investment Approach: This is the most common sustainable investment strategy, involving the consideration of ESG factors in investment practices, including screening, integration, thematic investing, and stewardship for risk/return optimization.

Impact Investment Approach: The term refers to a modern sustainable investment strategy that emerged in the early 2000s, and rather than solely focusing on ESG factors for risk and return optimization, this approach aims to generate positive and measurable environmental and social impact.

Planetary Boundaries: Refers to the biophysical thresholds in the Earth systems in which humanity and all living beings can survive and thrive.

Post-Growth Alternatives: The term refers to economic approaches that prioritize the well-being of humanity and the planet over economic growth, aiming to undo the damage caused by the current economic model.

Sustainable Investment Approach: The term refers to considering not only the financial returns of an investment but also its potential impact on environmental and social values, emphasizing the importance of ensuring that the invested company or project does not cause direct or indirect harm and instead contributes to creating long-term values.

Transformative Investment Approach: This a newly emerging investment approach arguing that investments should be directed to fields which can contribute to the transformation of the system in a way to eliminate the root causes of the systemic problems.

ENDNOTES

[1] The term "sustainable" refers to both reducing harm and doing no harm. Simply reducing harm is not enough now because our current way of living is exceeding the limits of what the planet can support. Thus, in this chapter, targeted sustainable practices mainly involve those that do not give harm to the environment and society.

[2] Signatories see their fiduciary role as acting in the best long-term interests of their beneficiaries. They evaluate environmental, social, and corporate governance issues as a risk parameter affecting the performance of investment portfolios(PRI, 2017).

[3] Assets under management (AUM), represent the total market value of the securities owned or managed by a financial institution (such as a bank, mutual fund, or hedge fund) on behalf of its clients.

[4] The ISSB was established on November 3, 2021. The Climate Disclosure Standards Board (CDSB) was incorporated into the IFRS Foundation to support the ISSB in January 2022, followed by the integration of the Value Reporting Foundation (VRF) in August 2022(The IFRS Foundation, 2023). The VRF was also formed in June 2021 through the merger of the International Integrated Reporting Council (IIRC) and the Sustainability Accounting Standards Board (SASB)(Anderson, 2024).

[5] The ISSB sustainability reporting standards are based on the TFCD, which has been disbanded as of November 2023 (FSB, 2023).

6   According to the Rockefeller Foundation, the term "impact investment" was first introduced at a conference in 2007 by the organization (The Rockefeller Foundation, 2015).

7   This figure excludes some type green bonds that are not held as part of a specific impact investment strategy, the impact of which cannot be measured and managed (Hand et al., 2022).

8   This estimate is very close to the GIIN's impact investment market size estimation in the same year, which is USD 502 billion AUM (Mudaliar & Dithrich, 2019).

Chapter 9
Which Fiscal Instruments Do Corrupt Governments Prefer During Fiscal Consolidation Episodes?

Kerim Peren Arin
https://orcid.org/0000-0002-6991-2468
Zayed University, UAE & CAMA, Australia

Elif Boduroğlu
https://orcid.org/0000-0003-1132-7159
Atilim University, Turkey

Esref Ugur Celik
https://orcid.org/0000-0001-9090-9346
Atilim University, Turkey

Nicola Spagnolo
Brunel University London, UK & University of Campania "Luigi Vanvitelli", Italy

ABSTRACT

This study investigates the fiscal policy choices of corrupt governments during periods of fiscal consolidation. By using the same dataset by Arin et al. (2011), our analysis of pooled observations for 18 OECD countries reveals two key findings: (i) corrupt governments tend to raise indirect taxes rather than reduce expenditures during fiscal adjustments, and (ii) they yield to political lobbying and pressure by lowering corporate taxes and increasing social benefits and subsidies during substantial fiscal adjustment episodes.

DOI: 10.4018/979-8-3693-5508-4.ch009

Copyright © 2025, IGI Global. Copying or distributing in print or electronic forms without written permission of IGI Global is prohibited.

1. INTRODUCTION

Modern governments prioritize economic stability and the effective management of public debt as crucial objectives. These goals significantly influence citizens' assessments of government performance. Therefore, governments aim to reduce budget deficits and promote economic growth through rigorous fiscal policies (Reinhart & Rogoff, 2010; Makhoba et al., 2021; Albu & Albu, 2021). However, keeping budget deficits and public debt at sustainable levels is a complex task, shaped by both economic and political factors. Governments often turn to strategies of tax or government spending to achieve fiscal consolidation in various forms (Blanchard & Perotti 2002; Ball et al., 2013; Afonso et al., 2021).

Many European Union countries began implementing Recovery and Resilience Plans in the late 2000s. The UK introduced Post-Brexit Fiscal Policies, while the US enacted the Bipartisan Budget Acts (2018, 2019, 2020) and the CARES Act (2020)[1]. However, despite these measures, not all efforts to reduce budget deficits have been successful. This has led researchers to explore which aspects of fiscal policy contribute to successful fiscal adjustments.

Previous literature, including works by Bohn (1991), Perotti (1996), Alesina & Ardagna (1998), Alesina & Perotti (1997), and Perotti, Strauch, & von Hagen (1998), suggests that successful fiscal adjustments often rely more on cutting government expenditures than on increasing tax revenues. Alesina & Perotti (1997) specifically argue that reducing government wages, salaries, and transfer payments is crucial for long-term deficit reduction. Recognizing the significance of the composition of fiscal adjustments, subsequent studies have examined the impact of political factors on fiscal policy. Alesina & Perotti (1996) suggest that budget institutions, including procedural rules and balanced budget laws, influence fiscal outcomes. They also argue that coalition governments are less effective at implementing fiscal adjustments due to internal conflicts. Huber, Kocher, & Sutter (2003) find that while the strength of coalition governments does not directly correlate with fiscal adjustment success, coalitions with equally strong partners tend to have higher budget deficits.

Corruption is another crucial political factor influencing fiscal policy. Theoretical studies by Chander & Wilde (1992) and Barreto & Alm (2003) emphasize the significant impact of corruption on fiscal administration. Mauro (1998) finds that corrupt governments often reduce spending on education. Volkerink & De Haan (1999) suggest that corrupt fiscal authorities prefer increasing indirect taxes while lowering income taxes. Arin et al. (2011) highlight that corrupt governments tend to raise taxes rather than cut expenditures, leading to failures in their budget consolidation efforts. Although it is well established that corrupt governments are more likely to increase taxes rather than reduce expenditures during fiscal adjustment episodes, there is still uncertainty about the specific types of taxes that are raised and the particular categories of spending that are altered during budget consolidations.

This study uses the same dataset as the seminal paper of Arin et al. (2011) to investigate the aforementioned question. Our analysis indicates that in countries with a higher rate of corruption, governments tend to rely more on indirect taxes for income generation and are less effective in reducing public expenditures. Analyzing the specific role of corruption levels in determining the types of taxes or public expenditures either increased or decreased during fiscal adjustment processes is crucial to gain a deeper understanding of how corruption affects fiscal policy and influences the effectiveness of fiscal adjustment. Therefore, it is essential for governments to reassess their anti-corruption strategies and formulate more efficient policies that enhance the efficacy of fiscal regulations.

The layout of the paper is the following: Section 2 reviews the literature; Section 3 describes the data used in the empirical analysis; Section 4 outlines the empirical framework and discusses the empirical results, including robustness checks; Section 5 offers some concluding remarks.

2. LITERATURE REVIEW

2.1 Fiscal Compositions and Budget Deficits

Milesi-Ferretti & Moriyama (2006) evaluated the fiscal measures of several European Union countries, using a balance sheet approach, and found that while these measures improved budget figures, they did not have a structural impact on government finances. They concluded that fiscal rules restricting the fiscal balance of government debt do not affect the government's net worth but do influence government objectives. In contrast, numerous studies indicate that the composition of fiscal adjustment efforts is more crucial than their magnitude.

For example, Bohn (1991) used an error correction model to analyze U.S. budget data from 1792 to 1988, demonstrating that cuts in government spending are essential for reducing budget deficits. Perotti (1996) supports this view, suggesting that successful fiscal adjustments rely on reducing social expenditures. Alesina & Perotti (1997) examined data from all OECD countries and found that adjustments based on tax increases, particularly direct taxes on households, often fail to permanently reduce public debt. Successful adjustments typically target government wages and employment. They also noted that coalition governments face challenges with fiscal adjustments due to internal conflicts. Ardagna (2004) analyzed data from OECD countries to assess the impact of fiscal contractions on the debt/GDP ratio and GDP growth. The results indicated that the greater the reduction in the fiscal deficit, the more likely it is that tight fiscal policies will lead to a decline in the debt-to-GDP ratio. The study argued that changes in fiscal policy, especially those involving reductions in public expenditures, lead to higher GDP growth rates. Yang et al. (2015) further explained this by showing that spending-based fiscal adjustments result in smaller output losses compared to tax-based fiscal adjustments.

Similarly, Von Hagen & Strauch (2001) documented that fiscal consolidations based on tax increases and reductions in public investment do not lead to long-term gains. Conversely, Heylen & Everaert (2000) argued that cutting the government wage bill is ineffective. Their findings indicated that fiscal adjustments in OECD countries depend on the composition of the adjustment program, with tax increases generally weakening success, except for corporate taxes, which can improve deficits. Heylen et al. (2013) analyzed 132 fiscal episodes in 21 OECD countries from 1981-2008, revealing that public debt reduction is more effective during fiscal consolidations that rely on spending cuts, particularly by efficient governments. However, they found that cuts to public investment are an exception, and labor market deregulation may be counterproductive.

Beyond the composition effects, the degree of centralization also significantly influences budget consolidation success. Schaltegger & Feld (2009) investigated the determinants of successful long-term budget deficit reduction using Swiss panel data from 1981-2001, finding that fiscal centralization significantly reduces the likelihood of successful fiscal consolidation. Buettner & Wildasin (2006), in an empirical study of dynamic fiscal policy adjustments in over 1,000 U.S. municipalities over 25 years using a vector error-correction model, revealed that fiscal imbalances are primarily addressed by future expenditure changes and subsequent grant adjustments. Intergovernmental grants were especially crucial for large cities in maintaining budget balance. Cogan et al. (2013) emphasized that to achieve successful fiscal consolidations, economic distortions caused by policy mistakes should be eliminated. They argued that to gain positive results from fiscal consolidation strategies, it is necessary to focus not only on fiscal measures but also on overall economic policies.

2.2 The Role of Corruption in Fiscal Administration

Corruption's impact on financial management in OECD countries has been extensively studied across various dimensions, particularly its effects on fiscal policies and budget management. Chander & Wilde (1992) utilized game theory to reveal that corruption leads to higher audit rates and reduced tax revenues in tax administration systems. Similarly, Barreto & Alm (2003) demonstrated that corruption in economies skews the optimal tax mix towards consumption taxes over income taxes, influencing fiscal priorities towards regressive taxation systems. Mauro (1998) highlighted corruption's distortion of government expenditure patterns, redirecting funds away from critical sectors like education. Volkerink & De Haan (1999) argued that political and institutional factors shape tax structures, with corrupt administrations often favoring indirect taxes, thereby compromising the integrity of direct taxation systems. Tanzi & Davoodi (2000) observed in developing countries that corruption diminishes income tax revenues due to negotiations with corrupt tax inspectors.

In the context of fiscal consolidation efforts, Arin et al. (2011) found that countries with higher corruption levels tend to rely less on spending cuts during consolidation initiatives, affecting the effectiveness of fiscal policies. Von Hagen & Strauch (2001) underscored the pivotal role of institutional frameworks and policy quality in achieving successful fiscal consolidations. Meanwhile, Chrysanthakopoulos & Tagkalakis (2023) emphasized the significance of well-designed fiscal rules and empowered fiscal councils in enhancing the likelihood of initiating and completing fiscal adjustments effectively. These studies collectively illustrate how corruption undermines fiscal integrity, distorts policy priorities, and erodes public trust in governance institutions, thereby hindering sustainable economic growth.

Political orientation also influences fiscal outcomes amidst corruption challenges. Tavares (2004) and Wiese et al. (2018) highlighted differing strategies employed by left-wing and right-wing governments in response to fiscal adjustments, with left-wing governments prioritizing spending cuts and right-wing governments favoring tax increases. Additionally, Chen & Neshkova (2019) demonstrated that higher financial transparency correlates with reduced corruption perceptions, underscoring the role of transparency in enhancing governance efficacy and accurately reflecting government spending. Furthermore, Doan et al. (2022) showed how corruption within tax administrations in transition economies can paradoxically stimulate innovation while compromising institutional integrity, presenting complex challenges for economic policy and governance. By examining these dynamics, this paper contributes to understanding the 'greasing the wheels' hypothesis and its impact on the success of fiscal adjustment programs.

This study has extensively examined the pivotal impacts of corruption on financial management, highlighting its detrimental effects on fiscal policies, budget management, and overall economic performance. From tax administration to expenditure patterns, and from fiscal consolidation efforts to policy instrument choices, corruption's pervasive effects seriously threaten sustainable fiscal integrity and public trust. Research underscores the importance of robust institutional frameworks, enhanced transparency measures, and effective policy interventions. Implementing these factors will be crucial in mitigating the adverse impacts of corruption on fiscal management, promoting economic growth, and strengthening the success of fiscal adjustment programs, thereby fostering a more resilient and equitable fiscal management environment.

3. DATA DESCRIPTION

The corruption index utilized in this study is derived from the International Country Risk Guide (ICRG). While the ethno linguistic fractionalization index is sourced from the original dataset of Mauro (1995), an updated version from Woldendorp (1993) is employed for the coalition dummy variable. Economic variables, including fiscal indicators, are obtained from the OECD Economic Outlook database.

The ICRG corruption index assesses the perception of foreign investors regarding the level of corruption in an economy. It considers various factors such as illicit payments and bribes associated with import and export licenses, exchange controls, tax assessments, police protection, and loans. Additionally, it accounts for practices like quid pro quo arrangements, clandestine party funding, and suspiciously close ties between political entities and businesses. This index ranges from 0 to 6, with 6 indicating the highest level of transparency in a country. The study sample covers yearly data for 18 OECD countries, which are listed in Table 1, spanning the period from 1984 to 2003.

Table 1. 18 OECD Countries

1. Australia	7. France	13. Norway
2. Austria	8. Greece	14. Portugal
3. Belgium	9. Iceland	15. Spain
4. Canada	10. Ireland	16. Sweden
5. Denmark	11. Italy	17. United Kingdom
6. Finland	12. Japan	18. United States

Control variables in the analysis include:

- Fiscal composition: Measured by changes in the revenue-to-expenditure ratio, following the approach of Baldacci, Cangiano, Mahfouz, & Schimmelpfennig (2001). This control is essential as suggested by Perotti (1996), Alesina & Perotti (1997), and Heylen & Everaert (2000) to evaluate the impact of economic and political variables on fiscal policy success.
- Openness of the economy: Included to capture its potential influence on current budget deficits. Mauro (1998) underscores the necessity of this control, albeit using a different measure of openness. Here, it is measured as the import/GDP ratio, aligning with Baldacci et al. (2001)'s approach.
- Monetary stance: Controls for the effect of monetary policy actions, measured by changes in real short-term interest rates, as per Baldacci et al. (2001)'s methodology.

- Coalition dummy: Reflects whether a coalition government exists post-election, based on findings from Alesina & Perotti (1997) indicating the challenges faced by coalition governments in fiscal consolidation.
- Ethno linguistic Fractionalisation: Recognized from previous studies, including Mauro (1995, 1998), as a significant factor influencing the fiscal response composition during consolidation episodes.
- Fiscal Success: The dependent variable is a dummy variable indicating fiscal success, defined as achieving a reduction in deficits. This measure follows Blanchard (1990), adjusted for unemployment rate stability to mitigate endogenous budget deficit increases during economic downturns. It excludes interest payments and incorporates gross capital accumulation to account for inflation effects, as recommended by Alesina & Perotti (1997).

These definitions and controls aim to provide a comprehensive framework for analyzing how corruption and other factors affect fiscal management and policy outcomes across OECD countries.

The Blanchard Measure of fiscal impulse (BFI) can be estimated as follow:

$$BFI = [g_t(u_{(t-1)}) - t(u_{(t-1)})] - (g_{t-1} - t_{t-1}) \qquad (1)$$

where $g_t(u_{(t-1)})$ and $t(u_{(t-1)})$ denote, respectively, unemployment-adjusted government spending and tax revenue. g_{t-1} and t_{t-1} are previous year's government expenditure and revenue respectively.

In order to calculate unemployment-adjusted expenditure, we regress government spending as a share of GDP (Gt) on two time trends (*TREND1* and *TREND2*) and on unemployment rate (Ut):

$$G_t = \alpha_0 + \alpha_1 TREND1 + \alpha_2 TREND2 + \alpha_3 U_t + \omega_t \qquad (2)$$

Subsequently, we utilize the coefficients obtained from this regression to estimate the level of government spending in period t under the assumption that unemployment remains unchanged from the previous year:

$$G(U_{t-1}) = \hat{\alpha}_0 + \hat{\alpha}_1 TREND1 + \hat{\alpha}_2 TREND2 + \hat{\alpha}_3 U_{t-1} + \hat{\omega}_t \qquad (3)$$

where the $\hat{\alpha}_i$'s are the estimated coefficients in equation (2) and $\hat{\omega}_t$ is the estimated residual in the same regression. We follow the same procedure to estimate unemployment-adjusted government revenues.

The fiscal policy response is categorized as follows based on the Budgetary Financial Instrument (BFI) as a percentage of GDP:

- Neutral: -0.5% < BFI < 0.5%
- Loose or small expansions: 0.5% < BFI < 1.5%
- Very loose or strong adjustment: BFI ≥ 1.5%
- Tight or small adjustment: -1.5% ≤ BFI ≤ -0.5%
- Very tight or strong adjustment: BFI ≤ -1.5%

Following Alesina & Perotti (1997), a successful adjustment in year *t* is characterized by achieving a "very tight" fiscal stance, where the gross debt/GDP ratio in year t+3 is at least 5 percentage points lower than in year t. Summary statistics for all variables are presented in Table 2 .

Table 2. Descriptive Statistics

Variables	Observation	Mean	Standard Deviation	Min	Max
Corruption Index	360	5.006	0.987	2	6.166
Ethno linguistic Fractionalisation	360	21.388	21.457	1	75
Openness (% of GDP)	360	0.267	0.138	0.021	0.850
Monetary Stance	355	-0.420	2.443	-13.05	31.025
Government Benefits (% of GDP)	360	13.607	3.899	5.674	23.677
Fixed Investment (% of GDP)	340	3.065	0.942	1.142	6.362
Other Transfers (% of GDP)	360	4.016	1.721	-3.955	7.654
Subsidies (% of GDP)	360	1.800	1.031	0.140	4.480
Total Expenditure (% of GDP)	360	47.008	8.125	31.067	73.039
Total Tax Revenues (% of GDP)	360	44.223	8.636	29.962	65.437
Labour Taxes (% of GDP)	360	21.024	6.698	6.962	35.431
Corporate Taxes (% of GDP)	340	2.940	1.261	0.562	9.050
Indirect Taxes (% of GDP)	360	13.547	3.122	7.194	23.173
Transfers (% of GDP)	300	17.442	4.250	7.957	26.689
Total Expenditure (Cyclically-adjusted, % of potential GDP)	360	44.279	8.920	26.803	63.051
Total Tax Revenues (Cyclically-adjusted, % of potential GDP)	360	43.628	8.976	29.666	64.906
Labour Taxes (Cyclically-adjusted, % of potential GDP)	340	21.912	6.291	6.829	35.189
Corporate Taxes (Cyclically-adjusted, % of potential GDP)	340	2.718	0.991	0.591	6.250
Indirect Taxes ((Cyclically-adjusted, % of potential GDP	340	13.577	3.326	7.194	23.184

Note: The sample covers 18 OECD countries spanning the period from 1984 to 2003.

4. EMPIRICAL ANALYSIS

The benchmark Ordinary Least Squares (OLS) regression equation estimated can be specified as follows:

$$F_{it} = \alpha_0 + \alpha_1 Corruption_t + \alpha_2 X_t + \omega_t \tag{4}$$

where F_{it} represents the change in fiscal instrument i during fiscal adjustment periods t. $Corruption_t$ denotes the level of corruption during these fiscal adjustment periods. X_t is the vector of control variables used, including openness, coalition dummy, ethno-linguistic fractionalization, and monetary stance.

4.1 Empirical Results

The pooled OLS results are presented in Table 3. Our empirical findings indicate that corrupt governments face challenges in consolidating their budgets for two primary reasons. Firstly, our analysis shows that corrupt governments often employ ineffective fiscal instruments during fiscal adjustment periods, such as increasing indirect taxes (Regression 2). This contrasts with established literature (including Bohn (1991), Perotti (1996), Alesina & Ardagna (1998), Alesina & Perotti (1997), Perotti, Strauch, & von Hagen (1998)), which consistently finds that successful fiscal adjustments hinge on reducing government expenditures rather than raising taxes. This underscores that the choice of fiscal instrument significantly influences the success of budget consolidation efforts.

Moreover, our investigation reveals a broader context. We find that corrupt governments yield to political pressures, particularly from large corporations, leading them to reduce corporate taxes and increase subsidies and social benefits during fiscal adjustment episodes (regressions 4, 9, and 10).

Table 3. Fiscal Instrument Selection by Corrupt Governments During Fiscal Adjustment Periods

Specification	Dependent Variable	Corruption	Openness	Coalition Dummy	Ethno-linguistic Fractionalization	Monetary Stance	Constant	N	R²	F-stat	Estimation Technique
(1)	ΔTotal Tax Revenue	-0.089 (0.158)	-2.362 (1.438)	-0.124 (0.316)	-0.009 (0.006)	0.104 (0.070)	**1.941 (1.041)***	62	0.106	2.07*	OLS with Robust Standard Errors
(2)	ΔIndirect Taxes	**-0.166 (0.062)*****	-0.007 (0.350)	-0.171 (0.140)	0.003 (0.002)	0.044 (0.035)	**0.868 (0.386)****	62	0.175	2.12**	OLS with Robust Standard Errors
(3)	ΔLabor Taxes	-0.064 (0.071)	-0.756 (0.803)	-0.091 (0.169)	-0.001 (0.003)	-0.031 (0.046)	**0.761 (0.436)***	58	0.032	0.40	OLS with Robust Standard Errors
(4)	ΔCorporate Taxes	**0.221 (0.073)*****	-0.389 (0.482)	0.071 (0.230)	-0.007 (0.004)	0.038 (0.033)	-0.530 (0.577)	58	0.117	2.92**	OLS with Robust Standard Errors
(5)	ΔTotal Government Expenditure	-0.194 (0.188)	**-2.533 (1.465)***	0.609 (0.410)	0.009 (0.007)	-0.040 (0.096)	-0.194 (1.046)	62	0.148	1.85	OLS with Robust Standard Errors
(6)	Δ Other Transfers	-0.015 (0.037)	**-0.339 (0.192)***	0.090 (0.082)	**0.002 (0.001)***	-0.008 (0.010)	-0.032 (0.191)	62	0.110	2.10*	OLS with Robust Standard Errors
(7)	ΔGovernment Transfers	-0.166 (0.128)	-0.955 (0.622)	0.016 (0.257)	0.002 (0.004)	**-0.197 (0.094)****	0.671 (0.772)	51	0.166	1.60	OLS with Robust Standard Errors

continued on following page

Table 3. Continued

Specification	Dependent Variable	Corruption	Openness	Coalition Dummy	Ethno-linguistic Fractionalization	Monetary Stance	Constant	N	R²	F-stat	Estimation Technique
(8)	ΔGovernment Wage Bill	-0.106 (0.080)	-0.046 (0.395)	-0.202 (-0.182)	-0.002 (0.003)	0.010 (0.021)	0.500 (0.555)	56	0.064	0.61	OLS with Robust Standard Errors
(9)	ΔGovernment Benefits	**-0.162 (0.095)***	-0.699 (0.596)	0.069 (0.174)	0.001 (0.002)	**-0.085 (0.043)***	0.712 (0.464)	62	0.148	1.96*	OLS with Robust Standard Errors
(10)	ΔGovernment Subsidies	**-0.070 (0.028)****	-0.212 (0.475)	0.020 (0.081)	0.001 (0.001)	-0.013 (0.031)	0.244 (0.188)	62	0.054	1.79	OLS with Robust Standard Errors

Notes: Dependent Variable: Change in Percentage Share of Fiscal Tools in GDP during Adjustment Episodes
Robust Standard Errors are shown in parentheses
* Significant at 10% level, ** Significant at 5% level, *** Significant at 1% level.

4.2 Robustness Check

It could be argued that our current estimation may not accurately capture the impact of corruption on fiscal policy tools during adjustment periods, as other significant factors such as the business cycle are not accounted for. To address this issue, we revisit our model by employing cyclically-adjusted fiscal variables (measured as a percentage of potential GDP) as dependent variables. However, due to data limitations, we focus our investigation on how corruption affects changes in total government expenditure, total tax revenue, labor taxes, corporate taxes, and indirect taxes (cyclically-adjusted and measured as a percentage of potential GDP) during fiscal adjustment periods. The empirical findings are presented in Table 4. Notably, when using cyclically adjusted fiscal variables, our results remain largely consistent with our previous findings.

Robustness Check

Table 4. Corrupt Governments' Choice of Fiscal Instrument during Fiscal Adjustment Episodes

Specification	Dependent Variable	Corruption	Openness	Coalition Dummy	Ethno-linguistic Fractionalization	Monetary Stance	Constant	N	R^2	F-stat	Estimation Technique
(1)	ΔTotal Tax Revenue	0.011 (0.135)	-1.718 (1.316)	-0.14 (0.272)	-0.007 (0.005)	0.059 (0.063)	1.064 (0.835)	62	0.061	1.32	OLS with Robust Standard Errors
(2)	ΔIndirect Taxes	**-0.122 (0.057)****	0.056 (0.344)	-0.136 (0.109)	0.001 (0.002)	0.024 (0.035)	**0.0713 (0.328)****	58	0.132	1.37	OLS with Robust Standard Errors
(3)	ΔLabor Taxes	-0.064 (0.071)	-0.756 (0.803)	-0.091 (0.169)	-0.001 (0.003)	-0.031 (0.046)	**0.761 (0.436)***	58	0.032	0.40	OLS with Robust Standard Errors
(4)	ΔCorporate Taxes	**0.182 (0.063)*****	-0.28 (0.375)	**0.195 (0.106)***	-0.0017 (0.002)	0.02 (0.027)	**-0.692 (0.303)****	58	0.194	2.07*	OLS with Robust Standard Errors
(5)	ΔTotal Government Expenditure	-0.196 (0.142)	**-2.336 (1.321)***	0.142 (0.274)	-0.005 (0.005)	-0.004 (0.061)	1.154 (0.77)	62	0.121		OLS with Robust Standard Errors

Dependent Dummy Variable: Change in Percentage Share of Cyclically-Adjusted Fiscal Tools in Potential GDP during Fiscal Adjustments Episodes
Robust Standard Errors are shown in parentheses
Notes: * Significant at 10% level, ** Significant at 5% level, *** Significant at 1% level.

5. CONCLUSION

This paper addresses a crucial gap in the literature by examining how corruption influences both the composition and outcomes of fiscal adjustment policies. Its aim is to deepen our understanding of these dynamics by investigating the fiscal instruments favoured by corrupt governments during periods of fiscal adjustment and their impact on the success of these policies.

Our research reveals that corruption significantly diminishes the success of fiscal adjustment endeavours. Specifically, we find that corrupt governments tend to increase indirect taxes rather than implementing spending cuts to reduce budget deficits. This inclination suggests that corrupt administrations prioritize short-term political gains through populist measures, thereby jeopardizing the long-term sustainability of fiscal adjustments.

Furthermore, our study highlights that while corruption directly undermines fiscal adjustment success, changes in government expenditure patterns can mitigate its impact. Corrupt governments are observed to avoid reducing public salaries and transfer payments during fiscal adjustment periods, opting instead to raise indirect taxes.

These findings underscore the importance for international organizations and policymakers to exercise caution when evaluating fiscal adjustment efforts in countries plagued by high levels of corruption. Without addressing corruption effectively, fiscal adjustment initiatives are likely to fail. Therefore, enhancing the effectiveness of fiscal governance requires robust anti-corruption strategies that promote transparency and accountability.

In conclusion, given the detrimental effects of corruption on fiscal policy outcomes, combating corruption and enhancing transparency are imperative for the success of fiscal adjustment efforts. This study contributes to advancing more resilient and effective fiscal governance strategies by shedding light on the nexus between corruption and fiscal policy. Policymakers are encouraged to integrate anti-corruption measures as integral components of fiscal regulatory frameworks.

REFERENCES

Afonso, A., Alves, J., & Jalles, J. T. (2021). (Non-)Keynesian Effects of Fiscal Austerity: New Evidence from a Large Sample. *Social Science Research Network*, 1-42. https://doi.org/DOI: 10.2139/ssrn.3761941

Albu, A., & Albu, L. (2021). Public debt and economic growth in euro area countries. a wavelet approach. *Technological and Economic Development of Economy*, 27(3), 602–625. DOI: 10.3846/tede.2021.14241

Alesina, A., & Ardagna, S. (1998). Tales of fiscal adjustment. *Economic Policy*, 13(27), 487–545. DOI: 10.1111/1468-0327.00039

Alesina, A., & Perotti, R. (1996). Budget deficits and budget institutions. *Working Paper Series (National Bureau of Economic Research)*, 5556, 1–40.

Alesina, A., & Perotti, R. (1997). Fiscal adjustments in OECD countries: Composition and macroeconomic effects. International Monetary Fund Working Paper, 44(2), 210-248. https://doi.org/DOI: 10.2307/3867543

Ardagna, S. (2004). Fiscal stabilizations: When do they work and why. *European Economic Review*, 48(5), 1047–1074. DOI: 10.1016/j.euroecorev.2003.09.010

Arin, K. P., Chmelarova, V., Feess, E., & Wohlschlegel, A. (2011). Why are corrupt countries less successful in consolidating their budgets? *Journal of Public Economics*, 95(7–8), 521–530. DOI: 10.1016/j.jpubeco.2011.01.007

Baldacci, E., Cangiano, M., Mahfouz, S., & Schimmelpfennig, A. (2001). The effectiveness of fiscal policy in stimulating economic activity: an empirical investigation. *IMF Annual Research Conference*, International Monetary Fund.

Ball, L., Furceri, D., Leigh, D., & Loungani, P. (2013). The distributional effects of fiscal consolidation. *IMF Working Paper*, 13(151), 1. DOI: 10.5089/9781475551945.001

Barreto, R. A., & Alm, J. (2003). Corruption, optimal taxation, and growth. *Public Finance Review*, 31(3), 207–240. DOI: 10.1177/1091142103031003001

Blanchard, O. (1990), Suggestions for a new set of fiscal indicators. OECD Economics Department Working Papers, No. 79, OECD Publishing, Paris, https://doi.org/DOI: 10.1787/18151973

Blanchard, O., & Perotti, R. (2002). An empirical characterization of the dynamic effects of changes in government spending and taxes on output. *The Quarterly Journal of Economics*, 117(4), 1329–1368. DOI: 10.1162/003355302320935043

Bohn, H. (1991). The sustainability of budget deficits with lump-sum and with income-based taxation. *Journal of Money, Credit and Banking*, 23(3), 580–604. DOI: 10.2307/1992692

Buettner, T., & Wildasin, D. E. (2006). The dynamics of municipal fiscal adjustment. *Journal of Public Economics*, 90(6–7), 1115–1132. DOI: 10.1016/j.jpubeco.2005.09.002

Chander, P., & Wilde, L. (1992). Corruption in tax administration. *Journal of Public Economics*, 49(3), 333–349. DOI: 10.1016/0047-2727(92)90072-N

Chen, C., & Neshkova, M. I. (2019). The effect of fiscal transparency on corruption: A panel cross-country analysis. *Public Administration*, 98(1), 226–243. DOI: 10.1111/padm.12620

Chrysanthakopoulos, C., & Tagkalakis, A. (2023). The effects of fiscal institutions on fiscal adjustment. *Journal of International Money and Finance*, 134(102853), 1–16. DOI: 10.1016/j.jimonfin.2023.102853

Cogan, J. F., Taylor, J. B., Wieland, V., & Wolters, M. H. (2013). Fiscal consolidation strategy. *Journal of Economic Dynamics & Control*, 37(2), 404–421. DOI: 10.1016/j.jedc.2012.10.004

Cooray, A., Dzhumashev, R., & Schneider, F. (2017). How does corruption affect public debt? An empirical analysis. *World Development*, 90, 115–127. DOI: 10.1016/j.worlddev.2016.08.020

Doan, H. Q., Vu, N. H., Tran-Nam, B., & Nguyen, N. A. (2022). Effects of tax administration corruption on innovation inputs and outputs: Evidence from small and medium sized enterprises in Vietnam. *Empirical Economics*, 62(4), 1773–1800. DOI: 10.1007/s00181-021-02072-w

Heylen, F., & Everaert, G. (2000). Success and failure of fiscal consolidation in the OECD: A multivariate analysis. *Public Choice*, 105(1), 103–124. DOI: 10.1023/A:1005130929435

Heylen, F., Hoebeeck, A., & Buyse, T. (2013). Government efficiency, institutions, and the effects of fiscal consolidation on public debt. *European Journal of Political Economy*, 31, 40–59. DOI: 10.1016/j.ejpoleco.2013.03.001

Huber, G., Kocher, M., & Sutter, M. (2003). Government strength, power dispersion in governments and budget deficits in OECD-countries. A voting power approach. *Public Choice*, 116(3/4), 333–350. DOI: 10.1023/A:1024860709516

Makhoba, B. P., Kaseeram, I., & Greyling, L. (2021). Asymmetric and threshold effects of public debt on economic growth in sadc: A panel smooth transition regression analysis. *African Journal of Economic and Management Studies*, 13(2), 165–176. DOI: 10.1108/AJEMS-04-2021-0146

Mauro, P. (1995). Corruption and growth. *The Quarterly Journal of Economics*, 110(3), 681–712. DOI: 10.2307/2946696

Mauro, P. (1998). Corruption and the composition of government expenditure. *Journal of Public Economics*, 69(2), 263–279. DOI: 10.1016/S0047-2727(98)00025-5

Milesi-Ferretti, G. M., & Moriyama, K. (2006). Fiscal adjustment in EU countries: A balance sheet approach. *Journal of Banking & Finance*, 30(12), 3281–3298. DOI: 10.1016/j.jbankfin.2006.05.010

Perotti, R. (1996). Fiscal Consolidation in Europe: Composition Matters. *The American Economic Review*, 86(2), 105–110. https://www.jstor.org/stable/2118105

Perotti, R., Strauch, R., & Von Hagen, J. (1998). *Sustainability of public finances*. CERP.

Reinhart, C., & Rogoff, K. (2010). Growth in a time of debt. *The American Economic Review*, 100(2), 573–578. DOI: 10.1257/aer.100.2.573

Schaltegger, C. A., & Feld, L. P. (2009). Are fiscal adjustments less successful in decentralized governments? *European Journal of Political Economy*, 25(1), 115–123. DOI: 10.1016/j.ejpoleco.2008.08.002

Tanzi, V., & Davoodi, H. R. (2000b). Corruption, Growth, and Public Finances. *IMF Working Paper*, 2000(182), 1–27. DOI: 10.5089/9781451859256.001

Tavares, J. (2004). Does right or left matter? Cabinets, credibility and fiscal adjustments. *Journal of Public Economics*, 88(12), 2447–2468. DOI: 10.1016/j.jpubeco.2003.11.001

Volkerink, B., & De Haan, J. (1999). Political and institutional determinants of the tax mix : an empirical investigation for OECD countries. Research Report 99E05, University of Groningen, Research Institute SOM (Systems, Organisations and Management), 1-43.

Von Hagen, J. (1998). Fiscal policy and intranational risk-sharing (No. B 13-1998). ZEI working paper. https://hdl.handle.net/10419/39528

Von Hagen, J., & Strauch, R. R. (2001). Fiscal consolidations: Quality, economic conditions, and success. *Public Choice*, 109(3), 327–346. DOI: 10.1023/A:1013073005104

Wiese, R., Jong-A-Pin, R., & De Haan, J. (2018). Can successful fiscal adjustments only be achieved by spending cuts? *European Journal of Political Economy*, 54, 145–166. DOI: 10.1016/j.ejpoleco.2018.01.003

Woldendorp, J., Keman, H., & Budge, I. (1993). Political data 1945-1990. Party government in 20 democraties. *European Journal of Political Research*, 24(1), 1–119.

Yang, W., Fidrmuc, J., & Ghosh, S. (2015). Macroeconomic effects of fiscal adjustment: A tale of two approaches. *Journal of International Money and Finance*, 57, 31–60. DOI: 10.1016/j.jimonfin.2015.05.003

ENDNOTES

[1] The Coronavirus Aid, Relief, and Economic Security (CARES) Act is a comprehensive federal stimulus package enacted in the United States on March 27, 2020, in response to the economic fallout from the COVID-19 pandemic. It was designed to provide fast and direct economic assistance to American workers, families, and businesses.

Chapter 10
Understanding Trends in Economic Development and Financial Dynamics

Feyza Ozdinc
https://orcid.org/0000-0002-0414-0575
Gaziantep University, Turkey

Sukriye Gul Reis
https://orcid.org/0000-0001-7654-4256
Gaziantep University, Turkey

ABSTRACT

Since economic activities require funds, the financial system is a crucial component of the economic system, with the development of the financial sector having a significant impact on an economy's overall financial health. This study focuses on the intersection of economic development and finance and identifies significant themes and new research directions in the distribution of articles on finance and economic development. It reviews 296 articles from the Web of Science and Scopus databases, focusing on the dynamic fields of economic development and finance. The data shows an increasing trend after 2013, with 101 articles on this issue between 2015 and 2021 and 99 between 2022 and 2024. The results offer new perspectives on how economic development and finance are changing, offering light on both historical precedents and future directions.

DOI: 10.4018/979-8-3693-5508-4.ch010

INTRODUCTION

J. M. Keynes called the Great Depression "The Great Slump of 1930." He employed some metaphors to elaborate on the economic conditions of the times. In his essay, he said, "We have magneto trouble. How, then, can we start up again?" and he pointed out the financial system as a crucial component of the economic engine, which we have little understanding of. He believed that policymakers lacked a comprehensive understanding of the intricacies of the economic system, resulting in incorrect measures and exacerbating the economic crisis (Keynes, 2010). While it is unfortunate, we have to admit that the statement made almost a century ago remains valid: the financial system continues to play a crucial role in the economic machine, and we cannot claim to have a complete understanding of this intricate process.

Since there is a limited source of factors of production and endless wants and needs have to be met, scarcity is the fundamental economic problem that all societies have to face. Only with economic development can nations overcome scarce resources and increase options for the majority of people. When the latest economic developments are examined, it is seen that there are strong relationships between financial dynamics and economic indicators. An advanced financial system offers its users wider and more flexible options. Fund creation, evaluation of funds, transfer of funds, and allocation of funds to productive areas are related to the development of the financial system. Since economic activities require funds, the financial system is an important component of the economic system, and the development of the financial sector has a significant impact on the economy. The development of capital markets in the financing needed to realize real investments with high added value required for economic development is related to the development and depth of the financial system. The factor that was effective in increasing the international trade volume after financial liberalization was again closely related to the development of countries due to the development of financial instruments and institutions. Therefore, the capital market in a developed economy affects the returns on real and financial assets. The impact of liberalization on capital movements on the quality of investment has been much stronger than any impact on the quantity of investment. Particularly in developing countries, accessibility to credit has been an important determinant of investment rates.

The earlier onset of the Industrial Revolution in the United Kingdom, the Netherlands, and the United States of America is associated with the development of the financial system in those economies. The relatively developed financial system was influential in their economic rise. Therefore, it is crucial to understand the link between economic development and financial dynamics for a myriad of reasons, such as understanding the growth mechanisms of countries, resource allocation, advancing development strategies, and financial stability. Additionally, since changes in financial regulations, monetary policies, and banking systems have a significant impact on economic outcomes such as employment, income distribution, and economic growth, the interaction between economic development and finance has consequential policy implications.

This study aims to explore trends in economic development and financial dynamics by employing a bibliometric analysis. To achieve this goal, a comprehensive overview of scholarly articles from two databases, Web of Science (WoS) and Scopus, will be reviewed, and key themes and emerging research trajectories will be determined. In this chapter, we explore the dynamic fields of economic development and finance to give readers a thorough understanding of the major themes, challenges, and opportunities influencing these critical fields. We seek to shed light on today's global world by thoroughly examining the historical background, contemporary trends, and future directions of economic development and financial dynamics by using keywords, mapping, and clustering techniques and examining the links between keywords, countries, authors, and other factors.

THEORETICAL FRAMEWORK

Historical Evaluation

Economic development refers to the transformation of economies from a state of scarce resources and options for the majority of people to one of significantly increased resources and choices. Economic development encompasses nearly all aspects of economics, albeit with adjustments to account for the unique circumstances of developing nations (Behrman, 2001).

In the history of capitalism, the first crisis was the Long Depression between 1873-97 (Fels, 1949). Economic historians widely recognize the financial crisis of 1873 as one of the earliest worldwide crises in modern capitalism, and some suggest the Great War happened because of its aftermath effects (Marichal, 2014). In the second quarter of the 19th century, the United Kingdom adopted the gold standard. After the Great War, by the late 1920s, the majority of countries had forsaken the gold standard (Gallarotti, 1995). In *The Economic Consequences of the Peace*, Keynes (1920) suggested that the war reparations of $5 billion for Germany were excessively exorbitant and would push Germany out of capitalism. His perspective was right, and Germany experienced a state of economic downturn as a result of war reparations, which subsequently facilitated the rise of Hitler and the Nazi party to power in Germany. After World War I, the USA became the hegemonic power in the world, taking over from the UK, Germany, and France. The Ottoman Empire collapsed after World War I. The Great Depression was the second big crisis of capitalism, and it took place between 1929 and 1935. The Great Depression precipitated a severe recession in the Western world, leading to unemployment rates soaring as high as 25%. Keynes' interventionist ideas provided solutions to the Great Depression and its consequences. After the Great Depression, in 1939, World War II started and continued until 1945. In 1944, the Bretton Woods meeting was held towards the end of World War II. With the collapse of the Bretton Woods System in the 1970s, the transition to floating exchange rates contributed significantly to the diversification of financial instruments (derivative instruments) in the management of exchange rate risk and interest rate risk and thus to the development of the financial system. Following this development, with many regulations brought by the 1980 liberalization, regulations to be made for the development of international trade have become inevitable in countries that want to achieve their economic development goals. While all these developments affected the economic structure as output, they necessitated a deepened financial system.

Globalization affects the economy in three main dimensions: international trade, international production, and international financial flows. As a development of globalization following the Second World War, the international trade dimension refers to the elimination of restrictions on the exchange of goods and services. The international production dimension refers to the realization of production by multinational companies in more than one place at the same time. The first traces of multinational companies can be found in American companies just after the Second World War. The financial globalization process, which is the most important dimension of globalization, emerged with foreign direct investments. Subsequently, the borders in the bond and stock markets disappeared, and finally, short-term capital movements, also known as "hot money" flows (Seyidoğlu, 2003). Thus, globalization has brought along a series of regulations consisting of liberalization of capital movements, privatization, deregulation, financial liberalization, and floating exchange rates. International financial institutions, particularly the IMF, have played an important role in the establishment of this new order.

Development economics, as a field of academic discipline, emerged after WWII. To become a developed economy, a nation should have effective government institutions (Acemoglu et al., 2001; Rodrik et al., 2004), protection of property rights (see, e.g., Xu, 2013; Asoni, 2008; Johnson et al., 2002), a less cumbersome regulatory/legal system (Petreski, 2014), human capital (Becker, 1994:24), eligible geography (Sachs, 2001), and openness to trade (Frankel & Romer, 1999). A strong financial system will make it possible to put these things in order.

Finance and Growth: Theory

Financial development refers to the elements, strategies, and organizations that contribute to efficient financial intermediation and markets, as well as widespread and comprehensive access to capital and financial services (World Economic Forum, 2012). The financial system plays a crucial role in obtaining and distributing funds for economic activities. The development of the financial sector has a significant impact on the overall financial well-being of an economy (Yiadom et al., 2023). According to Levine (2005), the financial sector plays a vital role in the economy through five distinct means. The functions encompassed are as follows: 1) providing comprehensive information regarding investments and allocation of capital; 2) overseeing investments and maintaining corporate governance to ensure that the funds allocated attain the desired objectives; 3) aiding in trading, diversification, and risk management; 4) mobilizing and consolidating savings; and 5) facilitating the exchange of goods and services.

The literature has provided a wealth of theoretical and empirical evidence linking finance and economic development. There is evidence that finance leads to economic development (see, e.g., Schumpeter, 1911; McKinnon, 1973; Shaw, 1973; Demetriades & Law, 2006) or that economic development leads to finance (Robinson, 1952). Following the endogenous growth theory, there are studies that provide various theoretical contributions on the impact of financial development on economic growth. Durusu-Ciftci et al. (2017) categorized these theoretical contributions into five groups. First, most of the models reveal the allocative role of financial systems. Second, firms use financial markets to diversify their portfolios and increase their liquidity in order to reduce their risk, and thus financial markets promote growth. Third, financial development increases the efficiency of financial intermediation. Fourth, financial markets encourage the application of new technologies and entrepreneurship. Fifth, these markets affect economic growth through changes in incentives for corporate control.

Apart from all these, according to neo-classical growth theory, the role of financial development on economic growth is attributed to the development of the stock market (Atje & Jovanovic, 1993). It has been argued that stock market development is a leading indicator of economic growth. This conclusion coincides with the utilization of the long-term fund raising power of the stock market in the financial system for financing high value-added investment projects. Thus, supporting capital investments through the stock market has an important place among the steps to be taken towards growth.

The allocation of resources by financial intermediaries to productive areas (such as financing high-value-added investment projects, and financing sustainable investments) will impact economic growth. In addition, with the diversity of instruments used in financial markets, it will be possible to bring savings into the economy. Given the importance of finance for economic growth, the inherent risks, and the huge economic costs of banking crises, it is unsurprising that the financial sector is on the policy agenda (Beck, 2012).

METHODOLOGY

This study investigates patterns in economic development and finance by employing a bibliometric analysis. In order to identify significant themes and new research directions, an extensive examination of scholarly publications from two databases, Web of Science (WoS) and Scopus, was conducted. Scopus and Web of Science were selected as the databases for data collection due to their recognized scientific competence.

For this purpose, the terms "economic development" and "financ*" were used as keywords. To encompass a broader range of topics, an asterisk is employed alongside the term "finance" due to its several conjugations and the results obtained are reported in Table 1.

Table 1. Search Terms

Database	Web of Science (WoS)	Scopus
Search terms	TS=("economic development" AND " financ*")	TITLE-ABS-KEY("economic development" AND "financ*")
N	227	318

As we can see from Table 1, a further investigation of the WoS database using the search terms "economic development" and "financ*" as keywords in the Title section gave 227 documents, and of the Scopus database using the search terms "economic development" and "financ*" as keywords in the Title-Abstract-Keyword section gave 318 documents in the English language.

Combining these two databases gives us a total of 389 documents after deleting 153 duplicate items. After checking the data set manually, documents that were found to be unrelated and/or missing critical information, such as keywords, were omitted.

Table 2. Arranged Data

Database	Web of Science (WoS) and Scopus
Type	Article (Published and Early Access):
Language	English

continued on following page

Table 2. Continued

Database	Web of Science (WoS) and Scopus
Combined	545
Manual Check	N: 296

Thereafter, a dataset of 296 documents that were going to be used for the bibliometric analysis in this study was obtained (See Table 2). Additionally, as we can see from Table 2, we used "articles" as the document type and "English" as the publication language. Typically, while conducting these analyses, researchers manually choose English as the language of publication as a factor in determining the significance of the study.

The steps taken to obtain the data set can be briefly summarized as assembling, arranging, and assessing, which are suggested by Paul et al. (2021). Since it would be difficult to evaluate different languages together and most of the papers are written in English, we only used papers written in English. Lastly, for the analysis, R-tool bibliometrix is used in this study for mapping purposes (Aria & Cuccurullo, 2017).

DATA

Main information on the results of the research conducted in these databases is as shown in Table 3. As we can see from Table 3, the timespan for this combined data set consists of 296 documents from 1987 to 2024. These 296 documents are from 202 sources, and only 82 of them are single-authored documents by 76 authors. There are 688 authors in total, and they used a total of 810 keywords.

Table 3. Main Information

Main Information About Data	
Timespan	1987:2024
Sources (Journals, Books, etc.)	202
Documents	296
Annual Growth Rate %	5.78
Document Contents	
Keywords Plus (ID)	647
Author's Keywords (DE)	810
Authors	
Authors	688

continued on following page

Table 3. Continued

Authors of single-authored docs	76
Authors Collaboration	
Single-authored docs	82
Co-Authors per doc	2.56
International co-authorships %	3.378
Document Types	
article	276
article; article	2
article; book chapter	14
article; early access	1
article; proceedings paper	2
article; retracted publication	1

FINDINGS

The analysis will concentrate on the yearly output of these articles, which classify and study financial and economic developments by country. Then, information about the most cited countries and the impact of sources and authors will be given. Additionally, the most significant sources, their impact, and the influence of authors over the years will be thoroughly examined using figures. Furthermore, this study will examine the predominant concepts and dimensions found in 296 papers on the intersection of economic development and finance. Lastly, the top fifteen keywords, construct a conceptual structure map on a multidimensional scale, conduct a word tree map and thematic change analysis, and construct conceptual structure maps will be investigated.

Figure 1. Annual Production

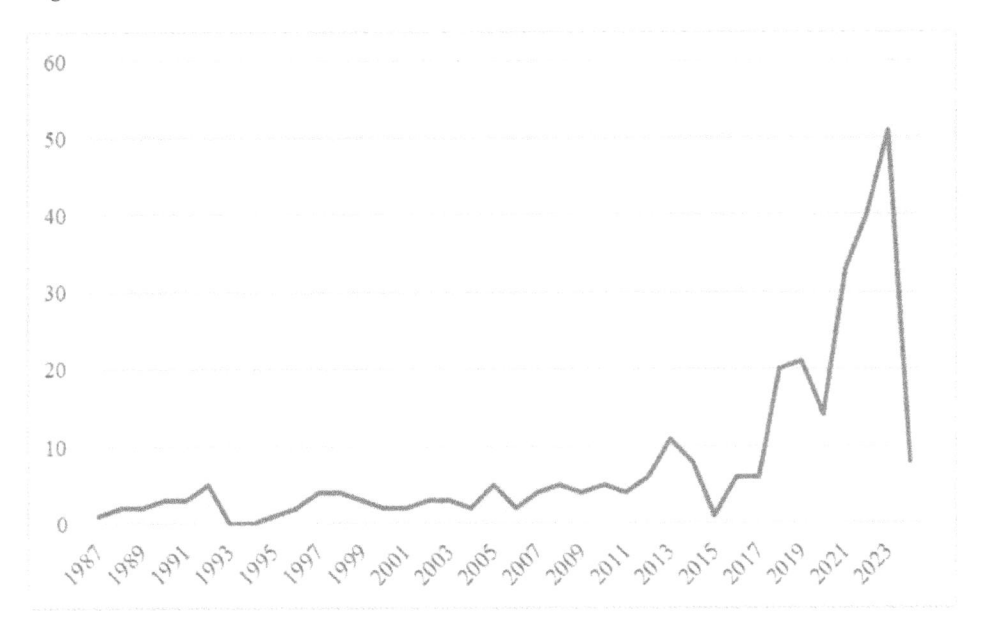

As we can see from Figure 1, even if there is a drop in the number of studies that address finance and economic development in 2015, there is an increasing trend after 2013. In fact, while the total number of articles on this issue for 1987-2014 period was 96, it was 101 for 2015-2021 period and 99 for 2022-2024 period.

Figure 2. Country Production

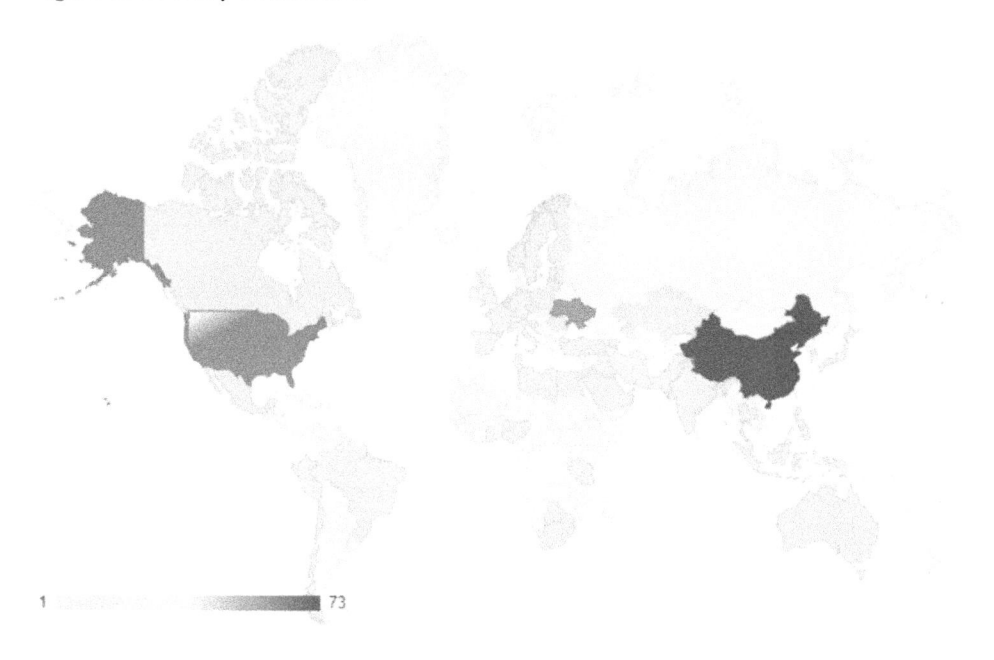

Figure 2 displays the geographical distribution of published researches by nation in the form of a map view. The indication chart employs a gradient of colors ranging from light blue to dark blue in order to classify countries according to their level, with lighter shades representing lower levels and darker shades representing higher levels. This map displays the scientific production of countries, which is represented by frequency and serves as a measure of the research output of various nations. The information provided covers various aspects, including citation analysis, research trends, impact and quality, and publication volume.

Table 4. Country Production Frequencies

Region	Freq.	Region	Freq.
China	73	Kazakhstan	2
USA	60	Lebanon	2
Ukraine	56	Peru	2
UK	26	Saudi Arabia	2
Malaysia	11	Azerbaijan	1
India	9	Belgium	1

continued on following page

Table 4. Continued

Region	Freq.	Region	Freq.
Japan	9	Botswana	1
Canada	8	Egypt	1
South Korea	8	Estonia	1
Pakistan	7	Finland	1
Brazil	5	Iran	1
Germany	5	Iraq	1
Indonesia	5	Jordan	1
Latvia	5	Kuwait	1
Nigeria	5	Libya	1
South Africa	5	Lithuania	1
Australia	4	Mexico	1
Croatia	4	Netherlands	1
Italy	4	Norway	1
Spain	4	Philippines	1
Chile	3	Romania	1
France	3	Singapore	1
Poland	3	Slovenia	1
Tunisia	3	Sweden	1
Turkey	3	Tanzania	1
Czech Republic	2	Thailand	1
Ghana	2	United Arab Emirates	1

According to the data in Figure 2 and Table 4, China has the highest frequency, with a count of 73, while the United States of America is second with a count of 60. Ukraine has 56, the United Kingdom has 26, Malaysia has 11, and India and Japan have 8 each.

Although it is not included in a table in this study, the country with the most corresponding authors is China with 61 articles, the United States of America with 27 articles, and the United Kingdom with 14 articles. As a result, it is not surprising that China is the nation with the most citations, as authors from this nation contributed to 61 out of 296 publications.

Table 5. Most Cited Countries

Country	TC	Average Article Citations
China	959	15.7

continued on following page

Table 5. Continued

Country	TC	Average Article Citations
United Kingdom	874	62.4
USA	706	26.1
India	147	24.5
Germany	126	31.5
Canada	100	33.3
Australia	72	18
Egypt	71	71
Netherlands	64	64
Saudi Arabia	58	29
Croatia	53	26.5
Pakistan	52	8.7
Morocco	44	44
Spain	43	21.5
Malaysia	39	4.9
Italy	34	8.5
France	30	15
Ukraine	21	1.8
Portugal	18	18
Estonia	14	14
Poland	13	13
Korea	12	2
Indonesia	11	2.8
Iran	10	5
Japan	10	2

It can be depicted from Table 5 that the average article citations within the two databases used in this study, WoS and Scopus, are remarkable for Egypt, the Netherlands, the UK, and Morocco, with 71, 64, 62.4, and 44, respectively.

Table 6 provides information on the effects of 202 sources, including 296 articles examined in this study. In bibliometric analysis, "Sources Impact" refers to the influence and importance of academic journals, conferences, and other publishing venues in a particular field. This impact is often calculated through various metrics that evaluate the productivity and citation performance of these sources. Understanding these metrics is important for researchers to identify the most influential journals to target for publication and to stay abreast of the latest research developments.

Table 6. Source Impact

Element	h-index	TC	NP
Environmental Science and Pollution Research	9	441	13
Sustainability (Switzerland)	6	103	12
World Development	4	300	4
Economic Research-Ekonomska Istrazivanja	3	30	4
Empirical Economics	3	16	3
Frontiers in Environmental Science	3	55	7
Resources Policy	3	273	4
Economic Inquiry	2	241	2
Economic Journal	2	514	2
Environmental Science and Policy	2	39	2
Financial and Credit Activity-Problems of Theory and Practice	2	8	7
International Journal of Energy Economics and Policy	2	8	3
International Journal of Environmental Research and Public Health	2	28	2
International Journal of Finance & Economics	2	231	2
International Journal of Social Economics	2	24	3
Journal of Coastal Research	2	11	4
Journal of Developing Areas	2	20	2
Journal of Emerging Market Finance	2	13	2
Journal of Environmental Engineering and Landscape Management	2	9	2
Macroeconomic Dynamics	2	5	2
Research in Economics	2	57	2
Technological Forecasting and Social Change	2	102	2
WSEAS Transactions on Business and Economics	2	15	3

Table 6 contains the h-index, total citation (TC) count and number of publications (NP) information of the relevant resources (Elements). A high h-index reflects both multiple publications and frequent citations; this shows the impact and relevance of the source. TC count provides information about the total number of citations of articles taken from a particular source. High total citations indicate that the articles in these sources are widely referenced and have a significant impact on the field.

Therefore, according to Table 6, the most relevant resources in the intercept of finance and economic development are as follows: Environmental Science and Pollution Research with 13 articles, Sustainability (Switzerland) with 12 articles, Financial and Credit Activity-Problems of Theory and Practice with 7 articles, Frontiers in Environmental Science with 7 articles, Applied Economics Letters with 4 articles, Economic Research-Ekonomska Istrazivanja with 4 articles, Handbook of Finance and Development with 4 articles, Journal of Coastal Research with 4 articles, Resources Policy with 4 articles, and World Development with 4 articles. Also Table 7 (below) provides detailed information about author impact.

Table 7. Author Impact

Element	h-index	TC	NP
Li C	4	29	4
Wang Y	3	14	4
Wu H	3	14	3
Zhang Y	3	22	3
Chen Z	2	11	2
Hall J	2	96	2
Ketkar K	2	20	2
Ketkar S	2	20	2
Khan A	2	68	2
Law S	2	216	2
Lee C	2	131	2
Li J	2	10	3
Li W	2	21	2
Lin J	2	22	2
Ma X	2	7	3
Mao Q	2	7	2
Nasir M	2	266	2
Paiders J	2	9	2
Paramati S	2	221	2
Shi L	2	7	2
Singh A	2	514	2

Table 7 shows the h-index, TC and NP that the researchers have as a result of their studies on the related economic development and finance. Although the number of publications were equal, Li C. ranked first and Wang Y. ranked second according to the h-index value.

In Figure 3, the top fifteen keywords are presented. Among the most frequent words, there are "economic development", "China", "finance", "economic growth", "carbon dioxide", "financial system", "sustainable development", "environmental economics", "investment", "growth" "green economy", "economic and social effects", "financial market", "carbon emission" and "banking".

Figure 3. Top Fifteen Keywords

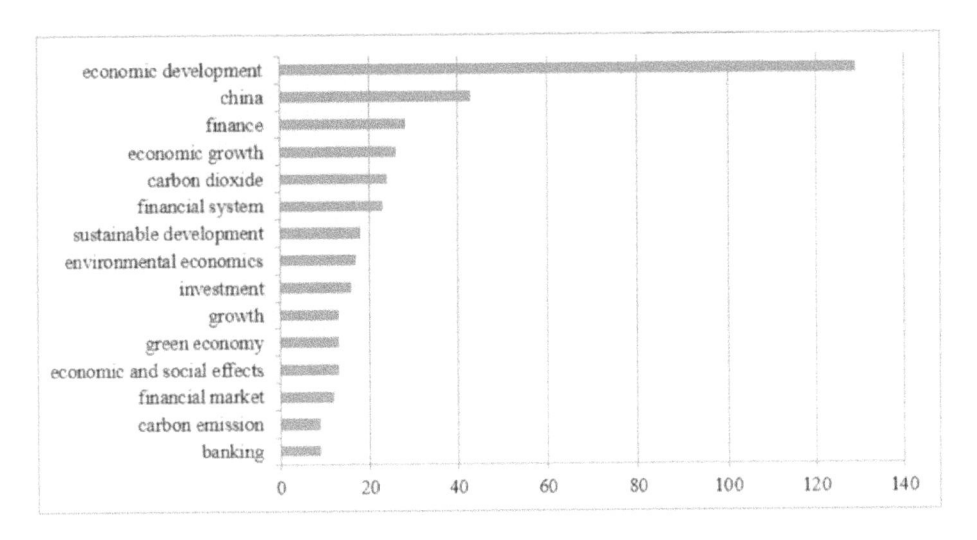

[Bar chart showing keyword frequencies from 0 to 140:
- economic development: ~130
- china: ~45
- finance: ~28
- economic growth: ~25
- carbon dioxide: ~22
- financial system: ~22
- sustainable development: ~18
- environmental economics: ~15
- investment: ~13
- growth: ~12
- green economy: ~11
- economic and social effects: ~10
- financial market: ~9
- carbon emission: ~7
- banking: ~6]

As shown in the Figure 3, since our main keywords are "economic development" and "financ*" it is expected that they will be two of the most frequent words/word pairs. Moreover, since this issue is studied mostly in China, China is the second most frequent word. This also implies that our analysis provides a wide range of issues relevant to the nexus of sustainability, finance, and economic development.

The presence of words and/or word pairs such as "carbon emission", "sustainable development", "environmental economics", "economic and social effects" and "green economy" shows the importance of studying economic and environmental issues globally. Thus, this perspective is important to address challenges such as climate change and achieve sustainable development goals.

Keywords like "green economy" and "carbon emission" are related to environmental sustainability, and this exposes the increasing importance of environmental considerations in economic development and financial decision-making.

Furthermore, the prominence of the keyword "sustainable development" underscores the alignment of our research with global agendas that are aimed at addressing the global challenges that our world faces.

A conceptual structure map created through the use of multiple correspondence analysis in bibliometric analysis is a visual depiction of the connections between different concepts, phrases, or subjects found in a collection of literature. This approach facilitates the identification and comprehension of the fundamental framework of study topics and their interconnectedness.

Figure 4. Multiple Correspondence Analysis

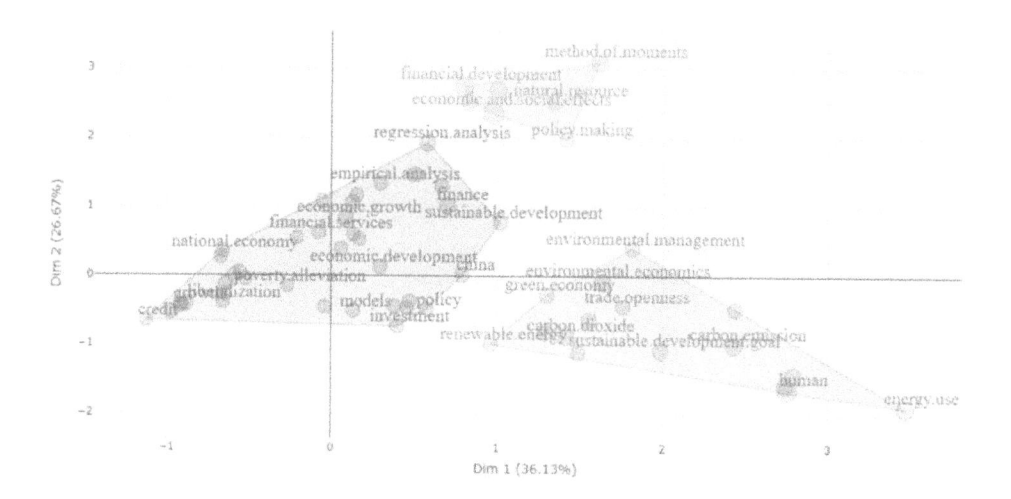

The red cluster in Figure 4 comprises phrases pertaining to conventional economic subjects such as "economic development", "finance", "investment", "policy" and "economic growth". This indicates a concentration on the study of economic theory, analysis of policies, and provision of financial services. The proximity of the terms "economic growth", "financial services" and "investment" in the red cluster emphasizes a key topic in economic research that centers around financial systems and economic policy.

The green cluster in Figure 4 encompasses terms such as "financial development", "policy formulation", "economic and social impacts" and "method of moments". This indicates an emphasis on quantitative methodologies and the wider impacts of financial and economic policies. The incorporation of phrases such as "policy making" and "economic and social effects" in the green cluster indicates research that connects economic theory with tangible policy implications, frequently employing quantitative methodologies.

The blue cluster in Figure 4 includes phrases pertaining to environmental and sustainable development subjects, such as "environmental economics", "carbon dioxide", "renewable energy", "green economy" and "carbon emission". This indicates a concentration on the convergence of economics and environmental concerns. The blue cluster's research area in environmental economics is strongly focused on "renewable energy", "carbon emission" and "sustainable development goal" with an emphasis on sustainability and environmental management.

Figure 5 shows that keywords are grouped into four areas as niche themes, motor themes, emerging or declining themes, and basic themes.

Figure 5. Thematic Map

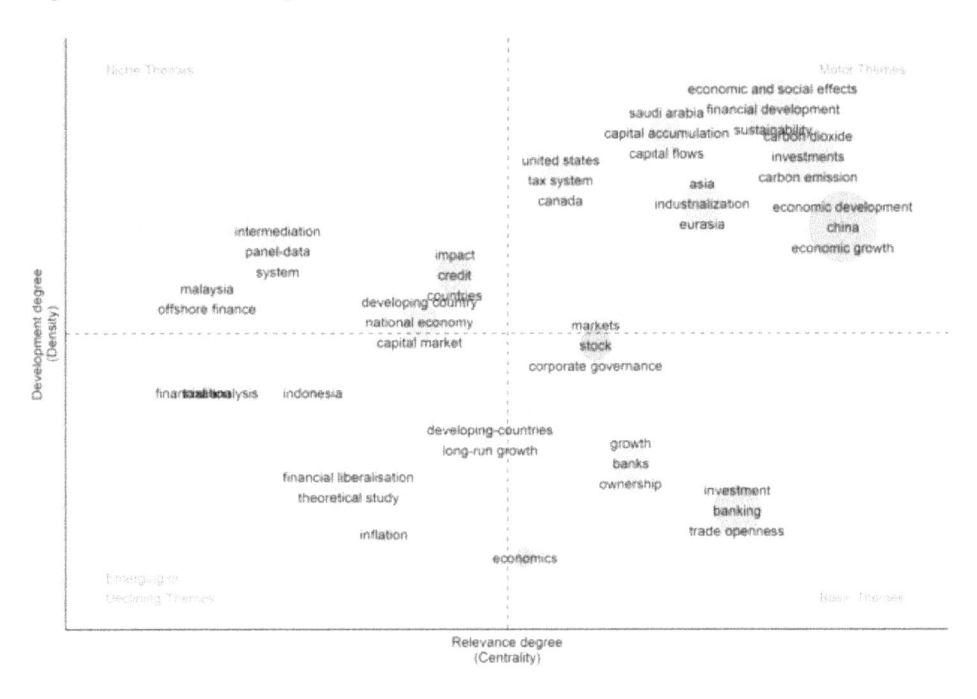

As shown in thematic map (in Figure 5), words in the basic themes area constitute the most basic keywords used in studies that examine economic development and financial dimensions together. The motor themes area shows the most commonly used and prominent keywords in the related research. Emerging or declining themes indicate both overused and newly used keywords. Niche themes indicate keywords that have not been taken into account when analyzing the economic development and finance dimensions and may be included in future studies.

Cobo et al. (2011) suggest that thematic evolution analysis (See Figure 6 below) can yield results that demonstrate the advancement and trajectory of development in a specific subject. Additionally, it can aid in forecasting future patterns in the relevant domain.

Figure 6. Thematic Evolution Analysis

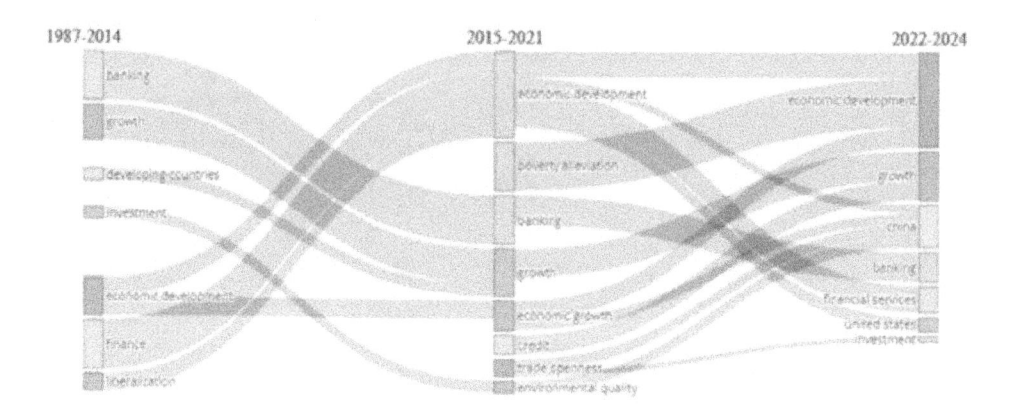

As shown in Figure 6, for thematic evolution analysis, we used the periods of 1987–2014, 2015–2021, and 2022–2024 to approximate the number of articles between the evolution periods. The total number of articles on this issue between 1987 and 2014 was 96; it was 101 between 2015 and 2021 and 99 between 2022 and 2024. The first period (1987–2014) shows the foundational themes in earlier research. The second period (2015–2021) indicates how themes evolved or new themes emerged. Lastly, the third period shows the current and emerging research trends.

These three periods show the keywords of most interest to researchers and how these keywords have evolved across the periods. Accordingly, "banking" maintained its importance throughout the analysis period. According to the intensity of usage, "finance", "economic development" and "liberalization" from keywords in the first period were grouped under "economic development" in the second period. The keywords "financial services", "economic development", "USA" and "China" took the place of "economic development" in the second period, in that order. "Growth" continued as "growth" in the next two periods. "Investments" turned into "environmental quality" in the second period and "China" in the third period. The "poverty alleviation" that emerged in the second period has evolved into "economic development". The word "credit" which intensified in the second period, evolved into the word "growth" in the third period. The words "China" and "investment" took the place of the word "trade openness" which gained importance in the second period. Finally, the word "developing countries" has evolved into "growth" in the second period.

RESULTS AND DISCUSSION

In conclusion, this study emphasizes the critical importance of comprehending the complex relationship between financial dynamics and economic development. Through a bibliometric analysis, this study attempts to explore the trends in finance and economic development. An exhaustive examination of scholarly publications was conducted utilizing data from reputable databases such as Web of Science and Scopus to identify significant subjects and emerging research areas. This research strives to give readers a comprehensive understanding of the important themes, possibilities, and difficulties that drive the dynamic disciplines of economic growth and finance. It does this by providing light on both historical precedents and future directions.

The results offer new perspectives on how economic development and finance are changing. The combined dataset includes scholarly articles spanning from 1987 to 2024 that reflect a wide range of perspectives. Particularly, some thematic trends emerge with a notable shift over time. The thematic evolution highlights the dynamic nature of the study in this field, moving from early focuses on fundamental studies of economic growth to more complex investigations of economic expansion, asset accumulation, and the role of finance in furthering sustainability.

The financial system and economic regulation play an important role in achieving the 17 Sustainable Development Goals by providing the necessary resources, investments and frameworks to support sustainable development efforts and address global challenges. The 193 member states of the United Nations have set 17 goals to be achieved by the end of 2030, which entered into force in January 2016 to eradicate poverty, protect planet Earth and ensure that all people live in peace and prosperity. The goals to be worked on in the process, called the "Decade of Action" because it covers the period between 2020 and 2030, include "no poverty, zero hunger, good health and well-being, quality education, gender equality, clean water and sanitation, affordable and clean energy, decent work and economic growth, industry, innovation and infrastructure, reduced inequality, sustainable cities and communities, responsible consumption and production, climate action, life below water, life on land, peace, justice and strong institutions, partnerships for the goals".

Overall, comprehending the correlation between economic development and finance is crucial for attaining the Sustainable Development Goals (SDGs). It guarantees that financial systems are in line with sustainable development priorities, mobilizes the required resources, promotes inclusive growth, supports climate action, and constructs resilient and fair economies. An integrated strategy is crucial for tackling the intricate and interrelated challenges described in the 2030 Agenda for Sustainable Development.

Indeed, the presence of terms like "green finance" and "sustainable development goals" indicates a growing understanding of the necessity of incorporating environmental factors into coordinating research endeavors with worldwide sustainability agendas. At this stage, the increase in sustainable investments also triggers the development of a diversity of green financial products to be used in financing investments. It would be appropriate to emphasize that the regulations to be made in this direction play an important role in the realization of economic development goals. China's frequent occurrence as a central theme highlights the country's significant influence on patterns of global economic activity and also indicates the growing awareness of the role that environmental sustainability plays in economic growth.

Additionally, our analysis results provide consistent information with the Economist's June 2024 issue. The June 2024 issue of the Economist presents two fundamental pieces of data that establish China's undeniable superiority. One of these factors is the quantity of citations received by China for its high-quality scientific works. Clarivate, a research business, has found that the number of citations for publications originating from China has exceeded those from the United States (US) and the European Union (EU). Nevertheless, during the early 2000s, papers originating from the United States were referenced 20 times more frequently than pieces from China. In response to criticism attributing the situation to Chinese scientists excessively citing each other's publications, the Economist highlighted the findings of the esteemed scientific institution known as the Nature Index. The Nature Index report featured a rigorous evaluation by a respected panel of referees to assess the quality of the papers. The report highlighted US-based articles three times more prominently than those from China and indicated that China's prominence is projected to increase by 2023 (Minton-Beddoes, 2024).

To sum up, this study contributes insightful information from a thorough bibliometric analysis to the continuing conversation on economic development and finance. In a highly interconnected global landscape, this research aims to inform policymakers and scholars by clarifying key themes, identifying emerging trends, and highlighting policy implications.

REFERENCES

Acemoglu, D., Johnson, S., & Robinson, J. A. (2001). The colonial origins of comparative development: An empirical investigation. *The American Economic Review*, 91(5), 1369–1401. DOI: 10.1257/aer.91.5.1369

Aria, M., & Cuccurullo, C. (2017). Bibliometrix: An R-tool for comprehensive science mapping analysis. *Journal of Informetrics*, 11(4), 959–975. DOI: 10.1016/j.joi.2017.08.007

Asoni, A. (2008). Protection of property rights and growth as political equilibria. *Journal of Economic Surveys*, 22(5), 953–987. DOI: 10.1111/j.1467-6419.2008.00554.x

Atje, R., & Jovanovic, B. (1993). Stock markets and development. *European Economic Review*, 37(2-3), 632–640. DOI: 10.1016/0014-2921(93)90053-D

Beck, T. (2012). The role of finance on economic development: benefits, risks, and politics. In Mueller, D. C. (Ed.), *The Oxford handbook of capitalism* (pp. 161–203). Oxford University Press. DOI: 10.1093/oxfordhb/9780195391176.013.0007

Becker, G. S. (1994). *Human capital: A theoretical and empirical analysis, with special reference to education* (3rd ed.). University of Chicago Press.

Behrman, J. (1977). 27. Development economics. In Weintraub, S. (Ed.), *Modern economic thought* (pp. 537–558). University of Pennsylvania Press., DOI: 10.9783/9781512808650-036

Cobo, M. J., Lopez-Herrera, A. G., Herrera-Viedma, E., & Herrera, F. (2011). An approach for detecting, quantifying, and visualizing the evolution of a research field: A practical application to the fuzzy sets theory field. *Journal of Informetrics*, 5(1), 146–166. DOI: 10.1016/j.joi.2010.10.002

Demetriades, P., & Law, S. H. (2006). Finance, institutions and economic development. *International Journal of Finance & Economics*, 11(3), 245–260. DOI: 10.1002/ijfe.296

Durusu-Ciftci, D., Ispir, M. S., & Yetkiner, H. (2017). Financial development and economic growth: Some theory and more evidence. *Journal of Policy Modeling*, 39(2), 290–306. DOI: 10.1016/j.jpolmod.2016.08.001

Fels, R. (1949). The long-wave depression, 1873–97. *The Review of Economics and Statistics*, 31(1), 69–73. DOI: 10.2307/1927196

Frankel, J. A., & Romer, D. H. (1999). Does trade cause growth? *The American Economic Review*, 89(3), 379–399. DOI: 10.1257/aer.89.3.379

Gallarotti, G. M. (1995). *The anatomy of an international monetary regime: The classical gold standard*. Oxford University Press. DOI: 10.1093/oso/9780195089905.001.0001

Johnson, S., McMillan, J., & Woodruff, C. (2002). Property rights and finance. *The American Economic Review*, 92(5), 1335–1356. DOI: 10.1257/000282802762024539

Keynes, J. M. (1920). *The economic consequences of the peace*. Harcourt, Brace, and Howe.

Keynes, J. M. (2010). The great slump of 1930. In *Essays in persuasion*. Palgrave Macmillan., DOI: 10.1007/978-1-349-59072-8_10

Levine, R. (2005). Finance and growth: Theory and evidence. In Aghion, P., & Durlauf, S. (Eds.), *Handbook of economic growth* (pp. 865–934). Elsevier.

Marichal, C. (2014). Historical reflections on the causes of financial crises: Official investigations, past and present, 1873–2011. *Investigaciones de Historia Económica-Economic. Historical Research*, 10(2), 81–91. DOI: 10.1016/j.ihe.2014.03.010

McKinnon, R. I. (1973). *Money and capital in economic development*. The Brookings Institution.

Minton-Beddoes, Z. (2024, June 15). The rise of Chinese science: Welcome or worrying? *The Economist*. https://www.economist.com/weeklyedition/2024-06-1

Paul, J., Lim, W. M., O'Cass, A., Hao, A. W., & Bresciani, S. (2021). Scientific procedures and rationales for systematic literature reviews (SPAR-4-SLR). *International Journal of Consumer Studies*, 45(4), 1–16. DOI: 10.1111/ijcs.12695

Petreski, M. (2014). Regulatory environment and development outcomes: Empirical evidence from transition economies. *Ekonomicky Casopis*, 62(3), 225–248.

Robinson, J. (1952). *The generalisation of the general theory, in the rate of interest, and other essays* (2nd ed.). Macmillan.

Rodrik, D., Subramanian, A., & Trebbi, F. (2004). Institutions rule: The primacy of institutions over geography and integration in economic development. *Journal of Economic Growth*, 9(2), 131–165. DOI: 10.1023/B:JOEG.0000031425.72248.85

Sachs, J. D. (2001). Tropical underdevelopment. *NBER Working Paper Series*, No. 8119. DOI: 10.3386/w8119

Schumpeter, J. (1911). *The theory of economic development*. Harvard University Press.

Seyidoğlu, H. (2003). Uluslararası mali krizler, IMF politikaları az gelişmiş ülkeler, Türkiye ve dönüşüm ekonomileri. *Doğuş Üniversitesi Dergisi*, 4(2), 141–156. DOI: 10.31671/dogus.2019.314

Shaw, E. S. (1973). *Financial deepening in economic development*. Oxford University Press.

World Economic Forum. (2012). *The financial development report 2012*. Reuttner, I., Glass, T., Drzeniek, H. M., Geiger, T., Koenitzer, M., Duffie, D., & Van Horen, N. https://www.weforum.org/publications/financial-development-report-2012/

Xu, G. (2013). Property rights, law, and economic development. *Law and Development Review*, 6(1), 117–142. DOI: 10.1515/ldr-2013-0004

Yiadom, E. B., Mensah, L., & Bokpin, G. A. (2023). Environmental risk and foreign direct investment: The role of financial deepening, access and efficiency. *Sustainability Accounting. Management and Policy Journal*, 14(2), 369–395. DOI: 10.1108/SAMPJ-12-2021-0552

ADDITIONAL READING

Carter, Z. D. (2020). *The price of peace: Money, democracy, and the life of John Maynard Keynes*. Random House.

Ferguson, N. (2009). *The ascent of money: A financial history of the world*. Penguin Books.

Kindleberger, C. P. (2005). *Manias, panics, and crashes: A history of financial crises*. WILEY. DOI: 10.1057/9780230628045

Krugman, P. R. (2009). *The return of depression economics and the crisis of 2008*. Penguin Books.

Shiller, R. J. (2012). *Finance and the good society*. Princeton University Press.

Wapshott, N. (2011). *Keynes Hayek: the clash that defined modern economics*. W.W. Norton & Co.

Chapter 11
Quantitative Measures and Moderating Power of Monetary Policies:
Insight from the Analysis of the Link between Equity Sector Indices with Money Supply

Orhan Özaydın
https://orcid.org/0000-0003-2585-1437
İstanbul Medipol University, Turkey

Edmund Ntom Udemba
Shanxi Technology and Business University, China

ABSTRACT

Re-evaluation of the critical macroeconomic indices behind the movement of money and other financial assets with respect to the flow and supply of money for the case of Türkiye is essential at this present economic situation of Türkiye. Türkiye's economic activities have been, and still passing through unstable development due to excessive inflation and poor performance of the foreign exchange rate. To this end, authors applied the monthly end price data from 2005 December to 2022 March to researched 10 different Istanbul Equity Indices (IEI) as dependent variable, to see whether they are related with Money supply for the case of Türkiye. From the quantitative analysis of the indices, all control variables including USD/TRY and BOND2Y coefficients are negatively correlated with equity indices and statistically

DOI: 10.4018/979-8-3693-5508-4.ch011

Copyright © 2025, IGI Global. Copying or distributing in print or electronic forms without written permission of IGI Global is prohibited.

significant. Furthermore, the impact of Central Bank reserves and deposits to the Central Bank (M1) and term deposits at banks (M2 minus M1) on sector indices is found to vary significantly across different sectors.

1. INTRODUCTION

Unstable situation and turbulence nature of Türkiye's economy calls for re-evaluation of the critical macroeconomic indices behind the movement of money and other financial assets with respect to the flow and supply of money. It has been established that macroeconomic factors impact the flow of money between firms and stock markets (Chen et al. 1986). Following the launching of the Arbitrage Pricing Model (APM) by Ross, (1976), scholars have tried to investigate with evidence the connectivity between stock prices and macroeconomic variables. For example, manufacturing sector is conceived to be a leading economic sector with a significant positive impact on stock and capital returns and prices, and since this sector predicts a significant positive impact on stock prices, it means that it will increase the profits of the companies in the sectors (Camilleri et al. 2019). However, an economy characterized by high inflation, can record both positive and negative impacts on stock returns due to inflation. A typical example is where a consumer prices impact interest rate, this will force the investors' demand for securities (bonds) to increase thereby spark a move to start removing stocks from their investment portfolios. This occurrence will instigate the firms to start searching for fund, and the easiest way to raise the fund is by issuing stocks in form of shares and debentures instead of bonds because of the high rate of market interest rate in the inflation environment. This will force the stock prices to fall due to selling pressure in the stock market (Quayes &Jamal, 2008)

Macroeconomic activities and performance of Türkiye's economy comprise the interaction of money supply and the performance of stock market and returns. This involves daily running of corporate bodies and the expected returns which connect to investors' decision on the profitable investments. The interactions between the money supply and stock return is complicated. The complexities are rooted in the power of money supply on the triangular nexus among inflation rates, interest rates, and aggregate demand. The increase on the influx of money through money supply create room for excess liquidity for the potential investors, and this surplus is channeled to the stock market for stock purchases. This can trigger inflation and push interest rates high, thus, the stock market begins to move downwards (Alatiqi & Fazel, 2008; Palmer, 1970). This has presented the study of macroeconomic with respect to stock prices, performance and returns as one of the hitting subjects in the financial literature. Stock price index fluctuate on daily basis through the instrument of macroeconomic indicators such as interest rate, inflation, money supply and demand.

The stock price mechanism is subject to the changes in the macroeconomic indicators (Hoque et al. 2019; Chang et al. 2021). Thus, the changes in money supply trigger volatility in stock market through the influence of interest rate and inflation (Sahu & Pandey, 2020). Increase in Money supply suggests decrease in the interest rate which drives the stock prices up due to the quest to invest on assets instead of holding money or keeping the savings in the bank, and vice versa. Additionally, expansion of stocks in form of shares and equities can be attributed to entrance of new issuers to the stock exchange market and corporate engagements in apportioning of the dividends and share transfer through convertible shares. The interaction of the macroeconomic indicators and the stock is partly determined by the available information to the investors and merchandise who rely on the information to trade on the available stocks and their prices. The information exposes the trajectory of the companies in the system with regards to their survivals and securities in the market for possible exploitation by the prospective investors. Investors needed this information as part of analytical tools to make timely decision on investments. Both the positive and negative values of the stock are made available through the information which the market reacts to (Jogiyanto, 2000).

Money supply of many countries have been researched with respect to their connectivity to the equity indices and stock prices. Studies on this aspect have often centered on the whole economy with individual perspectives as it concerns sectoral operation. Türkiye is among the emerging countries of the world faced with macroeconomic problems span on excessive money supply and declining of the interest rate. Türkiye's economy is faced with double digit inflation and catastrophic exchange problem which has generated different discussions on how to mitigate the macroeconomic problem of the country. On this premise, the present study aims to examine the connectivity that exist between the money supply and Istanbul sectoral base equity indices in Türkiye. As stated before, unstable situation and turbulence nature of Türkiye's economy calls for re-evaluation of the critical macroeconomic indices behind the movement of money and other financial assets with respect to the flow and supply of money. It has been established that macroeconomic factors impact the flow of money between firms and stock markets (Chen et al. 1986). Put succinctly, the main target of this study is to understand the existence of any relation between Istanbul sectoral base equity indices and money supply of Türkiye. Investigating the responses of the Türkiye's stock market and indices on its money supply through the interactions of the stock market and economic variables is essential at this point in time to both policymakers and investors. This will guide the authority in framing lasting monetary policies with the aim of stabilizing the economic situation of the country. By extension, the research work is expected to form a baseline for other economies passing through the same economic turbulence to frame a lasting monetary policy. The findings and policies derive from this study will aid in controlling the money supply and stabilizing the economic performance of any economy that deem them applicable to their economies. The study seeks to add to the finance literature by including nine (9) sectoral base stock indices to the existing indices such as BIST100 and BIST30. There are several past studies that have investigated macroeconomic variables and Istanbul Stock Exchange of Türkiye such as BIST100 and BIST30 (Tiryaki et al. 2019; He et al. 2023; Kassouri and Altıntas, 2020). Besides BIST100 index, including sectoral base 9 stock indices is the novelty of this paper.

The aim of this study is summarized as follows: i) to investigates the effects of Turkish monetary policy on sectoral stock indices in the context of monetary transmission theory on stocks ii) to expose how the money supply affects the sectors in the Istanbul stock market. iii) to quantitatively test the impact of the 9 different sector indices on Istanbul stock market, and the effect on money supply in Türkiye. The novelty of this study is based on its ability to reveal the relationship between the selected (9) different sector indices in the Istanbul stock market and the money supply in Türkiye, so that the effects of the money supply on a sectoral basis can be understood. This is very significant in the decision making in the mainstream of financial and monetary investment. The findings from this study are expected to be a beacon and roadmap towards policy framing by the authorities. As the method used in this study, we investigated the relationship between stock indices and money supply data by help of linear regression models. The suitability of the data and models is assured by unit root tests, heterodasticty tests, and tests of multicollinearity problems. A review of the literature, the data and methods, the study's findings, and conclusions follow.

2. THEORY AND LITERATURE

2.1 Central Bank and Monetary Policy

Monetary policy serves as a fundamental instrument employed by central banks to regulate economic conditions, maintain price stability, and affect levels of employment. Throughout the years, a multitude of theories and frameworks have emerged to elucidate the methodologies through which central banks implement monetary policy in pursuit of their macroeconomic goals. This segment examines the breadth of both theoretical and empirical literature pertaining to central bank monetary policies, with particular emphasis on the progression of monetary policy frameworks, the instruments utilized, and the empirical data that corroborates their efficacy.

The old view of monetary policy has been expressed, among others, by David Hume and Adam Smith; this is what has been referred to as the long-term neutrality of money. According to this school, changes in the money supply have effects only on nominal variables—for example, prices, wages—but not on real economic variables like output and employment. This view later found expression in the Quantity Theory of Money, which postulates a direct relation between changes in the money stock and changes in the price level.

Basically, the neoclassical framework uses classical ideas in asserting that the economy is self-correcting; therefore, all deviations from full employment are but temporary. In this view, monetary policy can have short-term effects on output and employment, but in the long run, the economy returns to its natural rate of unemployment, and monetary policy primarily influences inflation. Milton Friedman, a prominent neoclassical economist, argued that central banks should focus on controlling inflation through steady money supply growth, a view that influenced the development of monetarism (Friedman, 1968).

John Maynard Keynes developed Keynesian economics, which challenged the classical view by arguing that monetary policy may have significant effects on actual economic variables, at least in the short run. In fact, Keynes indicated that central banks are capable of using monetary policy to stimulate demand by lowering interest rates and increasing money supply during downturns. This view laid the foundation for modern concepts of countercyclical monetary policy (Keynes, 1936). The new Keynesian economics developed as a school toward the end of the 20th century, implementing the basics of Keynesian thinking with microeconomic foundations. Price and wage rigidities, which may lead to persistent deviations from full employment, are stressed by new Keynesians. They would support an active monetary policy stance in stabilizing the economy and lowering output fluctuations. The Taylor Rule, due to John Taylor, is an important policy rule suggesting that central banks should adjust interest rates in response to deviations of inflation and output from their targets (Taylor, 1993).

Throughout the second half of the 20th century, inflation targeting evolved into a dominant paradigm for monetary policy. Many central banks in advanced economies set specific targets for inflation, aiming to anchor expectations and help stabilize inflation but achieve price stability. It's very first implementation took place in New Zealand in 1990, only later to be adopted by other central banking structures, like the Bank of England and the European Central Bank. Research indicates that implementing inflation targeting has proven effective in mitigating inflation and stabilizing economic conditions. Investigations conducted by Bernanke et al. (1999) and Mishkin (2007) demonstrated that inflation targeting enabled central banks to attain lower and more stable inflation rates without compromising economic growth. The independence of central banks has become an important factor in establishing whether monetary policy is effective. Central banks that are independent have a greater tendency to resist political pressures aimed at actions with short-term benefits and limited long-term stability. As indicated, empirical evidence shows that central bank independence does lead to lower inflation and more stable levels of inflation (Cukierman, Webb, & Neyapti, 1992)

The global financial crisis of 2007-2008 and the subsequent recession set central banks on the road to unconventional monetary policies, as traditional policy tools, namely cuts in interest rates, were approaching their limit in that scenario. Quantitative easing, forward guidance, and negative interest rates formed axial parts of monetary policy in advanced economies. Quantitative easing is an extensive central bank purchase of assets aimed at enhancing liquidity within financial markets and lowering long-term interest rates. Joyce et al. (2012) and Gagnon et al. (2011) have shown that QE was successful in lowering the yields of government bonds and boosting economic activity. Forward guidance is an unconventional instrument that involves central banks expressing their future policy intentions to influence market expectations. Campbell et al. (2012) show that forward guidance can successfully shape expectations and influence long-term interest rates, particularly when the short-term rates are close to zero.

In recent years, there is increasing recognition of the role that financial stability can play in monetary policy. The Global Financial Crisis has underlined the risks coming from financial imbalances and seen the integration of macroprudential policy with conventional monetary policy. Macroprudential policy involves using regulatory tools to address systemic risks in the financial system. Claessens and Kose (2013) argue that macroprudential policy should complement monetary policy to achieve both price stability and financial stability. The coordination between these policies remains a subject of ongoing debate and research.

The literature on central-bank monetary policies has evolved over time, moving from classical and neoclassical theories, which emphasize the notion of money neutrality, to Keynesian and New Keynesian models that advocate active monetary intervention. Contemporary monetary frameworks are deeply indebted to the process of inflation targeting, central bank independence, and unconventional monetary policies. Considering emerging financial stability concerns, the integration of macroprudential policies with monetary policy has become an area of prime importance for future research.

2.2 Money Supply Channels

Monetary policy operates through several channels to influence the economy, with money supply channels being crucial in transmitting central bank actions to the real economy. Monetary policy is the set of policies that a central bank, for example, the Federal Reserve, uses to influence the country's money supply, interest rates, and inflation. All these may be directed towards attaining the macroeconomic objectives through traditional interest rate channels, credit channels, and asset price channels. The interest rate channel is the channel through which changes in the federal funds rate affect short-term interest rates and, in turn, long-term interest rates. These affect consumption and investment decisions through changing the costs of borrowing and the return on savings, influencing aggregate demand, and hence affecting inflation and economic growth (Mishkin, 1996). The credit channel operates through its effect on the lending behavior of banks and the creditworthiness of borrowers. A contraction in monetary policy would work further by reducing bank reserves, thereby reducing the amount of credit available and affecting borrowers dependent on bank credit, such as small businesses. Changes in monetary policy also have a constant impact on the balance sheet of firms and households and, hence, their borrowing capacity (Morris & Sellon, 1995). Interest rate also influences asset prices, and therefore the economy. Interest rate changes could affect stock and bond prices, which will have an influence on the wealth and investment decisions of households and companies. Higher interest rates might reduce stock prices and, thus, wealth and consumption (Chami et al., 1999). The risk-taking channel posits that low interest rates increase risk-taking by banks and investors. This may induce banks to lend in the direction of higher-risk borrowers to maintain profitability, and as such, magnify the effect of monetary policy on both financial stability and the level of economic activity (DeGroot, 2014). Monetary policy further channels into exchange rate, which affects net exports and aggregate demand. Normally, a currency's price will depreciate with a decrease in interest rates, thereby making exports cheaper and imports expensive to spark economic growth accordingly (McCredie et al., 2016). The capital structure channel could be seen as a process in which monetary policy transmits information regarding the decision of the firm to its debt-equity mix. For example, central bank quantitative easing, which lowers corporate bond yields, imparts incentives for the substitution of bank loans with bond debt, affecting bank lending behavior and firms' investment decisions (Grosse-Rueschkamp et al., 2018). In summary, there are many monetary policy transmission channels that affect different aspects of economic activity. The effectiveness of the management by a central bank in such channels is important for achieving goals and preserving stability in the economy.

Asset price channel is one of the important mechanisms in monetary policy transmission, with impacts on some key economic variables like consumption and investment. The channel works through changes in the prices of assets such as stock and real estate, which affect household wealth and corporate decisions for investment. To illustrate, if monetary authorities think it proper to adopt a course of accommodation, the central bank policy, in terms of lowering interest rates, could increase asset prices. Higher asset prices raise the wealth of households—thereby encouraging more consumption—and can also make equity financing more attractive for firms—thereby leading to increased investment (Horatiu, 2013). Another study underlines the role of Tobin's q—the ratio of a firm's market value to the replacement cost of its assets. A higher q, brought about by increased asset prices, raises the incentive of firms to invest more (Dan, 2013). Mathematically to understand the interest and stock price relations under the present value or discounted cash flow model, stock prices equal the present value of expected future dividends. When S is price of stock, K is the term, D is expected dividend and the assumption of a fixed discount rate (R), the stock price can be represented as Equation 1 which is a version of the present value model. According to this model's mechanism, a change in monetary policy can affect stock returns (Akay & Nargeleçekenler, 2009).

$$S_t = E_t\left[\sum_{j=1}^{K} \left(\frac{1}{1+R}\right)^j D_{t+j}\right] \tag{1}$$

Economic theory deals with the causes of the interaction between monetary policy and stock prices. The central bank (CB) influences interest rates by tuning the money supply. Increasing the money supply decreases the interest rates (Parasız, 2013). Thus, stock prices are being valued higher. Another practical example for monetary policy to stock channel that when the Central Bank implements an expansionary monetary policy, interest rates will decrease and the demand for stocks will increase as the bond yields will decrease, which will increase the price of stocks. Monetary policy plays an important role in determining the returns of securities by changing the discount rate used by market participants or by influencing the expectations of market participants who will participate in future economic activity. Actually, the discount rate used by market participants is just the market interest rate, and moreover, the Central Bank can influence the market interest rate. As a result, stock market participants must pay attention to the strategies of the monetary authority (Ioannidis & Kontonikas, 2008).

Monetary policy and stock price levels are widely interested by researchers in literature. To begin with the most prior one; Hashemzadeh, N.& Taylor, P. (1988) examine the statistical causality relationship between the money supply and stock price levels. Using Granger-Sims' test to determine one-way causality, they find in their research that the relationship between money supply and stock prices is that some changes in stock price levels are caused by the money supply and vice versa. Handoyo et al. (2015) investigate monetary policy on Indonesian Stock price as well as main sectors stock price such as agricultural, mining, manufacture, and financial sector indexes. Their method is the Monte Carlo algorithm to Near-SVAR models. They discover that both aggregated and sectoral stock prices respond positive to a monetary policy positive shock.

Nkechukwu et al. (2015) conduct a study to evaluate the effect of macroeconomic variables on stock market prices for Nigeria for the period 1980-2013. The findings show that M2 has a significant long-term positive effect on stock prices. Thus means, expansionary monetary policy has positively related with stock prices. Nwaogwugwu, (2018) empirically examines the impact of macroeconomic policy and stock market behavior in Nigeria with the help of ARDL model. He works with Broad Money, Interest Rate as indicators of macroeconomic policy. The results of the study show that the money supply and interest rate have statistically significant effects on the stock market in the short and long term. Thus, macroeconomic policy actions have significant effects on the stock market in Nigeria both in the short and long term. Nwaogwugwu suggests that in order to realize the full potential of stock market activity in countries, authorities shall use fiscal and monetary policy together, not independently of each other.

Studies have been conducted to investigate the effectiveness of the stock channel in Türkiye, and different results have been seen. Örnek (2009) tests the efficiency of the stock channel between 1990-2006 with the quarterly data of Türkiye. He applies the impulse response functions and variance decomposition method within the scope of VAR model. Findings reveal that the stock channel does not work effectively in Türkiye. He explains the reason that the stock market in Türkiye does not gain enough depth. Besides, Akay and Nargeleçekenler (2009) investigate how the monetary policy changes in Türkiye affect the stock prices with the help of structural VAR model. They show that the contractionary monetary policy shock has a reducing effect on stock prices in both the short and long run. Fattah and Kocabıyık (2020) explore the effects of macroeconomic factors on stock markets in Türkiye and the USA. As a result of the Toda-Yamamoto causality analysis for the US data, a one-way causality relationship is found from the money supply to the S&P500 Index. In Türkiye, a bidirectional causality has been determined between the money supply and the BIST100 index. In other words, if the BIST100 index changes, the money supply also changes, and if the money supply variable changes, the BIST100 index also changes.

The asset price channel is indirectly linked to the determination of the prices of sectoral stocks. Its effect is passed on through altering the price of real and financial assets that have differentiated effects on sectors. The basic conduit for this is through the alteration of interest rates under central bank monetary policy. The sensitivity of the movement of interest rates and other macroeconomic factors to sectoral stock prices will then determine the extent these price changes are picked up. Segal (2019) indicates that the differential impacts are derived from the way individual sectors address economic uncertainty and changes in monetary policy. Ewing et al. (2003), indicate that macroeconomic shocks also give rise to sector-specific responses. To illustrate, variables such as fluctuations in interest rates or inflationary pressures can elicit responses that are distinctive among certain sectors, which tend to exhibit greater responsiveness than others. Sectors such as technology and finance, for instance, may demonstrate a heightened sensitivity to such external influences. The asset price channel is essential to determine the performance of the different sectors; hence, knowledge of sector-specific impacts would be significant to policymakers and investors.

2.3 Sectoral Indices

Monetary policy-stock market indices relations, at both the aggregate and sectoral levels, have always received significant attention in the economic literature. Conventional wisdom in mainstream economic theories simply suggests that monetary policy, through mechanisms like interest rates, influences stock markets by changing borrowing costs and consumption expenditure and business investment. However, this may differ radically across sectors due to their idiosyncratic characteristics and different sensitivities to monetary policy actions.

Kreamer (2022) discusses the concept of sectoral heterogeneity, where different sectors demonstrate a ranging degree of sensitivity to interest rates, leading to suboptimal fluctuations in sectors for a single monetary policy. His model suggests that policymakers should consider the differing sensitivities of each sector to interest rates in developing monetary policies, tending to reduce sectoral volatility.

There have been several empirical studies aimed at measuring the effects of monetary policy on different sectoral indices. Tomar and Kesharwani (2022) conducted a study on the Indian stock market. This study found that the responses of monetary policy to different sectors are asymmetric. They used the Nonlinear Auto-Regressive Distributed Lag methodology and observed that inflationary pressures are more significant in the healthcare and power sectors compared to the metals sector. The study enables an understanding of the sector-specific responses to monetary policy changes, which are necessary for optimizing policy effectiveness.

Sova and Lukianenko (2020) make an invaluable contribution that is based on the use of not just a theoretical model but also an empirical analysis of the monetary policy-stock market indices nexus in several economies. While the stock markets in advanced economies exhibited clear sensitivity towards monetary policy changes, the responsiveness was relatively muted in emerging economies. This incongruence is attributed to the developing financial markets in developing nations, which show a decreased sensitivity to changes in short-term monetary policy.

Looking into the market of the US, Hammoudeh et al. (2015) observed the US monetary policy's outcomes over prices in various commodity sectors. The obtained results revealed that the positive interest rate shocks, in general, gave rise to breath taking responses over all the sub-sectors, including food and metals commodities, showing price-increasing persistence of foods and price-reducing of metals. This heterogeneity in the responses indicates the requirement of a sectoral approach to comprehend the broader consequences of monetary policy. Raddatz and Rigobón (2003) focus on the sector-specific effects of monetary policy during the high-tech crisis in the United States. They conclude that monetary policy led to a temporary boom in residential investment and durable consumption but had no significant impact on the high-tech sector.

Another important factor that shapes the sectoral response to monetary policy is the persistence of sectoral inflation. Ida (2020) investigates this by examining the welfare differential between timeless perspective and purely discretionary monetary policy. He shows that sectoral inflation persistence raises the complexity of the central bank's optimization problem, and in the process, the TP policy is more favorable in terms of stabilizing sectoral inflation rates. This means that it will be able to improve monetary policy if sectoral inflation persistence is addressed properly.

Sengupta (2014) examines the heterogeneous impact of monetary policy shocks across sectors in India. From the estimates using a VAR model, her findings show that Manufacturing, Mining, and Construction are the most responsive sectors to changes in monetary policy. In addition, interest rate channels are the most potent channel of monetary transmission, which makes it indispensable for a sector-specific policy. Medyawati and Yunanto (2021) also apply a Vector Error Correction Model (VECM) to investigate the impacts of monetary policy on the industrial sector in Indonesia. Results show that the industrial sector reflects a positive response to the changes in interest rate, but a negative reaction to the inflationary pressure. The research underlines the strong impact of inflation and foreign direct investment on the industrial sector. Alam and Waheed (2006) examine the sector-specific impact of monetary policy in the case of Pakistan and document heterogeneous distributional effects of these policy actions. According to them, different sectors have different responses to monetary shocks, with some sectors being more badly affected than others. Hamd (2022) discusses the circumscribed impact of monetary policy on the real sector in Iraq. Inhibiting factors, such as high interest rates and foreign exchange market speculations, are detected in the study, with the suggestion that monetary policy should include actions that help enhance national industries.

Fiordelisi, Galloppo, and Ricci (2014) study the effects of monetary policy steps adopted in the financial crisis in relation to the interbank markets, key equity indices, and world systemically important financial institutions. The main results indicate that unconventional monetary policy strategies had on stock markets much more influence than traditional interest rate decisions ever had. Chodorow-Reich (2014) investigates the effects of unconventional monetary policy on financial institutions and reveals that expansions implemented during the 2008-09 financial crisis had stabilizing effects on banks and life insurance firms. Unconventional measurements play a significant role during economic turmoil.

Prabu et al. (2020) study the impact of monetary policy surprises in India and the US on sectoral stock indices of India. They suggest that sectors such as banking and FS highly respond to monetary policy surprises; on the contrary, some other sensitive sectors, such as media and pharma, are less responsive. Rao (2011) examines the effect of monetary policy on the profitability of Indian banking; this paper finds how the banks change their lending and deposit rates to sustain profitability in between policy regulations. The paper finds that monetary policy crucially affects the financial sector. Jansen, Kishan, and Vacaflores (2013) investigate how changes in monetary policy impact the net sales of publicly traded U.S. firms across industries. The authors document the strongest responses to policy in industries such as Retailing and Wholesaling and find that firm size has a mitigating effect.

Arnold and Vrugt (2002) analyze whether monetary policy is transmitted uniformly countrywide to the different parts and sectors of the country. Their results confirm that sector-specific effects account for a lot of the variability in sensitivity rate estimates, thus emphasizing the role of industrial composition. Chouraqui, Driscoll, and Strauss-Khan (2013) perform a tight literature review in investigating the impact of monetary policy on real sector variables. This study assesses different analytic frameworks, including neo-Keynesian and monetarist frameworks, in the quest to explain the effect of monetary policy on real domestic sectors.

Main purpose of this study is to investigate the link between Istanbul sectoral base equity indices and money supply of Türkiye, and suggested attainable monetary policies that will help in moderating and stabilizing the stock market and the entire economy performance of Türkiye. There are several past studies that investigated about macroeconomic variables and Istanbul Stock Exchange about Türkiye such as BIST100 and BIST30. Besides BIST100 index, including sectoral base 9 stock indices is the novelty of this paper.

3. DATA AND METHODOLOGY

3.1 Data

We research 10 different IEI as dependent variable, whether they are related with Money supply. Our independent variables are Central Bank reserves and deposit to central bank (M1) and term deposit at banks (M2 minus M1). In fact, these variables are not mutually consisting same information, we assume there is no multicollinearity problem among independent variables, so we test already that. By help of that we can observe ZXCV Besides Money supply, we add some -most known in the literature- control variables most such that USD/TRY and 2 Years Government Bonds. All these data retrieve from www.investing.com as monthly end price data from 2005 December to 2022 March (Table 1). Because of necessity stationary series for constructing regression, we calculate percent of change (Equation 1), hence we get 195 sample return data. First, unit roots are tested for all return series.

Table 1. Data and Variable Descriptions

Abbr.	Description
BIST100	Istanbul Stock Exchange 100 Company Index
XUSIN	Industrial Stock Index
XGIDA	Food Stock Index
XTEKS	Textile Stock Index
XBANK	Bank Stock Index
XULAS	Transportation Stock Index
XTLKM	Telecommunication Stock Index
XHOLD	Equity Company (Holding) Index
XTCRT	Trade Company Stock Index
XTRZM	Tourism Stock Index
M1	Turkish Central Bank M1 Money Supply
M2_M1	M2 minus M1, Term Deposits
BOND2Y	2 Year Bond Interest Rates
USDTRY	USD-TRY Exchange Rate

3.2 Modeling

The empirical analysis is conducted within a structured econometric framework to ensure the robustness of the results derived from the analysis. The study is based on time series data, which required preliminary transformation to achieve stationarity.

Given that price data is often non-stationary, the data is first differenced into return data. This approach, as evidenced in the literature, maintains the information content while overcoming the stationarity issues identified in previous studies. Stationarity of the return data is checked through the Augmented Dickey-Fuller (ADF) (1979) and Phillips-Perron (PP) (1988) unit root tests. This is an important check to prevent spurious regressions, which are some of the common problems in time series econometrics when dealing with non-stationary data. After having checked for the stationarity, ten regression models are estimated that tested the relationships between dependent variables- Istanbul Sectoral Base Equity indices against the independent variables USD/TRY exchange rate, 2-year bond yields, and monetary aggregates M1 and M2-M1. Ordinary Least Squares estimation is the primary regression technique used evaluating magnitude and relations of the variables each other. The following diagnostic tests are conducted to confirm the validity of these regression models. The first is serial correlation; Durbin-Watson's statistic is used to check if the residuals are autocorrelated. The second is heteroscedasticity; the Arch-LM test is utilized to check if there is conditional heteroscedasticity within the residuals, specifically in terms of the ARCH effect. The last is multicollinearity; the probable problem of multicollinearity among the independent variables is checked with the VIF test.

Following the objective of this study, that is; to test the relationship between Istanbul sectoral base equity indices and money supply of Türkiye, the authors specify the scientific model showing the linear relationship of the selected variables. The final regression models control for USD/TRY exchange rates and 2-year bond yields, both of which have a negative relation to stock indices and thus confirm the literature on the impact of exchange rates and bond yields on equity markets. Monetary variables are controlled through M1 and M2-M1 to try to capture the money supply effect through the market transmission mechanism on stock prices. The established linear regression models are presented in equations from 2 to 11, with the dependent variable expressed in return transformation (R) as a function of the price index (Equation 1).

Return data, $R = (Price_t - Price_{t-1}) / Price_{t-1}$ (1)

$$R - BIST100 = C_{1t} + a_{11}M_{1t} + a_{12}M_{2t-}M_{1t} + a_{13}BOND2Y + a_{14}USD/TRY + \mu_t \quad (2)$$

$$R - XUSIN = C_{2t} + a_{21}M_{1t} + a_{22}M_{2t-}M_{1t} + a_{23}BOND2Y + a_{24}USD/TRY + \mu_t \quad (3)$$

$$R - XGIDA = C_{3t} + a_{31}M_{1t} + a_{32}M_{2t-}M_{1t} + a_{33}BOND2Y + a_{34}USD/TRY + \mu_t \quad (4)$$

$$R - XTEKS = C_{4t} + a_{41}M_{1t} + a_{42}M_{2t\_}M_{1t} + a_{43}BOND2Y + a_{44}USD/TRY + \mu_t \quad (5)$$

$$R - XBANK = C_{5t} + a_{51}M_{1t} + a_{52}M_{2t\_}M_{1t} + a_{53}BOND2Y + a_{54}USD/TRY + \mu_t \quad (6)$$

$$R - XULAS = C_{6t} + a_{61}M_{1t} + a_{62}M_{2t\_}M_{1t} + a_{63}BOND2Y + a_{64}USD/TRY + \mu_t \quad (7)$$

$$R - XTLKM = C_{7t} + a_{71}M_{1t} + a_{72}M_{2t\_}M_{1t} + a_{73}BOND2Y + a_{74}USD/TRY + \mu_t \quad (8)$$

$$R - XHOLD = C_{8t} + a_{81}M_{1t} + a_{82}M_{2t\_}M_{1t} + a_{83}BOND2Y + a_{84}USD/TRY + \mu_t \quad (9)$$

$$R - XTCRT = C_{9t} + a_{91}M_{1t} + a_{92}M_{2t\_}M_{1t} + a_{93}BOND2Y + a_{94}USD/TRY + \mu_t \quad (10)$$

$$R - XTRZM = C_{10t} + a_{101}M_{1t} + a_{102}M_{2t\_}M_{1t} + a_{103}BOND2Y + a_{104}USD/TRY + \mu_t \quad (11)$$

Where from the above Equations from 2 to 11, R - XUSIN, R - XGIDA, R - XTEKS, R - XBANK, R - XULAS, R - XTLKM, R - XHOLD, R - XTCRT and R – XTRZM represent Istanbul sectoral base equity indices returns and R - BIST100 represents Istanbul Stock Exchange 100 Company Index returns. For all equations above $M_1, M_{2\_}M_1, BOND2Y$ and USD/TRY represent Central Bank reserves, deposit to central bank (M1) and term deposit at banks (M2 minus M1), 2 Years Government Bonds and USD/TRY respectively. Also, a_{i1}, a_{i2}, a_{i3} and a_{i4} represent the coefficients of the variables.

4. RESULTS AND DISCUSSIONS

4.1 Findings

The econometric analysis is conducted by transforming price data into return data to achieve stationarity, performing unit root tests to confirm data suitability, and applying multiple diagnostic tests to validate the regression models. The price data is converted to return data, thereby ensuring the maintenance of information integrity while facilitating the generation of stationary data. For further insight, please direct your attention to Table 2, which presents a range of diagnostic statistical information. ADF and PP unit root tests are applied, resulting there is no unit root for all return data (Table 3).

Table 2. Descriptive statistics

Variable	Min	Mean	Med	Max	Std	Var	Skw	Kur
BIST100	-0.231	0.012	0.011	0.229	0.076	0.006	-0.086	3.281
XUSIN	-0.230	0.016	0.017	0.191	0.069	0.005	-0.380	3.869
XGIDA	-0.172	0.0118	0.008	0.207	0.071	0.005	0.082	2.903
XTEKS	-0.297	0.0186	0.018	0.261	0.085	0.007	-0.257	3.870
XBANK	-0.249	0.0086	0.007	0.390	0.101	0.010	0.352	3.593
XULAS	-0.328	0.0235	0.009	0.373	0.117	0.014	0.182	3.240
XTLKM	-0.223	0.0091	0.007	0.247	0.077	0.006	0.060	3.543
XHOLD	-0.298	0.0122	0.016	0.291	0.087	0.008	-0.024	3.941
XTCRT	-0.303	0.0176	0.014	0.237	0.070	0.005	-0.279	4.728
XTRZM	-0.291	0.0137	0.008	0.489	0.112	0.012	0.670	5.092
M1	-0.138	0.0157	0.017	0.219	0.045	0.002	0.207	5.316
M2_M1	-0.030	0.0155	0.013	0.145	0.020	0.000	2.051	13.20
BOND2Y	-0.220	0.0070	-0.004	0.288	0.095	0.009	0.306	3.483
USDTRY	-0.079	0.0137	0.005	0.403	0.055	0.003	3.122	20.25

Table 3. Unit Root Test

Variable	ADF-None		ADF-Drift		ADF-Trend		PP-Trend	
BIST100	**-9.356**	***	**-9.622**	***	**-9.677**	***	**-13.97**	***
XUSIN	-8.319	***	-8.796	***	-8.979	***	-12.68	***
XGIDA	-9.584	***	-9.979	***	-9.959	***	-17.07	***
XTEKS	-8.226	***	-8.656	***	-8.832	***	-13.01	***
XBANK	-9.978	***	-10.05	***	-10.02	***	-14.53	***
XULAS	-7.934	***	-8.310	***	-8.337	***	-13.38	***
XTLKM	-11.79	***	-12.05	***	-12.03	***	-16.91	***
XHOLD	-9.368	***	-9.555	***	-9.651	***	-13.26	***
XTCRT	-9.227	***	-9.967	***	-9.928	***	-13.92	***
XTRZM	-8.855	***	-9.003	***	-9.342	***	-13.05	***
M1	-8.451	***	-10.23	***	-10.23	***	-15.26	***

continued on following page

Table 3. Continued

Variable	ADF-None		ADF-Drift		ADF-Trend		PP-Trend	
BIST100	**-9.356**	***	**-9.622**	***	**-9.677**	***	**-13.97**	***
M2_M1	-5.542	***	-9.298	***	-9.429	***	-12.95	***
BOND2Y	-9.192	***	-9.236	***	-9.285	***	-11.98	***
USDTRY	-8.970	***	-9.697	***	-10.12	***	-12.76	***

Note, ***1%, ** 5%, 10 * % denote Significance levels
Source: Authors computation and compilation

After deploying ten regression models, residuals are controlled for serial correlation and heteroscedasticity. For serial correlation, Durbin-Watson test is applied, and seen all residuals are not autocorrelated each other at least %5 significant level, hence validating OLS assumption of no serial correlation as shown in Table 4. Arch-LM test deployed to test whether residual has arch effect or not. Except for the case of the XUSIN index, which had an ARCH effect at the 3rd lag at the level of significance of 1%, all other models indicated no significant heteroscedasticity, which further justifies that the models are appropriate for inference (Table 4). Multicollinearity were tested by variation Inflation factor test (VIF). All centered VIF results for independent variables less than 5, thus there is no multicollinearity problem among independent variables.

Table 4. Ten Istanbul Sectoral Indices Regression Models

Coefficient	BIST100	XUSIN	XGIDA	XTEKS	XBANK
C	0.007	0.005	0.009	0.012	0.017
Prob.	0.329	0.465	0.211	0.157	0.051
M1	(0.126)	(0.057)	(0.016)	0.043	**(0.243) ***
Prob.	0.262	0.604	0.889	0.748	**0.085**
M2_M1	1.005 **	1.251***	0.609	**0.963***	0.260
Prob.	0.019	0.003	0.154	0.060	0.625
BOND2Y	(0.305)***	(0.175)***	(0.213)***	(0.230)***	(0.471)***
Prob.	0.000	0.002	0.000	0.001	0.000
USDTRY	(0.472)***	(0.491)***	(0.333)**	(0.525)***	(0.380)*
Prob.	0.004	0.002	0.044	0.008	0.064
Stats. /Tests	BIST100	XUSIN	XGIDA	XTEKS	XBANK
R-Square	0.251	0.141	0.140	0.144	0.333
F-test Prob.	0.000	0.000	0.000	0.000	0.000

continued on following page

Table 4. Continued

DW-t	2.065	1.796 *	2.467	1.919	2.250
DW Prob.	0.671	0.074	0.991	0.282	0.959
ARCH-LM Lags	1	3**	1*	1	1
ARCH-LM Chi-Sq	0.263	11.12	3.080	2.340	0.446
ARCH-LM Prob.	0.608	0.011	0.079	0.126	0.504

Coefficient	XULAS	XTLKM	XHOLD	XTCRT	XTRZM
C	0.013	0.004	0.006	0.007	0.012
Prob.	0.243	0.627	0.456	0.283	0.269
M1	(0.109)	(0.079)	(0.142)	0.094	0.073
Prob.	0.556	0.521	0.282	0.390	0.686
M2_M1	1.462 **	0.825*	1.143 **	1.225***	0.539
Prob.	0.038	0.077	0.023	0.003	0.430
BOND2Y	(0.345)***	(0.243)***	(0.294)***	(0.160)***	(0.270)***
Prob.	0.000	0.000	0.000	0.005	0.004
USDTRY	(0.604)**	(0.326)*	(0.532)***	(0.652)***	(0.446)*
Prob.	0.025	0.069	0.006	0.000	0.089

Stats. /Tests	XULAS	XTLKM	XHOLD	XTCRT	XTRZM
R-Square	0.137	0.133	0.199	0.181	0.105
F-test Prob.	0.000	0.000	0.000	0.000	0.000
DW-t	1.938	2.409	1.866	2.101	1.772
DW Prob.	0.327	0.998	0.170	0.758	0.053
ARCH-LM Lags	1	1	1	1	1**
ARCH-LM Chi-Sq	1.154	0.181	1.046	0.224	4.746
ARCH-LM Prob.	0.283	0.671	0.307	0.636	0.029

Note, *** 1%, ** 5%, * 10% denote Significance levels
Source: Authors computation and compilation

As is widely known in the literature and theory, changes in money supply affect stock prices through the market transmission mechanism. Expansions in money supply increase the ability to loan through market channels, leading to lower interest rates and thus triggering an increase in equity investments (Tiryaki et al. 2019). The M2_M1 variable represents time deposits in the research models and is equivalent to the formula M2 minus M1. Results show that monetary expansion (contraction) in time deposits has a positive (negative) effect on BIST100, XUSIN, XTEKS, XU-LAS, XTLKM, XHOLD, XTCRT stock indices. These results are consistent with the general literature. However, although XGIDA, XBANK and XTRZM indices are positively related to M2-M1 on the models, statistically significant results are not obtained; they are indifferent to M2-M1. This may be due to the differences in the internal dynamics of the food, banking and tourism sectors. As a result, when monetary expansion in time deposits is carried out, it is more appropriate for investors to focus on stock indices covering the industrial, textile garment, transportation, telecommunication, holding and trade sectors. Among these sectors, transportation which its M2_M1 coefficient is 1.462, is the most affected sector from the time deposits expansion.

The coefficient of M1 narrow money supply in the models is significant and negatively correlated only with the XBANK index, which includes banks. Other stock indices do not have a significant relationship with M1. It is understandable for banks that narrow money supply (M1) has an impact on banks' stocks. This monetary transmission effect is likely to affect banks' market interest rates and thus banks' profitability. An increase in M1 money supply will trigger a fall in market interest rates because of abundant quantity of money. Investors would therefore expect bank profitability to fall and bank stocks to fall in value, and vice versa.

Respect to results, the coefficients of USDTRY and BOND2Y, which are control variables for all models, are negatively related to stock indices and statistically significant. Rising 2-year bond interest rates and an increase in the value of USD relative to TRY lead investors to flee stock indices (He et al., 2023; Kassouri and Altıntas, 2020).

4.2 Discussions

The results of this study align with the existing literature on the relationship between monetary policy and stock prices, particularly regarding the influence of changes in the money supply on sectoral stock indices. The study affirms the positive effects of monetary expansion with time deposits on some sectoral indices, thereby contributing to the field of knowledge in this area. This would apply, for instance, to industrial, textile garment, transportation, telecommunication, holding and trade sectors of Türkiye, similar to the trends observable in other economies. For example, Handoyo et al. (2015) conclude that both the aggregated and sectoral stock prices of Indonesia reacted positively to monetary policy shocks, which is in line with the positive effect of monetary expansion observed in this study. This clearly shows that the asset price channel works efficiently in triggering stock prices of various sectors, particularly those more interest rate and liquidity sensitive. However, results contradict with Örnek (2009). He evaluates the efficacy of the stock channel between 1990 and 2006 using quarterly data from Turkey. The findings indicated that the stock channel is not an effective conduit in Turkey. Contrary to general findings the food and tourism indices (XGIDA, XTRZM) seem to be quite indifferent to changes in the M2-M1 variable. Consequently, the expansion of time deposits (M2-M1), which is initiated by the Central Bank money policy, functions via the stock channel and affects the sectorial stock indices.

In contrast, the negative relationship between the narrow money supply (M1) and the XBANK index is noteworthy. This finding is in line with the argument that an increase in M1 leads to lower market interest rates, reducing bank profitability due to compressed margins, as suggested by Rao (2011) in his study on the profitability of banks in India (Rao, 2011). This effect is likely due to banks' reliance on interest income, making them vulnerable to changes in the money supply. The negative relationship between the narrow money supply (M1) and the XBANK index, found in this study, is also supported by the work of Ioannidis and Kontonikas (2008), who underline that changes in interest rates directly influence the market interest rate. Thus, interest rates effect bank profitability and hence indirectly stock price adjustments. An increase narrow money supply decreases the banking sector stock price. The risk-taking channel posits that low interest rates increase risk-taking by banks and investors. This may induce banks to lend in the direction of higher-risk borrowers to maintain profitability (DeGroot, 2014). This finding suggests that in Türkiye, banks are particularly vulnerable to changes in narrow money supply, which may alter their profit margins and stock performance.

The findings also show the impact of external variables, such as the exchange rate and the bond yield, that go on to cement the fact of stability in macroeconomic variables and investors' confidence is important for sectoral stock performance. Similar to the finding of He et al. (2023), Kassouri and Altıntas (2020), this research elaborates that an increase in bond yields and currency devaluation might trigger capital outflow from the equity market; therefore, monetary and fiscal policies should be coordinated to avoid fluctuation of the financial markets.

The sectoral impact depicts in this study also agrees with Segal (2019) and Ewing et al. (2003), which points out that some sectors, like technology and finance, are sensitive to shocks in macroeconomics. Therefore, different types of reactions by various sectors in Türkiye bring out the requirement of understanding the dynamics of the sectors while formulating monetary policy. While this would mean boosts to sectors like transportation, telecommunications and others, might require more targeted interventions in order to control the associated risks and ensure optimal performance.

This research, therefore, adds to the existing debate on the asset price channel, underlining the heterogeneity in monetary policy effects across sectors in Türkiye. This means that sectoral differences should inform monetary policy formulation by policymakers in a way that ensures a balanced approach toward growth and stability.

Deep factors underlying sectoral differences, especially regarding emerging markets, may become an important focus of attention in future research.

5. CONCLUSION AND POLICY SUGGESTION

The motivation behind this research work is to investigate the link between Istanbul sectoral base equity indices and money supply of Türkiye and suggests attainable monetary policies that will help in moderating and stabilizing the stock market and the entire economy performance of Türkiye. In order to add to the literature, the study is posed to reveal the relationship between the selected (9) different sectoral indices in the Istanbul stock market and the money supply in Türkiye, and this is considered as the novelty of the study. The present economic situation and the investment environment of Türkiye call for urgent and sustainable solution that are rooted on monetary and fiscal policies. Following this, the central objective is further broken down and structured as following: i) to investigates the effects of Turkish monetary policy on sectoral stock indices in the context of monetary transmission theory on stocks ii) to expose how the money supply affects the sectors in the Istanbul stock market. iii) to quantitatively test the impact of the 9 different sector indices on Istanbul stock market, and the effect on money supply in Türkiye. To ascertain the solution towards the present economic turbulence, it is essential to expose the root of the problem. The easiest way to expose economic problems is to identify which variables or indicators that are acting against the fundamentals of stable economic performance. Most of the macroeconomic variables are interwoven with the money supply and its impacts on the stock market. So, to have a comprehensive finding towards the achieving the objectives of this study, that is, to investigate the link between Istanbul sectoral base equity indices and money supply of Türkiye, it is necessary to identify which variables have the power to impact the manufacturing sectors, and by extension, the factors that affect stock returns. Based on this, authors applied the monthly end price data from 2005 December to 2022 March to researched 10 different IEI as dependent variable, to see whether they are related with Money supply. Our independent variables are Central Bank reserves and deposit to central bank (M1) and term deposit at banks (M2 minus M1). Besides Money supply, we add some -most known in the literature- control variables most such that USD/TRY and 2 Years Government Bonds.

From the quantitative analysis of the indices, the following findings are established: i) All control variables including USD/TRY and BOND2Y coefficients are negatively correlated with equity indices and statistically significant, ii) Increasing 2-year bond interest rates and USD value regarding to TRY tend investors to escape from all equity indices, iii) Increasing M1 money supply leads to decrease in price of the money –called interest rates, iv) Other equity indices are irrelevant to M1, v) When term deposits increase, credits also increase. From this finding, term deposit quantitative easing affects BIST100, XUSIN, XTEKS, XULAS, XTLKM, XHOLD, XTCRT equity indices positively, vi) However, XGIDA, XBANK, XTRZM are indifferent to M2-M1. As a result, investors should get attention to equity indices including industry, textile ready dress, transportation, telecommunication, holding and trade sector, when term deposit quantitative easing.

Following the findings from the quantitative estimations, the following policies are suggested for the stability of the troubled economy and boosting the investors' confidence. Moderation of the impact of selected variables to restore the benefits of stocks. This can be achieved by reducing the quantity of money supply in order to activate increase in the rate of return on the equity indices. There must be avenue to increase term deposit which will impact credit to activate increase in demands of the equity indices. There is a need to watch and moderate the unstable link of USD/TRY in attempt to restore the investors' confidence. This can be controlled through the instrumentality of central bank in managing its reserve.

Conclusively, this study is significant not only to the Türkiye, but to other emerging countries possessing the same features as Türkiye. However, there are limitations to this study that can be seen from the selection of the variables. There are other important variables missing from the model and the analysis. Instruments like institutions or government, foreign direct investment (FDI) and economic complexity are important to this kind of analysis, but they are missing. Subsequent study or analysis of this topic may need to employ these variables in the future research.

In conclusion, this study contributes to the ongoing discussion on the asset price channel by highlighting the varying impacts of monetary policy across different sectors in Türkiye. It suggests that policymakers should consider sectoral differences when designing monetary policy to achieve balanced growth and stability. Future research may need to focus on the underlying factors driving these sectoral differences, particularly in emerging markets.

REFERENCES

Akay, H. K., & Nargeleçekenler, M. (2009). Do monetary policy shocks affect stock prices? Turkish experience. *Marmara Üniversitesi İ.İ.B.F. Journal*, 17(2), 129–152.

Alam, T., & Waheed, M. (2006). Sectoral effects of monetary policy: Evidence from Pakistan. *Pakistan Development Review*, 45(4), 1103–1115.

Alatiqi, S., & Fazel, S. (2008). Can money supply predict stock prices? *The Journal of Economic Education*, 8(2), 54–59.

Arnold, I., & Vrugt, E. B. (2002). Regional effects of monetary policy in the Netherlands. *International Journal of Business and Economics*, 1(2), 123–134.

Bernanke, B. S., Laubach, T., Mishkin, F. S., & Posen, A. S. (1999). *Inflation targeting: Lessons from the international experience*. Princeton University Press.

Camilleri, S. J., Scicluna, N., & Bai, Y. (2019). Do stock markets lead or lag macroeconomic variables? Evidence from select European countries. *The North American Journal of Economics and Finance*, 48, 170–186. DOI: 10.1016/j.najef.2019.01.019

Campbell, J. R., Evans, C. L., Fisher, J. D., & Justiniano, A. (2012). Macroeconomic effects of Federal Reserve forward guidance. *Brookings Papers on Economic Activity*, 1(1), 1–54. DOI: 10.1353/eca.2012.0004

Chami, R., Cosimano, T., & Fullenkamp, C. (1999). The stock market channel of monetary policy. Organizations & Markets eJournal. https://doi.org/.DOI: 10.5089/9781451843958.001.A001

Chang, B. H., Bhutto, N. A., Turi, J. A., Hashmi, S. M., & Gohar, R. (2020). Macroeconomic variables and stock indices: An asymmetric evidence from quantile ARDL model. *South Asian Journal of Business Studies*, 10(2), 242–264. DOI: 10.1108/SAJBS-09-2019-0161

Chen, N. F., Roll, R., & Ross, S. A. (1986). Economic forces and the stock market. *The Journal of Business*, 59(3), 383–403. DOI: 10.1086/296344

Chodorow-Reich, G. (2014). Effects of unconventional monetary policy on financial institutions. *Brookings Papers on Economic Activity*, 2014(1), 155–227. DOI: 10.1353/eca.2014.0003

Chouraqui, J., Driscoll, M., & Strauss-Khan, M. (2013). The effects of monetary policy on the real sector: What do we know? *PSL Quarterly Review*, ●●●, 42.

Claessens, S., & Kose, M. A. (2013). Macroprudential policies: When and how to use them. *IMF Working Paper*, 2013(130).

Cukierman, A., Webb, S. B., & Neyapti, B. (1992). Measuring the independence of central banks and its effect on policy outcomes. *The World Bank Economic Review*, 6(3), 353–398. DOI: 10.1093/wber/6.3.353

Dan, H. (2013). The asset price channel and its role in monetary policy transmission. Econometric Modeling: Macroeconomics eJournal.

DeGroot, O. (2014). The risk channel of monetary policy. FEDS Working Paper No. 2014-31, Available at *SSRN*: https://ssrn.com/abstract=2434518 or DOI: 10.2139/ssrn.2434518

Dickey, D. A., & Fuller, W. A. (1979). Distribution of the estimators for autoregressive time series with a unit root. *Journal of the American Statistical Association*, 74(366, 366a), 427–431. DOI: 10.2307/2286348

Enamul Hoque, M., Soo Wah, L., & Azlan Shah Zaidi, M. (2019). Oil price shocks, global economic policy uncertainty, geopolitical risk, and stock price in Malaysia: Factor augmented VAR approach. Economic research-. *Ekonomska Istrazivanja*, 32(1), 3701–3733.

Ewing, B., Forbes, S., & Payne, J. (2003). The effects of macroeconomic shocks on sector-specific returns. *Applied Economics*, 35(2), 201–207. DOI: 10.1080/0003684022000018222

Fattah, A. S., & Kocabıyık, T. (2020). Impact of macroeconomic variables on stock markets: Türkiye and USA comparison. *Finansal Araştırmalar ve Çalışmalar Dergisi*, 12(22), 116–151. DOI: 10.14784/marufacd.691108

Fiordelisi, F., Galloppo, G., & Ricci, O. (2014). The effect of monetary policy interventions on interbank markets, equity indices, and G-SIFIs during financial crisis. *Journal of Financial Stability*, 11, 49–61. DOI: 10.1016/j.jfs.2013.12.002

Friedman, M. (1968). The role of monetary policy. *The American Economic Review*, 58(1), 1–17.

Gagnon, J., Raskin, M., Remache, J., & Sack, B. (2011). The financial market effects of the Federal Reserve's large-scale asset purchases. *International Journal of Central Banking*, 7(1), 3–43.

Grosse-Rueschkamp, B., Steffen, S., & Streitz, D. (2018). A capital structure channel of monetary policy. Econometric Modeling: Macroeconomics eJournal. DOI: 10.2139/ssrn.2988158

Hamd, B. A. (2022). The role of monetary policy in activation of the real sector in Iraq. Webology, 19(1).

Hammoudeh, S., Nguyen, D., & Sousa, R. (2015). US monetary policy and sectoral commodity prices. *Journal of International Money and Finance*, 57, 61–85. DOI: 10.1016/j.jimonfin.2015.06.003

Handoyo, R. D., Jusoh, M., & Zaidi, M. A. S. (2015). Impact of monetary policy and fiscal policy on indonesian stock market. Expert Journal of Economics. *Sprint Investify*, 3(2), 113–126.

Hashemzadeh, N., & Taylor, P. (1988). Stock prices, money supply, and interest rates: The question of causality. *Applied Economics*, 20(12), 1603–1611. DOI: 10.1080/00036848800000091

He, X., Gokmenoglu, K. K., Kirikkaleli, D., & Rizvi, S. K. A. (2023). Co-movement of foreign exchange rate returns, and stock market returns in an emerging market: Evidence from the wavelet coherence approach. *International Journal of Finance & Economics*, 28(2), 1994–2005. DOI: 10.1002/ijfe.2522

Horatiu, D. (2013). The asset price channel and its role in monetary policy transmission. *Annals of Faculty of Economics*, 1, 445–454.

Ida, D. (2020). Sectoral inflation persistence and optimal monetary policy. *Journal of Macroeconomics*, 65, 103215. DOI: 10.1016/j.jmacro.2020.103215

Ioannidis, C., & Kontonikas, A. (2008). The impact of monetary policy on stock prices. *Journal of Policy Modeling*, 30(1), 33–53. DOI: 10.1016/j.jpolmod.2007.06.015

Jansen, D. W., Kishan, R. P., & Vacaflores, D. E. (2013). Sectoral effects of monetary policy: The evidence from publicly traded firms. *Southern Economic Journal*, 79(4), 946–970. DOI: 10.4284/0038-4038-2011.040

Joyce, M., Lasaosa, A., Stevens, I., & Tong, M. (2012). The financial market impact of quantitative easing in the United Kingdom. *International Journal of Central Banking*, 7(3), 113–161.

Kassouri, Y., & Altıntaş, H. (2020). Threshold cointegration, nonlinearity, and frequency domain causality relationship between stock price and Turkish Lira. *Research in International Business and Finance*, 52, 101097. DOI: 10.1016/j.ribaf.2019.101097

Keynes, J. M. (1936). *The general theory of employment, interest, and money.* Palgrave Macmillan.

Kreamer, J. (2022). Sectoral Heterogeneity and Monetary Policy. *American Economic Journal. Macroeconomics*, 14(2), 123–159. Advance online publication. DOI: 10.1257/mac.20190248

McCredie, B., Docherty, P., Easton, S., & Uylangco, K. (2016). The channels of monetary policy triggered by central bank actions and statements in the Australian equity market. *International Review of Financial Analysis*, 46, 46–61. DOI: 10.1016/j.irfa.2016.04.008

Medyawati, H., & Yunanto, M. (2021). The impact of monetary policy on the industry sector in Indonesia. Journal Ekonomi dan Studi Pembangunan. .DOI: 10.17977/um002v13i22021p159

Mishkin, F. (1996). The channels of monetary transmission: lessons for monetary policy. NBER Working Paper Series. DOI: 10.3386/w5464

Mishkin, F. (2007). Inflation targeting: Lessons from the experience of developed and emerging market economies. *Comparative Economic Studies*, 49(3), 548–581.

Morris, C., & Sellon, G. (1995). Bank lending and monetary policy: Evidence on a credit channel. *Econometric Reviews*, 80, 59–75.

Nkechukwu, G., Onyeagba, J., & Okoh, J. (2015). Macroeconomic variables and stock market prices in Nigeria: A cointegration and vector error correction model tests. *International Journal of Scientific Research*, 4(6).

Nwaogwugwu, I. C. (2018). The effects of monetary and fiscal policy on the stock market in Nigeria. *Journal of Economics and Development Studies*, 6(1), 79–85.

Örnek, İ. (2009). Functioning of monetary transfer mechanism channels in Türkiye. *Maliye Dergisi*, 156, 104–125.

Palmer, M. (1970). Money supply, portfolio adjustments and stock prices. *Financial Analysts Journal*, 26(4), 19–22. DOI: 10.2469/faj.v26.n4.19

Parasız, İ. (2013). Theory and Policy: Macro Economics. Publisher: Ezgi. Bursa.

Phillips, P. C. B., & Perron, P. (1988). Testing for a unit root in time series regression. *Biometrika*, 75(2), 335–346. DOI: 10.1093/biomet/75.2.335

Prabu, A., Bhattacharyya, I., & Ray, P. (2020). Impact of monetary policy on the Indian stock market: Does the devil lie in the detail? *Indian Economic Review*, 55(1), 1–24. DOI: 10.1007/s41775-020-00078-2

Quayes, S., & Jamal, A. (2008). Does inflation affect stock prices? *Applied Economics Letters*, 15(10), 767–769. DOI: 10.1080/13504850600770871

Raddatz, C., & Rigobón, R. (2003). *Monetary policy and sectoral shocks: Did the Fed react properly to the high-tech crisis?* Monetary Economics. DOI: 10.3386/w9835

Rao, P. (2011). Monetary policy: Its impact on the profitability of banks in India. *The International Business & Economics Research Journal*, 5(3). Advance online publication. DOI: 10.19030/iber.v5i3.3465

Ross, S. A. (2013). The arbitrage theory of capital asset pricing. In Handbook of the fundamentals of financial decision making: Part I, p.11-30. DOI: 10.1142/9789814417358_0001

Sahu, T. N., & Pandey, K. D. (2020). Money supply and equity price movements during the liberalized period in India. *Global Business Review*, 21(1), 108–123. DOI: 10.1177/0972150918761084

Segal, G. (2019). A tale of two volatilities: Sectoral uncertainty, growth, and asset prices. *Journal of Financial Economics*, 134(1), 110–140. Advance online publication. DOI: 10.1016/j.jfineco.2019.03.002

Sova, Y., & Lukianenko, I. (2020). Theoretical and empirical analysis of the relationship between monetary policy and stock market indices. 2020 10th International Conference on Advanced Computer Information Technologies (ACIT), 708-711. DOI: 10.1109/ACIT49673.2020.9208926

Taylor, J. B. (1993). Discretion versus policy rules in practice. *Carnegie-Rochester Conference Series on Public Policy*, 39, 195–214. DOI: 10.1016/0167-2231(93)90009-L

Tiryaki, A., Ceylan, R., & Erdoğan, L. (2019). Asymmetric effects of industrial production, money supply and exchange rate changes on stock returns in Türkiye. *Applied Economics*, 51(20), 2143–2154. DOI: 10.1080/00036846.2018.1540850

Tomar, K., & Kesharwani, S. (2022). Asymmetric effect of monetary policy on Indian stock market sectors: Do monetary policy stimulus transpire the same effect on all sectors? *Cogent Economics & Finance*, 10(1), 1999058. Advance online publication. DOI: 10.1080/23322039.2021.1999058

KEY TERMS AND DEFINITIONS

Asset Price Channel: Part of monetary transmission that changes in monetary policy have on financial asset prices, such as equities and bonds. When interest rates are changed or the money supply is altered by a central bank, it changes asset prices, which then have effects on household wealth, consumption, and investments. Lower interest rates increase asset prices, thereby raising wealth and spending, whereas high interest rates reduce spending.

Central Bank: The main financial institution responsible for managing a country's monetary policy, regulating the money supply and overseeing the banking system. These institutions set policy rates, print money and act as lender of last resort to maintain stability in financial markets. This is in addition to implementing policies to control inflation, strengthen the currency and ensure economic growth.

M1 Narrow Money: A component of the money supply that includes liquid forms of money, such as currency in circulation and demand deposits at banks (such as current accounts). M1 is called "narrow" because it includes only those assets that can be spent easily and quickly for transactions, thus distinguishing it from larger measures of money, such as M2.

M2 Broad Money: M2 includes not only physical currency and demand deposits, but also, among other things, savings accounts, time deposits for Türkiye. This measure is more comprehensive than M1 and is therefore often used to assess monetary policy in terms of its impact on the economy in general and on inflation and financial markets in particular.

Monetary Policy: Monetary policy is the action taken by a country's central bank to control the money supply and interest rates to achieve its objectives, which may be to control inflation or stimulate employment. This can have a huge impact on share prices and investor behavior.

Monetary Transmission Channels: These are channels through which changes in central bank monetary policy impact the economy, especially output and inflation. Important channels concern interest rates, credit rate, exchange rate, and asset price money channels, all impacting consumer spending, business investment, and economic activity.

Money Supply: This is the amount of money in circulation in an economy at any given time. It includes cash, coins and balances held in current and savings accounts. Changes in the money supply affect inflation, interest rates and general economic activity.

Sectoral Stock Indices: These are stock indices that aim at sectors such as manufacturing, technology, or finance. They provide information on the state of that sector, usually regarding performance and the impact on the broader market.

Stock Market: The market where shares of public companies are bought and sold. It reflects the state of economic health by capturing and summarizing investor sentiment and influences at the macroeconomic level.

Chapter 12
Fostering Prosperity:
Unveiling the Impact of Governance Quality on GDP per Capita in OECD Nations

İhsan Erdem Kayral
https://orcid.org/0000-0002-8335-8619
Başkent University, Turkey

Hacer Pınar Altan
Atılım University, Turkey

Tiago Silveira Gontijo
https://orcid.org/0000-0003-2636-899X
Federal University of São João del-Rei, Brazil

ABSTRACT

This study aims to investigate the influence of the quality of governance on economic development among 38 OECD countries using a panel data approach. The data was gathered from the World Bank database for the period of 2002-2021 and consists of six governance indicators and two macroeconomic variables. The independent variables are the six governance indicators (WGI): control of corruption (CC), government effectiveness (GE), political stability and absence of violence/terrorism (PS), rule of law (RL), regulatory quality (RQ), and voice and accountability (VA). The dependent variable is the natural logarithm of GDP per capita, and inflation and real interest rates are control variables. The research identifies a direct and significant relationship between GDPPC and GE, PS, RL, RQ, and VA in OECD countries. These findings suggest that the existence of mechanisms for GE, PS, RL, RQ, and VA contribute positively to economic development. Moreover, interest rates and inflation are found to be significant and negatively related to GDPPC.

DOI: 10.4018/979-8-3693-5508-4.ch012

Copyright © 2025, IGI Global. Copying or distributing in print or electronic forms without written permission of IGI Global is prohibited.

1. INTRODUCTION

In recent years, the term "institutions" has become fashionable in social sciences, including economics. In particular, towards the end of the 20th century, institutions began to have an important mission in development economics and studies on the relationships between development economics and institutions increased accordingly. In this context, innovative institutional economics became popular in addressing the development failures of underdeveloped countries, and as it stands, institutions of poor quality considered as a critical factor in economic lagging. Despite the fact that the significance of institutions is widely accepted among researchers, their role and connections with the economy remain unclear (Jütting, 2003).

Terms such as *institutional development, governance reform,* and *good governance* are used interchangeably, and they have been supported by the International Monetary Fund (IMF) and the World Bank (WB) to embrace superior institutions to reinforce economic development since the 1990s (Chang, 2006; Chang, 2011). Consequently, institutions have been commonly used by the IMF and WB to assess the success of countries at many levels, such as social, political and economic (Albassam, 2013). Hereby, these two prominent organizations started to assign some *"governance related conditionalities"* that incorporate various articles about some economic institutions needed to be met by borrowing countries (Chang, 2011). Therefore, it is vital and inevitable that all countries support their economic development through good governance agents. For instance, AlShiab et al. (2020) mentioned in their study that countries with strong legal infrastructure tend to attract more capital from offshore economies. Similarly, many studies have shown that the institutional base is a key factor in the progress of many countries at different levels of revenue. According to Rodrik (2008), one of the main impacts of good institutions on economic development is their interaction with the global economic environment. On the other hand, many government administrators seem to defend against poor politics and institutions preventing economic growth, thereby causing excessive corruption. In this frame of reference, both poor politics and institutions seem to be the number one obstacle for most economies. For instance, interest groups usually see technological progress as a threat to their power and deliberately hinder some necessary technological changes, even though a large part of society and the development of the economy benefits from it (Snowdon & Vayne, 2012).

Within this framework, this chapter examines the relationship between governance quality and GDP per capita in OECD nations, focusing on key theoretical frameworks and citing relevant studies. It begins by defining governance quality and its theoretical underpinnings and then proceeds to summarize key studies that explore this theme. This chapter effectively integrates various perspectives and empirical findings to support its arguments, demonstrating a comprehensive understanding of the subject matter. Additionally, it identifies gaps in the existing research and outlines how the current study contributes to filling these gaps, thereby establishing a clear rationale for its approach and methodology.

The rest of this study is organized as follows: Section 2 covers a review of selected literature, Section 3 covers the data and methodology, Section 4 covers the results and discussions, and Section 5 concludes the study. It is mostly presumed that when there is a steadiness in political structure in an economy, it promotes a favorable hit.

This study is focuses on political institutions. Considering previous research indicating an adverse link between the quality of institutions (for some variables) and economic growth (Zhuo et al., 2020), this study aims to view the positive effects of stable and strong institutions on economic development. Therefore, the driving force of this study is to illustrate the potential negative impact of non-functioning political institutions in economies. The expected contribution of this chapter to the existing literature is to demonstrate how good governance can affect economic development in OECD countries. With this in mind, our humble contribution in this study is to offer a comprehensive perspective on the political institutions of OECD countries and their impacts on their respective economies.

2. LITERATURE REVIEW

Institutions are important tools for protecting states from future ambiguities, for this reason, it is crucial to have steady institutions to provide good economic, financial, and governmental practices. Disordered sluggish institutions are considered a source of underdevelopment in many economies (Shirley, 2008). As a result, many nations that have not embraced Anglo-American institutions are thought to have low-quality institutions (Chang, 2011). However, the ways in which economic institutions operate in various countries are distinct (Stiglitz, 1998). Countries are not at the same level of development worldwide, and the neoclassical growth model relates this to different production factors and aggregation choices among countries. However, when it comes to measuring economic progress, innovation, capital build-up, and education are only a fraction of the growth process; in reality, institutional structure matters the most (Acemoğlu et al., 2005). Institutions change continuously, and they are tools established by people to decrease the amount of volatility in trade and bring formation to the economic constitution. In this context, institutions frame the economy by guiding what order the economy will go to (North, 1991). Institutions have an explicit influence on earnings, but the fact remains that there are also unobservable effects of institutions on the development process (Jütting, 2003). Economic prosperity and growth expected to be the product of institutional traits and institutions can be grouped into four categories. They are economic, political, legal, and social institutions. Studies of political institutions usually employ variables that ptovide details about elections, electoral rules, the type of political system, the party composition of the opposition and governmental and political stability (Clarke et al., 2000).

Ultimately, institutional quality is an important means of improving the legal structure and reinforcing good governance objectives, which are at the core of the development process (Jacobs, 2010). The quality of institutions and good governance is vital for supporting economic growth (Adams & Bengisu, 2013).

Numerous studies have been conducted on economic development to pinpoint the fundamentals that have an affirmative impact on the level of development. Moreover, some studies show that the quality of the institutional structure is one of the leading elements in supporting the development process. For example, satisfactory institutions help countries harmonize with the global economy (Alshiab, 2020). Similarly, good governance provides institutions and rules that are more competent and powerful. All governments strive for what is best for their country; they desire richness, expansion, and development and take caution accordingly. Good governance is one of the critical elements for achieving all these factors and development. Most importantly, developed countries have good governance practices. Essentially, governance can be described as the conducting (political, economic, executive, etc.) of assets, capital, reserves of a country to accomplish the prosperity level that was an eventual objective (Sarhangi et al., 2021).

In the process of analyzing underdeveloped and developed countries, state involvement in economic affairs, arrangements, formations, the power, and influence of politics on economic activities come forward. In this sense, the term governance is interested in issues pertaining to democratic phenomena and the rule of law, such as equality before law, juridical autonomy, having a voice on political and social issues, elections based on worldwide standards, and freedom of expression (UNDESA; UNDP, 2012). While the IMF, UN, and WB emphasize the value of good governance, the importance of this concept dates back to decolonization after 1945. In those days, countries that had been previously colonized by Western Countries started to have political freedom to govern themselves. For better standards of living, freedom, and competitiveness on the international platforms, the importance of governance cannot be overlooked (Ashiku, 2016). Although countries' strategic positions and geography are important in good governance practices, the main component of ineffective governance in developing countries is fruitless structural adjustment programs[1]. For instance, many underdeveloped countries can not utilize the aid provided by international organizations to increase GDP per capita (Drake et al., 2001).

Governance phenomena have many dimensions, but six essential indicators have an especially important effect on the economic structure (Kaufmann et al., 1999). In the context of governance, the WB determined six governance indicators called *World Governance Indicators* (WGI): voice and accountability, political stability and absence of violence/terrorism, government effectiveness, regulatory quality, rule of law, and control of corruption (Ashiku, 2016; Zhuo et al., 2020). The economy is expected to move to a long-term constructive structure when there are favorable governance indicators in a country (Alshiab, 2020). Moreover, as political stability improves, countries become more developed (Kaufmann & Kraay, 2002). Despite various descriptions of governance, effective governance is the capability to utilize a country's means and interests (Zhuo et al., 2020). The WB describes good governance as "the manner in which power is exercised in the management of a country's economic and social resources for development" and the economic approach under the good governance body requires a market view that is different from the 1980s. At the heart, good governance is about improving the relationship between the state, society, and market (Drake et al., 2001). Additionally, Zhuo et al. (2020) found that there is a small but adverse relationship between government effectiveness, political stability, regulatory quality, and economic growth in OECD countries. This study highlights that while these governance indicators are generally seen as positive factors for economic development, their findings suggest that under certain conditions, these factors can have a nuanced negative impact on economic growth.

Some of the researches on governance and economic development are as follows: Abdiweli (2001), Ari and Veiga (2013), Campos and Nugent (1999), d'Agostino et al. (2012a, b), Mehanna et al. (2010), Nomor and Iorember (2017), Ramadhan et al. (2016), and Uddin et al. (2017). These studies shows that political stability is related to economic wellbeing.

Moreover, many studies highlight the positive impact of various governance indicators on economic growth. For instance, Kaufmann and Kraay (2002) demonstrated that political stability and the absence of violence are significantly correlated with economic growth. Likewise, government effectiveness, which includes the quality of public services and the degree of its independence from political pressures, has been shown to positively influence economic growth (Kaufmann et al., 1999). Regulatory quality, which refers to the ability of the government to formulate and implement sound policies and regulations, is positively associated with economic growth. Voice and accountability, indicating the extent to which a country's citizens are able to participate in selecting their government, also play a crucial role in fostering economic development (Uddin et al., 2017). Sarhangi et al. (2021) supports these findings, highlighting the critical role of governance in promoting economic stability and growth across diverse global contexts.

3. MATERIAL AND METHODS

3.1. Methodology

This study aims to investigate the impact of effective governance on economic development. Within this framework, this study examines the relationships between governance indicators and economic development in 38 OECD countries over the period of 2002-2021, utilizing a panel data approach. For this objective, we apply a static model and a dynamic model known as the first difference Generalized Method of Moments (GMM) model. To determine the static model, the Hausman Specification test was conducted. Based on test results, the appropriate model (either the fixed effect model or random effect model) was chosen and employed as the static model for further analysis.

3.1.1 Static Model

According to the static model, Equation (1) can be used to evaluate how governance affects economic growth in OECD countries:

$$\ln\text{GDPPC}_{it} = \alpha + \beta \text{WGI}_{it} + \gamma \text{Inflation}_{it} + \delta \text{Real Interest Rates}_{it} + \varepsilon_{it} \quad (1)$$

where ln is used for natural logarithm, i denotes the countries and t shows the time. GDPPC is GDP per capita in country, WGI are the estimates of the World Bank governance indicators, including control of corruption (CC), governance effectiveness (GE), political stability and absence of violence/terrorism (PS), rule of law (RL), regulatory quality (RQ), and voice and accountability (VA). We used two macroeconomic indicators as control variables. The first one, Inflation_{it}, displays the inflation rates of countries, while the second one, $\text{Real Interest Rates}_{it}$, shows the interest rates of the countries, α is constant, β is the coefficient of WGI, γ and δ are the coefficients of control variables, and ε_{it} is the error term.

In the context of the static model, we conducted the Hausman Specification Test (1978) to determine which method would be more efficient to apply in Ordinary Least Squares (OLS) models: fixed or random effects. Based on the results of the Hausman Specification Test, we determined the appropriate model to use for measuring the relationships among the variables.

3.1.2 Dynamic Model

In the context of the dynamic model, we implemented ther first-difference GMM model. According to dynamic model, Equation (2) can be used to evaluate how governance affects economic growth in OECD countries:

$$\ln GDPPC_{it} = \alpha + \theta \ln GDPPC_{it-1} + \beta WGI_{it} + \gamma Inflation_{it} + \delta Real\ Interest\ Rates_{it} \quad (2)$$

where ln is used for natural logarithm, i denotes the countries and t shows the time. $GDPPC_{it-1}$ refers to the GDP per capita of a country with a one-year lagged and θ is the coeffient of this variable. The remaining variables and coeffients are consistent with the static model.

In both the static and dynamic models, each step was repeated for all six models. Each of these models examines the relationship between economic growth and each WGI indicator and macroeconomic factors, such as inflation and interest rates. Governance indicators are expected to illustrate a positive relationship with economic growth across all models. Concerning macroeconomic control variables, however, it is expected that inflation rates and interest rates will be negative correlated with economic growth.

3.2. Data

We used panel data from 38 countries, and the data used in this study were gathered from the WB database for the period of 2002-2021. The data collected comprise the six governance indicators, independent variables, and two macroeconomic variables, inflation and real interest rates, as control variables, and the natural logarithm of GDP per capita as the dependent variable, for 38 OECD countries. The six governance indicators (WGI) considered were control of corruption (CC), governance effectiveness (GE), political stability and absence of violence/terrorism (PS), rule of law (RL), regulatory quality (RQ), and voice and accountability (VA). Summary information regarding the six WGI indicators are shown in Table 1.

Table 1. Summary Table (WGI)

Variable Name	Description (measurement of perceptions)	Range
CC	public power over: - exercised for private gain, including both petty and grand forms of corruption - quality of public services, - quality of the civil service	Between -2.5 and 2.5
GE	- degree of its independence from political pressures - quality of policy formulation and implementation, - credibility of the government's commitment to policies	Between -2.5 and 2.5
PS	- likelihood of political instability - politically-motivated violence - trust in and adhere the rules of society for agents, - the quality of contract enforcement for agents,	Between -2.5 and 2.5
RL	- property rights, - police and the courts, - likelihood of crime and violence.	Between -2.5 and 2.5
RQ	ability of the government: - formulate and implement policies - formulate and implement regulations to permit and promote private sector development	Between -2.5 and 2.5
VA	- a country's citizens selecting their government, - freedom of expression, - freedom of association, - a free media	Between -2.5 and 2.5

Source: World Bank (2024)

The descriptive statistics for the governance indicators, control variables, and dependent variables for the 38 countries are presented in Table 2.

Table 2. Descriptive Statistics

Variable	N	Mean	Std. Dev.	Min	Max
GDPPC (Dependent)	760	10.2193	0.7119	8.3053	11.6299
CC	760	1.1662	0.8199	-1.0016	2.4591
GE	760	1.2099	0.6051	-0.4879	2.3464
PS	760	0.6377	0.7137	-2.3760	1.7532
RL	760	1.1842	0.6709	-0.7997	2.1248
RQ	760	1.2236	0.4851	-0.2307	2.0866
VA	760	1.1020	0.4608	-0.8602	1.8009
Inflation	760	2.5412	2.9767	-4.5000	45.0000
Real Interest Rates	326	3.3481	3.2625	-12.5199	15.1473

Note: According to unit root test results, all variables are found stationary at level.

According to Table 2, the average GDP per capita was the highest, with a value of 10.2193. The control of corruption (CC) had the highest standard deviation of 0.8199 in the WGI. Political stability and the absence of violence/terrorism (PS) follow the second-highest standard deviation. However, the coefficient of variation (calculated as std. dev. divided by the mean) had the highest value. Therefore, PS can be described as the most volatile indicator within WGI.

Table 3. Unit Root Tests

Variable	ADF	PP	LLC	Bai & Ng	Peseran
GDPPC	-6.4697***	-12.8940***	-7.9973***	-5.3877***	-1.6086
CC	-7.1308***	-15.2631***	-5.8045***	-4.7248***	-1.6933
GE	-9.3925***	-18.5695***	-7.6231***	-4.5692***	-1.8539
PS	-11.5256***	-20.4519***	-10.7930***	-4.0223***	-1.8738
RL	-8.1127***	-16.3446***	-7.8880***	-5.5003***	-2.0514
RQ	-7.8978***	-17.1935***	-6.5877***	-4.6954***	-1.5905
VA	-11.8979***	-15.8139***	-13.8971***	-5.8668***	-1.9996
Inflation	-13.1221***	-21.6487***	-14.7865***	-8.7354***	-2.1994
Real Interest Rates	-6.7512***	-10.018***	-14.2986***	-[a]	-[a]

Note: Table 3 shows the panel unit root tests results. *** $p<0.01$, ** $p<0.05$. [a] We could not apply second generation panel unit root tests because there is no balanced panel for this variable.

We examined whether the variables used in our study meet the stationarity condition, unit root tests were applied, and the test results are presented in Table 3. The ADF, PP, and LLC tests are classified as first-generation panel unit root tests, while the Bai & Ng and Pesaran tests are considered second-generation panel unit root tests. First-generation panel unit root tests analyze under the assumption that series are cross-sectionally independent, whereas second-generation panel unit root tests account for cross-sectional dependence, thus introducing new testing methods under this assumption. Therefore, second-generation tests, which consider cross-sectional dependence, were also employed to examine the stationarity condition. For all tests (except the Pesaran test), rejecting the null hypothesis (the opposite for the Pesaran test) indicates that the variable meets the stationarity condition. Accordingly, it was found that all variables meet the stationarity condition with 99% confidence interval based on the unit root tests examined. Therefore, it was concluded that panel data analysis could be used with the aforementioned variables.

4. RESULTS AND DISCUSSIONS

In this study, we investigated the effect of governance on economic growth for 38 OECD countries using fixed effects and a dynamic model using the GMM estimator of Arellano and Bond (1991).

The Hausman test is significant in Table 4, showing that Hausman rejected the correlated statement. Therefore, we applied fixed-effects models to WGIs as static models.

Table 4. Fixed Effect Models for GDPCC: Static Models

VARIABLES	(1)	(2)	(3)	(4)	(5)	(6)
Constant	10.2917***	10.1722***	10.2046***	9.9995***	10.0480***	10.3077***
	(0.0363)	(0.0438)	(0.0185)	(0.0507)	(0.0395)	(0.0469)
CC	0.0476					
	(0.0333)					
GE		0.0625*				
		(0.0378)				
PS			0.0628***			
			(0.0251)			
RL				0.2267***		
				(0.0464)		
RQ					0.1695***	
					(0.0332)	
VA						0.0644*
						(0.0349)
Inflation	-0.0157***	-0.0157***	-0.0150*	-0.0164***	-0.0156***	-0.0162***
	(0.0028)	(0.0029)	(0.0029)	(0.0028)	(0.0028)	(0.0029)
Real Interest Rates	-0.0096***	-0.0108***	-0.0105***	-0.0119***	-0.0124***	-0.0162***
	(0.0021)	(0.0022)	(0.0021)	(0.0020)	(0.0020)	(0.0021)
Observations	326	326	326	326	326	326
Hausman Test	49.0027***	48.1630***	19.1831***	25.8246***	27.1059***	52.3120***

Note: Table 2 shows the result of pooled OLS, fixed effect. Values in parenthesis are the standard errors. *** $p<0.01$, ** $p<0.05$, * $p<0.1$. Note: Hausman Test Scores (Chi-square) are found between and ($p<0.01$). The p-values are less than 1% for all models. It means that the fixed effects estimator is more efficient for ordinary least square models.

In Table 4, government effectiveness (GE) in Model 2, political stability (PS) in Model 3, the rule of law (RL) in Model 4, regulatory quality (RQ) in Model 5 and voice and accountability (VA) in Model 6 are significant and positively correlated with GDPPC ($p<0.01$, $p<0.05$, and $p<0.10$, respectively). These findings suggest that the existence of components for government effectiveness, political stability, voice and accountability, and the rule of law contribute positively to economic development. Moreover in Models 1-6 real interest rates and inflation were found to be significant and negatively related to GDPPC.

Table 5 illustrates the GMM models for the GDPCC as dynamic models. As shown in Table 5, all indicators (independent variables as WGIs) were significant (except CC) and positively correlated with GDPPC (p<0.01 and p<0.05). Moreover in Models 1-6 real interest rates and inflation are found to be significant and negatively related to GDPPC, with the exception of Model 2, in which inflation is insignificant.

Table 5. GMM Models for GDPCC: Dynamic Models

VARIABLES	(1)	(2)	(3)	(4)	(5)	(6)
GDPPC$_{t-1}$	0.8802***	0.8837***	0.8736***	0.8717***	0.8738***	0.8633***
	(0.0080)	(0.0121)	(0.0084)	(0.0051)	(0.0011)	(0.0010)
CC	0.0081					
	(0.0130)					
GE		0.0274**				
		(0.0130)				
PS			0.0227***			
			(0.0036)			
RL				0.0149**		
				(0.0068)		
RQ					0.0237***	
					(0.0036)	
VA						0.0298***
						(0.0014)
Inflation	-0.0007*	0.0002	-0.0005*	-0.0005***	-0.0005***	-0.0006***
	(0.0004)	(0.0006)	(0.0003)	(0.0001)	(0.0001)	(0.0001)
Real Interest Rates	-0.0023***	-0.0032***	-0.0025***	-0.0024***	-0.0027***	-0.0023***
	(0.0003)	(0.0009)	(0.0007)	(0.0004)	(0.0001)	(0.0002)
Observations	289	289	289	289	289	289
Sargan's J test	18.7046	16.8443	18.1077	12.3341	17.9301	17.8085
AR (2)	-2.2667**	-2.5499**	-2.4337**	-1.5666*	-2.2516**	-2.2929**

Note: Values in parentheses are standard errors. *** p<0.01, ** p<0.05, * p<0.1. Note: Sargan-Hansen test (Sargan's J test) refers to the over-identification test for the restrictions in the estimation of GMM. AR (2) represents the test of Arellano Bond for the existence of autocorrelation of the second order.

Similarly, AlShiab (2016) found a positive effect between the quality of governance and the growth of the economy. Zhuo et al. (2020), found direct significant effect of rule of law, control of corruption, and voice and accountability on economic growth, the results of Sarhangi (2021) shows a positive relationship between the rule of law (RL) and economic growth (GDP) with financial development (FD) and Knack and Keefer (1997), Campos and Nugent (1999), Han et al. (2014) has similar findings.

The diagnostic tests (Sargan test for over-identification) in Table 5 show superior statistical performance, and AR (2) represents the test of Arellano Bond for the existence of autocorrelation of the second order.

5. CONCLUSION

The current investigation offers insights into the correlation between the quality of governance and economic development across 38 OECD countries from 2002 to 2021. According to WB governance, there are six elements: (i) the control of corruption; (ii) government effectiveness, (iii) political stability, (iv) control of corruption and regulatory quality, (v) voice and accountability, and (vi) the rule of law. The fundamental query leading this study is whether good governance quality affects economic development in OECD countries. With this purpose in mind, in addiction to the six worldwide governance indicators (WGI), two controlled variables such as inflation, and real interest rates, were provided through the WB's official database. Employing a panel data methodology, the study conducted analyses to assess the influence of governance quality on the economic development of OECD countries. For this purpose, used fixed effect model, first difference GMM model to examine the effect of governance on economic growth.

Considering previous research showing the adverse linkage between good governance and economic growth, this study aimed to examine the positive effects of stable and strong institutions on economic development. The current findings show that government effectiveness, political stability, and the rule of law are significantly and positively related to GDPPC. Similarly, in previous studies of AlShiab (2016), Campos and Nugent (1999), Han et al. (2014), Knack and Keefer (1997), Sarhangi (2021), and Zhou et al (2020), it is clear that there is a positive relationship between governance quality and economic growth.

In this study the results met most expectations per se. That is being said, the governance indicators, such as, government effectiveness, political stability, voice and accountability, and rule of law contribute positively to economic development and are vital for the economies of 38 OECD countries. These findings suggest that OECD countries should prioritize governance indicators for economic prosperity. The quality of the institutions is crucial for supporting economic welfare. The institutional quality of good governance, which serves to improve legal structure and reinforce alternative good governance objectives, is at the core of the economic development process. The quality of the institutional structure is one of the leading elements in supporting economic development and prosperity. Similarly, good governance provides both institutions and rules that are more competent and powerful. All governments strive for what is best for their country; they desire richness, expansion, and development in the economy and take cautions accordingly. Good governance is one of the critical factors for achieving all these factors and development; subsequently, all developed countries have good governance practices. Policemakers may need to engage in a broad improvement process that stimulates institutional development to boost the economic boom.

In future studies, a comparison can be conducted between the effects of political institutions on 32 developed OECD economies and six emerging OECD economies, aiming to discern the differences between these two distinct groups of countries. Furthermore, the inclusion of additional variables in the models can enhance the depth and scope of the analysis. While this chapter discusses the correlation between these variables and provides empirical evidence, future studies could benefit from a deeper analysis of causal pathways. Specifically, it would be interesting to investigate how other aspects of governance affect economic outcomes at the individual and societal levels. Thus, including case studies or comparative analyses of OECD nations that have undergone significant governance reforms could enrich our investigation by illustrating practical examples of policy interventions and their economic impacts.

Figure 1.

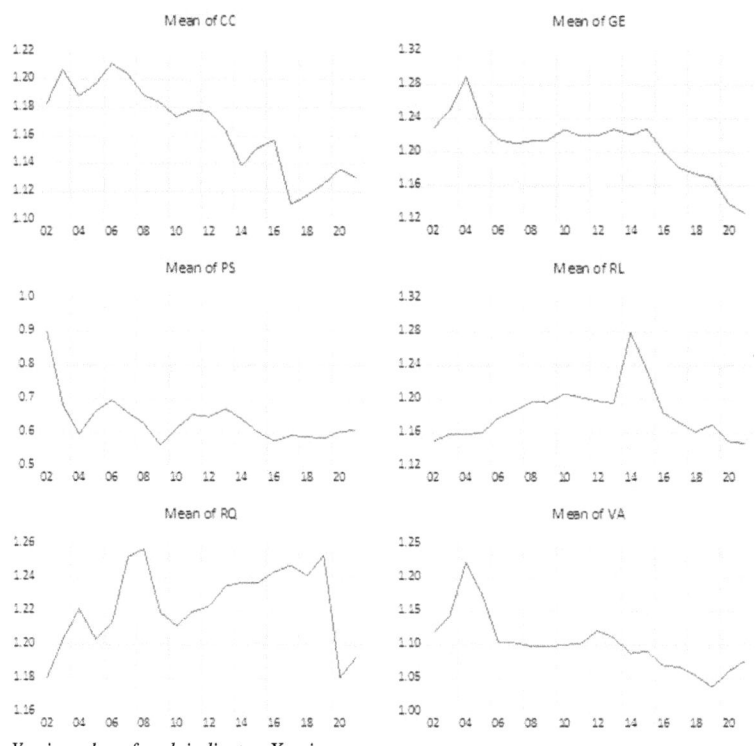

Note: *Y axis: value of each indicator, X axis: year*

REFERENCES

Abdiweli, A. (2001). Political instability, policy uncertainty, and economic growth: An empirical investigation. *Atlantic Economic Journal*, 29(1), 87–106. DOI: 10.1007/BF02299934

Acemoglu, D., Johnson, S., & Robinson, J. A. (2005). Institutions As A Fundamental Cause Of Long-Run Growth. Handbook of Economic Growth, Volume 1A. Doi: DOI: 10.1016/S1574-W84(05)OloW-3

Adams, S., & Mengistu, B. (2008). Privatization, governance and economic development in developing countries. *Journal of Developing Societies*, 24(4), 415–438. DOI: 10.1177/0169796X0902400401

Albassam, B. A. (2013). The Relationship Between Governance and Economic Growth During Times of Crisis. *European Journal of Sustainable Development*, 2(4), 1–18. http://ecsdev.org. DOI: 10.14207/ejsd.2013.v2n2p1

AlShiab, M. S. I., Al-Malkawi, H.-A. N., & Lahrech, A. (2020). Revisiting The Relationship between Governance Quality and Economic Growth. *International Journal of Economics and Financial Issues*, 10(4), 54–63. DOI: 10.32479/ijefi.9927

Ari, A., & Veiga, F. J. (2013). How Does Political Instability Affect Economic Growth. *European Journal of Political Economy*, 29, 151–167. DOI: 10.1016/j.ejpoleco.2012.11.001

Ashiku, M. (2016). Development Through Good Governance. *European Journal of Social Sciences Education and Research, 3,* (2). https://www.un.org/Docs/SG/Report98/con98.htm

Bai, J., & Ng, S. (2006). Confidence Intervals for Diffusion Index Forecasts and Inference for Factor-Augmented Regressions. *Econometrica*, 74(4), 1133–1150. DOI: 10.1111/j.1468-0262.2006.00696.x

Campos, N. F., & Nugent, J. B. (1999). Development Performance and the Institutions of Governance: Evidence from East Asia and Latin America. *World Development*, 27(3), 439–452. DOI: 10.1016/S0305-750X(98)00149-1

Chang, H. J. (2006). *Understanding The Relationship Between Institutions and Economic Development: Some Key Theoretical Issues. World Institute For Development Economics Research.* United Nations University.

Chang, H. J. (2011). Institutions and Economic Development: Theory, Policy and History. *Journal of Institutional Economics*, 7(4), 473–498. DOI: 10.1017/S1744137410000378

Clarke, G. R., Groff, A., Keefer, P., Beck, T., Clarke, G., & Walsh Beck, P. (2000). *New tools and new tests in comparative political economy: The Database of Political Institutions*. https://www.researchgate.net/publication/23549161

d'Agostino, G., Dunne, J. P., & Pieroni, L. (2016). Government Spending, Corruption and Economic Growth. *World Development*, 84, 190–205. DOI: 10.1016/j.worlddev.2016.03.011

Dickey, D. A., & Fuller, W. A. (1981). Likelihood Ratio Statistics for Autoregressive Time Series with a Unit Root. *Econometrica*, 49(4), 1057–1072. DOI: 10.2307/1912517

Drake, E., Malik, A., Xu, Y., Kotsioni, I., El-Habashy, R., & Misra, V. (2001). *Good Governance and the World Bank*. University of Oxford.

Han, X., Khan, H., & Zhuang, J. (2014). Do Governance Indicators Explain Development Performance? A Cross-Country Analysis. *ADB Economics Working Paper Series*, 17.

Jacobs, S. (2004). Regulatory İmpact Assessment And The Economic Transition to Markets. *Public Money & Management*, 5(24), 283–290. DOI: 10.1111/j.1467-9302.2004.00435.x

Jütting, J. (2003). *Institutions and Development: A Critical Review*. Oecd Development Centre.

Kaufmann, D., & Kraay, A. (2002) Growth Without Governance. World Bank Policy Research Working Paper 2928.

Kaufmann, D., Kraay, A., & Zoido-Lobaton, P. (1999). Governance Matters. The World Bank Development Research Group Macroeconomics and Growth and World Bank Institute. www.worldbank.org/html/dec/Publications/Workpapers/home.html

Knack, S., & Keefer, P. (1997). Does Social Capital Have an Economic Payoff? A Cross-Country Investigation. *The Quarterly Journal of Economics*, 112(4), 1251–1288. DOI: 10.1162/003355300555475

Levin, A., Lin, C., & Chu, S. C. (2002). Unit Root Tests in Panel Data: Asymptotic and Finite-Sample Properties. *Journal of Econometrics*, 108(1), 1–24. DOI: 10.1016/S0304-4076(01)00098-7

Mahran, H. A. (2023). The impact of governance on economic growth: Spatial econometric approach. *Review of Economics and Political Science*, 8(1), 37–53. DOI: 10.1108/REPS-06-2021-0058

Mehanna, R. A., Yazbeck, Y., & Sarieddine, L. (2010). Governance and Economic Development in MENA Countries: Does Oil Affect The Presence of A Virtuous Circle? *Journal of Transnational Management*, 15(2), 117–150. DOI: 10.1080/15475778.2010.481250

Nomor, D. T., & Iorember, P. T. (2017). Political Stability and Economic Growth in Nigeria. *IOSR Journal of Economics and Finance*, 08(02), 45–53. DOI: 10.9790/5933-0802034553

North, D. C. (1991). Institutions. *The Journal of Economic Perspectives*, 5(1), 97–112. DOI: 10.1257/jep.5.1.97

Pesaran, M. H. (2007). A Simple Panel Unit Root Test in the Presence of Cross Section Dependence. *Journal of Applied Econometrics*, 22(2), 265–312. DOI: 10.1002/jae.951

Phillips, P. C. B., & Perron, P. (1988). Testing for Unit Roots in Time Series Regression. *Biometrika*, 75(2), 335–346. DOI: 10.1093/biomet/75.2.335

Ramadhan, A. A., Jian, Z. H., Henry, K. K., & Pacific, Y. K. T. (2016). Does Political Stability Accelerate Economic Growth in Tanzania? A Time Series Analysis. *Global Business Review*, 17(5), 1026–1036. DOI: 10.1177/0972150916656652

Rodrik, D. (2008). The Real Exchange Rate and Economic Growth. *Brookings Papers on Economic Activity*, 2(2), 365–412. DOI: 10.1353/eca.0.0020

Sarhangi, K., Niya, M. J. M., Amiri, M., Sargolzaeı, M., & Sarvolia, E. H. E. (2021). The Impact of Effective Governance and Regulatory Quality on Financial Development Under Economic Conditions of the Mena Countries. *The Impact of Effective Governance and Regulatory Quality on Financial Development Under Economic Conditions of the Mena Countries*, 27(3). Advance online publication. DOI: 10.47750/cibg.2021.27.03.335

Shirley, M. M. (2008). Institutions and Development. In *Handbook of New Institutional Economics* (pp. 611–638). Springer Berlin Heidelberg., DOI: 10.1007/978-3-540-69305-5_25

Snowdon, B., & Vayne, H. (2012). *Modern Maroekonomi*. Efil Yayınevi.

Stiglitz, J. E., & Furman, J. (1998). Economic Crises: Evidence and Insights from East Asia. *Brookings Papers on Economic Activity*, •••, 2.

Uddin, A., Ali, H., Masih, M. (2017). Political Stability and Growth: An Application Of Dynamic GMM and Quantile Regression.Elseiver.com.

UNDESA, UNDP (2012). Governance and development. *UN System Task Team on the Post-2015 UN Development agenda.*

World Bank. (2024). Worldwide Governance Indicators. https://datacatalog.worldbank.org/search/dataset/0038026. Access date: 17th July 2024.

World Development Report. (2002). Building Institutions for Markets. Oxford University Press.

Zhuo, Z., O, A. S. M., Muhammad, B., & Khan, S. (2020). Underlying the Relationship Between Governance and Economic Growth in Developed Countries. *Journal of the Knowledge Economy*, 12(3), 1314–1330. DOI: 10.1007/s13132-020-00658-w

ENDNOTE

[1] Structural Adjustment Programmes (SAPs) are economic policies for developing countries that have been promoted by the World Bank and International Monetary Fund (IMF) since the early 1980s by the provision of loans conditional on the adoption of such policies. Structural adjustment loans are those made by the World Bank. They are designed to encourage the structural adjustment of an economy by, for example, removing "excess" government controls and promoting market competition as part of the neo-liberal agenda followed by the Bank. The Enhanced Structural Adjustment Facility is an IMF financing mechanism to support macroeconomic policies and SAPs in low-income countries through loans or low-interest subsidies (United Nations Economic and Social Commission for Western Asia, 2023).

Chapter 13
The Impact of Trade and Financial Globalization on Cross-Border Investments:
Perspective of Newly Industrialized Countries

Sinem Atıcı Ustalar
https://orcid.org/0009-0005-9476-8487
Ataturk University, Turkey

ABSTRACT

This study analyzes the impact of Newly Industrialized Countries (NICs) trade and financial globalization on bilateral financial asset trade. The analysis is carried out using the financial gravity model. The model is estimated with the PPML estimator using bilateral portfolios, debt securities, and equity investments of 120 countries between 2001-2022. De facto and de jure trade and financial openness variables are used to control globalization in model estimation. Estimation results show that the impact of trade and financial openness on financial asset trade in NICs is higher than the world average. When compared with G7 countries, show that the openness of NICs' goods and capital markets is not yet at the level of industrialized countries.

DOI: 10.4018/979-8-3693-5508-4.ch013

1. INTRODUCTION

Newly Industrialized Countries (NICs) are typically characterized by rapid industrialization, urbanization, and economic growth. These countries often have a strong manufacturing sector, export-oriented industries, and a growing middle class (Er, 1997). Additionally, NICs often have expanding stock and bond markets. This offers companies the opportunity to increase their capital and investors to diversify their portfolios (Haggard, 1986). Moreover, policymakers and international organizations facilitate the smooth flow of global trade and investment (Boddin, 2016). The place of NICs in the international economy is remarkable. While the share of NICs in the world's total portfolio investments was 0.32% in 2001, this rate increased to 2.36% in 2022. The share of these countries in foreign trade increased from 14.2% to 23.7% from 2001 to 2022.[1]

Considering these features of NICs, their integration with world financial markets is expected to be high. However, Ustalar (2023) found that home bias in international stock portfolio investments of these countries is high with the International Capital Asset Pricing Model. This finding of the author shows that NICs' financial market integration is low. Furthermore, it is seen that the distribution of cross-border portfolio investments varies between countries although the barriers to international trade in goods and financial assets have decreased significantly due to the impact of globalization. This situation arises from cultural (Bellofatto, 2017), institutional (Beck & Levine, 2003), legal system (La Porta *et al.*, 1998), and information (Portes & Rey, 2005) differences between countries. Another important reason is that the trade and financial globalization of countries is different. In this context, the level of globalization of NICs and bilateral financial investments may cause them to differ from other industrialized countries. The study aims to analyze the impact of trade and financial globalization on the bilateral financial asset trade in NICs.

In the study, the impact of trade and financial globalization of NICs' bilateral financial asset trade is examined with the financial gravity model of Okava and van Wincoop (2012). Brazil, China, Mexico, South Africa, Philippines, Malaysia, Thailand, Türkiye, India, and Indonesia are considered as NICs in the analysis. The financial gravity model is estimated using bilateral portfolio, debt securities, and equity investments of 120 countries in 2001-2022. In estimating the financial gravity model, countries' trade and financial openness are used to measure the impact of globalization. There is evidence in the literature that the impact of openness on financial investments differs according to de facto and de jure measurement. Therefore, the model is estimated separately using de facto and de jure trade and financial openness. The model results show that trade and financial openness are determinants of portfolio, debt securities, and equity investments across countries. Rising trade and financial openness increase bilateral financial asset trade. Furthermore, the effects of trade and financial openness differ according to de facto and de jure measures. Investors take into consideration de jure openness measures in their international portfolio choices.

In the financial gravity model, the effect of trade and financial openness on financial investments in NICs is estimated with interaction variables. The interaction coefficients obtained from the model estimation show that the effect of trade and financial openness on financial investments in NICs is different from the world average. The estimation results reveal that the rise in trade and financial openness increases portfolio, debt securities, and equity investments in NICs. The interaction coefficients are compared with G7 countries, the effect of trade and financial openness is higher in G7 countries. This may be due to institutional factors in NICs. Although NICs have economic growth potential, they are politically unstable countries (O'Neill, 1984) compared to G7 countries. The rule of law for the years 2001-2022 is 1.20 for G7 countries, while it is -0.41 for NICs[2]. In addition, NICs have younger financial markets compared to G7 countries. Therefore, especially in terms of trade openness, the relationship between real and financial markets is lower compared to G7 countries.

There are no studies in the relevant literature addressing the impact of NICs' trade and financial openness on bilateral asset trade. Additionally, studies considering trade and financial openness as determinants of bilateral portfolio investments are limited in the literature. In this respect, it is expected that the findings of the study will contribute to the literature.

In the following section of the study, the relevant literature is presented. Then, the empirical equations of the financial gravity model are presented and the model results are discussed. The last section is the conclusion.

2. LITERATURE REVIEW

Economic globalization is defined as the process of liberalization and integration of goods and factor markets of national economies (Das, 2004). Alternatively, it is defined as the integration of goods and factor markets, which operated separately until globalization (Conley, 2000). UNCTAD (1994) classifies this definition of globalization as "shallow integration". In addition, UNCTAD (1994) classifies the integration of national economies with international financial markets, as well as commodity and factor markets, as "deep integration". As can be understood from this classification of UNCTAD (1994), two important types of economic globalization are trade and financial integration. Trade integration includes trade agreements, reduced trade barriers, and increased cross-border flows of goods and services that facilitate advances in transportation and communications technologies (Das, 2004).

Financial integration involves the integration of financial markets and institutions on a global scale by allowing the free movement of capital, investments, and financial services between countries (Baele et al., 2004). Additionally, financial integration can be defined as the absence of location-based discrimination in access to financial markets (Weber, 2006).

Globalization of trade increases the cross-border flow of goods and services (Das, 2004). Heathcote and Perri (2013) showed that there is a positive relationship between trade openness and international portfolio diversification with a two-good international business cycle model. Additionally, Aizenman and Noy (2009), and Peter (2012) revealed that financial asset trade between countries with high trade openness is high. The first channel explaining the relationship between trade openness and financial asset investments is the information costs channel. In this context, countries with high trade openness also have high trade in goods and services with partner countries. Portes and Rey (2005) state that the flow of information is high between countries with tighter trade relations. With the help of their increased information due to high goods trade, investors calculate the financial asset risk of the partner country lower (Okava & van Wincoop, 2012) and financial asset trade between partner countries increases. The second channel explaining the relationship between trade openness and financial asset investments is also trade costs channel.

Considering goods trade as an information channel in cross-border financial asset investments has been based on the gravity model approach in the literature from the very first moment. Aviat and Cœurdacier (2007) discussed the relationship between goods trade and equity investments with a simultaneous equation approach. The analysis using the gravity model was conducted only for 2001 with 62 countries. Estimation results show that a 10 percent increase in imports between country pairs increases bilateral equity investments by 6-7 percent. With the addition of imports to the gravity model, it was observed that the negative effect of geographical distance representing information flow decreased by 60 percent. De Santis (2010) analyzed the determinants of equity and government bond investments among European Union countries. He stated that investors will prefer the trading partner with whom they have close commercial relations by accelerating the information flow. The author concluded that the effect of trade in goods and services is stronger on bilateral equity investments. Chitu et al. (2014) analyzed historical ties on the determinants of US government bond investments and revealed that countries with tight trade relations have historically had more information about each other, which reduces financial market frictions and increases bilateral government bond investments.

Mehigan (2016) analyzed the impact of trade on bilateral bank flows of developed countries before and during the global financial crisis. The analysis using the gravity model covers the years 2005-2009. Model results show that growing imports increase bank flows between countries. The positive impact of imports was calculated higher before the Global Financial Crisis. Mercado (2018) analyzed whether bilateral trade have a push and pull effect on bilateral capital flows. He modeled capital flows between 10 developed countries and 186 trading partners for the years 2000-2016 with the gravity model. According to the model results, the impact of gravitational factors such as geographical distance, common language, similarity of legal systems and the tight bilateral trade relationship on bilateral capital flows is strongly significant. Trade in goods is a pull factor for bilateral capital flows.

The second channel explaining the relationship between trade openness and bilateral financial investments is the trade cost channel. Obstfeld and Rogoff (2001) state that friction in good trade increases the local investor's demand for local stocks. This situation is called home bias in international financial asset trade (Tesar & Werner, 1995). The decreasing trade costs between partner countries cause rising trade openness. In this case, local investors' demand for foreign assets will increase and financial asset investment between partner countries will also rise. In other words, countries with high trade openness will have low home bias in their financial markets. Lane and Milesi-Ferretti (2004), following Obstfeld and Rogoff (2001), reveal that the differentiation of countries' trade costs with partner countries changes international portfolio allocation. On the contrary, Coeurdacier (2009) demonstrated with his two-good general equilibrium model that trade costs do not create home bias in equity investments. However, the increase in trade costs increases foreign bias in equity investments. Similarly, Van Wincoop and Warnock (2010) investigated the impact of trade costs on the US's portfolio investments with 21 industrialized countries using the general equilibrium approach. Model findings show that the increase in trade costs does not cause home bias in portfolio investments. However, unlike Obstfeld and Rogoff (2001) and Lane and Milesi-Ferretti (2004), Coeurdacier (2009) and Wincoop and Warnock (2010) considered trade costs as fluctuations in the real exchange rate.

The level of financial market integration is important for investors to calculate expected returns in international financial markets. The expected returns are determined by a combination of local and global risk sources (Karolyi & Stulz, 2003). In this case, the more open a country's financial markets are, the more local investors will be able to eliminate local risks through international portfolio diversification. Thus, financial investments between countries will increase. Daude and Fratzscher (2008) examined the hierarchy of cross-border investments in 77 countries and found that financial openness increased FDI, equity, debt, and loan investments. The gravity model findings show that financial openness affects FDI the most. Wildmann (2011) investigated the determinants of portfolio choices of German banks in emerging capital markets (ECMs) for the period March 2002-December 2007. The study findings show that financial openness decreased German banks' equity investments in ECMs and increased their bond investments. Mercado and Park (2011) examined the determinants of the volatility of capital inflows to 50 emerging countries for the period 1980-2009 and found that financial openness increased the volatility of FDI and FPI inflows. The model was also estimated for developing Asian countries. According to the estimation results, the increment in financial openness increases the volatility of FDI and FPI inflows in Asian countries. However, the effect of financial openness on FPI is insignificant. Peter (2012) examined the relationship between asset holdings, trade flows, and financial openness for the years 2001 and 2007 with the help of a three-country stochastic general equilibrium model. The author calculated the effects of de facto and de jure financial openness separately in the model. According to the estimation results, the effects of de jure and de facto financial openness on asset holdings are positive in 2001 and 2007. However, the positive effect of financial openness decreased in 2007. Increasing financial openness is one of the factors that increment foreign portfolio investments between countries.

The relevant literature focuses on the theoretical and empirical relationship between trade and financial asset investments. However, studies examining the impact of financial openness on bilateral asset investments are limited. In the following section, empirical gravity model equations measuring the impact of trade and financial openness on bilateral investments are presented.

3. METHODOLOGY

In this section, the empirical models and methods to be estimated to test the impact of globalization on NICs' cross-border investments will be presented and discussed. First, benchmark models will be created that measure the average expected impact of trade and financial openness, which represents globalization, on cross-border investments. In light of these model results, I will focus on NICs.

It is important to control information costs in international financial investments in creating benchmark models. Empirical studies in the literature on information costs have used the financial gravity model from the very beginning. Structurally, the study uses a financial gravity model created by the theoretical approach of Okava and van Wincoop (2012). The financial gravity model is a powerful tool for analyzing the determinants of investments between countries.

In the study, panel data with cross-sectional and t time sections consisting of source and destination country pairs (ji) was used to estimate the financial gravity model. The panel data set used includes portfolio, debt securities, and equity investments made by 120 countries (Annex 1: Country List) in 119 countries (120*119) in the data set, excluding themselves, between 2001 and 2022. However, in the data set used, 57.30% of bilateral portfolio investments are missing and 19.40% are zero,

57.49% of debt instrument investments are missing and 23.44% are zero, 52.98% of stock investments are missing and 28.50% are zero.

It is known that log-linear methods used with OLS and similar estimators create a deviation in the gravity model resulting in the presence of zero trade flows in the data set. If observation values take the value of zero, especially for small or distant countries, when the logarithms of these values are taken, information about small or distant countries is systematically lost in the estimation (Frankel, 1997). Balancing the panel by removing country pairs with zero trade flows from the data set or estimating the model by changing the value of the dependent variable from 0 to 1 (log 1=0) are frequently applied methods for the solution, but are theoretically inconsistent (Yotov et al., 2016) and gives deviated estimates (Santos Silva & Tenreyro, 2006). Santos Silva and Tenreyro (2006, 2011) state that it is appropriate to estimate bilateral flows in multiplicative form, without taking their logarithm, under the assumption that they have a Poisson distribution.

Based on this, the empirical gravity equations used in the study were estimated in multiplicative form following the suggestion of Santos Silva and Tenreyro (2006, 2011). First, benchmark models were created based on the theoretical approach of Okawa and van Wincoop (2012). Relevant literature shows that the impact of openness on asset trade differs according to de facto and de jure measurement methods. For this reason, de facto and de jure trade and financial openness measurements were taken into account when creating benchmark models. First, Model (1) and Model (2) test the expected average impact of trade openness on bilateral financial asset trade for the years 2001-2022, according to de facto and de jure measurement methods, respectively. Model (1) and Model (2) are defined as follows.

(Model 1)

$$FAT_{jit} = \exp(\alpha_1 lnMCAP_{jt} + \alpha_2 lnMCAP_{it} + \alpha_3 lnD_{ji} + \alpha_4 BORDER_{ji} + \alpha_5 LANG_{ji} + \alpha_6 COL_{ji} + \alpha_7 lnROL_{it} + \alpha_8 lnRTS_{it} + \alpha_j + \alpha_i + \alpha_t + \varepsilon_{jit})$$

(Model 2)

$$FAT_{jit} = \exp(\alpha_1 lnMCAP_{jt} + \alpha_2 lnMCAP_{it} + \alpha_3 lnD_{ji} + \alpha_4 BORDER_{ji} + \alpha_5 LANG_{ji} + \alpha_6 COL_{ji} + \alpha_7 lnROL_{it} + \alpha_8 lnTARIFF_{it} + \alpha_j + \alpha_i + \alpha_t + \varepsilon_{jit})$$

In Model (1) and Model (2), FAT_{jit} shows the investments made by country j (source country) in the financial assets of country i (destination country) in period t. The FAT_{jit} variable includes portfolio, debt securities, and equity investments between countries. $MCAP_{jt}$ and $MCAP_{it}$ are market capitalization as indicators of the financial size of source and destination countries, respectively. As the financial size of countries increases, financial investments between them rise. Essentially, four different interest variables were added to the model to measure information costs. The first of these is the distance variable (D_{jt}), which shows the geodesic distances[3] between two countries. The other three are dummy variables that are expected to increase investments by reducing information costs. The dummy variable $BORDER_{jt}$ represents the common border and takes the value of 1 if two countries have common border, and 0 otherwise. The variable $LANG_{jt}$ is defined as 1 if a common language is spoken in both countries and 0 if not. COL_{ji} controls the colonial ties between the two countries that have existed from past to present ($COL_{ji}=1$).

In a country where the rule of law prevails, the enforcement of public rules is impartial and effective, thanks to the laws, government policies, and regulations that regulate economic activities. In addition, public information infrastructure such as accounting, auditing, and financial rating is highly reliable and transparent (Wu et al., 2012). For this reason, the rule of law is an important institutional variable in foreign financial investments. Because it ensures both the protection of foreign investors and the fairness and transparency of transactions in the investment process (Akişik, 2020). For this purpose, the effect of the rule of law on bilateral financial investments was controlled in Model (1) and Model (2). In the models, the ROL_{it} variable represents the rule of law of country i in period t. As the rule of law increases in the destination country, it is expected to have a positive impact on cross-border investments.

Gygli *et al.* (2019) divided the measure of globalization into de jure and de facto. De jure globalization is a measure of the policies that allow and control flows (goods, capital, people, and information) and activities. De facto globalization is a measure that represents actual flows and activities (Leal et al., 2021). In the study, trade and financial openness were used to measure globalization in the goods and capital markets, respectively. Aizenman and Noy (2009) revealed in their study that there is an endogenous relationship between trade and financial openness. Countries with high trade openness also have high financial openness, and vice versa. Therefore, the financial gravity model was estimated separately for each openness measure.

In Model (1), the impact of de facto trade openness on bilateral investments is measured by the RTS_{it} variable. RTS_{it} represents the real trade shares of country i in period t. To measure de facto trade openness, real trade shares were calculated following Alcala and Ciccone (2004). Real trade shares are calculated as the ratio of the trade volumes of 120 countries to real GDP. The effect of the RTS_{it} variable on bilateral financial investments is expected to be calculated positively.

For de jure trade openness in the model (2), tariff rates of 120 countries were calculated, following Gräbner et al. (2018). De jure trade openness is calculated as 100 minus the tariff rate, which is an average of the applied weighted mean and most favored nations' tariff rates. Since increasing tariff rates means increasing barriers to foreign trade, and rising trade costs, so the coefficient of the $TARIFF_{it}$ variable is expected to be calculated negatively.

In Model (1) and Model (2), α_j and α_i are fixed effect variables belonging to countries j and i, respectively. Fixed effects for countries j and i are used to estimate the model without bias as an indicator of multilateral resistancein financial costs (Okawa & van Wincoop, 2012). Fixed effects also help measure the impact of interest variables without bias by controlling country heterogeneity due to time-invariant characteristics specific to countries j and i. Finally, α_t is a time dummy variable and controls for global shocks, including price changes.

Model (3) and Model (4) were created to test the effect of de facto and de jure financial openness on bilateral investments, respectively.

(Model 3)

$$FAT_{jit} = \exp(\alpha_1 lnMCAP_{jt} + \alpha_2 lnMCAP_{it} + \alpha_3 lnD_{ji} + \alpha_4 BORDER_{ji} + \alpha_5 LANG_{ji} + \alpha_6 COL_{ji} + \alpha_7 lnROL_{it} + \alpha_8 lnLMF\_OPEN_{it} + \alpha_j + \alpha_i + \alpha_t + \varepsilon_{jit})$$

(Model 4)

$$FAT_{jit} = \exp(\alpha_1 lnMCAP_{jt} + \alpha_2 lnMCAP_{it} + \alpha_3 lnD_{ji} + \alpha_4 BORDER_{ji} + \alpha_5 LANG_{ji} + \alpha_6 COL_{ji} + \alpha_7 lnROL_{it} + \alpha_8 lnKAOPEN_{it} + \alpha_j + \alpha_i + \alpha_t + \varepsilon_{jit})$$

In model (3), LMF_OPEN_{it} represents the de facto financial openness of country i in period t. The LMF_OPEN_{it} variable was calculated as a percentage of total foreign assets and total foreign liabilities as a percentage of GDP, following Lane and Milessi-Ferretti (2017). In Model (4), de jure financial openness is represented by the kaopen variable. $KAOPEN_{it}$ variable is a variable calculated by Chinn and Ito (2008), taking into account the presence of multiple exchange rates, restriction on current and capital account transactions, and the requirement of the surrender of export proceeds. When rising financial openness increases bilateral investments, the coefficients of the LMF_OPEN_{it} and $KAOPEN_{it}$ variables are expected to be calculated positively.

Once the benchmark models were established, the impacts of trade and financial openness on financial asset investments in the NICs were considered in the analysis. Interaction variables were used to separate the effect of trade and financial openness in NICs from world average. In addition, interaction variables were used to compare the impact of globalization on investments in NICs with G7 countries. For this purpose, interaction variables were added to Models 1, 2, 3, and 2, which are the benchmark model.

(Model 1a)

$$FAT_{jit} = \exp(\alpha_1 lnMCAP_{jt} + \alpha_2 lnMCAP_{it} + \alpha_3 lnD_{ji}$$
$$+ \alpha_4 BORDER_{ji} + \alpha_5 LANG_{ji} + \alpha_6 COL_{ji} + \alpha_7 lnROL_{it}$$
$$+ \alpha_8 lnRTS_{it} + \alpha_9 lnRTS_{it}*dNIC_i + \alpha_{10} lnRTS_{it}*dG7_i + \alpha_j + \alpha_i + \alpha_t + \varepsilon_{jit})$$

(Model 2a)

$$FAT_{jit} = \exp(\alpha_1 lnMCAP_{jt} + \alpha_2 lnMCAP_{it} + \alpha_3 lnD_{ji}$$
$$+ \alpha_4 BORDER_{ji} + \alpha_5 LANG_{ji} + \alpha_6 COL_{ji} + \alpha_7 lnROL_{it} + \alpha_8 lnTARIFF_{it}$$
$$+ \alpha_9 lnTARIFF_{it}*dNIC_i + \alpha_{10} lnTARIFF_{it}*dG7_i + \alpha_j + \alpha_i + \alpha_t + \varepsilon_{jit})$$

(Model 3a)

$$FAT_{jit} = \exp(\alpha_1 lnMCAP_{jt} + \alpha_2 lnMCAP_{it} + \alpha_3 lnD_{ji}$$
$$+ \alpha_4 BORDER_{ji} + \alpha_5 LANG_{ji} + \alpha_6 COL_{ji} + \alpha_7 lnROL_{it} + \alpha_8 lnLMF\_OPEN_{it}$$
$$+ \alpha_9 lnLMF\_OPEN_{it}*dNIC_i + \alpha_{10} lnLMF\_OPEN_{it}*dG7_i + \alpha_j + \alpha_i + \alpha_t + \varepsilon_{jit})$$

(Model 4a)

$$FAT_{jit} = \exp(\alpha_1 lnMCAP_{jt} + \alpha_2 lnMCAP_{it} + \alpha_3 lnD_{ji}$$
$$+ \alpha_4 BORDER_{ji} + \alpha_5 LANG_{ji} + \alpha_6 COL_{ji} + \alpha_7 lnROL_{it} + \alpha_8 lnKAOPEN_{it}$$
$$+ \alpha_9 lnKAOPEN_{it}*dNIC_i + \alpha_{10} lnKAOPEN_{it}*dG7_i + \alpha_j + \alpha_i + \alpha_t + \varepsilon_{jit})$$

$dNIC_i$ in the equations takes the value of 1 if the destination country is a NIC country, and 0 otherwise. Brazil, China, Mexico, South Africa, Philippines, Malaysia, Thailand, Türkiye, India, and Indonesia were considered as NICs in the analysis. $DG7_i$ is a dummy variable that takes the value of 1 if the destination country is a G7 country, and 0 otherwise. The impact of de facto and de jure trade and financial openness on investments in NIC is measured by interaction variables, which are the multiplication the openness variables with the $dNIC_i$ dummy variable. In models (1a) and (2a), $lnRTS_{it}*dNIC_i$ and $lnTARIFF_{it}*dNIC_i$ measure the impact of de facto and de jure trade openness on financial investments in NICs. The effect of the $lnRTS_{it}*dNIC_i$ variable on investments in NICs is expected to be calculated as positive, while the effect of $lnTARIFF_{it}*dNIC_i$ is expected to be calculated as negative. In Models (3a) and (4a), the $lnLMF\_OPEN_{it}*dNIC_i$ interaction variable measures the effect of de facto financial openness and the $lnKAOPEN_{it}*dNIC_i$ variable measures the effect of de jure financial openness on financial investments in NICs. Financial openness is expected to increase investments in NICs.

Portfolio, debt securities, and equity investments, which constitute the dependent variable, were obtained from *the IMF's Coordinated Portfolio Investment Survey (CPIS)* database, and market capitalization variables were obtained from *the World Bank's World Development Indicators* database. The geographical distance variable and dummy variables (common border, colonial relations and common language) used as a measure of information costs in the model were taken from *CEPII's Gravity* database. According to the definition of CEPII, for two countries to be considered to have a common language, at least 9 percent of their populations must speak this language. The rule of law variable was obtained from *the World Bank's World Governance Indicators (WGI)* database. The real trade share and tariff rates were calculated with data obtained from *the IMF's DOTS* and *the World Bank's World Development Indicators* database. The data used in the calculation of the LMF_OPEN_{it} open variable was obtained from *The External Wealth of Nations* database by Lane and Milessi-Ferretti (2017).

4. EMPIRICAL RESULTS

PPML estimator results for Models (1), (2), (3) and (4) are shown in Table 1. All models are estimated for equity (EQ_{jit}), debt securities (DS_{jit}), and portfolio (FPI_{jit}), investments. Country-fixed effects and time-fixed effects of source and destination countries are included in all models. According to the results of all models, the financial market size of the countries is positive and significant as expected. Increasing financial market size supports investments between countries. Consistent with the results of studies in the literature, the significant effect of geographical distance is negative on bilateral financial investments. This supports the hypothesis that geographically close countries have easier access to information about bilateral equity, debt securities, and portfolio investments and incur lower information costs. According to the results of Model (1), the effect of the common border variable on bilateral financial investments is positive and significant as expected. Having a common border increases bilateral equity investments between countries by 85%($e^{0.619}$), debt securities by 87%($e^{0.630}$), and portfolio investments by 79%($e^{0.584}$). The $BORDER_{ji}$ affects bilateral financial investments positively and significantly in Models (2), (3) and (4). Lower information costs for financial markets between neighboring countries increase bilateral financial investments.

Other information cost variables are colony relationship and common language variables. These variables represent cultural closeness and are expected to increase their bilateral financial investment. Looking at the Model (1)'s estimation results, if the country speaks the same language, it increases bilateral equity investments by 11%($e^{0.102}$), while it increases debt securities and portfolio investments by 22%($e^{0.198}$)

and 14%($e^{0.131}$), respectively. The fact that the two countries have colonial ties in the past increases bilateral equity investments by 16%($e^{0.152}$), debt securities by 27%($e^{0.237}$) and portfolio investments by 29%($e^{0.253}$). The effect of common language and colonial ties on bilateral financial investments is also positive and significant in Models (2), (3) and (4). Additionally, when colony and language variables are added to the model, the significance of the border effect decreases in all model results. This result is not surprising, considering the abundance of historical and linguistic shares between neighboring countries.

In countries where the rule of law is high, the protection of foreign investors is high and transactions in the investment process are more transparent and fair (Akişik, 2020). Therefore, the rule of law is an important institutional variable for foreign investors. In all models, the $lnROL_{it}$ variable shows that the increase in the rule of law in destination countries increases bilateral financial investments. Countries with high rule of law are more preferred by foreign investors.

In model (1), the coefficient of real trade shares ($lnRTS_{it}$), which measures the effect of de facto trade openness on bilateral investments, is positive and significant. A 1% increase in real trade shares increases bilateral equity investments by 0.57%, debt securities by 0.47% and portfolio investments by 0.46%. The change in real trade shares affect bilateral equity investments the most, in line with the literature. In Model (2), the effect of tariff rates ($lnTARIFF_{it}$), used as a de jure measurement of trade openness, on bilateral investments is measured. Increases in tariff rates reduce financial investments between countries. A 1% increase in tariff rates reduces bilateral equity investments by 0.59%, while it reduces debt securities and portfolio investments by 0.98% and 0.75%, respectively.

The fact that the coefficients of the real trade shares and tariff rates variables are significant indicates that these two variables can be used to represent trade openness in the analysis of the determinants of financial asset trade. Additionally, the estimation results of Models (1) and (2) show that the impact of de facto and de jure measures of trade openness on bilateral financial investments is different like Gygli et al. (2019). De jure trade openness affects bilateral investments more than de facto measure. In addition, the increase in the trade openness of the destination country affects financial asset trade both through the trade cost channel, as shown by Obstfeld and Rogoff (2001), and through the trade information channel, as revealed by Portes and Rey (2005).

Table 1. The impact of trade and financial openness on bilateral financial investments

Dependent Variables	Model 1			Model 2			Model 3			Model 4		
	(1) EQ_{jit}	(2) DS_{jit}	(3) FPI_{jit}	(4) EQ_{jit}	(5) DS_{jit}	(6) FPI_{jit}	(7) EQ_{jit}	(8) DS_{jit}	(9) FPI_{jit}	(10) EQ_{jit}	(11) DS_{jit}	(12) FPI_{jit}
$\ln MCAP_{jt}$	0.615*	0.253*	0.420*	0.618*	0.255*	0.429*	0.611*	0.258*	0.418*	0.611*	0.249*	0.443*
	(0.016)	(0.085)	(0.083)	(0.099)	(0.088)	(0.075)	(0.013)	(0.086)	(0.085)	(0.089)	(0.074)	(0.064)
$\ln MCAP_{it}$	0.850*	0.684*	0.771*	0.852*	0.685*	0.772*	0.857*	0.681*	0.777*	0.897*	0.671*	0.768*
	(0.039)	(0.022)	(0.032)	(0.045)	(0.025)	(0.036)	(0.045)	(0.023)	(0.037)	(0.038)	(0.025)	(0.035)
$\ln D_{ji}$	-0.447*	-0.549*	-0.508*	-0.483*	-0.498*	-0.523*	-0.485*	-0.540*	-0.542*	-0.335*	-0.507*	-0.464*
	(0.054)	(0.055)	(0.044)	(0.058)	(0.053)	(0.046)	(0.055)	(0.054)	(0.043)	(0.047)	(0.059)	(0.045)
$BORDER_{ji}$	0.619**	0.630**	0.584**	0.393**	0.192**	0.235**	0.635**	0.242**	0.387**	0.469**	0.250**	0.228**
	(0.016)	(0.025)	(0.062)	(0.045)	(0.099)	(0.081)	(0.096)	(0.071)	(0.073)	(0.193)	(0.200)	(0.182)
$LANG_{ji}$	0.102*	0.198*	0.131*	0.206*	0.241*	0.234*	0.185*	0.206*	0.220*	0.392*	0.165*	0.348**
	(0.061)	(0.037)	(0.045)	(0.078)	(0.042)	(0.055)	(0.068)	(0.032)	(0.047)	(0.144)	(0.146)	(0.137)
COL_{ji}	0.152*	0.237*	0.253*	0.198*	0.186*	0.137*	0.193*	0.171*	0.139*	0.192*	0.212*	0.147*
	(0.065)	(0.063)	(0.048)	(0.077)	(0.063)	(0.062)	(0.068)	(0.059)	(0.050)	(0.138)	(0.173)	(0.150)
$\ln ROL_{it}$	0.682*	0.508*	0.674*	0.415*	0.346*	0.342*	0.821*	0.476*	0.969*	0.443*	0.218*	0.340*
	(0.075)	(0.074)	(0.058)	(0.087)	(0.086)	(0.067)	(0.077)	(0.070)	(0.061)	(0.077)	(0.085)	(0.058)
$\ln RTS_{it}$	0.568*	0.473*	0.464*									
	(0.076)	(0.095)	(0.057)									
$\ln TARIFF_{it}$				-0.594*	-0.978*	-0.748*						
				(0.056)	(0.084)	(0.044)						

continued on following page

Table 1. Continued

Dependent Variables	Model 1			Model 2			Model 3			Model 4		
	(1) EQ_{jit}	(2) DS_{jit}	(3) FPI_{jit}	(4) EQ_{jit}	(5) DS_{jit}	(6) FPI_{jit}	(7) EQ_{jit}	(8) DS_{jit}	(9) FPI_{jit}	(10) EQ_{jit}	(11) DS_{jit}	(12) FPI_{jit}
$lnLMF\_OPEN_{it}$							0.246*	0.142*	0.213*			
							(0.013)	(0.010)	(0.012)			
$lnKAOPEN_{it}$										0.657*	0.676*	0.888*
										(0.027)	(0.041)	(0.094)
Constant	31.627*	15.366*	22.497*	11.643*	10.248*	14.594*	28.562*	13.698*	22.188*	10.390*	12.987*	11.951*
	(2.862)	(2.256)	(2.172)	(1.908)	(1.615)	(1.306)	(2.923)	(2.136)	(2.352)	(0.441)	(0.124)	(0.763)
Observations	82,247	67,237	79,019	61,788	51,968	59,630	76,570	62,687	73,575	75,878	61,962	72,945
R^2	0.789	0.793	0.759	0.762	0.797	0.773	0.772	0.797	0.745	0.903	0.839	0.849
a_j	Yes	Yes	Yes	Yes	Yes	Yes	Yes	Yes	Yes	Yes	Yes	Yes
a_i	Yes	Yes	Yes	Yes	Yes	Yes	Yes	Yes	Yes	Yes	Yes	Yes
a_t	Yes	Yes	Yes	Yes	Yes	Yes	Yes	Yes	Yes	Yes	Yes	Yes

Note: * $p<0.01$, ** $p<0.05$, *** $p<0.1$ indicate 1%, 5% and 10% statistical significance levels, respectively. Values in parentheses are robust standard errors.

The estimation results of Model (3) and Model (4) are also presented in Table (1). Model (3) estimates the impact of de facto financial openness on bilateral financial investments. The effect of the $lnLMF\_OPEN_{it}$ variable, which was used following Lane and Milessi-Feretti (2017) to represent de facto financial openness, is positive and significant. A 1% rise in $lnLMF\_OPEN_{it}$ results in a 0.25% increase in bilateral equity investments, a 14% increase in debt securities and a 0.21% increase in portfolio investments. The de facto financial openness of the destination country affects the stock market the most. This shows that the endogenous learning process defined by Van Nieuwerburgh and Veldkamp (2009) is valid in financial asset trade. The high share of foreign financial assets in the portfolios of domestic investors provides investors with information about the relevant financial assets and the market. In other words, investors invest in financial assets about which they have high information, and at the same time, they have higher information about these assets because they invest highly in these financial assets. Van Nieuwerburgh and Veldkamp (2009) define this process as the endogenous learning process.

Finally, in Model (4), the effect of the $lnKAOPEN_{it}$ variable, which represents de jure financial openness, on bilateral investments was calculated. The impact of the $lnKAOPEN_{it}$ variable on bilateral financial investments was found to be positive and significant. A 1% increment in $lnKAOPEN_{it}$ increases bilateral equity investments by 0.66%, debt securities by 0.68% and portfolio investments by 0.89%. The significant effects of $lnLMF\_OPEN_{it}$ and $lnKAOPEN_{it}$ variables on bilateral financial investments indicate that these two variables are suitable for analysis. Increasing financial openness shows that countries' integration with world financial markets is also growing. In this case, as Karolyi and Stulz (2003) state, investors in international financial markets price both country-specific risks and global risks. The estimation results of Models (3) and (4) show that with increasing financial openness, local investors can eliminate local risks and increase their investments through international portfolio diversification.

The results in Table (1) show the average effect of the variables for all countries. The results of Table (1) show that information costs and institutional factors are important determinants of bilateral financial investments. Investors view markets where their information is incomplete and the rule of law is low as riskier. This causes them to keep higher risk premiums regarding markets where their information and rule of law is low. For this reason, they give more weight in their portfolios to assets of countries where information costs are lower and the rule of law is higher. Moreover, the results in Table (1) show that trade and financial openness are important determinants of bilateral financial asset trade. Investors especially prefer the financial assets of destination countries with high trade and financial openness.

In Table (2) and (3), the possible differing effects of trade and financial openness for Newly Industrializing Countries (NICs) were analyzed and for this purpose, the coefficient estimates of the interaction variables added to the model were focused on, keeping the number of countries in the database constant. The interaction variables in Table (2) first measure the impact of de facto and de jure trade openness on investments in the NICs and G7 countries. Table (2) first presents the estimation results of Model (1a). Model (1a) is an extended version of Model (1) with interaction variables. According to the estimation results, the coefficient estimates of financial market size, information costs and rule of law variables on bilateral financial investments are compatible with the literature and are meaningful.

First, Model (1a) investigates whether the effect of de facto trade openness on financial investments in NICs is different from the average. Interaction variable estimates show that the impact of real trade shares ($lnRTS_{it}*dNIC_j$) on equity, debt secorities and portfolio investments in NICs from other countries is significant. It can be seen that the effect of real trade shares on NIC's bilateral financial investments with other countries differs from the world average. Similar findings also apply to G7 countries. The interaction coefficient of real trade shares with NIC countries ($lnRTS_{it}*dNIC_j$) is 0.43 for equity investments, 0.20 for debt securities, and 0.34 for portfolio investments. A 1% increase in the real trade shares creates an rise of 0.67% in equity investments, 0.63% in debt securities, and 0.46% in portfolio investments in NIC countries. In addition, the increase in the real trade shares rises the equity, debt securities, and portfolio investments in G7 countries by 0.99%, 0.97%, and 0.88%, respectively. However, the change in real trade shares affects investments to G7 countries more than the NICs.

Table 2. The interactive effect of trade openness on NIC's investments

Dependent Variables	Model 1a			Model 2a		
	(1) EQ_{jit}	(2) DS_{jit}	(3) FPI_{jit}	(4) EQ_{jit}	(5) DS_{jit}	(6) FPI_{jit}
$\ln MCAP_{jt}$	0.495*	0.402*	0.474*	0.466*	0.455*	0.455*
	(0.091)	(0.083)	(0.072)	(0.085)	(0.079)	(0.062)
$\ln MCAP_{it}$	0.475*	0.480*	0.489*	0.401*	0.487*	0.494*
	(0.092)	(0.070)	(0.064)	(0.069)	(0.068)	(0.069)
$\ln D_{ji}$	-0.351*	-0.437*	-0.375*	-0.371*	-0.437*	-0.378*
	(0.073)	(0.046)	(0.044)	(0.075)	(0.050)	(0.050)
$BORDER_{ji}$	0.606*	0.125*	0.333**	0.419***	0.125**	0.262***
	(0.047)	(0.132)	(0.151)	(0.024)	(0.034)	(0.045)

continued on following page

Table 2. Continued

Dependent Variables	Model 1a			Model 2a		
	(1) EQ_{jit}	(2) DS_{jit}	(3) FPI_{jit}	(4) EQ_{jit}	(5) DS_{jit}	(6) FPI_{jit}
$LANG_{ji}$	0.242*	0.584*	0.419*	0.213*	0.586*	0.405*
	(0.051)	(0.108)	(0.124)	(0.049)	(0.011)	(0.031)
COL_{ji}	0.163*	0.324**	0.217***	0.341*	0.313**	0.225***
	(0.047)	(0.133)	(0.112)	(0.046)	(0.136)	(0.121)
$\ln ROL_{it}$	0.268*	0.126*	0.128*	0.170*	0.141**	0.140**
	(0.073)	(0.055)	(0.082)	(0.064)	(0.157)	(0.164)
$\ln RTS_{it}$	*0.225**	*0.192**	*0.120**			
	(0.065)	*(0.070)*	*(0.043)*			
$\ln RTS_{it} * dNIC_{i}$	*0.433**	*0.203**	*0.340**			
	(0.004)	*(0.081)*	*(0.008)*			
$\ln RTS_{it} * dG7_{i}$	*0.766**	*0.773**	*0.757**			
	(0.061)	*(0.038)*	*(0.091)*			
$\ln TARIFF_{it}$				*-0.263**	*-0.882**	*-0.683**
				(0.059)	*(0.003)*	*(0.094)*
$\ln TARIFF_{it} * dNIC_{i}$				*-0.171**	*-0.301**	*-0.304**
				(0.015)	*(0.017)*	*(0.089)*
$\ln TARIFF_{it} * dG7_{i}$				*-0.493**	*-0.939**	*-0.551**
				(0.004)	*(0.094)*	*(0.066)*
Constant	-9.499*	-8.229*	-9.041*	-11.102*	-13.278*	-10.606*
	(1.599)	(2.611)	(1.362)	(0.624)	(1.075)	(3.206)
Observations	66,934	66,114	72,206	56,019	54,874	53,792
R^2	0.804	0.878	0.838	0.800	0.874	0.870
α_j	Yes	Yes	Yes	Yes	Yes	Yes
α_i	Yes	Yes	Yes	Yes	Yes	Yes
α_t	Yes	Yes	Yes	Yes	Yes	Yes

Note: * p<0.01, ** p<0.05, *** p<0.1 indicate 1%, 5%, and 10% statistical significance levels, respectively. Values in parentheses are robust standard errors.

Model (2a) presented in the last three columns of Table (2) was estimated by expanding Model (2) with interaction variables. The interaction of tariff rates with NICs ($lnTARIFF_{it} * dNIC_{i}$) and G7 ($lnTARIFF_{it} * dG7_{i}$) countries are added to model (2a). First, according to the estimation results, the impacts of financial market size, information costs, and rule of law variables on bilateral financial investments are significant. The model results show that the interaction variables are significant so that the impact of tariff rates diverges from the world avarege in the NICs and

G7 countries. According to the interaction coefficient, a 1% increase in tariff rates reduces equity investments by 0.43%, while it reduces debt securities and portfolio investments in NICs by 1.18% and 0.99%, respectively. The interaction coefficients demonstrate that the change in tariff rates affects investments to G7 countries more than the NICs. Rising tariff rates have more negative impact on NICs.

The estimation results of models (1a) and (2a) show that trade openness are determinant of financial investments in NICs and G7 countries. Investors prefer the financial assets of NICs, which have high trade openness. The fact that the coefficients of the interaction variables obtained for these countries are higher than the average shows that investors consider the openness of the goods markets in their preferences for the financial assets of these countries. The fact that NIC's interaction coefficients are below those of G7 countries emphasizes that the trade openness level of these countries has not yet reached the G7 level. In addition, de jure trade openness has a higher impact on financial investments in NICs and G7 countries. This shows the importance of legal trade openness over actual openness, especially for foreign investors.

The interaction variables in Table (3) measure the impact of de facto and de jure financial openness on investments in the NICs and G7 countries. Model (3a) is an extended version of Model (3) with interactions between the NICs and G7 countries with de facto financial openness. The estimation results of Model (3a) are presented in the first three columns of Table (3). The estimation results of the Model (3a) show that the effects of financial market size, information costs, and the rule of law on bilateral financial investments are significant. In the model, the interaction coefficients of the $lnLMF\_OPEN_{it}$ variable, which represents de facto financial openness, with NICs and G7 countries are significant. The impact of de facto financial openness on financial investment in the NICs and G7 countries is different from the world average. A 1% increase in the $lnLMF\_OPEN_{it}$ variable increases equity investments in NIC countries by 0.32%, debt securities by 0.42%, and portfolio investments by 0.34%. In G7 countries, the coefficients of interaction variables are higher than those of NICs.

Model (4a) is the addition of the interaction variables of de jure financial openness with NIC and G7 countries to Model (4). The results of Model (4a) are included in the last three columns of Table (3). Estimation results reveal that the effects of financial market size, information costs, and the rule of law on bilateral financial investments are calculated significantly. Estimates show that the impact of the $lnKAOPEN_{it}$ variable, which indicates de jure financial openness, on financial investments in NIC and G7 countries is different from the world average. A 1% accrete in $lnKAOPEN_{it}$, equity investments, debt securities and portfolio investments in NICs countries react with an increase of 0.95%, 0.85%, and 1.16%, respectively. The interaction coefficients are higher for G7 countries than NICs.

In the estimation results of models (3a) and (4a), the effect of interaction variables was calculated to be higher than the world average for NICs. This shows that, in addition to trade openness, the openness of these countries' capital markets is an important determinant in foreign investors' financial investment preferences in NICs. However, the impact of de facto and de jure financial openness on investments in the NICs is different. However, the model results show that foreign investors pay more attention to de jure financial openness in their investments in NICs' financial markets. As in trade, investors in financial markets are increasingly taking legal measures of financial openness into account in their investment choices.

Table 3. The interactive effect of financial openness to NIC's investments

Dependent Variables	Model 3a			Model 4a		
	(1) EQ_{jit}	(2) DS_{jit}	(3) FPI_{jit}	(4) EQ_{jit}	(5) DS_{jit}	(6) FPI_{jit}
$\ln MCAP_{jt}$	0.476*	0.395*	0.358*	0.454*	0.483*	0.391*
	(0.085)	(0.082)	(0.071)	(0.090)	(0.084)	(0.066)
$\ln MCAP_{it}$	0.455*	0.473*	0.280*	0.252*	0.556*	0.403*
	(0.094)	(0.071)	(0.064)	(0.096)	(0.064)	(0.075)
$\ln D_{ji}$	-0.350*	-0.441*	-0.375*	-0.396*	-0.449*	-0.402*
	(0.073)	(0.046)	(0.044)	(0.083)	(0.049)	(0.051)
$BORDER_{ji}$	0.615*	0.107*	0.334*	0.558**	0.132**	0.336***
	(0.248)	(0.129)	(0.152)	(0.275)	(0.135)	(0.174)
$LANG_{ji}$	0.235*	0.590*	0.413*	0.241*	0.583*	0.420*
	(0.150)	(0.106)	(0.123)	(0.158)	(0.111)	(0.132)
COL_{ji}	0.165*	0.327*	0.218*	0.359*	0.307**	0.217**
	(0.148)	(0.131)	(0.112)	(0.156)	(0.140)	(0.121)
$\ln ROL_{it}$	0.231*	0.138*	0.101*	0.244*	0.131**	0.144**
	(0.074)	(0.054)	(0.079)	(0.077)	(0.052)	(0.071)
$\ln LMF\_OPEN_{it}$	*0.102**	*0.107**	*0.104**			
	(0.058)	*(0.085)*	*(0.076)*			
$\ln LMF\_OPEN_{it}*dNIC_i$	*0.220**	*0.252**	*0.234**			
	(0.126)	*(0.085)*	*(0.193)*			
$\ln LMF\_OPEN_{it}*dG7_i$	*0.604**	*0.711**	*0.653**			
	(0.510)	*(0.157)*	*(0.209)*			
$\ln KAOPEN_{it}$				*0.637**	*0.558***	*0.873**
				(0.298)	*(0.269)*	*(0.328)*

continued on following page

Table 3. Continued

Dependent Variables	Model 3a			Model 4a		
	(1) EQ_{jit}	(2) DS_{jit}	(3) FPI_{jit}	(4) EQ_{jit}	(5) DS_{jit}	(6) FPI_{jit}
$lnKAOPEN_{it}*dNIC_i$				0.312*	0.288**	0.291*
				(0.561)	(0.428)	(0.677)
$lnKAOPEN_{it}*dG7_i$				0.847*	0.922*	0.836*
				(0.281)	(0.560)	(0.233)
Constant	-9.253*	-7.720*	-10.142*	-12.741*	-12.573*	-12.563*
	(3.527)	(2.607)	(2.293)	(3.889)	(2.385)	(2.691)
Observations	64,868	63,923	69,935	62,737	62,262	67,701
R^2	0.805	0.881	0.840	0.794	0.878	0.845
α_j	Yes	Yes	Yes	Yes	Yes	Yes
α_i	Yes	Yes	Yes	Yes	Yes	Yes
α_t	Yes	Yes	Yes	Yes	Yes	Yes

Note: * p<0.01, ** p<0.05, *** p<0.1 indicate 1%, 5%, and 10% statistical significance levels, respectively. Values in parentheses are robust standard errors.

The findings obtained from the empirical analysis of the study first show that one reason for the variation in the level of bilateral financial asset trade between countries is the difference in the level of openness. Second, the impact of de facto and de jure measures of trade and financial openness on bilateral financial investments differs. Investors are paying more attention to de jure measurements in international financial investments. This shows that investors prefer countries with high legal globalization in financial asset investments. Thirdly, the estimation results show that the level of trade and financial openness is important for financial investments in NICs. The high trade and financial openness causes investors' demand for the financial assets of NICs to be higher than the world average. Finally, it appears that the goods and capital markets of the NICs are not as globalized as the industrialized G7 countries and these economies have still developing markets. Therefore, in addition to industrialization, regulations aimed at rising the integration of goods and capital markets in NICs will lead to an increase in financial asset trade in these countries.

5. CONCLUSION

Globalization has increased interconnectedness between economies, creating more opportunities for cross-border investments. This situation provides investors with access to wider investment opportunities and diversification of their portfolios. However, the impact of globalization on cross-border investments is not the same for all countries. Because of globalization, investors are exposed to new risks such as volatility in global markets and economic and political uncertainty in different countries.

This study examines the impact of globalization on financial asset investments in Newly Industrialized Countries (NICs). For this purpose, the financial gravity model, which takes into account the geographical distribution of information and is considered to work well in the analysis of bilateral economic flows, is used. With the help of the financial gravity model, the average effect of openness variables on bilateral financial asset trade and the change of this effect in NICs and G7 countries were investigated with interaction terms. Thus, a comparison was made of the impact of trade and financial openness on financial asset trade between NICs and G7 countries.

The analysis, which is carried out with the PPML estimator for the heteroskedasticity problem caused by zero trade flows, covers equity, debt securities, and portfolio investments of 120 countries between 2001-2022. In the empirical analysis, the average impact of trade and financial openness, which represent globalization, on bilateral financial investments is first examined by controlling information costs and the rule of law. The impact of de jure and de facto measures of trade and financial openness is considered separately in the analysis due to the endogenous relationship.

The first stage estimation results show that trade and financial openness are important determinants of bilateral investments of 120 countries. The effect of trade and financial openness differs according to de facto and de jure measurements. The estimation results indicate that investors prefer destinations with high trade and financial openness in their portfolio preferences. In addition, investors pay more attention to de jure openness in their destination country preferences.

In the second stage of the analysis, the focus is on the effect of globalization on financial investments made in NICs. For this purpose, interaction variables of trade and financial openness variables with NICs were created and estimated. In addition, the coefficients obtained for NICs were compared with G7 countries. According to the analysis results, the effect of trade and financial openness on financial asset investments in NICs differs from the world average. Investors take into account the trade and financial openness of these countries when choosing the financial assets of NICs. Similar to the estimation results in the first stage, the effect of de jure trade and financial openness on financial investments in NICs is higher. The interaction coefficients obtained are higher than the world average, which shows that investors take trade and financial openness into consideration more when investing in NICs compared to other countries. When the interaction coefficients are compared with G7 countries, it is seen that NICs are not yet as open as G7 countries.

Although there are many findings in the relevant literature on the impact of globalization on cross-border investments, no such finding has been found for NIC countries. The study findings show that trade and financial openness are important for NIC countries to attract financial investments. Any regulation that will strengthen trade and financial integration with world markets will support financial asset investments in these countries. In this respect, the study is expected to contribute to the literature.

REFERENCES

Aizenman, J., & Noy, I. (2009). Endogenous financial and trade openness. *Review of Development Economics*, 13(2), 175–189. DOI: 10.1111/j.1467-9361.2008.00488.x

Akisik, O. (2020). The impact of financial development, IFRS, and rule of LAW on foreign investments: A cross-country analysis. *International Review of Economics & Finance*, 69, 815–838. DOI: 10.1016/j.iref.2020.06.015

Alcala, F., & Ciccone, A. (2004). Trade and productivity. *The Quarterly Journal of Economics*, 119(2), 613–646. DOI: 10.1162/0033553041382139

Aviat, A., & Coeurdacier, N. (2007). The geography of trade in goods and asset holdings. *Journal of International Economics*, 71(1), 22–51. DOI: 10.1016/j.jinteco.2006.02.002

Baele, L., Ferrando, A., Hördahl, P., Krylova, E., & Monnet, C. (2004). Measuring financial integration in the Euro Area. *ECB Occasional Paper*, 1, 6-20.

Beck, T., & Levine, R. (2003). Legal institutions and financial development. *World Bank Policy Research Working Paper*, 3136, 1–42.

Bellofatto, A. (2017). How does language impact foreign investment in a multilingual country? Available on *SSRN* at 3001825.00000.

Boddin, D. (2016). The role of newly industrialized economies in global value chains. *IMF Working Paper*, 207, 1–38.

Chinn, M., & Ito, H. (2008). A new measure of financial openness. *Journal of Comparative Analysis*, 10(3), 309–322.

Chitu, L., Eichengreen, B., & Mehl, A. (2014). History, gravity, and international finance. *Journal of International Money and Finance*, 46, 104–129. DOI: 10.1016/j.jimonfin.2014.04.002

Coeurdacier, N. (2009). Do trade costs in goods market lead to home bias in equities? *Journal of International Economics*, 77(1), 86–100. DOI: 10.1016/j.jinteco.2008.10.005

Conley, T. (2000). Defining and understanding economic globalisation. *Policy. Organizações & Sociedade*, 19(1), 87–115.

Das, D. K. (2004). Trade and global integration. In *The Economic Dimensions of Globalization*. Palgrave Macmillan. DOI: 10.1057/9781403938671_4

Daude, C., & Fratzscher, M. (2008). The pecking order of cross-border investment. *Journal of International Economics*, 74(1), 94–119. DOI: 10.1016/j.jinteco.2007.05.010

De Santis, R. A. (2010). The geography of international portfolio flows, international CAPM, and the role of monetary policy frameworks. SSRN *Electronic Journal*, 6(2), 147-197.

Er, H. A. (1997). Development patterns of industrial design in the third world: A conceptual model for newly industrialized countries. *Journal of Design History*, 10(3), 293–307. DOI: 10.1093/jdh/10.3.293

Frankel, J. (1997). *Regional trading blocs in the world economic system*. Institute for International Economics.

Gräbner, C., Heimberger, P., Kapeller, J., & Springholz, F. (2018). Measuring economic openness, *wiiw. Working Paper*, 157, 1–39.

Gygli, S., Haelg, F., Potrafke, N., & Sturm, J. E. (2019). The KOF globalisation index—Revisited. *The Review of International Organizations*, 14(3), 543–574. DOI: 10.1007/s11558-019-09344-2

Haggard, S. (1968). The Newly industrializing countries in the international system. *World Politics*, 38(2), 343–370. DOI: 10.2307/2010241

Heathcote, J., & Perri, F. (2013). The international diversification puzzle is not as bad as you think. *Journal of Political Economy*, 121(6), 1108–1159. DOI: 10.1086/674143

Karolyi, G. A., & Stulz, R. M. (2003). Are financial assets priced locally or globally? In Constantinides, G. (Ed.), *Handbook of the Economics of Finance*. North Holland.

La Porta, R., Silanes, F., Shleifer, A., & Vishny, R. W. (1998). Law and finance. *Journal of Political Economy*, 106(6), 1113–1155. DOI: 10.1086/250042

Lane, P. (2000). International investment positions: A cross-sectional analysis. *Journal of International Money and Finance*, 19(4), 513–534. DOI: 10.1016/S0261-5606(00)00019-X

Lane, P., & Milesi-Ferretti, G. (2017). International financial integration in the aftermath of the global financial crisis. *IMF Working Paper*, 115(115), 1–53. DOI: 10.5089/9781484300336.001

Lane, P., & Milesi-Ferretti, G. M. (2004). International investment patterns. *IMF Working Paper*, 134(134), 1–46. DOI: 10.5089/9781451855630.001

Leal, P. H., Marques, A. C., & Shahbaz, M. (2021). The role of globalization, de jure and de facto, on environmental performance: Evidence from developing and developed countries. *Environment, Development and Sustainability*, 23(5), 7412–7431. DOI: 10.1007/s10668-020-00923-7

Mehigan, C. (2016). Bilateral adjustment of bank assets: boom and bust. *Trinity Economics Papers*, No. 0616.

Mercado, R. (2018). Bilateral capital flows: gravity, push, and pull. *The South East Asian Central Banks (SEACEN) Research and Training Centre Working Paper*, No. 5.

Mercado, R. V. Jr, & Park, C. Y. (2011). What drives different types of capital flows and their volatilities in developing Asia? *International Economic Journal*, 25(4), 655–680. DOI: 10.1080/10168737.2011.636628

O'Neill, H. (1984). HICs, MICs, NICs and LICs: Some elements in the political economy of graduation and differentiation. *World Development*, 12(7), 693–712. DOI: 10.1016/0305-750X(84)90082-2

Obstfeld, M., & Rogoff, K. (2001). The six major puzzles in international macroeconomics. Is there a common cause? *NBER Macroeconomics Annual*, 15, 339–390. DOI: 10.1086/654423

Okawa, Y., & van Wincoop, E. (2012). Gravity in international finance. *Journal of International Economics*, 87(2), 205–215. DOI: 10.1016/j.jinteco.2012.01.006

Peter, A. (2012). Bilateral trade, openness, and asset holdings. *Open Economies Review*, 23(4), 713–740. DOI: 10.1007/s11079-011-9211-7

Portes, R., & Rey, H. (2005). The determinants of cross-border equity flows. *Journal of International Economics*, 65(2), 269–296. DOI: 10.1016/j.jinteco.2004.05.002

Santos-Silva, J. M. C., & Tenreyro, S. (2006). The log of gravity. *The Review of Economics and Statistics*, 88(4), 641–658. DOI: 10.1162/rest.88.4.641

Santos-Silva, J. M. C., & Tenreyro, S. (2011). Further simulation evidence on the performance of the poisson pseudo-maximum likelihood estimator. *Economics Letters*, 112(2), 220–222. DOI: 10.1016/j.econlet.2011.05.008

Tesar, L. L., & Werner, I. M. (1995). Home bias and high turnover. *Journal of International Money and Finance*, 14(4), 467–492. DOI: 10.1016/0261-5606(95)00023-8

UNCTAD. (1994). *World investment report 1994: Transnational corporations, employment and the workplace*. United Nations.

Ustalar, S. A. (2023). Gelişmiş ve gelişmekte olan ülkelerin finansal piyasa entegrasyonlarının düzeyine ilişkin bir inceleme. *Eskişehir Osmangazi Üniversitesi Sosyal Bilimler Dergisi*, 2(2), 499–517. DOI: 10.17494/ogusbd.1309475

Van Nieuwerburgh, S., & Veldkamp, L. (2009). Information immobility and the home bias puzzle. *The Journal of Finance*, 64(3), 1187–1215. DOI: 10.1111/j.1540-6261.2009.01462.x

Van Wincoop, E. V., & Warnocak, F. E. (2010). Can trade costs in goods explain home bias in assets? *Journal of International Money and Finance*, 29(6), 1108–1123. DOI: 10.1016/j.jimonfin.2009.12.003

Weber, A. A. (2006). *European financial integration and (its implications for) monetary policy*. The Annual General Meeting, Amsterdam, Netherlands.

Wildmann, C. (2011). What drives portfolio investments of German banks in emerging capital markets? *Financial Markets and Portfolio Management*, 25(2), 197–231. DOI: 10.1007/s11408-011-0158-x

Wu, J., Li, S., & Selover, D. D. (2012). Foreign direct investment vs. foreign portfolio investment the effect of the governance environment. *MIR. Management International Review*, 52(5), 643–670. DOI: 10.1007/s11575-011-0121-0

Yotov, Y., Pıermartını, R., Monteıro, J., & Larch, M. (2016). *An advanced guide to trade policy analysis: the structural gravity model*. WTO Publications. DOI: 10.30875/abc0167e-en

KEY TERMS AND DEFINITIONS

Financial Gravity Model: A theoretical model that states that financial asset trade between countries depends on the economic or financial size of the countries and bilateral financial frictions. Financial asset trade between countries with similar economic or financial sizes is high. In the model, bilateral financial frictions are generally considered as information costs between countries. High information costs between countries reduce bilateral financial asset investments.

Financial Integration: It refers to the process of integration of financial markets and institutions globally. The high level of financial integration indicates that investors face similar transaction processes and costs in international markets and have equal access to financial instruments and services.

Globalization: The increasing integration of economic, social, cultural and technological processes worldwide and the decreasing importance of national borders. Economically, globalization can be defined as the increasing integration of countries' goods, capital and labor markets with world markets.

Information Costs: Information costs in international financial markets are all costs that investors incur to access accurate and timely information. Information costs include information acquisition costs, processing costs, communication costs, and risk management costs. Increasing information costs negatively affect market participation and efficiency.

International Portfolio Investments: It refer to the investment in cross-border financial assets of investors. International portfolio investments include financial instruments such as stocks, bonds, investmend funds and derivatives. International portfolio investments are affected by factors such as investors' risk preference, volatility of global financial markets, exchange rate risk, transaction and information costs and political risk of countries.

Newly Industrialized Countries: A group of countries that are among the developing economies and whose industrialization rate is faster than other countries. Newly industrialized countries are countries that have developed in heavy industry as well as agriculture and service sectors, technology, infrastructure investments, trade competitiveness and education levels.

Trade Integration: It can be defined as the free movement of goods and services across borders. The high level of trade globalization indicates that countries face low trade barriers in international trade.

ENDNOTES

[1] Calculations are made by the author with data obtained from the CPIS and DOTS database of the IMF.

[2] Calculated by the author from the World Bank's World Government Indicators (WGI) database. According to the WGI's methodology, the rule of law takes values between -2.5 and +2.5. Higher values indicate better governance.

[3] Geodesic distances are calculated according to the great circle formula, which uses the latitudes and longitudes of the most important cities.

APPENDIX

Country List

No.	Country	No.	Country	No.	Country
1	Albania	41	Finland	81	Nicaragua
2	Algeria	42	France	82	Niger
3	Angola	43	Georgia	83	Nigeria
4	Argentina	44	Germany	84	North Macedonia
5	Armenia	45	Ghana	85	Norway
6	Australia	46	Greece	86	Oman
7	Austria	47	Guatemala	87	Pakistan
8	Azerbaijan	48	Guinea	88	Papua New Guinea
9	Bahrain	49	Honduras	89	Peru
10	Bangladesh	50	Hong Kong SAR, China	90	Philippines
11	Belarus	51	Hungary	91	Poland
12	Belgium	52	Iceland	92	Portugal
13	Benin	53	India	93	Romania
14	Bolivia	54	Indonesia	94	Russian Federation
15	Bosnia and Herzegovina	55	Ireland	95	Saudi Arabia
16	Botswana	56	Israel	96	Senegal
17	Brazil	57	Italy	97	Singapore
18	Brunei Darussalam	58	Jamaica	98	Slovak Republic
19	Bulgaria	59	Japan	99	Slovenia
20	Cambodia	60	Jordan	100	South Africa
21	Cameroon	61	Kazakhstan	101	Spain
22	Canada	62	Kenya	102	Sri Lanka
23	Chad	63	Korea, Rep.	103	Sudan
24	Chile	64	Kuwait	104	Sweden
25	China	65	Kyrgyz Republic	105	Switzerland
26	Colombia	66	Latvia	106	Tajikistan
27	Congo, Rep.	67	Libya	107	Tanzania
28	Costa Rica	68	Lithuania	108	Thailand
29	Cote d'Ivoire	69	Luxembourg	109	Togo
30	Croatia	70	Malawi	110	Trinidad and Tobago
31	Cyprus	71	Malaysia	111	Tunisia

continued on following page

Country List (continued)

No.	Country	No.	Country	No.	Country
32	Czech Republic	72	Mali	112	Türkiye
33	Denmark	73	Malta	113	Uganda
34	Dominican Republic	74	Mexico	114	Ukraine
35	Ecuador	75	Moldova	115	United Kingdom
36	Egypt, Arab Rep.	76	Morocco	116	United States
37	El Salvador	77	Mozambique	117	Uruguay
38	Estonia	78	Namibia	118	Venezuela, RB
39	Eswatini	79	Netherlands	119	Zambia
40	Fiji	80	New Zealand	120	Kosovo

Chapter 14
Uneven Human Development:
Revisiting Economic, Environmental, and Political Determinants in OECD

Özge Kozal
https://orcid.org/0000-0002-5542-6290
Ege University, Turkey

ABSTRACT

This study examines the factors influencing uneven human development in OECD countries from 1995 to 2021, focusing on industrial structure, governance, and environmental degradation while controlling for income inequality, trade openness, and unemployment. The MMQR analysis reveals that increasing industrial output alone does not enhance human development; however, medium and high-technology manufacturing exports significantly boost HDI. Additionally, CO_2 emissions per capita negatively impact HDI, highlighting the need for zero-carbon industrialization. Democracy improves HDI in lower quantiles, while income inequality negatively affects HDI, particularly in higher quantiles. Trade openness supports HDI. The study suggests that OECD countries should pursue high-tech industrialization, reduce CO_2 emissions, strengthen democratic governance, address income inequality, and manage trade openness for sustainable and equitable human development, requiring integrated policies to connect economic, social, and environmental aspects.

DOI: 10.4018/979-8-3693-5508-4.ch014

1. INTRODUCTION

The contemporary era is characterized by a multitude of interrelated crises, which collectively pose a significant challenge to the world. On the one hand, there is a deepening of inequalities, while on the other, we are confronted with health crises such as the COVID-19, economic crises, and, perhaps most importantly, environmental challenges. Some of these crises have a long historical precedent; historical capitalism inherently tends to produce crises that allow it to reproduce itself, and inequalities constitute just one outcome (Nölke, 2022). However, some crises, such as the current pandemic, are novel and have caught the world unprepared. The impact of these crises varies significantly across countries. While some countries, particularly those that are developed, may identify new opportunities, others are likely to encounter significant challenges. Furthermore, it is insufficient to concentrate exclusively on intercountry variations in the consequences; even within countries, there are considerable disparities in the impact of crises. Those in vulnerable groups in developed, developing, and less developed countries are particularly at risk of marginalization, facing increased inequality across economic, social, and political domains (Simona-Moussa & Ravazzini, 2019). In this context, ensuring macroeconomic stability is of vital importance, but it is also crucial to consider the quality of life with a human and planet-centric development view during this time.

In the field of development theory, the concept of uneven development—frequently discussed in relation to combined development—offers a comprehensive framework for understanding the differentiation in development processes within and across countries (Dunford and Liu, 2018). This conceptual approach is particularly useful for analyzing the diverse patterns of economic, social, and political change that occur in different regions and countries (Beblawi and Salma, 1987). It examines the intricate nuances of these disparities in conjunction with regional spatial divisions of labor, the industrial composition of societies, crisis formation, patterns of urbanization and regionalization, and gentrification (Anderson et al., 1983; Peck et al., 2023). In essence, unequal development is regarded as a fundamental aspect of the contemporary capitalist system, akin to an inherent and inescapable reality. The historical development of capitalism is predicated on the perpetuation of disparities through the operation of economic and ideological mechanisms. The creation of inequalities is regarded as a primary source of both these mechanisms (Wallerstein, 2006).

The concept of uneven development encompasses not only the mode of production, and the backwardness experienced by societies, but also the superstructures that shape and influence these processes (Makki, 2015). This approach permits the simultaneous consideration of both the mode of production and its relationship with superstructures, thereby providing a tool for the comprehension of inequalities. In this study, we adopt the term "uneven human development" to describe the intricate interrelationship of factors influencing human development disparities across countries. Fundamentally, this phenomenon arises from the systemic inequalities intrinsic to capitalist modes of production and global economic structures. These inequities manifest in disparate rates of economic growth, industrial structures, access to resources, social services, institutional capacity, and overall quality of life across diverse regions and population groups.

What are the reasons for reconsidering the issue of uneven human development? The multidimensional crises, such as those related to the environment, health, and economics, have served to exacerbate existing problems in the global economy, widening and deepening inequalities worldwide. This situation has reinvigorated interest in uneven development as a pivotal research agenda within economics, prompting a resurgence of attention in the academic literature. In light of this framework, the objective of this study is to gain insight into the dynamics of uneven development, with a particular emphasis on human development in OECD countries, which exhibit considerable heterogeneity in economic and political structures. Nevertheless, elucidating the underlying causes of uneven development is a complex undertaking that demands significant effort. One significant challenge is establishing a standardized methodology for evaluating the extent of uneven development. While modern economics frequently employs numerical metrics to quantify and assess various phenomena, this methodology has been critiqued for its reductionist nature. Nevertheless, as an aggregate measure, the Human Development Index (HDI) provides a useful starting point for reflecting variations in uneven human development, despite its limitations. The fundamental premise of the HDI is an equally weighted assessment of income, education, and health aspects of human development. Map 1 depicts the global patterns of human development in 2022, exhibiting notable regional variations, with a range of human development index values between 0.380 and 0.967. The map illustrates the distribution of high, low, and moderate human development across the region. In order to elucidate these discrepancies, it is essential to examine the historical underpinnings of the countries' economic development stages and to analyze them in relation to a multitude of factors, including the availability of natural resources, the social and political structures, and the intricate foundation and the transformation of the modes of production. Nevertheless, this is a challenging task. Alternatively, an econometric analysis framework can be employed to ascertain the correlation between specific factors and uneven human development, which is the approach adopted in this study.

Figure 1. Map 1: Regional Variations in Human Development Index (2022)

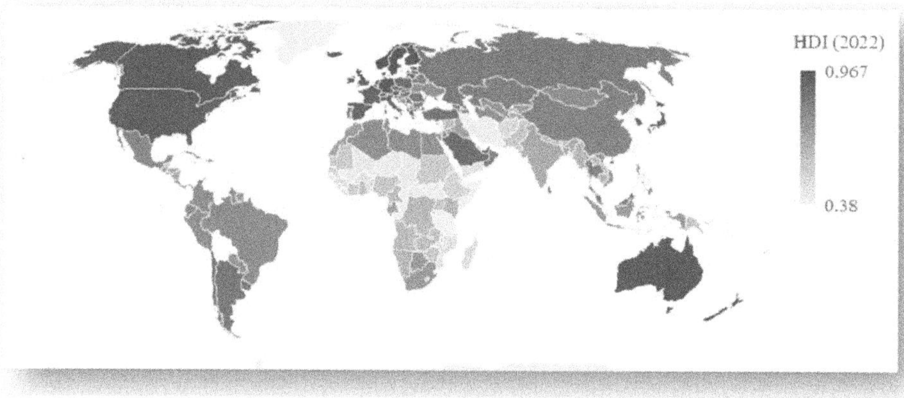

Source: UNDP

The principal objective of this study is to examine the impact of industrial structure, governance, and environmental challenges on human development in OECD countries, while accounting for three main macroeconomic variables: the unemployment rate, trade openness, and income inequality, with a particular emphasis on extreme income concentration. The OECD case is selected due to the diversity in economic, political, and structural conditions, which enables the capture of the variations in human development over the 1995-2021 period.[1]

The study proceeds as follows: next section will discuss the changes in the capitalist mode of production in relation to industrialization, globalization, and environmental challenges. Following that, an empirical analysis will be conducted on the factors affecting the HDI in OECD countries from 1995 to 2021 and then concludes.

2. A DISCUSSION ON INDUSTRIALIZATION, GOVERNANCE AND ENVIRONMENTAL CHALLENGES

From the 18th century to the 21st century, the world economy has undergone a series of cycles, influenced by technological developments, economic policies, and shifts in production patterns. These cycles have shaped the growth and development trajectories of nations. It is a challenging task to provide a comprehensive account of the various turning points in economic history. In this section, we will endeavor to synthesize the emergence and decline of three pivotal concepts that have shaped the foundations of the human development paradigm, which serve as the basis for our empirical analysis: industrialization, governance, and environmental degradation.

Rise and Demise of Industrialization

The first Industrial Revolution resulted in a crucial turning point in the development of capitalism. It brought in new ways of producing goods and sparked subsequent revolutions in energy, materials, and leading industries across various countries. Especially the phase of the capitalist mode of production after the World War II created a significant shift in industrialization, largely driven by the Fordist mode of production. This period was the era of increasing production quantitatively and the pursuit of large-scale operations, particularly championed by the US economy, until the late 1960s (Atkinson and Lind, 2018:7). This was not only a shift in capital accumulation dynamics in production side, but also consumption patterns of the individuals have also greatly change. This paradigm shift was known as golden age of capitalism, characterized by conditions like full employment, abundant international credit, and minimal labor and capital pressures, industrialization was seen as essential for growth and development in both practical and theoretical discussions (Kaldor, 1966; Cornwall, 1977; Chereny, 1982; Szirmai and Verspangen, 2015).

World War II triggered the golden age of capitalism and shaped all dimensions of the world economy through a new institutional perspective led by IMF and World Bank -in 1995 WTO jointed to the club-. However, during this period, mainstream economics did not prioritize environmental concerns and inequality. Industrialization was a major aim for countries seeking growth, development, and modernization. In the 1960s, many countries pursued industrialization, with economic planning presented as a policy prescription comprising various measures to achieve this goal. But this age of prosperity did not last forever. By the end of the 1960s, the real sector experienced a diminishing profit rate, following the first and second petroleum shocks in the 1970s. These crises catalyzed another shift in the economic paradigm. The new neoliberal era, characterized by the rise of the finance capital, aimed to eradicate barriers to capital flows through deregulation, privatization, and liberalization. This program, advocated by developed nations, was recommended to developing countries as a means to 'climb the ladder towards the league of developed nations.' Unlike previous era, the focus was on financial stability and ending financial repression, with industrialization dramatically falling out of favor. Later, these policies were seen as tools of "kicking away the ladder," as argued by Chang (2002). Chang contends that today's developed countries did not follow the same policies they now recommend to developing nations. Instead, they employed a variety of protectionist and interventionist strategies to develop their own economies. Only after achieving a certain level of development did, they adopt more liberal, free-market policies, contrary to their policy suggestions to developing countries.

In the regulation of neoliberal policies, on one side, there was a rise of finance capital and the demise of industrialization; on the other side, there was another call for trade liberalization. The expectation was that markets, opened to international competition, would participate in the race and consequently achieve product quality at international standards in both production and marketing. They were also expected to make infrastructural and institutional arrangements that would create cost advantages and increase their capacity for innovation. However, when viewed from the conditions of today's global economy, it is evident that the liberalization applied in the 1980s, particularly for developing countries or those with weak integration into the international economy, has resulted in failure. This failure is attributed to both the insufficiency of the internal dynamics of these countries and the roles imposed on them by the international division of labor. Forcing a developing country into a free trade regime through neoliberal policies, making it compete with the goods of countries that had gained competitive power long before, has at times led to significant social and economic crises at both local and regional levels. Neoliberal policies implemented under the leadership of the IMF were expected to provide financial support for the development of the economy and particularly employment in these countries for macroeconomic stability. However, with the liberalization policies of financial markets, developing countries have become open to all kinds of speculative capital movements. As a result, these volatile funds rapidly left the country at the slightest sign of economic or political instability, turning these economies into even more unstable and fragile ones than before (Barbaros and Kozal, 2017: 108).

In the 1990s, the deep inequalities created by neoliberal policies led to another paradigm shift in economics called sustainable human development. This shift called for a rethinking of development, placing human beings at the center of economic policy. This new paradigm defined a three-dimensional approach: connectiveness of economy, ecology, and society. The concept of "inclusive growth," and the main policy rhetoric centered on the concept of "no one left behind" became prominent (Agarwal, 2023). This marked an important turning point in the economics of development. However, the importance of industrialization and new approaches to it were still not on the agenda; instead, the focus remained on the macroeconomic stability of economies, particularly those experiencing underdevelopment and uneven development.

The question is whether; to sustain human development, we must return to and focus on industrialization. There is no doubt that neglecting industrialization and the rise of finance capital has severed the ties between the real sector and financialization. The uncontrolled massive growth of financial markets and the delinking of the real sector from industrialization had reached an alarming state. Varoufakis (2014) highlighted the increasing importance of the finance sector for capitalism as "a mythical role". The 2008 economic crisis prompted a return to basics: reindustrialization, particularly in Europe, under the new name "Industry 4.0," became a priority. The 2008 global economic crisis was a sign of the unsustainability of this relationship. It was not merely a mortgage crisis in the USA; it also led to questioning the global capital accumulation process. Crises can reshape the world economy, and capitalism often finds ways to create new opportunities to mitigate the negative effects of these crises. Three years later, a new industrial cycle debate emerged, first in Germany and then in early industrialized countries like the USA and the UK. Industrialization, seen as the most important source of value production, was brought back to the agenda in these countries with a different understanding of production organization. This process, identified with the concept of Industry 4.0, describes the automation of all parts of value chains and the integration of all actors in the process. This integration essentially refers to connecting all steps, from production to the final consumer, allowing for real-time and continuous communication (Lasi et al., 2014). With this new cycle, which will reshape production and consumption patterns, central countries have found a way out of the 2008 crisis, where the limits of growth based on financial capital became visible. Reindustrialization is now on the agenda for creating sustainable human development while also addressing environmental challenges (Westkämper and Walter, 2014).[2]

Historically, countries that experienced premature deindustrialization and deindustrialization (Rodrik, 2016) continue to face deep poverty, high import dependency, high income inequality, and macroeconomic instability. This is why countries need to rethink industrialization policies with regard to regional specialization structures once again.

Rising Environmental Concerns

In the period following World War II, the phenomenon of the "Great Acceleration" resulted in a considerable intensification of the pressure on Earth's systems and a notable increase in human-induced environmental degradation (McNeill and Engelke, 2016). While capitalism has resulted in significant capital accumulation, it has also caused substantial environmental damage, both directly and indirectly affecting life on Earth. The first prominent discussion of environmental concerns was in the "Limits to Growth" report, which projected that growth would be impeded within 100 years if environmental degradation continued unchecked (Meadows et al., 1972). In 5-16 June 1972, Declaration of the United Nations Conference on the Human Environment emphasized the importance of starting of a dialogue between industrialized and developing countries on the link between economic growth, the pollution of the air, water, and oceans and the well-being of people around the world and that was the first global conference to prioritize environmental issues on a significant scale covering 26 principles (UN, 1972) This marked a critical point in the history of economic development, bringing environmental challenges to the forefront.

The Brundtland Report with the title of Our Common Future articulated a widely accepted definition of sustainable development: "Sustainable development is development that meets the needs of the present without compromising the ability of future generations to meet their own needs" (Brundtland and Khalid, 1987; Hajian and Kashani, 2021). This new understanding of development, contrasting with the previously dominant idea of unlimited growth, set boundaries on growth and led to the search for a model that integrates social, ecological, economic, spatial, and cultural dimensions of economic growth and development. Initially focused on meeting the needs of the current generation without compromising future generations, the concept evolved in the early 2000s into a paradigm aimed at not exceeding "planetary boundaries" as emphasized by Röckstrom et al. (2009).

The current understanding acknowledges the intricate interdependence between environmental sustainability, economics, and human well-being (Tyagi et al., 2014). The economic and social consequences of environmental degradation are of paramount importance, particularly in terms of their direct impact on human well-being. The deterioration of the natural environment has a detrimental impact on human health, impairs access to clean water and air, and heightens vulnerability to natural disasters. These challenges have a particularly adverse impact on the poor and marginalized, exacerbating existing inequalities and impeding overall socio-economic progress. Consequently, sustainable development is not merely an environmental imperative; it is also a crucial element in attaining economic stability and improving human well-being. In light of the realities of 21st-century industrialization, it is evident that industrial production plays a significant role in environmental degradation. A review of the empirical literature reveals a multitude of studies examining the negative impact of industrialization on environmental degradation focusing on the different countries (Destek et al. 2024; Prempeh, 2024; Quito et al. 2023) which shows production patterns of the todays world continue to create massive pressure on Earth-systems. In light of these findings, it is imperative to rethink approaches to income generation, placing a strong emphasis on environmental sustainability as a prerequisite for improving human well-being and fostering economic growth.

Institutions, Democracy and Governance

The role of institutions in economic growth and development is a topic of significant interest in both theoretical and empirical literature (Acemoglu and Robinson, 2008; Addi and Abubakar, 2024; Barra et. al., 2022). There is a consensus that the institutional capacity of countries, democracy and governance have a positive effect on economic growth and development. The work of Acemoğlu and Robinson

(2012) on the topic of "Why Nations Fail" has greatly contributed to this literature by introducing the concept of inclusive governments and institutions, as well as exploitative institutions. In contrast to inclusive institutions, extractive institutions are not conducive to economic growth and development. They primarily serve the interests of elite groups. To achieve inclusive growth and development, it is imperative to establish inclusive political structures that facilitate and support liberties and broad political participation.

Although the concept of governance is employed to explain the relationship between the state and the individual, and good governance is equated with high institutional capacity, the term itself had a different meaning at the outset. As previously stated, the 1990s witnessed a paradigm shift in the approach to human development, with a focus on the organization of economic and environmental aspects. The term governance was introduced to organize the institutional background of the state-individual relationship. However, the term "governance" gained prominence in international aid circles at the end of the 1980s. Doornbos (2003) posited that the concept of governance emerged as a discourse among donors, seemingly as unexpectedly as the fall of the Berlin Wall, which occurred shortly before. These two developments appear to be somewhat related. Prior to this period, aid agencies and other development institutions did not evaluate their program relationships with counterparts based on good governance criteria. The twofold goal of governance reform is to create more effective public policies and to establish procedures that are legitimate and accountable to the public. The term "good governance" is often associated with efforts to combat corruption. However, in this study, we utilize the term "governance" in accordance with the definition proposed by Rose-Ackerman (2017), which encompasses all institutional structures that facilitate both desirable substantive outcomes and public legitimacy.

Regardless of how the concept of institution is defined, it is clear that there is a very close relationship between the realization of human development in a country and basic institutional structure such as democratic governance, the relationship between civil society and the state, and the accountability of the government and other institutions. Issues closely related to human development, such as how countries generate income, how they redistribute it, what kind of industrial strategy they pursue, whether they are party to environmental agreements or not, are all determined within the framework in which the boundaries of the game are drawn, that is, by institutions. Therefore, to discuss human development in the 21st century, it is necessary to go beyond basic variables such as income to discuss how the rules that determine the environment in which people realize themselves are set and monitored.

3. WHAT DO DATA SAY?

The aim of the study is not to conduct a complex econometric analysis to understand the dynamics of uneven human development, but rather to identify the factors affecting HDI in OECD countries for 1995-2021 period. Unlike linear regression techniques, which rely on assumptions such as normality, no multicollinearity, and homoscedasticity—assumptions already violated in our model—we apply fixed effect method of moments quantile regression (MMQR) technique proposed by Machado and Silva (2019). This method can capture distributional heterogeneity and nonnormality of data, as well as provide robust results in the presence of outliers in the sample. In addition to its technical advantages, this method allows for the parameters among different quantiles of the dependent variable, which is the natural logarithm of HDI, to be analyzed. This enables a more nuanced analysis of different settings of HDI. Table 1 presents the data, descriptions, and their sources. All the data are used in their natural logarithmic forms except PDEM.

First, let us explain the dataset and why these variables are included in the model. Manufacturing value added in GDP (MANVA) is used as a proxy for industrialization and it is expected that industrialization contributes to human development. Yet the study covers the period from 1995 to 2021, during which the composition and technology intensity of manufacturing became increasingly important for development. Therefore, we also included the share of medium and high-tech exports share in manufacturing exports (HIGHTECH). This variable is not correlated with MANVA and allows us to assess both structure of the industrialization and the technology intensity of export within the same model, expecting a positive correlation. Democracy is a crucial component of development, though it is not captured in the basic HDI. To examine the correlation between the level of democracy and HDI, we included the participatory democracy index (PDEM), which ranges from 0 to 1, indicating a spectrum from poor to good democracy, expecting a positive correlation. Environmental degradation is a major global challenge affecting both production and consumption patterns. Therefore, we added CO_2 emissions (metric tons per capita) as a proxy for environmental degradation. The relationship between CO_2 emissions and HDI can be either positive or negative. A positive relationship might indicate that higher CO_2 emissions correlate with increased industrial activity and energy consumption, driving economic growth and improving living standards, income, and access to health services and education, which contribute positively to HDI. Conversely, a negative relationship would suggest that environmental degradation jeopardizes human well-being through various channels such as negative health impacts, an increasing number of natural disasters hampering economic activity, and exacerbating inequalities affecting vulnerable populations.

Finally, three important control variables are added, addressing major macroeconomic issues in OECD countries. Trade openness (OPEN) is one of the most common proxies for globalization and a good proxy to capture the integration level of the world economy through trade. In this respect, the share of trade in GDP is included in the model. Pre-tax national income shares of the top 10% (TOP10), to capture the relationship between extreme income concentration and HDI is added. And last is the unemployment rate (UNEMP), for which we expect a negative correlation with HDI.

Table 1. Data and Description

Name	Data Description	Data Source
HDI	Human Development Index (0-100)	UNDP
MANVA	Manufacturing, value added (% of GDP)	World Bank
HIGHTECH	Medium and high-tech exports (% manufactured exports)	World Bank
CO2	CO_2 emissions (metric tons per capita)	World Bank
OPEN	Trade (% of GDP)	World Bank
PDEM	To what extent is the ideal of participatory democracy achieved? Interval, from low to high (0-1)	V-dem Project
TOP10	Pre-tax national income, top 10% share	World Inequality Database
UNEMP	Unemployment, total (% of total labor force)	World Bank

Source: Compiled by Authors.

Table 2. Descriptive Statistics

Variable	Obs	Mean	Std. Dev.	Min	Max	Pr(skewness)	Pr(kurtosis)	JB
HDI	1026	4.454	0.081	4.132	4.57	0.0000	0.0000	0.0000
MANVA	1026	2.672	0.342	1.516	3.555	0.0000	0.0075	0.0000
HIGHTECH	1026	3.896	0.413	2.046	4.447	0.0000	0.0000	0.0000
CO2	1026	1.934	0.579	0.144	3.243	0.0000	0.0001	0.0000
OPEN	1026	4.357	0.522	2.797	5.961	0.1046	0.0571	0.0444
TOP10	1026	3.606	0.211	3.225	4.217	0.0000	0.0160	0.0000
UNEMP	1026	7.74	4.087	1.81	27.47	0.0000	0.0000	0.0000
PDEM	1026	0.606	0.093	0.175	0.81	0.0000	0.0000	0.0000

Source: Authors calculation.

Descriptive statistics of the variables are presented in Table 2, which shows the non-normality of the data based on skewness, kurtosis, and Jarque-Bera normality test probability values. Table 3 presents the correlation matrix.

Table 3. Correlation matrix

Variables	(1)	(2)	(3)	(4)	(5)	(6)	(7)	(8)
(1) HDI	1.000							
(2) MANVA	-0.011	1.000						
(3) HIGHTECH	0.126	0.435	1.000					
(4) CO2	0.302	-0.098	0.16	1.000				
(5) OPEN	0.175	0.102	0.087	-0.047	1.000			
(6) TOP10	-0.52	-0.191	-0.184	-0.293	-0.372	1.000		
(7) UNEMP	-0.327	0.008	0.07	-0.119	-0.061	0.044	1.000	
(8) PDEM	0.523	0.148	0.043	0.09	0.242	-0.566	-0.046	1.000

Source: Authors calculation.

The Breusch-Pagan LM Test for cross-sectional dependency, as shown in Table 2, indicates the presence of cross-sectional dependency. According to the slope homogeneity test by Pesaran and Yamagata (2008), Table 3 reveals the presence of country-specific heterogeneity, demonstrating that the regression parameters differ for each individual cross-sectional unit at the 1% significance level. Consequently, the second-generation panel root test (CIPS) by Pesaran (2007) is used. All variables, except TOP10, became stationary at the first difference, while TOP10 is already stationary at level.

Table 4. Breusch-Pagan LM Cross Sectional Dependency Test

	Chi2	Probability
HDI	chi2(703) = 15516.659	0.0000

Source: Authors calculation

Table 5. Testing for Slope Homogeneity

		Delta	p-value
HDI	$\tilde{\Delta}$	22.144	0.0000
	$\tilde{\Delta}_{adj}$	27.141	0.0000

Source: Authors calculation.

Table 6. Pesaran (2007) CIPS panel unit root test results

	Level (with intercept)	Level (intercept and trend)	First difference (with intercept)	First difference (with intercept and trend)	Level of integration
HDI	-1.864	-2.357	-4.433***	-4.487***	I(1)
MANVA	-1.882	-2.011	-4.208***	-4.412***	I(1)
HIGHTECH	-1.898	-2.138	-4.464***	-4.729***	I(1)
OPEN	-1.966	-2.201	-3.952***	-4.070 ***	I(1)
TOP10	-2.212*	-2.949***	-	-	I(0)
CO2	-1.390	-2.367	-4.866***	-5.012***	I(1)
UNEMP	-1.880	-3.052***	-3.428***	-3.671***	I(1)
PDEM	-1.751	-2.360	-4.337***	-4.337***	I(1)

Note: Critical values are -2.04, -2.11 and -2.23 for 10%, 5% and 1% respectively for the unit root test with constant. -2.54, -2.61, and -2.73 for 10%, 5% and 1% respectively for the unit root test with constant and trend.
Source: Authors calculation.

For benchmark comparison, pooled, fixed effect, and random effect OLS regressions are first estimated, as shown in Table 7. Regarding industrialization, it can be concluded that no statistically significant correlation between HDI and industrialization is found. However, the share of medium and high technology-intensive exports in total manufacturing exports is positively correlated with HDI only in the pooled OLS estimation. CO_2 emissions have a relatively strong positive correlation with HDI, consistent across all estimation methods. Trade openness contributes positively to HDI in OECD countries. Extreme income concentration appears to be positively correlated with HDI, but this relationship is not robust, and the magnitude of the coefficient is very small. An increase in the unemployment rate decreases HDI, while participatory democracy contributes positively to HDI in all three estimations.

Table 7. Baseline Estimation based on Linear Regression Techniques

	(1)	(2)	(3)
	Pooled	Fixed Effect	Random Effect
MANVA	-.0003	.0012	.0008
	(.0032)	(.0031)	(.0031)
HIGTECH	.0052**	.0035	.004
	(.0026)	(.0025)	(.0025)
CO2	.0148***	.0176***	.0169***
	(.0024)	(.0023)	(.0023)
OPEN	.0089***	.0073***	.0077***

continued on following page

Table 7. Continued

	(1)	(2)	(3)
	(.0025)	(.0024)	(.0024)
TOP10	.002***	-.0017	.0015
	(.0008)	(.0032)	(.0014)
UNEMP	-.0007***	-.0007***	-.0007***
	(.0001)	(.0001)	(.0001)
PDEM	.0337***	.037***	.0366***
	(.0113)	(.0109)	(.0109)
_cons	-.0024	.0112	-.0004
	(.0028)	(.0115)	(.0049)
Observations	988	988	988

Standard errors are in parentheses. *** p<.01, ** p<.05, * p<.1. Robust standard errors are used in fixed effect estimation.

Source: Authors calculations.

However, the statistical insignificance of some variables and the lack of robust correlations across estimations may result from violations of the basic assumptions of OLS estimation. For this reason, a fixed effect MMQR regression model is applied, with the regression coefficients presented in Table 8. To apply this technique first a fixed effect panel is written as in Equation 1 and transform into Equation 2. In the Equation 2, X'_{it} covers the matrix of all the explanatory variables as stated in Equation 3. In addition to these, β represents coefficients of the variables', individual fixed effect is shown as α_i, for country i, δ_i represents the quantile-specific fixed effect (Machado and Silva, 2019) in the Equation 2.

$$HDI_{i,t} = \beta_0 + \beta_1 MANVA + \beta_2 HIGHTECH + \beta_3 CO2 + \beta_4 PDEM + \beta_5 OPEN$$

$$+ \beta_6 TOP10 + \beta_7 UNEMP + \alpha_i + \varepsilon_{it} \quad (1)$$

$$HDI_{it} = \alpha_i + X'_{it}\beta + (\delta_i + W'_{it}\gamma) \quad (2)$$

$$X'_{it} = \begin{bmatrix} MANVA_{it} & HIGHTECH_{it} & CO2_{it} & PDEM_{it} & OPEN_{it} & TOP10_{it} & UNEMP_{it} \end{bmatrix}' \quad (3)$$

Table 8. Fixed Effect MMQR Regression Estimation Results

Dependent Variable: HDI			Quantiles				
	Location	Scale	0.1	0.25	0.5	0.75	0.9
MANVA	-.1352***	.0067	-.146***	-.141***	-.1348***	-.129***	-.1255***
	(.008)	(.0049)	(.0129)	(.0102)	(.008)	(.0079)	(.0089)
HIGTECH	.0618***	-.0078*	.0744***	.0685***	.0612***	.0545***	.0504***
	(.0072)	(.0044)	(.0115)	(.0091)	(.0071)	(.007)	(.0079)
CO2	-.0317***	.0002	-.0321***	-.0319***	-.0317***	-.0315***	-.0314***
	(.0063)	(.0038)	(.0101)	(.0079)	(.0062)	(.0062)	(.007)
OPEN	.1123***	-.0042	.1191***	.1159***	.112***	.1083***	.1061***
	(.0067)	(.0041)	(.0108)	(.0085)	(.0066)	(.0066)	(.0074)
PDEM	.0507	-.0445**	.1224**	.0889**	.0477	.0094	-.0139
	(.0323)	(.0198)	(.052)	(.041)	(.0321)	(.0318)	(.0359)
TOP10	-.0406**	-.0035	-.035	-.0376	-.0408**	-.0438**	-.0456**
	(.0193)	(.0118)	(.031)	(.0244)	(.019)	(.019)	(.0214)
UNEMP	-.0014***	.0003	-.0019***	-.0017***	-.0014***	-.0011***	-.001**
	(.0004)	(.0002)	(.0006)	(.0005)	(.0004)	(.0004)	(.0004)
constant	4.2732***	.0851*	4.1358***	4.1999***	4.2788***	4.3522***	4.3968***
	(.0776)	(.0474)	(.1249)	(.0983)	(.0769)	(.0764)	(.0862)

Standard errors are in parentheses. *** $p<.01$, ** $p<.05$, * $p<.1$.
Source: Authors calculations.

The analysis reveals several interesting findings, beginning with the unexpected negative correlation between industrialization, proxied by the manufacturing value-added share in GDP, and HDI. This counterintuitive result suggests that simply increasing industrial output does not necessarily lead to better human development outcomes. However, a deeper examination shows that medium and high-technology exports within the manufacturing sector have a significant positive impact on HDI, particularly in the lower quantiles of HDI. This indicates that the type of industrialization matters greatly; specifically, industrialization driven by middle and high technology is more beneficial for human development than that based on low technology. This conclusion is crucial for OECD countries, emphasizing that while industrialization remains necessary for enhancing human development, it should focus on high-tech industries. For a clearer focus, Figure 1 highlights countries such as Chile, Australia, New Zealand, Greece, Iceland, Colombia, Latvia, Turkey, Portugal, and Lithuania, which had the lowest levels of high-tech exports in 2021 and relatively low level of HDI compared the rest of the country in the OECD. Although the study did not use the medium and high-tech manufacturing value-added in GDP due to collinearity issues, it is examined to understand the general picture of high and medium-tech industrial production among OECD countries. Notably, in 2021,

Switzerland, South Korea, Germany, Denmark, Japan, Hungary, and Ireland were leading in producing medium and high-tech products, with Switzerland and Ireland achieving highest shares of 68% and lowest share 54.37%, respectively. These countries also had the highest HDI levels in the same year. Even in the raw data, there is similar trend between share of medium a high technology industrial production share in GDP, the share of medium and high technology export in manufactured total export and HDI.

Figure 2. Human Development Index (2021)

Source: UNDP

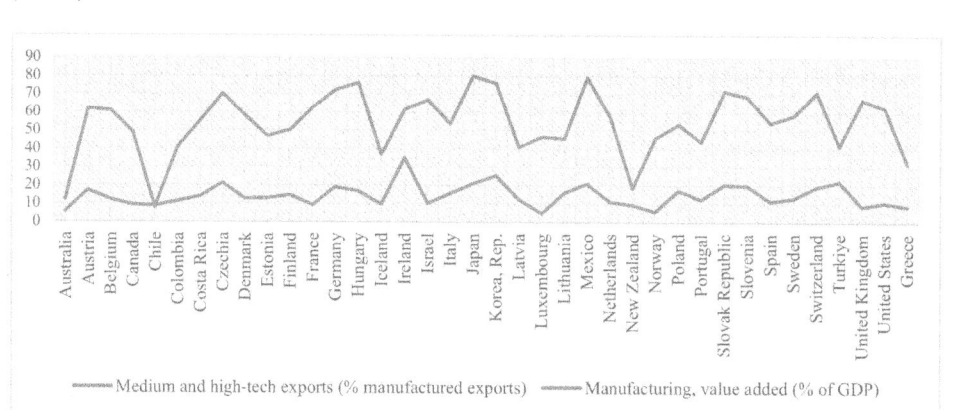

Figure 3. Medium and High Technology Export and Manufacturing Value Added (2021)

Source: UNDP

Figure 4. Medium and high-tech manufacturing value added (% manufacturing value added)

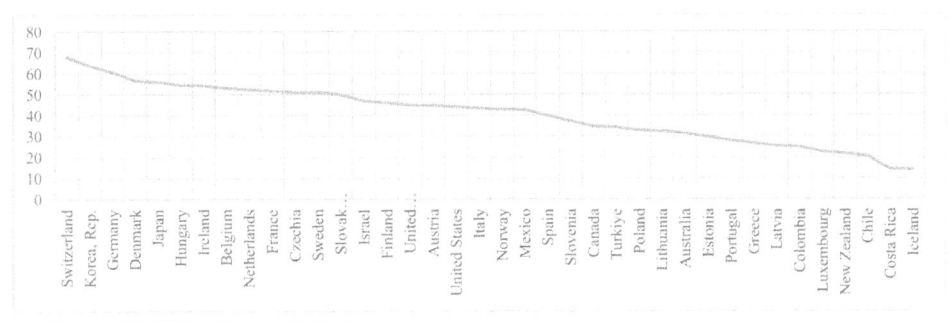

Source: World Development Indicators

The study further finds that an increase in CO2 emissions per capita negatively impacts HDI across all quantiles. This suggests that reducing CO2 emissions is crucial for achieving higher HDI levels, consistent with the broader literature on how climate change exacerbates multidimensional inequalities. Given that industrial production is a major source of CO2 emissions, transitioning to zero-carbon industrialization aligns with both improving HDI and complying with the Paris Climate Agreement. Figure 4 presents the CO2 emissions per capita as of 2021 among OECD countries. OECD countries have significantly higher per-capita CO2 emissions than most other regions, averaging 8.3 tons per person in 2019, whereas the rest of the world averaged 4.4 tons per person (OECD, 2019). missions in OECD countries reached their peak in 2007 and gradually declined by 9% by 2017. The COVID-19 pandemic led to a further 9% reduction in emissions by 2020 due to decreased human activities. However, emissions rebounded by 4% in 2021 (OECD, 2023). As of 2021 Australia, Canada, United States, Luxembourg and Korea have the highest level of CO2 emissions per capita with a value of above 10 metric tons as in at Figure 5.

Figure 5. CO2 emissions (metric tons per capita, 2021)

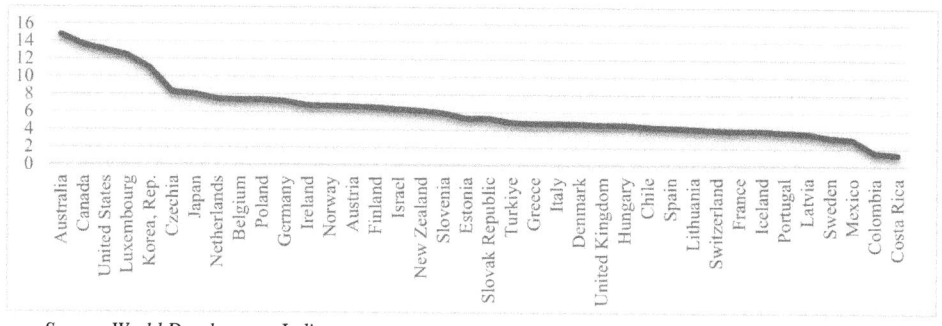

Source: World Development Indicators

Interestingly, democracy, which is not a component of the basic Human Development Index, contributes to HDI only in the 0.10 and 0.25 quantiles. This may be due to the heterogeneous levels of participatory democracy among OECD countries. It seems that the countries with low level of HDI can achieve a higher level of HDI by increasing governance capacity. But the countries with already higher levels of HDI this is not the case.

Figure 6. Participatory Democracy Index (2021)

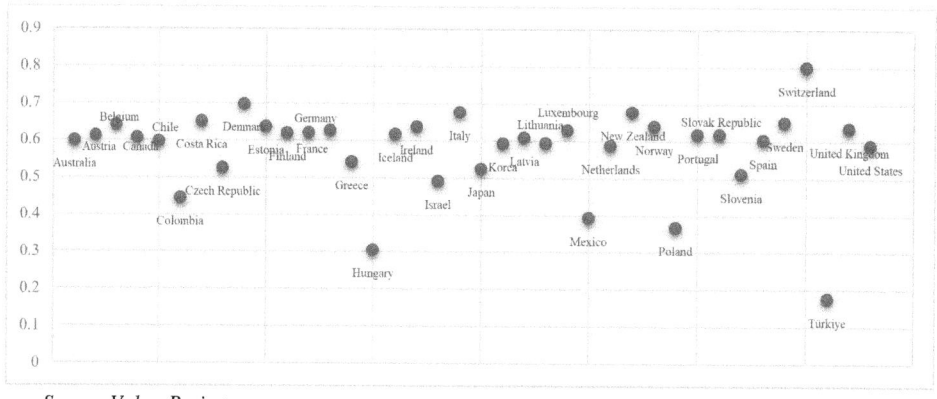

Source: V-dem Project

Income inequality, on the other hand, has a significant negative impact on HDI, particularly in the higher quantiles (0.5-0.75 and 0.90). This implies that in regions with above-average HDI, addressing extreme income concentration is essential for further improving human well-being.

Three additional macroeconomic variables, extreme income concentration, unemployment and trade openness, are also examined. The study highlights the dramatic increase in income inequality since the 1980s, driven by neoliberal policies, and the negative impact of unemployment on HDI across all quantiles. Following the 2008 global economic crisis and the COVID-19 pandemic, unemployment rates have risen in OECD countries, particularly affecting developing nations. To improve HDI, OECD countries should implement macroeconomic policies aimed at reducing unemployment and extreme income concentration, emphasizing the importance of redistributive policies.

Figure 7. Pre-tax national income Top 10% share

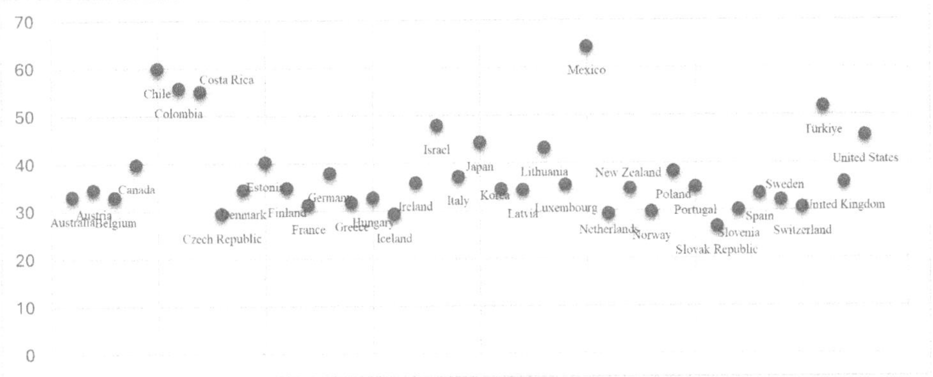

Source: World Inequality Database

Trade openness, used as a proxy for globalization, also contributes positively to HDI. While there is no direct link between HDI and trade openness, human development dimensions, particularly income per capita, are closely related to trade openness. This supports the idea that trade drives economic growth, which in turn enhances human development (Kabadayi, 2013; Hamdi and Hakimi, 2021). The positive impact of trade openness is more pronounced in the lower quantiles of HDI. In conclusion, the study suggests that while trade openness can enhance HDI, it should be managed carefully to avoid potential negative impacts from pollution-intensive trade. By focusing on high-tech industrialization, mitigating CO_2 emissions, reducing income inequality, and addressing unemployment, OECD countries can create a more sustainable and equitable path to human development.

CONCLUSION

This study analyzes the determinants of uneven human development by focusing on industrial structure, governance and environmental degradation by controlling income inequality, trade openness and unemployment in OECD countries for 1995-2021. Evidence from the MMQR analysis uncovers several key findings. Firstly, contrary to expectations, negative correlation between manufacturing value added share in GDP shows that merely increasing industrial output does not necessarily lead to improved human development outcomes. However, findings from further examination reveals that medium and high-technology manufacturing export significantly enhance HDI. This underscores the importance of the structure of industrialization, highlighting that high-tech industrialization has potentially create more benefits for human development than low-tech one. Especially for countries like Chile, Australia, New Zealand, Greece, Iceland, Colombia, Latvia, Turkiye, Portugal, and Lithuania, which had low levels of high-tech exports and relatively low HDI in 2021, should prioritize policies that foster technological advancement and innovation. In addition to this, negative association between CO_2 emission per capita and HDI also underscores the necessity for OECD countries to transition to zero-carbon industrialization, which would not only improve HDI but also support the objectives of the Paris Climate Agreement. Policymakers should implement strategies to reduce CO_2 emissions, focusing on sustainable industrial practices.

Democracy, although not a component of the basic HDI, contributes to HDI in the lower quantiles (0.10 and 0.25), suggesting that enhancing governance capacity can improve human development in countries with lower HDI. However, for countries with already high HDI levels, impact of governance capacity is less pronounced. Thus, OECD countries with lower HDI should focus on strengthening democratic institutions and governance as part of their development strategy.

Income inequality significantly negatively impacts HDI, particularly in the higher quantiles of HDI. This highlights the importance of addressing extreme income concentration to further improve well-being in regions with above-average HDI. The dramatic rise in income inequality since the 1980s, driven by neoliberal policies, and the negative impact of unemployment on HDI across all quantiles, call for macroeconomic policies that reorganize labor market conditions and needs for a policy change for reducing income inequality compatible with the Sustainable Development Agenda of 2050. Redistributive policies and efforts to create inclusive economic growth are essential for enhancing human development. Lastly, trade openness positively contributes to HDI, especially in the lower quantiles, supporting the notion that trade drives economic growth, which in turn enhances human development. However, the risk of creating pollution of trade should not neglect. Trade policies should be managed to mitigate potential negative impacts from pollution-intensive activities as well.

To sum up, OECD countries can achieve sustainable and equitable human development by focusing on high-tech industrialization, reducing CO2 emissions, enhancing democratic governance, addressing income inequality, and managing trade openness. From a policy standpoint, OECD countries need a comprehensive and multidimensional development plan to address both macroeconomic and environmental challenges together to cope with uneven human development. There is also a need for a roadmap for planning reindustrialization strategies in these countries to create more resilience. In the 21st century, in the world economy everything is more interconnected than ever before. It is not only about the integration of the world economies but also defining strong linkages between economy-society and ecology regarding both intergenerational wellbeing and the health of the planet. This requires more integrated policies to empower civil society, increase technology intensive industrial production without creating environmental degradation.

REFERENCES

Acemoglu, D., & Robinson, J. (2008). *The role of institutions in growth and development* (Vol. 10). World Bank.

Acemoglu, D., & Robinson, J. A. (2012). *Why nations fail: The origins of power, prosperity, and poverty*. Crown Business.

Addi, H. M., & Abubakar, A. B. (2024). Investment and economic growth: Do institutions and economic freedom matter? *International Journal of Emerging Markets*, 19(4), 825–845. DOI: 10.1108/IJOEM-07-2021-1086

Agarwal, R. (2023). Industrial policy and the growth strategy trilemma. IMF Finance and Development, March.

Atkinson, R. D., & Lind, M. (2018). *Big is beautiful: Debunking the myth of small business*. MIT Press. DOI: 10.7551/mitpress/11537.001.0001

Barbaros, R. F., & Kozal, Ö. E. (1980). Planlamanın Başarısızlığı: Kalkınma Miti ve Sanayileşmenin Düşüşü. In Barbaros, E. R., & Zurcher, E. J. (Eds.), *Modernizmin Yansımaları* (pp. 105–160).

Barra, C., Ruggiero, N., & Zotti, R. (2020). Short-and long-term relation between economic development and government spending: The role of quality of institutions. *Applied Economics*, 52(9), 987–1009. DOI: 10.1080/00036846.2019.1646884

Brundtland, G. H., & Khalid, M. (1987). Our common future. Oxford University Press, Oxford, GB.

Chang, H.-J. (2002). *Kicking away the ladder: Development strategy in historical perspective*. Anthem Press.

Chenery, H. B. (1982). Industrialization and Growth: The Experience of Large Countries. (No. SWP539, p. 1). The World Bank.

Coppedge, M., Gerring, J., Knutsen, C. H., Lindberg, S. I., Teorell, J., Altman, D., Angiolillo, F., Bernhard, M., Borella, C., Cornell, A., Fish, M. S., Fox, L., Gastaldi, L., Gjerlow, H., Glynn, A., Good God, A., Grahn, S., Hicken, A., Kinzelbach, K., . . . Ziblatt, D. (2024). V-Dem [Country-Year/Country-Date] Dataset v14. Varieties of Democracy (V-Dem) Project. https://doi.org/DOI: 10.23696/mcwt-fr58

Cornwall, J. (1977). *Modern Capitalism. Its Growth and Transformation*. St. Martin's Press.

Destek, M. A., Hossain, M. R., & Khan, Z. (2024). Premature deindustrialization and environmental degradation. *Gondwana Research*, 127, 199–210. DOI: 10.1016/j.gr.2023.06.006

Doornbos, M. (2003). "Good Governance": The Metamorphosis of a Policy Metaphor. *Journal of International Affairs*, 57(1), 3–17. https://www.jstor.org/stable/24357910

Dunford, M., & Liu, W. (2018). Uneven and combined development. In *Transitions in Regional Economic Development* (pp. 123–150). Routledge. DOI: 10.4324/9781315143736-7

Hajian, M., & Kashani, S. J. (2021). Evolution of the concept of sustainability. From Brundtland Report to sustainable development goals. In *Sustainable resource management* (pp. 1–24). Elsevier. DOI: 10.1016/B978-0-12-824342-8.00018-3

Hamdi, H., & Hakimi, A. (2021). Trade Openness, Foreign Direct Investment, and Human Development: A Panel Cointegration Analysis for MENA Countries. *The International Trade Journal*, 36(3), 219–238. DOI: 10.1080/08853908.2021.1905115

Kabadayi, B. (2013). Human Development and Trade Openness: A Case Study on Developing Countries. *Advances in Management & Applied Economics*, 3(3), 193–199.

Kaldor, N. (1966). *Causes of the Slow Rate of Growth of the United Kingdom*. Cambridge University Press.

Lasi, H., Fettke, P., Kemper, H. G., Feld, T., & Hoffmann, M. (2014). Industry 4.0. *Business & Information Systems Engineering*, 6(4), 239–242. DOI: 10.1007/s12599-014-0334-4

Le Monde. Europe's reindustrialization: A challenging work in progress https://www.lemonde.fr/en/economy/article/2024/05/09/europe-s-reindustrialization-a-challenging-work-in-progress_6670854_19.html#, Published on May 9, 2024

Machado, J. A., & Silva, J. S. (2019). Quantiles via moments. *Journal of Econometrics*, 213(1), 145–173. DOI: 10.1016/j.jeconom.2019.04.009

Makki, F. (2015). Reframing development theory: The significance of the idea of uneven and combined development. *Theory and Society*, 44(5), 471–497. DOI: 10.1007/s11186-015-9252-9

McNeill, J. R., & Engelke, P. (2016). *The great acceleration: An environmental history of the Anthropocene since 1945*. Harvard University Press. DOI: 10.2307/j.ctvjf9wcc

Meadows, D., Randers, J., & Meadows, D. (2013). The Limits to Growth (1972). In Robin, L., Sörlin, S., & Warde, P. (Eds.), *The Future of Nature: Documents of Global Change* (pp. 101–116). Yale University Press., DOI: 10.2307/j.ctt5vm5bn.15

Nölke, A. (2022). Introduction: Confronting a Multidimensional Crisis of Capitalism. In Post-Corona Capitalism (pp. 1-8). Bristol University Press.

North, D. C. (2003). The role of institutions in economic development. UN.

OECD. (2019). Environment at a glance indicators. https://www.oecd.org/environment/environment-at-a-glance/

Peck, J., Werner, M., & Jones, M. (2023). A dialogue on uneven development: A distinctly regional problem. *Regional Studies*, 57(7), 1392–1403. DOI: 10.1080/00343404.2022.2116417

Pesaran, M. H. (2007). A simple panel unit root test in the presence of cross-section dependence. *Journal of Applied Econometrics*, 22(2), 265–312. DOI: 10.1002/jae.951

Pesaran, M. H., & Yamagata, T. (2008). Testing slope homogeneity in large panels. *Journal of Econometrics*, 142(1), 50–93. DOI: 10.1016/j.jeconom.2007.05.010

Prempeh, K. B. (2024). The role of economic growth, financial development, globalization, renewable energy and industrialization in reducing environmental degradation in the economic community of West African States. *Cogent Economics & Finance*, 12(1), 2308675. DOI: 10.1080/23322039.2024.2308675

Quito, B., del Río-Rama, M. D. L. C., Álvarez-García, J., & Durán-Sánchez, A. (2023). Impacts of industrialization, renewable energy and urbanization on the global ecological footprint: A quantile regression approach. *Business Strategy and the Environment*, 32(4), 1529–1541. DOI: 10.1002/bse.3203

Rockström, J., Steffen, W., Noone, K., Persson, Å., Chapin, F. S.III, Lambin, E., Lenton, T. M., Scheffer, M., Folke, C., Schellnhuber, H. J., Nykvist, B., de Wit, C. A., Hughes, T., van der Leeuw, S., Rodhe, H., Sörlin, S., Snyder, P. K., Costanza, R., Svedin, U., & Foley, J. (2009). Planetary boundaries: Exploring the safe operating space for humanity. *Ecology and Society*, 14(2), art32. DOI: 10.5751/ES-03180-140232

Rodrik, D. (2011). *Akıllı küreselleşme: küresel piyasalar, devlet ve demokrasi neden birlikte var olamazlar?* Efil Yayınevi.

Rodrik, D. (2016). Premature deindustrialization. *Journal of Economic Growth*, 21(1), 1–33. DOI: 10.1007/s10887-015-9122-3

Rose-Ackerman, S. (2017). What does "governance" mean? *Governance: An International Journal of Policy, Administration and Institutions*, 30(1), 23–27. DOI: 10.1111/gove.12212

Simona-Moussa, J., & Ravazzini, L. (2019). From one recession to another: Longitudinal impacts on the quality of life of vulnerable groups. *Social Indicators Research*, 142(3), 1129–1152. DOI: 10.1007/s11205-018-1957-5

Szirmai, A., & Verspagen, B. (2015). Manufacturing and Economic Growth in Developing Countries, 1950-2005. *Structural Change and Economic Dynamics*, 34, 46–59. DOI: 10.1016/j.strueco.2015.06.002

Tyagi, S., Garg, N., & Paudel, R. (2014). Environmental degradation: Causes and consequences. European researcher, 81(8-2), 1491.

United Nations Development Programme. (1972), United Nations Conference on the Human Environment, 5-16 June 1972, Stockholm, https://www.un.org/en/conferences/environment/stockholm1972

Varufakis, Y. (2014). *Küresel Minotauros* (Kohen, F., Trans.). Encore Yayınları.

Wallerstein, I. (2006). *Tarihsel Kapitalizm*. Metis Yayınları.

Westkämper, E., & Walter, F. (2014). Towards the re-industrialization of Europe. A Concept for Manufacturing for, 2030, 1-111.

World Bank. World Development Indicators, https://databank.worldbank.org/source/world-development-indicators, accessed: 30.05.2024

World Inequality Database. https://wid.world/data

Yeldan, E. (2008). Türkiye'nin Ekonomi Politiği. Ankara: Orion Kitabevi. United Nations Development Programme, https://hdr.undp.org/data-center/human-development-index#/indicies/HDI

KEY TERMS AND DEFINITIONS

Deindustrialization: Deindustrialization refers to the decline of the manufacturing sector in an economy, typically in terms of its share of total employment or GDP.

Great Acceleration: These include a sharp rise in population, industrialization, and resource consumption, as well as a rapid expansion of human activity and its environmental consequences since mid-twentieth century.

Human Development Index: An index that defines and ranks countries according to their "level of human development". It basically focuses on income, educational attainment, and life expectancy at birth. Even though there is a lot of criticism about this aggregate measurement, this can be accepted as a broader reflection rather than the focus on GDP per capita.

Inclusive Growth: Inclusive growth refers to economic growth that benefits all segments of society. It emphasizes equitable distribution of wealth, social inclusion and long-term environmental sustainability. It aims to ensure that the opportunities created by economic progress can be accessed by all. In sum, inclusive growth is the embodiment of the principle that wealth creation, economic freedom and equal opportunity can exist in harmony.

Industrialization: In the classical view, industrialization refers to a transformation from an agrarian society to an industrialized society. However, in this chapter, industrialization reflects the broader concept that encompasses all of the socio-economic, political, and cultural aspects of the transformation.

Planetary Boundaries: This concept identifies nine critical environmental limits that humanity must stay within to maintain Earth's resilience, including climate change, biodiversity loss, biogeochemical fluxes (nitrogen and phosphorus cycles), land system change, freshwater use, ocean acidification, atmospheric aerosol loading, stratospheric ozone depletion, and the release of novel entities (such as chemical pollution).

Uneven Human Development: The term introduced by the author to describe multidimensional unequal development in economic, social and political terms in the historical capitalism.

ENDNOTES

[1] In 1995, HDI value were ranging from 0.886 (United States) to Turkiye (0.623), as of 2021 Colombia (0.752) to Switzerland (0.965) which shows variations in the levels of HDI.

[2] There has been a renewed emphasis on industrialization, especially in developed countries. For example, today this resurgence was highlighted in prominent publications such as Le Monde, which on May 9, 2024, featured an article titled "Europe's Reindustrialization: A Challenging Work in Progress."

Chapter 15
Sustainable Finance Practices for Handling Climate Change:
The Case of Türkiye

Bakhtiyar Garayev
Anadolu University, Turkey

Aslı Afşar
 https://orcid.org/0000-0001-7031-1419
Anadolu University, Turkey

ABSTRACT

Global climate change has emerged as one of the world's most urgent issues, with climatic catastrophes having significant economic and environmental impacts. These challenges play a crucial role in Türkiye's development strategies and policies. Financing the necessary transformation to reduce carbon emissions and adapt is vital in the fight against climate change. Integrating environmental, social, and governance (ESG) criteria into investment processes promotes sustainable development and the achievement of environmental goals. Consequently, sustainable finance practices have gained importance, supported by good practices from various organizations and banks in Türkiye. This research examines Türkiye's position in international climate agreements and its actions aligned with sustainable development goals. Additionally, the study analyzes the integrated reports of eight banks that are members of the UN Global Compact, exploring their sustainability strategies.

DOI: 10.4018/979-8-3693-5508-4.ch015

Copyright © 2025, IGI Global. Copying or distributing in print or electronic forms without written permission of IGI Global is prohibited.

INTRODUCTION

Global climate change is one of the most serious and complicated challenges confronting the global community. Climate change has far-reaching environmental, societal and economic consequences. The primary source of these changes is the emission of greenhouse gases into the atmosphere as a result of fossil fuel burning, deforestation and industrial activities. In this framework, tackling global warming not only represents an environmental necessity, but also essential to social fairness and financial sustainability.

Global climate change has a number of consequences, including sea level rise, increased extreme weather events, diminished biodiversity, ecosystem degradation, and food security concerns. These changes have a significant influence on human societies, particularly the most vulnerable groups. As a result, solving climate change involves a matter of human rights and equitable globalization. Climate change mitigation measures consist of reducing greenhouse gas emissions, improving carbon dioxide capture and storage technology, converting to renewable energy, boosting energy efficiency, and implementing laws that promote sustainable development. Effective collaboration at the national and international levels are required to effectively execute these policies.

The globally community has pledged to take action against climate change with significant initiatives such as the Paris Agreement. However, greater effort is required to meet these promises and reach the objective of reducing global warming to 1.5 degrees Celsius. In such an environment, research and innovation, policy making, financial systems, and broad societal engagement are critical components of this global issue. The Kyoto Protocol, signed in 1997, was a step towards making the fight against climate change and global warming a mandatory obligation for all countries. The agreement, which imposes responsibilities on developed countries to reduce greenhouse gas emissions, including specific steps towards sustainable development, is a protocol similar to the objectives of the Framework Convention on Climate Change in terms of financial sanctions, but with legal sanctions.

The banking and finance sector also contributes significantly to the fight against climate change. Sustainable finance and investment are crucial for funding environmentally friendly initiatives and technology. Green bonds, sustainable loans, and ESG-compliant investments may all contribute to achieve sustainable development goals.

Preventing climate change is a complicated and pressing issue that necessitates the development of effective measures within a global context. In this context, sustainable financial methods play an important role in lowering greenhouse gas emissions, supporting green technology, and financing climate change adaption strategies. In academic literature, sustainable finance is described as a combination of financial tools and policies that ensure that economic growth is compatible with environmental and social issues. In this paradigm, sustainable climate finance practices have emerged as a critical study field at both the conceptual and operational levels.

This study aims to analyze the comprehensive annual reports that Turkish banks that operate in the market produce with respect to sustainability. These publications provide an explanation of the environmental initiatives that banks undertake, their methods for assessing sustainability initiatives, and the future sustainability-related advantages that banks will offer.

The study is organized into three major sections. Environmental, Social, and Governance (ESG) concepts and the fundamentals of sustainable finance are covered first. These principles describe how environmental, social, and governance issues are addressed while making financial decisions. Sustainable financial products such as green bonds, social bonds and sustainable loans are discussed in the second section. In this section, the types and characteristics of products used in the financing of sustainable projects are discussed and how these products can be used in combating climate change is evaluated.

Additionally, sustainable financing strategies and their implications for the banking industry are examined, as well as Türkiye's climate change condition. The sustainability of Türkiye's financial sector is discussed as part of the Sustainable Financing Practices framework. The sustainability integration reports of eight Turkish banks are analyzed to evaluate their sustainability activities and reporting systems. These assessments explain Türkiye's current condition in terms of sustainable funding and make recommendations for future initiatives.

1. FUNDAMENTALS OF SUSTAINABLE FINANCE

Sustainable finance involves including environmental, social, and governance (ESG) factors into financial service and investment decisions. The term "ESG" refers to investments made by investors based on environmental, social, and governance concerns (European Commission, 2020). This integration is required to boost long-term investment returns while lowering financial risk. Sustainable finance in the context of climate change involves financing tools that favour low- or neutral-level initiatives. Green bonds, permanent credits, green funds, and carbon trading systems are all valuable financial tools in this industry.

Sustainable banking and finance principles stimulate the development of environmentally ecologically conscious funding ventures. While the notion of sustainable finance is regarded as a duty of governmental authorities, the private sector is equally involved in the process of achieving sustainable development goals (UN 2030). There is little question that sustainable banking and finance practices established by banks, particularly those operating in developing countries, help to drive their growth. Supporting sustainable finance need strong policy and regulatory frameworks. These frameworks compel financial institutions to include ESG factors into their decision-making processes and to promote the creation of green finance products. At the international level, accords such as the Paris Agreement and the Sustainable Development Goals emphasize the importance of sustainable financing and encourage participating countries to take measures towards it. In 2015, the United Nations (UN) adopted the Sustainable Development Goals (SDGs) and the Paris Climate Agreement. These developments marked an important turning point in the international community in combating climate change and sustainability. The agreements encouraged countries to take concrete steps to reduce greenhouse gas emissions and transition to a lower-carbon economy. These global efforts also had a significant impact on the financial sector. Decisions have started to be taken to ensure that financial transactions proceed in line with climate-compatible and low-carbon development. In this context, the European Green Deal (EGC) published by the European Union (EU) in 2019 was a prominent development.

The main applications of sustainable finance market goods include green bonds, green loans, social bonds, sustainable development bonds, sustainable development-related bonds and loans, transition bonds, and bonds connected to sustainable development goals. The concentration on sustainability in international agreements to alleviate the environmental, social, and economic consequences of global climate change has sparked renewed interest in sustainable finance. Perpetual bonds and loans are designed to support proactive environmental and social impact-oriented efforts and act as crucial instruments for sustainable finance (ISO, 2021)

Sustainable finance is financial decision-making that takes into account environmental, social and governance (ESG) criteria. This requires investors and other financial actors to pay attention not only to profitability but also to the long-term social and environmental impacts of their investments. Since there is an international emphasis on the establishment of sustainable development goals with global climate change, it is necessary to provide the necessary financing to the private sector in line with these goals (Schoenmaker & Willem, 2019).

The concept of sustainable finance, which is of great importance in terms of achieving a more sustainable economy as well as combating global climate change, is also extremely important in terms of achieving the UN Sustainable Development Goals. In recent years, the European Commission has focussed on promoting sustainable finance practices as a cornerstone of sustainable growth. To this end, the "Action Plan on Financing Sustainable Growth" was published in 2018. This plan aims to define the scope of sustainable economic activities and categorise their environmental sustainability by establishing the EU Taxonomy. The action plan focuses on three main objectives (European Commission, 2018).

1. **Guiding Sustainable Investments:** The plan aims to channel capital flows in a way that promotes sustainable and inclusive growth. This includes promoting the development and use of sustainable financing instruments such as green bonds and investments aligned with sustainable development goals (SDGs).
2. **Managing Financial Risks:** The action plan also aims to manage financial risks arising from climate change, resource scarcity, environmental degradation and social problems. This includes encouraging financial institutions to improve their capacity to assess and manage these risks and to use tools such as stress tests.
3. **Transparency and Long-Termism:** The Plan also aims to promote transparency and long-term thinking in financial and economic activities. This includes encouraging companies and investors to better disclose their sustainability performance and prioritise long-term investments.

Conference of the Parties28 (COP28), held in Dubai, UAE, is one of the most important climate conferences since the Paris Agreement. One of the highlights of COP28 was the finalisation of the first Global Stocktake (GST), a mid-term assessment of progress towards the 2015 Paris Agreement goals. In addition to CO2, the conference established ambitious goals for drastically lowering non-CO2 emissions, particularly methane, by the year 2030. The conference confirmed the commitment to the Paris Agreement's 1.5°C warming target and agreed to provide developing countries with a new $250 billion fund for adaptation (https://www.cop28.com/). Conference of the Parties29 (COP 29), which will take place in Baku, Azerbaijan between 11-22 November 2024, has the potential to be a critical turning point in the fight against the threat of global warming. Some of the important events affecting the development of sustainable finance in the world are listed below:

1992 Rio Conference
UN Environment Programme Finance Initiative (UNEP FI)
UN Framework Convention on Climate Change (UNFCC)
Kyoto Protocol
Dow Jones Sustainability Index
Paris Climate Agreement
UN Agenda 2030
European Green Deal

Sustainable finance addresses how finance interacts with economic, social and environmental issues. The main task of the financial system is to allocate finance to the most efficient use. Finance can play a leading role in allocating investment in sustainable companies and projects and thus accelerate the transition to a low-carbon, circular economy (Schoenmaker, 2017).

Table 1. Sustainable Finance Typology.

Sustainable Finance Typology	Value Created	Ranking of Factors	Appearance
Sustainable Finance 1.0	Shareholder Value	F > S and E	Short Term
Sustainable Finance 2.0	Stakeholder Value	T = F + S + E	Medium Term
Sustainable Finance 3.0	Common Good Value	S and E > F	Long Term

Source: *Schoenmaker, 2017*

The table shows the apparent values of sustainable finance in the short, medium and long term. F = financial value; S = social impact; E = environmental impact; T = total value. In traditional finance, the shareholder aims to maximise profits from a combination of appropriately valued financial return and risk, with an eye to the short term. However, the shareholder needs to take a long-term view for sustainable finance. The United Nations' Sustainable Development Goals state that government, companies and citizens should act together.

1.1. Environmental, Social and Governance (ESG) principles

Sustainable finance advocates the integration of ESG principles in financial decision-making, aiming to achieve economic growth together with social justice and environmental protection. ESG principles form the basis of sustainable finance. Companies are encouraged to comply with these principles, fulfil their social responsibilities, reduce their environmental impact and adopt good governance practices.

The term environmental, social and governance investment (ESG) was first coined in the 2004 report of The Global Compact (UN Global Compact), which brought together 20 of the world's largest financial institutions (Hill, 2020). ESG is a concept that has come to the fore in recent years and attracted the attention of investors. Considering environmental, social and corporate governance principles, ESG investment aims to integrate sustainability and responsibility principles into investments with a long-term perspective.

Financial actors are realising that achieving long-term and sustainable financial returns depends on well-managed social, environmental and economic systems (Shiller, 2013). Therefore, interest in investments based on Environmental, Social and Governance (ESG) principles is growing rapidly. Although there are different estimates of the size of the global ESG market today, Bloomberg Intelligence and the Global Sustainable Investment Alliance (GSIA) estimate it to be approximately $40 trillion. This figure is expected to increase further by 2025 (Schwartzkopff & Kishan, 2022).

Sustainable investments are investments that take into account environmental, social and governance (ESG) principles and aim for long-term sustainability. Although the size and criteria of these investments vary, their importance is increasing with global climate change and international climate agreements.

Table 2 shows the topics addressed by major financial institutions and companies within the scope of ESG criteria in different aspects

Table 2. ESG Criteria - Major Index Providers.

	Thomson Reuters	**MSCI**	**Bloomberg**
Environmental	Resource utilisation Innovation Emission	Natural resources Climate change Pollution and waste Environmental opportunities	Carbon emissions Climate change impacts Pollution Waste management Renewable energy Resource depletion
Social	Labour Force Human rights Community Product liability	Product liability Human capital Stakeholder engagement Social opportunities	Supply chain Discrimination Political contributions Diversity Human rights Community relations
Governance	Administration Shareholders CSR strategy	Corporate governance Corporate behaviour	Cumulative voting Executive compensation Shareholders' rights Takeover defences Staggered board Independent directors
Metrics	186	34	>120

Source: Boffo & Patalano, 2020

International climate agreements and sustainability are indispensable elements of the development agenda of countries today. Considering the intersection of environment and economy, developed countries prioritise the environment in their development plans. Sustainable finance is shaped by sensitising companies to the environmental impacts of their production processes. Environmental finance forms the basis of this understanding by supporting objectives such as adaptation to and mitigation of climate change, protection of biodiversity, minimising environmental risks and pollution. Sustainable finance is a critical tool for the common future of environment and development. It can build a healthier environment and a more prosperous economy.

In the fight against global climate change, the environmental (E) assessment pillar of ESG criteria plays a critical role. Environmental scoring helps investors make informed decisions about the transition to low carbon by measuring the environmental impact, carbon footprint and resource utilisation of investments (OECD,

2020). The environmental criterion of sustainable finance aims to ensure that the economic process operates in harmony with nature and based on environmental sensitivities. In this context, investments are made in low-carbon technologies and sustainable flexible infrastructure. These investments can stimulate growth and economic recovery, address inequalities and accelerate the transition to climate-resilient economies (United Nations, 2021).

The social factor (S) of the sustainable finance criteria (ESG) refers to the social relations-oriented criteria of finance for achieving the goals of a sustainable economy and sustainable development. These criteria assess sensitivities to companies' social relationships with people and organisations, as distinct from environmental and governance factors (UNPRI, 2017). The social criterion covers not only basic elements such as employee rights and job security, but also issues such as community integration, employee welfare, human rights and equality. As a result, the social criterion of sustainable finance is an important tool for building a more just and inclusive society. In this way, the social responsibility of companies can be increased and the quality of human life can be improved. Finance should be sustainable in terms of social engagement and its impact on investment decision-making. This is important not only as a question of sustainable development in an ecological sense, but also, perhaps more importantly, in terms of social responsibility and the sustainability of social bonds (Lagoarde-Segot & Paranque, 2018).

The governance criteria (G) of sustainable finance include the basic principles that ensure the sustainable management of a company or an economy with a budget. These criteria assess corporate behaviour and the general character of decisions affecting the governance dimension of companies. The governance component of sustainable finance aims to ensure that corporate governance becomes more long-term and that sustainability is embedded in management processes. In this way, the long-term success of companies and the welfare of stakeholders can be ensured (Johnson etc., 2020).

Although ESG criteria do not have a fixed framework, it is a dynamic process of discovery that connects organisations beyond purely financial expectations to evolving ethical, moral and sustainable superiority expectations (Krishnamoorthy, 2021).

In recent years, the need for a single global standard for sustainability reporting has become increasingly important. This need has been expressed by both the Conference of the Parties (COP) and the European Commission. At the COP26 Conference of the Parties, an important step towards this goal was taken and the International Sustainability Standards Board (ISSB) was established. The ISSB aims to enable companies to report their sustainability performance in a more transparent and comparable manner by developing and implementing global standards. This initiative represents a significant advance in sustainability reporting. The implementation of a single standard provides clearer and more consistent information for investors, regulators and other stakeholders, making it easier for companies to better assess their sustainability efforts.

2. SUSTAINABLE FINANCIAL PRODUCTS

Sustainable financial products are financial products designed and developed with environmental, social and governance (ESG) criteria in mind. These products ensure that investors and borrowers make financial decisions that contribute to sustainable development.

Environmental, social and economic threats caused by global climate change have brought the concept of sustainability to the forefront. In this context, sustainable finance has become an important tool. Sustainable finance aims to direct financial resources towards environmentally and socially responsible projects. In this way, it contributes to sustainable development goals such as combating global warming, promoting social justice and improving corporate governance. One of the important instruments of sustainable finance is sustainable bonds and loans. Such financial products are used to finance sustainability-oriented programmes such as renewable energy investments, environmentally friendly technologies and social development projects (Seville etc., 2021).

Sustainable bonds and loans, one of the main instruments of sustainable finance, constitute an important source for investing in environmentally and socially responsible projects. These products contribute to combating global warming and building a more liveable world by financing critical investments in areas such as renewable energy, energy efficiency, clean water and waste management. Another important element of sustainable finance is the adoption of corporate governance principles. Ethical and transparent management of companies, in addition to their environmental and social responsibilities, is the key to long-term success and investor confidence. In order for sustainable finance to develop and become widespread, governments, financial institutions and investors need to act in a joint effort. In this context, incentives and regulations for sustainable financial products should be developed, and investors should be informed and raised awareness about these products.

2.1. Green Bonds

Green bonds are a debt instrument specifically designed to finance environmentally sensitive projects. The funds obtained from these bonds are invested in projects operating in areas such as renewable energy, energy efficiency, clean water, waste management and sustainable agriculture. The main feature that distinguishes green bonds from other debt instruments is that the use of funds is strictly controlled. By purchasing green bonds, investors can be assured that the funds will only be allocated to projects that enhance environmental sustainability (Seville & Holmes, 2021).

The Green Bond Principles, developed by the International Capital Markets Association (ICMA), is a framework to ensure transparency, consistency and accountability in the green bond market. These principles consist of four main elements:

1. **Use of Proceeds:** Green bond issuers are required to ensure that funds raised from the sale of bonds are allocated only to pre-defined green projects. These projects can operate in areas such as renewable energy, energy efficiency, clean water, waste management and sustainable agriculture.
2. **Project Evaluation and Selection Process:** Green bond issuers should subject the projects to be financed to a rigorous evaluation and selection process. This process should assess the environmental benefits, viability and financial sustainability of the projects.
3. **Management of Revenues:** Green bond issuers need to ensure that funds raised from the sale of bonds are independently tracked and managed. These funds should be transparently allocated to pre-defined green projects.
4. **Reporting:** Green bond issuers are required to prepare and publicise regular reports showing the environmental impact of the bond and the utilisation of funds. These reports help to increase the confidence of investors and other stakeholders in green bonds.

The Green Bond Principles have contributed to the rapid growth and development of the green bond market. By providing investors with a framework for assessing the environmental impact of green bonds, these principles have increased interest in these products. Green bond markets, which have become increasingly important in recent years due to the effects of global climate change, are currently developing. Accordingly, cumulative green bond issuance, which reached USD 1.2 trillion in 2021, reached USD 1.7 trillion in 2022 (CBI, 2022).

2.2. Social Bonds

Social bonds are a type of loan instrument that is used to fund initiatives with the goal of providing social benefits. Funds from these bonds are used to support programs in education, health, housing, employment, and social inclusion. The primary distinction between social bonds and regular bonds is that the usage of money is rigorously limited. By acquiring social bonds, investors may be confident that the funds will be utilized solely to meet defined social impact goals. The 4 types of social bonds determined within the scope of Social Bond Principles are as follows (ICMA, 2020):

Standard social themed bond
Social income bonds
Social project bonds
Social asset-backed securities and mortgage-backed bonds

2.3. Sustainability Bonds

Sustainable bonds are an instrument used to finance green and social projects. These bonds are critical to achieving the Sustainable Development Goals (SDGs). The SDGs include global goals such as eradicating poverty, reducing inequality and protecting the environment (ICMA, 2018).

Green, social and sustainability bonds have shown rapid growth in recent years, creating a market volume of USD 1 trillion. These bonds are an important tool for achieving sustainable development goals (Climate Bonds Initiative and others, 2021).

2.4. Green Loans

Green loans, like green bonds, are used to support and finance green projects. These loans aim to promote sustainable economic activities by acting on the principle of environmental sensitivity. The Green Loan Principles (GLP) is a framework established to encourage the financing of environmentally beneficial projects. Under these principles, some of the categories recognised as green projects are as follows (LMA, 2021):

Renewable energy: Projects for the production of renewable energy sources such as solar energy, wind energy, geothermal energy and hydroelectric energy.
Energy efficiency: Renovation or retrofit projects that save energy in existing buildings or facilities.
Sustainable management of natural resources: Development and promotion of sustainable practices in areas such as forestry, agriculture and water resources management.
Clean transport: Development of public transport systems, transition to electric vehicles and construction of alternative transport infrastructure such as bicycle paths.
Adaptation to climate change: Developing infrastructure and systems that are resilient to the impacts of climate change, such as droughts, floods and extreme weather events.

Eco-efficient products and green buildings: Design and construction of products and buildings that cause less damage to the environment at the production stage and throughout their lifecycle.

2.5. Sustainability Loans

Social loans are specialised credit instruments used to finance projects that contribute to social development, such as facilitating access to basic services such as education, health, social housing, creating employment and ensuring food security. These loans are aimed at improving the living conditions of disadvantaged groups of society and building a fairer society. Social loans are a technique that helps communities grow and improves financial institutions' reputations. They can assist achieve long-term development goals, improve relationships with target audiences, and gain access to new markets. Social lending has great promise for a more inclusive and equitable financial system (APLMA, 2021).

3. HANDLING CLIMATE CHANGE IN TÜRKİYE

Türkiye is among the countries where the concrete impacts of climate change are being experienced more intensely every day. Climate changes such as increasing temperatures, increasing frequency of extreme weather events (heavy rainfall or drought) negatively affect our critical sectors such as agriculture, water resources, energy, tourism and ecosystems. Therefore, Türkiye urgently needs to take measures to combat climate change and realise its sustainable development goals. The impacts of climate change in Türkiye can have major consequences not only on the environment but also on economic and social dimensions.

A decrease in agricultural productivity, shortage of water, soaring costs of energy production, frequency and severity of natural disasters and coastal erosion is slowing down economic growth in this country as well as increasing social inequalities. Therefore, combating climate change and sustainability have emerged as the most important issues on Turkey's agenda. Turkey demonstrates its sensitivity to this issue by signing international climate agreements and developing different strategies and action plans at national level. The main thrust of these approaches include increasing renewable energy sources, improving energy efficiency, promoting sustainable transportation, investing in sustainable finance and protecting forests together with afforestation.

Sustainable financial techniques for mitigating climate change are equally essential at the national and global levels. Türkiye is taking significant measures to mitigate climate change, particularly via investments in renewable energy and increased energy efficiency. In this framework, a scholarly analysis of Türkiye's sustainable funding practices and their role in addressing climate change will assist us better grasp the country's challenges and prospects.

Furthermore, Türkiye has increased its efforts to secure long-term finance sources for climate change mitigation efforts. Financial tools such as green bonds and credit mechanisms are used to finance environmentally beneficial operations. This type of investment encourages sustainable development and accelerates Türkiye's transition to a low-carbon economy. Turkey actively participates in the United Nations Framework Convention on Climate Change (UNFCCC) and other global forums, in addition to making contributions to international climate policies. Within this context, Türkiye commits to assist developing countries in areas such as technology transfer and capacity building.

Türkiye signed the Paris Climate Agreement in 2015 and it was ratified by the Grand National Assembly of Türkiye in 2021. Under the agreement, Türkiye committed to reduce greenhouse gas emissions by 21% by 2030. This target demonstrates the determination of Türkiye to fulfil its international responsibilities in the fight against climate change. Türkiye's climate change plan seeks to minimize greenhouse gas emissions, promote the use of renewable energy, and boost energy efficiency. Sustainable funding techniques are critical for achieving these aims.

Türkiye has developed a number of policies and action plans to tackle climate change. "Climate Change Mitigation Strategy and Action Plan (2024-2030" and "Adaptation Strategy and Action Plan (2011-2023)" are two of the most important policy publications in the subject. These documents propose climate-friendly policies for energy, transportation, agriculture, forestry, and industry (T.R. Ministry of Environment and Urbanization, 2023).

Climate change is a worldwide danger, and it is critical that governments throughout the world work together to combat it. Türkiye joined international organizations aimed at protecting the environment and the ozone layer, such as the Vienna Convention and the Montreal Protocol, and continues to participate in crucial accords negotiated in subsequent years. Many international environmental accords, treaties, and partnerships are indirectly linked to global climate change. Türkiye continues to meet its international climate change duties by participating in the United Nations Framework Convention on Climate Change, the Kyoto Protocol, and the Paris Agreement, the three most major initiatives in this sector.

3.1. Sustainable Financing Implementation in Türkiye

Türkiye's sustainable financing is seen in its investments in green energy projects, particularly green bonds and green loans. With its recent rise, Türkiye's renewable energy sector has emerged as a prominent player in sustainable financing. Investments in solar and wind energy projects have sparked widespread interest. Türkiye's geographical location gives it a high potential for solar and wind energy, making sustainable energy investments even more fascinating. Climate change policy is addressed in Turkish development plans, as is research on sustainability strategies and action plans, and investment in this subject has increased in recent years.

However, the establishment of the Borsa İstanbul Sustainability Index is an essential step toward promoting the growth of sustainable finance in Türkiye. The goal of index is to identify firms that satisfy sustainability requirements and encourage investor interest in these companies. In addition, several Turkish banks promote sustainable finance practices by providing unique financing choices for projects that complete ESG criteria. Another significant achievement in sustainable finance in Türkiye was the signing of a statement by eight United Nations Global Compact member banks. Türkiye's acceptance of the Paris Agreement and the United Nations Sustainable Development Principles in 2015 accelerated sustainability research, and the country issued its first green bond in 2016. The Global Compact Türkiye Declaration on Sustainable Finance, signed by seven institutions for the first time in 2017, is a significant step toward developing sustainable finance practices in Türkiye. Today, eight banks signed the proclamation. The signatories to the Declaration have committed to establishing a system and model for assessing environmental and social risks and taking them into account in their lending processes. In this way, they aim to lend in a sustainable and responsible manner and fulfil their environmental and social responsibilities (UN, 2018).

The updated declaration in 2021 defined more comprehensive principles for taking into account environmental and social factors in sustainable finance and credit assessment processes. With this update, environmental and social sensitivities as well as climate change have been brought to the forefront. The statement also emphasises the commitment to improving incentives for sustainable investments and financing products and to mainstreaming practices in this area. In this way, it is aimed to contribute to a more sustainable future and fulfil environmental and social responsibilities (UN, 2021).

In order to take full advantage of the promise of sustainable finance, the financial industry should support investments based on ESG (environmental, social, and governance) norms, as well as raise knowledge and competencies in green finance and sustainable investment initiatives. In this process, collaboration between governments, the financial industry, and non-governmental organizations (NGOs) is crucial for developing laws and regulations that will enhance a sustainable financial environment.

Sustainable finance continues to develop in Türkiye. Among the leading organisations in this field are the Banking Regulation and Supervision Agency (BDDK) and the Capital Markets Board (CMB). In recent years, the Turkish banking sector has also started to pay more attention to sustainability and significant developments have taken place in this context.

Published in 2014 by the Banks Association of Türkiye, "The Sustainability Guidelines for the Banking Sector" has been an important guide for the banking and finance sector in achieving sustainable development goals in Türkiye. This guideline, which is based on environmental and social sensitivities, was prepared with the contributions of a wide range of stakeholders such as the public, civil society and the academy, and was updated in 2021 and remains up-to-date. Sustainability Guidelines for the Banking Sector contains sustainable principles for the banking and finance sectors in Türkiye (TBB, 2014).

Sustainability indices are an important tool that demonstrates companies' commitment to their environmental and social responsibilities to investors. These indices contribute to a more sustainable business world by encouraging companies to focus not only on their financial performance but also on their environmental and social risk management. In Türkiye, the Borsa Istanbul Sustainability Index (BIST Sustainability) was established in 2014 with this awareness. The main purpose of the index is to improve the understanding, knowledge and practices of sustainability among companies traded on BIST. BIST Sustainability assigns scores to companies by evaluating their performance in areas such as corporate governance, environmental and social responsibility and sustainability strategies. According to this index, the companies with the highest scores are included in the index (BIST, 2014). The BIST Sustainability Index is an important tool for both companies and investors. By improving their sustainability performance through this index, companies can gain a competitive advantage and achieve long-term success. Investors can use this index to invest in companies that comply with sustainability principles and attach importance to environmental and social responsibilities.

Sustainable banking aims to ensure that the financial sector continues its activities and contributes to sustainable development by taking into account its environmental, social and governance (ESG) responsibilities. In this context, the Sustainable Banking Strategy Plan to be implemented in Türkiye between 2022 and 2025 includes important targets and actions. The main objectives of the Plan include developing sustainable financing, promoting sustainable loans, facilitating banks' access to funds for sustainability purposes and promoting sustainable investments. To this end, efforts will be carried out to ensure and disseminate the necessary standards by taking ESG elements into account. Analysing financial risks arising from climate change and supporting banks against these risks are also among the important elements of the plan. In addition, the plan also addresses the sustainable finance vision and mission of the Banking Regulation and Supervision Agency (BDDK).

Climate change risks present a significant risk for banks. The pricing of these risks and the spread of their effects encourage banks to offer green loans in line with sustainable development and sustainable finance. Green loans contribute to the mitigation of climate change by being granted to projects that are beneficial to the environment and society. In recent years, banks in Türkiye have been encouraging clean energy investments, with a particular focus on green loans for the energy sector. In this way, it is aimed to reduce carbon emissions and ensure energy security. Green loans are both environmentally and economically beneficial. These loans can create new job opportunities and ensure sustainable development.

Many banks in Türkiye contribute to the fight against global warming by offering various products within the scope of sustainable finance. These products and activities are developed in line with the objectives of international agreements. Banks aim to provide benefit both the environment and the economy by developing innovative practices. In this way, they will be able to contribute to building a more sustainable future.

3.2. Sustainable Banking

Retail banking can be defined as the banking system that includes retail and commercial banking products for individuals and households. These include loans, mortgages, credit card services, travellers' cheques, bank transfers, overdraft protection, cash management, insurance and more. Products and services are those in the retail banking sector (UNEP Finance Initiative, 2007).

Financing projects that meet the standards set by financial resource owners such as the World Bank are the most important feature that distinguishes green loans from other loans. Banks provide low-cost loans to finance environmental projects. The main sustainable products and services developed in the retail banking sector are as follows (Güler & Tufan, 2015):

> green mortgages,
> green car loans,
> green credit cards
> green deposits

Corporate and investment banks are banks that provide financial services to large-scale organisations. They operate in areas such as complex banking products and services, derivative transactions and foreign currency trading according to the demands of companies. Climate change offers new opportunities for investments, enabling these banks to diversify their investment and loan portfolios. In this way, banks can both contribute to sustainability goals and increase their profitability.

European Bank for Reconstruction and Development (EBRD) categorises green investments into seven categories (Alfsen, 2013):

Energy Efficiency: Projects that save energy in buildings and industries.
Clean Energy: Investments in renewable energy sources such as solar, wind and geothermal.
Water Management: Projects for efficient use of water and prevention of water pollution.
Waste Management: Infrastructure investments for recycling and disposal of waste.
Sustainable Living: Implementation of sustainability principles in buildings and cities.
Environmental Services: Services for pollution prevention and environmental protection.
Sustainable Public Transport: Development of public transport systems and investments in electric vehicles.

EBRD strongly criticises projects that lead to environmental degradation. In this context, it emphasises that investments such as fossil fuel production, nuclear energy and the production and trade of products containing hazardous substances should be reduced.

The banking sector plays an important role in the development of sustainability and sustainable development goals. The importance of banks in this field has increased because financing is an important tool, especially for projects using renewable and environmentally friendly energy sources. One year after the European Investment Bank issued the world's first green bond in 2007, the World Bank issued its first green bond in November 2008, setting the blueprint for today's green bond market (World Bank Group, 2024). Banks then provided green loans to help combat, mitigate and adapt to global climate change. In particular, after 2015, Turkey has focussed on sustainability due to the introduction of the UN Sustainable Development Goals, the Paris Agreement and the inclusion of sustainability targets in its strategy and development plans. In the current context, many private banks in Turkey are producing important products in the field of sustainable finance and developing new practices to comply with the targets of international agreements against global climate change.

3.2.1. Akbank

Founded in 1948, Akbank is a pioneering Turkish bank in the field of sustainability. Since 2009, the bank has been publishing sustainability reports in accordance with Global Reporting Initiative (GRI) standards and is the longest operating bank in this field in Türkiye. Integrating sustainability into its business model and processes, Akbank focuses on reducing its environmental footprint. In this context, Akbank became the first Turkish bank to sign the UN Global Compact in 2007. In addition, Akbank launched the Carbon Disclosure Project (CDP) in 2010 and became a founding member of the UN Environment Programme Finance Initiative's Commitment to Financial Health and Inclusion in 2021. In 2021, Akbank published the Sustainable Financing Framework and started to categorise its sustainable financing projects based on green and social criteria. In this way, Akbank strengthened its green loan portfolio by offering 16 sustainable financing products as of 2022. The Bank aims to provide TL 200 billion in financing to sustainable projects and sustainable investment funds reaching TL 15 billion by 2030. (Akbank, 2023).

Akbank's sustainability efforts are also recognised internationally. In 2022, Akbank won the GlobalFinance sustainable financing awards in Türkiye. In the ESG risk rating determined by Sustainalytics, Akbank was assessed as low risk with 16.1 points (Global Finance, 2022; Sustainalytics, 2024). In 2021, Akbank provided "Green foreign trade credit" to foreign trade clients for foreign trade transfers that adhered to sustainability and environmental sensitivity as part of its suite of green finance services. The renewable energy portfolio comprised a total installed capacity of 4,722 MW. In addition, the bank spent USD 1.321 billion in renewable energy projects, reducing carbon emissions by 3.8 million tons. (Akbank, 2021).

Since 2016, Akbank has been focusing exclusively on renewable energies in energy production and assuming a pioneering role in this field. As of 2020, 5.8 million tonnes of emissions were prevented with the loan support of USD 1,577 million provided to renewable energy projects. In this way, renewable energy generation projects increased their share in Akbank's total energy generation portfolio to 84% (Akbank, 2021).

Akbank marked a first by prioritising sustainability in its syndication transactions in 2021 and maintained this principle in 2022. With the renewed syndication loan, Akbank contributed to the Turkish economy by providing a source of 700 million USD and took an important step by including sustainability performance criteria in the transaction. This syndication, which was realised with the participation of 32 banks from 15 different countries, confirms Akbank's commitment to sustainability and its prominent position in this field (Akbank Investor Relations, 2022).

Akbank took an important step for the development of sustainable finance in Türkiye by linking the interest rate of the 2022 syndicated loan to 3 different ESG performance indicators. These indicators cover sustainable development goals such as gender equality, use of renewable energy and not lending to coal-fired power plants. In this way, Akbank leads the sector by channelling its financial resources in a way to promote sustainable development. This innovative approach will contribute to further mainstreaming sustainability in the banking sector and to achieving sustainable development goals in Türkiye. (Deutsche Bank, 2021).

3.2.2. The Industrial Development Bank of Türkiye (TSKB)

Industrial Development Bank of Türkiye (TSKB) played a prominent role in this field by issuing Türkiye's first green/sustainable bond in 2016. In this way, TSKB strengthened its position as one of the leading banks in the field of sustainability. In the environmental, social and governance (ESG) risk assessment conducted by Sustainalytics, an international assessment organisation, TSKB achieved a score of 7.00, placing it among the lowest risk banks in Türkiye. This high score is an indication of the strong commitment of TSKB to sustainability and its successful practices in this area (Sustainalytics, 2024). In 2016, TSKB completed a green/sustainable bond offering for USD 300 million, a first in Türkiye. This 5-year bond was a huge success, generating more than 13 times its target amount. TSKB's move contributed significantly to the Turkish private sector's transition to a low-carbon economy and represented a watershed moment in the development of sustainable finance in Türkiye. Green bond issuance pioneered the industry by drawing investors' attention to green finance and generating awareness about it. (TSKB, 2016).

Established in 1950 with the support of the Central Bank of the Republic of Türkiye and the World Bank, TSKB stands out as Türkiye's first private development and investment bank. Since its establishment, TSKB has made significant contributions to the development of the country by providing credit support to many areas such as the domestic automotive and rubber sectors. TSKB has not only focussed on economic development, but has also adopted the principles of sustainability. TSKB is the first Turkish bank to establish an Environmental Management System compliant with the ISO 14001 standard and continues to be a pioneer in this field. TSKB also demonstrated its environmental responsibility by publishing the first GRI-approved sustainability report and becoming the first Turkish bank to receive a greenhouse gas verification certificate. In 2020, during the COVID-19 pandemic, TSKB contributed to the health sector by issuing the first lease certificate to the food sector and providing resources to the market. Demonstrating its commitment to sustainability by being included in the BIST Sustainability Index, TSKB has been working in line with its development and sustainability goals for more than 70 years (TSKB, 2023).

In 2021, TSKB achieved a significant success by securing a syndicated loan totalling USD 194 million with the participation of 14 banks. This syndicated loan was indexed to three different sustainability criteria, demonstrating TSKB's sensitivity and commitment in this area. The loan, which has a 367-day maturity and an annual interest rate of 175 basis points, has also achieved a remarkable success with a renewal rate of 130%. With this syndicated loan, TSKB met its financing needs in line with sustainability principles and contributed to the development of green and sustainable finance in Türkiye (TSKB,2021a).

TSKB clearly demonstrates its commitment to renewable energy with its decision not to invest in coal power plants. The bank, which derives most of its electricity generation portfolio from renewable energy, reinforced its commitment in this area by including energy and resource efficiency projects in its loan themes in the 2010s. By the end of 2020, 88% of TSKB's total energy portfolio consisted of renewable energy projects. In this way, TSKB plays a prominent role in the transition of Türkiye to a sustainable energy future and makes significant contributions to the environment and the economy (TSKB, 2021b).

TSKB is the leader in this field, financing 15% of the renewable energy capacity of Türkiye. Thanks to these investments, the Bank has also earned the title of being the first Turkish bank to achieve carbon neutrality by reducing approximately 12.8 million tonnes of CO_2 emissions in Türkiye every year (TSKB, 2022).

3.2.3. İşbank

Founded in 1924, İşbank assumed a pioneering role in the sector with its environmental and social management strategy launched in 2013. Within the scope of this strategy, the Bank has taken important steps to control and manage its environmental and social impacts. In 2017, İşbank signed the Global Compact Türkiye Financing Declaration prepared by the Global Compact Türkiye Sustainable Banking and Finance Working Group and committed to assessing environmental and social risks in credit processes for investments of USD 10 million or more. The Bank continues to develop its sustainability perspective comprehensively in the fields of environment, social and governance under the "sustainable management system" established in 2015. İşbank also attaches importance to digitalisation and offers innovative solutions to its customers by developing products and services such as Pay for the future, İşcep, personal banking assistant maxi, maximum mobile, maximum workplace, digital loans, commercial virtual card and digital safe deposit box. In 2019, İşbank realised the first green bond issue in Türkiye and used the funds obtained from this bond to finance renewable energy and environmental projects (İş Bankası, 2023).

İşbank clearly demonstrates its commitment to environmental, social and governance (ESG) principles by being ranked in the low-risk category with a score of 18.1 according to the assessment conducted by the independent organisation Sustainalytics. This score is an indicator of İşbank's strong performance in sustainability and its attention to risk management (Sustainalytics, 2022). In addition to the BIST Sustainability Index, İşbank, which carries its success in sustainable finance to international platforms, is also included in the FTSE4Good Emerging Markets Index, an important index for ESG investments. In this respect, İşbank stands out as a pioneering institution that contributes to sustainable development not only in Türkiye but also on a global scale (İş Bankası 2020).

As a member of the UN Global Compact sustainable finance working group, İşbank has accelerated its lending activities for sustainable projects in recent years. In 2021, the bank's sustainable bond framework was expanded to include credit transactions. In this way, İşbank can carry out green, social and sustainability-themed loan transactions through Eurobond issuances. With the funds to be obtained from these loans;

> Projects that create environmental impact
> Women entrepreneurship projects
> SMEs in less developed regions can be financed and thus create a positive impact both environmentally and also socially (İş Bankası 2020).

The energy sector in Türkiye is a significant source of carbon emissions. Being aware of this situation, İşbank has focused on renewable energy since 2015 and directed its new project financing for electricity generation investments to this field. In 2020, it contributed to the net zero goal in this sector by ceasing to provide financing support for thermal power plant investments based on fossil fuels such as coal and natural gas (İş Bankası, 2021).

In addition to the financing support, it also provides for renewable energy, Türkiye İş Bankası also offers various loan products to encourage the transition to a green economy. With these loans, you can both contribute to the environment and gain economic advantages. Some of the green loan products offered by İşbank are as follows:

> Protection the Seas Loan: With this loan, you can make energy efficiency and emission-reducing investments in your marine vehicles.
> Green Vehicle Loan: You can use this loan to purchase electric, hybrid or zero emission vehicles.

Environmentally Friendly Workplace Loan: You can finance investments in energy efficiency and waste management in your business with this loan.

Environmentally Friendly Housing Loan: You can choose this loan to buy a house in energy-efficient buildings or to make your existing house energy-friendly.

Environmentally Friendly Personal Loan: It is a type of loan that you can use to purchase environmentally friendly products such as solar panels and bicycles.

3.2.4. Garanti BBVA

Garanti BBVA is one of the pioneers of sustainable finance in Türkiye. Garanti BBVA, one of the first banks to implement the first practices in this area, also offered the first green loan of USD 10 million in 2018(Garanti BBVA, 2018) Showing its commitment to sustainability on international platforms, Garanti BBVA is included in important indices such as the Dow Jones Sustainability Index, FTSE4Good and BIST Sustainability Index. The Bank is also a founding member of UNEP FI and pioneers the development of sustainable finance in Türkiye. As of 2022, Garanti BBVA scored 21.1 points in the ESG risk assessment conducted by Sustainalytics and is in the medium-risk banks category (Sustainalytics, 2024). In addition to green and environmentally friendly loans, Garanti BBVA also contributes to the UN Sustainable Development Goals and developed 91 different sustainable loans and products in 2020 and 50 different sustainable loans and products in 2021(ESG Analyst Data & Presentation, 2021).

Renewable energy expenditures are becoming increasingly important in order to meet global warming and environmental targets. Garanti BBVA, one of the main banks in this industry, provides a variety of financing options. The Bank provides loans to help realise renewable energy projects such as solar, hydroelectric, and wind energy. In 2020, Garanti BBVA received USD 700 million in investment from overseas markets as part of the ESG Linked Syndicated Loan, making it one of largest green syndicated loans in Türkiye. In 2021, the Bank inked a new syndicated loan with 34 banks from 18 countries and plans to grow its sustainable financing volume to TL 2 billion in 2022 (Garanti BBVA, 2021).

3.2.5. Halkbank

Founded in 1938, Halkbank has adopted the mission of protecting not only tradesmen and craftsmen but also the environment. Accordingly, the Bank aims to contribute to a sustainable future by integrating climate crisis and other environmental risks into its business processes. The Bank implements various sustainability practices such as environmental impact assessment report, green building certificate, ISO Environmental Management Certificate, carbon emission assessment, occupational health and safety assessment and consumer rights sensitivity assessment. In addition to complying with environmental laws within the scope of the ISO Environmental Management System and ISO 50001 Energy Management System, Halkbank also carries out activities to reduce energy, water and paper use and waste management. Another important mission of Halkbank is to encourage women entrepreneurship. To this end, Halkbank established the Women Entrepreneurs Department, the first and only banking unit in Türkiye, and offers special advantageous services to women entrepreneurs. In this way, Halkbank aims to contribute to the Turkish economy, social welfare and gender equality (Halk Bankası,2023).

According to an assessment conducted by Sustainalytics, Halkbank's sustainability performance is in the medium-risk category with a score of 22.5. This indicates that the bank carries some significant risks in terms of its environmental and social responsibilities, corporate governance practices and risks in these areas. Halkbank can take steps to improve its ESG risk rating, such as reducing its environmental impact, protecting employee rights, increasing transparency and accountability, and strengthening corporate governance practices (Sustainalytics, 2024).

3.2.6. VakıfBank

Founded in 1954, Vakıfbank has been publishing sustainability reports since 2014, demonstrating its transparency and commitment in this area. Stating that it complies with the guidelines of the GRI's G4 in its first report, the bank believes that the source of development and growth is renewable energy and sustainable projects that create added value. In 2018, Vakıfbank became the first bank in Türkiye to obtain the Occupational Health and Safety Management System Certificate. Participating in many principles and initiatives with its pioneering efforts in the field of sustainability, Vakıfbank also achieved the success of being the first public bank in this sector. Vakıfbank is one of the participants of the United Nations Global Compact (UN Global Compact) and the first Turkish public institution to sign the Women's Empowerment Principles (WEPs). In addition, within the scope of TurSEFF loans developed by the European Bank for Reconstruction and Development (EBRD), Vakıfbank has taken concrete steps by financing 868 projects totalling more than EUR 122 million in energy efficiency, renewable energy, supplier and vendor loans since 2010(Türkiye Vakıflar Bankası, 2023).

Vakıfbank has officially documented its performance in this area by being included in the BIST Sustainability Index. In the ESG risk assessment conducted by Sustainalytics, the Bank scored 18.6 points, indicating that it is at a low-risk level. This clearly indicates that Vakıfbank's sustainability efforts and practices are in line with international standards and that the Bank is a pioneer in this field (Sustainanltycs,2024).

3.2.7. Yapı Kredi

Founded in 1944, Yapı Kredi Bank has made it its mission to contribute to a sustainable future by undertaking the environmental and social responsibilities of the finance sector since its establishment. In line with this awareness, the Bank has been one of the signatories of the United Nations Global Compact (UN Global Compact) and signed the Global Compact Türkiye Sustainable Financing Declaration as a founder in 2017. The Bank has implemented the Environmental and Social Risk Assessment System to improve its sustainability management system. In this way, it aims to identify risks in advance by assessing the environmental and social impacts of investments and to support sustainable projects. The success of Yapı Kredi in the field of sustainability was recognised by its inclusion in the FTSE4Good Emerging Markets Index, one of the leading global sustainability indices of the London Stock Exchange (Yapı Kredi Bank, 2023).

Yapı Kredi Bank officially documents its performance in this sector by being included in the BIST Sustainability Index. However, it should be noted that it is not at a low-risk level with a score of 14.8 in the ESG risk assessment conducted by Sustainalytics. This shows that the bank's sustainability efforts and practices do not fully comply with international standards and that improvements are needed in this sector (Sustainanltycs, 2024).

The Sustainability approach of the Bank includes not only economic development, but also social welfare and environmental protection. In this context, Yapı Kredi focuses on creating long-term value in all areas and for all stakeholders.

3.2.8. Ziraat Bank

Ziraat Bank is a well-established organisation that has been operating since 1863 and pioneering the issue of sustainability. Since 2013, the Bank has published a Sustainability Report every year, demonstrating its commitment to the principles of transparency and accountability. It is stated that the reports comply with the Global Reporting Initiative (GRI) principles and level A content. The Bank has adopted a comprehensive sustainability policy, taking into account the environmental and social impacts of its lending activities. The sustainability reports for the period 2013-2020 include topics such as greenhouse gas emissions, energy efficiency, waste management and education. One of the concrete steps in this area is the reduction in greenhouse gas emissions. In 2018, the Bank's greenhouse gas emissions amounted to 75,856.9-tCO2e, a decrease of 13.47% compared to the previous year. The

Bank continues to support the reduction in greenhouse gas intensity and to achieve effective energy management targets (Ziraat Bankasi, 2023).

CONCLUSION

Technological advances have made the scientific evidence of global climate change clearer. This situation has mobilised governments and the business world and encouraged them to develop sustainable solutions. The need for financing to realise this transformation has also increased. The 2015 Paris Climate Agreement aims to prevent climate disasters by limiting global warming. The signatory countries, including Türkiye, are in a common endeavour to achieve this goal.

The idea of sustainable development was first introduced in Türkiye in the 1990s in the Seventh Five-Year Development Plan. Within this framework, targets such as regional development and environmental protection were set. In 2000, with the impact of the Millennium Development Goals of the United Nations and the UN Global Compact in 2005, efforts gained momentum. Climate change started to be addressed in the Eighth Five-Year Development Plan and has continued to be an important issue in development plans since then.

In recent years, global warming has started to be given more importance in development plans and strategies prepared by ministries in Türkiye. Targets are set to reduce emissions in sectors with a large share in greenhouse gas emissions such as energy, industry, agriculture and waste. In line with these goals, renewable energy, innovation in agriculture and technological transformation in transport are becoming priorities.

Innovative methods are being developed to finance a sustainable transformation in Türkiye. In this way, it will be possible to achieve the Sustainable Development Goals faster. Institutions and ministries such as the Banks Association of Türkiye (TBB), Borsa Istanbul (BIST), Capital Markets Board (CMB), and Banking Regulation and Supervision Agency (BRSA) are working on this issue. As of 2022, 65 companies were included in the BIST Sustainability Index and the number of companies preparing sustainability reports is increasing. An important function of sustainable finance is to incentivise companies that comply with Environmental, Social and Governance (ESG) criteria. In this way, companies pay more attention to reducing carbon emissions and fulfilling their social responsibilities. This contributes to increasing environmental and social awareness and achieving the Sustainable Development Goals. For a sustainable future, investments that are environmentally sensitive and support mitigation activities are needed. These investments are critical in combating climate change and achieving the Sustainable Development Goals.

Sustainability reports are an important tool for banks. Thanks to these reports, banks can get ahead of the competition and strengthen their image and reputation by presenting their sustainability activities in a transparent manner. Stakeholders, investors and other interested parties can use these reports to comprehensively evaluate banks' corporate performance and make risk analyses for the future.

Many banks now prefer to prepare integrated annual reports that present financial and non-financial information in a single report. In this way, stakeholders can follow the financial performance of banks as well as their sustainability efforts in a single report. The increasing number of banks publishing integrated annual reports leads to an increase in support for sustainable development. This encourages banks to develop environmentally sensitive products, services and funds.

In addition to their role in the economy, banks have an important responsibility in the field of sustainability. By providing money and credit to businesses, they can encourage them to operate in a more sustainable manner and thus shape the future and society. Banks can contribute to the fight against climate change by using their loans to support environmentally friendly investments and practices. They can also help build a more just and inclusive society by financing socially responsible firms and projects. This power and capability of banks is vital for a sustainable future. By adopting policies and practices that promote sustainability, banks can take an important step towards a more sustainable world.

Turkish banks operate responsibly by developing sustainability practices in three main areas: environment, economy and society. This comprehensive approach demonstrates that banks recognise the importance of sustainability and are taking concrete steps in this sector. Banks that are making the necessary efforts to develop sustainable banking and finance have made significant progress in this area. In this way, the Turkish banking sector is contributing to a more sustainable future.

Sustainable financial practices are critical in the fight against climate change both in Türkiye as well as around the world. The goal of the study are to review sustainability initiatives of the banks, ascertain their degree of knowledge of the problem, and determine potential for the future. In this research, the integrated reports of eight banks that are members of the UN Global Compact are examined and the relationship between sustainability strategies and financial performance of these banks is analysed. According to the report, Turkish banks have used a variety of techniques to meet their sustainability goals, and these tactics help to reduce their environmental effect while also supporting their long-term financial performance.

Green finance and investing strategies based on environmental, social, and governance (ESG) standards are particularly prominent in the reports of the banks under consideration. Banks make a direct contribution to the battle against climate change by lending to initiatives that assist the transition to a low-carbon economy and establishing sustainable investment funds. Furthermore, banks' use of techniques such as energy efficiency and the usage of renewable energy in their operational operations are regarded as significant events toward corporate sustainability.

In conclusion, the adoption of sustainable finance practices by Turkish banks in combating climate change not only helps them fulfil their environmental responsibilities but also improves their financial performance. In this environment, enhancing banks' sustainability practices and developing novel financial instruments will make major contributions to climate change mitigation at both the national and international levels. The acceleration of sustainability-oriented reform in Turkish financial industry will help the country move to a low-carbon economy. For future studies, it is recommended to conduct content analysis after examining the integrated reports of the banks within the scope of the research. Additionally, besides the banking sector, it is possible to address other areas within the scope of Fintech.

REFERENCES

Akbank. (2020). Entegre Raporu. İstanbul: Akbank.

Akbank. (2021). Entegre Faaliyet Raporu. İstanbul: Akbank.

Akbank. (2021). Sürdürülebilir Finans Çerçevesi. İstanbul: Akbank.

Akbank. (2023). Entegre Faaliyet Raporu. İstanbul: Akbank

Alfsen, H. K. (2013). *EBRD Second Opinion*. CICERO Center For International Climate and Environmental Research., https://www.ebrd.com/downloads/capital/CICERO.pdf

APLMA. LMA, LSTA. (2021). Social Loan Principles. United Kingdom: Loan Market Association, Asia Pacific Loan Market Association, Loan Syndications & Trading Association.

Boffo, R., & Patalano, R. (2020). *ESG Investing: Practices, Progress and Challenges*. OECD.

CBI. (2022). Sustainable Debt Market Summary Q1 2022. Climate Bonds Initiative, https://www.climatebonds.net/files/reports/cbi_susdebtsum_q12022_01e.pdf

Climate Bonds Initiative and Others. (2021). *How to Issue Green Bonds, Social Bonds and Sustainability Bonds*. Climate Bonds Initiative.

Deutsche Bank. (2021) Deutsche Bank executes its first ESG-linked repo transaction globally with Turkey's Akbank https://country.db.com/news/detail/20210812- 104 deutsche bank-executes-its-first-esg-linked-repo-transaction-globally-with-turkey-sakbank?language_id=1

ESG Analyst Data & Presentation. (2021). https://www.garantibbvainvestorrelations.com/en/images/pdf/ESG-Analyst-Data-ENG2021.pdf etkinlikler.html

European Commission. (2018). Action Plan: Financing Sustainable Growth. Brussels: European Commission European Commission. (2020). Overview of sustainable finance. European Commission website. https://ec.europa.eu/info/business-economy-euro/banking-andfinance/sustainable-finance/overview-sustainable-finance_en

European Union. (2020). Regulation (EU) 2020/852 of the European Parliament and of the Council of 18 June 2020 on the establishment of a framework to facilitate sustainable investment, and amending Regulation (EU) 2019/2088. Official Journal of the European Union, L 198, https://eur-lex.europa.eu/eli/reg/2020/852/oj

Garanti, B. B. V. A. (2018). Garanti BBVA'dan Zorlu Enerji'ye Türkiye'nin ilk "Yeşil Kredi"si. https://surdurulebilirlik.garantibbva.com.tr/surdurulebilirlikblog/garanti-bbva-dan-zorlu-enerji-ye-turkiye-nin-ilk-yesil-kredi-si/

Garanti, B. B. V. A. (2021). *Entegre Faaliyet Raporu*. Garanti BBVA.

Global Compact, U. N. (2018). *Global Compact Türkiye Sürdürülebilir Finansman Bildirgesi*. Global Compact Network Türkiye.

Global Finance. (2022).Sustainable Finance Awards. https://d2tyltutevw8th.cloudfront.net/media/document/sustainable-finance-awards-2022- regional-winners-1654089494.pdf

Güler, O., & Tufan, E. (2015). Yeşil Bankacılık ve Yeşil Krediler: Antalya'daki 4-5 Yıldızlı Otel İşletmelerinin Bakış Açıları Üzerine Bir Araştırma. *Anatolia: Turizm Araştırma Dergisi*, 26(1), 80–86.

Halkbank (2023).www.halkbank.com.tr/tr/bankamiz/surdurulebilirlik/surdurulebilirlik/raporlarve

Hill, J. (2020). ESG, SRI, and impact investing-Chapter 2. *Environmental, Social, and Governance (ESG) Investing*, 13-27.

ICMA. (2017). *Green Bond Principles. Zürih*. International Capital Market Association.

ICMA. (2018). *Green Bond Principles*. ICMA Group.

ICMA. (2020). *Sustainability-Linked Bond Principles*. The International Capital Market Association.

İş Bankası. (2021). *2021 Entegre Faaliyet Raporu*. Türkiye İş Bankası.

İş Bankası. (2023) https://www.isbank.com.tr/bankamizi-taniyin/raporlarimiz

ISO. (2021). *Green and sustainable finance*. International Organization for Standardization Central Secretariat.

Johnson, E. C., Stout, J. H., & Walter, A. C. (2020). Profound Change. *Business Lawyer*, 75(4), 2567–2608.

Krishnamoorthy, R. (2021). Environmental, Social, and Governance (ESG) Investing: Doing Good to Do Well. *Open Journal of Social Sciences*, 9(7), 189–197. DOI: 10.4236/jss.2021.97013

Lagoarde-Segot, T., & Paranque, B. (2018). Finance and sustainability: From ideology to utopia. *International Review of Financial Analysis*, 55, 80–92. DOI: 10.1016/j.irfa.2017.10.006

LMA. (2021). *Green Loan Principles*. Loan Market Association, Asia Pacific Loan Market Association, Loan Syndications & Trading Association.

OECD. (2020). *Business and Finance Outlook 2020: Sustainable and Resilient Finance*. OECD Publishing., DOI: 10.1787/eb61fd29-

Schoenmaker, D. (2017). From risk to opportunity: A framework for sustainable finance. *RSM series on positive change, 2*.

Schoenmaker, D., & Schramade, W. (2018). *Principles of sustainable finance*. Oxford University Press.

Schwartzkopff, F., & Kishan, S. (2022). bloomberg.com: https://www.bloomberg.com/news/articles/2022-02-10/funds-managing-1-trillion-strippedof-esg-tag-by-morningstar

Seville, D., & Holmes, J. (2021). https://www.mondaq.com/canada/financial-services/1050064/green-bonds-and-beyondsustainable-finance-in-the-capital-markets

Seville, D. A., Holmes, J., & Murphy, M. (2021). Green bonds and beyond: sustainable finance in the capital markets. Torys LLP. https://www.torys.com/ourlatest-thinking/publications/2021/03/green-bonds-and-beyond-sustainable-finance-in-thecapital-markets

Shiller, R. J. (2013). Reflections on Finance and the Good Society. *The American Economic Review*, 103(3), 402–405. DOI: 10.1257/aer.103.3.402

Sustainanltycs. (2024). https://www.sustainalytics.com/esg-ratings

TBB. (2014). *Bankacılık Sektörü İçin Sürdürülebilirlik Kılavuzu*. Türkiye Bankalar Birliği.

T.R. Ministry of Environment and Urbanization. (2023), Adaptation Strategy and Action Plan (2024-2030), Ankara T.R. Ministry of Environment and Urbanization (2023), Climate Change Mitigation Strategy and Action Plan (2024-2030), Ankara

TSKB. (2021). *Konsolide Ara Dönem Faaliyet Raporu*. Türkiye Sınai Kalkınma Bankası A.Ş.

TSKB. (2021a). *Entegre Faaliyet Raporu*. Türkiye Sınai Kalkınma Bankası.

TSKB. (2021b). *İklim Riskleri Raporu*. Türkiye Sınai Kalkınma Bankası.

TSKB. (2023). *Türkiye Sınai Kalkınma Bankası*. Sürdürülebilir Bankacılık.

Türkiye Vakıflar Bankası. (2023)https://www.vakifbank.com.tr/surdurulebilirlik-raporlari.aspx?pageID=1254

UNEP Finance Initiative İnnovative Financing for Sustainability. (2007), "Green Financial Products and Services Report:Current Tredns And Future Oppourtunities in North America, https://www.unepfi.org/fileadmin/documents/greenprods_01.pdf

UNFCCC. (2021). *The Paris Agreement*. United Nations Framework Convention on Climate Change.

United Nations. (2021). Inter-agency Task Force on Financing for Development, Financing for Sustainable Development Report 2021. New York: United Nations publication.

United Nations. (2021). Inter-agency Task Force on Financing for Development, Financing for Sustainable Development Report 2021. New York: United Nations publication.

UNPRI. (2017). *Esg Integration: How Are Social Issues Influencing Investment Decisions*. The UN Principles for Responsible Investment.

World Bank Group. (2024). IBRD Funding Program. https://treasury.worldbank.org/en/about/unit/treasury/ibrd/ibrd-green-bonds

Ziraat Bankası, T. C. (2023), "Raporlar", https://www.ziraatbank.com.tr/tr/bankamiz/surdurulebilirlik/raporlarimiz

KEY TERMS AND DEFINITIONS

Climate Change: Climate change describes the long-term changes in temperature patterns and air conditions.
ESG: Abbreviation for Environmental, Social and Governance factors and is a framework for assessing the sustainability performance of a company or investment.
Green Bonds: Green bonds are a debt instrument specifically designed to finance environmentally sensitive projects.
Sustainable Banking: Sustainable banking refers to the implementation of financial services in a way that supports environmental and social sustainability.
Sustainable Development Goals: The Sustainable Development Goals are a universal call to action that outlines the objectives member states of the United Nations aim to achieve by 2030.

Sustainable Finance: Financial activities that take into account environmental, social and governance (ESG) factors.

Chapter 16
Spatial Analysis of Environmental Degradation:
The Role of International Trade and Democracy

Elif Korkmaz Tümer
Ege University, Turkey

Erol Türker Tümer
Dokuz Eylul University, Turkey

ABSTRACT

This paper explores the drivers of environmental degradation by using spatial panel data models to account for spatial interdependence among countries. Despite a large body of literature investigating the relationship between international trade, democracy, and the environment, previous studies have produced mixed results, partly due to the conceptualizations of variables and methodological limitations. This paper addresses these limitations by proposing alternative measures of trade openness and democracy while accounting for spatial dependence between countries. The results reveal that income, economic complexity, democracy, energy intensity, and agricultural land contribute to CO2 emissions, while forest area is negatively associated with environmental degradation. The results also reveal that while trade openness has statistically significant and positive direct effects, there are strong spillover effects as well. Indeed, the negative spillover effects of trade openness outweigh the direct effects, leading to a mitigating impact on environmental degradation.

DOI: 10.4018/979-8-3693-5508-4.ch016

Copyright © 2025, IGI Global. Copying or distributing in print or electronic forms without written permission of IGI Global is prohibited.

1. INTRODUCTION

Environmental degradation refers to the deterioration of the environmental systems and can take many forms, including the depletion of natural resources, water and air pollution, and the extinction of wildlife (Patterson, 2021). Due to the vital role of the environment in human life, each of these problems can lead to serious social, economic and political consequences. Among them, problems closely related to environmental changes such as migration, health, inequality and sustainable development have begun to come to the fore on the political agenda in recent years. Therefore, monitoring environmental systems and determining the factors contributing to environmental degradation are considered essential for understanding the nature of these problems and designing policies to protect environmental quality.

There is a growing body of literature investigating the drivers of environmental degradation and environmental quality. However, many aspects of this topic still require further scrutiny due to its importance. For instance, a strand of the literature focuses solely on the relationship between economic growth and environmental pollutants, through testing the Environmental Kuznets Curve (EKC) (Grossman and Krueger, 1991; Grossman and Krueger, 1995). The EKC hypothesis implies that in the initial stages of economic development, environmental quality tends to be considered as a luxury good, leading developing countries to make a choice between a clean environment and economic growth. However, as countries reach a certain level of development, environmental quality becomes a normal good. As a result, the opportunity cost of implementing more stringent environmental policies decreases that makes a clean environment preferable to economic growth (Bernauer, Kalbhenn, Koubi and Spilker, 2010). The EKC hypothesis, while making significant implications regarding the relationship between income and environmental quality, is frequently criticized for its reliance on a relatively simplified relationship that does not allow for the differentiation of the impact of income from other factors. Empirical studies indicate that the relationship between environmental degradation and income levels does not follow a standard pattern as proposed by the EKC hypothesis. Instead, it varies depending on the selected countries and environmental indicators such as CO_2 and SO_2 (Bernauer et al., 2010; Stern, 1998).

A second strand of the literature, on the other hand, focuses on the political economy of environmental degradation and discusses the possible effect of democracy and political institutions on environmental degradation. However, the majority of previous studies report mixed results regarding this effect. In one of the earliest studies on the topic, Congleton (1992) suggests that in addition to economic considerations and policies, deterioration of the environment is closely related to the type of political systems and institutions.

In democratic governments, the marginal cost of environmental protection is observed to be lower compared to authoritarian regimes. Besides this, democratic governments have greater respect for individual fundamental rights and freedoms and are more successful in safeguarding these rights. Moreover, the core values of democracy, including individual rights and freedoms, are closely related to environmental policy and conservation (Fredriksson and Gaston, 2000). For instance, media freedom and freedom of expression facilitate public access to accurate information about environmental issues. Accordingly, environmentalists can freely express their thoughts, convey their demands to policymakers, and transform these ideas into environmental policy. In this respect, governments elected through democratic processes are expected to be more sensitive to public demands regarding environmental issues, as they tend to be more responsive to the needs expressed by the public (Midlarsky, 1998).

On the contrary, authoritarian regimes may choose to make decisions independently of public demands and preferences regarding environmental protection (Neumayer, 2002a). Given the political power of the ruling elite, authoritarian governments can dictate their political agenda without considering environmental consequences and concerns. Hence, authoritarian regimes, compared to their democratic counterparts, are expected to be less successful in controlling environmental pollution. Although it is theoretically expected that democracies tend to generate better environmental outcomes compared to autocracies, the empirical evidence on the mitigating impact of democracy on emissions is weak (Lindvall and Karlsson, 2023). In a recent study, Rydén et al. (2020) provide a comprehensive review of the literature on democracy and biodiversity conservation, confirming the ambiguity. The study asserts that this ambiguity primarily arises from the lack of high-quality data, which results in the use of different proxies to measure biodiversity and democracy. Bättig and Bernauer (2009) also suggest that although the relationship between democracy and levels of political commitment to climate change mitigation is positive, it is ambiguous when it comes to policy outcomes such as emissions reductions.

Several studies indicate that higher levels of democracy are associated with reductions in carbon emissions and/or carbon emission growth rates (Lu et al., 2022). Mak Arvin and Lew (2009) also shows that, although the impact varies across different environmental quality measures, income groups, and regions, less democratic countries tend to have worse environmental conditions and outcomes. On the other hand, Povitkina (2018) demonstrates that democracy-environment nexus is conditional on the levels of corruption and democracies tend to generate better environmental outcomes in countries where corruption is low. Midlarsky (1998) analyzes the impact of democracy on different environmental degradation variables and concludes that there is no uniform relationship. The analysis of three different environmental indicators —deforestation, carbon dioxide emissions, and soil erosion by water— reveals a significant negative relationship between democracy and environmental preservation while the relationship is positive when the protected land area is considered.

In addition to political institutions, the impact of international trade on the environment has also been extensively studied in the literature. A significant body of research supports the view that the trade-environment linkage is non-linear, necessitating consideration of the heterogeneous impact of trade on the environment, as these impacts vary across different income groups (Wang and Zhang, 2021). Some studies suggest that international trade and trade intensity, through mechanisms such as innovation and product differentiation, can mitigate CO_2 emissions and enhance environmental quality (Leitão, 2021a; Leitão, 2021b). Conversely, other studies provide evidence that trade openness significantly increases CO_2 emissions (Dou, Malik, and Dong, 2021; Ahmed, Rehman, and Ozturk, 2017; Ansari, Haider, and Khan, 2020). Only a few recent studies consider the spillover effects of trade openness in literature. Ragoubi and Mighri (2021) analyze the spillover effects of trade openness on CO_2 emissions in middle-income countries, finding that the direct effects of openness are positive, while the indirect effects are negative. Conversely, other studies, such as Lv and Li (2021), report that both the direct and indirect effects of trade openness are insignificant.

The empirical evidence for the effect of trade openness on environmental degradation is mixed because of the differences in conceptualization of the freedom variable, country selection and/or methodological choices. For instance, the most commonly used indicator for trade openness in the empirical literature, is the ratio of total trade to GDP. However, trade freedom indices based on the ratio of trade (total, exports, or imports) to national income calculations should be used carefully as they can lead to serious measurement errors (Gräbner, Heimberger, Kapeller ve Springholz, 2021). For this reason, this paper uses alternative trade openness variables to avoid potential endogeneity problems and measurement errors.

There is a significant amount of empirical support for the effect of international factors and interdependence between countries on environmental performance and policy-making process. For example, it is a well-known fact that environmental degradation is heavily influenced by the actions of trade partners of a country because of the ecological footprints embodied in imports and exports. Moreover, environmental degradation is also affected by proximate countries and neighbors due to spillover effect. That is, environmental issues have transboundary impacts, where negative externalities from economic activities in one country can cross borders and cause environmental damage in others. Previous studies show that the determinants of environmental degradation including financial development (Lv and Li, 2021), urbanization (Li, Wu and Wu, 2022), energy prices (Li, Fang and He, 2020), globalization (You and Lv, 2018) and several other economic variables show spatial spillover effects. That is, environmental degradation is not only correlated in time but also space due to several factors including the geographical and socio-economic linkages between nation-states (Bolea, Espinosa-Gracia and Jimenez, 2024). However, the majority of empirical studies on the determinants of environmental degradation solely focus on the temporal aspect while overlooking the importance of the spatial factors (Jeetoo and Chinyanga, 2023). Accordingly, the analysis of environmental degradation should encompass the economic, political and/or geographical interactions among countries to be able to obtain reliable results. The current paper basically aims to consider such interactions and thus provide empirical support for the possible spillover effects.

Considering all these facts, this study applies a spatial panel econometric analysis to answer some important questions such as, whether there exists a spatial autocorrelation for environmental degradation across the countries and how democratic institutions, trade openness and economic complexity affect environmental quality. Additionally, the paper addresses the indirect impacts of explanatory variables on environmental degradation by revealing spatial linkages. Ignoring spatial dependence can lead to biased and inconsistent estimates as it violates the independence assumption between observations (LeSage & Pace, 2009).

This study employs a comprehensive strategy that considers spatial effects as well as both domestic and international factors to overcome some of the methodological shortcomings in previous studies and thus contribute to the existing literature on the topic in several ways. Previous research on environmental problems largely ignored the possible spillover effects between the neighbors. In addition, the selection of the spatial model in previous research is often made arbitrarily without conducting the necessary diagnostic tests (e.g., Wang and Zhou, 2021). By employing spatial econometric techniques to account for spatial dependency, this study examines the direct and indirect (spillover) effects of explanatory variables, providing a more comprehensive assessment of their impact on environmental degradation.

Methodologically, the choice of an appropriate spatial econometric model in the studies by You and Lv (2018), Li et al., (2020), Lv and Li (2021) and Li et al., (2022) is similar to the strategy used in this paper. Li et al., (2020) follows the strategy proposed by Elhorst (2014) for model selection; however, their study focuses on Chinese provinces for the years between 2002 and 2016. Li et al., (2022) also analyze the China's largest provincial economy, Guangdong province. On the other hand, Lv and Li (2021) cover 97 countries over the period of 2000–2014 to examine the impact of financial development on CO_2 emissions. Given these considerations, our study includes a more extensive set of countries and employs more recent data by using a global sample of 120 countries from 1995 to 2018.

Finally, it is suggested that the mixed results regarding the impact of trade openness on environmental degradation arise from the methodological choices and the conceptualization of the trade openness indicator. To further investigate the environment-trade nexus, this study employs alternative indicators of trade openness that cover different dimensions of trade liberalization. The econometric methodology adopted in this study investigates both the direct and spillover effects of trade openness, enabling a comprehensive analysis of the trade openness-CO2 emissions relationship.

The remainder of this study is organized as follows: Section 2 describes the methodology; Section 3 presents the data used for the empirical analysis; Section 4 discusses the empirical findings; Section 5 concludes.

2. METHODOLOGY

Analyzing environmental degradation requires models that account for the strategic interactions between nation-states. One of the most critical details about such models is considering the interaction between units and incorporating them into the model (Anselin, 1988, p.16). Weight matrices -or interaction matrices- can be used to model various interactions between units including geographical, economic, financial, or cultural proximity.

Briefly, a weight matrix is an *nxn* square matrix that represents the degree of spatial relationship between units (LeSage & Pace, 2009, pp.9). When forming spatial models, the first step is creating these matrices and then determining the appropriate spatial model based on the weight matrix and the type of interaction between units. Types of interactions can be classified into three groups: endogenous interaction effects among the dependent variable, exogenous interaction effects among the independent variables, and interaction effects among the error terms (Elhorst, 2014b). The general nesting spatial (GNS) model is the general model that contains all types of interaction effects and has the following form:

$$y_t = \rho W y_t + \alpha_{In} + X_t \beta + W X_t \theta + u_t, \quad u_t = \lambda W u_t + \varepsilon_t \tag{1}$$

where, $W y_t$ and $W X_t$ represents endogenous and exogenous interaction effects respectively and $W u_t$ is the interaction effect among error terms. ρ is the spatial autoregressive coefficient and λ is the spatial autocorrelation coefficient where β and θ denote the vectors of unknown parameters (Elhorst, 2014b). In this paper, we follow the model selection procedure described in LeSage and Pace (2009) and Elhorst (2010), which starts with the Spatial Durbin Model (SDM) and tests for the alternative models such as the spatial autoregressive (SAR) model and spatial error model (SEM). Then, SDM can be tested against the spatial autocorrelation (SAC) model by using the Akaike information criterion, and the appropriate model can be selected out of these for alternative models.

Following this procedure, this paper uses the Spatial Durbin Model (SDM) and it has the following form:

$$y_t = \rho W y_t + \alpha_{In} + X_t \beta + W X_t \theta + \varepsilon_t \ \ \varepsilon_t \sim N(0, \sigma^2 I_n) \tag{2}$$

The interpretation of the parameter estimates from the spatial models is different from the interpretation of the classical linear regression parameters because of the potential interactions between units. In spatial models, parameter estimates are more comprehensive and contain more information than the coefficients obtained in classical regression analysis because the information set of an observation is not only affected by explanatory variables but also by neighboring units (LeSage and Pace, 2009, p.33). These effects can be demonstrated using the SDM model as follows:"

$$y_t = \rho W y_t + \alpha_{In} + X_t \beta + W X_t \theta + \varepsilon_t$$

$$(I_N - \rho W) y_t = X_t \beta + W X_t \theta + \alpha_{In} + \varepsilon_t \tag{3}$$

For $S_r(W) = V(W)(I_N \beta_r + W \theta_r)$ and $V(W) = (I_N - \rho W)^{-1}$, we can rewrite this equation as follows:

$$y_t = \sum_{r=1}^{k} S_r(W) X_{tr} + V(W) \alpha_{In} + V(W) \varepsilon_t \tag{4}$$

The diagonal elements of the *nxn* matrix Sr(W) represent the direct effects, and off-diagonal elements represent indirect impacts where the direct effects can be calculated by taking the average of the diagonal elements of S_r (LeSage and Pace (2009). Finally, for robust and consistent results, the maximum likelihood estimation method is employed to estimate the SDM model.

3. DATA

This study uses data from a global sample of 120 countries from 1995 to 2018. The choice of sample period and countries included in the analysis is determined by data availability. Specifically, economic complexity variables limit the number of countries included in the dataset, as the index is calculated for around 130 countries.

Additionally, we excluded small island nations and countries with populations of less than one million, as these generally have relatively low levels of emissions and could lead to biased estimates. The dataset includes various explanatory variables of environmental degradation, namely, income, economic complexity, democratic institutions, natural resources, energy intensity, and trade openness. In empirical literature, environmental degradation is primarily measured by ecological footprint and CO2 emissions along with other greenhouse gas (GHG) emissions. In this paper, environmental degradation is measured by the logarithm of CO2 emissions per capita, which is one of the most common proxies used for environmental degradation in the literature (Anwar et al., 2023; Burki and Tahir, 2022; Hatmanu et al., 2021; Mak Arvin and Lew, 2009; Shaheen et al., 2020; Zhang et al., 2019). The data are expressed in metric tons per capita and derived from the World Bank. Table 1 below presents the definitions and sources of all variables used in the analysis.

The natural logarithm of the real GDP per capita (mil. 2017US$) is included into model to analyze the impact of income on environmental degradation. There is broad consensus in the literature that it is one of the most significant factors affecting environmental outcomes. Besides income, we use The Atlas of Economic Complexity index to analyze the impact of the industrial structure of a country. Briefly, economic complexity expresses the composition of a country's productive output. Hence, it captures how diversified and ubiquitous a country's export basket is (Hausman et al., 2014). The economic complexity of a country is directly related to the environmental quality of the country as the composition of the goods produced is associated with natural resources and energy consumption (Kaufman et al., 1998). Hausman et al., (2014) assert that the index reflects the productive knowledge and capabilities of a country, which can easily facilitate resource-efficient, cleaner, and environmentally friendly production processes. On the other hand, complex products primarily result from industrial manufacturing or chemical sectors, which operate with high levels of energy intensity (Neagu, 2020). Therefore, the marginal effect of economic complexity on environmental degradation will depend on the relative strength of these opposing influences.

Table 1. Variables and Definitions

Variable	Definition	Source
Dependent Variable		
CO_2	Natural logarithm of the CO2 emissions (kt) per capita.	World Bank
Independent Variables		
GDPP	Natural logarithm of the real GDP per capita (mil. 2017US$).	Penn World Table, version 10.0

continued on following page

Table 1. Continued

Variable	Definition	Source
COMPLEXITY	Economic Complexity Index	The Atlas of Economic Complexity index
DEMOCRACY	14–(POLITICAL+CIVIL) where POLITICAL is political rights and CIVIL is civil liberties.	Freedom House, 2021
ENERGY	Energy intensity level of primary energy (MJ/$2011 PPP GDP)	World Bank
AGRICULTURE	Natural logarithm of the Agricultural land (% of land area)	World Bank
FOREST	Natural logarithm of the Forest area (% of land area)	World Bank
TRADEOPEN	Natural logarithm of the ratio of total external trade to GDP.	World Bank
TRADEGLOBAL	Natural logarithm of the KOF Trade Globalization Index	KOF Swiss Economic Inst, 2018
TRADEFREEDOM	Freedom to trade internationally	Fraser Institute, 2021

In literature, the level of democracy is generally (but not always) represented by a dummy variable that is relatively constant over time. Although slowly evolving, the quality and the structure of institutions can change in time. There are also several composite indices that measure the level of democracy and the strength of democratic institutions within a country. The Varieties of Democracy (V-Dem) by the V-Dem project is a widely used index in literature to measure the quality of democracy. V-Dem aims to conceptualize democracy by recognizing five major principles: electoral, liberal, participatory, egalitarian, and deliberative (Coppedge, 2023). In addition to that, Polity which is developed by the Center for Systemic Peace also provides a comprehensive dataset covering 167 countries, enabling cross-country comparisons over time. The Polity score of a country reflects the authority characteristics of states based on six component measures of executive recruitment, constraints on executive authority and political competition (Marshall, and Gurr, 2020). In contrast, Freedom in the World database provided by Freedom House focuses on a different aspect of democracy through two intermediary indices: political rights and civil liberties, without aiming for a comprehensive conceptualization of democracy. Given that different indices assess various dimensions and aspects of democracy, researchers can select the most relevant index to the aims of their study to derive appropriate inferences and policy implications. Lastly, comparative analyses of these democracy indices indicate that the pairwise correlations between them are high, decreasing the possibility of selection bias in empirical studies (Niño-Zarazúa et al., 2020). Following Tümer (2019), this study uses the political rights and civil liberties indices from the Freedom House to construct a democracy variable that reflects political changes in a country over time. Similarly, Mak Arvin and Lew (2009) use an average of these ratings to analyze the impact of democracy on environmental quality.

The energy intensity variable, which is included in the model to control cross-country differences in energy needs, indicates how much energy is used to produce one unit of economic output. Basically, this variable is used as a proxy for the level of energy usage and is expected to have a positive sign in regressions due to the close relationship between energy consumption and emissions.

The agriculture variable measures agricultural development and shows the percentage of agricultural land in the total land area of a country. Agricultural activities can cause various environmental problems including emissions, deforestation, biodiversity loss, and soil degeneration. More than that, in countries where agricultural activities are relatively high, it becomes more difficult to take strict legal measures to protect the environment (Egger et al., 2011). Because of that, we expect a positive relationship between agricultural development and environmental degradation (Balogh, 2022). The second environmental variable is the forest area, measured as the percentage of a country's total land area. We expect an increase in forest area to decrease environmental degradation, as forests play a significant role in mitigating climate change by acting as a "carbon sink" that absorbs billions of tons of CO_2 per year (UNDP, 2023).

Table 2. Descriptive Statistics

Variable	Obs.	Mean	Std. Dev.	Minimum	Maximum
CO2	2,880	0.8461	1.4927	-4.1158	3.8649
GDPP	2,880	2.2111	0.1347	1.7047	2.4868
COMPLEXITY	2,880	0.0907	0.9853	-2.6959	2.8589
DEMOCRACY	2,880	7.3889	3.7091	0	12
ENERGY	2,880	1.7285	0.5134	0.6473	4.0602
AGRICULTURE	2,880	3.4924	0.7647	0.9586	4.4484
FOREST	2,880	2.9495	1.4706	-4.7794	4.5229
TRADEOPEN	2,880	4.2874	0.6222	-1.7873	6.0807
TRADEGLOBAL	2,880	3.9772	0.3577	2.5482	4.5744
TRADEFREEDOM	2,880	7.1157	1.3318	1.4450	10

This paper uses three different measures of trade openness. The first measure is the traditional measure of trade openness, calculated as the natural logarithm of the ratio of total external trade to GDP and published by the World Bank. The second measure is the Trade Globalization Index published by the Swiss Economic Institute (KOF), which serves as an alternative measure of trade openness. This index is calculated using variables that account for both the de facto and de jure dimensions of trade freedom, including trade volume as a share of GDP, trade partner diversity, trade regulations, trade taxes, tariff rates, and free trade agreements (Gygli et al., 2019). The third measure of trade freedom is the sub-index of the Economic Freedom Index published by the Fraser Institute, which measures the freedom to trade internationally. This sub-index evaluates a wide range of trade restrictions, including tariffs, quotas, hidden administrative restraints, and controls on exchange rates and capital movement (Gwartney, J., Lawson, R., Murphy, R., 2023). Table 2 presents descriptive statistics of the variables employed in the regression analysis.

We use a row-standardized spatial weights matrix based on inverse distance to measure the spatial dependence between countries. In order to compute the distances, we use latitude and longitude data obtained from CEPII (Centre d'Etudes Prospectives et d'Informations Internationales). For the distance d_{ij} between countries i and j, the inverse distance weights matrix is defined as follows:

$$W = 1/d_{ij} \qquad (2)$$

Before proceeding to spatial econometric analyses, we use Moran's I statistic to assess spatial autocorrelation. Moran's I statistic ranges from -1 to 1, with values closer to 1 indicating positive autocorrelation, where similar values are spatially clustered. On the other hand, values closer to -1 indicate negative autocorrelation, where neighboring units are dissimilar (Anselin, 1995).

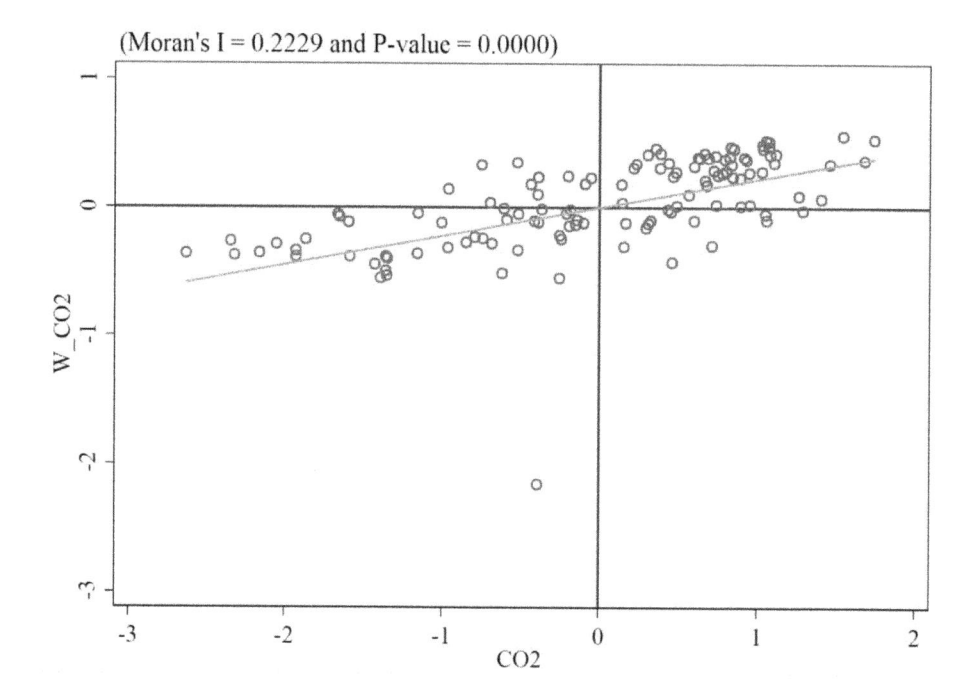

Figure 1a. Moran's I Scatter Plot for 1990

(Moran's I = 0.2229 and P-value = 0.0000)

Figure 1b. Moran's I Scatter Plot for 2018

(Moran's I = 0.2672 and P-value = 0.0000)

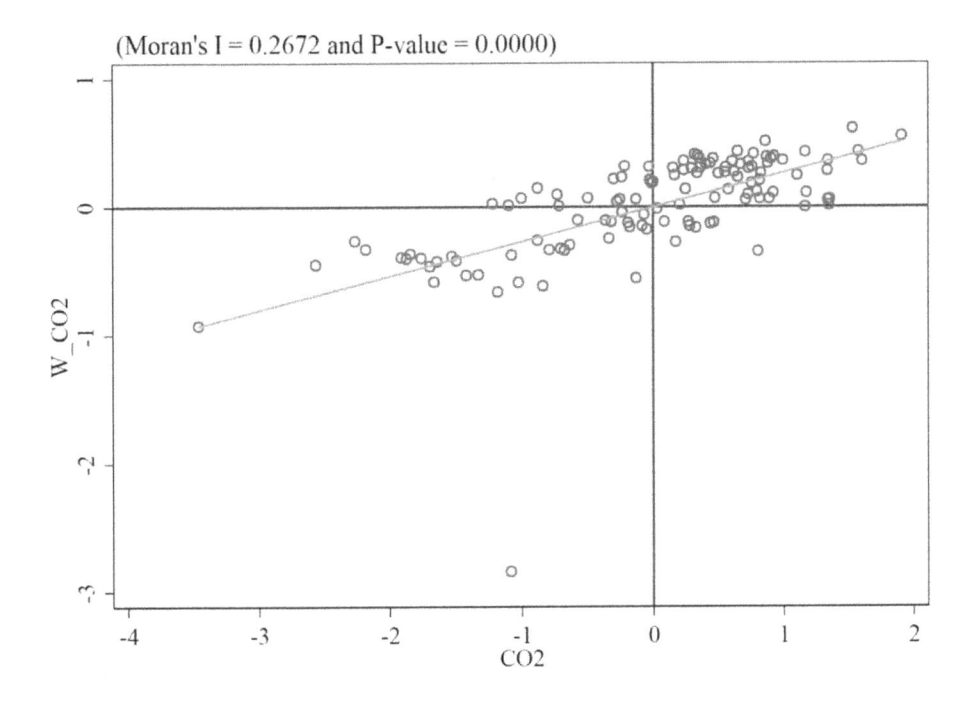

Figure 1 (a) and (b) display Moran's I scatter plots in the years 1995 and 2018, respectively. In each of these figures, the x-axis represents the standardized values of per capita emissions, whereas the y-axis shows the spatially weighted values of the same variable. Accordingly, these scatter plots help us to visualize global spatial autocorrelation and detect spatial clusters in emissions. As the data portrayed above shows, spatial autocorrelation is positive and statistically significant in both scatter plots. Also, comparing two graphs implies that the spatial autocorrelation coefficient is higher in 2018 (Moran's I=0.2672) than in 1990 (Moran's I=0.2229). These two findings suggest that environmental degradation tends to cluster geographically, and the degree of spatial dependence increases over time. Therefore, the preliminary analysis here provides evidence supporting the importance of spatial effects and the transboundary nature of environmental problems.

4. EMPIRICAL RESULTS

This section examines the determinants of environmental degradation using spatial econometric models. As explained in the methodology section, an initial step is to implement diagnostic tests to determine the appropriate spatial model. Starting from the SDM and then comparing it with the SAR and SEM models by using the Wald test show that SDM is the best model that fits the data. In addition to this, a comparison of the Akaike information criterion, which is used to compare SDM with the SAC as an alternative model, reveals that SDM is the most appropriate choice to analyze spatial effects. After deciding on the SDM model, this paper employed the Hausman Test to decide between fixed or random effects. As the results provided in Table 3 imply, the null hypothesis, which states that the preferred model is random effects, is rejected at conventional significance levels. Thus, the Hausman test reveals that the preferred model should be a fixed effects model.

Table 3. Estimation of SDM using geographical distance matrix

	(1)	(2)	(3)	(4)	(5)	(6)
GDPP	1.6326***	1.5464***	1.9477***	2.017***	1.9843***	1.8761***
	(.1212)	(.1225)	(.1241)	(.1237)	(.1214)	(.125)
COMPLEXITY	.0989***	.0955***	.0803***	.0828***	.0814***	.0775***
	(.0147)	(.0147)	(.0143)	(.0142)	(.014)	(.0142)
DEMOCRACY		.0146***	.0123***	.0091***	.0111***	.0115***
		(.0035)	(.0033)	(.0033)	(.0033)	(.0033)
ENERGY			.2204***	.2282***	.2083***	.2232***
			(.0222)	(.022)	(.0217)	(.0221)
AGRICULTURE			.2334***	.2267***	.2175***	.2331***
			(.0401)	(.0398)	(.0393)	(.04)
FOREST			-.3623***	-.3489***	-.3599***	-.3592***
			(.0628)	(.0622)	(.0616)	(.0625)
TRADEOPEN				.0824***		
				(.0124)		
TRADEGLOBAL					.2953***	
					(.0271)	
TRADEFREEDOM						.0191***
						(.0062)
W_GDPP	-.2649	-.1451	.8461**	.8707**	1.0255***	.8142***

continued on following page

Table 3. Continued

	(1)	(2)	(3)	(4)	(5)	(6)
	(.1867)	(.1988)	(.3358)	(.3424)	(.345)	(.3364)
W_COMPLEXITY	.1728**	.1653**	.0234	-.0044	-.0242	.0208
	(.0791)	(.0791)	(.0775)	(.077)	(.0759)	(.0773)
W_DEMOCRACY		-.021	.0034	.015	.0227	.0009
		(.0128)	(.0131)	(.0136)	(.0154)	(.0131)
W_ENERGY			.0354	-.0152	-.0118	-.0490
			(.0793)	(.0795)	(.0786)	(.0801)
W_AGRICULTURE			.2587	.2151	.2955	.300
			(.2464)	(.2468)	(.2475)	(.2462)
W_FOREST			-.7645***	-.8872***	-.7666***	-.6624**
			(.2867)	(.2877)	(.2888)	(.2876)
W_TRADEOPEN				-.2193***		
				(.0699)		
W_TRADEGLOBAL					-.5848***	
					(.1127)	
W_TRADEFREEDOM						-.0407
						(.0293)
Spatial rho (ρ)	.6168***	.6223***	.4634***	.4768***	.48***	.4583***
	(.0442)	(.0441)	(.0527)	(.0523)	(.0516)	(.0528)
Variance: sigma2_e	.0319***	.0317***	.0293***	.0288***	.028***	.029***
	(.0008)	(.0008)	(.0008)	(.0008)	(.0007)	(.0007)
Observations	2880	2880	2880	2880	2880	2880
R-squared	.6805	.6619	.3103	.3097	.3367	.3313
Hausman:	chi2(15) = 32.49 Prob>=chi2 = 0.0055						

SDM vs SAR: 29.76***
SDM vs SEM: 107.58***
SDM vs SAC: AIC_SDM=-1985.245, AIC_SAC=-1972.691
Standard errors are in parentheses *** p<.01, ** p<.05, * p<.1

As can be seen from Table 3, the spatial autoregressive coefficient (ρ) is positive and statistically significant at a 5% significant level across all models, ranging between 0.4583 and 0.6168. These findings prove that there are strong spatial interactions among countries and confirm the relevance of the SDM. The presence of this spatial dependence in environmental degradation aligns with previous findings in the related literature (Bolea, Espinosa-Gracia and Jimenez, 2024; Lv and Li, 2021; Ragoubi and Mighri, 2021; Wang and Zhou, 2021).

As mentioned above, the interpretation of parameter estimates is quite different in spatial models than in classical linear regression. To analyze the impact of a particular variable on the dependent variable within its own economy, it is necessary to calculate the direct effects. To test for the presence of spatial spillovers, indirect effects must be calculated. Table 4 presents the results of these calculations for both the direct and indirect effects.

Table 4. Direct and Indirect Effects

	Direct Effects			Indirect Effects		
	(1)	(2)	(3)	(4)	(5)	(6)
GDPP	2.062***	2.033***	1.916***	3.425***	3.722***	3.022***
	(0.125)	(0.123)	(0.127)	(0.675)	(0.692)	(0.604)
COMPLEXITY	0.083***	0.081***	0.078***	0.080	0.042	0.117
	(0.013)	(0.013)	(0.013)	(0.144)	(0.142)	(0.140)
DEMOCRACY	0.009***	0.012***	0.012***	0.037	0.054*	0.011
	(0.003)	(0.003)	(0.003)	(0.025)	(0.029)	(0.023)
ENERGY	0.230***	0.210***	0.226***	0.171	0.161	0.272*
	(0.021)	(0.020)	(0.021)	(0.147)	(0.146)	(0.146)
AGRICULTURE	0.234***	0.226***	0.242***	0.634	0.782	0.770
	(0.038)	(0.038)	(0.038)	(0.490)	(0.493)	(0.474)
FOREST	-0.369***	-0.377***	-0.373***	-2.001***	-1.798***	-1.519***
	(0.062)	(0.061)	(0.063)	(0.574)	(0.578)	(0.543)
TRADEOPEN	0.078***			-0.338**		
	(0.013)			(0.138)		
TRADEGLOBAL		0.285***			-0.841***	
		(0.028)			(0.222)	
TRADEFREEDOM			0.020***			0.092*
			(0.006)			(0.053)

Standard errors are in parentheses *** p<.01, ** p<.05, * p<.1

Table 4 reveals that per capita GDP has positive and statistically significant direct and indirect effects in all models, meaning that an increase in national income accelerates environmental degradation both in the home country and in neighboring countries. In addition to that, the magnitude of the indirect effects of per capita income is considerably high, proving strong evidence for the existence of spatial spillovers. Previous research on the relationship between environmental degradation and income presents similar findings regarding the significance of the direct and indirect effects, including the magnitude of the spillover effects (Abdo et al., 2022;

Wang and Zhou, 2021). Therefore, the evidence shows that the level of economic development is one of the major contributors to environmental degradation.

In line with previous literature, the analysis indicates evidence of a positive correlation between economic complexity and environmental degradation (Aluko et al., 2023; Boleti et al., 2021; Neagu, 2020; Wang et al., 2023). Despite having non-significant indirect effects, Table 4 shows that economic complexity has positive and statistically significant direct effects at a 5% level of significance across all models. In other words, economic complexity leads to increased pollution, which in turn, contributes to environmental degradation. However, this result does not necessarily mean that increasing diversification and sophistication of the product mix is a threat to environmental quality in every circumstance. Instead, it is known that the development of production capabilities can be aligned with the advancement of production processes that promote environmental-friendly practices. For instance, Can and Gozgor (2017) report that, in the long run, economic complexity reduces CO_2 emissions in France, in line with the expectation that economic complexity lowers CO_2 emissions in high-income countries by reshaping production processes through structural transformation and the adoption of advanced technologies. Therefore, the result presented in Table 4 can be interpreted as a policy implication rather than a simple correlation: countries should adopt new sustainable practices that mitigate environmental impacts as they transition to a more complex production system. Otherwise, increased complexity relying on the current production techniques might worsen the environmental outcomes.

It is well-documented that democratic governments are more inclined to join international environmental agreements and adopt environmental laws, policies, and regulations (Congleton, 1992; Egger et al., 2011; Fredriksson and Gaston, 2000; Murdoch and Sandler, 1997; Neumayer, 2002a; Neumayer, 2002b; Payne, 1995; Sauquet, 2014; Von Stein, 2008; Yamagata et al., 2017). However, the empirical evidence linking democratic governance to CO_2 emission reductions is relatively weak (Bättig and Bernauer, 2009; Rydén et al., 2020). This weakness can be attributed to the prevalence of corruption and the inefficiency of state institutions in some democracies, which hinders the effective implementation of environmental policies (Lindvall and Karlsson, 2023; Povitkina, 2018).

The results provided above show that although the direct impact of democracy is statistically significant, there are no spillover effects of democracy. Additionally, the magnitude of the direct and indirect effects of democracy on environmental degradation is relatively low compared to all other factors. Therefore, the high emissions observed in democracies are not solely due to the level of democracy but are also influenced by other economic and trade-related variables. Our results align with prior research, such as that of Lindvall and Karlsson (2023), who suggest that other factors, namely, economic growth, income distribution, energy mix, and corruption, may influence environmental performance more than democracy.

The empirical results for the impact of energy intensity on environmental performance are mostly in line with a priori expectations: the direct impact of this variable is statistically significant and positive, with a considerably high coefficient in magnitude. Therefore, the estimations based on the SDM model reveal that higher energy intensity contributes to CO_2 emissions, confirming the results of previous research (Danish et al., 2020; Shahbaz et al., 2015). Given the strong and close link between economic growth, production, and energy consumption, one can roughly interpret this finding as the need to reduce energy usage to lower the level of emissions. However, this finding may also point to the need to increase the share of renewable energy sources in the national energy mix to control the negative effects of production on environment.

Agricultural activities are one of the main contributors to GHG emissions. According to recent data, agriculture contributes 25–30% of global GHG emissions which rises to around one-third when all agricultural products are included (Ritchie, 2021). Our results align with some prior research that identified agricultural development and agricultural machinery use stimulates CO_2 emissions (Balogh, 2022). Given that agriculture is the primary source of food production, a well-functioning agricultural sector and the implementation of sustainable agricultural practices are essential to minimizing negative ecological impacts while ensuring food security. In line with previous research, this study shows that increasing forest area can substantially decrease environmental degradation (Waheed et al., 2018). Forest area has also statistically significant indirect effects, meaning that an increase in forest area in one country negatively affects the CO_2 emissions of neighboring countries, hence improving overall environmental quality.

As can be seen from Table 4, trade openness variables are statistically significant at the 1% significance level and have a positive relationship with environmental degradation in all three models. In other words, increased trade liberalization increases environmental degradation in the target country through rising CO_2 emissions. The direct impacts are particularly large in the second model where we measure trade openness through the KOF trade globalization index. Moreover, all three trade openness variables also have statistically significant indirect effects. Except for the third model, indirect effects are negative and much higher than the positive direct effect. As a result, trade openness has a significantly negative total effect, implying that an increase in trade freedom in neighboring countries positively influences the target country's environmental quality. That is to say, trade openness leads to better environmental outcomes when significant spillover effects are taken into account. These findings regarding the impact of trade openness are similar to those of Ragoubi and Mighri (2021). However, instead of considering different dimensions of trade liberalization, their study only uses the trade-to-GDP ratio as an openness indicator, which solely indicates the relative importance of international trade in the economy.

5. CONCLUSION

This paper explores the drivers of environmental degradation by using spatial panel data models to account for spatial interdependence among countries. Despite a large body of literature investigating the relationship between international trade, democracy, and the environment, previous studies have produced mixed results, partly due to the conceptualizations of variables and methodological limitations. This paper aims to address these limitations by proposing alternative measures of trade openness and democracy while accounting for spatial dependence between countries, which is shown to have a significant impact on empirical findings.

In sum, empirical findings provided here support the existence of spatial dependence on CO_2 emissions, which highlights the significance of considering spatial interactions between countries. Besides this, the findings of the study are generally consistent with those in the literature and confirm the validity of the identified national factors. The results reveal that income, economic complexity, democracy, energy intensity and agricultural land contribute to CO_2 emissions, while forest area is negatively associated with environmental degradation. Additionally, the findings from all regression models indicate significant spillover effects of exogenous variables on environmental degradation. For example, income has a significant positive spatial effect, whereas forest area and trade openness have negative spatial effects on CO_2 emissions.

The results also reveal that while trade openness has statistically significant and positive direct effects, there are strong spillover effects as well. Indeed, the negative spillover effects of trade openness outweigh the direct effects, leading to a mitigating impact on environmental degradation. As previously mentioned, models that do not account for spatial effects and strategic interactions have been inadequate in identifying these indirect impacts of trade openness on environmental degradation, limiting the ability of empirical models to fully investigate the trade-environment relationship.

From a policy perspective, these findings offer important insights into mitigating climate change and environmental degradation. Firstly, the results highlight the close relationship between macroeconomic conditions and environmental quality. It is found that having higher income levels can have negative environmental impacts, which implies that policy makers should consider environmental consequences of their development plans rather than solely focusing on numbers and increasing material well-being. Secondly, the negative relationship between institutional quality and environmental outcomes reported here carries an implicit message to all governments: political institutions and practices should be reformed so that they can transmit environmental concerns and demands of society to policymakers. That means, institutions and political processes should more pro-environment.

The results also show that transitioning to more efficient production technologies, protecting and expanding forest areas, and reducing agricultural emissions can yield positive effects in the short term. The variables of economic complexity and energy intensity highlight the importance of transforming production systems and deploying low-carbon technologies as crucial steps towards achieving net zero emissions.

In addition to these implications, the results clearly demonstrate that sustainable development goals can only be achieved through global collaboration. International cooperation and supporting countries in their efforts to tackle climate change are essential due to the geographical dependence of environmental degradation. Policy choices in one country have far-reaching effects, influencing not only domestic outcomes but also those of neighboring states. The significant and substantial indirect effects of income, forest area, and trade openness must be carefully considered due to their potential impact on surrounding countries. As suggested by Antweiler et al. (2001), free trade can benefit the environment depending on the scale, technique, and composition effects. The results of this study also reveal that increased trade openness in neighboring countries positively affects environmental quality in the home country, proving that the technique effect dominates by facilitating a transition to cleaner techniques with lower emissions intensity. In this respect, it is fair to say that although increased economic activity and international trade may be harmful, it is possible to mitigate their negative environmental impacts by following sustainable and inclusive green growth policies and strategies.

REFERENCES

Abdo, A. B., Bin, L., Zhang, X., Saeed, M., Qahtan, A. S. A., & Ghallab, H. M. H. (2022). Spatial analysis of financial development's effect on the ecological footprint of belt and road initiative countries: Mitigation options through renewable energy consumption and institutional quality. *Journal of Cleaner Production*, 366, 132696. DOI: 10.1016/j.jclepro.2022.132696

Ahmed, K., Rehman, M. U., & Ozturk, I. (2017). What drives carbon dioxide emissions in the long-run? Evidence from selected South Asian Countries. *Renewable & Sustainable Energy Reviews*, 70, 1142–1153. DOI: 10.1016/j.rser.2016.12.018

Aluko, O. A., Opoku, E. E. O., & Acheampong, A. O. (2023). Economic complexity and environmental degradation: Evidence from OECD countries. *Business Strategy and the Environment*, 32(6), 2767–2788. DOI: 10.1002/bse.3269

Ansari, M. A., Haider, S., & Khan, N. A. (2020). Does trade openness affects global carbon dioxide emissions: Evidence from the top CO2 emitters. *Management of Environmental Quality*, 31(1), 32–53. DOI: 10.1108/MEQ-12-2018-0205

Anselin, L. (1988). *Spatial Econometrics: Methods and Models*. Springer Netherlands., DOI: 10.1007/978-94-015-7799-1

Anwar, A., Chaudhary, A. R., & Malik, S. (2023). Modeling the macroeconomic determinants of environmental degradation in E-7 countries: The role of technological innovation and institutional quality. *Journal of Public Affairs*, 23(1), e2834. DOI: 10.1002/pa.2834

Balogh, J. M. (2022). The impacts of agricultural development and trade on CO2 emissions? Evidence from the Non-European Union countries. *Environmental Science & Policy*, 137, 99–108. DOI: 10.1016/j.envsci.2022.08.012

Bättig, M. B., & Bernauer, T. (2009). National Institutions and Global Public Goods: Are Democracies More Cooperative in Climate Change Policy? *International Organization*, 63(2), 281–308. DOI: 10.1017/S0020818309090092

Bernauer, T., Kalbhenn, A., Koubi, V., & Spilker, G. (2010). A comparison of international and domestic sources of global governance dynamics. *British Journal of Political Science*, 40(3), 509–538. DOI: 10.1017/S0007123410000098

Bolea, L., Espinosa-Gracia, A., & Jimenez, S. (2024). So close, no matter how far: A spatial analysis of CO2 emissions considering geographic and economic distances. *World Economy*, 47(2), 544–566. DOI: 10.1111/twec.13424

Boleti, E., Garas, A., Kyriakou, A., & Lapatinas, A. (2021). Economic complexity and environmental performance: Evidence from a world sample. *Environmental Modeling and Assessment*, 26(3), 251–270. DOI: 10.1007/s10666-021-09750-0

Burki, U., & Tahir, M. (2022). Determinants of environmental degradation: Evidenced-based insights from ASEAN economies. *Journal of Environmental Management*, 306, 114506. DOI: 10.1016/j.jenvman.2022.114506 PMID: 35051821

Can, M., & Gozgor, G. (2017). The impact of economic complexity on carbon emissions: Evidence from France. *Environmental Science and Pollution Research International*, 24(19), 16364–16370. DOI: 10.1007/s11356-017-9219-7 PMID: 28547378

Congleton, R. D. (1992). Political Institutions and Pollution Control. *The Review of Economics and Statistics*, 74(3), 412–421. https://about.jstor.org/terms. DOI: 10.2307/2109485

Coppedge, M. (2023). V-Dem's conceptions of democracy and their consequences. *V-Dem Working Paper, 135*.

Danish, U., Ulucak, R., & Khan, S.-U.-D. (2020). Relationship between energy intensity and CO2 emissions: Does economic policy matter? *Sustainable Development (Bradford)*, 28(5), 1457–1464. DOI: 10.1002/sd.2098

Dou, Y., Zhao, J., Malik, M. N., & Dong, K. (2021). Assessing the impact of trade openness on CO2 emissions: Evidence from China-Japan-ROK FTA countries. *Journal of Environmental Management*, 296, 113241. DOI: 10.1016/j.jenvman.2021.113241 PMID: 34265664

Egger, P., Jeßberger, C., & Larch, M. (2011). Trade and investment liberalization as determinants of multilateral environmental agreement membership. *International Tax and Public Finance*, 18(6), 605–633. DOI: 10.1007/s10797-011-9169-9

Elhorst, J. P. (2010). Applied spatial econometrics: Raising the bar. *Spatial Economic Analysis*, 5(1), 9–28. DOI: 10.1080/17421770903541772

Elhorst, J. P. (2014). Spatial Econometrics from Cross-Sectional Data to Spatial Panels. Springer. https://www.springer.com/series/10096

Elhorst, J. P. (2014b). Spatial panel models. *Handbook of regional science, 3*.

Fredriksson, P. G., & Gaston, N. (2000). Ratification of the 1992 Climate Change Convention: What Determines Legislative Delay? *Public Choice*, 104(4), 345–368. https://www.jstor.org/stable/30026432. DOI: 10.1023/A:1005129300402

Gräbner, C., Heimberger, P., Kapeller, J., & Springholz, F. (2021). Understanding economic openness: A review of existing measures. *Review of World Economics*, 157(1), 87–120. DOI: 10.1007/s10290-020-00391-1

Grossman, G. M., & Krueger, A. B. (1991). Environmental Impacts of a North American Free Trade Agreement. National Bureau of Economic Research Working Paper Series, No, 3914.

Grossman, G. M., & Krueger, A. B. (1995). Economic growth and the environment. *The Quarterly Journal of Economics*, 110(2), 353–377. DOI: 10.2307/2118443

Gwartney, J., Lawson, R., & Murphy, R. (2023). *Economic Freedom of the World: 2023 Annual Report*. Fraser Institute. DOI: 10.53095/88975012

Gygli, S., Haelg, F., Potrafke, N., & Sturm, J. E. (2019). The KOF globalisation index–revisited. *The Review of International Organizations*, 14(3), 543–574. DOI: 10.1007/s11558-019-09344-2

Hatmanu, M., Cautisanu, C., & Iacobuta, A. O. (2021). On the relationships between CO2 emissions and their determinants in Romania and Bulgaria. An ARDL approach. *Applied Economics*, 54(22), 2582–2595. DOI: 10.1080/00036846.2021.1998328

Hausmann, R., Hidalgo, C. A., Bustos, S., Coscia, M., & Simoes, A. (2014). *The atlas of economic complexity: Mapping paths to prosperity*. Mit Press. DOI: 10.7551/mitpress/9647.001.0001

Jeetoo, J., & Chinyanga, E. R. (2023). A spatial econometric analysis of the environment Kuznets curve and pollution haven hypothesis in Sub-Saharan Africa. *Environmental Science and Pollution Research International*, 30(20), 58169–58188. DOI: 10.1007/s11356-023-26306-9 PMID: 36973630

Kaufmann, R. K., Davidsdottir, B., Garnham, S., & Pauly, P. (1998). The determinants of atmospheric SO2 concentrations: Reconsidering the environmental Kuznets curve. *Ecological Economics*, 25(2), 209–220. DOI: 10.1016/S0921-8009(97)00181-X

Kelejian, H. H., & Prucha, I. R. (2010). Specification and estimation of spatial autoregressive models with autoregressive and heteroskedastic disturbances. *Journal of Econometrics*, 157(1), 53–67. DOI: 10.1016/j.jeconom.2009.10.025 PMID: 20577573

Leitão, N. C. (2021). The Effects of Corruption, Renewable Energy, Trade and CO_2 Emissions. *Economies*, 9(2), 62. DOI: 10.3390/economies9020062

Leitão, N. C. (2021). Testing the Role of Trade on Carbon Dioxide Emissions in Portugal. *Economies*, 9(1), 22. DOI: 10.3390/economies9010022

LeSage, J., & Pace, R. K. (2009). *Introduction to Spatial Econometrics*. CRC Press. DOI: 10.1201/9781420064254

Li, K., Fang, L., & He, L. (2020). The impact of energy price on CO2 emissions in China: A spatial econometric analysis. *The Science of the Total Environment*, 706, 135942. DOI: 10.1016/j.scitotenv.2019.135942 PMID: 31846876

Li, Z., Wu, H., & Wu, F. (2022). Impacts of urban forms and socioeconomic factors on CO2 emissions: A spatial econometric analysis. *Journal of Cleaner Production*, 372, 133722. DOI: 10.1016/j.jclepro.2022.133722

Lindvall, D., & Karlsson, M. (2023). Exploring the democracy-climate nexus: A review of correlations between democracy and climate policy performance. *Climate Policy*, 24(1), 87–103. DOI: 10.1080/14693062.2023.2256697

Lu, Z., Mahalik, M. K., Mallick, H., & Zhao, R. (2022). The moderating effects of democracy and technology adoption on the relationship between trade liberalisation and carbon emissions. *Technological Forecasting and Social Change*, 180, 121712. DOI: 10.1016/j.techfore.2022.121712

Lv, Z., & Li, S. (2021). How financial development affects CO2 emissions: A spatial econometric analysis. *Journal of Environmental Management*, 277, 111397. DOI: 10.1016/j.jenvman.2020.111397 PMID: 33039704

Mak Arvin, B., & Lew, B. (2009). Does democracy affect environmental quality in developing countries? *Applied Economics*, 43(9), 1151–1160. DOI: 10.1080/00036840802600277

Marshall, M.G. and Gurr, T.R. (2020). 'Polity5: Political regime characteristics and transitions, 1800-2018: Dataset Users' Manual'.

Midlarsky, M. I. (1998). Democracy and the Environment: An Empirical Assessment. *Journal of Peace Research*, 35(3), 341–361. DOI: 10.1177/0022343398035003005

Murdoch, J. C., & Sandler, T. (1997). The voluntary provision of a pure public good: The case of reduced CFC emissions and the Montreal Protocol. *Journal of Public Economics*, 63(3), 331–349. DOI: 10.1016/S0047-2727(96)01598-8

Neagu, O. (2020). Economic complexity and ecological footprint: Evidence from the most complex economies in the world. *Sustainability (Basel)*, 12(21), 9031. DOI: 10.3390/su12219031

Neumayer, E. (2002a). Do Democracies Exhibit Stronger International Environmental Commitment? A Cross-Country Analysis. *Journal of Peace Research*, 39(2), 139–164. DOI: 10.1177/0022343302039002001

Neumayer, E. (2002b). Does trade openness promote multilateral environmental cooperation? *World Economy*, 25(6), 815–832. DOI: 10.1111/1467-9701.00464

Niño-Zarazúa, M., Gisselquist, R. M., Horigoshi, A., Samarin, M., & Sen, K. (2020), Effects of Swedish and International Democracy Aid, EBA Report 2020:07. Appendix II. Comparative Analysis of Democracy Indices. The Expert Group for Aid Studies (EBA), Sweden. https://eba.se/wp-content/uploads/2020/12/Appendix_II_webb.pdf

Patterson, W. R. (2021). Ecological Degradation. In Romaniuk, S., & Marton, P. (Eds.), *The Palgrave Encyclopedia of Global Security Studies*. Palgrave Macmillan., DOI: 10.1007/978-3-319-74336-3_395-1

Payne, R. A. (1995). Freedom and the Environment. *Journal of Democracy*, 6(3), 41–55. DOI: 10.1353/jod.1995.0053

Povitkina, M. (2018). The limits of democracy in tackling climate change. *Environmental Politics*, 27(3), 411–432. DOI: 10.1080/09644016.2018.1444723

Ragoubi, H., & Mighri, Z. (2021). Spillover effects of trade openness on CO_2 emissions in middle-income countries: A spatial panel data approach. *Regional Science Policy & Practice*, 13(3), 835–877. DOI: 10.1111/rsp3.12360

Ritchie, H. (2021). How much of global greenhouse gas emissions come from food? Published online at OurWorldInData.org. Retrieved from: 'https://ourworldindata.org/greenhouse-gas-emissions-food' [Online Resource]

Rydén, O., Zizka, A., Jagers, S. C., Lindberg, S. I., & Antonelli, A. (2020). Linking democracy and biodiversity conservation: Empirical evidence and research gaps. *Ambio*, 49(2), 419–433. DOI: 10.1007/s13280-019-01210-0 PMID: 31236785

Sauquet, A. (2014). Exploring the nature of inter-country interactions in the process of ratifying international environmental agreements: The case of the Kyoto Protocol. *Public Choice*, 159(1–2), 141–158. DOI: 10.1007/s11127-012-0033-y

Shahbaz, M., Solarin, S. A., Sbia, R., & Bibi, S. (2015). Does energy intensity contribute to CO_2 emissions? A trivariate analysis in selected African countries. *Ecological Indicators*, 50, 215–224. DOI: 10.1016/j.ecolind.2014.11.007

Shaheen, A., Sheng, J., Arshad, S., Muhammad, H., & Salam, S. (2020). Forecasting the determinants of environmental degradation: A gray modeling approach. *Energy Sources. Part A, Recovery, Utilization, and Environmental Effects*, •••, 1–21. DOI: 10.1080/15567036.2020.1827090

Stern, D. I. (1998). Progress on the environmental Kuznets curve? *Environment and Development Economics*, 3(2), 173–196. DOI: 10.1017/S1355770X98000102

Tumer, E. T. (2019). Institutions and World Income Distribution. *Ekonomik Yaklasim*, 30(113), 43. Advance online publication. DOI: 10.5455/ey.17008

UNDP. (2023). Forests can help us limit climate change – here is how. UNDP Global Climate Promise. 'https://climatepromise.undp.org/news-and-stories/forests-can-help-us-limit-climate-change-here-how' [Online Resource]

Von Stein, J. (2008). The international law and politics of climate change: Ratification of the United Nations framework convention and the Kyoto protocol. *The Journal of Conflict Resolution*, 52(2), 243–268. DOI: 10.1177/0022002707313692

Waheed, R., Chang, D., Sarwar, S., & Chen, W. (2018). Forest, agriculture, renewable energy, and CO2 emission. *Journal of Cleaner Production*, 172, 4231–4238. DOI: 10.1016/j.jclepro.2017.10.287

Wang, Q., Yang, T., & Li, R. (2023). Economic complexity and ecological footprint: The role of energy structure, industrial structure, and labor force. *Journal of Cleaner Production*, 412, 137389. DOI: 10.1016/j.jclepro.2023.137389

Wang, Q., & Zhang, F. (2021). The effects of trade openness on decoupling carbon emissions from economic growth–evidence from 182 countries. *Journal of Cleaner Production*, 279, 123838. DOI: 10.1016/j.jclepro.2020.123838 PMID: 32863606

Wang, X., & Zhou, D. (2021). Spatial agglomeration and driving factors of environmental pollution: A spatial analysis. *Journal of Cleaner Production*, 279, 123839. DOI: 10.1016/j.jclepro.2020.123839

Yamagata, Y., Yang, J., & Galaskiewicz, J. (2017). State power and diffusion processes in the of global environmental treaties, 1981–2008. *International Environmental Agreement: Politics, Law and Economics*, 17(4), 501–529. DOI: 10.1007/s10784-016-9332-y

You, W., & Lv, Z. (2018). Spillover effects of economic globalization on CO2 emissions: A spatial panel approach. *Energy Economics*, 73, 248–257. DOI: 10.1016/j.eneco.2018.05.016

Zhang, Y., Khan, S. A. R., Kumar, A., Golpîra, H., & Sharif, A. (2019). Is tourism really affected by logistical operations and environmental degradation? An empirical study from the perspective of Thailand. *Journal of Cleaner Production*, 227, 158–166. DOI: 10.1016/j.jclepro.2019.04.164

KEY TERMS AND DEFINITIONS

Economic Complexity: A holistic measure that shows how diverse and sophisticated a country's export basket is.

Economic Development: A process of advancing a society's economic, political, and social conditions.

Energy Intensity: The amount of energy required to produce one unit of economic output.

Environmental Degradation: The deterioration of environmental systems, including the depletion of natural resources, water and air pollution, and the extinction of wildlife.

Institutions: A set of rules and constraints that form incentive mechanisms and shape the nature of human interactions in social, political, and economic areas.

Trade Freedom: A measure that assesses the freedom to trade internationally. The term accounts for trade restrictions, including tariffs, quotas, hidden administrative barriers, and controls on exchange rates and capital movement.

Trade Openness: A measure that evaluates the extent to which a country engages in international trade.

Chapter 17
Green Industrial Policies and Sustainable Economy Approaches Ensuring Industrial Growth and Environmental Balance

Tuğba Koyuncu Çakmak
https://orcid.org/0000-0002-2721-1313
İstanbul Esenyurt University, Turkey

ABSTRACT

The aim of this chapter is to analyses the effects of industrial growth on environmental degradation in terms of green industrial policies. The relationship between environmental pollution and economic growth has been explained from two different perspectives. The first approach points to the existence of a potential duality between economic growth and environmental protection and the existence of a trade-off relationship in terms of achieving economic growth or reducing environmental pollution. The second approach claims that the negative impact of economic growth on environmental pollution can be corrected by green industrial policies. Numerous empirical studies and country-level data in the literature suggest that economic growth also stimulates the development of sustainable technologies and innovations that can enhance environmental protection. Recent evidence, especially from developed countries, shows that there is a decoupling between environmental pollution and economic growth, and, thanks to green industry policy measures, between economic growth and emissions. This draws attention to the fact that while economic growth increases thanks to green policy measures, environmental pollution decreases at the same time. Therefore, it is pointed out that it is possible to reduce carbon emissions

DOI: 10.4018/979-8-3693-5508-4.ch017

Copyright © 2025, IGI Global. Copying or distributing in print or electronic forms without written permission of IGI Global is prohibited.

without compromising economic growth. Therefore, it is very important for policy makers and decision makers to support green industrial policies in the fight against climate change and global warming.

1. INTRODUCTION

Industrialization has played a critical role in the economic and social development of modern societies. However, especially in the 1990s and afterwards, the negative effects of industrialization on environmental pollution have become increasingly important and have been studied by many researchers. Industrialization may also lead to problems such as depletion of natural resources, environmental pollution and climate change, which may cause deterioration of the environmental balance. Therefore, the concepts of sustainable industrialization and environmental sustainability aim to prevent environmental degradation while ensuring industrial growth. For this reason, the phenomenon of "sustainable industrialization" has recently started to take place increasingly in the environment-economy literature. Sustainable industrialization refers to the realization of industrial activities in accordance with the principle of sustainability in environmental, economic and social dimensions. Sustainable industrialization aims to ensure sustainable use of natural resources, reduce environmental pollution and increase social welfare. Along with industrial growth, a balance needs to be established between environmental protection and conservation of natural resources.

Balancing the environmental impacts of industrial growth faces several challenges. First, there is the potential dichotomy between economic growth and environmental protection. This implies that countries or economic communities have a trade-off relationship in terms of achieving economic growth or reducing environmental pollution. The environmental literature shows that there is a positive relationship between economic growth and environmental degradation, but this relationship becomes negative after countries reach a certain level of prosperity. In other words, the growth of industry can often lead to overuse of natural resources and environmental pollution. However, economic growth can also stimulate the development of environmental technologies and innovations, which can increase environmental protection. Moreover, recent evidence from EU countries and some developed countries shows that there is a decoupling between environmental pollution and economic growth through environmentally sound policy measures taken. That is, green policy measures increase economic growth while at the same time reducing environmental pollution. This makes it possible to reduce carbon emissions without compromising economic growth. As the level of development of countries increases, green industrialisation and the increase in the share of the service sector in GDP are also effective in the decrease in environmental damage. In addition to the transition to green industry, green technology and innovation, the decrease in the share of the industrial sector in GDP and the increase in the service sector are also very effective in reducing carbon emissions.

Secondly, the long-term environmental costs of short-term economic gains may be ignored. While many industrial activities may provide immediate profitability, they may cause environmental damage in the long run. Therefore, sustainable industrialization strategies aim to integrate the principle of sustainability into economic decision-making processes. Thirdly, policy uncertainties at national and international level can hinder sustainable industrialization. Incompatibilities between the environmental standards and policies of different countries can make it difficult for industries to comply with environmental regulations and hinder the achievement of environmental balance. Green industrial policies and strategies are important tools used to promote sustainable production practices and reduce the environmental impact of industries. Many of these policies include environmental regulations, tax incentives, subsidies and R&D investments in environmentally friendly technologies. For example, many countries offer incentives to industries to improve their environmental performance. These incentives support projects to increase energy efficiency and reduce waste and emissions, thereby reducing environmental costs and promoting economic benefits. In addition, R&D investments in green technologies are also an important way to support sustainable industrialization. Government-funded R&D programs encourage the development of environmentally friendly technologies and provide innovative solutions to reduce the environmental impact of industry.

This chapter addresses the concepts of sustainable industrialization and environmental sustainability, focusing on the challenges of achieving a balance between industrial growth and environmental protection. The aim of this chapter is firstly to examine the trade-off between economic growth and environmental pollution and to explain alternative ways of achieving this balance. It also discusses how green industrial policies and strategies promote sustainable production practices and contribute to resource efficiency and waste reduction in industries. Moreover, it discusses how sustainable economy approaches can be applied in industries and how they enable more efficient utilization of resources. Considering the environmental impacts of industrial activities, it is evaluated in terms of the ecological footprint concept. Factors such as industrial production processes, energy consumption, water use, waste generation and carbon emissions play an important role in environmental sustainability. Reducing these negative impacts is one of the main objectives of sustainable industrialization. On the other hand, sustainable production practices and technologies are an important tool to reduce the environmental impacts of industrial activities. Therefore, sustainable production practices and technologies such as energy efficiency, waste reduction, recycling and renewable energy use play an important role in achieving sustainable production targets. In addition, green industrial policies and strategies are another factor aiming to reduce the environmental impacts of industrial activities. These policies include environmental regulations, tax incentives, subsidies and R&D investments in environmentally friendly technologies. Effective implementation of green industrial policies plays an important role in ensuring sustainable industrialization.

2. INDUSTRIAL DEVELOPMENT AND ENVIRONMENTAL DEGRADATION: THE ROLE OF CARBON EMISSIONS

Increases in carbon emissions reduce air quality and cause environmental degradation. Energy consumption resulting from the use of fossil fuels and economic activities lacking environmental sensitivity lead to the accumulation of greenhouse gas emissions (GHG) in the atmosphere, causing air pollution and consequently global warming and climate change. Greenhouse gas emissions into the atmosphere (Carbon dioxide: CO_2, Methane: CH_4, Nitrous Oxide: N_2O, Hydrofluoride carbons: $HFCs$, Perfluoro carbons: $PFCs$, Sulphurhexa fluoride: SF_6) have an important share among the factors causing air pollution. Among the greenhouse gas emissions into the atmosphere, the share of carbon dioxide emissions is quite high. The IPCC (2023) report shows that global warming triggered by greenhouse gas emissions is 1.5 °C above pre-industrial levels (Calvin et al., 2023). This situation underlines the urgency and importance of the measures needed to combat climate change and environmental degradation.

Global CO_2 emissions have followed a continuously increasing trend up to the present, according to the NASA (2024) data in Figure 1. It is noteworthy that this rate of increase has gained momentum especially after the 1990s. The fact that the increase in emissions causes global warming and reduces air quality has led many researchers in the environmental and economic literature to focus on identifying economic activities that cause carbon emissions. The Kuznets curve (1955) hypothesis, which claims that there is an 'inverted U' shaped relationship between GDP and income inequality, has been revised in terms of environmental degradation and the relationship between CO_2 emissions and GDP has been empirically tested. The Environmental Kuznets Curve (EKC) developed by (Grossman & Krueger, 1991) claims that there is an inverted U-shaped relationship between economic growth (GDP) and environmental pollution (CO_2), that is, economic growth will increase CO_2 emissions until countries reach a certain level of prosperity, but after this level of prosperity, CO_2 emissions will decrease with environmentally sensitive policy measures and technological developments.

Figure 1. Change in world CO_2 emission by period of 1958/3- 2024/3

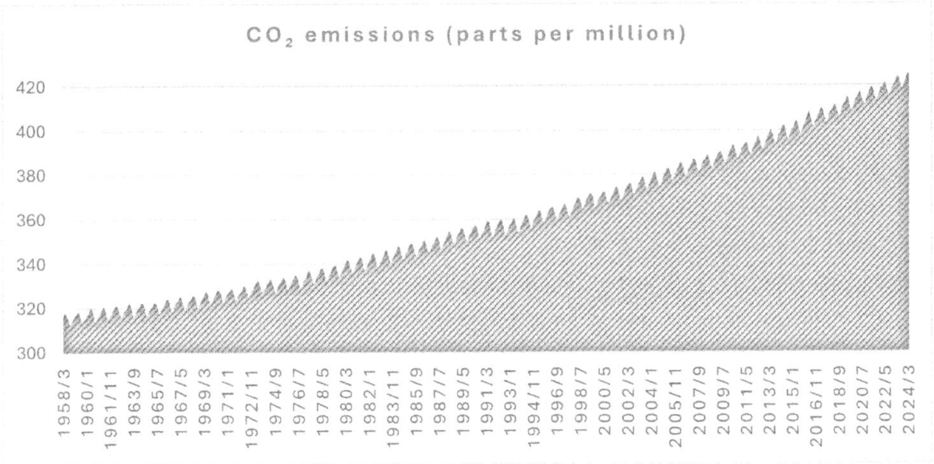

Source: *NASA, 2024*

Empirical studies show that increases in gross domestic product, hence economic growth, have a positive effect on CO_2 emissions (Leitão et al., 2022); (de Bruyn et al., 1998); (Jiang et al., 2019); (He et al., 2014). (Sharma et al., 2021), who investigated the effect of changes in GDP per capita on CO_2 emissions in South and Southeast Asian countries over the period 1976-2015, found that increases in GDP cause environmental degradation, but the square of GDP is negatively related to CO_2 emissions. This evidence suggests that after reaching the turning point of economic growth, environmental degradation will decrease in South and South-East Asian countries. In the study investigating the relationship between coal consumption, industrial production and CO_2 emissions in China and India for the period 1971-2011, empirical findings show that there is an inverted U-shaped relationship between industrial production and CO_2 emissions for India, while it cannot be accepted in China (Shahbaz vd., 2015). On the other hand, the impact of economic growth on industrial pollution in Mediterranean countries has been investigated in three groups with different human development indices: European, Euro-Asian and African-Mediterranean countries. Considering several relevant human development variables such as health effects, political rights, civil liberties, civil liberties, schooling rate and adult literacy rate, the impact of increases in welfare and industrial development on environmental degradation is analyzed. The results show that while Northern Mediterranean countries show improvements in terms of industrial pollution, environmental degradation increases in Southern Mediterranean countries where human development indicators are weak (Gürlük, 2009). These findings supported that environmental pollution resulting from industrial activities is successful in reducing pollution intensity through strict environmental regulations (Cole, 2004). However, for industrialization-induced air quality deterioration, it is important to implement strict industrialization development strategies to reduce emissions depending on economic growth (Zafar et al., 2020). On the other hand, evidence on the decoupling of greenhouse gas (GHG) emissions and economic growth from developed countries, especially the European Union (EU) countries, which have recently implemented rigid environmental policies to combat fossil fuel use and environmental pollution, is promising for combating global warming and climate change above 1.5 °C.

(Papież et al., 2021); (Naqvi, 2021); (Madaleno & Moutinho, 2018); (Karmellos et al., 2021), observed in their studies that there is a decoupling between GHG emissions and economic growth in EU countries, and while economic growth increased in EU countries during the periods examined, significant reductions in GHG emissions were observed gradually, especially in the years after the Kyoto commitment came into force. This decoupling accelerated after 2005, when the EU adopted a stringent energy policy to reduce the use of fossil fuel-based energy. This evidence shows that emissions can be reduced through environmentally sound policy measures while at the same time ensuring industrial production and economic growth. These are promising findings in the fight against global warming and climate change in line with the Sustainable Development Goals (SDGs) to reduce warming above 1.5 °C.

3. ECOLOGICAL FOOTPRINT AND ENVIRONMENTAL CHANGE: HOW IS THE BALANCE OF NATURE BEING DISTURBED?

CO2 emissions and greenhouse gas emissions have been used in many empirical studies in the past and present to represent environmental pollution. However, these variables are not sufficient to represent the entirety of environmental degradation. Because carbon dioxide and other greenhouse gas emissions reflect air pollution. Considering that deterioration in air quality has a significant contribution to global warming and climate change, it cannot be said that it is wrong to use carbon dioxide and other greenhouse gas emissions as a variable representing environmental pollution. However, the ecological footprint provides data on environmental pollution, including emissions, which determine how much burden the consumption habits and lifestyles of a particular country or community place on nature. The ecological footprint consists of Built-up Land footprint, Carbon footprint, Cropland footprint, Fishing Grounds footprint, Forest Products footprint and Grazing Land footprint (Global Footprint Network, 2024). The carbon footprint created by carbon emissions resulting from the combustion of fossil fuels makes a significant contribution to the ecological footprint. As a result of the combustion of fossil fuels, a large amount of carbon dioxide is released into the atmosphere, causing global warming and climate change with the effect of greenhouse gas emissions. For this reason, the ecological footprint better represents the environmental degradation caused by the production and consumption activities of a society or population in direct relation to climate change and global warming.

Figure 2. Ecological footprint and change in biological capacity in the world from 1961 to 2022

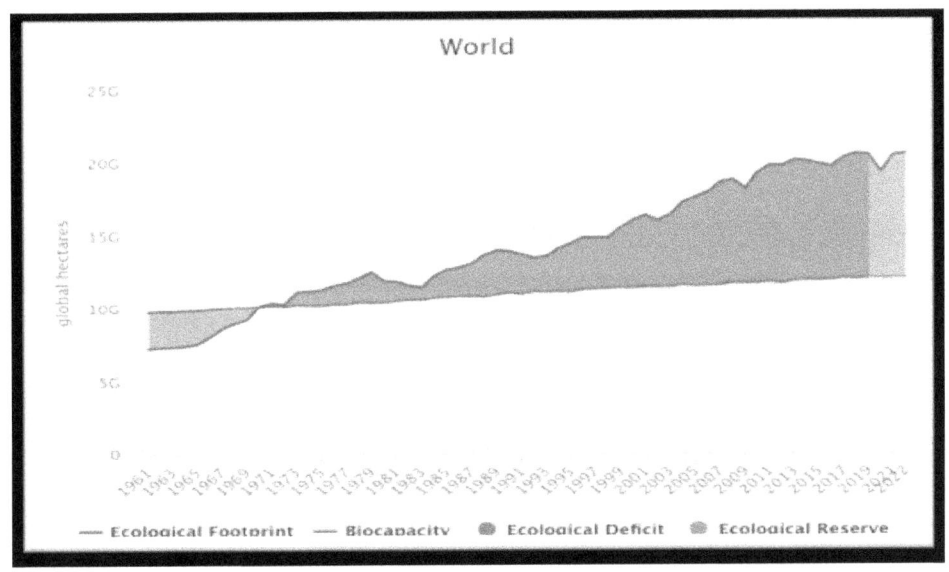

Source: *Global Footprint Network, 2024*

Figure 2 shows the change in ecological footprint and biological capacity in the world from 1961 to 2022. According to these current data obtained from the Global Footprint Network, it is observed that the biological capacity has decreased worldwide, especially after the 1970s, and the ecological deficit continues to increase rapidly with the increase in the ecological footprint. Figure 3 shows the status of ecological deficit and reserves according to countries. It is seen that the ecological footprint is intense especially in developed and developing countries where industrial activities are intense. This situation draws attention to the importance of environmental strategies in combating climate change and global warming.

Figure 3. Ecological deficit/reserve status by country in the world

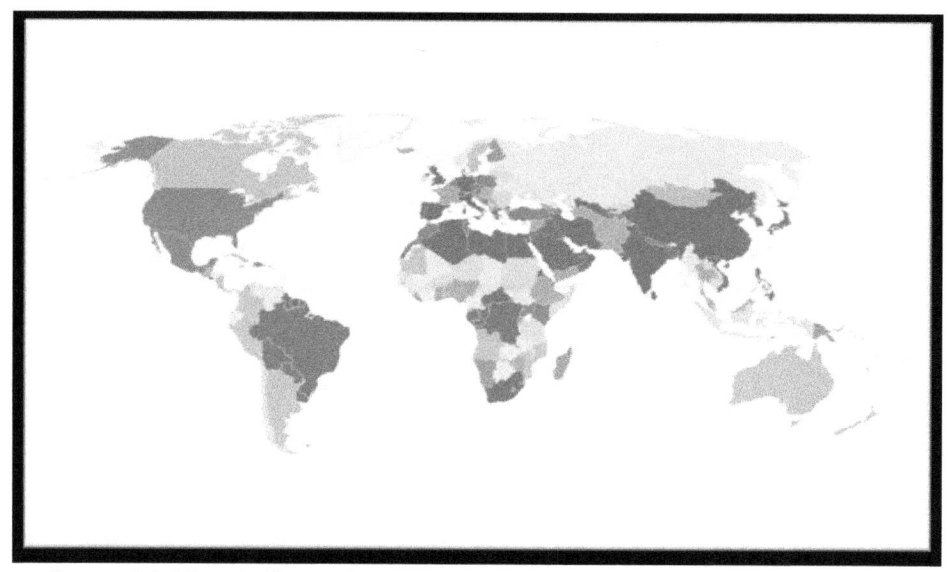

Source: *Global Footprint Network, 2024*

Recent evidence from the environmental economics literature suggests that the ecological footprint represents environmental degradation more comprehensively. (Destek & Sarkodie, 2019) investigated the relationship between economic growth and ecological footprint in 11 newly industrialized countries and found that there is an inverted U-shaped relationship between economic growth and ecological footprint. These results support the EKC hypothesis in terms of ecological footprint representing environmental pollution. Evidence from Turkey for the period 1990-2015 in the study by (Koyuncu et al., 2021), from Thailand for the period 1975Q1-2018Q4 in the study by (Adebayo et al., 2024) and from China for the period 1960-2019 in the study by (Magazzino, 2024) show that economic growth triggers ecological footprint and thus environmental degradation. Excessive consumption of natural resources as a result of industrial activities causes environmental degradation. Therefore, while realizing economic growth and production activities, environmental sustainability strategies in the consumption of natural resources are important for policy makers and researchers (Amer et al., 2024).

4. ENERGY CONSUMPTION AND ENVIRONMENTAL POLLUTION: ENERGY USE FROM RENEWABLE AND FOSSIL FUEL CONSUMPTION

The demand for energy is increasing rapidly every day, driven by the world's growing population, economic growth and technological development. Especially in various industrial production sectors such as steel, chemistry, cement, automotive and textile, there is a high demand for heat and electrical energy up to 1500 °C - 2000 °C in the process of processing raw materials into commercial products. Depending on these energy-intensive industrial production activities, energy consumption, especially from fossil fuels, is among the important factors causing environmental pollution. (Sumaira & Siddique, 2023) analyzed the impact of industrialization and fossil fuel-based energy consumption on environmental degradation in South Asian countries for the period 1984-2016. Unfortunately, the findings show that there is a long run cointegration between industrialization, energy consumption and environmental pollution and that industrialization and energy consumption are the causes of pollution. In addition, the importance of policies for the development of energy efficient technologies in the industrial sector was emphasized. On the other hand, (Miao et al., 2020) investigated the effects of energy consumption and environmental pollution on the technological innovation performance of industrial enterprises in China for the years 2009-2016. Empirical findings show that technological innovation and increasing energy efficiency of industrial enterprises have a significant driving effect on reducing emissions. These results also support the findings of the study by (Sumaira & Siddique, 2023). In addition to these technological developments that provide energy efficiency, the use of alternative renewable energy sources also has an important share in reducing carbon emissions and environmental pollution.

(Simionescu, 2024) investigated the impact of renewable energy consumption on environmental pollution in Poland, Czech Republic, Hungary and Slovakia in the period 1996-2022 and found that the consumption of renewable energy sources reduces carbon dioxide emissions. Moreover, (Kongkuah, 2024), who examined the impact of both the consumption of renewable energy sources and fossil fuel-based energy consumption on environmental degradation, found that there is a negative relationship between renewable energy consumption and ecological footprint, while non-renewable energy consumption has a positive effect on ecological footprint. These results clearly show that renewable energy improves the quality of the environment, while non-renewable energy consumption deteriorates the quality of the environment. Moreover, it is claimed that there may be a decoupling between CO_2 emissions and economic growth through green industrial policies and sustainable economic growth approaches. According to this view, while economic growth will continue to increase thanks to technological developments and green industrial policies, it is thought that greenhouse gas emissions that cause deterioration in environmental quality will decrease at the same time.

(Jiang et al., 2019) examined the relationship between economic growth and CO_2 emissions in China between 1995 and 2014 and emphasized that there is a weak decoupling effect between economic growth and CO_2 emissions, and that renewable energy use and low-carbon technical advances are effective in this result. (Chen et al., 2020) investigated whether there is a decoupling between energy consumption and economic growth in 89 countries in 2000-2016 and concluded that there is a strong decoupling in 18 countries. On the other hand, (Karmellos vd., 2021) investigated the decoupling effect between CO_2 emissions and economic growth in EU-27 countries for the period 2013-2018, (Dai et al., 2016) in BRICS (Brazil, Russia, India, China and South Africa) countries for the period 1995-2014. It was found that there is a strong decoupling between CO_2 emissions and economic growth in EU-27 countries, while there is a weak decoupling in BRICS countries. This empirical evidence from developed (EU-27) and developing (BRICS) countries shows that with the increase in the level of prosperity, it is possible to correct the deterioration in the environmental quality of green industrial policies taken in the fight against climate change and global warming. In addition, fossil fuel-based energy production and use hinder decoupling with economic growth, while renewable energy consumption promotes decoupling (Zhou et al., 2024); (Wang & Kim, 2024).

Figure 4. According to periods of 1990-2022 change in per capita CO_2 emissions and GDP

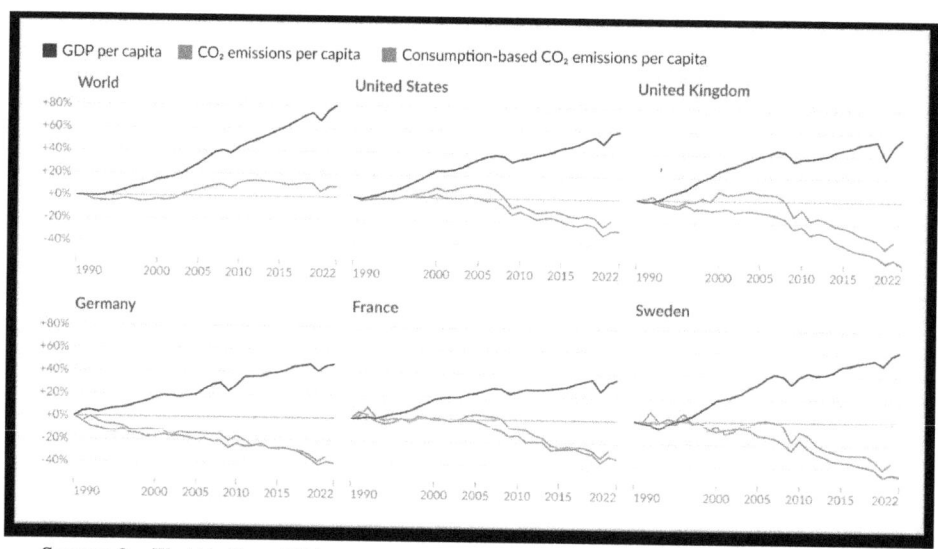

Source: *Our World in Data, 2024*

Figure 4 shows the change in CO_2 emissions per capita and Gross Domestic Product per capita in some developed countries and the world between 1990-2022. According to this graph, while decoupling is observed in the USA after 2010, it is observed that the UK, France, Germany and Switzerland have entered the process of decoupling since the 2000s. The implementation of the decisions taken in the Kyoto Protocol (1997) by the EU countries in reducing CO_2 emissions and environmental degradation without compromising economic growth for sustainable development and combating climate change is critical in ensuring this decoupling.

5. DISCUSSION AND CONCLUSION

The fight against global warming and climate change is an issue that has attracted attention especially after the 1990s due to the increasing negative impact of industrialization on the deterioration of environmental quality. Numerous studies in the literature provide empirical evidence that non-renewable energy consumption and economic growth deteriorate environmental quality. The environmental and economic literature suggests that increases in GDP exacerbate environmental pollution. However, contrary to this, recent evidence suggests that there may be a decoupling between environmental pollution and economic growth.

This section analyses the effects of industrial growth on environmental degradation. Two different perspectives on the relationship between environmental pollution and economic growth are explained, supported by qualified empirical studies in the literature. According to the first approach, there is a potential duality between economic growth and environmental protection. This means that countries have a trade-off relationship in terms of achieving economic growth or reducing environmental pollution. In other words, there is a positive relationship between economic growth and environmental degradation. The amount of greenhouse gas emissions increases due to excessive and uncontrolled use of natural resources. The second approach supports the negative impact of economic growth on environmental pollution, but argues that this negative impact can be corrected by green industrial policies. In addition, economic growth can also stimulate the development of environmental technologies and innovations that can increase environmental protection. Recent evidence, especially from EU countries and some developed countries, shows that there is a decoupling between environmental pollution and economic growth, and between economic growth and emissions, thanks to green industrial policy measures. That is, green policy measures increase economic growth while at the same time reducing environmental pollution. This implies that it is possible to reduce carbon emissions without compromising economic growth.

The green industrial growth policy measures taken in the Kyoto Protocol (1997) have led to significant reductions in emissions in EU countries since the 2000s. Therefore, green industrial policies and strategies have improved the deterioration of environmental quality by providing sustainable growth. In addition, resource efficiency and waste minimization in industries should also be supported. On the other hand, sustainable production practices, green energy and industrial policies, technological advances, economic structures and international co-operation are important tools to reduce the environmental impacts of industrial activities. Therefore, sustainable production practices and technologies such as energy efficiency, waste minimization, recycling and renewable energy use play an important role in achieving sustainable production targets. In addition, green industry policies and strategies are another factor aiming to reduce the environmental impacts of industrial activities. These policies include environmental regulations, tax incentives, subsidies and R&D investments in environmentally friendly technologies. Effective implementation of green industrial policies plays an important role in ensuring sustainable industrialization. Therefore, it is important that policy makers and decision makers support green industrial policies in the fight against climate change and global warming.

REFERENCES

Adebayo, T. S., Pata, U. K., & Akadiri, S. S. (2024). A comparison of CO2 emissions, load capacity factor, and ecological footprint for Thailand's environmental sustainability. *Environment, Development and Sustainability*, 26(1), 2203–2223. DOI: 10.1007/s10668-022-02810-9

Amer, E. A. A. A., Meyad, E. M. A., Meyad, A. M., & Mohsin, A. K. M. (2024). The impact of natural resources on environmental degradation: A review of ecological footprint and CO2 emissions as indicators. *Frontiers in Environmental Science*, 12, 1368125. Advance online publication. DOI: 10.3389/fenvs.2024.1368125

Calvin, K., Dasgupta, D., Krinner, G., Mukherji, A., Thorne, P. W., Trisos, C., Romero, J., Aldunce, P., Barrett, K., Blanco, G., Cheung, W. W. L., Connors, S., Denton, F., Diongue-Niang, A., Dodman, D., Garschagen, M., Geden, O., Hayward, B., Jones, C., . . . Péan, C. (2023). *IPCC, 2023: Climate Change 2023: Synthesis Report. Contribution of Working Groups I, II and III to the Sixth Assessment Report of the Intergovernmental Panel on Climate Change [Core Writing Team, H. Lee and J. Romero (eds.)]. IPCC, Geneva, Switzerland.* (First). Intergovernmental Panel on Climate Change (IPCC). DOI: 10.59327/IPCC/AR6-9789291691647

Chen, X., Shuai, C., Zhang, Y., & Wu, Y. (2020). Decomposition of energy consumption and its decoupling with economic growth in the global agricultural industry. *Environmental Impact Assessment Review*, 81, 106364. DOI: 10.1016/j.eiar.2019.106364

Cole, M. A. (2004). Trade, the pollution haven hypothesis and the environmental Kuznets curve: Examining the linkages. *Ecological Economics*, 48(1), 71–81. DOI: 10.1016/j.ecolecon.2003.09.007

Dai, S., Zhang, M., & Huang, W. (2016). Decomposing the decoupling of CO2 emission from economic growth in BRICS countries. *Natural Hazards*, 84(2), 1055–1073. DOI: 10.1007/s11069-016-2472-0

de Bruyn, S. M., van den Bergh, J. C. J. M., & Opschoor, J. B. (1998). Economic growth and emissions: Reconsidering the empirical basis of environmental Kuznets curves. *Ecological Economics*, 25(2), 161–175. DOI: 10.1016/S0921-8009(97)00178-X

Destek, M. A., & Sarkodie, S. A. (2019). Investigation of environmental Kuznets curve for ecological footprint: The role of energy and financial development. *The Science of the Total Environment*, 650, 2483–2489. DOI: 10.1016/j.scitotenv.2018.10.017 PMID: 30293003

Grossman, G. M., & Krueger, A. B. (1991). *Environmental Impacts of a North American Free Trade Agreement* (Working Paper 3914). National Bureau of Economic Research. DOI: 10.3386/w3914

Gürlük, S. (2009). Economic growth, industrial pollution and human development in the Mediterranean Region. *Ecological Economics*, 68(8), 2327–2335. DOI: 10.1016/j.ecolecon.2009.03.001

He, C., Huang, Z., & Ye, X. (2014). Spatial heterogeneity of economic development and industrial pollution in urban China. *Stochastic Environmental Research and Risk Assessment*, 28(4), 767–781. DOI: 10.1007/s00477-013-0736-8

Jiang, J.-J., Ye, B., Zhou, N., & Zhang, X.-L. (2019). Decoupling analysis and environmental Kuznets curve modelling of provincial-level CO2 emissions and economic growth in China: A case study. *Journal of Cleaner Production*, 212, 1242–1255. DOI: 10.1016/j.jclepro.2018.12.116

Karmellos, M., Kosmadakis, V., Dimas, P., Tsakanikas, A., Fylaktos, N., Taliotis, C., & Zachariadis, T. (2021). A decomposition and decoupling analysis of carbon dioxide emissions from electricity generation: Evidence from the EU-27 and the UK. *Energy*, 231, 120861. DOI: 10.1016/j.energy.2021.120861

Kongkuah, M. (2024). Impact of Belt and Road countries' renewable and non-renewable energy consumption on ecological footprint. *Environment, Development and Sustainability*, 26(4), 8709–8734. DOI: 10.1007/s10668-023-03068-5

Koyuncu, T., Beşer, M. K., & Alola, A. A. (2021). Environmental sustainability statement of economic regimes with energy intensity and urbanization in Turkey: A threshold regression approach. *Environmental Science and Pollution Research International*, 28(31), 42533–42546. DOI: 10.1007/s11356-021-13686-z PMID: 33813705

Kuznets, S. (1955). Economic Growth and Income Inequality. *The American Economic Review*, 45(1), 1–28.

Leitão, J., Ferreira, J., & Santibanez-González, E. (2022). New insights into decoupling economic growth, technological progress and carbon dioxide emissions: Evidence from 40 countries. *Technological Forecasting and Social Change*, 174, 121250. DOI: 10.1016/j.techfore.2021.121250

Madaleno, M., & Moutinho, V. (2018). Effects decomposition: Separation of carbon emissions decoupling and decoupling effort in aggregated EU-15. *Environment, Development and Sustainability*, 20(1), 181–198. DOI: 10.1007/s10668-018-0238-4

Magazzino, C. (2024). Ecological footprint, electricity consumption, and economic growth in China: Geopolitical risk and natural resources governance. *Empirical Economics*, 66(1), 1–25. DOI: 10.1007/s00181-023-02460-4

Miao, C., Meng, X., Duan, M., & Wu, X. (2020). Energy consumption, environmental pollution, and technological innovation efficiency: Taking industrial enterprises in China as empirical analysis object. *Environmental Science and Pollution Research International*, 27(27), 34147–34157. DOI: 10.1007/s11356-020-09537-y PMID: 32557046

Naqvi, A. (2021). Decoupling trends of emissions across EU regions and the role of environmental policies. *Journal of Cleaner Production*, 323, 129130. DOI: 10.1016/j.jclepro.2021.129130

Papież, M., Śmiech, S., & Frodyma, K. (2021). The role of energy policy on the decoupling processes in the European Union countries. *Journal of Cleaner Production*, 318, 128484. DOI: 10.1016/j.jclepro.2021.128484

Shahbaz, M., Farhani, S., & Ozturk, I. (2015). Do coal consumption and industrial development increase environmental degradation in China and India? *Environmental Science and Pollution Research International*, 22(5), 3895–3907. DOI: 10.1007/s11356-014-3613-1 PMID: 25277709

Sharma, R., Shahbaz, M., Kautish, P., & Vo, X. V. (2021). Does energy consumption reinforce environmental pollution? Evidence from emerging Asian economies. *Journal of Environmental Management*, 297, 113272. DOI: 10.1016/j.jenvman.2021.113272 PMID: 34280860

Simionescu, M. (2024). Pollution and renewable energy consumption in the V4 countries. *Environmental Science and Pollution Research International*, 31(2), 1954–1963. DOI: 10.1007/s11356-023-31223-y PMID: 38049692

Sumaira, & Siddique, H. M. A. (2023). Industrialization, energy consumption, and environmental pollution: Evidence from South Asia. *Environmental Science and Pollution Research*, 30(2), 4094-4102. DOI: 10.1007/s11356-022-22317-0

Wang, Z., & Kim, M.-K. (2024). Decoupling of CO2 emissions and income in the U.S.: A new look from EKC. *Climatic Change*, 177(3), 52. DOI: 10.1007/s10584-024-03706-5

Zafar, A., Ullah, S., Majeed, M. T., & Yasmeen, R. (2020). Environmental pollution in Asian economies: Does the industrialisation matter? *OPEC Energy Review*, 44(3), 227–248. DOI: 10.1111/opec.12181

Zhou, Z., Zeng, C., Li, K., Yang, Y., Zhao, K., & Wang, Z. (2024). Decomposition of the decoupling between electricity CO2 emissions and economic growth: A production and consumption perspective. *Energy*, 293, 130644. DOI: 10.1016/j.energy.2024.130644

KEY TERMS AND DEFINITIONS

Carbon Emissions: The term refers to carbon-based gases released into the atmosphere, in particular carbon dioxide (CO_2) and carbon monoxide (CO).
Climate Change: It is a term that refers to global warming and changes in the world's climate system.
Environmental Pollution: It is a term that refers to the pollution of natural resources such as air, water, soil and the damage to ecosystems due to human activities.
Green Growth: It is a concept used to describe sustainable economic growth and ways to prevent environmental pollution.
Industrial Growth: It is a term that refers to the growth and expansion of sectors of an economy such as manufacturing, mining, construction, energy production, more production capacity, application of new technologies, increase in labour force and increase in economic output.
Renewable Energy: It is the term that refers to the energy obtained from energy sources that are constantly renewed and inexhaustible by nature.
Sustainable Growth: It is a term that refers to ensuring the sustainability of natural resources through the development of technology and innovation while ensuring economic growth.

ENDNOTE

[*] Department of Business Administration, İstanbul Esenyurt University, İstanbul, Turkey, tugbakoyuncu@esenyurt.edu.tr, ORCID: 0000-0002-2721-1313.

Chapter 18
Environmental Policies in Global Economies and Environmental Concern in Regional Sustainable Production:
Environmental Sustainable Production

Aslı Öztopcu
https://orcid.org/0000-0001-6419-2425
Maltepe University, Turkey

ABSTRACT

Today, rapidly growing population, industrialization, and urbanization are causing global environmental problems to become an ever-greater threat. Globally, there is an increasing demand for sustainable development due to issues including air pollution, water resource depletion, biodiversity reduction, and climate change. This chapter looks at how regionally implemented environmental policies contribute to the global economies' sustainable development objectives. With examples from projects in developed and developing countries, this article tries to understand the environmental policies and practices implemented for sustainable development. The findings demonstrate that international cooperation is necessary to ensure the world's sustainability. Nonetheless, a significant determinant of the sufficiency of efforts is a nation's degree of social and economic development. The outputs of

DOI: 10.4018/979-8-3693-5508-4.ch018

Copyright © 2025, IGI Global. Copying or distributing in print or electronic forms without written permission of IGI Global is prohibited.

this study can provide insights into regional environmental problems, cooperation against environmental risks, and the global implications of advances in environmental sustainability.

INTRODUCTION

Developing countries were aiming for rapid and stable growth to reach the level of development of developed countries. Yet economic development ignored the alternative costs of economic growth, such as protecting the natural environment and natural resources, preventing pollution, and providing clean water and food. The need to leave a habitable environment for future generations then added these strategies. New growth and development strategies started to emerge within the historical process. Ultimately, the goal of all countries was to improve the conditions for sustainable development.

When we look at the rapid modernization process, we see that countries invested in areas such as education, roads, and communication. From the early 1900s until today, we can say that countries in the global economy have turned towards rapid industrialization. At the same time, export-oriented growth has been one of the policies adopted by many countries. Since the 1960s, countries such as South Korea, Taiwan, Hong Kong, and Singapore have implemented various incentives and reforms to increase exports and become competitive in the global market. This strategy led to their rapid economic growth. Following the economic changes spearheaded by Deng Xiaoping in 1978, China became more open and embraced an export-led growth model. This made China one of the world's largest economies. Today, many trade partnerships, such those with the EU (European Union), have helped countries grow their economies. However, as countries have focused on increasing production and economic growth, they have faced the destruction of scarce resources. As a result of the world's hegemony over nature in the socio-economic development process and the effort to use nature as if it were an inexhaustible resource, many life-threatening negativities have emerged. Global warming and many related threats have shown that they will make life difficult for future generations. For this reason, production ecology, which includes environmental factors in the new understanding of economic growth, has come to the agenda.

Production has the potential to degrade the environment as well as improve it. Sometimes innovations that lead to an increase in costs are not of interest to firms. This indifference means consuming the environment more quickly. The effects of production can be easily observed, especially in industrial-intensive regions. Therefore, production incentives should focus on industrialization that does not harm the environment. While increasing production to meet human needs today, it should also be able to meet the needs of future generations. Sustainable production will be realized if clean production and environmentally friendly products (recycled products or packaging) are included in production standards. Moreover, regional variations in the economy, environment, and society complicate the use of industrial development strategies. Reduced waste, pollution, and energy use will all directly affect people's quality of life. Different practices are needed to strengthen the link between the environment and the economy, especially in rural areas. In addition, the first step to sustainability is productivity. For productivity, it is important to have accessible raw materials, improved working conditions, the elimination of wage inequalities, and high technology. Today, many companies do not have these conditions. In this context, production is also not sustainable.

Sustainable development refers to social, economic, and cultural importance in terms of society and ecological importance in terms of natural resources. This study aims to examine the macroeconomic impact of sustainable regional development activities. Although there are many studies on the subject in the literature, there are not many studies that examine the relationship between production and the environment at the regional level. For example, Kahramanoğlu et al. investigated the relationship between regional ecology and production index through the example of Perm region, one of the industrial centers of the Russian Federation. The relationship between industrial production and the environment was found to be negative (Kahramanoğlu et al., 2023). Xu & Zhang (2022) also contributed to the literature by showing the importance of the relationship between regional energy economy and environment. Finally, Amasawa et al. (2023) analyzes the link between consumption and production in terms of sustainability. According to the results, there is a need for political will and strong regulators. Although these and similar studies emphasize the relationship between regional production and the environment, they do not reveal its importance at the macro level. In this context, strategies and practices developed to protect the environment and natural resources in regional policies have been investigated. In the first part of the study, the understanding of sustainable development in mainstream economics from growth theories until today has been reviewed. In the second part, the understanding of sustainable regional development is clarified and development policies are emphasized. The last section focuses on examples of regional environmental policies. The outputs of this study provide insights into regional environmental problems, cooperation against environmental risks, and the global implications of advances in environmental sustainability.

FROM PAST TO PRESENT IN THE PERSPECTIVE OF SUSTAINABLE DEVELOPMENT

In the early 19th century, we could not talk much about sustainable development as countries preferred industrial-oriented growth. According to the invisible hand theory of classical economists, it was assumed that natural resources would replenish themselves or even not be depleted, but this was not possible. In a world that focuses only on growth, we have a global problem. With the forecast of the impending climate catastrophe, the idea of sustainability entered our lives. Throughout economic history, the importance of sustainable development policies has increased, especially in the middle of the 20th century. In this situation, we have to deal with the depletion of our limited resources due to irrational production and consumption practices. This is the danger of the destruction of future lives. This concern requires global cooperation to achieve sustainable environmental conditions.

The first movement that comes to mind about sustainable development was the United Nations conference in Stockholm (Switzerland) in 1972. The conference aimed to attract the attention of countries to raise environmental awareness with the phrase "Only One Earth" (UN, 2024). In 1974, in Cocoyoc (Mexico), UNEP and UNCTAD (United Nations Organization for Trade Agreements) discussed the use of resources (UN Environment Programme, 1974). A year later, the Mediterranean Action Plan (1975) brought together Mediterranean neighboring countries for cooperation. In 1976, at the United Nations Conference on Human Settlements (Habibat) in Vancouver, talks persisted (UN, 1972). The relationship between the environment and development took on a worldwide scope with the publication of the Brundtland Report in 1987, starting in 1982.

The 1992 Earth Summit and the 1992 UN Conference on Environment and Development in Rio helped to increase awareness of the significance of international collaboration (UNCED, 1992). The "Framework on Climate Change" was decided upon during this conference. Sustainable development and housing issues were linked during the 1996 Istanbul, Turkey-hosted second United Nations Conference on Human Settlements (Habitat II). Kyoto, Japan, established goals in 1997 to lower greenhouse gas emissions. In a similar vein, New York reexamined its framework of roles related to sustainable development.

The Millennium Declaration was endorsed at the United Nations Millennium Summit (2000), with 147 countries joining 187 member states (UN, 2024). The United Nations Summit on Sustainable Development took place in Johannesburg, South Africa, in 2002. Reorganized in 2012, the Rio Conference was finalized as a development blueprint. The idea of a global green economy was first presented during this meeting in 2012. The Green New Deal program in the US prioritized energy efficiency, clean energy investments, and sustainable infrastructure (Markey & Ocasio-Cortez, 2019). As a follow-up, the Agenda 2030 SDGs (Sustainable Development Goals) were adopted in New York in 2015. In Europe, the Europen Green Deal, which started in 2019, includes measures such as reducing carbon emissions, circular economy, and protecting biodiversity (European Commission, 2021). In 2020, the Paris Climate Agreement, the successor to the Kyoto Protocol, was signed (UNFCCC, 2020). The focus of this agreement was on greenhouse gas emissions and climate change.

The World Commission on Environment and Development (WCED) defines sustainable development as development that can readily meet the demands of future generations (Bruthland report, 1987). Sustainable development policies are strategies and measures that ensure environmental protection and social equity while ensuring economic growth. Since environmental problems and their harmful effects will restrict daily life, the search for alternative solutions to these problems has begun (Figure 1).

Figure 1. Effects of environmental degradation on life

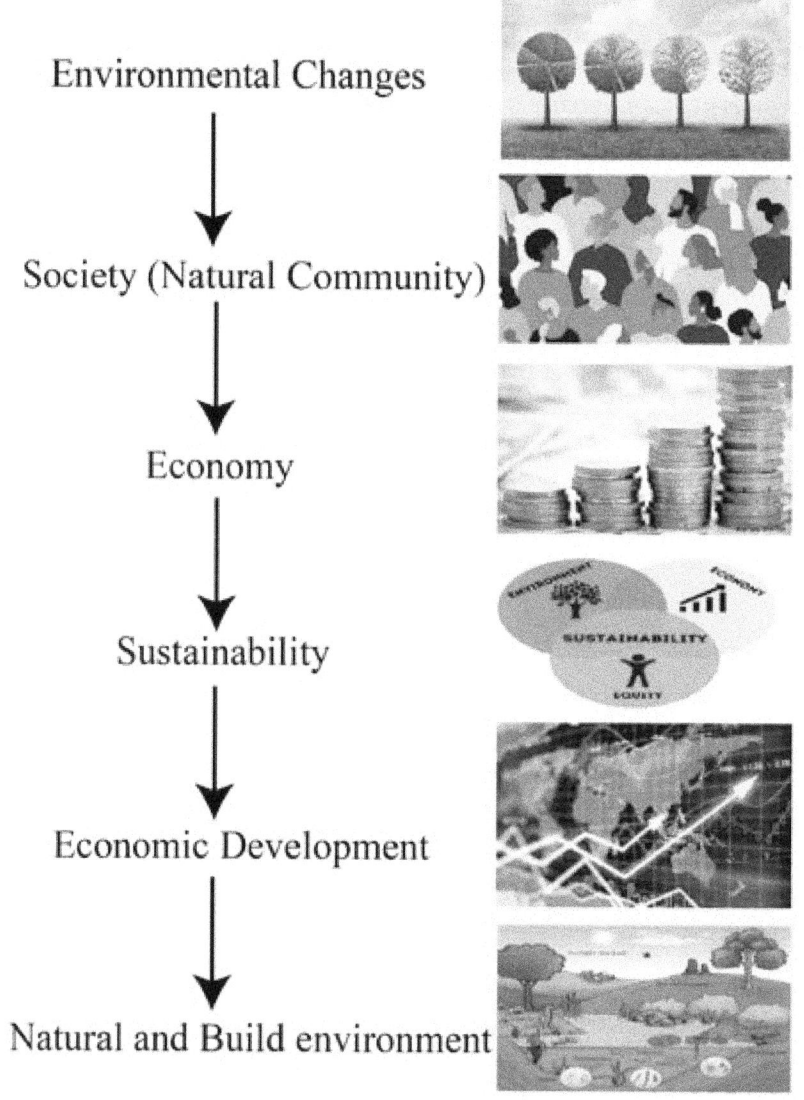

Environmental Changes
↓
Society (Natural Community)
↓
Economy
↓
Sustainability
↓
Economic Development
↓
Natural and Build environment

Source: Zhang et al., (2022). Globalization, Green Economy and Environmental Challenges: State of the Art Review for Practical Implications. Frontiers in Environmental Science, 10.

As can be seen, the movement that started in the 1970s has gradually increased, and projects have been increased to solve the most important global problem today. In this process, concepts such as "Green Economy", "Green Growth", and "Green Chemistry" have started to be used. Different projects are being developed all over the world in the context of the SDGs. Some of these offer short-term solutions, and some offer long-term solutions. For example, in the 1940s, Mexico started to support small farmers through land reform. In the 1980s, China started to increase productivity in the agricultural sector by switching to individual production. As a result, living standards in rural areas began to rise. Similarly, according to the World Bank report, Costa Rica is making significant efforts with sustainable development policies such as renewable energy use, forest protection, and eco-tourism (World Bank, 2020).

Conservation of natural resources at the local level is social capital for low-income people (Turner, 2008). Environmental protection is the sharing of knowledge that can be passed on from generation to generation. This transfer is significantly influenced by the reciprocal relationships that exist between humans and the natural environment (Bhattacharya, 2024). Thus, the emphasis should be on ingraining sustainable local consciousness to fulfill the objectives of sustainable development. Nations' respect for nature, urbanization, the design of living spaces, and the way they protect greenery show their relationship with sustainable development (Harvey, 2009). The purpose of the effort to protect the environment is to ensure that life can continue today and tomorrow in a healthy and safe environment. The task of fulfilling this purpose belongs to human beings. Environmental awareness is a process that continues with family education and school education. The establishment of production and consumption awareness may require more than this. Therefore, we need some rules in our lives. It is obvious that a society with conscious human behavior will provide more benefits to future generations.

Looking at world environmental statistics, it will be easier to understand why this mobility is increasing. For example, 2023 was the hottest year on record. Hurricanes have increased in frequency as ocean temperatures have risen. Living along the coast has become particularly dangerous. The increase in greenhouse gas emissions has resulted in further global warming. The number of disaster-related mortality is also predicted to rise as the number of flood incidents increases. It is predicted that 14.5 million people may die by 2050 due to weather-related causes (Ritchie et al., 2024). In the December 2023 IICEC World Conference on Changing Energy Geopolitics, Climate Crisis & Turkey, it was stated that even under the assumption that all expected measures in the industry are fulfilled, the world needs at least 20 years to recover. These predictions and statistics make it clear that urgent measures must be taken to ensure sustainable living.

Today, the most important issues that sustainable development is usually related to are social, economic and environmental (WCED report, 1987). The social dimension of sustainable development aims to ensure equality and sufficiency in social services such as education, health and justice. It also focuses on issues such as improving the sociocultural structure, gender equality, and removing social barriers (Kaya & Ek, 2021). While the environment refers to the characteristics of physical elements that affect daily life, the social issue addresses both social events and the economy together (Estoque, 2020: 2). The economic dimension is the feasibility and success of the economy, aiming to improve the quality and quantity of society. Reducing risks in the production and consumption process, protecting natural resources and the environment, increasing renewable energies and waste management are the most discussed issues (Kaya & Ek, 2021). Even though this study focuses on the relationship between production and the environment, processes and events have both social and economic consequences.

In the literature, after the second quarter of the twentieth century, the structural deterioration of ecosystems has led economists to focus on the environmental problems. The main objective of the new process called sustainable development is to protect the environment and support economic development. Research on sustainable development is constantly increasing in line with the studies conducted by governments and organizations such as the UN, OECD and the World Bank. We can emphasize some studies in the context of our research topic. Economic policies and sustainable development debate in the context of ecology (Mol, 2002), the importance of green infrastructure in sustainable urban development (Benedict & McMahon, 2006) and the need to accelerate sustainable development due to food shortages, energy crisis, global warming and other natural phenomena (Shi, Han, Yang, & Gao, 2019). For example, bacterial techniques used to clean up oil waste or the production of technologies to produce goods with less environmental impact can have a positive impact on the environment (Alagöz, 2007). In this context, environmental factors need to be addressed in more detail in the context of development.

ENVIRONMENTAL FACTORS IN SUSTAINABLE DEVELOPMENT

Sustainability is one of the mainstream debates of the 21st century. Sustainable development environment and economy and to ensure that the needs of future generations are met without fully depleting natural resources. Therefore, continuity of the process is important (Kaya & Ek, 2021).

Environmental sustainability also provides economic sustainability. In other words, it is thought to carry out studies by focusing on the environment. The factors affecting the sustainability of the environment are industrialization, population growth, and urbanization. Rapid technological change has also been added to these. The first concerns that led to the increase in these studies in recent years have been climate change, reduction of water resources, rapid population growth, and destruction of the ozone layer. The renewal of resources is not immediate. The amount of pollutants is better in this process. Therefore, there should not be enough waste in nature to make renewal difficult. Human health, biodiversity, water, and soil quality, and the relationship between animal-soil-nature should not be disturbed. In addition, due to urbanization, industrialization, and population growth, natural resource consumption is expected to be 60% higher by 2060 than in 2020 (Economic Forum, 2024).

Natural disasters affect all living things, so the problem is spreading faster now. For example, the United Nations' Intergovernmental Panel on Climatic Change (IPCC) said that CO_2 emissions are the principal cause of climate change (2007). The detrimental consequences of external causes, such as increasing traffic and noise, on the environment and people have become apparent. Countries have recognized how natural disasters affect conflict, trade, migration, and consumerism. Conservation of natural resources, preservation of biodiversity, irrigation techniques, protection of surrounding agricultural lands and farms, and protection of natural areas such as seas, streams, and lakes from production wastes have become priority topics of discussion regarding environmental events. They also began to incorporate methods such as lowering CO_2 emissions, regulating trash that causes air pollution, eliminating the use of chemicals that harm the ozone layer, utilizing renewable energy, and reducing the use of fossil fuels in their manufacturing operations.

The ongoing rise in industry is one of the factors contributing to the environment's growing significance in development. Some of the producers see the environment as a repository of waste and garbage. Lack of awareness has caused serious damage to the ecosystem. However, in recent years, there have been new dimensions in the consumption of limited natural resources in production. For example, the global pandemic or the supply problems experienced during Russia's invasion of Ukraine served as a warning about access to resources. Research in this field has revealed the need to re-evaluate production processes. For example, food consumption has emerged as the main cause of ecological footprints (Galli, 2023). This means that people's soil, water, and carbon emissions are much lower than the food they consume. Carbon dioxide in the world has reached its ecological limit. Global warming is leading to rising water levels, increased storms, and coastal erosion. This danger negatively affects everyone, especially the poor (Kaypak, 2011). The economic loss caused by these disasters is constantly increasing.

Figure 2. Economic losses from climate, weather, and water-related disasters between 1970 and 2019

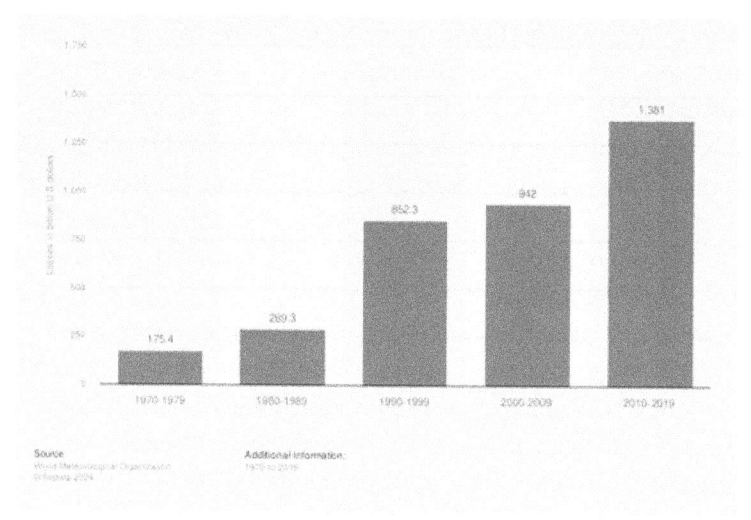

Source: Statisca (2024).

Climate change has resulted in additional expenditures such as lowering greenhouse gas emissions, battling pollution, and greening living environments. These expenditures continue to stymie attempts, particularly in underdeveloped countries. Argentina and Costa Rica, for example, rank high on the sustainability index, whereas Pakistan and Kenya rank worse (Sustainable Development Report, 2023). The EU's environmental protection programs have adopted six fundamental viewpoints. The EU's environmental criteria are enshrined in legislation, such as the free movement of products (Complementarity), the establishment of new environmental protection standards to safeguard the environment, and the implementation of emergency measures to protect the environment even when forecasts are met. Add to taking measures before hazards occur, responding immediately to environmental damage, and prioritizing technologies to reduce pollution.

Thus far, the European Union has been the site of the majority of environmental efforts that meet these requirements (European State of the Climate, 2023). For example, the EU Green Deal and the Farm to Fork Plan are helping to move the EU towards more sustainable food systems and society. Significant statistical data started to emerge on Earth Overshoot Day. The Global Footprint Network sets the agenda for numerous problems. In this way, countries are moving towards making new decisions. When researched on a sectoral basis, we can see that some sectors are rapidly progressing in environmentalist approaches. For example, recent developments in automobile production are making progress in terms of environmentalism.

In sectors such as the paint industry or textiles, however, progress is slower than in the automotive industry. In addition, the impact of environmentalist developments may be reduced in less developed regions. Therefore, it is understood that different practices are needed in sector-intensive regions of a country's economy.

In the literature, there are many studies evaluating the relationship between sustainable development and the environment from various perspectives. Examples of such studies include Faucheux & O'Connor (1998), which analyzes the environmental aspects of sustainable development, Dinda (2004), which explains the relationship between the environment and development, Davies et al. (2015), which examines the contributions of green infrastructure to sustainable living, and Anderson (2019), which explains natural resource management from a sustainable environment perspective.

Increased industrialization meets our needs but can endanger both today and tomorrow. Environmental improvement requires that production conditions and the characteristics of final products are environmentally friendly. Moreover, there are different views on the perception of the environmental quality of products. More regulation may be needed to ensure production with high environmental quality (Palacios-Argüello et al., 2020; Ullah, 2024).

CIRCULAR ECONOMY (CE) AND ENVIRONMENT IN PRODUCTION

Environmental policies in production encompass ideas and procedures designed to lessen the environmental impact of manufacturing processes. These tactics are centered on increasing productivity. If production and consumption continue as they have in the past, the earth's lifespan will shrink. According to the 2023 annual European State of the Climate Report, the continuously increasing temperature has caused many problems (European State of the Climate 2023). In the future, droughts will increase and water will become scarcer, making agriculture increasingly difficult.

The circular economy ensures that resources remain in a continuous cycle by extending the life of products, recycling, and reusing them. In this context, the circular economy provides systems to improve the relationship between production and the environment (Valencia et al., 2023).

Research shows that businesses are eager to establish their ecosystem (Tronvoll et al., 2020). Moreover, these collaborations and other regulations are reflected in the processes of companies (Stabler et al., 2024). The new producer responsibility legislation (EPR) addresses circular practices with features such as material waste, recycling, and recovery (Dong et al., 2021).

Figure 3. Circular economy and waste hierarchy

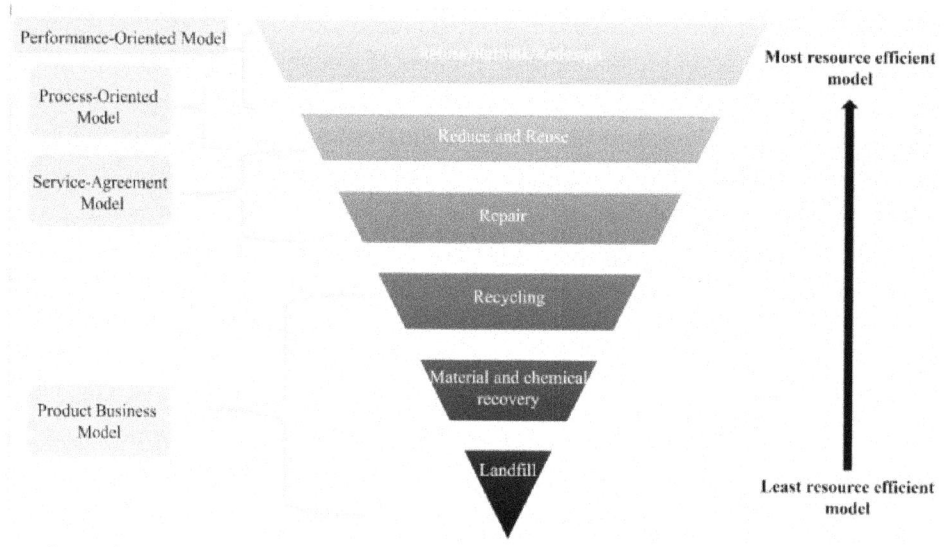

[Figure: Inverted pyramid showing waste hierarchy from top (most resource efficient) to bottom (least resource efficient): Reuse/Refurbish/Redesign, Reduce and Reuse, Repair, Recycling, Material and chemical recovery, Landfill. Left side labels: Performance-Oriented Model, Process-Oriented Model, Service-Agreement Model, Product Business Model.]

Source: Dong et al., 2021; Stabler et al., 2024.

Many performance standards have been developed to ensure that products do not harm the environment. Examples include newly developed product models, new production standards and regulations developed by sector, or the development of new labels to be used for environmental sustainability (Handfield, 2002; Palacios-Argüello, et al., 2020).

In addition to these, in the literature, Şahzeben et al. (2023) evaluated sustainable production and consumption together in circular economy. Kazakova & Lee (2022) focused on creating a circular economy process with supply chain, materials, management and production. Saari et al. (2024) analyzed the issues that determine the inclusion of manufacturing firms in the circular economy matrix. Antonioli et al. (2022). (2022) investigated the evidence of the relationship with the circular economy on an original set of 3000 Italian manufacturing firms.

Circular Economy focuses on reducing environmental footprints. In this context, circular city systems will have reached an environmentally friendly system with the correct and minimum use of materials and energy. To avoid these problems, issues are addressed in the direction of technological and digitalization in existing production techniques (Varriale et al., 2024). Although there are changes in existing initiatives, it is thought that new initiatives will have the strongest connection with the environment (Dean & McMullen, 2007; Jha & Pande, 2024). Sustainable business models in manufacturing and the proliferation of circular supply chains are emphasized (Geissdoerfer et al., 2018). The relationship between production and the environment is evaluated in various categories. These are clean production, industrial symbiosis, green chemistry, and waste management.

Clean Production

Cleaner production refers to operations that limit negative impacts while focusing on resource efficiency. In other words, it prioritizes issues like energy efficiency, water conservation, and waste reduction (Van Berkel 2010). Businesses strive to make products with less waste by utilizing less water, raw materials, energy, and chemicals. In this context, UNIDO (United Nations Industrial Development Organization) and UNEP (United Nations Environment Programme) work with governments, businesses, and other organizations to build National Cleaner Production Centers (NCPC). NCPCs strive to offer four services. The initial step is to disseminate knowledge and raise awareness, followed by expanded training, factory implementation, and policy guidance.

Industrial Symbiosis

Using waste from one business as a source of raw materials for another is known as industrial symbiosis. By doing this, waste production and the requirement for raw materials are both decreased (Chertow, 2000; Demartini et al., 2022). Eco-industrial parks are needed for industrial symbiosis. Because the implementation of this method requires the physical proximity of enterprises and their cooperation. In other words, this method helps companies achieve global results. There are countries in the world that have successfully implemented this system. For example, in Kalundorg (Denmark), partner firms share wastewater, electricity, steam, and water. The results show an increase in environmental and economic efficiency (Grann, 1997; Krugman, 1991). In this business model, industrial symbiosis focuses on extracting value from both sharing and waste. Therefore, one company's waste can meet the input needs of another company.

Various tactics are used to achieve industrial symbiosis. Popular methodologies include Agent Tanbalı, Material Flow Analysis, Network Analysis, and Mixed Integer Linear Programming (Demartini et al., 2022). However, it is also clear that long-term planning is required to adopt these ideas. Although they can be used in any country or sector, eco-industrial parks, in particular, require additional funding.

Green Chemistry

The green chemistry technique, like other approaches, aims to minimize environmental impact while designing processes. Special emphasis is placed on reducing the use of harmful chemicals and utilizing renewable raw materials. Green chemistry is basically based on 12 principles. These are as follows.

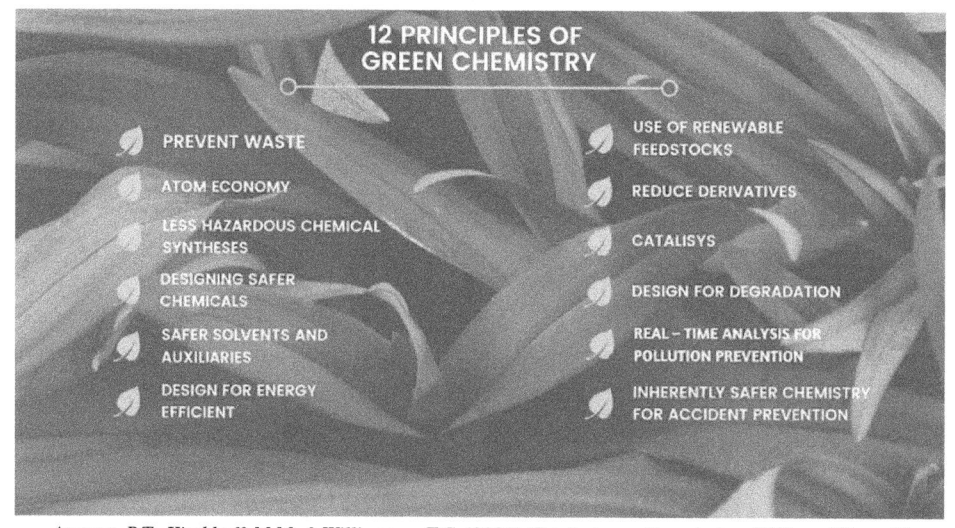

Figure 4. 12 principle of green chemistry

Anastas, P.T., Kirchhoff, M.M. & Williamson, T.C. (2001). Catalysis as a Foundational Pillar of Green Chemistry. Applied Catalysis A: General, 22, pp. 3-13.

The green chemistry approach, like other approaches, focuses on reducing environmental impacts in the design of processes. Particular emphasis is placed on reducing the use of toxic chemicals and using renewable raw materials. In the first place, it works by preventing pollution from occurring. The principles of environmentally friendly chemistry are important for the use of more efficient reactions with non-hazardous starting materials, the use of renewable resources, the conservation of energy and the production of reusable, recyclable or - degradable waste.

Chemical waste, toxic and polluting properties of chemical products, and fossil raw materials make green chemistry mandatory. First of all, it is predicted that there is a need for trained workers in the sector (Etzkorn & Ferguson, 2023). On the other hand, green chemistry practices are needed for the realization of sustainable chemistry. In this approach, the use of green chemistry, raw material processing, production process, and economy will also be included. In this way, a holistic picture can be seen (Martínez et al., 2022).

Priority issues for green chemistry in the industrial field include energy sustainability, resource footprint efficiency, product toxicity, and recycling. For example, it is important to reduce dependence on fossil fuels for chemical and fuel production in a production process. It is necessary to have renewable raw materials. Reducing the environmental footprint in a circular economy can also reduce the persistence of chemicals (Ganesh et al., 2021).

Waste Management and Recycling

The amount of waste produced and consumed has increased in tandem with population growth. Waste management in the production process guarantees that waste is reduced, reused, and recycled. These regulations safeguard natural resources while also preventing environmental contamination. On the other side, the customer bears significant responsibility for waste. The increase in domestic waste and its negative effects on nature pose a danger to future generations (Tulebayeva et al., 2020). Each waste has a different treatment process. It is necessary to cover the wastes with soil to prevent them from being blown by the wind due to weather conditions, flying animals, pests and odors from harming nature and living things again. The most effective solution without harming living beings and the natural environment is to eliminate waste at its source. Therefore, knowledge, education and rules are very important in waste management (Çetin, 2021).

While waste management is carried out on the one hand, efforts are made to ensure zero waste on the other. The aim of zero waste is to prevent waste, to use resources in a beneficial way, to reveal the cause of waste generation and to recover it. For this purpose, it is important to establish public and private sector cooperation. It requires separate studies to be carried out according to sectors (Çetin, 2021).

The wastes that threaten us in daily life are multifaceted. Wastes leaking into sewers left in nature and thrown into the sea harm both human health and the ecological system (M. Mahgoub et al., 2020). Wastes that mix with drinking or irrigation water re-enter our homes through agricultural products. It also damages habitat during agriculture. Construction and demolition waste has also reached almost 70% of the total waste generated globally (Ferronato et al., 2023).

Sustainable development goals (SDGS) prioritize prevention, recycling, and reuse. In this context, preventing and minimizing waste is the primary goal. At the same time, the reuse of waste will provide the desired results in the circular economy. For example, the increase in methane emissions from landfilling in solid waste management causes climate change. Thanks to the measures to be taken for these emissions, they can be taken at low carbon cost (Veral, 2019). Research shows that solid waste management also has an impact on reducing greenhouse gas emissions (Sharma & Chandel, 2017).

ENVIRONMENTAL IMPACT ASSESSMENT (EIA)

EIA normally seeks to examine the environmental repercussions of big projects in advance and then take steps to mitigate negative effects. In 1970, the National Environmental Policy Act (USA) established the Environmental Impact Assessment. It is a popular environmental management tool around the world. The EIA creates a good environmental model while limiting negative impacts. As a result, numerous new initiatives are being developed. Projects can be carried out in many sectors. Generally, it has become mandatory in large-scale infrastructure projects, power plants, and mining enterprises. The savings, benefits, and social interaction in production and consumption contribute to the circular economy. Thus, it serves sustainable development through the protection of natural resources and ecosystems.

EIA is carried out in several stages. First, screening is used to assess the nature of a project and its relationship with the environment. This is followed by scoping. In this process, factors related to the environment are identified, and all stakeholders are informed. The environmental implications of the project are thoroughly investigated during the impact assessment phase. Mitigation and management come next. At this stage, measures are determined to eliminate or minimize the negative impacts identified according to the reports. The stage where everything is written down and a clear idea is obtained is decision-making. At this stage, it becomes clear whether the authorized units will approve or not. The process continues for approved projects. Controls are made to ensure that the measures are done correctly (Joseph et al., 2015; Morgan, 2012).

As may be seen, the EIA procedure is completed in several stages. It is mandatory in the USA (NEPA, 1970) and the European Union (2011/92/EU) (Almeida & Montaño, 2017). Many countries, including Australia, Canada, and New Zealand, have adopted it as an official practice (Morgan 2012). The majority of United Nations member nations have signed a legal agreement implementing EIA (Morgan, 2012). Thanks to this obligation, many benefits arise in the sustainable development approach. First of all, social awareness increases as a result of involving and informing the public (1). Natural resources and ecosystems can be protected (2) and projects comply with environmental laws at the macro level (3). However, there are sometimes limitations or uncertainties in the content and implementation of EIA. EIA has a long history of contributing to sustainable development and it is clear that it needs to be continuously improved (Tetlow & Hanusch, 2012; Morgan, 2012).

STUDIES ON SUSTAINABLE DEVELOPMENT APPROACH

As environmental problems worsen, so do anxieties about the future. While national economies strive for economic progress, they also strive to ensure the country's long-term viability. For this goal, legislation, procedures, and projects are developed in collaboration with the government, municipalities, non-governmental organizations, businesses, and the general population. In addition to the cooperation of individual enterprises and eco-industrial parks, new initiatives are being implemented all over the world, particularly in industrialized countries such as the European Union, the United States, Japan, and Australia.

Energy Efficiency Policies

Energy efficiency is critical on a worldwide scale for both environmental and economic reasons. Energy efficiency initiatives aim to lessen the environmental effect of manufacturing operations by decreasing energy use. Various laws and procedures are being implemented around the world to increase energy efficiency.

The European Union (EU) focused on energy efficiency and savings with the Energy Efficiency Directive (EED) in 2012. To this end, they have turned to renewable energy sources and made the conditions necessary to improve the environmental performance of products mandatory. For example, an additional 11.7% reduction in energy consumption is required by 2030 (Energy Efficiency Directive, 2023). Therefore, not only large manufacturers but also small and medium-sized enterprises (SMEs) with energy-saving potential will need to conduct energy audits.

Under the Climate Change Action Plan, the United States has implemented new measures to reduce greenhouse gas emissions and improve energy efficiency. Measures have also been taken to cut energy consumption in federal buildings. Energy-saving production is encouraged in order to improve energy efficiency. The Inflation Reduction Act, the government's most comprehensive legislation, is set to take effect in 2022, with a focus on investments in clean energy and electric vehicles. Greenhouse gas emissions have now been cut by around 50% compared to 2005 levels. Action was also taken through the American Innovation and Manufacturing Act to reduce high pollutants such as hydrofluorocarbons (HFCs) and methane. In addition, after 2035, passenger cars are required to emit zero emissions (Lashof, 2024).

The Chinese government passed a law in 2005 to improve energy efficiency. After 2006, it became one of the important countries in renewable energy resources. In 2009, important results were achieved with the law developed (Schuman & Lin, 2012). In particular, it has taken an important step by doubling its energy production. Subsidies and tax reductions are applied for renewable energy production and use. Looking at the values between 2020-2024, it is seen that China has problems achieving some targets (Civillini, 2024). However, its leadership in energy continues.

A National Energy Efficiency Mission has been developed under India's National Action Plan on Climate Change (NAPCC). New standards have been developed to increase efficiency. Energy Saving Certificates are encouraged. This certificate aims to reduce energy consumption in energy-intensive industries. According to 2017 data, 31 million tons of carbon emission reduction were achieved. In the 2024-2025 period, work has been initiated on pulp, paper, and textiles in sectors such as iron and steel and oil refineries. In addition, consumers are informed about energy-efficient products (New & Renewable Energy Department, India, 2024).

Japan enacted the Energy Conservation Law, which covers new standards and measures. The Top Runner Program (1999) developed standards for energy-intensive products such as household appliances and motor vehicles. This system is also applied to importing companies sending goods to Japan (Top Runner Program, 2024). Smart Grid Technologies (SGAM) are also being developed (EU-Japan, 2022).

Waste Management Policies

Waste Management policies vary from region to region. However, cooperated policies and strategies can be grouped under some headings. These are waste minimization, recycling, composting, energy recovery, hazardous waste management, landfills, and pollution prevention. Many countries are engaged in projects and initiatives related to these issues.

In countries with large populations such as the USA and Japan, the "Zero Waste Cities" project aims to reduce waste generation and increase recycling (Zero Waste Cities, 2024). The most frequently adopted and implemented project in developing countries is "Waste Recycling Programs" (Free Recycling Programs, 2024; Municipal Waste Recycling Program, 2024; Külekçi & Güvendi, 2023). It is carried out for the safe recycling of electronic waste. In Melbourne, Australia, the "Zero Waste House" can be given as an example. This house is built from recycled materials. The house also has a smart system powered by solar energy. Sample applications have been made to reduce waste in the house. For example, there are different technologies such as composting systems, charcoal tanks, and water oxygen systems (A Zero-Waste Home, 2021). In Thailand, various projects on both waste management and recycling have been started with the Phuket Zero Waste initiative. Similarly, recycling projects are being carried out in Hanoi, Vietnam.

We said that projects are more common in European countries. The European Union has launched projects promoting the circular economy. It aims to keep the product life cycle long and reduce the amount of waste. Apart from this, in the Netherlands, Boyat Slat strives to collect and recycle plastic waste in the oceans with "The Ocean Cleanup" project (The Ocean Cleanup, 2024). In the Netherlands, the "Precious Plastic" project, which encourages the alteration of plastic waste into novel goods in recycling machines, allows citizens to create their own recycling machines (Precious Plastic Universe, 2024). In France, laws have been passed requiring supermarkets to donate unsold food (France's Food Waste, 2024). In addition, discounts are provided in supermarkets for products approaching their expiry date. Similarly, vegan waste restaurants such as FREA have started to open in Berlin (Zero Waste Restaurant, 2019). The project started with the aim of avoiding unnecessary packaging and waste. We can also give a different example from Denmark. Bornholm Island has taken action to become a "zero waste island" by 2032. It has started to implement recycling and garbage disposal technologies using a new waste separation system (Bornholm Island, 2019).

Other Sustainability Projects

In the perspective of sustainable development, there are many different projects and initiatives related to environmental policies other than energy efficiency and waste management projects. It is not easy to categorize all of the projects focusing on different environmental aspects as it is a very broad topic. However, we can say that there are many new studies that are being added every day.

Innovative projects are being implemented in Singapore to protect water resources. For example, the NEWwater project uses advanced treatment techniques to transform waste water into drinking water (Lee & Tan, 2016). China is the world's leading solar energy generator. It invests in sustainable energy by establishing solar farms, especially on the Tibetan Plateau. (Murray, 2021). Similarly, in Bangladesh, the "Barind Tract Water Management Project" aims to protect water resources to combat drought (Islam et al., 2020).

India has lagged behind many countries in terms of hygiene conditions. The Indian government has started to improve general cleanliness and hygiene conditions. New toilets, clean water, environmental cleanliness, and waste management are being worked on. In addition, the "Namami Gange Project" has been launched to clean the Ganges River in India (Simon & Joshi, 2022).

We can also give an example from Indonesia. Initiatives such as the "Bali Plastic Exchange" have been launched to combat plastic waste pollution. They are also working on the collection, sorting, and recycling of existing plastic waste (Franken et al., 2019).

South Korea includes Smart City Projects. Especially in Seoul, energy efficiency and clean transportation solutions are implemented (Choi, 2020). Similarly, in Thailand, Green Transportation Projects are implemented in big cities such as

Bangkok to reduce traffic and increase electric buses, and bicycle sharing programs (Kokkaew & Rudjanakanoknad, 2017).

The Mangrove Forest Conservation Project was developed in the Philippines. It aims to protect the shoreline, erosion, and marine ecosystems (Garcia et al. 2013). In Malaysia, numerous programs are being developed to protect forests and biodiversity. For instance, the "Heart of Borneo" project aims to preserve rainforests on Borneo Island (Sabran et al., 2014).

CONCLUSION

Regional strategies and policies help global economies mitigate environmental concerns. This chapter has explored the awareness, concerns, common problems and alternative solutions of various countries in the context of environmental policies. It was found that regional environmental policies would be more effective if they were tailored to regional needs and demands.

Exemplary practices and laws can serve as models for other locations and practices on a global scale. Partnerships between the public and private sectors, as well as community engagement, are critical for the success of regional sustainability programs. Furthermore, education and awareness activities are vital to ensuring that all parts of society participate in this process. Although economics plays an important role in these issues, it is not effective in the formulation of environmental policies. Therefore, political economy and academic cooperation is important for stable environmental policy. When environmental projects are analyzed, we can say that almost all countries are in cooperation. However, it is seen that more initiatives and faster results are achieved in countries with high economic power and developed countries. In developing countries, it is understood that projects are still being developed to improve basic living conditions. Although environmental destruction and recovery first show a regional impact, it is seen that different incentives and investments are needed to accelerate the initiatives of developing countries as they affect the other parts of the world. In this context, it can be said that the quality framework for production stages and products in developing countries should be revisited. New regulations and sanctions to improve unfavorable conditions are needed. Re-evaluation of the process on a sectoral basis and its execution by the Ministry of Environment within the framework of government policies will make it easier to achieve expectations.

As a result, global economies need to develop strong and integrated policies at the regional level to ensure environmental sustainability. These policies, which consider each region's unique ecological, economic, and social dynamics, will serve as an important lever in achieving global sustainable development goals.

REFERENCES

Alagöz, M. (2007). The environmental factor in sustainable development: a theoretical perspective. Akademik Bakiş Uluslararası Hakemli Sosyal Bilimler E-Dergisi (Academic Bakış International Refereed Social Sciences E-Journal), 11, pp. 1-12.

Almeida, M., & Montaño, M. (2017). The effectiveness of environmental impact assessment systems in São Paulo and Minas Gerais states. *Ambiente & Sociedade*, 20(2), 77–104. DOI: 10.1590/1809-4422asoc235r2v2022017

Amasawa, E., Kişita, Y., & Muhammed, A. F. (2023). Envisioning the Linkages Between Consumption and Production for Sustainability: Outcomes from Expert Workshops in Malaysia. *Circular Economy and Sustainability*, 4(1), 733–753. DOI: 10.1007/s43615-023-00308-8

Anastas, P. T., Kirchhoff, M. M., & Williamson, T. C. (2001). Catalysis as a Foundational Pillar of Green Chemistry. *Applied Catalysis A, General*, 22(1-2), 3–13. DOI: 10.1016/S0926-860X(01)00793-1

Anderson, D. A. (2019). *Environmental Economics and Natural Resource Management* (5th Edition). Published: Routledge DOI: 10.4324/9781351121477

Antonioli, D., Ghisetti, C., Mazzanti, M., & Nicolli, F. (2022). Sustainable production: The economic returns of circular economy practices. *Business Strategy and the Environment*, 31(5), 2603–2617. DOI: 10.1002/bse.3046

Benedict, M. A., & McMahon, E. T. (2006). *Green infrastructure: Linking landscapes and communities*. Island Press.

Bhattacharya, S. (2024). Indigenous knowledge for sustainable development: A case study of Kurmi Mahatos. *Indian Journal of History of Science*, 59(2), 192–203. Advance online publication. DOI: 10.1007/s43539-024-00120-9

Business, E. U. in Japan (2024). Smart Grid & Smart City. Retrieved from https://www.eu-japan.eu/eubusinessinjapan/sectors/energy/smart-grid-smart-city (accessed: 03.06.2024).

Çetin, A. S. (2021). *Waste management*. Pearson Journal of Social Sciences & Humanities., DOI: 10.46872/pj.121

Charlton, E. (2024). Centre for nature and climate in World Economic Forum. https://www.weforum.org/agenda/2024/03/sustainable-resource-consumption-urgent-un/

Chertow, M. R. (2000). Industrial symbiosis: Literature and taxonomy. *Annual Review of Energy and the Environment*, 25(1), 313–337. DOI: 10.1146/annurev.energy.25.1.313

Choi, Y. S. (2020). Smart city development projects in the Republic of Korea. *R-Economy*, 6(1), 40–49. DOI: 10.15826/recon.2020.6.1.004

Civillini, M. (2024). China's energy efficiency goal looks unlikely. Climate Home News. Retrieved from https://www.climatechangenews.com/2024/03/06/china-steps-away-from-2025-energy-efficiency-goal/ (access: 07.06.2024).

Dean, T. J., & McMullen, J. S. (2007). Toward a theory of sustainable entrepreneurship: Reducing environmental degradation through entrepreneurial action. *Journal of Business Venturing*, 22(1), 50–76. DOI: 10.1016/j.jbusvent.2005.09.003

Demartini, M., Tonelli, F., & Govindan, K. (2022). An investigation into modelling approaches for industrial symbiosis: A literature review and research agenda. *Cleaner Logistics and Supply Chain*, 3, 100020. DOI: 10.1016/j.clscn.2021.100020

Dinda, S. (2004). Environmental Kuznets curve hypothesis: A survey. *Ecological Economics*, 49(4), 431–455. DOI: 10.1016/j.ecolecon.2004.02.011

Dong, L., Liu, Z., & Bian, Y. (2021). Match circular economy and urban sustainability: Re-investigating Circular Economy Under Sustainable Development Goals (SDGs). *Circular Economy and Sustainability*, 1(1), 243–256. DOI: 10.1007/s43615-021-00032-1

Estoque, R. C. (2020). A Review of the Sustainability Concept and the State of SDG Monitoring Using Remote Sensing. *Remote Sensing (Basel)*, 12(11), 1–22. DOI: 10.3390/rs12111770

Etzkorn, F. A., & Ferguson, J. L. (2023). Integrating green chemistry into chemistry education. *Angewandte Chemie International Edition*, 62(2), e202209768. Advance online publication. DOI: 10.1002/anie.202209768

European Commission energy, climate, environment (2023). Energy efficiency directive. Retrieved from https://energy.ec.europa.eu/topics/energy-efficiency/energy-efficiency-targets-directive-and-rules/energy-efficiency-directive_en (access: 07.06.2024).

European Commission Report (2023). European state of the climate. Retrieved from https://climate.copernicus.eu/esotc/2023 (access: 04.06.2024).

Europen Commission. (2021). The European green deal. https://commission.europa.eu/strategy-and-policy/priorities-2019-2024/european-green-deal_en

Faucheux, S., O'Connor, & Straaten, J. (1998). Sustainable development: Concepts, rationalities and strategies. Published: Springer Nature.

Ferronato, N., Moresco, L., Guisbert Lizarazu, G. E., Gorritty Portillo, M. A., Conti, F., & Torretta, V. (2023). Comparison of environmental impacts related to municipal solid waste and construction and demolition waste management and recycling in a Latin American developing city. *Environmental Science and Pollution Research International*, 30(4), 8548–8562. DOI: 10.1007/s11356-021-16968-8

France's law for fighting food waste. (2020). Zero Waste Europe. https://zerowasteeurope.eu/library/france-law-for-fighting-food-waste/(access: 07.06.2024).

Franken, M., de Jong, W., Iongh, Z., & Marsbergen, A. (2019). Research into Bali's plastic polluted rivers and designs of suitable collection structures for rivers to mitigate the plastic discharge into the ocean. Civil Engineering Consultancy Project | CIE4061-09. Delft University of Technology. DOI: 10.13140/RG.2.2.25445.14560

Free recycling programs. (2024). Terracycle free recycling programs. Retrieved from https://www.terracycle.com/en-US/brigades (access: 02.06.2024).

Fundingsland Tetlow, M., & Hanusch, M. (2012). Strategic environmental assessment: The state of the art. *Impact Assessment and Project Appraisal*, 30(1), 15–24. DOI: 10.1080/14615517.2012.666400

Ganesh, K. N., Zhang, D., Miller, S. J., Rossen, K., Chirik, P. J., Kozlowski, M. C., Zimmerman, J. B., Brooks, B. W., Savage, P. E., Allen, D. T., & Voutchkova-Kostal, A. M. (2021). Green chemistry: A Framework for a sustainable future. *Organometallics*, 40(12), 1801–1805. DOI: 10.1021/acs.organomet.1c00343

Garcia, K., Gevaña, D., & Malabrigo, P. (2013). Philippines' mangrove ecosystem: Status, threats, and conservation. In Mangrove Ecosystems of Asia: Status, Challenges and Management Strategies (pp.81–94). Springer Nature. DOI: 10.1007/978-1-4614-8582-7_5

Gattermayr, S. (2021). Zero-waste home in the middle of Melbourne's Federation Square! Retrieved from https://thedesignfiles.net/2021/02/sustainabledesign-joost-bakker-greenhouse-federation-square (access: 10.06.2024).

Geissdoerfer, M., Morioka, S. N., de Carvalho, M. M., & Evans, S. (2018). Business models and supply chains for the circular economy. *Journal of Cleaner Production*, 190, 712–721. DOI: 10.1016/j.jclepro.2018.04.159

Grann, H. (1997). *The Industrial Green Game: Implications for Environmental Design and Management*. The National Academies Press., DOI: 10.17226/4982

Gunn, K. (2019) Bornholm Island, Denmark is going trash free—By recycling all of its waste. Retrieved from https://www.nationalgeographic.com/environment/article/bornholm-island-denmark-goes-trash-free-by-recycling (access: 09.06.2024).

Handfield, R., Walton, S. V., Sroufe, R., & Melnyk, S. A. (2002). Applying environmental criteria to supplier assessment: A study in the application of the Analytical Hierarchy Process. *European Journal of Operational Research*, 141(1), 70–87. DOI: 10.1016/S0377-2217(01)00261-2

Harvey, B. (2009). Indigenous knowledge, sustainable development and the environment: Implications for research, education and capacity building. In *Indigenous knowledges, development and education* (pp. 57–71). Brill., DOI: 10.1163/9789087906993_005

Islam, M., Jahan, C., Rahaman, M., & Mazumder, Q. (2020). Governance status in water management institutions in Barind Tract, Northwest Bangladesh: An assessment based on stakeholder's perception. *Sustainable Water Resources Management*, 6(2), 21. Advance online publication. DOI: 10.1007/s40899-020-00371-1

Jha, V. K., & Pande, A. S. (2024). Making sustainable development happen: Does sustainable entrepreneurship make nations more sustainable? *Journal of Cleaner Production*, 440, 140849. DOI: 10.1016/j.jclepro.2024.140849

Joseph, C., Gunton, T., & Rutherford, M. (2015). Good practices for environmental assessment. *Impact Assessment and Project Appraisal*, 33(4), 1–17. DOI: 10.1080/14615517.2015.1063811

Kahramanoğlu, A., Glezman, L., & Fedoseeva, S. (2023). Analysis of the Relationship Between Regional Indices of Industrial Production and the Environmental Profile. Digital Transformation in Industry Conference Paper. DOI: 10.1007/978-3-031-30351-7_13

Kaya, F., & Ek, N. H. (2021). Kalkınmanın Çevre Sorunları Üzerine Etkisi: Sürdürülebilir Kalkınma Kavramına Bütüncül Bir Bakış. *City Health Journal Chj*, 2(2), 79–84.

Kaypak, Ş. (2011). Küreselleşme sürecinde sürdürülebilir bir kalkınma için sürdürülebilir bir çevre. A Sustainable Environment for A Sustainable Development in the Process of Globalization). *Journal of Karamanoğlu Mehmetbey University Social and Economics Research*, 2011(1), 19–33.

Kazakova, E., & Joosung, L. (2022). Sustainable manufacturing for a circular economy. *Sustainability (Basel)*, 14(24), 17010. Advance online publication. DOI: 10.3390/su142417010

National Mission on Enhanced Energy Efficiency. (2024). New & Renewable Energy Department in India. Retrieved from https://hareda.gov.in/about-department/national-mission-on-enhanced-energy-efficiency/

Nguyen, H.-Q., Toan, T., Dang, P., Phuong, L., Anh, T., Quang, N., Dao, Q., Quoi, L., Hanington, P., & Sea, W. (2017). Conservation of the Mekong Delta wetlands through hydrological management. *Ecological Research*, 33(1), 87–103. DOI: 10.1007/s11284-017-1545-1

Palacios-Argüello, L., Gondran, N., Nouira, I., Girard, M.-A., & Gonzalez-Feliu, J. (2020). Which is the relationship between the product's environmental criteria and the product demand? Evidence from the French food sector. *Journal of Cleaner Production*, 244, 118588. Advance online publication. DOI: 10.1016/j.jclepro.2019.118588

Precious Plastic Universe. (2024). Say hi to the precious plastic universe. Retrieved from https://preciousplastic.com//(accessed: 02.06.2024).

Ritchie, H., Rosado, P., Samborska, V., & Roser, M. (2024). Climate change. Our World in Data. https://ourworldindata.org/climate-change

Saari, L., Valkokari, K., Martins, J. T., & Acerbi, F. (2024, June 28). martins, J. T., & Acerbi, F. (2024). Circular Economy Matrix Guiding Manufacturing Industry Companies towards Circularity—A Multiple Case Study Perspective. *Circular Economy and Sustainability*. Advance online publication. DOI: 10.1007/s43615-024-00385-3

Sabran, S., Nilus, R., Pereira, J., Sugau, J., & Kugan, F. (2014). Contribution of the heart of Borneo (hob) initiative towards botanical exploration in Sabah, Malaysia. *Reinwardtia*, 14(1), 137. DOI: 10.14203/reinwardtia.v14i1.406

Şahzabeen, A., Ghosh, A., Pandey, B., & Shekhar, S. (2023). *Circular economy and sustainable production and consumption in circular economy and sustainable production and consumption.*, DOI: 10.1007/978-3-031-40304-0_3

Schuman, S., & Lin, A. (2012). China's Renewable Energy Law and its impact on renewable power in China: Progress, challenges and recommendations for improving implementation. *Energy Policy*, 51, 89–109. DOI: 10.1016/j.enpol.2012.06.066

Sharma, B. K., & Chandel, M. K. (2016). Life cycle assessment of potential municipal solid waste management strategies for Mumbai, India. Waste Management & Research. *Waste Management & Research*, 35(1), 79–91. Advance online publication. DOI: 10.1177/0734242X16675683

Shi, L., Han, L., Yang, F., & Gao, L. (2019). The Evolution of Sustainable Development Theory: Types, Goals, and Research Prospects. *Sustainability (Basel)*, 11(24), 7158. DOI: 10.3390/su11247158

Kokkaew, N., & Rudjanakanoknad, J. (2017). Green assessment of Thailand's highway infrastructure: A Green Growth Index approach. *KSCE Journal of Civil Engineering*, 21(7), 2526–2537. DOI: 10.1007/s12205-017-0923-0

Krugman, P. (1991). Increasing returns and economic geography. *Journal of Political Economy*, 99(3), 483–499.

Külekçi, G., & Güvendi, A. (2023). Waste management and recycling programs empowering environmental sustainability: The case of Gümüşhane. *Atras Journal*, 9(52), 57–66. DOI: 10.5281/zenodo.10402418

Lashof, D. (2024). Tracking progress: Climate action under the biden administration. Retrieved from https://www.wri.org/insights/biden-administration-tracking-climate-action-progress (access: 04.06.2024).

Lee, H., & Tan, T. (2016). Singapore's experience with reclaimed water: Newater. *International Journal of Water Resources Development*, 32(4), 1–11. DOI: 10.1080/07900627.2015.1120188

Mahgoub, M. S., Shehata, R. M., El-Ela, F. L. A., Farghali, A., Zaher, A., & Mahmoud, K. (2020). Sustainable waste management and recycling of Zn–Al layered double hydroxide after adsorption of levofloxacin as a safe anti-inflammatory nanomaterial. *RSC Advances*, 10(46), 27633–27651. DOI: 10.1039/D0RA04898D

Markey, E., & Ocasio-Cortez, A. (2024). Reintroduce green new deal resolution | U.S. Senator Ed markey of Massachusetts. Retrieved from https://www.markey.senate.gov/news/press-releases/markey-and-ocasio-cortez-reintroduce-green-new-deal-resolution(access: 04.06.2024).

Martínez, J., Cortés, J. F., & Miranda, R. (2022). Green chemistry metrics, A review. *Processes (Basel, Switzerland)*, 10(7), 1274. Advance online publication. DOI: 10.3390/pr10071274

Mol, A. P. J. (2002). Ecological modernization and the global economy. *Global Environmental Politics*, 2(2), 92–115. DOI: 10.1162/15263800260047844

Morgan, R. K. (2012). Environmental impact assessment: The state of the art. *Impact Assessment and Project Appraisal*, 30(1), 5–14. DOI: 10.1080/14615517.2012.661557

Municipal Waste Recycling Program. (2024). Municipal Waste Recycling Program key results and impacts. Retrieved from https://urban-links.org/project/municipal-waste-recycling-program-mwrp/(access: 04.06.2024).

Murray, J. (2021). Profiling the five largest solar power plants in China. NS Energy. https://www.nsenergybusiness.com/analysis/largest-solar-plants-china/

Simon, M., & Joshi, H. (2022). *Story of the Ganga River: Its pollution and rejuvenation*. Springer., DOI: 10.1007/978-3-030-87067-6_2

Stabler, D., Hakala, H., Huikkola, T., & Mention, A. L. (2024). Aligning servitization and circularity: The role of institutional confluence in sustainable business models. *Journal of Cleaner Production*, 462, 142666. DOI: 10.1016/j.jclepro.2024.142666

Sustainable Development Report (2023). Implementing the SDG stimulus. Retrieved from https://dashboards.sdgindex.org/ (accessed: 10.06.2024).

The Ocean Cleanup. (2024). The Ocean Cleanup. Retrieved from https://theoceancleanup.com/

The Paris Agreement/UNFCCC. (2015). Retrieved from https://unfccc.int/process-and-meetings/the-paris-agreement (accessed: 10.06.2024).

Top Runner Programme. (2019). IEA. Retrieved from https://www.iea.org/policies/1945-top-runner-programme (accessed: 09.06.2024).

Tronvoll, B., Sklyar, A., Sörhammar, D., & Kowalkowski, C. (2020). Transformational shifts through digital servitization. *Industrial Marketing Management*, 89, 293–305. DOI: 10.1016/j.indmarman.2020.02.005

Tulebayeva, N., Yergobek, D., Pestunova, G., Mottaeva, A., & Sapakova, Z. (2020). Green economy: Waste management and recycling methods. E3S Web of Conferences, 159, 01012. DOI: 10.1051/e3sconf/202015901012

Turner, N. J. (2008). *The earth's blanket: Traditional teachings for sustainable living*. D & M Publishers.

Ullah, A., Ghani, H. U., & Gheewala, S. H. (2024). Green public procurement and ecolabels towards sustainable consumption and production. Encyclopedia of Sustainable Technologies (Second Edition), 1, pp. 368-381. DOI: 10.1016/B978-0-323-90386-8.00087-5

UN Conference on Environment and Development – UNCED. (1992). IISD earth negotiations bulletin. Retrieved from http://enb-test.iisd.org/negotiations/un-conference-environment-and-development-unced (access: 01.06.2024).

United Nations. (1972). United Nations Conference on the Human Environment, Stockholm, 1972. United Nations; United Nations. Retrieved from https://www.un.org/en/conferences/environment/stockholm1972 (access: 04.06.2024).

United Nations Environment Programme. (1974). The Cocoyoc Declaration adopted by the participants in the UNEP/UNCTAD Symposium on & quot; Patterns of Resource Use, Environment and Development Strategies" held at Cocoyoc, Mexico, https://digitallibrary.un.org/record/838843

Valencia, M., Bocken, N., Loaiza, C., & De Jaeger, S. (2023). The social contribution of the circular economy. *Journal of Cleaner Production*, 408, 137082. DOI: 10.1016/j.jclepro.2023.137082

Van Berkel, R. (2010). Evolution and diversification of national cleaner production centres (NCPCs). *Journal of Environmental Management*, 91(7), 1556–1565. DOI: 10.1016/j.jenvman.2010.02.032

Varriale, V., Cammarano, A., Michelino, F., & Caputo, M. (2024). The role of digital technologies in production systems for achieving sustainable development goals. *Sustainable Production and Consumption*, 47, 87–104. DOI: 10.1016/j.spc.2024.03.035

Veral, E. S. (2019). An evaluation on the circular economy model and the loops design in the Context of Waste Management. *European Journal of Science and Technology*, 15(18). Advance online publication. DOI: 10.31590/ejosat.479333

WCED report, (1987). World Commission on Environment and Development Brundtland Report. Retrieved from https://www.are.admin.ch/dam/are/en/dokumente/nachhaltige_entwicklung/dokumente/bericht/our_common_futurebrundtlandreport1987.pdf.download.pdf/our_common_futurebrundtlandreport1987.pdf (accessed: 26.11.2023).

World Bank. (2024). The World Bank in Costa Rica. Retrieved from https://www.worldbank.org/en/country/costarica/overview (accessed: 05.06.2024).

World Commission on Environment and Development. (1987). Report of the World Commission on Environment and Development: Note: by the Secretary-General. https://digitallibrary.un.org/record/139811 (accessed: 10.06.2024).

Xu, C., & Zhang, J. (2022). Dynamic analysis of the coupling relationship between regional energy economy and environment based on big data. *Energy Reports*, 8, 13293–13301. DOI: 10.1016/j.egyr.2022.09.137

Zero Waste Cities. (2024). Zero Waste Cities in Europe. Retrieved from https://zerowastecities.eu/ (access: 28.05.2024).

Zero Waste Restaurant. (2024). Lessons from FREA. Retrieved from https://www.foodunfolded.com/article/zero-waste-restaurant-lessons-from-frea (accessed: 10.06.2024).

Zhang, L., Xu, M., Chen, H., Li, Y., & Chen, S. (2022). Globalization, Green Economy and Environmental Challenges: State of the Art Review for Practical Implications. *Frontiers in Environmental Science*, 10, 870271. Advance online publication. DOI: 10.3389/fenvs.2022.870271

KEY TERMS AND DEFINITIONS

Circular Economy: A market economy that seeks to keep natural resources in the economy for as long as possible and preserves the value of physical resources, minimizing consumption, waste and risks.

Environmental Concern: Concern that life will deteriorate due to climate change and increased disasters.

Environmental Impact Assessment: Determining the positive and negative environmental impacts of planned projects, mitigating them to prevent damage to the environment, taking measures and developing alternative projects.

Sustainability: Meeting today's needs so that future generations can meet their own needs.

Sustainable Development: The common denominator in the economic and social development goals of countries is sustainability.

Sustainable Production: Products that protect the natural environment both directly and indirectly.

Waste Management: It is the process of collecting, storing and recycling wastes that arise after production activities and threaten environmental health.

Chapter 19
Empirical Analysis of the Relationship Between Inclusive Green Growth and Agricultural Added Value:
The Case of Türkiye

Başak Özarslan Doğan
https://orcid.org/0000-0002-5126-7077
Gelisim University, Turkey

ABSTRACT

In this study, the relationship between inclusive green growth and agricultural added value in Türkiye for the period 1990-2020 was examined with the help of the ARDL bounds test. In order to represent inclusive green growth, the inclusive green growth index was created using the Principal Component Analysis method. In addition, the effects of inclusive green growth, as well as the effects of total labor force and temperature increase on agricultural added value, were also examined in the study. According to the findings, inclusive green growth in Türkiye positively affects agricultural added value and the coefficient is statistically significant. In addition, in the study, the effect of the total labor force on agricultural added value was found to be positive and the coefficient was statistically significant. While the effect of temperature increase on agricultural added value is found to be negative, the coefficient is statistically insignificant.

DOI: 10.4018/979-8-3693-5508-4.ch019

1. INTRODUCTION

The emergence of many problems such as national and international inequalities, environmental deformations, and problems in accessing clean food and water has caused the understanding of growth and development to change and develop. Although pure economic growth provides the condition for increased welfare of the society, it is insufficient to eliminate poverty and inequality for all segments of society. The fact that the opportunities created by growth are not spread equally throughout society has turned attention from pure economic growth to inclusive economic Growth (Avcı ve Tonus, 2020).

The growth model that provides an increase in welfare for the entire population of a society and distributes all material and non-material welfare components homogeneously is defined as inclusive Growth (Keyifli vd., 2022: 41). Problems such as global monetary crises, unfair income distribution, unemployment and poverty cause countries to re-plan their economic growth policies by spreading them equally across the society. In order for economic growth in a country to be inclusive and sustainable, the income of every segment of the society as well as their opportunities in education, health and social fields must be increased.

Inclusive growth ensures the balance between sustainable development and economic growth. While providing this balance, unlike traditional growth models, it does not focus only on the amount of output, but on the equal distribution of the amount of output. When evaluated from this perspective, inclusive growth is at the center of the economic policies discussed in recent years, as it allows both economic and social goals to be evaluated in one pot (Özgün, 2021: 274).

Following the announcement of the Sustainable Development Goals (SDGs), many countries began to implement new development strategies focused on inclusive green growth, which were put forward to focus the world's attention on both green and inclusive growth. At this point, inclusive green growth can be summarized as economic growth that provides greater access to sustainable socioeconomic opportunities for a greater number of people, regions or countries, while protecting the vulnerable, and all of this is done in a fair environment. Promoting inclusive green growth plays a critical role in achieving sustainable development goals, considering the economic, environmental and social dimensions of sustainable development (Desalegn ve Tangl, 2022).

The agricultural sector is one of the key sectors in achieving sustainable development and growth goals. Factors such as temperature increase and climate change due to the effect of greenhouse gases that occur as a result of excessive production and consumption pose a threat to developing countries such as Turkiye.

Floods, storms and heat waves that occur due to these factors also create negative effects in areas such as agricultural production and animal husbandry. Therefore, in countries where environmental impacts are felt intensely, advanced agricultural methods need to be applied to increase output. As a result of advanced agricultural methods that cannot be applied, agricultural production and the share of agriculture in the country's income will decrease. This situation will cause countries to face a decrease in their national income.

The agricultural sector, one of the most basic sectors, is of great importance in the development of the country's economy and the rural development of the country. Although the share of the agricultural sector in GDP in Turkey has decreased compared to the 1980s, real production has increased steadily. For example, while the agricultural sector constituted approximately 25% of GDP in 1980, the contribution of the agricultural sector to GDP was calculated as 4.8% in 2022. The most important reason for this is thought to be the effect of export-based macroeconomic policies followed in the 1980s (Ministry of Trade of the Republic of Turkiye, 2024).

Figure 1 below shows the development of agricultural added value per worker, calculated by dividing the amount of economic value obtained from agriculture in Turkiye by the number of people working in agriculture, between 1991 and 2019. When looking at the agricultural added value per worker, it is seen that there is an increase over the years. it is seen that the agricultural value added per worker, which was 6,388 USD in 1991, doubled to 12,336 USD in 2019.

Figure 1. Agriculture value added per worker

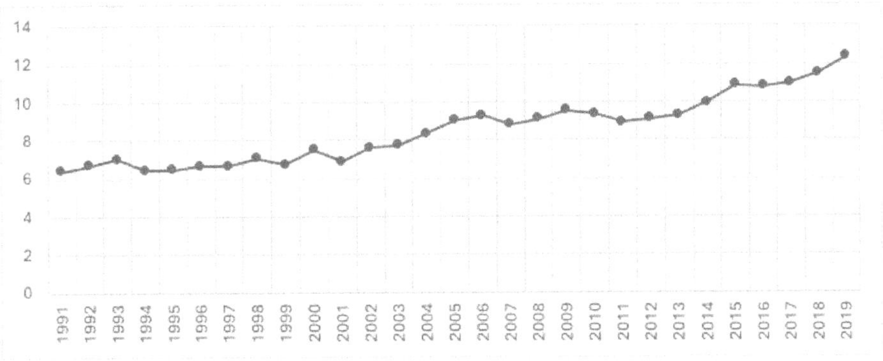

Source: Our World in Data, 2024.

As we can see at Turkiye's agricultural product exports, agricultural product exports have increased over the years. Figure 2 below shows Türkiye's agricultural and total export values. According to Figure 2, agricultural exports, which were 4.07 billion dollars in 2001, increased approximately 5 times to 20.71 billion dollars in 2020.

Figure 2. Türkiye Agriculture and Total Export Values(Million dollars)

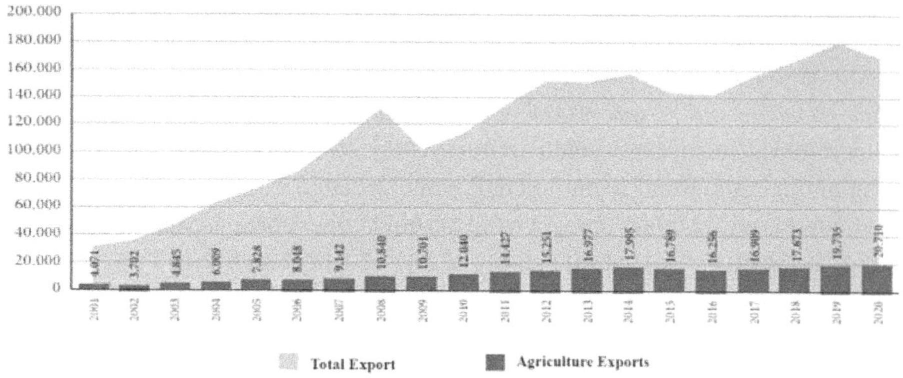

Source: Ministry of Agriculture and Forestry, 2021.

Figure 3 shows the share (%) of Türkiye's Agricultural Exports in Total Exports between 2001-2020. Accordingly, while the share of agricultural products exports in general exports was approximately 12% in 2001, it is seen that it had the lowest share in 2008 with approximately 8%.

Figure 3. Share of Türkiye's Agricultural Exports in Total Exports between 2001-2020 (%)

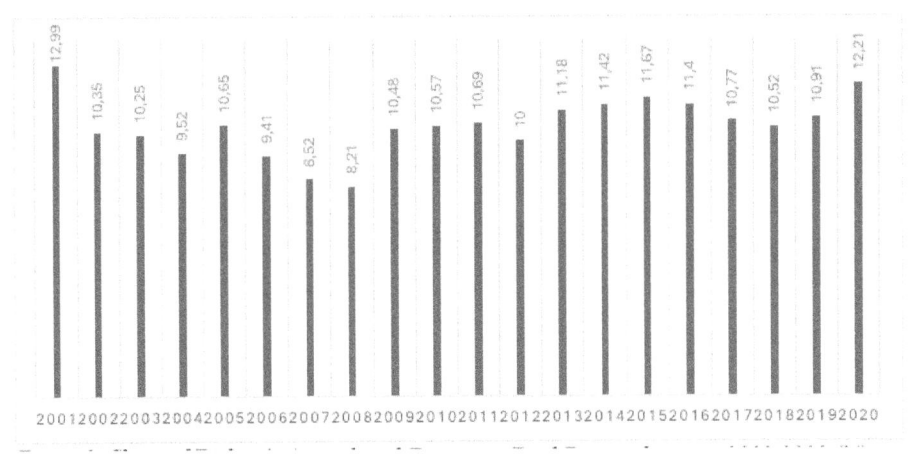

Source: Ministry of Agriculture and Forestry, 2021.

The aim of this study is to empirically test the relationship between inclusive green growth and agricultural added value in Türkiye for the years 1990-2020. In this context, the study first created an inclusive green growth index using the Principal Component Analysis (PCA) method to represent inclusive green growth for Türkiye. In addition, also inclusive green growth, the study also investigated the effects of technology, total labor force and temperature increase variables on agricultural added value. In the study, the ARDL Bounds test method was applied as the main model to measure the relationship between inclusive green growth and agricultural added value.

2. LITERATURE

This study, which examines the relationship between agricultural added value and inclusive green growth, contributes to the literature through two different channels. Firstly, this study is one of the first studies to calculate inclusive green growth for Türkiye. Secondly, there are very limited studies in the literature examining the relationship between inclusive green growth and agricultural added value. Therefore, the literature part of the study consists of two stages. In the first stage, empirical studies examining the relationship between agricultural production and economic growth were included and these studies are expressed in Table 1. In the second stage, international studies that are thought to be important specifically for inclusive growth are listed in Table 2.

Table 1. Summary of selected literature examining the relationship between agricultural production and economic growth

Author (s)	Term	Country	Method	Result
Özbay (2023)	1994-2019	Türkiye	ARDL bound test	A negative relationship was found between economic growth and agricultural production in the short term, and a positive relationship between economic growth and agricultural production in the long term.
Ertürkmen (2023)	1984-2021	MIST Countries	Panel data analysis	The effect of economic growth on agricultural production was found to be negative and statistically significant.
Baoua (2023)	1991-2020	Nigeria	ARDL bound test	In the long term, agricultural production, agricultural exports and agricultural imports affect economic growth positively and statistically significantly.
Kılınç and Kılınç (2021)	2009-2017	Türkiye	Panel data analysis	A positive relationship was found between agricultural production and GDP per capita. In other words, as agricultural production increases, GDP per capita also increases.
Kopuk and Meçik (2020)	1998Q1-2020Q1	Türkiye	Johansen cointegration And Granger causality test	A unidirectional causality relationship from the agricultural sector to GDP has been found, and evidence has also been demonstrated that investments in the agricultural sector will increase economic growth.
Canbay and Kırca (2020)	1961-2017	Türkiye	Johansen cointegration and Granger causality test	It has been stated that economic growth affects the agricultural sector negatively, while the agricultural sector affects economic growth positively.
Anwar et al. (2015)	1975-2012	Pakistan	OLS method	Findings have been obtained that there is a positive and significant relationship between economic growth and agriculture.
Xie and Awokuse (2014)	1980-2011	9 developing countries	Johansen and Juselius (1990) cointegration tests, ARDL, DAG	It was determined that the driving force of growth for the sample period was agricultural production.
Işıksal and Chmeze (2016)	1997-2012	Nigeria	Johansen Cointegration Analysis	The study found that there is a positive and significant relationship between Agriculture and GDP and that GDP and agricultural production affect each other bidirectionally.

continued on following page

Table 1. Continued

Author (s)	Term	Country	Method	Result
Sheikh et al. (2012)	1980-2010	Pakistan	Johansen cointegration test and ECM	Agricultural production in Pakistan has a positive and significant impact on economic growth in the short and long term.

In addition to Table 1, the study by Awan and Vashma (2014) is one of the important studies in this field. The authors examined the main determinant of the agricultural sector and the relationship between agricultural economic development and GDP with data for the period 1980-2010 for Pakistan. According to the study findings, increasing agricultural production is one of the main determinants of GDP in Pakistan. In their study, Asom and UshahembaIjirshar (2016) examined the effect of agricultural added value on the growth of the Nigerian economy for the period 1981-2015. The study result showed that agricultural value added had a positive but insignificant impact on the growth of the Nigerian economy in both the short and long term during the sample period considered in Nigeria. When the studies in Table 1 are examined in general, it is seen in the economic literature that agricultural production creates a driving force on the country's income and has a generally positive effect on GDP. On the other hand, Table 2 summarizes empirical studies on inclusive growth.

Table 2. Summary of selected literature on inclusive growth

Author(s)	Term	Country	Method	Result
Pham et al. (2024)	2011-2021	Top 10 Asian countries with the highest income	CS-ARDL	Study findings provide evidence that financial development accelerates inclusive growth.
Xu et al. (2024)	1990-2019	35 OECD countries	CS-ARDL, FMOLS, DOLS ve AMG estimators	Technological development, energy efficiency, renewable electricity and human capital have a positive impact on inclusive growth.
Yang et al. (2023)	2009-2017	72 countries	GMM	It has been found that inclusive growth contributes to financial development by increasing economic freedom.
Ngounou et al. (2023)	1995-2020	48 African countries	Driscoll and Kraay, generalized least squares, robustness via Lewbel two-stage least squares, and system GMM	Findings have been obtained that urbanization will accelerate inclusive growth.

continued on following page

Table 2. Continued

Author(s)	Term	Country	Method	Result
Keyifli et al. (2022)	1985-2019	8 major emerging market economies	Bootstrap Panel Rolling Window causality approach	It has been determined that in India, Indonesia, Mexico and South Africa, inclusive growth causes public sector size, and in Turkey, public sector size causes inclusive growth.
Sarpong and Nketiah-Amponsah (2022).	2004-2018	Sub-Saharan African Countries	Arellano–Bover/ Blundell–Bond system GMM	In Sub-Saharan Africa, a one-unit increase in the use of financial products and services increases inclusive growth by 0.03 units.
Altunç and İşlek (2022)	1995-2011	MENA countries	Panel Fourier Toda Yamamoto causality analysis	There is a bidirectional causality relationship between financial openness and inclusive growth.
Can et al. (2019)	1991-2015	Türkiye	ARDL bound test	Inclusive growth accelerates globalization in the sample period.
Whajah vd. (2019)	2000-2016	54 African Countries	Fixed effects regression method	The effect of public sector size on inclusive growth is positive, while the effect of public debt on inclusive growth is negative.
Kamran vd. (2022)	2008-2018	11 selected developing countries	Principal components analysis	Authors who examine the relationship between sustainable development and inclusive growth state that it will be effective to develop inclusive growth as a policy strategy to further increase sustainable development in developing countries.

There are important theoretical studies in the literature regarding inclusive growth. In this context, Avcı and Tonus (2020) drew a broad framework of inclusive growth by gathering the definitions made by various institutions and organizations. Thus, they clearly revealed the similarities and differences of the implemented inclusive growth policies by emphasizing the points that countries and institutions emphasize when defining inclusive growth. Another important study in this field is Berber et al. (2024)'s study. Berber et al. (2024) in their study, they created inclusive growth indices for Turkiye's sub-regions for 2014 and 2021, taking McKinley's (2010) study as a reference. According to the findings, the inclusive growth index for Türkiye in general will increase in 2021 compared to 2014.

3. DATA SET, MODEL AND METHOD

3.1. Data Set

In this study examining the relationship between agricultural added value and inclusive green growth, firstly, the inclusive green growth index was created to represent inclusive green growth, based on some studies based on green growth (Ofori et al., 2023; Acosta et al., 2019; OECD, 2017). In this context, the variables in question were selected to include the socio-economic and environmental components of green growth and are expressed in table 3 below.

Table 3. Variables Used to Create the Inclusive Green Growth Index

Socio-Economic Indicators	Environmental Indicators
GDP per capita	Woodland
Population density	Farmland
GINI coefficient	Carbon emissions
Human capital	Fossil fuel consumption
Financial development	Clean water
Infant mortality rate	
Schooling rate	

The comprehensive green growth index created for Türkiye within the framework of selected indicators covers the years 1990-2020. The variables used to create the index were obtained from the World Bank database and the index was created with the help of the Principal Components Analysis (PCA) method.

Principal component analysis method is one of the frequently preferred methods in the field of multivariate data analysis. This method is also known as the variable analysis reduction method, and thanks to this method, what is meant by a data set containing many variables can be expressed with a smaller number of components (Dunteman, 1989: 8).

The suitability of variables for PCA analysis is determined by the Kaiser-Meyer-Olkin (KMO) coefficient and Bartlett Test. The Kaiser-Meyer-Olkin (KMO) criterion refers to the index value that tests the suitability of the sample mass for factor analysis by comparing the significance levels of the observed correlation coefficient and partial correlation coefficients (Kellekçi and Berköz, 2006; Avcu and Yayla, 2021: 72). Bartlett's test is performed to see whether there is a relationship between the variables and whether it is necessary to apply principal component analysis to the data, and if there is a relationship between the variables, to understand whether they are important or not. Table 4 below shows the Kaiser-Meyer-Olkin (KMO) and Bartlett Chi-Square Tests applied.

Table 4. KMO and Bartlett Chi-Square Test Results

KMO Test	O,81
Barlett Chi-Square	472,55 (0.0000)

According to Table 4, it is seen that the KMO test value is 0.81. This value indicates that the variables are very well suited to principal component analysis. On the other hand, according to the Bartlett Chi-Square Test, it is seen that the variables are suitable for principal component analysis.

The analysis period of the study, which examines the relationship between agricultural added value and inclusive green growth, consists of 1990-2020 annual data, and the variables and explanations included in the model are listed in Table 5.

Table 5. Variables and Explanations

Variables	Descriptions	Sources
AGRGDP	Agriculturel added value	WDI
LABOR	Total labor force	WDI
TEMP	Temperature	General Directorate of State Meteorology- annual average temperature
IGG	Inclusive green growth index	Created by the author using the PCA method

3.2. Model and Method

In this study, it is aimed to empirically examine the relationship between agricultural added value and inclusive green growth in Turkey for the period 1990-2020. In this context, the model used to analyze the data was created as in equation 1:

$$LAGRGDP_t = \beta_0 + \beta_1 IGG_t + \beta_2 TEMP_t + \beta_3 LLABOR_t + \varepsilon_t \qquad (1)$$

In the model, AGRGDP is the dependent variable, agricultural added value, IGG, the inclusive green growth index, TEMP, the dependent variable, global warming, LLABOR, the logarithm of the natural state of the total labor force, and ε_t, the error term. In addition, the t index in the model indicates that the variables are time series and β's indicate the parameter coefficients.

The long-term relationship between inclusive green growth and agricultural value added was examined with the ARDL bounds test.

3.2.1. Unit Root Tests

In the study, first, the stationarity degrees of the series used in the model were determined to avoid obtaining misleading results in the estimation of the model. For this purpose, in the study, Augmented Dickey Fuller (ADF) (1981) and Phillips-Peron (PP) (1988) unit root tests, which are frequently used stationarity tests in the literature, were conducted and the test results obtained are shown in Table 6.

Table 6. ADF and PP Unit Root Test Statistics Results

Variables	ADF	PP
LAGRGDP	-1.368(0.848)	-2.372(0.385)
DLAGRGDP	-9.823(0.000)***	-27.628(0.000)***
IGG	-1.680 (0.734)	-2.380(0.381)
D(IGG)	-7.868 (0.000)***	-7.758(0.000)***
LLABOR	-1.739(0.708)	-1.789(0.684)
D(LLABOR)	-4.275(0.010)**	-4.317(0.009)***
TEMP	-6.017(0.000)***	-6.121(0.000)***

Note: Note: *** sign indicates 1%, ** sign indicates 5% significance level.

In the test results shown in Table 6, it is seen that the variables LAGRGDP, IGG and LLABOR become stationary when the first difference is taken, that is, the degree of stationarity is I(1), while the TEMP variable is stationary at the level, that is, the degree of stationarity is I(0).

3.2.2. ARDL Bounds Test

ARDL (Autoregressive distributed lag) bounds test method is one of the frequently used methods to detect the short and long-term relationship between economic variables. The model was first introduced by Pesaran, Shin and Smith (2001) to investigate the relationship between series combined in the order I(0) and I(1). In an ARDL bounds test for cointegration, there are two steps to determine the relationship between variables: The first step involves determining the long-term relationship through bounds testing. If the test shows the existence of long-term cointegration, the next step is to evaluate the short-term model (Anand et al., 2019). Equation 2 below expresses the general equation of the ARDL model:

$$\Delta Y_t = \beta_o + \sum_{i=1}^{n}\beta_1 \Delta Y_{t-i} + \sum_{i=0}^{n}\beta_2 \Delta X_{t-i} + \varphi_1 Y_{t-1} + \varphi_2 X_{t-1} + \varepsilon_t \qquad (2)$$

In Equation 1, Y_t is the independent variable at time t, Δ is the first difference operator, β_0 is the constant term, β_1 and β_2 are the short-term coefficients, φ_1 and φ_2 are the long-term coefficients, and finally ε_t is the error term.

If we substitute the variables in the study into the equation above, we get equation 3:

$$\Delta LAGRGDP_t = \beta_o + \sum_{i=1}^{n}\beta_1 \Delta LAGRGDP_{t-i} + \sum_{i=0}^{n}\beta_2 \Delta IGG_{t-i}$$

$$+\sum_{i=0}^{n}\beta_3 \Delta LLABOR_{t-i} + \sum_{i=0}^{n}\beta_4 \Delta TEMP_{t-i} + \varphi_1 LAGRGDP_{t-1} + \varphi_2 IGG_{t-1}$$

$$+\varphi_3 LLABOR_{t-1} + \varphi_4 TEMP_{t-1} + \varepsilon_t \tag{3}$$

In the model in Equation 2, the lag length is determined as (1,0,1,0) through the Akaike Information Criterion (AIC), and the hypotheses whose validity was tested are stated below.

$$H_0 = \varphi_1 = \varphi_2 = \varphi_3 = \varphi_4 = 0$$
$$H_0 \neq \varphi_1 \neq \varphi_2 \neq \varphi_3 \neq \varphi_4 \neq 0$$

Before examining the long-term relationship in the ARDL model, it should be examined whether there is a cointegration relationship between the variables. For this, Peseran, et al. (2001) critical values are used. These critical values are compared with the calculated F statistics values. If the calculated F statistics value is greater than the critical values, it can be said that there is a cointegration relationship between the variables.

Table 7. Cointegration Test Results

K	F statistic	Lower Limit 5%	Upper Limit 5%
3	8.19	2.79	3.67

According to the cointegration results expressed in Table 7, it is seen that the F statistic value (8.19) is greater than both the critical lower limit and the upper limit. Accordingly, the hypothesis stating that there is no long-term relationship between the variables is rejected. In other words, there is a long-term cointegration relationship between agricultural added value, temperature increase, total labor force and inclusive green growth considered in the analysis.

After estimating long-run cointegration with the bounds test, the next stage is to estimate the long-run ARDL model. In this context, equation 4 below expresses the long-term coefficients of the model.

$$LAGRGDP_t = \varphi_1 LAGRGDP_{t-1} + \varphi_2 IGG_{t-1} + \varphi_3 LLABOR_{t-1} + \varphi_4 TEMP_{t-1} + \varepsilon_t \quad (4)$$

ARDL long-term coefficients are expressed in Table 8. The findings show that inclusive green growth and total workforce have a positive and significant impact on Turkey's agricultural added value. According to the results, a 1% increase in inclusive green growth increases agricultural added value by 0.11 percent in the long run, and this result is statistically significant. Inclusive green growth, defined as economic growth that provides greater access to sustainable socioeconomic opportunities for a greater number of people, regions or countries, while also protecting the vulnerable, supporting the environment and doing all of this in a fair environment, leads to an increase in both the factors of production and the productivity of these factors. It is opening. The increase in inclusive green growth requires the sustainability of sectors that are the basic dynamics of the economy, especially the agricultural sector. On the other hand, thanks to technological developments, the correct and efficient use of agricultural production capacity also increases the efficiency of the sector in question. The abundance of clean water, agricultural land and forest lands, which are among the environmental indicator components of inclusive green growth, increases according to the development level of the countries. In other words, countries that attach importance to development want to have cleaner water, more agricultural land and forest land. Therefore, the increase in inclusive green growth contributes positively to agricultural added value by increasing the tendency to own more agricultural land and use these lands in the most efficient way.

Similarly, a 1% increase in the total labor force increases the agricultural added value in Turkey by 0.59 percent and the coefficient is statistically significant. Agricultural value-added performance depends on the total workforce and especially the education level, age and productivity of the workforce, as well as the geographical characteristics of the country (Popescu et al., 2021). Since it is known that the production factors in economic analysis theories are labor force, land and capital (Schumpeter, 1954), it is expected that the increase in the total labor force will positively affect the agricultural added value. On the other hand, the TEMP variable in the model negatively affects the agricultural added value, and the coefficient is seen to be statistically insignificant.

Table 8. ARDL Long-Term Coefficients

Variables	Coefficient	Std Error	T Statistic	Prob
IGG	0.115228	0.022230	5.183324	0.0000***
LLABOR	0.592588	0.135030	4.388551	0.0002***
TEMP	-0.010773	0.010857	-0.992235	0.3310

continued on following page

Table 8. Continued

Variables	Coefficient	Std Error	T Statistic	Prob
C	15.16117	2.291221	6.617071	0.0000

Note: *** sign indicates 1% significance level.

After analyzing the long-term parameters, the next stage of the study is to obtain the short-term dynamics. For this purpose, the following ECM model is estimated.

$$\Delta LAGRGDP_t = \beta_o + \sum_{i=1}^{n} \beta_1 \Delta LAGRGDP_{t-i} + \sum_{i=0}^{n} \beta_2 \Delta IGG_{t-i}$$

$$+ \sum_{i=0}^{n} \beta_3 \Delta LLABOR_{t-i} + \sum_{i=0}^{n} \beta_4 \Delta TEMP_{t-i} + \lambda ECM_{t-1} + \varepsilon_t$$

Here, β_o, β_1, β_2, β_3, β_4 the short-term coefficient parameters, ECM_{t-1}, error correction term, λ represents the error correction coefficient.

Table 9. Error correction model test results

Variables	Coefficient	Std Error	T Statistic	Prob
DLLABOR (-1)	0.087340	0.184833	0.472534	0.6408
ECT (-1)	-0.991580	0.143406	-6.914502	0.0000

As can be seen in Table 9, the error correction coefficient lies between 0 and -1 and is statistically significant. This means that the variables move together and similarly towards long-term equilibrium (Anand et al., 2019). Accordingly, the ECT value in the model is -0.99. This means that a 0.9% deviation from long-term equilibrium each year is corrected by the model.

According to the diagnostic and evaluation test statistics results in Table 10, the Breusch-Godfrey LM test, which investigates the existence of autocorrelation, indicates that there is no autocorrelation problem in the model, while the Breusch-Pagan Godfrey test result shows that there is no heteroskedasticity problem in the model.

Table 10. Diagnostic test statistics for the model

R^2	0.565
Log likelihood	63.806
Breusch Godfrey LM Testi	1.334(0.51)
Breusch Pagan Godfrey	6.360(0.272)
Jarque-Bera	0.721(0.697)

Note: Values in parentheses indicate probability values.

The stability of the model is measured by (CUSUM) and (CUSUMQ) tests. If the graphs of both tests remain within the 5% upper and lower limits, it can be said that there is no structural break and the model is stable. Figure 4 below shows the (CUSUM) and (CUSUMQ) tests.

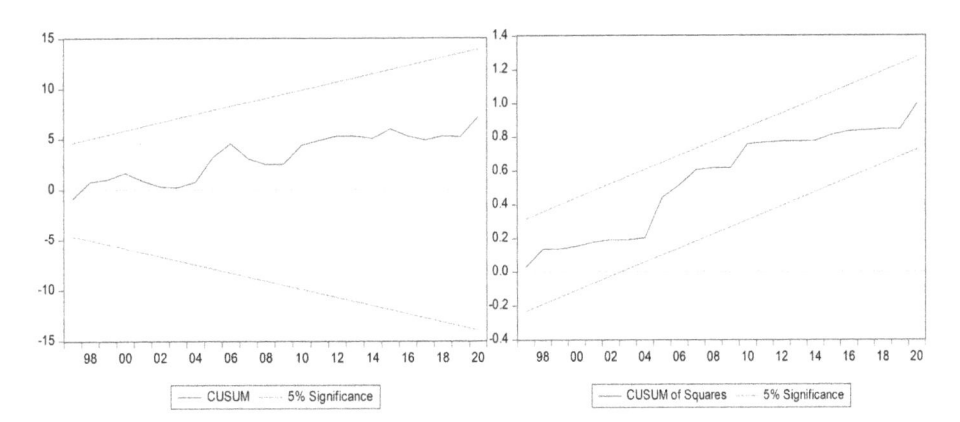

Figure 4. (CUSUM) and (CUSUMQ) Tests

CONCLUSION

Throughout the history of humanity until today, agriculture has been one of the most basic sectors of the economy to obtain food products and ensure food security in meeting the consumption needs of the population. On the other hand, the agricultural sector also provides raw materials to other sectors related to agriculture, which form the basis of the economy. Therefore, productivity in the agricultural sector has a large share in the production costs of other related sectors.

Today, in many developed countries, especially in the European Union member countries, agricultural products are used in the sustainable development of rural communities, in more efficient production while protecting the environment, in the fight against climate change and global warming, in meeting the demands of the society regarding healthy and balanced nutrition, and in keeping up with increasing scientific and technological developments. Great importance is given to productivity and innovation. This contributes to the increase in agricultural added value in these countries.

The aim of this study is to empirically examine whether inclusive green growth increased agricultural added value in Turkey during the 1990-2020 period. In this direction, to represent inclusive green growth, the inclusive green growth index was created by taking into account socio-economic and environmental indicators using the principal component analysis method. Then, the effects of inclusive green growth, total labor force and temperature increase on agricultural added value were examined with the ARDL bounds test method. According to the findings, inclusive green growth has a positive and statistically significant effect on agricultural added value. Sustaining economic growth and sharing it fairly among all segments of the society is only possible if all sectors that meet the needs of the society are supported efficiently, productively and homogeneously within the country. Increasing inclusive green growth will increase the productivity of the country's workforce and natural resources, and thus lead to the development of a production method that creates added value in the agricultural sector, as in other sectors. On the other hand, in the study, the effect of total labor force and temperature increase on agricultural added value was found to be positive, and among these variables, the total labor force variable is statistically significant, but the temperature increase is statistically insignificant.

This study offers a number of policy recommendations as follows.

1. Policies regarding sustainable food systems should be developed to increase agricultural added value within the framework of inclusive green growth.
2. On the other hand, for the efficiency of agricultural production, it is necessary to support the institutional infrastructure that will keep up with technological development.
3. Finally, the areas used in agricultural production should be increased and the energy needs arising during the agricultural production phase in question should be supported by renewable energy sources.

REFERENCES

Acosta, L. A., Maharjan, P., Peyriere, H., Galotto, L., Mamiit, R. J., Ho, C., ... & Anastasia, O. (2019). Green growth index: Concepts, methods and applications (No. 5). GGGI technical report.

Abdou Baoua, M. M. (2023). Tarım Sektörünün Ekonomik Büyümeye Etkisi: Nijer Cumhuriyeti İçin Ampirik Bir Çalışma (1991-2020). Selçuk Üniversitesi, Sosyal bilimler enstitüsü, Doktora tezi.

Altunç, Ö. F., & İşlek, H. (2022). Finansal Dışa Açıklık ve Kapsayıcı Büyüme İlişkisi: MENA Ülkeleri Örneği. *Bingöl Üniversitesi İktisadi ve İdari Bilimler Fakültesi Dergisi*, 6(2), 323–347. DOI: 10.33399/biibfad.1129995

Anand, V., Nizamani, M. Q., & Nizamani, F. Q. (2019). Macroeconomic determinants of inclusive growth in Pakistan: An ARDL approach. *Global Economic Review*, 4(2), 105–118.

Anwar, M. M., Farooqi, S., & Khan, G. Y. (2015). Agriculture Sector Performance: An Analysis Through The Role of Agriculture Sector Share in GDP. Journal of Agricultural Economics. *Extension and Rural Development*, 3(3), 270–275.

Asom, S. T., & Ijirshar, V. U. (2016). Impact of agriculture value added on the growth of Nigerian economy. *Nigerian Journal of Management Sciences, 5 (1), 239, 245.*

Avcı, B. S., & Tonus, Ö. (2020). Kapsayıcı Büyüme Üzerine Bir Değerlendirme. *Anadolu Üniversitesi İktisadi ve İdari Bilimler Fakültesi Dergisi*, 21(4), 37–55.

Avcu, N., & Yayla, N. (2021). Türkiye'de Kırsal Kalkınma ve Göç İlişkisi: Bir Panel Veri Analizi. *Uluslararası İktisadi ve İdari İncelemeler Dergisi*, (32), 67–86.

Awan, A.G. & Vashma Anum. "Impact of Infrastructure Development on Economic Growth", *Journal of Development and Economic Sustainability*; 2(5): 1- 15, 2014

Awokuse, T. O., & Xie, R. (2015). Does agriculture really matter for economic growth in developing countries?. *Canadian Journal of Agricultural Economics/ Revue canadienne d'agroeconomie, 63*(1), 77-99.

Berber, M., Yıldız, B., & Yılmaz, M. S. (2024). Türkiye'de bölgesel düzeyde kapsayıcı büyüme indeksi. *Gazi İktisat ve İşletme Dergisi*, 10(1), 159–178.

Can, Z.G.,Can, U., ve Bal, H. (2019). Kapsayıcı Büyüme ve Küreselleşme: Türkiye Örneği Inclusive Growth and Globalization: The Case of Turkey. *On Eurasian Economies 2019*, 197.

Can, Z. G., Can, U., & Bal, H. (2019). Kapsayıcı büyüme ve küreselleşme: Türkiye örneği. In International Conference on Eurasian Economies, Gaziosmanpaşa, KKTC.

Canbay, Ş., & Kırca, M. (2020). Türkiye'de sanayi ve tarım sektörü faaliyetleri ile iktisadi büyüme arasındaki ilişkiler: Kaldor büyüme yasasının analizi. *İnsan ve Toplum Bilimleri Araştırmaları Dergisi, 9*(1), 143-170.

Desalegn, G., & Tangl, A. (2022). Enhancing green finance for inclusive green growth: A systematic approach. *Sustainability (Basel)*, 14(12), 7416. DOI: 10.3390/su14127416

Dunteman, G. H. (1989). *Principal Components Analysis, Quantitative Applications in the Social Sciences*. Sage Publications. DOI: 10.4135/9781412985475

Ertürkmen, G. (2023). Doğrudan Yabancı Yatırımlar ve Ekonomik Büyümenin Tarım Sektörü Üzerine Etkisi: MIST Ülkeleri İçin Panel Veri Analizi. *Türk Tarım ve Doğa Bilimleri Dergisi*, 10(2), 283–291. DOI: 10.30910/turkjans.1219267

https://www.oecd-ilibrary.org/environment/green-growth-indicators-2017_9789264268586-en

Işıksal, A. Z., & Chimezie, O. J. (2016). Impact of Industrialization in Nigeria. *European Scientific Journal*, 12(10), 328–339. DOI: 10.19044/esj.2016.v12n10p328

Kamran, M., Rafique, M. Z., Nadeem, A. M., & Anwar, S. (2023). Does inclusive growth contribute towards sustainable development? Evidence from selected developing countries. *Social Indicators Research*, 165(2), 409–429. DOI: 10.1007/s11205-022-03020-6

Kellekçi, Ö. L., & Berköz, L. (2006). Konut ve Çevresel Kalite Memnuniyetini Yükselten Faktörler, İtü Dergisi/a, Cilt:5, Sayı:2. *Kısım*, 1, 167–178.

Keyifli, N., Karakurt, B., & Şentürk, S. H. (2022). Kamu Kesimi Büyüklüğü ve Kapsayıcı Büyüme İlişkisi: Yükselen Piyasa Ekonomileri Üzerine Ekonometrik Bir Çalışma. *Sayıştay Dergisi*, 33(124), 39–69. DOI: 10.52836/sayistay.1110377

Kılınç, E. C., & Kılınç, Ş., N. (2021). Türkiye'de Tarımsal Üretim-Gelir İlişkisi: Düzey-2 Bölgeleri Üzerine Bir Uygulama. *Verimlilik Dergisi*, 2, 177–192.

Kopuk, E., & Meçik, O. (2020). Türkiye'de imalat sanayi ve tarım sektörlerinin ekonomik büyüme üzerine etkisi: 1998-2020 dönemi analizi. *Yönetim ve Ekonomi Dergisi*, 27(2), 263–274. DOI: 10.18657/yonveek.693387

McKinley, T. (2010). Inclusive growth criteria and indicators: an inclusive growth index for diagnosis of country progress. Sustainable Development Working Paper Series, ADB, No: 14.

Ngounou, B. A., Tekam Oumbe, H., Ongo Nkoa, B. E., & Noubissi Domguia, E. (2024). Inclusive growth in the face of increasing urbanization: What experience for African countries? *Review of Development Economics*, 28(1), 34–70. DOI: 10.1111/rode.13026

Our World in Data. 2024. (https://ourworldindata.org/grapher/agriculture-value-added-per-worker-wdi?time=2019)

Özbay, Ü. (2023). Türkiye'de Sanayileşme, CO2 Emisyonu, Ekonomik Büyüme ve Tarımsal Üretim İlişkisi: Ampirik Bir Uygulama. *Tarım Ekonomisi Dergisi*, 29(2), 79–91. DOI: 10.24181/tarekoder.1311715

Özgün, F. (2021). Kapsayıcı büyümenin bir unsuru olarak "üretken istihdam" kavramı ve Türkiye üzerine bir değerlendirme. *Ekonomi İşletme ve Maliye Araştırmaları Dergisi*, 3(3), 273–295. DOI: 10.38009/ekimad.994260

Pesaran, M. H., Shin, Y., & Smith, R. J. (2001). Bounds testing approaches to the analysis of level relationships. *Journal of Applied Econometrics*, 16(3), 289–326.

Pham, T. H. A., Lin, C. Y., Moslehpour, M., Van Vo, T. T., Nguyen, H. T., & Nguyen, T. T. H. (2024). What role financial development and resource-curse situation play in inclusive growth of Asian countries. *Resources Policy*, 88, 104498. DOI: 10.1016/j.resourpol.2023.104498

Popescu, A., Dinu, T. A., Stoian, E., & Serban, V. (2021). Efficiency of labor force use in the European Union's agriculture in the period 2011-2020. Scientific Papers Series "Management. *Economic Engineering in Agriculture and Rural Development*, 21(3), 659–672.

Sarpong, B., & Nketiah-Amponsah, E. (2022). Financial inclusion and inclusive growth in sub-Saharan Africa. *Cogent Economics & Finance*, 10(1), 2058734. Advance online publication. DOI: 10.1080/23322039.2022.2058734

Schumpeter, J. A. (1987). *1954, History of Economic Analysis*. Published Routledge.

Sheikh, S. M., Ahmed, M., Shahan, S., & Khan, M. Z. (2012). Importance of Agricultural Sector in Pakistan. *Interdisciplinary Journal of Contemporary Research in Business*, 3(12), 421.

Tarım ve Orman Bakanlığı. (2021). (https://www.tarimorman.gov.tr/TAGEM/Belgeler/yayin/TARIMSAL%20DI%C5%9E%20T%C4%B0CARET%20SPB%202021-2025.pdf)

Ticaret Bakanlığı, T. C. (2024). https://ticaret.gov.tr/data/5b8700a513b8761450e18d81/Genel%20Tar%C4%B1m%20Sekt%C3%B6r%C3%BC%20Raporu.pdf

Whajah, J., & Godfred, A. B. (2019). Government Size, Public Debt and Inclusive Growth in Africa. *Research in International Business and Finance*, 49, 225–240. DOI: 10.1016/j.ribaf.2019.03.008

Xu, H., Ahmad, M., Aziz, A. L., Uddin, I., Aljuaid, M., & Gu, X. (2024). The linkages between energy efficiency, renewable electricity, human capital and inclusive growth: The role of technological development. *Energy Strategy Reviews*, 53, 101414. DOI: 10.1016/j.esr.2024.101414

Yang, Z., Vitenu-Sackey, P. A., Hao, L., & Tao, Y. (2023). Economic freedom, inclusive growth, and financial development: A heterogeneous panel analysis of developing countries. *PLoS One*, 18(7), e0288346. https://ticaret.gov.tr/data/5b870 0a513b8761450e18d81/Genel%20Tar%C4%B1m%20Sekt%C3%B6r%C3%BC%20 Raporu.pdf. DOI: 10.1371/journal.pone.0288346 PMID: 37432915

KEY TERMS AND DEFINITIONS

Agricultural Value Added: It is the numerical difference between the total outputs created in the agricultural sector and the inputs.

Green Growth: New and different growth strategy that adapts to changing conditions without harming the environment, minimizes ecological risks, and considers future generations.

Inclusive Growth: It is growth that gives the population as a whole the chance of increasing their welfare and allows all the components of welfare, whether monetary or non-monetary, to be distributed fairly throughout society.

Inclusive Green Growth: Economic growth that provides greater access to sustainable socio-economic opportunities for more people, regions or countries, protects the vulnerable and does so in an equitable environment.

Sustainable Development Goals: It is a universal call to action expressing the goals aimed to be achieved by the end of 2030 by the member states of the United Nations.

Chapter 20
Sustainable Development and Ecological Footprint in Türkiye

Hüseyin Naci Bayraç
Faculty of Economics and Administrative Sciences, Eskisehir Osmangazi University, Turkey

Fatih Çemrek
https://orcid.org/0000-0002-6528-7159
Faculty of Science, Eskisehir Osmangazi University, Turkey

ABSTRACT

The ecological footprint serves as a devised methodology aimed at quantifying the impact of human endeavors on ecosystems. Sustainability, in this context, entails the augmentation of biologically productive areas, fortification of their capacity for self-regeneration, and preservation thereof. The ecological footprint framework emerges as a numerical tool pivotal for fostering the sustainable utilization of resources. The principal objective of this research is to identify the determinants contributing to the ecological footprint within the framework of sustainable development, focusing on selected indicators for Türkiye, namely Ecological Footprint per Capita, CO_2 Emissions per Capita, GDP per Capita, Energy Consumption per Capita. The chapter aims to explore the interrelationships among these variables through cointegration and causality analyses.

DOI: 10.4018/979-8-3693-5508-4.ch020

1. INTRODUCTION

The increase in the world population, rapid changes in industry and technology, international competition, deforestation, agricultural development, urbanization, unlimited and unconscious consumption mentality cause the rapid destruction of nature by human hands. As a result of this destruction, a wide range of environmental problems arise, such as a decrease in biological diversity, global warming, acid rain, water, soil and air pollution, unplanned urbanization and depletion of natural resources. Ecological footprint is a method developed to measure the impact of human activities on ecosystems. All products produced as a result of people's physiological, economic and social activities constitute the ecological footprint.

Ecological footprint, used as an indicator of sustainability, carries the idea of leaving a protected environment to the next generations. Sustainability envisages increasing biologically existing productive areas, their ability to renew themselves and the maintenance of their renewal capacity. In order to sustain vital activities, individuals must organize their economic activities, especially their living conditions, by taking into account the biological carrying capacity of the earth.

The ecological footprint indicator is a numerical method used to ensure sustainable use of resources. This method represents a whole of ecological economics and sustainability concepts, which state that ecological resources have economic values. Calculating the ecological footprint is of great importance in terms of creating ecological awareness and developing ecological awareness. Institutions that reduce their ecological footprint can contribute to a sustainable movement.

The concept of ecological footprint; It was defined by Wackernagel and Rees to estimate the ecological area covered by the human race on a local, regional and global scale. The ecological footprint is compared with the total productive area in terms of living diversity and reveals whether the area in question continues its vital activities within its own borders. If the footprint as a result of the calculation is greater than the total productive area in terms of living diversity, it means that the economy of this area consumes more forests, cultivated land and other resources than it can handle, and this area produces waste above its digestion capacity.

An economy's or population's critical need for natural capital relative to biologically productive areas is represented by its ecological footprint. Ecological footprint is determined depending on population size, material living standards, technology used and ecological productivity (Mızık and Avdan, 2020: 457).

The work of the World Commission on Environment and Development, established by the United Nations, indicates that solutions to environmental problems are possible by adopting and implementing the principle of sustainable development. The report titled Our Common Future, prepared by the Commission, aims to disseminate the understanding of sustainability throughout the world. Sustainable development aims to achieve development without destroying or damaging natural resources and causing damage to the ecological cycle. Since the ecological footprint takes into account indicators of sustainability, it is a usable tool for environmental policy and management.

The main purpose of this study is to determine the factors that constitute the ecological footprint in the sustainable development process, the indicators selected for Turkey (Ecological Footprint per Capita (global hectare), CO2 Emission per Capita, GDP per Capita and Energy Consumption per Capita (kg oil equivalent)) variables. The aim is to investigate the relationships between them through cointegration and causality analysis. Annual data for the period 1999-2022 will be used in the study. Then, the results obtained and the strategies and policies implemented to reduce the ecological footprint will be discussed.

2. SUSTAINABLE DEVELOPMENT

The concept of sustainability refers to the sustainability of the functioning of a society, ecosystem or a continuous system without interruption and deterioration, without excessive use, damaging the vital connections of resources or overloading them (Yıldız, 2024; 31). Today, the world's resources are being depleted at a rate above sustainable levels, and humanity has to meet the needs of the present while also taking care of the needs of the future. Sustainability refers to the efficient transfer of natural resources to future generations, and ecological footprint data is used to monitor this efficiency.

Sustainable development aims to protect the world with limited resources on the one hand, and to ensure development on the other hand, in order to leave a sustainable world to future generations. In 1987, the United Nations World Commission on Environment and Development published the report "Our Common Future", also known as the Brundtland Report. According to the report, the concept of sustainable development is defined as development that enables future generations to meet their current needs without compromising their ability to meet their own needs. More broadly, sustainable development; It can also be defined as a process of change in which the use of resources, direction of investments, technological developments and institutional changes are in harmony and will increase the current and future potential to meet human needs and desires.

The sustainable development process has an "egalitarian and balanced" nature. Therefore, in order for development to continue indefinitely, the interests of groups of people of the same and different generations must be balanced, and at the same time the economic, social and environmental dimensions must be realized in an interconnected manner. Here, it is aimed that economic and social developments will provide a better quality of life for current and future generations, in a way that preserves the current natural balance of the world.

Sustainable development has a multidimensional and dynamic structure. Wealth, development and success, usually measured by the level of GDP, need to be renewed to include social and environmental indicators. To measure the degree of sustainable development, each country has different index systems that reflect the green economy approach of international organizations, public and private research institutions. Among these, the Global Footprint Index indicator has become increasingly popular in recent years. Existing biocapacity is of great importance in using the ecological footprint as a sustainability indicator. If the footprint is more than the biocapacity for an area examined, then ecological deficit; If it is less, there is an ecological surplus. While the first situation does not allow sustainability, the second is a prerequisite for ensuring sustainability (Pearce and Barbier, 2000: 127).

Ecological footprint; as a basic indicator of sustainable development, it can be used to see the changes that changes in human activities and consumption habits will create on the environment and to establish a relationship between global footprints and local activities. The main contribution of ecological footprint measurements to sustainable development is that it reveals the dimensions of the pressure on the ecosystem and has an important role in spreading environmental awareness by creating ecological difference.

3. ECOLOGICAL FOOTPRINT

Climate change, which is affected by factors such as rapid population growth in the world economy, globalization, urbanization, industrialization, and advances in technological activities, global warming, depletion and depletion of the ozone layer, melting of glaciers, greenhouse gas emissions, deterioration in environmental factors such as air pollution, excessive precipitation, hot weather, etc. Problems such as air waves, food and water scarcity negatively affect ecosystems and societies. Environmental degradation also negatively affects macroeconomic factors such as human health, workforce, productivity and sustainable growth. The main source of these negative developments is the activities carried out by human beings. The concept of ecological footprint deals with humankind's degradation of nature and the resulting environmental problems, and gives the balance of resources provided by the ecosystem against the demands of people.

Ecological footprint is one of the most widely used indicators of sustainability worldwide in recent years. This concept, which aims at environmental sustainability and is in line with the purpose of strong sustainability, was introduced to the literature in the 1990s with the work of William Rees and Mathis Wackernagel. Ecological footprint is an area-based indicator that measures the intensity of natural resource use and waste assimilation activity in a certain area. The ecological footprint also shows how much biologically productive space an economy with a given population needs to produce the resources it consumes using existing technology and to ensure the absorption of the waste it creates into nature.

Following the Rio Summit in 1992, the idea of ecological footprint has gained widespread acceptance worldwide as a sustainability-oriented approach. Today, humanity consumes much more than the world's production. Therefore, humanity's ecological footprint is 25% greater than the world's resource capacity today. It takes approximately one year and three months for the world to reproduce one year's consumption of humanity. Global overshoot threatens the sustainability of both humanity and biodiversity. If the limit exceedance, which increases the pressure of the ecological footprint on resources, continues, there will be permanent decreases in the world's resource supply/productivity. Preventing limit exceeding is possible by realizing the ecological boundaries of the world and the ecological footprint within these boundaries (Demirel, 2020: 967).

The strength of the ecological footprint is that it reduces all human impacts related to the use of natural resources and the environment to a single dimension, the need for space to enable their maintenance. An important strength of the ecological footprint is that it reduces the vast extent of environmental data into a single measure that can easily compare the carrying capacity of countries.

Ecological footprint emerged when humanity started to produce and consume the world's resources and expresses how much people use the world's resources during their life cycles. This concept provides information about the sustainability of the world by calculating the resources of the world with its ecological footprint and providing information about our resource stock. Having an ecological footprint lower than total resources is of great importance in terms of sustainability for the world.

In ecological footprint calculations, the main basis of footprint calculations is the observation of consumed resources and the resulting wastes and the measurement of the biologically productive area required to eliminate the wastes. Ecological footprints created based on these foundations show the biological productive area used by people in the production and consumption cycle.

National scale calculation formula of ecological footprint calculated in terms of area; It is expressed as Ecological Footprint (hectare) = Consumption x Production Area x Population. The unit of measurement is expressed in a common unit called the global hectare. It is calculated as 1 hectare = 2.47 acres or 10,000 square meters.

The equation created by Tiezzi et al. for ecological footprint calculation;

$$EF = \frac{\sum T_i}{Y_w} * AQF_i \qquad (1)$$

Ti: annual consumption rate by a nation for product i,
Yw: World average yield value for product i,
AQFi: Refers to the equivalence factor for product i.

Ecological footprint is calculated for the individual, society, city, region and planet. The balance between ecological footprint and biological capacity is important in the calculation. The low or high level between them shows what kind of production and consumption should be done. The ecological footprint calculation formula is used as an important tool in understanding the environmental impacts of individuals or societies and developing strategies to ensure continued sustainability.

WWF (World Wildlife Fund) calculates the ecological footprint by taking into account 6 types of land use that produce or provide resources for use by humans. These are agricultural areas, pastures, forests for timber and fuelwood, fishing areas, infrastructure and other construction areas, and forest areas necessary for the absorption of carbon emissions. The sum of the footprint calculated for each area constitutes the ecological footprint (Ulucak, 2015: 120).

i. *Carbon Footprint;* It is the total amount of CO_2 emissions accumulated directly or indirectly by a product resulting from human activities throughout its lifetime. When calculating CO_2 emissions, carbon released from fossil and non-fossil fuel use, electricity use and other activities are taken into account using the IEA's database. The largest part of the ecological footprint is the carbon footprint. Since greenhouse gases released into the atmosphere are considered waste, carbon footprint constitutes the only type of waste used in calculating the ecological footprint. The most general and simple carbon footprint calculation formula: Carbon Footprint = Fuel Consumption x Emission Factor.

ii. *Agricultural Lands Footprint;* It covers the areas where all products such as agricultural products, animal feed, and mowed meadows that are consumed or stocked by humans are grown. Data for these are obtained from FAO's product and trade statistics and national databases. Agricultural footprint is an indicator that shows the size and productivity of the land used to grow consumed agricultural products. Since the amount of agricultural products consumed should not exceed the amount produced, the footprint of agricultural areas should not exceed the biological capacity of agriculture. When calculating the Agricultural Land Footprint, unsustainable practices such as excessive or incorrect use of pesticides, fertilizers and water, and product selection that is not suitable for climate and soil structure are not included in the calculations as they will negatively affect agricultural production.

iii. *Grassland Footprint;* Grasslands that are demanded to feed animals and fall within the scope of commercial activities are taken into account. The areas where plants produced for feed and product residues that can be used for animals will be obtained are largely obtained from FAO's database. Grassland footprint; It refers to the pastures used for people's demands for animal products such as meat, milk, leather and wool. However, in this calculation, factors such as inefficiency and erosion of pasture lands as a result of excessive and misuse were not taken into account.
iv. *Fishing Areas Footprint;* It is based on production estimates required to carry out fishing activities and shows the fishing demand equivalent to the water area that will enable the country to fish sustainably. FAO's fish statistics are used for marine and freshwater products.
v. *Forest Areas Footprint;* This trace, which represents humankind's demand for forests, is calculated based on the amount of timber, cellulose, wood products and trees to be burned. The sum of domestic resources and products obtained from abroad constitutes the national forest footprint. FAO database is used for this calculation based on IPCC methodology.
vi. *Construction Areas Footprint;* human beings' housing, transportation, industrial production, dams, etc. It takes into account the infrastructure and superstructure formations, and considering that people generally occupy productive areas, these areas are considered to represent productive areas. Databases of WRI and BP are used.

This six-footprint calculation is considered a more detailed indicator than indicators measuring the level of environmental degradation (Destek and Sarkodie, 2019; 2484). Examining the ecological footprint in detail among different species allows identifying areas where ecological deficit is concentrated, monitoring changes over time, and making more accurate plans for the effective use of resources. Knowing and monitoring the ecological footprint distribution of individuals and decision makers in different consumption categories in society contributes to determining in which areas consumption should be balanced.

Among these components, carbon footprint is the fastest growing factor, not only greater than the sum of the effects of all other components. Since the carbon footprint constitutes approximately 60% of the global ecological footprint, scientists primarily pay attention to the carbon footprint to reduce the ecological footprint. The main policies to be implemented to reduce the ecological footprint are:

i. *Improving energy production;* carbon footprint, which is one of the most important ones responsible for the ecological footprint, occurs as a result of burning fossil fuels. In order to transition to a carbon-free economy, investments in renewable energy sources that reduce dependence on fossil fuels, improvement of production and consumption habits, and practices and policies that consider energy saving and efficiency should be followed.

ii. *Ensuring balanced use of natural resources;* agricultural areas, pastures, forests, wetlands and seas designated as production areas should be used efficiently by realizing that they are limited. In addition to using natural resources in a renewable, clean and healthy way, it is also necessary to minimize the waste generated.

iii. *Control of the population;* population growth rate is a very important factor that directly affects the ecological footprint. There is a human capacity that a city, region, country or the whole world can handle. This limit, which has already been exceeded, poses a great threat for the coming years. Practices should be initiated to prevent population growth by raising people's awareness.

iv. *Expanding recycling;* recycling policies should be expanded to ensure the renewability of natural resources, reduce waste, increase production efficiency, reduce the use of resources that production demands from the environment, and reduce carbon emissions generated during the production and transportation stages.

v. *Using substances that nature can transform;* it will reduce waste and carbon emissions. Biodegradable and recyclable products should be preferred instead of heavy metals, toxic substances, plastic and synthetic materials.

vi. *Local governments should take ecological values into account when planning cities;* protecting the habitats where animal and plant populations and beneficial organisms live, monitoring policies such as bioenergy use, recycling efforts, and encouraging public transportation are among the main duties of local administrators.

vii. *Practices aimed at developing ecological awareness;* it is one of the fundamental values that should spread from the individual to the family, from the city to the society and the country.

Depletion of biological resources that support ecological life is called "ecological limit exceedance". Consuming natural resources faster than their renewal period causes nature to exceed its own capacity. The world economy has begun to experience ecological overshoot since the early 1970s.

In order to reduce ecological limit exceedance; Including the ecological footprint factor in development plans, informing the citizens of the state on issues such as ecological footprint, biodiversity and climate change and making international collaborations, encouraging renewable energy sources to reduce carbon emissions, commissioning rainwater collection and integrated water treatment systems, It is necessary to implement mechanisms for recycling and minimizing waste, efficient use of production resources, reducing the population growth rate, protecting production areas, and implementing practices to prevent waste and excessive use.

4. LITERATURE REVIEW

Studies investigating the relationships between ecological footprint, CO2 emissions and economic growth and other macroeconomic variables are included in the following paragraphs.

Acar and Aşıcı (2017) investigated the income-environment relationship in Turkey within the framework of the Environmental Kuznets Curve (EKC) and the components of the ecological footprint indicator. In the analysis for the period 1961-2008, cointegration techniques were used. It was concluded that there is an inverse U-shaped relationship between production footprint and income. It has been determined that consumption, import and export footprints increase monotonously with income. In addition, it was stated that the import footprint is not sufficient to close the biocapacity gap in Turkey, which causes a continuous decrease in domestic biocapacity.

Doğan et al. (2020), in this study, investigated the validity of the ICC hypothesis for BRICST countries using the ecological footprint. As a result of the analysis made with the annual data covering the period 1980-2014, it was stated that the ICC hypothesis was not valid and that energy density and energy structure were important determinants of environmental degradation.

Kongbuamai et al. (2020) investigated the effects of economic growth, energy consumption, tourism, and natural resources on the ecological footprint of natural resources in ASEAN countries for the period 1995-2016. Cross sectional dependency test, second generation unit root test and Westerlund cointegration test were used in the analysis of the data. As a result of the study, it was stated that there is an inverted U-shaped ECC behavior in ASEAN countries, so there is a negative relationship between tourism and natural resources and ecological footprint.

In his study, Kılınç (2021) used panel data methods of the effects of energy R&D and demonstration expenditures on the ecological footprint using the data of OECD countries for the period 2002-2016. According to the results obtained from the study, it was determined that the ecological footprint decreased with the increase in energy, R&D and demonstration expenditures. In addition, it has been concluded that it increases the ecological footprint with the increase in energy use and GDP per capita.

Karaaslan and Çamkaya (2022) investigated the effects of economic growth (GDP), health expenditures (HE), renewable (REC) and non-renewable energy consumption (NREC) on CO2 emissions for Turkey. In the study, ARDL method was used to examine long and short-term effects and Toda-Yamamoto causality test was used to determine causality. According to the results of the ARDL method, it was determined that there was a cointegration relationship between the variables examined. According to the Toda-Yamamoto causality test, it was concluded that there is a one-way causality relationship from GDP, HE, REC and NREC to CO2.

Kutlu (2023) investigated the effect of tourism and economic growth on CO2 emissions by examining the period between 1992 and 2020 regarding the 10 countries that attract the most tourists in the world. In the study, the data were analyzed by panel data analysis method. When the results obtained from the study were examined, it was determined that there was a long-term relationship between CO2 emissions, gross domestic product (GDP) and tourism income series according to the results of the Pedroni and Westerlund cointegration tests. By applying Panel Dynamic Least Squares (DOLS) and Fully Corrected Least Squares (FMOLS) methods, it was concluded that the effect of tourist numbers and tourism revenues on CO2 emissions was negative and GDP had a positive effect.

Ullah et al. (2023) investigated the impact of natural resources, urbanization, biological capacity, and economic growth (EG) on ecological footprint (EFP) in Turkey between 1970 and 2018. ARDL method was used to investigate the short and long-term effects. According to the results, it was determined that EG and biological capacity increased EFP in both the short and long term. When the long-term results were evaluated, it was stated that the Environmental Kuznets Curve (ECC) hypothesis is valid for Turkey and urbanization has a negative effect on EFP. The Vector Error Correction Model (VECM) was applied to determine the relationship between the variables and in the short term, from EG to EFP; It has been determined that there is a one-way causality relationship from urbanization to economic growth, from biological capacity to EG. According to the results of long-term causality analysis, it was observed that there was a bidirectional causality relationship between EFP, urbanization and biological capacity series.

Şahin Kutlu and Kutlu (2022) investigated the impact of tourism activities on the ecological footprint in Turkey using the data of the period 1970-2017 (primary energy consumption, per capita income, tourism expenditure, tourism income, and total natural resource rent) with the ARDL boundary test approach. For this purpose, the variables used in the study are; primary energy consumption, per capita income, tourism expenditures, tourism revenues and total natural resource rent. Analysis results; It shows that energy consumption and tourism expenditures have a positive effect on the ecological footprint in the long run. In addition, the impact of per capita income and tourism revenues on ecological footprint in the long run has been reported negatively. However, it has been determined that the total natural resource rent affects the ecological footprint only in the short term.

5. DATA, METHODOLOGY AND ANALYSIS

In this study, using the annual data between the period 1999-2022, it is investigated whether there is a causal relationship between EFP (Ecological Footprint; global hectares/capita), CO_2 emissions (metric tons/capita) and GDP (2015 constant prices US$/capita) time series for Turkey with the Johansen cointegration test. Ecological footprint data is prepared by the Global Footprint Foundation and can be found on the (https://data.footprintnetwork.org/) website; CO2 emission and GDP data were also obtained from the official website of the World Bank (https://databank.worldbank.org/home.aspx).

5.1. Unit Root Tests

In order to be able to apply the cointegration tests used to determine whether there is a long-term relationship between the time series, it is necessary that the time series under study be stable to the same degree. Whether the time series are stationary or to what degree they are stationary is determined by unit root tests. The most commonly used tests are DF and ADF (Augmented Dickey and Fuller) (Dickey and Fuller, 1979; 1981), PP (Phillips and Perron, 1988), KPSS (Kwiatkowski et al. 1992). In this study, ADF and PP unit root tests were applied. In unit root tests, zero and absence hypotheses are expressed as follows.

H_0: The series is not stationary (the serial unit contains roots)
H_1: The series is stationary (there are no unit roots in the series) (Enders, 2004).

The results obtained from the unit root test are given in Table 1. When Table 1 is examined; While EFP, CO2 and GDP are at the level of time series, the H_0 hypothesis could not be rejected (It was determined that the series were not stationary. If the time series examined were taken with a difference of one degree, the series in question became stationary (both series are stationary in the first order) and the series is expressed as I (1). After the unit root tests are performed, it is investigated whether the linear combination of these two time series is stationary (I (expressed as 0)).

Table 1. ADF Unit Root Tests Results

	ADF			Phillips-Perron		
	None	Intercept	Trend and Intercept	Unfixed, No Trend	Fixed, No Trend	Fixed, Trendy
EFP (LEVEL)	1,632 (-1.956)	-0,822 (-3,021)	-2,208 (-3.633)	3,923 (-1.956)	-0,696 (-2.998)	-2,338 (-3.622)
CO2 (LEVEL)	1,708 (-1.956)	-1,074 (-3,012)	-2,904 (-3,633)	4,388 (-1.956)	-0,818 (-2.998)	-3,108 (-3.622)
GDP (LEVEL)	4,485 (-1.956)	-1,019 (-2,998)	-3,315 (-3,633)	6,117 (-1.956)	1,618 (-2.998)	-2,219 (-3.622)
EFP (1'st Difference)	-5,496 (-1.957)	-4,646 (-3,020)	-4,542 (-3.658)	-5,402 (-1.957)	-5,946 (-3,005)	-5,829 (-3.633)
CO2 (1'st Difference)	-4,653 (-1.957)	-5,258 (-3,012)	-5,141 (-3,645)	-4,653 (-1.957)	-6,970 (-3,005)	-6,625 (-3,633)
GDP (1'st Difference)	-2,514 (-1.957)	-3,906 (-3,005)	-4,197 (-3,633)	-2,514 (-1,95)	-3,829 (-3,005)	-4,174 (-3,633)

5.2. Cointegration Analysis

Johansen cointegration analysis, which are used to determine whether there is a long-term relationship between time series, are described in the following sections.

In econometric analyses of time series, cointegration is defined as the long-term movement of at least two or more time series variables in the same direction. First, in the approach proposed by Engle and Granger in 1987, cointegration relationships are estimated with the help of regression analysis. In the case of cointegration between the time series variables under consideration, the deviation from the equilibrium relationship is less than the 0th degree. It is defined as being integrated (static). In a 1993 study, Banerjee et al. defined cointegration as the statistical expression of the general structure of equilibrium-shaped relationships. If the degree of integration of two time series denoted as X_t and Y_t is not the same, it is understood that there is no long-term relationship between these two time series. In other words, it is said that the error term that arises as a result of a linear relationship between these two time series is not stationary. This can also be defined as these two time series not moving together or moving away from each other (Maddala and Kim, 1998).

If a time series under study does not deviate from the mean without taking the first difference (it is stationary), this time series is called stationary at the level, and this time series is shown as I(0). The linear combination of two time series, X and Y, which are different from the first order, is I(1). However, sometimes a linear combination of two time series variables that are stationary in the first order can also produce a variable that is stationary at the level. Thus, such time series are called cointgrated series. In other words, if two time series such as Xt and Yt are in the case of I(1) and

$$\varepsilon_t = Y_t - \alpha X_t \tag{2}$$

In the equation, ε_t if the error level is stationary, the time series variables Xt and Y_t are cointegrated and are defined by the notation CI(1,1). The coefficient in the equation is called $\alpha$the cointegration coefficient. In the case of more than two time series variables, the expression is called $\alpha$the cointegration vector (Cromwell et al., 1994). In 1987, Engle and Granger first introduced a one-equation two-stage cointegration analysis.

Johansen (1988) proposed a test based on the maximum likelihood method in the Vector Autoregression (VAR) model to determine the multiple cointegration vectors that can occur between two or more time series. This approach, also known as the Johansen method, is used to determine the maximum possible number of cointegration vectors among the time series variables under investigation and to obtain maximum likelihood estimates of the adjustment parameters of this cointegration vector (Holden and Thompson, 1992).

In the cointegration test, zero and opposite hypotheses are expressed as follows:

H0: There is no cointegration relationship between the series (r=0)
H1: There are at most r cointegration vectors.

The results of the Johansen Cointegration analysis for Turkey are given in Table 2.

When the results in Table 2 are examined, the null hypothesis, which is expressed as no cointegration between the EFP, CO2 AND GDP time series (r=0) according to the Trace test and the Greatest Eigenvalue Statistic, is rejected. From this, it can be stated that the EFP, CO2 and GDP series are related to each other in the long run.

Table 2. Johansen Cointegration Test Results

H_0	H_1	Test Statistics	% 95 Critical Value	Prob	Eigenvalue
Trace Test					
r=0	r=1	50.99009	42.91525	0.0064	0.774645
r<=1	r=2	18.20836	25.87211	0.3301	0.508259
r<=2	R=3	2.592670	12.51798	0.9210	0.111169
Largest Eigenvalue (λ_{max})					
r=0	r=1	32.78173	25.82321	0.0051	0.774645

continued on following page

Table 2. Continued

H₀	H₁	Test Statistics	% 95 Critical Value	Prob	Eigenvalue
r<=1	r=2	15.61569	19.38704	0.1625	0.508259
r<=2	r=3	2.592670	12.51798	0.9210	0.111169

Note: r: is the number of cointegration vectors.

Tablo 3. *VEC Model Resutls*

Causality Equation	Coefficient	Standard Mistake	t value	Adjusted R^2
ΔGDP_{-1}	4.92E-05	6.1E-05	0.81297	
ΔGDP_{-2}	4.458E-06	6.0E-05	0.07388	
$\Delta CO2_{-1}$	-0.151038	0.16760	-0.90119	
$\Delta C=2_{-2}$	-0.431079	0.14623	-2.947595	
$EC1_{-1}$	-1.334979	0.64296	**-2,07630**	0.218908
Dependent Variable: $\Delta CO2$				
$\Delta EFP-1$	-0.197685	1.60732	-0.12299	
$\Delta EFP-2$	1.418183	1.36282	1.04062	
$\Delta GDP-1$	-5.72E-05	0.00020	-0.28574	
$\Delta GDP-2$	-9.81E-05	0.00020	-0.49339	
EC t-1	0.832395	2.12361	0.40610	0.344585
Dependent Variable: ΔGDP				
$\Delta CO2-1$	-577.3110	828.103	-0.69715	
$\Delta CO2-2$	-2317.052	722.522	-3.20690	
$\Delta EFP-1$	2055.688	2404.52	0.85493	0.276305
$\Delta EFP-2$	4418.974	2038.75	2.16749	
EC t-1	-5087.550	3176.87	-1.60143	

From the results in Table 3; If the EFP variable is the dependent variable, it is seen that the error correction term shown as ECt-1 in the model provides statistical significance. If the GDP variable is the dependent variable, it is seen that the ECt-1 coefficient is not statistically significant. If the CO2 variable is the dependent variable, it is seen that the ECt-1 coefficient is not statistically significant. Hence; In the short run, there is a causal relationship between EFP and the CO2 and GDP time series.

6. CONCLUSION

The main argument of the ecological footprint concept is to emphasize sustainability by leaving a protected environment for future generations. Sustainability envisages increasing living productive areas in terms of quality and quantity, ensuring that these areas renew themselves and maintaining their renewal capacity.

Calculating the ecological footprint is of great importance in terms of creating ecological awareness and consciousness, as it reveals negative attitudes and behaviors developed towards the ecosystem. The ecological footprint allows making a prediction about how much the world's carrying capacity has been exceeded, rather than precise and absolute expressions.

In this study, it was investigated whether there is a relationship between ecological footprint and CO2 emissions and economic growth for Turkey. As a result of the analyzes, it was determined that the EFP, CO2 and GDP time series move with each other in the long term.

According to the results of the VEC model, it was determined that there was a causality relationship between EFP and CO2 and GDP time series in the short term. When the results obtained are examined economically, it will be possible to reduce CO2 emissions, reduce the use of fossil fuels and use other alternative energy sources more in order to reduce the ecological footprint indicator, and thus achieve economic growth.

When the results obtained from this study are evaluated, it is thought that different studies can be carried out by changing the period of the data used in the analysis or by adding other related series. It is thought that the results obtained from the study will open new horizons for energy and economy managers/decision-makers and researchers who will work in this field.

The fact that the rate of consumption of natural resources in Turkey is faster than the rate of production is increasing the ecological gap. According to the WWF report, while the ecological footprint of per capita consumption in Turkey is equal to the world average, its per capita biocapacity is below the world average. This situation shows that Turkey has a higher ecological debt than the world average. Turkey's Ecological Footprint value is 3.4 global hectares, according to the 2016 calculations of the Global Footprint Network. In addition, the biocapacity value, which is of great importance in the sustainability of ecological resources, is 1.5 global hectares, according to the 2016 calculations of the Global Footprint Network. The difference between Ecological Footprint and biocapacity is (-) 1.9 global hectares, which indicates a gap in ecological resources.

The ecological trade deficit is gradually increasing due to the fact that the amount of natural resources that Turkey imports from abroad is greater than what it exports. If the current situation continues like this, in the coming years we will face a gradually decreasing biological capacity problem in response to an ever-growing ecological footprint. Informing its citizens and making international collaborations on issues such as biodiversity and climate change for reducing the ecological footprint and a sustainable future, encouraging renewable energy sources, commissioning rainwater collection and integrated water treatment systems, implementing mechanisms for recycling and minimizing waste. It is necessary to implement practices aimed at reducing the population growth rate and preventing waste and overuse.

REFERENCES

Acar, S., & Aşıcı, A. A. (2017). Nature and Economic Growth in Turkey: What Does Ecological Footprint Imply? *Middle East Development Journal*, 9(1), 101–115. DOI: 10.1080/17938120.2017.1288475

Banerjee, A., Dolado, J. J., Galbraith, J. W., & Hendry, D. (1993). *Co-integration, error correction, and the econometric analysis of non-stationary data.* Oxford university press.

BP, (2021), BP Statistical Review of World Energy, June 2022.

Cromwell, J. B., Hannan, M. J., Labys, W. C., & Terraza, M. (1994). *Multivariate Tests for Time Series Models.* Sage Publications Inc. DOI: 10.4135/9781412985239

Demirel, M. (2022). Ecologic Footprint Makes History: Earth Overshoot Day. *Journal of Economics and Administrative Sciences*, 23(4), 963–980.

Dergıades, T., Martınopoulos, G., & Tsoulfıdıs, L. (2013). Energy Consumption and Economic Growth: Parametric and Non-Parametric Causality Testing for the Case of Greece. *Energy Economics*, 36, 686–697. DOI: 10.1016/j.eneco.2012.11.017

Destek, M. A., & Sarkodie, S. A. (2019). Investigation of Environmental Kuznets Curve for Ecological Footprint: The Role of Energy and Financial Development. *The Science of the Total Environment*, 650, 2483–2489. DOI: 10.1016/j.scitotenv.2018.10.017 PMID: 30293003

Dickey, D. A., & Fuller, W. A. (1979). Distribution of the Estimators for Autoregressive Time Series with a Unit Root. *Journal of the American Statistical Association*, 74, 427–431.

Dickey, D. A., & Fuller, W. A. (1981). Likelihood Ratio Statistics for Autoregressive Time Series With Unit Root. *Econometrica*, 49(4), 1057–1073. DOI: 10.2307/1912517

Doğan, E., Ulucak, R., Kocak, E., & Isik, C. (2020). The Use of Ecological Footprint in Estimating the Environmental Kuznets Curve Hypothesis For BRICST by Considering Cross-Section Dependence and Heterogeneity. *The Science of the Total Environment*, 723, 723. DOI: 10.1016/j.scitotenv.2020.138063 PMID: 32217396

Enders, W. (2004), Applied Econometric Time Series, 2'nd Edition John Wiley&Sons Inc. USA.

Engle, R. F., Granger, C., & Willaim, J. (1987). Co-Integration and Error Correction Representation, Estimation, and Testing. *Econometrica*, 55(2), 251–276. DOI: 10.2307/1913236

Erdoğan, S., & Gürbüz, S. (2014). The Relationship between Energy Consumption and Economic Growth in Turkey: Time Series Analysis with Structural Breaks. *Selçuk University Social Sciences Institute Journal*, 32, 79–87.

Georgantopoulos, A. G., & Tsamıs, A. (2011). The Relationship Between Energy Consumption and GDP: A Causality Analysis on Balkan Countries. *European Journal of Scientific Research*, 61(3), 372–380.

Holden, K., & Thompson, J. (1992). Co-Integration: An Introductory Survey. *British Review of Economic Issues*, 14(33), 1–55.

Jakovac, P. (2013). Empirical Analysis on Economic Growth and Energy Consumption Relationship in Croatia. *Ekonomska Istrazivanja*, 26(4), 21–42. DOI: 10.1080/1331677X.2013.11517628

Karaaslan, A., & Çamkaya, S. (2022). The Relationship Between CO_2 Emissions, Economic Growth, Health Expenditure, and Renewable and Non-Renewable Energy Consumption: Empirical Evidence From Turkey. *Renewable Energy*, 190, 457–466. DOI: 10.1016/j.renene.2022.03.139

Keskin, R. (2017). The Relationship Between Economic Growth and Oil Consumption in Turkey Under Structural Breaks. *Management and Economics*, 24(3), 877–892.

Kılınç, E. C. (2021). The Relationship between Ecological Footprint and Energy R&D Expenditures. *The Case of OECD Countries, Ömer Halisdemir University Journal of the Faculty of Economics and Administrative Sciences*, 14(2), 527–541.

Kongbuamai, N., Bui, Q., Yousaf, H., & Liu, Y. (2020). M.,A., U.,Liu, Y. (2020), The Impact of Tourism and Natural Resources on The Ecological Footprint: A Case Study of Asean Countries. *Environmental Science and Pollution Research International*, 27(16), 19251–19264. DOI: 10.1007/s11356-020-08582-x PMID: 32253690

Kutlu, D. (2023). The Impact of Tourism and Economic Growth on Carbon Dioxide Emissions. *Journal of Current Tourism Research*, 7(2), 427–444.

Kwiatkowski, D., Phıllıps, P. C. B., Schımdt, P., & Yongcheol, S. (1992). Testing the Null Hypothesis of Stationarity Against the Alternative of A Unit Root. *Journal of Econometrics*, 54(1-3), 59–178. DOI: 10.1016/0304-4076(92)90104-Y

Maddala, G.S. and Kim In-Moo. (1998), Unit Roots, Cointegration and Structural Change, Cambridge University Press, United Kingdom.

Mızık, E. T., & Avdan, Z. Y. (2020). The Cornerstone of Sustainability: Ecological Footprint, Artvin Çoruh University Natural Disasters Application and Research Center. *Journal of Natural Disasters and Environment*, 6(2), 451–467.

Öztürk, İ., & Acaravcı, A. (2011). The Causal Relationship Between Energy Consumption and GDP in Albania, Bulgaria, Hungary and Romania: Evidence from ARDL Bound Testing Approach. *Applied Energy*, 87(6), 1938–1943. DOI: 10.1016/j.apenergy.2009.10.010

Pearce, D., & Barbier, E. (2000). *Blueprint for a Sustainable Economy*. Earthscan Publications. DOI: 10.4324/9781849774239

Pejović, B., Karadžić, V., Dragašević, Z., & Backović, T. (2021). Economic Growth, Energy Consumption and CO2 Emissions in the Countries of the European Union and the Western Balkans. *Energy Reports*, 7, 2775–2783. DOI: 10.1016/j.egyr.2021.05.011

Phillips, P. C. B., & Perron, P. (1988). Testing for A Unit Root In Time Series Regression. *Biometrika*, 75(2), 335–346. DOI: 10.1093/biomet/75.2.335

Şahin Kutlu, Ş., & Kutlu, M. (2022, January-June). The Impact of Tourism Activities on Ecological Footprint: The Case of Turkey. *The Journal of Finance*, 182, 233–249.

Şanlı, F. B., & Tuna, K. (2014). Analysis of the Relationship Between Oil Consumption and Economic Growth in Turkey. *Finance and Finance Articles*, 102, 43–58.

Terzi, H., & Pata, U. K. (2016). The Effect of Oil Consumption on Economic Growth in Turkey. *Doğuş University Journal*, 17(2), 225–240. DOI: 10.31671/dogus.2018.53

Tsanı, S. Z. (2010). Energy Consumption and Economic Growth: A Causality Analysis for Greece. *Energy Economics*, 32(3), 582–590. DOI: 10.1016/j.eneco.2009.09.007

Uçak, S., & Usupbeyli, A. (2015). Causal Relationship Between Oil Consumption and Economic Growth in Turkey. *Ankara University SBF Journal*, 70(3), 769–787.

Ullah, A., Tekbaş, M., & Doğan, M. (2023). The Impact of Economic Growth, Natural Resources, Urbanization and Biocapacity on the Ecological Footprint: The Case of Turkey. *Sustainability (Basel)*, 15(17), 12855. DOI: 10.3390/su151712855

Yıldız, S. R. (2024). Effect of Macroeconomic Variables on Ecological Footprint: Panel Data Analysis on OECD Countries, 9 Eylül University, Institute of Social Sciences, Master's Thesis.

Žiković, S., & Vlahinic-Dizdarević, N. (2011). Oil Consumption and Economic Growth Interdependence in Small European Countries. *Ekonomska Istrazivanja*, 24(3), 15–32. DOI: 10.1080/1331677X.2011.11517465

KEY TERMS AND DEFINITIONS

Biocapacity: Refers to the capacity of a given biologically productive area to generate an on-going supply of renewable resources and to absorb its spillover wastes.

Cointegration: is a technique used to find a possible correlation between time series processes in the long term.

Ecological Footprint Indicator: Numerical method used to ensure sustainable use of resources.

Ecological Footprint: The only metric that measures how much nature we have and how much nature we use.

Global Hectares: Both the Ecological Footprint and biocapacity are expressed in global hectares.

Sustainable Development: It is how we must live today if we want a better tomorrow, by meeting present needs without compromising the chances of future generations to meet their needs.

Unit Root: It is a stochastic trend in a time series that is frequently referred to as a random walk with drift.

Chapter 21
Structural, Configurational, Relational, and Instrumental Dimensions of Entrepreneurship Ecosystems

José G. Vargas-Hernandez
https://orcid.org/0000-0003-0938-4197
Tecnológico Nacional de México, ITS Fresnillo, Mexico

Francisco J. González-Ávila
Tecnológico Nacional de México, ITS Fresnillo, Mexico

Omar C. Vargas-González
https://orcid.org/0000-0002-6089-956X
Tecnológico Nacional de México, Ciudad Guzman, Mexico

Selene Castañeda-Burciaga
https://orcid.org/0000-0002-2436-308X
Universidad Politécnica de Zacatecas, Mexico

Omar A. Guirette-Barbosa
https://orcid.org/0000-0003-1336-9475
Universidad Politécnica de Zacatecas, Mexico

DOI: 10.4018/979-8-3693-5508-4.ch021

Copyright © 2025, IGI Global. Copying or distributing in print or electronic forms without written permission of IGI Global is prohibited.

ABSTRACT

This study aims to analyze the structural, configurational, relational, and instrumental dimensions of entrepreneurship ecosystems. The analysis departs from the assumption that the entrepreneurship ecosystem is a focal multidimensional paradigm including several dimensions in its formation. The method employed is the meta-analytical descriptive and reflective based on conceptual, theoretical, and empirical literature review. The study concludes that the formation of any entrepreneurship ecosystem incorporates several dimensions, among others, the configurational, structural, relational, instrumental, and operational.

INTRODUCTION

The concept of business ecosystems can be understood from several dimensions that reflect how companies interact within a complex and dynamic environment in order to adapt to it and maximize their sustainability. Likewise, the importance of the business ecosystem is reflected in the competitiveness and growth of companies within a particular environment, which, in turn, is related to innovation and development issues, market expansion, risk management, etc.

On the other hand, entrepreneurship ecosystem is a focal multidimensional paradigm to analyze the phenomenon through the individual and organizational contexts (Schmutzler *et al.*, 2019). Different consistent perspectives on entrepreneurial ecosystems contribute to enlarge the scope of the phenomenon to analyze its multidimensionality in depth (Roundy & Fayard 2019). A systemic entrepreneurship dimension is incorporated into entrepreneurship ecosystems analysis. The taxonomic entrepreneurship ecosystem perspective builds up on the context of the multidimensional shift of entrepreneurship level.

However, entrepreneurship ecosystems literature reviews of configurational and relational approaches reveal the relevance of connections between the diverse elements (Alvedalen & Boschma, 2017; Cao & Shi, 2020; Fernandes & Ferreira, 2022; Theodoraki *et al.*, 2022). The entrepreneurship ecosystems literature has been using terms in reference to entrepreneurship system, entrepreneurship infrastructure, regional entrepreneurship systems (Van de Ven, 1993; Spilling, 1996; Neck *et al.* 2004; Qian *et al.* 2013; Cohen, 2006; Mack & Qian, 2016). Likewise, ecological studies contributions to entrepreneurship interplay between the structural, compositional, and functional entrepreneurship ecosystems.

The analysis of entrepreneurship ecosystems connected to research on business, innovation, and platform ecosystems, benefits the collaboration relationships, connectivity levels, flows of resources and quantities across the various stages creating the conditions to foster outcomes (Spigel & Harrison, 2018). Entrepreneurship use the entrepreneurial skills to create a company, start projects, innovate processes, models, structures, etc.

It should be noted that, the research model has formative indicators such as university ecosystem, entrepreneurship commitment, and evaluation of formative measurement models including convergent validity, multicollinearity analysis, significance, and relevance (Hair *et al.*, 2017). Research on the context of entrepreneurship ecosystem is in line with the qualitative case studies that provide constructs and elements without information on how they are related to the entrepreneurship outcomes.

Therefore, the entrepreneurship ecosystem level of analysis enriches the examination of the components, interrelationships and instrumental dynamics change which may trigger the shifts of creation and evolution of the involved firms, although research remains limited (Elia *et al.*, 2020; Nambisan, 2017). The use of latent cluster analysis and qualitative comparative analysis methods improve the study of entrepreneurship ecosystems (Schrijvers *et al.*, 2021).

Prior research connects relationships between entrepreneurship processes and entrepreneurship ecosystems suggesting that the formation entrepreneurial ecosystems formation centered on an opportunity co-evolution process (O'Shea *et al.*, 2021). For example, research in the sports industry on entrepreneurial ecosystems carried out by González-Serrano et al., (2021), found that creativity, technology, infrastructure, business, and human capital lead to high levels of shared sport-related GDP.

In the same sense, research on operational management supported by the digital transformation of knowledge, which impacts entrepreneurship ecosystems, stands out (Lanzolla *et al.*, 2018; Frank *et al.*, 2019). Research on habitual serial entrepreneurship, on the other hand, has distinctive characteristics of the novice entrepreneur, i.e., the first-time entrepreneur, and the portfolio entrepreneur, who runs several operations at the same time (Westhead & Wright, 1998).

Another research that takes up the entrepreneurial ecosystem is carried out by Valente (2024), who conducted a study on the relationship between early entrepreneurial activity and the entrepreneurial ecosystem in Latin America during the period 2010-2022, the author used a descriptive analysis and an Ordinary Least Squares model. His main results highlight the importance of government policies, as well as entrepreneurial education in early stages, which foster the development of entrepreneurship; likewise, the need for effective management of knowledge and technology transfer to foster innovation is also pointed out.

Also noteworthy is the study by Soto-Ortigoza and Prato-Zuluaga (2024), who analyzed Neo-Management and intelligent business ecosystems. The authors, through the application of surveys and in-depth interviews with the subjects that make up the companies, found that 62.5% of the participants expressed that business ecosystems should provide clear and transparent information on their operations, finances and governance. Likewise, it was found that 50% are in favor of business ecosystems taking responsibility for their actions and decisions, ensuring compliance with applicable laws and regulations. In terms of sustainability, it is imperative that business ecosystems evaluate the impact of their activities, with 56.3% of respondents prioritizing this action. The authors point out that companies must reorganize themselves through a neo-managerial philosophy towards the achievement of organizational networks, creating collaborative scenarios, in order to promote intelligent business ecosystems based on innovation, entrepreneurship strategies and competitiveness transfers.

In accordance with the above, it is possible to recognize that the information related to the entrepreneurial ecosystem is not unified, because the available bibliography presents the information from a particular context, likewise, there are few empirical studies that allow an analysis from an empirical approach. Therefore, the main objective of this study is to analyze the dimensions of entrepreneurial ecosystems, taking up the analysis of the structural dimension, as well as the configurational, relational, instrumental and operational dimensions. This is done through the descriptive and reflexive meta-analytical method, based on the review of conceptual, theoretical and empirical literature. Finally, some conclusions based on the literature review are presented.

STRUCTURAL DIMENSION

Entrepreneurship ecosystems are open systems, dependent and sensitive to outside conditions in nestedness positions phenomena leading to substantial heterogeneity in similar structures. Entrepreneurship ecosystems are dependent on specific conditions of structural complexity and organizational diversity framing the variation on conditions changing the entrepreneurship ecologies and instrumental factors. A structural model entailing entrepreneurship ecosystem with instruments that are divergent context-dependent to exploit the available resources.

Geography is critical to entrepreneurship as supporting structures are spatially organized with networking and non-local geographically concentrated (Johannisson, 2000). Entrepreneurship ecosystems research focuses on spatial dimensions with regional proximity and the technological digital context (Acs *et al.*, 2017; Brown & Mason, 2017). The regional spin-off processes bring the emergence of local institutions to develop training through the collective action of the entrepreneurship community lading to encourage the formation and nurture new firms, solving problems of firms and attracting skilled labor (Wolfe & Gertler, 2004).

Entrepreneurship ecosystem research focus on the structure beyond the geographical borders. The biotic and abiotic components interacting on natural ecosystems, people, infrastructure and culture in entrepreneurial ecosystem (Isenberg, 2016). Entrepreneurship culture is a common attribute categorized from the ecosystem actors and positioned as an aggregate dimension beyond the regulatory dynamics and the ecosystem development framework. Entrepreneurship culture is a dimension that concerns with the motivational orientation and the cultural attitude of workers.

On the other hand, commercial and professional infrastructures facilitate the emergence of new organizational businesses (Lee *et al.*, 2011). The debate on geographical determinants focuses on rural and urban market structures, university centered entrepreneurship and variations. The university-centered entrepreneurship ecosystems frameworks propose the formative entrepreneurial process and opportunity evolution influencing the ecosystem emergence. Universities use mechanisms to trigger the transformation of entrepreneurship ecosystems to integrate entrepreneurship. A university oriented by entrepreneurship is responsible for the formation of highly employable graduates, placements and occupational integration.

Across geographical boundaries, digital entrepreneurship ecosystems facilitate the network structure to connect entrepreneurship actors and consolidate the heterogeneous and dispersed stakeholders (Nambisan *et al.*, 2019b). Digital entrepreneurship takes place within an ecosystem supported by infrastructure. The digital entrepreneurship ecosystems use digital structures around entrepreneurship clusters around the interactions of actors including entrepreneurs, stakeholders, users, network participants, etc. Enabled organizational agility lead to the emergence of new work structures supported by digital infrastructure (Sambamurthy *et al.*, 2003; Nambisan *et al.*, 2019a). The digital entrepreneurship ecosystem is based on the dimensions represented by digital actors, activities, motivations and organization in a construct as collective intelligence system (Elia *et al.* 2020).

Entrepreneurship ecosystems consist of varied entrepreneurial attitudes, abilities, aspirations, and a vast variation of elements such as organizations, roles, people, infrastructure, events, etc. (Ács *et al.*, 2014; Regele & Neck, 2012). Infrastructures are at the center of the entrepreneurship ecosystem with individuals influencing the emergence of regional and local dynamics. Experiences, values, knowledge, and achievements must be communicated to become meaningful through narrative and storytelling structures to create coherent experiences in chronical sequences (Smith, 2009; Kvale, 1996; Roundy, 2016)

The presence of physical and service infrastructures is critical in entrepreneurial activities to avoid barriers to launch new business organizations (Ács *et al.*, 2014; Ghani *et al.*, 2014; Urbano *et al.* 2020). Physical infrastructure as compositional elements are combined with functional demand leading to entrepreneurial output. Entrepreneurship is related positively to service infrastructures but not to physical structures. The commercial and professional infrastructures are the professional support services to establishing a new business that allow entrepreneurship to concentrate capabilities and competences (Hechavarría & Ingram, 2019; Levie & Autio, 2008; Lee *et al.*, 2011).

Infrastructure is a significant factor that facilitates or limits entrepreneurship including public endowment funds for research and development of scientific knowledge and for the development of a financial system to facilitate financial requirements (Van de Ven, 1993). Entrepreneurship ecosystems may not afford infrastructure and information and communication technology. The entrepreneurship finance is absent in the literature review of entrepreneurship ecosystems turning to build on previous knowledge looking into the processors, where also the financial dimension has not a dominant position (Landström, 2017).

Therefore, the development of a universal construct for the elements of entrepreneurial ecosystems from a wide variety of dataset sources is required to compose accurate and credible metrics. Several metrics of regional entrepreneurship ecosystems focus on themes related sch as the regional competitiveness measured by the Regional Competitiveness Index (RCI) including factors of infrastructure and human capital (Annoni & Dijkstra, 2019). Entrepreneurship growth of nodes proliferate with start-up accelerators and increasing entrepreneurship infrastructure in Silicon Valley, London, Berlin, etc., in hybrid forms and less dynamic entrepreneurship ecosystems (Clarysse *et al.*, 2015).

The academic spin-off at local universities has a crucial role in facilitating entrepreneurship resources of financing, support structures, public sector services, etc. (Meoli et al., 2019; Brown & Mason, 2017). New actors within universities are getting involved in entrepreneurship ecosystems, creation of new structures responsible to offer courses and conferences, employment, occupational placement, and integration. Employment in in high-tech multinational firms, entrepreneurship delivers experience for the potential individuals gaining knowledge moving into entrepreneurship process and evolving in the organizational structure. Intrapreneurs operate within companies as employees, as well as independent entrepreneurs create, develop and renew management and production structures and processes (Scott Kundel, 1991; Formichella 2004).

The new models create new structures and links with local communities and cross-border diverse local actors in networks linking elements. Implementing intrapreneurship and entrepreneurship in academic settings of universities is concerned the capacity to adapt and reduce asymmetries with organizational structures and methods in entrepreneurship ecosystems while fostering a strong entrepreneurship orientation (Belitski & Heron, 2017).

Private universities possess strengths of developing entrepreneurship infrastructures (Powers & McDougall, 2005). Less full-time faculty challenges higher education to fulfill their mandates represents a shortcoming in engaging to establish an entrepreneurial culture overcoming organizational initiatives to establish industry-university interactions. This type of structures may not be able to enhance the organizational culture conducive to entrepreneurship (Rubens *et al.*, 2017). Stimulation of university entrepreneurial behavior requires organizational structures able to increase teaching, research, entrepreneurship, and management activities (Guerrero & Urbano, 2012; Marzocchi *et al.*, 2019).

Reentry to new venture following the failure focuses on dimensions include the entrepreneurship learning and experience career and psychological constructs such as resilience, motivation, and mindfulness (Tipu, 2020). Using semi-structured interviews and think-aloud verbal protocol discover the differences of ventures between novice and experienced entrepreneurs (Engel *et al.*, 2020).

Now, taking up the information previously mentioned regarding the structural dimension of business ecosystems, it is possible to highlight that this dimension refers to the way in which the different elements within the ecosystem are organized and distributed. This includes hierarchy, roles, power and authority relationships and the general arrangement of the ecosystem components. In other words, the structural dimension of the business ecosystem provides the organizational and functional framework that allows the different actors to work collaboratively and efficiently. It also establishes the basis for coordination, the flow of information and the creation of alliances. All these elements allow for the development and evolution of the entrepreneurial ecosystem.

CONFIGURATIONAL DIMENSION

The ecological research reframes the regional entrepreneurship ecosystems to focus on the entrepreneurship processes configured to influence the change of regional dynamics. The temporal dimension of the entrepreneurship ecosystems could evolve reconfiguring and adapting in recognition to its thriving new technologies (Mason *et al*, 2002; Harrison *et al*, 2004; Shavinina, 2004; Novakowski & Tremblay, 2007; Mason, 2008). The dynamic nature of the entrepreneurship ecosystems model value to identify the generic features emerging as a set of circumstances fully formed and without change conditions but ignores the time dimension. Entrepreneurship ecosystems discussions lack the time dimension leading to preconditions for the emergence and uncertainty in establish a momentum which is necessary to resolve casualty issues.

The level of maturity of the configuration elements tend to produce levels and types of outputs (Brown & Mason, 2017). Large defense companies tend to configure the nature of the entrepreneurship context and shape entrepreneurship ecosystems (Adams, 2011; WEF, 2014; Spigel, 2015).

Entrepreneurship is critical for clusters formation and configuration considered as complex adaptive systems (Feldman *et al.*, 2005). Entrepreneurship ecosystems form through bottom-up processes making futile to impose formation through top-down processes (Thompson *et al.*, 2018). A systemic approach of clusters of entrepreneurship lead to the configuration analysis of networks in entrepreneurship ecosystems. Analysis of entrepreneurship ecosystems has focused on regions and cluster of entrepreneurship ecosystems without the comparative and multi-scalar approaches. Cluster formation in dynamic and emergent agglomeration influenced by entrepreneurship ecosystem formed by start-ups, networks, actors, and agents with knowledge linkages that enable the local firms and propels exogenous uncertainty (Li, 2018).

It should be noted that, the geographical advantages of the entrepreneurship ecosystems declined during the pandemic during which the organizations adapted to the external shocks by developing a digital emerging model focusing on geographic distribution of entrepreneurship networks and clusters aimed to become more resilient. Founding firms at an early stage in cluster development has different consequences that the founding of firms in established clusters (Bresnahan *et al.* 2001).

An archetypal region of entrepreneurship ecosystems is the Sylicon Valley with large number of dealmakers and former entrepreneurship investing in a range of firms in a network and high-tech clusters acting as mentors, becoming a serial entrepreneurship and dealmaking investments in other firms (Feldman & Zoller, 2012; Mason et al., 2002; Callaghan & Charbonneau, 2004; Mason & Brown, 2014). Traditional cluster and innovation systems perspectives differ in their use affected by regional contexts (Ylinenpää, 2009).

Entrepreneurship has opportunities with clusters such as the labor market specialization and knowledge spillovers geographically localized (Rocha & Sternberg 2005; Delgado *et al.* 2010). Traditional entrepreneurship ecosystem policymaking has a distinction with the growth-oriented entrepreneurship ecosystem policymaking in terms of enterprise policies is that the main unit of focus in the traditional is on specific actors including individuals, entrepreneurs and geographic cluster of firms while the growth-oriented policymaking focuses on specific types of entrepreneurship, entrepreneurs networks and temporary clusters.

Policy making approaches adopted stimulate entrepreneurship ecosystems that are different from industrial clusters and support established small- and medium-sized firms. The Entrepreneurial Ecosystem Index is used to determine the regional entrepreneurship ecosystem elements confirming by the representation of clusters.

Weak or strong vertical levels of interactions on inter-actor networks between start-ups, large growing firms and sources of growth capital can be exposed configuring on the entrepreneurship ecosystems architecture and the levels of entrepreneurial orientation. Modularity adapts resource configurations to enable flexibility and facilitate entrepreneurship processes in value creation (Nambisan *et al.*, 2019b). Funding is not always present in late-stage configurations.

For example, adequate university configuration potentializes entrepreneurship in faculty and students (Ács *et al.*, 2009; Bercovitz & Feldman, 2004; Huyghe & Knockaert, 2015). Graduate students play a role in the establishment, development and growth of spin-off companies and reconfiguration over time.

Therefore, the configurational dimension of the business ecosystem focuses on how the resources and capabilities within the ecosystem are organized to maximize its efficiency and effectiveness. In other words, this dimension deals with how the elements of the ecosystem are configured to facilitate collaboration and the achievement of common goals among the companies that make up the ecosystem, to optimize the functioning of the ecosystem and achieve strategic objectives. Such configuration can occur within the business environment or even within the university environment.

RELATIONAL DIMENSION

The entrepreneurship ecosystem is defined in terms of actors and factors that have an impact on entrepreneurship activities over the relational factors explaining the interactions among the ecosystem elements (Alvedalen & Boschma, 2017; Ghio *et al.*, 2019; Stam, 2015). The emergence of an entrepreneurship ecosystem requires nurturing bottom-up relationships to develop shared conventions and meanings for subsequent structured relationships and activities (Thompson *et al.*,2018).

Findings in entrepreneurship ecosystems governance led to a relational model rather than hierarchical driving the dynamic interaction collaboration and contributing to the co-creation of supporting and regulatory infrastructures (Colombelli, *et al.*, 2019).

The relational factors that mediate entrepreneurship define the ecosystems. A universal model that optimizes the entrepreneurship ecosystem value created and strict relationship patterns driving entrepreneurship. Regional entrepreneurship ecosystem varies in categories and configurations of entrepreneurship relationships change. Measuring elements of entrepreneurship ecosystems is an essential input for ex-ante diagnosis in a benchmark of weaknesses and strengths relative to relevant regions. Dynamic local entrepreneurship ecosystems give attention to the initial processes of inter-relationships between actors (Mason & Brown, 2014).

Entrepreneurship connections support entrepreneurship ecosystems by mediating relationships with the ecosystem actors including founders, investors, mentors, partners, among others. The relationships in the entrepreneurship ecosystems between the entrepreneurs and the ecosystem actors attract and lead to startups scaling into large firms acquired and undertaken in public offering (Brown & Mason, 2017; Saxenian, 1996).

Thus, entrepreneurship is related to the willingness to commit resources to create and develop uncertain opportunities. Similarly, ecosystem entrepreneurship enhances relationships with the community and the territory, which facilitates obtaining financial resources through various mechanisms such as crowdfunding (Giudici *et al.*, 2018).

On the other hand, the bioecological view on entrepreneurship establishes structural relationships in the entrepreneurship ecosystem. Cultural values are related to cultural practices in relevant cultural dimensions for entrepreneurship. Entrepreneurship opportunities are diverse in relation to the different cultures. The national culture has positive and negative influence in the individual entrepreneurial behavior (Hayton *et al.*, 2002).

National culture related to individual entrepreneurship behavior is a manifestation of belonging to a specific culture supporting the potential and development of entrepreneurship practices and activities. The entrepreneurship ecosystem integrative capabilities tend to moderate relationships between cross-cultural entrepreneurship and the ecosystem of innovation (Shen, *et al.* 2023). Cross-cultural entrepreneurship has a positive relationship with the entrepreneurship ecosystem. Concentration of immigrants is related to entrepreneurship development (Kshetri, 2014). Entrepreneurship and innovation ecosystems are discussed in relation to the heterogeneous productive entrepreneurship *(*Audretsch *et al., 2019;*Wurth *et al.*, 2021; Estrin *et al.*, 2013).

Formal and informal relationships among family and friends, and networking between groups provide intangible resources and organizational, administrative, technological, administrative and commercial capabilities, to nascent entrepreneurship (Romano *et al.*, 2017). Entrepreneurship maintains the founders identity through relationships that develop into a shared identity (Bouncken & Kraus, 2022). The networks of stakeholders are intrinsic to entrepreneurship ecosystems with an impact on the configuration, evolution, and outcomes of entrepreneurial ecosystems identified in contextual, institutional, relational, organizational, and structural dimensions (Fernandes & Ferreira, 2022). For example, Microsoft has developed

Seattle into a dynamic hub driven by around 148 Microsoft-related spin-offs for software, computer, and processing development (Mayer, 2013).

Entrepreneurial self-efficacy is a mediator on the relationship between entrepreneurship ecosystem shaping entrepreneurial intention (Ali *et al.* 2019). Entrepreneurship self-efficacy in ecosystem shape the entrepreneurial intention including the integration as the mediator in the analysis of the relationship between the entrepreneurship ecosystem and the entrepreneurship intention (Ali *et al.*, 2019). The entrepreneurship intention levels are related to the serial entrepreneurship fast rate of venture creation (Kautonen *et al.*, 2015; Krueger *et al.*, 2000). The concept of path dependency is related to the conditions that intentionally determine the election and following of certain specific developments over others but do not determine specific outcomes (David, 1988; Arthur, 1989; Henning *et al.*, 2013).

On the other hand, deterioration of job satisfaction leads to the need for independence driving movement into entrepreneurship relevant for the relationship between entrepreneurship mentoring and intentions (Nooderhaven *et al.*, 2004; Kerr & Armstrong-Stassen, 2011; Stephens & Hegarty, 2022; Baluku *et al.*, 2019).

Now, entrepreneurial ecosystems have relationship with entrepreneurial initiative. Entrepreneurship initiatives within a short-term horizon may lead to misguided conclusions, such as the research that fails to identify a relationship between activities targeting student entrepreneurship (Alves *et al.*, 2019; Endeavor, 2017). Research and development spending in large corporations and government agencies with technology transfer and diffusion among firms are related to entrepreneurial development (Ahmad & Hoffmann, 2008; Kshetri, 2014). Technology transfer within and between firms is related to convocation and graduations (Gertler, 2010).

The entrepreneurship ecosystem relation with entrepreneurship initiatives in a systematic approach through a comparative tool such as the entrepreneurship ecosystem taxonomy leading to establish different profiles and identify similar and divergent entrepreneurship initiatives determinants. The diversity initiatives are related to the inclusion of different and divergent cultural subgroups and small groups not represented by the majority culture, which are not necessarily involved to achieve competitive advantages and more favorable results.

Differentiation between embryonic and scale-up entrepreneurship ecosystems is the close bonds to transnational entrepreneurship growth nodes and connections to resources, relationships with business angels, entrepreneurship dealmaking, etc. The analyze the factors affecting the contributions of entrepreneurship ecosystem to startup development providing a positive impact on the relationships (Zaidi, *et al.* 2023). The presence of service providers, accountants, lawyers, business consultants, recruitment agencies, etc. that meet the needs of firms in entrepreneurship ecosystems in supporting new startups, avoiding perform non-core activities and stumbling blocks in the expected long-term relations.

The relationship between ten elements of entrepreneurship ecosystems and productive entrepreneurship output measure concluding that there is not a distinction that correspond to composition, structure, and functions, claiming that the entrepreneurship ecosystem elements are mutually interdependent and co-evolving in a territory (Stam & Van de Ven, 2021). Entrepreneurship ecosystems dependency on the context is related to a bundle of actors to analyze their interrelationships within their constituents (Mack & Mayer, 2016; Acs et al. 2008; Cao & Shi, 2020).

On the other hand, it is recognized that, the genesis of entrepreneurship ecosystem is a process emphasized by intellectual capital from a perspective of collective intelligence supporting human capital, structural capital, and relational capital. Human capital or human talent is an input linked to firm formation for entrepreneurship ecosystems (Acs & Armington, 2004; Glaeser et al., 2010). Deviating from the traditional entrepreneurship ecosystem model in new firm formation, leading into the contextual determinants of faculty engagement in processes of corporate entrepreneurship.

There is a relationship between human capital ecosystems and entrepreneurial ecosystems. Specific human capital in entrepreneurship is related to the valuable education, training, and experiences to entrepreneurship activities. Human capital has a nexus with entrepreneurial ecosystems. The entrepreneurship beliefs are related to the commitment in entrepreneurship education regarding responsibilities to support the activities at the entrepreneurship ecosystem (Hopkins & Feldman, 1989).

Entrepreneurship ecosystems favors the creation and management of intellectual capital, human capital, relational capital, and structural capital subject to conditions of diversity of actors with different expertise and competencies and use of mechanisms to share and combine individual contributions to be implemented. Qualifications of managers and workers are related to the productivity of firms (Grossman et al., 2017).

The entrepreneurship ecosystem is related to the digital knowledge capability (DKC). Human capital and the ability of serial entrepreneurship is related to innovative business models. The enablers of intellectual capital (IC) in entrepreneurial ecosystems organizational dynamics have the purposes to regenerate the intangible resources for entrepreneurship through model development to capture the interdependencies across human, relational and organizational capital (Grande, et al. 2023).

Public entrepreneurship evolving ecosystem architectures need to create the conditions for cooperation to support collaborative relationships. Public ecosystem architecture must promote the emergence of entrepreneurship ecosystems focusing on the creating the conditions for participants and actors to form embryonic relationships, shared identity, and mechanisms for interactions.

The business model captures an entire entrepreneurial action in its complex relationship between the firms' value creation and appropriation (Zott et al., 2011). Seriality in entrepreneurship is affected by the conditions of causal ambiguity of the action-outcome relationship making difficult to evaluate courses of action (Levitt & March, 1988). There is an inverse relationship in serial entrepreneurship between innovativeness and new venture success (Boyer & Blazy, 2014; Hyytinen et al., 2015; Reid & Smith, 2000).

Indirect effects of serial entrepreneurship occur after direct effects related to grief have been digested and reflected on learning to propose recovery strategies (Shepherd, 2003). The value of ventures sold by serial entrepreneurship is related to intellectual property rights, innovation, and employment (Cotei & Farhat, 2017). Employees are related to lifestyle entrepreneurship by replacing lost wages in growth firms occurring recycling through mobility from declining firms into innovative start-up and scale-up firms.

The formation of university ecosystems is self-reinforcing by strengthening the faculty's commitment to the entrepreneurial event. University entrepreneurship ecosystem fosters intellectual capital in the context of international related activities though identified human, relational, and organizational capital enablers differentiated in explorative and exploitative facets. There is a positive relation between university entrepreneurship ecosystems and the faculty with strong entrepreneurial experience engaged with entrepreneurship activities of individuals (Salati et al., 2020). Universities aiming at developing student and faculty entrepreneurship need some internal changes more related to behavioral transformation than to firm creation.

There is a positive relation between university ecosystems development and faculty engagement in entrepreneurship activities with more entrepreneurship experience. The bidirectional relationships within university entrepreneurship ecosystems remain limited within the context of academic entrepreneurship. Private universities have strong relationships between academic ecosystems and the faculty commitment to entrepreneurship activities (Hair et al., 2018). Private universities have string relationship between the faculty commitment and the academic entrepreneurship ecosystems to support entrepreneurship activities.

Based on the above information, the relational dimension of the entrepreneurial ecosystem focuses on how the different actors in the ecosystem relate to each other. This includes the nature and quality of these relationships, as well as communication mechanisms and conflict management; in other words, cooperation between all the elements that make up the ecosystem. Relationships can be between companies, customers, strategic partners, or even competitors in certain contexts. Likewise, relationships can be developed from the university and academic sectors. It should be noted that an effective approach to the relational dimension can contribute to the efficiency of operations and processes, increase customer satisfaction and enhance growth opportunities.

INSTRUMENTAL AND OPERATIONAL

Entrepreneurship ecosystem operations have an essential role in shaping the entrepreneurial intentions (Donaldson, 2019). Operationalization of the elements of the entrepreneurship ecosystem into measurable dimensions at geographical level. Location preferences are relevant in emerging entrepreneurship ecosystems in areas of high-density residences for early entrepreneurs in quality of life considerations operating in localities when started business. Regional entrepreneurship ecosystem focuses on regional changing conditions of instrumental response to change, which can be differentiated by the stabilized and disturbed responses of a holistic ecology perspective.

The boundaries discussion of an entrepreneurial ecosystem determines the level of analysis, the data sources, and operational measures of the ecosystem elements. Formal professional networking organizations may operate in various forms, membership, rules, regulations, etc. as for example allow entry only to established entrepreneurship that fulfills requirements of business size, turnover level, etc. For example, collaboration between academia and industry based on specific need of entrepreneurship drive instrumental human resources development in international agencies. The university entrepreneurship ecosystems framework is extended beyond evolution opportunities of entrepreneurship process to commercialize within as an inherent risk involving multiple parties with divergent goals operating across organizational networks.

The operation costs of business angels' networks as dating agencies enable to search and find for financial sources to support (Harrison & Mason, 1996). The operating costs of business angel networks enable investments and entrepreneurship seeking finance from programs connecting (Mason, 2009; Walshok *et al.* 2002; Audretsch, 2015)

On the other hand, the digital entrepreneurship ecosystem acquires identity at a system level with an intangible culture that supports cooperation (Du *et al.*, 2018). Digital technology transformation on entrepreneurship is an enabler, moderator and even the outcome of entrepreneurial operations and business model (Steininger, 2018). Institutional adaptation towards entrepreneurial operations is hindered (Fisher 2015).

Considering the previous information, it is necessary to detail that the instrumental dimension of the business ecosystem is related to the tools, technologies, systems and resources used to facilitate and support the operations and processes within the ecosystem. This dimension allows the elements within the system to efficiently develop all their activities. For example, information systems facilitate the collection, storage, processing and transmission of information among the elements of the ecosystem. Meanwhile, technological and digital tools encourage innovation and facilitate the performance of processes.

The operational dimension of the business ecosystem refers to the processes, procedures and practices that ecosystem members use in their daily operations. This dimension ensures that operations are effective, efficient and aligned with the ecosystem's objectives. Aspects such as operations management, quality management and continuous improvement and risk management stand out. In general terms, it can be said that the instrumental dimension of the business ecosystem focuses on the tools and technologies needed to support and facilitate operations, while the operational dimension focuses on the processes and procedures that enable the ecosystem to function.

DISCUSSION

According to the descriptive and reflective meta-analytical analysis based on the review of conceptual, theoretical and empirical literature, it is possible to determine the specific aspects that integrate the dimensions of the entrepreneurial ecosystem. Emphasizing the importance of their application within the business context, since these dimensions must be present for an adequate performance of the ecosystem. Table 1 shows a comparative analysis between the structural dimensions, as well as the configurational, relational, instrumental and operational dimensions.

Table 1. Comparative analysis of the dimensions of the entrepreneurial ecosystem

DIMENSION	DESCRIPTION	OBJECTIVE AND APPROACH	EXAMPLE OF PERFORMANCE WITHIN THE ENTREPRENEURIAL ECOSYSTEM
Structural	It reflects the general organization and hierarchy of actors in the business ecosystem.	Define how the different actors within the entrepreneurial ecosystem are organized and structured.	Structure of strategic alliances and market positions. For example, an ecosystem includes a supplier, a manufacturer, a distributor and a retailer, with a clear hierarchy of influence and authority among them.
Configurational	Refers to the arrangement and configuration of resources and capabilities within the ecosystem to maximize value and efficiency.	Optimize the disposition and use of resources and capabilities to create value within the ecosystem to meet strategic objectives.	For example, the configuration of collaborative platforms, supplier networks, with which logistics and information exchange are optimized.
Relational	It examines the relationships and interactions between the different elements that make up the ecosystem, such as customers, suppliers, competitors and partners.	Facilitate cooperation and effective interaction among the various members of the ecosystem.	This can be seen in collaborative networks and relationships between companies in a value chain, such as strategic alliances.
Instrumental and operational	The instrumental dimension analyzes the tools, technologies and systems used to facilitate interaction and management within the business ecosystem. The operational dimension focuses on the processes that facilitate the day-to-day operation and effective interaction between ecosystem stakeholders.	The objective of the instrumental dimension is to provide the necessary tools and systems for effective operation and management within the ecosystem. While, the purpose of the operational dimension is to ensure the effective implementation of processes that facilitate the interaction and functioning of the ecosystem.	Examples of applications include the use of data analysis tools (specialized software), as well as standardized processes that facilitate interaction between elements of the business ecosystem.

On the other hand, some important theoretical elements of entrepreneurial ecosystems are highlighted, such as the consideration that these are open entrepreneurial systems (Johannisson, 2000; Acs et al., 2017; Brown & Mason, 2017); the importance of geography and spatial context (Johannisson, 2000; Wolfe & Gertler, 2004). Similarly, entrepreneurial ecosystems have a close relationship with university ecosystems and human capital (Ács et al., 2009; Bercovitz & Feldman, 2004; Salati Marcondes de Moraes, 2020). Likewise, it is necessary to highlight digital ecosystems and technological adaptation of entrepreneurial ecosystems (Du et al., 2018; Steininger, 2018).

CONCLUSIONS

This study analyzes the structural, configurational, relational and instrumental dimensions of entrepreneurship ecosystems, supported from the assumption that the entrepreneurship ecosystem is a focal multidimensional paradigm including several dimensions in its formation. The study concludes that the formation of any entrepreneurship ecosystem incorporates several dimensions, among others, the configurational, structural, relational, instrumental and operational.

The knowledge findings on entrepreneurship ecosystems are depository of structural change of top management of firms in the production paradigms to encourage the organizational stakeholders to improve their abilities to acquire, assimilate and implement external knowledge to develop organizations. Commercial and professional, physical, and service infrastructures have intensive impacts on entrepreneurial activities.

Entrepreneurship ecosystems lack of a holistic approach focusing on the inter-relations between the networks and entrepreneurship. The elements of the entrepreneurship ecosystems are related to entrepreneurship outputs. Entrepreneurship is determined to overcome obstacles related to the creation and development of firms.

The relational forms support the network building through the development of connections between entrepreneurship actors, institutional priorities alignment fostering peer-based interactions. Connectivity increases and intensifies involving entrepreneurship ecosystems giving rise to challenge the existing collaborative learning and relating stakeholders and actors among business and innovation platform ecosystem to create value collectively and capture competitiveness. Entrepreneurship role models play a relevant role in educating ecosystem to identify problems and solutions related to disruptions, innovation to enlarge the market size, getting support from government at all levels to back organizations, etc.

Entrepreneurship ecosystems emerge, operate, and evolve responding in combination to specific circumstances triggered by contractions and closure of the firm without the influence of policy. A pragmatic approach of entrepreneurship can overcome regulatory barriers and create regulatory covers and jurisdiction to operate.

Micro-foundations of entrepreneurship ecosystems research may be able to outsource resources and organizational capabilities to implement flexible organizational structures of local entrepreneurship that enable to have access to collective resources which are potential source of competitive advantages. The temporal local dimension of the analysis of entrepreneurship ecosystems reveals there is intra-mobility distribution in cross-sectional values

Research on serial entrepreneurship can explore new venture successful teams, networks and external relationships of assistance and support such as venture capitals, banks, businesses, etc.

REFERENCES

Ács, Z., Braunerhjelm, J., Audretsch, D., & Carlsson, B. (2009). The knowledge spillover theory of entrepreneurship. *Small Business Economics*, 32(1), 15–30. DOI: 10.1007/s11187-008-9157-3

Acs, Z., Desai, S., & Hessels, J. (2008). Entrepreneurship, economic development, and institutions. *Small Business Economics*, 31(3), 219–234. DOI: 10.1007/s11187-008-9135-9

Acs, Z.J., Armington, C. (2004). The impact of geographic differences in human capital on service firm formation rates. *J. Urban Econ.* 56, 244–278. ttps://.DOI: 10.1016/j.jue.2004.03.008

Ács, Z. J., Autio, E., & Szerb, L. (2014). National systems of entrepreneurship: Measurement issues and policy implications. *Research Policy*, 43(3), 476–494. DOI: 10.1016/j.respol.2013.08.016

Acs, Z. J., Stam, E., Audretsch, D., & O'Connor, A. (2017). The lineages of the entrepreneurial ecosystem approach. *Small Business Economics*, 49(1), 1–10. DOI: 10.1007/s11187-017-9864-8

Adams, S. B. (2011). Growing where you are planted: Exogenous firms and the seeding of Silicon Valley. *Research Policy*, 40(3), 368–379. DOI: 10.1016/j.respol.2010.12.002

Ahmad, N., & Hoffmann, A. N. (2008), *A framework for addressing and measuring entrepreneurship*, OECD Statistics Working Paper, Paris, January, available at: www.olis.oecd.org/olis/2008doc.nsf/LinkTo/NT000009FA/$FILE/JT03239191.PDF

Ali, I., Ali, M., & Badghish, S. (2019). Symmetric and asymmetric modeling of entrepreneurial ecosystem in developing entrepreneurial intentions among female university students in Saudi Arabia. *International Journal of Gender and Entrepreneurship*, 11(4), 435–458. DOI: 10.1108/IJGE-02-2019-0039

Alvedalen, J., & Boschma, R. (2017). A critical review of entrepreneurial ecosystems research: Towards a future research agenda. *European Planning Studies*, 25(6), 887–903. DOI: 10.1080/09654313.2017.1299694

Alves, A., Fischer, B., Schaeffer, P., & Queiroz, S. (2019). Determinants of student entrepreneurship: An assessment on higher education institutions in Brazil. *Innovation & Management Review*, 16(2), 96–117. DOI: 10.1108/INMR-02-2018-0002

Annoni, P. & Dijkstra, L. (2019). *The EU Regional Competitiveness Index.*

Arthur, W. B. (1989). Competing technologies, increasing returns, and lock-in by historical events. *Economic Journal (London)*, 99(394), 116–131. DOI: 10.2307/2234208

Audretsch, D. B. (2015). *Everything in its place: Entrepreneurship and the strategic Management of Cities, regions, and states*. Oxford University Press. DOI: 10.1093/acprof:oso/9780199351251.001.0001

Audretsch, D. B., Cunningham, J. A., Kuratko, D. F., Lehmann, E. E., & Menter, M. (2019). Entrepreneurial ecosystems: Economic, technological, and societal impacts. *The Journal of Technology Transfer*, 44(2), 313–325. DOI: 10.1007/s10961-018-9690-4 PMID: 30956392

Baluku, M. M., Leonsio, M., Bantu, E., & Otto, K. (2019). The impact of autonomy on the relationship between mentoring and entrepreneurial intentions among youth in Germany, Kenya, and Uganda. *International Journal of Entrepreneurial Behaviour & Research*, 25(2), 170–192. DOI: 10.1108/IJEBR-10-2017-0373

Belitski, M., & Heron, K. (2017). Expanding entrepreneurship education ecosystems. *Journal of Management Development*, 36(2), 163–177. DOI: 10.1108/JMD-06-2016-0121

Bercovitz, J., & Feldman, M. (2004). *Academic entrepreneurs: Social learning and participation in university technology transfer*. University of Toronto.

Bouncken, R. B., & Kraus, S. (2022). Entrepreneurial ecosystems in an interconnected world: Emergence, governance, and digitalization. *Review of Managerial Science*, 16(1), 1–14. DOI: 10.1007/s11846-021-00444-1

Boyer, T., & Blazy, R. (2014). Born to be alive? The survival of innovative and non-innovative French micro-startups. *Small Business Economics*, 42(4), 669–683. DOI: 10.1007/s11187-013-9522-8

Bresnahan, T., Gambardella, A., & Saxenian, A. (2001). 'Old economy' inputs for 'new economy' outcomes: Cluster formation in the new Silicon Valleys. *Industrial and Corporate Change*, 10(4), 835–860. DOI: 10.1093/icc/10.4.835

Brown, R., & Mason, C. (2017). Looking inside the spiky bits: A critical review and conceptualisation of entrepreneurial ecosystems. *Small Business Economics*, 49(1), 11–30. DOI: 10.1007/s11187-017-9865-7

Callaghan, J., & Charboneau, K. (2004). The role of venture capital in building technology companies in the Ottawa region. In Shavinina, L. V. (Ed.), *Silicon Valley North: Technology, Innovation, Entreprenuership and Competitve Capacity* (pp. 169–201). Emerald. DOI: 10.1108/S1479-067X(2004)0000009010

Cao, Z., & Shi, X. (2020). A systematic literature review of entrepreneurial ecosystems in advanced and emerging economies. *Small Business Economics*, ●●●, 2020.

Clarysse, B., Wright, M., & VanHove, J. (2015). *A look inside accelerators*. Nesta.

Cohen, B. (2006). Sustainable valley entrepreneurial ecosystems. *Business Strategy and the Environment*, 15(1), 1–14. DOI: 10.1002/bse.428

Colombelli, A., Paolucci, E., & Ughetto, E. (2019). Hierarchical and relational governance and the life cycle of entrepreneurial ecosystems. *Small Business Economics*, 52(2), 505–521. DOI: 10.1007/s11187-017-9957-4

Cotei, C., & Farhat, J. (2017). The M&A exit outcomes of new, young businesses. *Small Business Economics*, 50(3), 545–567. DOI: 10.1007/s11187-017-9907-1

David, P. A. (1988). *Path-dependence: Putting the past into the future of economics. Institute for Mathematical Studies in the Social Sciences Technical Report No. 533*: Stanford University Press.

Delgado, M., Porter, M. E., & Stern, S. (2010). Clusters and entrepreneurship. *Journal of Economic Geography*, 10(4), 495–518. DOI: 10.1093/jeg/lbq010

Donaldson, C. (2019). Intentions resurrected: A systematic review of entrepreneurial intention research from 2014 to 2018 and future research agenda [September.]. *The International Entrepreneurship and Management Journal*, 15(3), 953–975. DOI: 10.1007/s11365-019-00578-5

Du, W. D., Pan, S. L., Zhou, N., & Ouyang, T. (2018). From a marketplace of electronics to a digital entrepreneurial ecosystem (DEE): The emergence of a meta-organization in Zhongguancun, China. *Information Systems Journal*, 28(6), 1158–1175. DOI: 10.1111/isj.12176

Elia, G., Margherita, A. & Passiante, G. (2020). Digital entrepreneurship ecosystem: how digital technologies and collective intelligence are reshaping the entrepreneurial process *Technol. Forecast. Soc. Chang.*, 150. Article 119791

Endeavor. (2017). *Pesquisa empreendedorismo nas universidades brasileiras 2016.* http://info.endeavor.org.br/eub2016

Engel, Y., van Werven, R., & Keizer, A. (2020). How novice and experienced entrepreneurs name new ventures. *Journal of Small Business Management*, ●●●, 1–31. DOI: 10.1080/00472778.2020.1738820

Estrin, S., Korosteleva, J., & Mickiewicz, T. (2013). Which institutions encourage entrepreneurial growth aspirations? *Journal of Business Venturing*, 28(4), 564–580. DOI: 10.1016/j.jbusvent.2012.05.001

Feldman, M., & Zoller, T. D. (2012). Dealmakers in place: Social capital connections in regional entrepreneurial economies. *Regional Studies*, 46(1), 23–37. DOI: 10.1080/00343404.2011.607808

Feldman, M. P., Francis, J., & Bercovitz, J. (2005). Creating a cluster while building a firm: Entrepreneurs and the formation of industrial clusters. *Regional Studies*, 39(1), 129–141. DOI: 10.1080/0034340052000320888

Fernandes, A. J., & Ferreira, J. J. (2022). Entrepreneurial ecosystems and networks: A literature review and research agenda. *Review of Managerial Science*, 16(1), 1–59. DOI: 10.1007/s11846-020-00437-6

Fisher, J. E. (2015). Challenges in determining whether creativity and mental illness are associated. *Frontiers in Psychology*, 6, 163. DOI: 10.3389/fpsyg.2015.00163 PMID: 25750632

Formichella, M. M. (2004). *El concepto de emprendimiento y su relación con la educación, el empleo y el desarrollo local*. Tres Arroyos.

Frank, , Dalenogare, L. S., & Ayala, N. F. (2019). Industry 4.0 technologies: Implementation patterns in manufacturing companies. *International Journal of Production Economics*, 210, 15–26. DOI: 10.1016/j.ijpe.2019.01.004

Gertler, M. (2010). Rules of the Game: The Place of Institutions in Regional Economic Change. *Regional Studies*, 44(1), 1–15. DOI: 10.1080/00343400903389979

Ghani, E., Kerr, W. R., & O'Connell, S. (2014). Spatial determinants of entrepreneurship in India. *Regional Studies*, 48(6), 1071–1089. DOI: 10.1080/00343404.2013.839869

Ghio, N., Guerini, M., & Rossi-Lamastra, C. (2019). The creation of high-tech ventures in entrepreneurial ecosystems: Exploring the interactions among university knowledge, cooperative banks, and individual attitudes. *Small Business Economics*, 52(2), 523–543. DOI: 10.1007/s11187-017-9958-3

Giudici, G., Guerini, M., & Rossi-Lamastra, C. (2018). Reward-based crowdfunding of entrepreneurial projects: The effect of local altruism and localized social capital on proponents' success. *Small Business Economics*, 50(2), 307–324. DOI: 10.1007/s11187-016-9830-x

Glaeser, E. L., Kerr, W. R., & Ponzetto, G. A. M. (2010). Clusters of entrepreneurship. *Journal of Urban Economics*, 67(1), 150–168. DOI: 10.1016/j.jue.2009.09.008

González-Serrano, M. H., Crespo-Hervás, J., Pérez-Campos, C., & Calabuig, F. (2021). Entrepreneurial ecosystems for developing the sports industry in European Union countries. *Journal of Business Research*, 136(July), 667–677. DOI: 10.1016/j.jbusres.2021.07.060

Grande, S., Bertello, A., De Bernardi, P., & Ricciardi, F. (2023). Enablers of explorative and exploitative intellectual capital in entrepreneurial ecosystems. *Journal of Intellectual Capital*, 24(1), 35–69. DOI: 10.1108/JIC-07-2021-0197

Grossman, G. M., Helpman, E., & Kircher, P. (2017). Matching, Sorting, and the Distributional Effects of International Trade. *Journal of Political Economy*, 125(1), 224–264. DOI: 10.1086/689608

Guerrero, M., & Urbano, D. (2012). The development of an entrepreneurial university. *The Journal of Technology Transfer*, 37(1), 43–74. DOI: 10.1007/s10961-010-9171-x

Hair, J. F., Hult, G. T. M., Ringle, C. M., & Sarstedt, M. (2017). *A primer on partial least squares structural equation modeling (PLS-SEM)*. Sage.

Hair, J. F., Sarstedt, M., Ringle, C. M., & Gudergan, S. P. (2018). *Advanced issues in partial least squares structural equation modeling (PLS-SEM)*. Sage.

Harrison, R. T., Cooper, S. Y., & Mason, C. M. (2004). Entrepreneurial activity and the dynamics of technology-based cluster development: The case of Ottawa. *Urban Studies (Edinburgh, Scotland)*, 41(5-6), 1045–1070. DOI: 10.1080/00420980410001675841

Harrison, R. T., & Mason, C. M. (Eds.). (1996). *Informal Venture Capital: Evaluating the Impact of Business Introduction Services*. Prentice Hall.

Hayton, J. C., George, G., & Zahra, S. A. (2002). National culture and entrepreneurship: A review of behavioral research. *Entrepreneurship Theory and Practice*, 26(4), 33–52. DOI: 10.1177/104225870202600403

Hechavarría, D. M., & Ingram, A. E. (2019). Entrepreneurial ecosystem conditions and gendered national-level entrepreneurial activity: A 14-year panel study of GEM. *Small Business Economics*, 53(2), 431–458. DOI: 10.1007/s11187-018-9994-7

Henning, M., Stam, E., & Wenting, R. (2013). Path dependence research in regional economic development: Cacophony or knowledge accumulation? *Regional Studies, 47*(8), 1348–1362. . 2012. 750422DOI: <ALIGNMENT.qj></ALIGNMENT>10.1080/ 00343404

Hopkins, T., & Feldman, H. (1989). Changing entrepreneurship education: Finding the right entrepreneur for the job. *Journal of Organizational Change Management*, 2(3), 28–40. DOI: 10.1108/09534818910145066

Huyghe, A., & Knockaert, M. (2015). The influence of organizational culture and climate on entrepreneurial intentions among research scientists. *The Journal of Technology Transfer*, 40(1), 138–160. DOI: 10.1007/s10961-014-9333-3

Hyytinen, A., Pajarinen, M., & Rouvinen, P. (2015). Does innovativeness reduce startup survival rates? *Journal of Business Venturing, 30*(4), 564–581. https://doi.org/ vent.2014.10.001DOI: 10.1016/j.jbus

Isenberg, D. J. (2016). Applying the ecosystem metaphor to entrepreneurship: Uses and abuses. *Antitrust Bulletin*, 61(4), 564–573. DOI: 10.1177/0003603X16676162

Johannisson, B. (2000). Networking and Entrepreneurial Growth. In Sexton, D. L., & Landström, H. (Eds.), *The Blackwell Handbook of Entrepreneurship* (pp. 368–386). Blackwell.

Kautonen, T., Van Gelderen, M., & Fink, M. (2015). Robustness of the theory of planned behavior in predicting entrepreneurial intentions and actions. *Entrepreneurship Theory and Practice*, 39(3), 655–674. DOI: 10.1111/etap.12056

Kerr, G., & Armstrong-Stassen, M. (2011). The bridge to retirement: Older workers' engagement in post-career entrepreneurship and wage- and- salary employment. *The Journal of Entrepreneurship*, 20(1), 55–76. DOI: 10.1177/097135571002000103

Krueger, N. F.Jr, Reilly, M. D., & Carsrud, A. L. (2000). Competing models of entrepreneurial intentions. *Journal of Business Venturing*, 15(5–6), 411–432. DOI: 10.1016/S0883-9026(98)00033-0

Kshetri, N. (2014). *Global Entrepreneurship: Environment and Strategy*. Routledge. DOI: 10.4324/9781315795607

Kvale, S. (1996). *Interviews: An Introduction to Qualitative Research Interviewing*. Sage Publications.

Landström, H. (2017). *Advanced Introduction to Entrepreneurial Finance*. Edward Elgar Publishing, Inc.

Lanzolla, G., Lorenz, A., Miron-Spektor, E., Schilling, M., Solinas, G., & Christopher, T. (2018). Digital transformation: What is new if anything? *Academy of Management Discoveries*, 4(3), 378–387. DOI: 10.5465/amd.2018.0103

Lee, S.-H., Yamakawa, Y., Peng, M. W., & Barney, J. B. (2011). How do bankruptcy laws affect entrepreneurship development around the world? *Journal of Business Venturing*, 26(5), 505–520. DOI: 10.1016/j.jbusvent.2010.05.001

Levie, J., & Autio, E. (2008). A theoretical grounding and test of the GEM model. *Small Business Economics*, 31(3), 235–263. DOI: 10.1007/s11187-008-9136-8

Levitt, B., & March, J. G. (1988). Organizational learning. *Annual Review of Sociology*, 14(1), 319–338. DOI: 10.1146/annurev.so.14.080188.001535

Li, P. (2018). A tale of two clusters: Knowledge and emergence. *Entrepreneurship and Regional Development*, 30(7–8), 822–847. DOI: 10.1080/08985626.2018.1462857

Mack, E., & Mayer, H. (2016). The evolutionary dynamics of entrepreneurial ecosystems. *Urban Studies (Edinburgh, Scotland)*, 2016(53), 2118–2133. DOI: 10.1177/0042098015586547

Mack, E. A., & Qian, H. (Eds.). (2016). *Geographies of Entrepreneurship*. Routledge Studies in Human Geography. New York: Routledge. DOI: 10.4324/9781315686653

Marzocchi, C., Kitagawa, F., & Sánchez-Barrioluengo, M. (2019). Evolving missions and university entrepreneurship: Academic spin-offs and graduate start-ups in the entrepreneurial society. *The Journal of Technology Transfer*, 44(1), 167–188. DOI: 10.1007/s10961-017-9619-3

Mason, C. (2008). Entrepreneurial dynamics and the origin and growth of high-tech clusters. In Karlsson, C. (Ed.), *Handbook of Research on Innovation and Clusters: Cases and Policies* (pp. 33–53). Edward Elgar. DOI: 10.4337/9781848445079.00010

Mason, C., & Brown, R. (2014). *Entrepreneurial ecosystems and growth oriented entrepreneurship*. Paris: Final Report to OECD http://lib.davender.com/wp-content/uploads/2015/03/Entrepreneurial-ecosystems-OECD.pdf

Mason, C., Cooper, S., & Harrison, R. (2002). Venture capital and high technology clusters: the case of Ottawa. In Oakey, R., During, W., & Kauser, S. (Eds.), *New Technology-Based Firms in the New Millennium* (Vol. II, pp. 261–278). Pergammon.

Mason, C. M. (2009). Public policy support for the informal venture capital market in Europe a critical review. *International Small Business Journal*, 27(5), 536–556. DOI: 10.1177/0266242609338754

Mayer, H. (2013). Entrepreneurship in a Hub and Spoke Industrial District: Firm Survey Evidence from Seattle's Technology Industry. *Regional Studies*, 47(10), 1715–1733. DOI: 10.1080/00343404.2013.806792

Meoli, M., Paleari, S., & Vismara, S. (2019). The governance of universities and the establishment of academic spin- offs. *Small Business Economics*, 52(2), 485–504. DOI: 10.1007/s11187-017-9956-5

Nambisan, S. (2017). Digital entrepreneurship: Toward a digital technology perspective of entrepreneurship. *Entrepreneurship Theory and Practice*, 41(6), 1029–1055. DOI: 10.1111/etap.12254

Nambisan, S., Wright, M., & Feldman, M. (2019a). The digital transformation of innovation and entrepreneurship: Progress, challenges, and key themes. *Research Policy*, 48(8), 103773. DOI: 10.1016/j.respol.2019.03.018

Nambisan, S., Zahra, S. A., & Luo, Y. (2019b). Global platforms and ecosystems: Implications for international business theories. *Journal of International Business Studies*, 50(9), 1464–1486. DOI: 10.1057/s41267-019-00262-4

Neck, H., Meyer, D., Cohen, B., & Corbett, A. (2004). An entrepreneurial system view of new venture creation. *Journal of Small Business Management*, 42(2), 190–208. DOI: 10.1111/j.1540-627X.2004.00105.x

Nooderhaven, N., Thurik, R., Wennekers, S., & van Stel, A. (2004). The role of dissatisfaction and per capita income in explaining self- employment across 15 European countries. *Entrepreneurship Theory and Practice*, 28(5), 447–466. DOI: 10.1111/j.1540-6520.2004.00057.x

Novakowski, N., & Tremblay, R. (2007). *Perspectives on Ottawa's High-Tech Sector*. P.I.E.- Peter Lang.

O'Shea, G., Farny, S., & Hakala, H. (2021). The buzz before business: A design science study of a sustainable entrepreneurial ecosystem. *Small Business Economics*, 56(3), 1097–1120. DOI: 10.1007/s11187-019-00256-4

Powers, J. B., & McDougall, P. (2005). Policy orientation effects on performance with licensing to start-ups and small companies. *Research Policy*, 34(7), 1028–1042. DOI: 10.1016/j.respol.2005.05.014

Qian, H., Acs, Z. J., & Stough, R. R. (2013). Regional systems of entrepreneurship: The nexus of human capital, knowledge, and new firm formation. *Journal of Economic Geography*, 13(4), 559–587. DOI: 10.1093/jeg/lbs009

Regele, M. D., & Neck, H. M. (2012). The entrepreneurship education sub-ecosystem in the United States: Opportunities to increase the entrepreneurial activity. *Journal of Business and Entrepreneurship*, (Winter), 25.

Reid, G. C., & Smith, J. A. (2000). The impact of contingencies on management accounting system development. *Management Accounting Research*, 11(4), 427–450. DOI: 10.1006/mare.2000.0140

Rocha, H. O., & Sternberg, R. (2005). Entrepreneurship: The role of clusters theoretical perspectives and empirical evidence from Germany. *Small Business Economics*, 24(3), 267–292. DOI: 10.1007/s11187-005-1993-9

Romano, M., Nicotra, M., & Schillaci, C. (2017). Nascent Entrepreneurship and Territorial Social Capital: Empirical Evidences from Italy. In Cunningham, J. A., & O'Kane, C. (Eds.), *Technology-Based Nascent Entrepreneurship: Implications for Economic Policymaking* (pp. 71–93). Palgrave Macmillan US., DOI: 10.1057/978-1-137-59594-2_4

Roundy, P., & Fayard, D. (2019). Dynamic Capabilities and Entrepreneurial Ecosystems: The Micro-Foundations of Regional Entrepreneurship. *The Journal of Entrepreneurship*, 2019(28), 94–120. DOI: 10.1177/0971355718810296

Roundy, P. T. (2016). Start-up community narratives: The discursive construction of entrepreneurial ecosystems. *The Journal of Entrepreneurship*, 25(2), 232–248. DOI: 10.1177/0971355716650373

Rubens, A., Spigarelli, F., Cavicchi, A., & Rinaldi, C. (2017). Universities' third mission and the entrepreneurial university and the challenges they bring to higher education institutions. *Journal of Enterprising Communities: People and Places in the Global Economy*, 11(3), 354–372. DOI: 10.1108/JEC-01-2017-0006

Salati Marcondes de Moraes, G. R., Brandão Fischer, B., & Leite Campos, M. (2020). University Ecosystems and the Commitment of Faculty Members to Support Entrepreneurial Activity BAR. *BAR - Brazilian Administration Review*, 17(2), e190013. Advance online publication. DOI: 10.1590/1807-7692bar2020190013

Sambamurthy, V., Bharadwaj, A., & Grover, V. (2003). Shaping agility through digital options: Reconceptualizing the role of information technology in contemporary firms. *Management Information Systems Quarterly*, 27(2), 237–263. DOI: 10.2307/30036530

Saxenian, A. (1996). *Regional advantage*. Harvard University Press.

Schmutzler, J., Andonova, V., & Diaz-Serrano, L. (2019). How context shapes entrepreneurial self-efficacy as a driver of entrepreneurial intentions: A multilevel approach. *Entrepreneurship Theory and Practice*, 2019(43), 880–920. DOI: 10.1177/1042258717753142

Schrijvers, M., Stam, E., & Bosma, N. (2021). Figuring it out: Configurations of high-performing entrepreneurial ecosystems in Europe. Utrecht University School of Economics (U.S.E.). *Working Paper Series*, 21(05). https://www.uu.nl/sites/default/files/REBO_USE_WP_21-05.pdf

Scott Kundel, S.W. (1991). *El impacto de la estructura de la estrategia y de la industria en nuevo funcionamiento de la empresa*. Doctoral Dissertation, University of Georgia, Dissertation Abstracts International, 52-06A, # 2205.

Shavinina, L. V. (Ed.). (2004). *Silicon Valley North: A High-Tech Cluster of Innovation and Entrepreneurship*. Elsevier. DOI: 10.1108/S1479-067X(2004)9

Shen, R., Guo, H., & Ma, H. (2023). How do entrepreneurs' cross-cultural experiences contribute to entrepreneurial ecosystem performance? *Journal of World Business*, 58(2), 101398. DOI: 10.1016/j.jwb.2022.101398

Shepherd, D. A. (2003). Learning from business failure: Propositions of grief recovery for the self-employed. *Academy of Management Review*, 28(2), 318–328. DOI: 10.2307/30040715

Smith, R. (2009). Mentoring and perpetuating the entrepreneurial spirit within family business by telling contingent stories. *New England Journal of Entrepreneurship*, 12(2), 27–40. DOI: 10.1108/NEJE-12-02-2009-B003

Soto-Ortigoza, M., & Prato-Zuluaga, R. (2024). Neo management and intelligent business ecosystems. *Revista Global Negotium*, 7(2). 167-185. http://publishing.fgu-edu.com/ojs/index.php/RGN/article/view/458/868

Spigel, B. (2015). The relational organization of entrepreneurial ecosystems. *Entrepreneurship Theory and Practice*. Published online first DOI: .DOI: 10.1111/etap.12167

Spigel, B., & Harrison, R. (2018). Toward a process theory of entrepreneurial ecosystems. *Strategic Entrepreneurship Journal*, 12(1), 151–168. DOI: 10.1002/sej.1268

Spilling, O. R. (1996). The entrepreneurial system: On entrepreneurship in the context of a mega-event. *Journal of Business Research*, 36(1), 91–103. DOI: 10.1016/0148-2963(95)00166-2

Stam, E. (2015). Entrepreneurial ecosystems and regional policy: A sympathetic critique. *European Planning Studies*, 23(9), 1759–1769. https://doi.org/. 10614 84DOI: 10. 1080/09654 313.2015

Stam, E., & Van De Ven, A. H. (2021). Entrepreneurial Ecosystems Elements. *Small Business Economics*, 56(2), 809–832. DOI: 10.1007/s11187-019-00270-6

Steininger, D. M. (2018). Linking information systems and entrepreneurship: A review and agenda for IT associated and digital entrepreneurship research. *Information Systems Journal*, 29(2), 363–407. DOI: 10.1111/isj.12206

Stephens, S., & Hegarty, C. (2022). Retirees from public service: The journey to small enterprise ownership. *Small Enterprise Research*, 29(1), 52–67. DOI: 10.1080/13215906.2021.1901141

Theodoraki, C., Dana, L. P., & Caputo, A. (2022). Building sustainable entrepreneurial ecosystems: A holistic approach. *Journal of Business Research*, 140, 346–360. DOI: 10.1016/j.jbusres.2021.11.005

Thompson, T. A., Purdy, J. M., & Ventresca, M. J. (2018). How entrepreneurial ecosystems take form: Evidence from social impact initiatives in Seattle. *Strategic Entrepreneurship Journal*, 12(1), 96–116. DOI: 10.1002/sej.1285

Tipu, S. A. A. (2020). Entrepreneurial re-entry after failure: A review and future research agenda. *Journal of Strategy and Management*, 13(2), 198–220. DOI: 10.1108/JSMA-08-2019-0157

Urbano, D., Audretsch, D., Aparicio, S., & Noguera, M. (2020). Does entrepreneurial activity matter for economic growth in developing countries? The role of the institutional environment. *The International Entrepreneurship and Management Journal*, 16(3), 1065–1099. DOI: 10.1007/s11365-019-00621-5

Valente, Y. (2024) *Actividad emprendedora temprana y el ecosistema empresarial en América Latina periodo 2010 - 2022.*(Tesis de Pregrado) Universidad Nacional de Chimborazo, Riobamba, Ecuador. http://dspace.unach.edu.ec/handle/51000/13165

Van de Ven, H. (1993). The development of an infrastructure for entrepreneurship. *Journal of Business Venturing*, 8(3), 211–230. DOI: 10.1016/0883-9026(93)90028-4

Walshok, M. L., Furtek, E., Lee, C. W., & Windham, P. H. (2002). Building regional innovation capacity: The San Diego experience. *Industry and Higher Education*, 16(1), 27–42. DOI: 10.5367/000000002101296063

WEF. (2014). Entrepreneurial ecosystems and around the globe and early-stage company growth dynamics an entrepreneurs perspective. Davos: World Economic Forum. http://www3.weforum.org/docs/WEF_II_EntrepreneurialEcosystemsEarlyStageCompany_Report_2014.pdf

Westhead, P., & Wright, M. (1998). Novice, portfolio, and serial founders: are they different? *Journal of Business Venturing, 13*(3), 173–204. https://doi.org/ 90002-1DOI: 10.1016/S0883-9026(97)

Wolfe, D. A., & Gertler, M. S. (2004). Clusters from the Inside and Out: Local Dynamics and Global Linkages. *Urban Studies (Edinburgh, Scotland)*, 41(5/6), 1071–1093. DOI: 10.1080/00420980410001675832

Wurth, B., Stam, E., & Spigel, B. (2021). Toward an entrepreneurial ecosystem research program. *Entrepreneurship Theory and Practice*. Advance online publication. DOI: 10.1177/1042258721998948

Ylinenpää, H. (2009). Entrepreneurship and innovation systems: Towards a development of the ERIS/IRIS concept. *European Planning Studies*, 17(8), 1153–1170. DOI: 10.1080/09654310902981011

Zaidi, R. A., Khan, M. M., Khan, R. A., & Mujtaba, B. G. (2023). Do entrepreneurship ecosystem and managerial skills contribute to startup development? *South Asian Journal of Business Studies*, 12(1), 25–53. DOI: 10.1108/SAJBS-07-2020-0233

Zott, C., Amit, R., & Massa, L. (2011). The business model: Recent developments and future research. *Journal of Management*, 37(4), 1019–1042. DOI: 10.1177/0149206311406265

ADDITIONAL READING

Bullón-Solís, O., Méndez-Gutiérrez, L., Gutiérrez-Justo, K., & Valero-Palomino, F. (2024). Entrepreneurship in a Bibliometric study from 2011 to 2021 in Scopus. *Revista San Gregorio*, 1(58), 46–55. DOI: 10.36097/rsan.v1i58.2466

Lozano, M. (2018). Business ecosystem. *Estudios De La Gestión: Revista Internacional De Administración*, (2), 61–86. DOI: 10.32719/25506641.2017.2.3

Montoya-Restrepo, L., & Montoya-Restrepo, I. (2022). Organizational restoration, an emerging strategy as a metaphor for the adaptation of business ecosystems. *Criterio Libre*, 20(36), e459084. DOI: 10.18041/1900-0642/criteriolibre.2022v20n36.9084

Novo Castro, S., Stable Rodríguez, Y., & Ortiz Núñez, R. (2023). Scientific production on innovation in business ecosystems from the Web of Science. GECONTEC: *Revista Internacional De Gestión Del Conocimiento Y La Tecnología, 11*(1), 112–127. DOI: 10.5281/zenodo.7928022

Ramírez-Campos, Á., Marcelino-Aranda, M., Domínguez-Aguirre, L., & Camacho, A. (2020). Analysis of the scientific production on Business Ecosystems. *Revista Española de Documentación Cientifica*, 43(3), e271.

KEY TERMS AND DEFINITIONS

Configurational Dimension: Refers to the arrangement and configuration of resources and capabilities within the ecosystem to maximize value and efficiency. It aims to optimize the disposition and use of resources and capabilities to create value within the ecosystem in order to meet strategic objectives.

Dimensions of the Entrepreneurship Ecosystem: are the dimensions that allow the formation of any entrepreneurship ecosystem, among them, the configurational, structural, relational, instrumental and operational dimensions; which, as a whole, allow approaching the entrepreneurial ecosystem through an integral and complementary vision.

Entrepreneurship Ecosystems: refers to the dynamic environment through which companies interact, with the aim of enhancing their development and adapting to changes; likewise, the factors that influence the interaction of the elements that make up the ecosystem, the resources and the applicable regulations are taken up.

Instrumental Dimension: The instrumental dimension analyzes the tools, technologies and systems used to facilitate interaction and management within the business ecosystem. The objective of the instrumental dimension is to provide the necessary tools and systems for effective operation and management within the ecosystem.

Operational Dimension: The operational dimension focuses on the processes that facilitate the day-to-day operation and effective interaction between ecosystem stakeholders. The purpose of the operational dimension is to ensure the effective implementation of processes that facilitate the interaction and functioning of the ecosystem.

Relational Dimension: It examines the relationships and interactions between the different elements that make up the ecosystem, such as customers, suppliers, competitors and partners. Its main focus is to facilitate cooperation and effective interaction between the different members of the ecosystem.

Structural Dimension: It reflects the general organization and hierarchy of actors in the business ecosystem. Its objective is to define how the different actors in the entrepreneurial ecosystem are organized and structured.

About the Contributors

Oytun Meçik works at the Department of Economics, at Eskisehir Osmangazi University. He does research in Macroeconomics, Labor Economics, Economic and Social Networks, Structural Transformation, and Industrial Innovation. Meçik, a member of the Turkish Economic Association, serves as editor and editorial board member in journals and publishers.

* * *

Hacer Pınar Altan successfully graduated from University of North Carolina at Greensboro, USA. She majored in International business and minored in Economics. She received both masters and Ph. D degrees from Atılım University at Ankara, Türkiye and her masters degree is in European Union and PhD degree in Political Economics. Following her graduation, she worked at POSH Company, and PSC Med Supply as an administartive emloyee at Greensboro, NC. After upon her return to Türkiye, respectively she worked at GÜRİŞ Holding company and TATLICI Holding company as an adminsitrative employee. She worked at Siirt University as an expert/academician. Presently she has been working at Company as an expert in human resources department. So far she has been written five articles in Political Economy area and some other articles at different fields.

Sinem Atıcı Ustalar graduated from Dokuz Eylül University, Faculty of Economics and Administrative Sciences, Department of Economics. She completed her master's degree in the Financial Economics and Banking program at the same University in 2017 and completed his doctorate in Economics in 2023. The author's doctoral study was conducted on the effect of investors' information level on financial market risk. Dr. Sinem ATICI USTALAR started working at Atatürk University as a research assistant in 2019 and will continue to work as an Assistant Professor in the Department of Economic Theory at the same university in 2024.

H. Naci Bayraç, graduated from Anadolu University, Faculty of Economics and Administrative Sciences, Department of Economics in 1986. He completed his master's degree in 1988 and his doctorate in 1999 at Anadolu University, Institute of Social Sciences, Department of Economics. He is working as a faculty member of Faculty of Economics and Administrative Sciences, Department of Economics in Eskişehir Osmangazi University. His fields of study are Economic Development and International Economics, Economic Integration, EU Economics, Turkish Economy, Energy Economics, Regional Economics, New Economy, Agricultural Economics. He became an associate professor in 2019.

Fatih Çemrek was born in Konya in 1977. He graduated from Arts and Science Faculty of Osmangazi University in 1998. From this time to 2001, he attended Master's program in Institutes of Science of Osmangazi University and graduated from Ph.D. Program of Institutes of Science of Eskişehir Osmangazi University in 2006. To date from 1999, he is working as a faculty member of Applied Statistics in Arts and Science Faculty of Eskişehir Osmangazi University. He is interested in studies of Time Series Analysis, Econometric Time Series Analysis, Multivariate Statistical Analysis, and Applied Statistics. He became an assistant professor in 2008 and became an associate professor in 2015. He is married and has one girl and one boy children

Fatih Ceylan is a research assistant (PhD) at Usak University, Faculty of Economics and Administrative Sciences, Department of Economics, Economic Policy. He completed his undergraduate and graduate education at Ege University and his PhD at Dokuz Eylul University, Türkiye. His research focuses on economic complexity, financial markets, crypto assets, financial econometrics, macroeconomic environment, and policies His studies to date consist of 16 articles published in journals indexed, 11 proceedings, and 3 book chapters. Usak University, Faculty of Economics and Administrative Sciences, Department of Economics Economic Policy Division, ORCID: 0000-0002-3685-2032

Birol Erkan is a professor of department of economics at İskenderun Technical University in Turkey. He received his doctorate in department of international economics at Manisa Celal Bayar University in Turkey. His works areas are macroeconomics, international economics, international trade, export competitiveness, comparative advantages and logistics.

Bakhtiyar Garayev I was born on 22.05.1997 in the city of Baku. I graduated from school in 2014, then I won the Business Administration department at the Faculty of Business Administration of the Turkic World. In 2015, I transferred to SABAH groups, where the state provided more opportunities, after the exam and interview. During my university years, I had short-term internships at 'Azersun Holding' and 'Intex Audit' companies. In 2018, I attended the 'Sustainable Development: Problems and Perspectives' held at the Azerbaijan State University of Economics, where I studied in 2018. After graduating from university, I earned a master's degree in Finance at Anadolu University in the same year. During my master's degree, I published an article and attended a conference. In 2021, I started my PhD in Finance. Within the framework of this period, I took an active role in the Youth Branch of the Eskişehir Azerbaijanis Association and I work as an editor in Üç Çizgi Magazine, which is the publication organ of the association. I actively continue my academic activities along with volunteering activities. Within the framework of these activities, I published 3 articles and participated in 4 conferences.

Tiago Silveira Gontijo PhD in Production Engineering from UFMG in the research line "Stochastic Modeling and Simulation". Participated in the Academic Doctorate for Innovation (DAI) Program from CNPq. Master's and Bachelor's degrees in Production Engineering. Bachelor's degrees in Administration and Economics. Interrupted PhD in Public Health from the Faculty of Medicine at UFMG. Has 10 years of teaching experience and in educational management. Currently an adjunct professor at the Federal University of São João del-Rei (UFSJ). Developed teaching activities at institutions such as UFOP, PUC-MG, UNIBH, UNA, and Izabela Hendrix. Has articles published in various journals. Has experience in data analysis and applied statistics, with emphasis on biostatistics, renewable energies, systematic literature review, and time series. Proficient in the R language.

Omar Guirette-Barbosa Bussines Management Ph D. Experience in quality systems based on ISO standards such as 9001, 17025, etc. Consultant on accreditation and certification issues, as well as on the application of continuous improvement tools and industrial engineering.

İhsan Erdem Kayral graduated from the Department of Economics at Hacettepe University as the top student of the faculty and department. He received his MSc. and Ph.D. degrees in the field of Finance in the Department of Business Administration at the same university. Completing his studies, Assoc. Prof. İhsan Erdem Kayral started to work in TUBITAK (The Scientific and Technological Research Council of Turkey) as a Chief Expert in 2010 and he served there for over 8 years. He worked in the Department of Economics and Department of International Trade and Business Administration at Konya Food and Agriculture University for approximately 4 years. Assoc. Prof. Kayral worked as a faculty member in the International Trade and Finance Department (served as Director of Graduate School of Social Sciences almost one year) at OSTIM Technical University for 2 years. Currently, he works as Assoc. Prof. in the Department of Business Administration at Başkent University. He has written several papers and book chapters about finance and forecasting the macroeconomic data. Assoc. Prof. Ihsan Erdem Kayral has lots of awards in various fields. He also receives a National Tubitak Master's Degree Scholarship and Turkish Economics Association Achievement Grant at Bachelor's Degree Level.

Ezgi Kopuk is a doctor of economics. Her fields of study are international economics, industrial economics, innovation, employment, competition, economic development and energy.

Tuğba Koyuncu Çakmak, she received her bachelor's and master's degrees in economics. She completed her PhD in economics at Eskişehir Osmangazi University with a thesis consisting of three papers titled 'Three Essays on the Relationship between Unemployment, Employment and Environmental Pollution: Environmental Phillips Curve and Environmental Employment Curve Approaches'. Koyuncu Çakmak conducts econometric modelling research on sustainable economic growth, climate change, environmental pollution, employment and investment.

|**Ozge Kozal** is currently working at Ege University, Department of Economics. Her research interests include political economy of economic development, industrialization and ecological economy.

Başak Özarslan Doğan completed her undergraduate education at Anadolu University, Department of Economics, in 2012. Dr. Başak Özarslan Doğan received her master's degree in Economics from Eskişehir Osmangazi University Social Sciences Institute in 2017. In 2021, she received her doctorate from Anadolu University, Institute of Social Sciences, Department of Economics..Dr. Özarslan Doğan has many articles published in international peer-reviewed journals in macroeconomics, papers presented at international scientific meetings, and book chapters.

Orhan Özaydın is adept at combining theoretical knowledge with practical experience. With fifteen years of experience in the real sector and a background in the finance departments of international companies, his areas of expertise include budgeting, accounting, controlling, banking, and treasury. He holds a Ph.D. in Financial Economics, M.S. in MBA, and B.S. in Mathematics. Additionally, he is a Certified Management Accountant (CMA) from IMA, USA. His areas of financial expertise include risk management, corporate finance, accounting, financial modelling, time-series econometrics, R coding, data analysis, data science, and advanced Excel. He teaches undergraduate and postgraduate courses in Turkish and English, and his research interests financial economics, financial markets, corporate finance, econometric analysis, and quantitative modelling.

Feyza Ozdinc She has been working at the Department of Economics at the Faculty of Economics and Administrative Sciences at Gaziantep University since 2013. Feyza Özdinç, who completed her Ph.D. in Economics at Hacettepe University, holds a Master's Degree in Economics from the University of North Carolina in the USA and a Bachelor's Degree in Economics from Gaziantep University. During her doctoral thesis, she conducted research as a Ph.D. Fellow at the World Institute for Development Economics Research (UNU-WIDER). Özdinç's research areas include Behavioral Economics, Experimental Economics, Development, Poverty, and Gender Inequality. She is a member of the Turkish Economic Association and the American Economic Association.

Aslı Öztopcu received her Bachelor's degree from Anadolu University, Faculty of Business Administration and her Master's degree in Business Administration from Eskişehir Osmangazi University. She received her PhD degree from Maltepe University, Department of Economics. Since 2005, she has been a full-time faculty member at Maltepe University. He teaches economics and business administration courses. Öztopçu's articles are mainly in the field of economics. His research interests include sustainable development, behavioral economics and environmental economics. Simultaneously with his academic work, he is a consultant in the fields of business, marketing, communication and management.

Sukriye Reis In 2007, I started as a research assistant at Gaziantep University, Faculty of Economics and Administrative Sciences, Department of Business Administration. I started my doctoral education in finance at Anadolu University. I completed my doctoral dissertation titled "Liquidity, Performance And Return Relatıonshıp In Terms Of Instıtutıonal Investors: An Example Of Borsa Istanbul". I have been working as an associate professor at Gaziantep University in the same department since 2022 and continue my research on financial markets, behavioral finance, portfolio management, and sustainability.

Burcu SAVAŞ ÇELİK completed her undergraduate education at Giresun University, department of Economics, in 2012. Dr. Burcu SAVAŞ ÇELİK received her master's degree in Economics from Karabük University in 2015. She received her doctorate from Karadeniz Technical University, Institute of Social Sciences Department of Economics in 2021. Dr. Savaş Çelik has many articles international peer-reviewed journals in macroeconomics, papers presented at international scientific meetings and book chapters.

Nicola Spagnolo holds a Ph.D. in Economics from the University of London. He is currently a Reader at Brunel University London, Professor at Universita' degli Studi della Campania "Luigi Vanvitelli" and Research Associate with the Centre for Applied Macroeconomic Analysis at Australian National University. His research interests are in finance, statistical methods and applied econometrics. He has published extensively on the following topics: i) analysis of financial risk, ii) Markov switching models, iii) modelling energy prices, iv) financial crises determinants, v) risk management, vi) modelling structural breaks in financial variables, and vii) climate risk and financial markets. He has contributed, among others, to the following journals: Economics Letters, Energy Economics, Energy Journal, Energy Policy, European Journal of Finance, Journal of Economics and Behavioural Organisation, Journal of Empirical Finance, Journal of International Money and Finance, Journal of Macroeconomics, Journal of Population Economics, Journal of Time Series Analysis, Organisational Research Methods.

Omar Vargas-González Professor, research assistant and former Head of Computer Systems Department at Tecnológico Nacional de México Campus Ciudad Guzmán, professor at Telematic Engineering at Centro Universitario del Sur Universidad de Guadalajara with a master degree in Computer Systems. Has been trained in Innovation and Multidisciplinary Entrepreneurship at Arizona State University (2018) and a Generation of Ecosystems of Innovation, Entrepreneurship and Sustainability for Jalisco course by Harvard University T.H. Chan School of Health. At present conduct research on diverse fields such as Entrepreneurship, Economy, Statistics, Mathematics and Information and Computer Sciences. Has collaborated in the publication of many scientific articles and conducted diverse Innovation and Technological Development projects.

Sureyya Yigit is a Professor of Politics and International Relations at the School of Politics and Diplomacy at New Vision University in Tbilisi, Georgia. He has lectured at several universities in Scandinavia, Turkey, and Central Asia. He is an Editorial Board member of the IGI Book Series Conflict Management - 3 Volumes, an International Academic Board member of RIPEA - Journal of Argentine Foreign Policy Research, an Associate Editor on the Editorial Board of the International Journal of Green Business, a member of the Editorial Board of AcademCraft - Open access journal of education research and case studies and an Editorial Advisory Board Member for IGI Global Cases on Security, Safety and Risk Management. He is also the senior consultant to ZDS – Women's Democracy Network Public Fund, a non-governmental organisation based in Bishkek, Kyrgyz Republic, and a consultant to Aeropodium, a London-based business.

Index

A

Africa 2, 3, 4, 14, 15, 16, 17, 18, 19, 22, 23, 25, 26, 27, 28, 30, 39, 44, 67, 92, 93, 100, 102, 110, 111, 112, 115, 116, 153, 188, 191, 202, 269, 332, 340, 358, 441, 456, 466, 500, 511, 512

Agricultural Value Added 495, 499, 502, 512

ARDL Bounds Test 139, 493, 497, 503, 508

B

Bibliometric Analysis 261, 264, 265, 270, 273, 277, 278

BRICS+ 41, 44, 45, 55, 456, 459

Budget Deficit 31, 244, 247

C

Climate Change 91, 134, 158, 214, 217, 218, 273, 377, 386, 387, 388, 389, 390, 391, 393, 395, 396, 397, 398, 399, 400, 401, 402, 403, 411, 412, 413, 416, 417, 421, 428, 437, 438, 439, 440, 443, 444, 448, 450, 452, 453, 456, 457, 458, 459, 462, 463, 466, 467, 470, 471, 472, 477, 479, 480, 488, 491, 494, 507, 516, 520, 528

Cointegration 100, 106, 112, 118, 143, 144, 193, 194, 196, 199, 307, 308, 383, 455, 498, 499, 503, 504, 513, 515, 521, 522, 523, 524, 525, 526, 530, 532

Correlations 71, 72, 73, 77, 89, 98, 103, 374, 427, 442

Corruption 16, 17, 21, 22, 25, 30, 46, 242, 243, 244, 245, 246, 247, 248, 249, 250, 252, 253, 254, 255, 256, 257, 313, 314, 317, 318, 319, 320, 324, 328, 369, 421, 435, 436, 441

D

Decision-making Process 43

Demand for Labor 183

Developing Countries 1, 2, 7, 10, 11, 14, 15, 23, 25, 28, 29, 34, 36, 37, 40, 42, 43, 45, 47, 48, 49, 50, 51, 52, 53, 56, 58, 59, 63, 68, 88, 90, 95, 100, 102, 117, 118, 124, 126, 127, 128, 149, 160, 163, 164, 165, 182, 245, 260, 277, 316, 327, 330, 365, 366, 367, 383, 385, 390, 391, 399, 420, 442, 453, 463, 464, 480, 482, 494, 498, 500, 509, 510, 512, 560

Development 2, 4, 5, 6, 10, 13, 15, 16, 17, 20, 22, 25, 27, 28, 29, 30, 33, 35, 38, 39, 43, 47, 48, 50, 52, 53, 55, 57, 59, 63, 93, 94, 117, 124, 125, 126, 127, 128, 129, 132, 134, 135, 136, 137, 138, 139, 140, 141, 147, 148, 149, 150, 151, 152, 153, 154, 155, 157, 158, 160, 161, 162, 164, 167, 173, 174, 175, 178, 179, 180, 182, 186, 188, 190, 191, 193, 204, 205, 211, 221, 223, 227, 233, 237, 255, 256, 259, 260, 261, 262, 263, 264, 266, 267, 271, 272, 273, 274, 275, 276, 277, 278, 279, 280, 281, 283, 287, 305, 308, 313, 314, 315, 316, 317, 318, 320, 323, 324, 325, 327, 328, 329, 330, 341, 353, 354, 355, 361, 362, 363, 364, 365, 366, 367, 368, 369, 370, 371, 375, 378, 379, 380, 381, 382, 383, 384, 385, 386, 387, 388, 389, 390, 391, 392, 393, 394, 395, 396, 397, 398, 399, 400, 401, 402, 403, 405, 406, 407, 408, 409, 410, 411, 412, 417, 420, 422, 423, 428, 435, 436, 437, 438, 439, 440, 442, 443, 445, 447, 448, 449, 450, 451, 452, 455, 457, 459, 460, 461, 462, 463, 464, 465, 466, 467, 469, 470, 471, 472, 473, 474, 475, 477, 478, 479, 481, 482, 483, 484, 485, 486, 487, 488, 489, 490, 491, 494, 495, 499, 500, 501, 505, 507, 508, 509, 510, 511, 512, 513, 514, 515,

516, 520, 529, 532, 534, 535, 537, 538, 539, 540, 541, 542, 543, 544, 545, 546, 549, 550, 551, 554, 555, 556, 557, 560, 561, 562

Dumitrescu and Hurlin 185, 196, 199, 200

E

Ecological Footprint 384, 426, 439, 442, 444, 449, 452, 453, 454, 455, 459, 460, 461, 513, 514, 515, 516, 517, 518, 519, 520, 521, 522, 523, 527, 528, 529, 530, 531, 532

Economic Development 27, 33, 47, 93, 127, 135, 136, 155, 162, 178, 179, 180, 182, 204, 255, 259, 260, 261, 262, 263, 264, 266, 267, 271, 272, 273, 274, 275, 276, 277, 278, 279, 280, 281, 313, 314, 315, 316, 317, 318, 323, 324, 325, 327, 328, 329, 363, 368, 382, 383, 384, 405, 410, 420, 435, 445, 460, 463, 464, 470, 499, 550, 554

Economic Growth 4, 7, 10, 11, 12, 13, 15, 41, 47, 50, 118, 124, 125, 126, 128, 129, 138, 139, 140, 148, 149, 150, 151, 152, 153, 157, 158, 159, 160, 161, 162, 164, 165, 167, 169, 175, 177, 180, 181, 182, 183, 185, 186, 190, 191, 199, 200, 201, 202, 203, 204, 205, 208, 209, 210, 211, 231, 234, 238, 242, 245, 255, 257, 261, 263, 264, 272, 274, 277, 278, 279, 280, 288, 289, 310, 314, 315, 316, 317, 318, 319, 322, 324, 327, 328, 329, 330, 332, 333, 363, 367, 368, 369, 370, 379, 380, 382, 384, 385, 386, 389, 392, 398, 420, 436, 441, 444, 447, 448, 449, 450, 451, 452, 454, 455, 456, 457, 459, 460, 461, 462, 464, 467, 494, 497, 498, 499, 505, 508, 509, 512, 521, 522, 527, 529, 530, 531, 560

Energy Consumption 82, 370, 426, 428, 436, 439, 449, 450, 455, 456, 457, 459, 460, 461, 479, 480, 513, 515, 521, 522, 529, 530, 531

Entrepreneurship Ecosystems 533, 534, 535, 536, 537, 538, 539, 540, 541, 542, 543, 544, 545, 546, 549, 562

Environment 6, 10, 14, 16, 17, 25, 125, 127, 149, 158, 186, 213, 230, 235, 238, 245, 280, 284, 303, 314, 355, 356, 363, 367, 368, 369, 384, 385, 388, 391, 393, 397, 398, 399, 400, 402, 404, 406, 407, 408, 412, 413, 416, 419, 420, 421, 422, 424, 428, 436, 437, 438, 439, 441, 442, 443, 448, 455, 459, 460, 464, 465, 466, 467, 469, 470, 471, 472, 473, 474, 475, 477, 478, 482, 483, 484, 486, 489, 490, 491, 494, 505, 507, 510, 512, 514, 515, 516, 517, 520, 521, 527, 529, 530, 534, 541, 552, 555, 560, 562

Environmental Concern 463, 491

Environmental Degradation 15, 25, 208, 361, 364, 367, 368, 370, 371, 380, 383, 384, 385, 391, 403, 419, 420, 421, 422, 423, 424, 426, 428, 431, 432, 433, 434, 435, 436, 437, 438, 439, 440, 443, 444, 445, 447, 448, 450, 451, 452, 453, 454, 455, 457, 459, 461, 484, 516, 519, 521

Equity Investments 300, 331, 332, 333, 334, 335, 336, 337, 341, 342, 345, 346, 348

ESG 207, 213, 214, 216, 217, 218, 219, 220, 221, 222, 224, 226, 228, 232, 235, 237, 387, 388, 389, 390, 392, 393, 394, 395, 400, 401, 404, 405, 407, 408, 409, 410, 411, 412, 414, 415, 416, 417, 418

ESG Investment 213, 216, 217, 219, 221, 237, 392

F

Financial Capital 124, 125, 128, 129, 130, 132, 133, 134, 136, 137, 139, 140, 141, 147, 148, 149, 155, 367

Financial Dynamics 259, 260, 261, 277

Financial Globalization 262, 331, 332

Financial Stability 33, 34, 35, 37, 38, 40, 50, 52, 133, 134, 153, 185, 186, 187, 188, 190, 191, 192, 193, 197, 200,

201, 202, 203, 204, 205, 261, 288, 289, 306, 365
Fiscal Adjustment 241, 242, 243, 245, 249, 250, 252, 253, 254, 255, 256, 257, 258
Fourier Toda-Yamamoto 107, 108

G

G7 25, 45, 95, 96, 97, 98, 101, 331, 333, 339, 340, 346, 347, 348, 349, 350, 351, 352
G-20 Countries 99, 102, 112
GDP 26, 44, 55, 93, 129, 130, 131, 140, 190, 191, 197, 198, 199, 200, 211, 243, 244, 246, 247, 248, 251, 252, 253, 313, 314, 316, 318, 319, 320, 324, 338, 339, 370, 371, 375, 376, 380, 385, 386, 422, 426, 427, 428, 429, 434, 437, 448, 449, 450, 451, 457, 495, 498, 499, 501, 509, 513, 515, 516, 521, 522, 523, 524, 525, 526, 527, 530, 531, 535
GDP per Capita 313, 314, 316, 318, 319, 320, 386, 426, 451, 498, 501, 513, 515, 521
Global Energy Prices 7, 61, 63, 64, 68, 69
Global Food Prices 61, 64, 65, 68, 70, 71, 74, 78, 83, 91
Global Geopolitical Risks 61, 63, 67, 98
Globalisation 57, 202, 353, 354, 441
Global Supply Chain 61, 63, 64, 66, 69, 74, 92, 93, 94, 98
Governance 17, 19, 20, 21, 22, 23, 25, 26, 27, 28, 29, 30, 33, 34, 35, 36, 37, 38, 40, 41, 43, 47, 48, 49, 50, 51, 52, 54, 55, 56, 57, 58, 59, 207, 211, 212, 213, 218, 236, 237, 238, 245, 254, 263, 313, 314, 315, 316, 317, 318, 319, 320, 322, 324, 325, 327, 328, 329, 330, 341, 356, 357, 361, 364, 368, 369, 378, 380, 381, 383, 385, 387, 389, 390, 392, 393, 394, 395, 400, 401, 405, 406, 407, 409, 411, 412, 415, 417, 418, 435, 439, 461, 486, 536, 541, 551, 552, 556
Governance Reform 36, 40, 41, 56, 58, 314, 369

Granger Causality 67, 68, 99, 100, 101, 102, 106, 107, 108, 112, 115, 119, 121, 140, 196, 498
Green Finance 278, 390, 400, 404, 405, 412, 510
Green Industrial Policy 457

H

Human Capital 16, 22, 123, 124, 125, 127, 128, 129, 130, 132, 134, 135, 136, 137, 138, 139, 140, 141, 147, 148, 149, 150, 151, 152, 153, 154, 155, 157, 158, 159, 161, 162, 164, 165, 166, 167, 168, 169, 170, 172, 174, 177, 178, 179, 180, 182, 183, 184, 262, 279, 393, 499, 501, 512, 535, 538, 544, 548, 550, 557
Human Development 136, 137, 138, 154, 361, 363, 364, 366, 367, 369, 370, 371, 375, 378, 379, 380, 381, 383, 386, 451, 460

I

IMF 2, 3, 4, 5, 6, 10, 11, 12, 13, 14, 15, 25, 26, 27, 28, 30, 31, 33, 34, 35, 36, 37, 38, 39, 40, 41, 42, 43, 44, 45, 46, 47, 48, 49, 50, 51, 52, 53, 54, 55, 56, 57, 58, 59, 74, 92, 93, 102, 138, 141, 152, 193, 200, 255, 257, 262, 281, 306, 314, 316, 330, 341, 353, 354, 357, 365, 366, 382
Impact Investment 207, 213, 216, 220, 221, 224, 228, 229, 232, 237, 239
Inclusive Governance 34
Inclusive Green Growth 28, 426, 493, 494, 497, 501, 502, 504, 505, 508, 510, 512
Income Inequality 38, 95, 161, 209, 361, 364, 367, 378, 379, 380, 381, 450, 460
Industrialization 5, 128, 129, 139, 149, 160, 332, 350, 357, 361, 364, 365, 366, 367, 368, 370, 373, 375, 377, 379, 380, 381, 382, 384, 385, 386, 448, 449, 450, 452, 455, 457, 458, 461, 463, 464, 470, 471, 473, 510, 516
Industrialized Countries 3, 123, 124, 125,

128, 132, 136, 137, 138, 147, 148, 149, 155, 331, 332, 335, 351, 354, 357, 367, 454, 479

Industrial Policies 25, 135, 155, 447, 448, 449, 450, 455, 456, 457, 458

Industrial Sector 123, 125, 126, 136, 137, 138, 139, 140, 148, 149, 154, 155, 173, 293, 449, 455

Inflation 2, 7, 9, 10, 12, 26, 31, 38, 41, 61, 62, 63, 64, 65, 66, 67, 68, 69, 70, 71, 74, 75, 76, 78, 79, 80, 81, 82, 83, 84, 85, 86, 87, 88, 89, 90, 91, 92, 93, 94, 95, 96, 97, 98, 99, 100, 101, 102, 105, 106, 107, 108, 109, 110, 112, 113, 116, 117, 118, 119, 120, 121, 133, 185, 186, 190, 191, 192, 193, 199, 200, 201, 202, 203, 247, 283, 284, 285, 287, 288, 289, 293, 299, 305, 307, 308, 310, 313, 318, 319, 320, 321, 322, 323, 324, 479

Inflation Rate 65, 100, 101, 109, 110, 112, 116, 120, 186

Institutions 1, 6, 8, 11, 13, 14, 15, 17, 19, 20, 22, 30, 31, 33, 35, 36, 39, 48, 51, 56, 124, 133, 134, 136, 137, 138, 152, 157, 163, 168, 175, 176, 177, 185, 186, 187, 188, 201, 203, 212, 214, 221, 222, 223, 224, 242, 245, 255, 256, 260, 262, 277, 279, 280, 294, 304, 305, 310, 314, 315, 316, 324, 325, 327, 328, 329, 330, 334, 353, 356, 368, 369, 380, 382, 384, 385, 390, 391, 392, 393, 395, 398, 400, 411, 420, 422, 423, 426, 427, 435, 438, 439, 440, 444, 445, 486, 500, 514, 516, 536, 550, 552, 553, 558

Instrumental Dimension 546, 547, 562

Interest Rate 95, 99, 100, 101, 102, 108, 109, 110, 111, 112, 116, 118, 120, 185, 186, 190, 191, 192, 193, 199, 200, 201, 204, 262, 284, 285, 289, 290, 291, 293, 294, 301, 302, 405, 406

International Institutions 6, 33, 36, 39

International Monetary Fund 1, 2, 11, 31, 33, 37, 46, 53, 54, 55, 57, 58, 92, 102, 133, 134, 152, 153, 255, 314, 330

International Trade 62, 94, 260, 262, 332, 357, 383, 419, 422, 437, 438, 445, 554

L

Long-term Government Bond Yields 190, 199, 201

M

monetary policies 9, 15, 62, 63, 82, 89, 90, 100, 117, 133, 185, 187, 201, 261, 283, 285, 286, 288, 292, 294, 303

money supply 2, 31, 283, 284, 285, 286, 287, 289, 290, 291, 292, 294, 295, 296, 300, 301, 302, 303, 304, 305, 307, 308, 309, 310

N

NEET 170, 171, 172, 183

NICs 331, 332, 333, 336, 339, 340, 346, 347, 348, 349, 350, 351, 352, 355

O

OECD 5, 6, 7, 9, 10, 12, 14, 15, 25, 26, 28, 38, 56, 139, 140, 167, 170, 171, 182, 185, 186, 187, 190, 191, 192, 197, 200, 208, 218, 232, 235, 241, 243, 244, 246, 247, 248, 255, 256, 257, 313, 314, 315, 317, 318, 319, 322, 324, 325, 328, 361, 363, 364, 370, 371, 373, 375, 376, 377, 378, 379, 380, 381, 384, 393, 414, 416, 439, 470, 499, 501, 510, 521, 530, 531, 550, 556

OECD Countries 10, 26, 140, 167, 170, 186, 187, 190, 191, 192, 200, 241, 243, 244, 246, 247, 248, 255, 257, 313, 315, 317, 318, 319, 322, 324, 361, 363, 364, 370, 371, 373, 375, 376, 377, 378, 379, 380, 381, 439, 499, 521, 530, 531

Overeducation 163, 165, 166, 170, 175, 176, 179, 180, 182, 184

P

Panel Analysis 178, 191, 512
Panel Data 55, 99, 101, 102, 103, 104, 107, 108, 109, 110, 112, 116, 118, 119, 123, 125, 142, 148, 158, 185, 192, 193, 198, 204, 244, 313, 318, 319, 321, 324, 328, 336, 419, 437, 443, 498, 521, 522, 531
Panel Data Analysis 55, 104, 123, 125, 148, 185, 192, 193, 198, 204, 321, 498, 522, 531
Portfolio Investments 332, 333, 335, 336, 341, 342, 345, 346, 348, 351, 356, 357
Post Growth 207, 231, 232, 234
Principal Component Analysis 106, 493, 497, 501, 502, 508
Production 12, 17, 31, 63, 64, 66, 67, 68, 69, 89, 98, 124, 125, 126, 127, 128, 132, 134, 137, 140, 148, 149, 151, 155, 158, 160, 161, 167, 173, 174, 180, 209, 214, 216, 226, 228, 234, 260, 262, 268, 277, 309, 315, 362, 363, 364, 365, 366, 367, 368, 370, 371, 376, 377, 393, 397, 398, 403, 404, 426, 435, 436, 438, 439, 442, 444, 449, 450, 451, 452, 453, 454, 455, 456, 458, 460, 461, 462, 463, 464, 465, 466, 469, 470, 471, 472, 473, 474, 475, 476, 477, 478, 479, 482, 483, 485, 486, 488, 489, 490, 491, 494, 495, 497, 498, 499, 505, 507, 508, 517, 518, 519, 520, 521, 527, 538, 549, 553, 561

Q

Quality of Human Capital 137, 159, 161, 162, 168, 184
Quantity of Human Capital 161, 162, 184

R

Relational Dimension 541, 545, 562

S

Scopus 259, 261, 264, 270, 277, 561
Skills 52, 124, 127, 132, 134, 135, 137, 138, 150, 155, 157, 158, 161, 162, 163, 165, 166, 167, 168, 169, 170, 173, 174, 175, 176, 177, 179, 180, 184, 535, 561
Spatial Econometric Models 432
Stabilisation 6, 7, 11, 12, 13, 31
Structural Adjustment 1, 2, 4, 5, 6, 10, 11, 12, 13, 14, 26, 27, 28, 30, 31, 38, 316, 330
Structural Dimension 536, 539, 562
Structural Reforms 33, 35, 36, 38, 40, 41, 50, 52, 117, 134, 135
Structural Shifts 120
Supply of Labor 184
Sustainability 9, 10, 29, 123, 124, 127, 132, 133, 137, 178, 181, 209, 211, 213, 214, 219, 226, 233, 234, 235, 236, 237, 238, 254, 256, 257, 271, 273, 274, 277, 278, 281, 355, 368, 383, 386, 387, 388, 389, 390, 391, 392, 393, 394, 395, 396, 397, 398, 400, 401, 402, 403, 404, 405, 406, 407, 408, 409, 410, 411, 412, 413, 414, 415, 416, 417, 442, 448, 449, 454, 459, 460, 462, 463, 464, 465, 466, 470, 472, 474, 477, 481, 482, 483, 484, 486, 487, 488, 491, 505, 509, 510, 513, 514, 515, 516, 517, 518, 527, 530, 531, 534, 536
Sustainable Development 29, 30, 33, 126, 154, 157, 158, 174, 221, 233, 237, 272, 273, 274, 277, 278, 327, 368, 380, 383, 387, 388, 389, 390, 391, 392, 394, 395, 397, 398, 399, 400, 401, 402, 403, 405, 407, 408, 411, 412, 417, 420, 438, 440, 452, 457, 463, 464, 465, 466, 467, 469, 470, 472, 473, 477, 478, 479, 481, 482, 483, 484, 485, 486, 488, 489, 490, 491, 494, 500, 507, 510, 512, 513, 514, 515, 516, 532
Sustainable Development Goals 158, 174, 221, 237, 273, 277, 278, 383, 387, 388,

389, 390, 391, 392, 395, 397, 398, 401, 403, 405, 408, 411, 417, 438, 452, 467, 477, 482, 484, 490, 494, 512

Sustainable Finance 207, 212, 214, 215, 216, 232, 233, 387, 388, 389, 390, 391, 392, 393, 394, 395, 398, 400, 401, 402, 403, 405, 406, 407, 408, 411, 413, 414, 415, 416, 418

Sustainable Production 449, 450, 458, 463, 465, 474, 483, 488, 490, 491

T

Total Labor Force 371, 493, 497, 502, 504, 505, 508

Trade Globalization 357, 427, 428, 436

Trade Liberalisation 6, 7, 10, 17, 28, 442

Transformative Investment 207, 213, 224, 225, 226, 227, 228, 231, 233, 236, 238

U

Unemployment 6, 26, 31, 37, 38, 69, 93, 126, 157, 163, 165, 168, 169, 171, 173, 175, 176, 180, 181, 182, 183, 184, 209, 247, 262, 287, 361, 364, 371, 373, 379, 380, 494

W

Web of Science 259, 261, 264, 277, 561

World Bank 1, 2, 3, 5, 6, 7, 8, 10, 11, 12, 13, 14, 15, 16, 17, 18, 19, 20, 22, 23, 25, 26, 27, 30, 31, 39, 47, 54, 56, 57, 58, 141, 150, 151, 154, 187, 188, 200, 205, 306, 313, 314, 318, 320, 328, 330, 341, 353, 357, 365, 371, 382, 385, 402, 403, 405, 417, 426, 427, 428, 469, 470, 490, 501, 523

Z

Z-score 185, 186, 187, 188, 190, 191, 193, 199, 200, 201, 205